Inspiration and Interpretation:

SEVEN SERMONS PREACHED BEFORE
THE UNIVERSITY OF OXFORD:

WITH PRELIMINARY REMARKS:

BEING AN ANSWER TO A VOLUME ENTITLED

"Essays and Reviews."

By the same Author.

A PLAIN COMMENTARY ON THE FOUR HOLY GOSPELS. 7 vols. Fcap. 8vo.

NINETY SHORT SERMONS FOR FAMILY READING. 2 vols. Fcap. 8vo.

THE PORTRAIT OF A CHRISTIAN GENTLEMAN: A MEMOIR OF P. F. TYTLER, ESQ. (2nd. Ed.) 1859. Crown 8vo.

Inspiration and Interpretation:

SEVEN SERMONS PREACHED BEFORE
THE UNIVERSITY OF OXFORD:

WITH PRELIMINARY REMARKS:

BEING AN ANSWER TO A VOLUME ENTITLED

"Essays and Reviews."

BY THE

REV. JOHN WILLIAM BURGON, M.A.,
FELLOW OF ORIEL COLLEGE, AND SELECT PREACHER.

I CANNOT HOLD MY PEACE, BECAUSE THOU HAST HEARD, O MY SOUL,
THE SOUND OF THE TRUMPET, THE ALARM OF WAR.

DEAN BURGON SOCIETY PRESS
Box 354
Collingswood, New Jersey 08108

Oxford & London:
J. H. AND JAS. PARKER.
1861.
ISBN 1-888328-04-5

Printed by Messrs. Parker, Cornmarket, Oxford.

TO THE REVEREND

WILLIAM SEWELL, D.D.,

FELLOW OF EXETER COLLEGE: LATE PROFESSOR OF MORAL PHILOSOPHY
IN THE UNIVERSITY OF OXFORD; AND LATE WARDEN
OF ST. PETER'S COLLEGE, RADLEY.

MY DEAR FRIEND,

Let me have the satisfaction of inscribing this volume to yourself. I know of no one who has more faithfully devoted himself to the sacred cause of Christian Education: no one to whom those blessed Truths are more precious, which of late have been so unscrupulously assailed, and which the ensuing pages are humbly designed to uphold in their integrity.

Affectionately yours,

JOHN W. BURGON.

Published by

**The Dean Burgon Society Press
Box 354
Collingswood, New Jersey 08108
U.S.A.
Phone: 609-854-4452**
February, 1999

Copyright, 1999
All Rights Reserved

ISBN #1-888328-04-5

Foreword

The Publishers. This book, *Inspiration and Interpretation*, is published by the Dean Burgon Society, Incorporated (DBS). The Society takes its name from Dean John William Burgon (1813-1888), a conservative Anglican clergyman. The DBS is recognized by the I.R.S. as a non-profit, tax exempt organization. All contributions are tax deductible. The Society's main purpose is stated in its slogan, **"IN DEFENSE OF TRADITIONAL BIBLE TEXTS."** The DBS was founded in 1978, and, since then, has held its annual two-day conference in the United States and Canada. During this time, many excellent messages defending the King James Bible and its underlying Hebrew and Greek texts are presented. The messages are available in three forms: (1) video cassettes; (2) audio cassettes, and (3) the printed message books. For information on receiving any of the above, plus a copy of the *"THE ARTICLES OF FAITH, AND ORGANIZATION"* of the Dean Burgon Society, please write or phone the office at **609-854-4452**. You may use your CREDIT CARD if you wish, and send your order by **FAX** at **609-854-2464** or by E-Mail at **DBSN@Juno.Com**.

The Dean Burgon News. The Society has a paper called *The Dean Burgon News*. It comes out from time to time, as the Lord provides the time and the funds. Within its pages the *News* proclaims:

"The DEAN BURGON SOCIETY, INCORPORATED proudly takes its name in honor of John William Burgon (1813-1888), the Dean of Chichester in England, whose tireless and accurate scholarship and contribution in the area of New Testament Textual Criticism; whose defense of the Traditional Greek Text against its many enemies; and whose firm belief in the verbal inspiration and inerrancy of the Bible, we believe, have all been unsurpassed either before or since his time!"

The Present Reprint. The DEAN BURGON SOCIETY, INCORPORATED is pleased to present, in this form, another of Dean John William Burgon's most convincing books, *Inspiration and Interpretation*. This is our fifth reprint of one of Dean Burgon's books. The first book was *The Last Twelve Verses of Mark*, available as **#1139** for a GIFT of **$15 + $4** for postage and handling. The second book was *The Revision Revised*, available as **#611** for a GIFT of **$25 + $5** for postage and handling. The third book was *The Traditional Text of the Holy Gospels*, available as **#1159** for a GIFT of **$16 + $4**. The fourth book, *The Causes of Corruption*, is page for page like the original book written in 1896 by Dean Burgon, and edited after his death by Rev. Edward Miller. It is Volume II of this subject as a continuation of *The Traditional Text*. This fifth book, *Inspiration and Interpretation*, was written by Dean Burgon in 1861. In the **APPENDIX** you will find a 52-page summarization of the main points brought out in the book. It is fully indexed for easy reference. You might want to begin by reading the **APPENDIX** first.

The Importance of *Inspiration and Interpretation*. In this book Dean Burgon delivers seven sermons preached to his students at the University of Oxford. In the sermons, he defended the inerrancy of the Bible--down to the very words, syllables, and letters of it. He also gives sound principles of Biblical interpretation. Before these seven constructive sermons, the Dean makes a 228 page answer to *Essays and Reviews*. In this answer he shows himself a champion of Bible believing truth and an opponent of every heresy and heretic attempts to dishonor God's inerrant Word.

Other Books by Dean Burgon. For those wanting to read four other excellent reprints, the following can be ordered from THE DEAN BURGON SOCIETY.

1. *The Last Twelve Verses of Mark*, 400 pages, perfect bound book for a gift of **$15.00**.
2. *The Revision Revised*, 640 pp. hardback for a gift of **$25.00**.
3. *The Traditional Text of the Holy Gospels*, 384 pages, hardback for a gift of **$16.00**.
4. *The Causes of Corruption*, 360 pages, hardback for a gift of **$15.00**.

Please add **$4.00** or **15%** (whichever is greater) for postage & handling.

Future Reprints. As funds permit, the DEAN BURGON SOCIETY soon hopes to bring into reprint form other important books "IN DEFENSE OF TRADITIONAL BIBLE TEXTS."

Sincerely for God's Written Words,

DAW/w   Pastor D. A. Waite, Th.D., Ph.D.
            President, THE DEAN BURGON SOCIETY

The
Dean Burgon
Society
In Defense of Traditional Bible Texts
Box 354
Collingswood, NJ 08108, U.S.A.

**Dean John William Burgon
(1813--1888)**

ΔΕΙ ΓΑΡ ΚΑΙ ΑΙΡΕΣΕΙΣ ἘΝ ὙΜΙΝ ΕΙΝΑΙ, ἹΝΑ ΟΙ ΔΟΚΙΜΟΙ
ΦΑΝΕΡΟΙ ΓΕΝΩΝΤΑΙ ἘΝ ὙΜΙΝ.

Ac si diceret: Ob hoc hærescôn non statim divinitus eradicantur auctores, ut probati manifesti fiant; id est, ut unusquisque quam tenax, et fidelis, et fixus Catholicæ fidei sit amator, appareat. Et revera cum quæque novitas ebullit, statim cernitur frumentorum gravitas, et levitas palearum: tunc sine magno molimine excutitur ab arcâ, quod nullo pondere intra aream tenebatur.—VINCENTIUS LIRINENSIS, *Adversus Hæreses*, § 20.

PREFACE.

I AM unwilling that this volume should go forth to the world without some account of its origin and of its contents.

I. Appointed last year, (without solicitation on his part,) to the office of Select Preacher, the present writer was called upon at the commencement of the October Term to address the University. His Sermon, (the first in the volume,) was simply intended to embody the advice which he had already orally given to every Undergraduate who had sought counsel at his hands for many years past in Oxford; advice which, to say the truth, he was almost weary of repeating. Nothing more weighty or more apposite, at all events, presented itself, for an introductory address: nor has a review of the current of religious opinion, either before or since, produced any change of opinion as to the importance of what was on that first occasion advocated.

Another, and another, and yet another preaching turn unexpectedly presented itself, in the course of the same Term; and the IInd, IIIrd, and IVth of the ensuing Sermons, (preached on alternate Sundays,) were the result. The study of the Bible had been advocated in the first Sermon; but it was urged from a hundred quarters that a considerable amount of unbelief prevailed respecting that very Book for which it was evident that the preacher claimed entire perfection and absolute supremacy. The singular fallacy of these last days, that Natural Science, in some unexplained manner, has already demolished,—or is inevitably destined to demolish[a],—the Book of Divine Revelation, appeared to be the fallacy which had emerged into most offensive prominence; and to this, he accordingly addressed himself.—It will not, surely, be thought by any one who reads the IInd of these Sermons that its author is so weak as to look with jealousy on the progress of Physical Science. His alarm does not arise from the cultivation of the noblest study but one,—viz. the study of GOD's Works; but from the prevalent *neglect of the noblest study of all*, —viz. *the study of GOD's Word*. His quarrel is not with the Professors of Natural Science, but with those who are mere *Pretenders* to it. Moreover, he makes no secret of his displeasure at the undue importance which has of late been claimed for Natural Science; and which is sufficiently implied by the prevalent fashion of naming it without any distinguishing epithet,—as "Science," absolutely: just as if *Theology* were not a Science also[b]!

It is not necessary to speak particularly of the contents of the next two Sermons; except to say that the train of thought thus started conducted the author inevitably over ground which was already occupied in the public mind by a volume which had already

---

[a] The reader is invited to refer to the passages cited in the present volume, at pp. lxxxvii. and lxxxviii.

[b] See p. 47 to p. 50. Also Appendix (B.)

obtained some notoriety, and which has since become altogether infamous. Enough of the contents of that unhappy production I had read to be convinced that in a literary, certainly in a *Theological* point of view, it was a most worthless performance; and I recognized with equal sorrow and alarm that it was but the matured expression of opinions which had been fostering for years in certain quarters: opinions which, occasionally, had been ventilated from the University pulpit; or which had been deliberately advocated in print[e]; and which it was now hinted were formidably maintained, and would be found hard to answer. Astonished, (not by any means for the first time in my life,) at the apathy which seemed to prevail on questions of such vital moment, I determined at all events not to be a party to a craven silence; and denounced from the University pulpit with hearty indignation that whole system of unbelief, (if system it can be called,) which has been growing up for years among us[d]; and which, I was and am convinced, must be openly met,—not silently ignored until the mischief

---

[e] In illustration of what is meant, may be particularized a highly objectionable Sermon which Dr. Temple preached before the University some years ago, and which occasioned no small offence to many who heard it,—as all in Oxford well remember. It was almost as unsound as the same writer's Essay "On the Education of the World," which, to the best of my remembrance, it strongly resembled.—A printed Sermon by Dr. Temple may also be referred to, "preached on Act-Sunday, July 1, 1860, before the University of Oxford, during the Meeting of the British Association," entitled "*The present Relations of Science to Religion.*"—Professor Jowett's handling of the Doctrine of the Atonement, needs only to be referred to.

[d] Page 80 to 82.

becomes unmanageable: met, too, by building up men in THE TRUTH: above all, by giving Theological instruction to those who are destined to become Professors of Theological Science, and are about to undertake the cure of souls. . . . . In this spirit, I asserted the opposite fundamental verities; and so, would have been content to dismiss the "Essays and Reviews" from my thoughts for ever.

But in the meantime, the respectability of the authors of that volume had attracted to their work an increasing share of notice. An able article in the 'Westminster Review' first aroused public attention. A still abler in the 'Quarterly' awoke the Church to a sense of the enormity of the offence which had been committed. It was not that *danger* was apprehended. There could be but one opinion as to the essential impotence of the attack. But the circumstances which aroused public indignation were twofold. First,— Here was a *conspiracy* against the Faith. Seven Critics had *avowedly combined* "to illustrate the advantage derivable to the cause of Religious and Moral Truth from a free handling, in a becoming spirit, of" what they were pleased to characterize as "subjects peculiarly liable to suffer by the repetition of conventional language, and from traditional modes of treatment[e]." They prefixed to their joint labours the expression of a "hope that their volume would be received as an attempt" to do this. That their allusion was to the Creeds, Articles, Book of Common Prayer and Administration of the Sacraments,—was obvious. Equally obvious was the *un*-becoming spirit, the arro-

[e] "To the Reader," prefixed to *Essays and Reviews*.

gance and the hostility,—with which all those sacred things were handled by those seven writers.

Secondly,—"Essays and Reviews" attracted notice because six of its authors were *Ministers of the Church of England.* Here were six Clergymen openly making light of their sacred profession, and apparently worse than regardless of their Ordination vows. As an infidel but certainly in this instance most truthful as well as able Reviewer, remarked concerning the work in question,—"In their ordinary, if not plain sense, there has been discarded the Word of GOD, the Creation, the Fall, the Redemption, Justification, Regeneration, and Salvation, Miracles, Inspiration, Prophecy, Heaven and Hell, Eternal punishment and a Day of Judgment, Creeds, Liturgies, and Articles, the truth of Jewish History and of Gospel narrative; a sense of doubt thrown over even the Incarnation, the Resurrection, and Ascension, the Divinity of the Second Person, and the personality of the Third. It may be that this is a *true* view of Christianity; but we insist, in the name of common sense, that it is a *new* view. Surely it is waste of time to argue that it is agreeable to Scripture, and not contrary to the Canons'!"

' 'Neo-Christianity' in the *Westminster Review,* No. 36.—How true is what follows:—"The Bible is one; and it is too late now to propose to divide it. We shall only point out that *the moral value of the Gospel teaching becomes suspicious* when the whole miraculous element is discarded.

"We certainly do think that the Gospels assert a miraculous Incarnation, Resurrection, and Ascension; and that the Epistles teach Original Sin, and a vicarious Sacrifice. If this be doubted by our authors, it is sufficient for us to say that such is the impression they have created on all ages of Christians."

"We desire that if the Bible, or any part of it be retained as

This twofold phenomenon, which has shocked the public conscience and perplexed common sense, has been *the sole* cause of the amount of attention "Essays and Reviews" has excited. Laymen might have combined to produce this volume, almost unheeded. An obscure Clergyman might possibly have published any one of these seven papers; and with a rebuke for his immorality or his insolence, he would probably have been unnoticed by the world. But here is a combination of Doctors of Divinity; Professors; Fel-

Holy Writ, it be defended as a miraculous gift to Man, and not by distorting the principles of modern Science. Let the Essayists be assured that there exists *no middle course;* that there is no Inspiration more than is natural, yet not supernatural; *no Theology which can abandon its doctrines and retain its authority."*

Lastly, with what sickening and almost Satanic power, does the same writer invite the Essayists and Reviewers to make shipwreck of their souls in the following terrible passage. And yet, who sees not that *on their principles* absolute and professed unbelief is *inevitable?* He says:—"How long shall this last? Until men have the courage to bury their dead convictions out of sight, and the greater courage to form new. All honour to these writers for the boldness with which they have, at great risk, urged their opinions. *But what is wanted is strength* not merely to face the world, but *to face one's own conclusions.* We know the cost. It must be endured. Let each who has thought and felt for himself, ask himself first what he *does not* believe, and then, if wise or needful, avow it. Next let him ask himself what he *does* believe, and pursue it to its true and full conclusions. Neither loose accommodation nor sonorous principles will long give them rest. It is of as little use to surrender the more glaring contradictions of Science as it is to evaporate discredited doctrine into a few vague precepts. That end will not be attained by our authors by subliming Religion into an emotion, and making an armistice with Science. It will not be obtained by any unreal adaptation; *nor by this, which is, of all recent adaptations,* at once the most able, the most earnest, and *the most suicidal."*

lows, nay Heads of Colleges; Instructors of England's Youth; Teachers of Religion; Chaplains to Royal and noble personages!

The Jesuitical notice prefixed to the book, (deprecating the idea that its authors should be held responsible, except severally for their several articles,) completed the scandal. As if seven men, each armed with his own appropriate weapon of violence, breaking into a house, and spreading ruin around them, could "readily be understood," (to quote their own language,) to incur each a limited responsibility! . . . . . Charity doubtless would have rejoiced to spread her mantle over any one or more of the number, "who, on seeing the extravagantly vicious manner in which some of his associates had performed their part, had openly declared his disgust and abhorrence of such unfaithfulness, and had withdrawn his name[g],"—with some expression of sorrow for the irreparable mischief which he had actively helped to occasion. But long before *nine* editions of "Essays and Reviews" had appeared, it became apparent that each of the living authors, (for one, alas, has already gone to his account!) has made himself responsible for the *whole* work[h]. Nay, there are some of the number who

---

[g] The Bishop of Exeter to Dr. Temple.

[h] The Bishop of Manchester exactly expressed the general opinion, when he said,—"Nor will I for a single moment, however my personal feelings might interfere, conceal my deliberate conviction that every partner in that work is equally guilty."—(*Guardian*, Ap. 10, 1861, p. 341.) But the most faithful language of all came from the Bishop of Exeter in his crushing reply to an inquiry put to him by Dr. Temple. "I avow that I hold every one of the seven persons acting together for such an object to be alike re-

make no secret of their satisfaction at what has happened; and seem desirous only that their volume should obtain a yet wider circulation[1].

"Essays and Reviews," as already stated, with the turn of the year, experienced a vast increase of notoriety. The entire Bench of Bishops condemned the book; and both Houses of Convocation endorsed the Episcopal censure. A very careful perusal of the volume became necessary; and it proved to be infinitely weaker in point of ability, infinitely more fatal in point of intention, than could have been suspected from the known respectability and position of its authors. A clamour also arose for a Reply to these Seven Champions,—not exactly of Christendom.

---

sponsible for the several acts of every individual among them in executing their avowed common purpose."

[1] A letter from Dr. Rowland Williams, which has appeared in the newspapers, contains the following language with reference to the American reprint of "Essays and Reviews:"—"I confess myself personally gratified that my own work, and that of my far more distinguished coadjutors, with whom it is sufficient honour for me to be included in the same volume, should have obtained the honour of a reprint in another hemisphere. Still more would I hail the circumstance as an auspicious token of the sympathy which should prevail between kindred nations, as regards subjects of the highest import, and as a sign of the prospects of Christian freedom beyond the Atlantic. . . . .

"I have not yet discovered any community or individual possessing the right to cast the first stone at those who interpret the Bible in freedom, and who subordinate its letter to its spirit, or its parts to its whole. Even if Holy Scripture were, as is popularly fancied, the foundation,—and not, as I believe, the expression and the memorial,—of Religious Truth in man, it would be absurd to render it honours essentially different from those which it claims for itself, or to make it a master, where it claims only to be a servant."

"You *condemn:* but why do you not *reply?*"—became quite a popular form of reproach.

It was useless to urge, in private, such considerations as the following:—To reply to a volume of 433 pages, each of which contains a fallacy or a falsity,—while some pages are packed full of both,—is a serious undertaking.—Besides, the book *has been* replied to already; for there is scarcely an objection urged within its pages which was not better urged, and effectually disposed of, in the last century. Nay, every good Review of "Essays and Reviews" has *answered* the book: for what signify the details, if the fundamental lie has been detected, and unrelentingly exposed? The man who plants his heel on the serpent's head, and refuses to withdraw it, can afford to disregard the tortuous writhings of the long supple body.—Again. These attacks are seven. Must seven men *with* "concert and comparison,"—with leisure and inclination too,—be procured to *demolish* this flimsy compound of dogmatism and unbelief? to disperse these cloudy doubts, and to analyse and repel these many ambiguous statements?—Once more. A fool can assert, and in a moment, that 'There is no God.' But it requires a wise man to refute the lie; and his refutation will probably demand a volume.—I say, it was in vain to urge such considerations as these. "Why does no one *reply* to these 'Essays and Reviews?'" was asked,—till, I apprehend, pens enough have been unsheathed to do the work effectually.

It struck me, in the meantime, that I should be employing myself not unprofitably at such a juncture, if (laying aside all other work for a month or two)

I were to attempt a short reply to the volume in question, myself; and to combine it with the publication of the Sermons I had already preached; and which I had the comfort of learning had not only been favourably received by some of those who heard them, but had attracted some slight notice outside the University also. Accordingly, with not a little reluctance, in the month of February I began. The *Destructive* part of the argument, I determined to address to the younger members of my own College,—men with whom I live in daily intimacy, and on terms of private friendship; and whom, above all, I desired to protect against the influence of that "moral poison," (as the Bishop of Exeter describes it,) of which the world has lately heard so much. The *Constructive* part of the argument, I resolved to complete as opportunities might offer, in my Sermons. One such opportunity presented itself early in Lent; of which I availed myself to establish some fundamental truths relative to the Interpretation of Holy Writ[k]. By favour of the Vice Chancellor, the promise of yet another preaching turn was obtained. It appeared best to avail myself of the opportunity to consider the chief objections which have been brought against the Bible from the *marvellous* character of some of its contents[l]. An University Sermon preached exactly ten years ago, (on the Doctrine of Accommodation,) supplied an important link in the argument. . . . Thus the unscientific shape in which the present volume appears, is explained; and its want of exact method is accounted for. Let me add, that but for

[k] Serm. V.   [l] See Sermon VII.

the forward state of what I like to regard as the *Constructive* part of the present volume,—(and which I am not without a humble hope will secure for the rest a more than ephemeral interest,)—I should have been slow indeed to undertake the distasteful task of answering a work of which I have long since been heartily weary.

II. And now, for a few words on the general question which has called out these "Sermons" and "Preliminary Remarks."

At the root of the whole mischief of these last days lies *disbelief in the Bible* as *the Word of God.* This is the fundamental error. Dangerous enough is it to the moral and intellectual nature of Man, when the authority of the Church is doubted: or rather, this is *the first* downward step. Not to believe that CHRIST bequeathed to His Church a Divine form of polity: not to believe that He set officers over His Kingdom, of which He is Himself the sole invisible Head: not to believe that He invested His Apostles with authority to delegate to others the Commission He had Himself conveyed to them; and that, by virtue of such transmitted powers, the Church has authority in the Ministration of GOD's Word and Sacraments: not to believe that He vouchsafed to His Church extraordinary guidance at the first, and that He vouchsafes to His Church effectual guidance still:—an utter want of faith in the Church and her Ordinances, is the first step, I repeat, in a soul's downward progress.

Next comes an impatience of Creeds. It has been falsely asserted by an Essayist and Reviewer that

"Constantine inaugurated the principle of doctrinal limitation ᵐ;" by which is meant that definitions of Faith date from the Council of Nicæa, A.D. 325: the truth being that the famous Œcumenical Council which was then held did but rule the consubstantiality of the SON with the FATHER: whereas elaborate Creeds exist of a far earlier date; as all are aware. Creeds indeed are coeval with Christianity itselfⁿ. What need to add that when the decree of the first Œcumenical Council concerning the true faith in the adorable Trinity has been set at nought, all other decisions of the Church are disregarded also?

That marvellous concrete fact, the Bible,—has next to be encountered. Unmethodical as it seems to be, the Bible arrests a man in his impatient course with many a significant History,—many an unmanageable precept. Much of its contents, it is true, are of such a nature that they may be glossed over,—explained away,—ignored,—set aside. The reading is doubtful: or there are two opinions, (perhaps twenty,) concerning it: or the language may be figurative: or the words are not to be pressed too closely: or a perverse logic may pretend to find in it agreeable confirmation, instead of stern reproof. Not a few places there are, however, which defy any such handling; stubborn rocks which refuse to yield a single trace of the wished-for vegetation, in return for the most determined husbandry. Nothing of the kind ever will or can be made to germinate upon them. They are absolutely unmanageable, and hopelessly in the way of the man who is determined to cast off restraint,—

ᵐ *Essays and Reviews*, p. 166.   ⁿ See p. clxxvii. to p. clxxxiii.

whether spiritual, intellectual, or moral. He is for being lawless; or at least, without law: but *the Bible* is unmistakably *an external Law*, and is opposed to him. The Bible is his enemy, and the Bible claims to be Divine. . . . What need to state that to deny the Inspiration of the Bible, and to undermine its authority, and to explain away its statements, becomes the next object of the unbeliever? It is precisely at this stage of his downward progress that public attention is excited, and public indignation aroused. The Church, (like its Divine Author,) may be outraged, and few will be found to remonstrate. The Creeds may be assailed, (especially "one unhappy Creed!"), and it is hinted that these are speculative matters, on which none should pronounce too dogmatically. But (thank GOD!) Englishmen yet love their Bible; and Common Sense is able to see that an uninspired Bible is *no Bible at all*. At the assault upon the Bible, therefore, as I said, an indignant outcry is raised,—as *now*.

Systematically to cope with such irreverence, such entire ignorance rather of all the questions at issue, from the pulpit, would be clearly impracticable. Men require to be taught "which be the first principles." They require to be educated in Divinity. And thus we come back to the fontal source of all the mischief of our own Day. We, in Oxford, give no systematic training to our Candidates for Holy Orders. We do not even attempt it. Nay, incredible to relate, *we do not give them any training at all.* And the fatal consequences of this omission are to be seen on every side. A youth no sooner gets through "the Schools," and graduates in Arts, than he inquires for a Curacy. During the three months, perhaps six, of interval, he makes himself sufficiently acquainted with the Alphabet of Divinity to enable him to satisfy the very modest requirements of the Bishop's examination; after which he finds himself at once actively engaged in the Bishopric of souls and the profession of Theology. It is probable that the realities of the Ministerial calling, and the eminently practical nature of such an one's daily life, will keep *this* man from error. Not so his—more, shall I say, or less?—fortunate fellow-student; who, by hard self-relying labour, having obtained distinction in the Schools, finds himself in the enjoyment of a fellowship, and straightway engages in the work of tuition. This man, whose fellowship is his "title" for orders, studies Divinity, or neglects it, at pleasure: and if he studies it, he studies it in his own way. He has read a little of heathen Ethics with great care; or he has trained himself to the exactness of mathematical inference. With the purest idiom of ancient Greece he has also made himself very familiar. He is besides a Master of Arts. What need to add that such an one is not therefore a Master of *Divinity?* possesses no qualification which authorizes him to dogmatize about any one department of *Theological Science?*

The plain truth is, (and it is really better to speak plainly,)—the plain truth is, that the offensive Sermons one sometimes hears from the University pulpit, —the offensive Essays and Reviews which have lately occasioned so much public scandal,—are the work of men who discuss that which they do not understand;

profess that which they were never, at any time of their life, taught. Their method of handling a text is altogether unique and extraordinary. Their remarks concerning Divine things are even puerile. Their very citations of Scripture are incorrect. Their cool affectation of superiority of knowledge, their claim to intellectual power, would be laughable, were the subject less solemn and important. Speculations so feeble that they sound like the cries of an infant in the dark, are insinuated to be the sublime views of a bold and original thinker, who "*has by a Divine help been enabled to plant his foot somewhere beyond the waves of Time!*"—Doubts so badly expressed that they read like the confused utterance of one in his sleep, claim to be regarded as the legacy of one who is about to "*depart hence before the natural term, worn out with intellectual toil*°*!*" ... In a word,—Men who have never been taught and trained, but have grown up in a miserable self-evolved system of their own,—(with a little of Hegel, and a little of Schleiermacher, and a little of Strauss,)—cannot *but* trouble the peace of the Church. They deny her authority. (They are not aware of her claims.) They cavil at her Creeds. (They are not acquainted with their history.) They doubt the authenticity of the very Bible. (They know wondrous little about it.)—How did the Bible attain its actual shape? They cannot tell. How has it been guarded? They are careless to inquire. How does it come to us as 'the Bible,'—*the* Book of all books? It is best not to discuss a question which must infallibly bring forward *the Church* as "a wit-

° Mr. Jowett in *Essays and Reviews*, p. 433.

ness and a keeper of Holy Writ[p]." Men are even impatient to publish their private prejudice that it is to be interpreted like any other book; that it is inspired in no other sense than Sophocles and Plato. "The principle of private judgment," (it is said,) "puts Conscience between us and the Bible, making Conscience *the supreme interpreter*[q]." "Hence," it is said, "we use the Bible,—some consciously, some unconsciously,—not to override, but to evoke the voice of Conscience." (p. 44.) "The Book of this Law," (as Hooker phrases it,) is dethroned; and Man usurps the vacant seat, and becomes a Law unto himself! God Himself is dethroned, in effect; and Man becomes his own god.

To cope systematically with all this from the University pulpit, as already remarked, is plainly impossible. The preacher must take up the question at some definite stage, and arrest the false teachers *there*. "That wicked,"—or rather "THE LAWLESS ONE," (ὁ ἄνομος, as he is called in 2 Thess. ii. 8,)—must be bound, hand and foot, *somewhere* in his career of lawlessness; and in these Sermons *the threshold of the Bible* has been chosen as the place for the conflict. My life for his life. I will slay or be slain on the very portal of Holy Scripture. With the young, you begin at the beginning,—"the Creed, the Lord's Prayer, the Ten Commandments;" and they must be further instructed in the Church Catechism. But the foundation cannot be laid afresh with the full-grown. It is idle to talk about the authority of *the Church* to men who do not believe in the Bible. It is useless

---

[p] Article XX.   [q] *Essays and Reviews*, p. 45.

to dispute about Creeds with men who know nothing of the origin and history of Christianity. Reserving the *true* method of teaching for those who alone are capable of being taught, we are constrained to argue with men of full age about *the Inspiration and Interpretation of the Bible.*—If in the ensuing Sermons the principles handled are so very elementary, it is because the available limits were so very narrow,—while the field over which Unbelief has spread itself, is so very broad.

III. When a few words have been added concerning the manner in which I have executed my task, this Preface shall be brought to a close.—If the style of the present SERMONS,—considering the auditory, and above all considering the subject, — shall be thought by competent judges not sufficiently dignified in parts, I will bow to their decision without remonstrance. Everybody can divine the defence which would be set up; but perhaps it may not be quite a valid defence. A man feels strongly and warmly; writes fast and freely; is determined to be clearly understood: is weary of the dignified conventionalities under which Scepticism loves to conceal itself when it comes abroad. Perhaps some expressions which may be permitted in delivery, ought to be remodelled when a Sermon is sent to the press.

But with regard to the ensuing PRELIMINARY REMARKS, I shall not so easily be persuaded to think that I am mistaken as to the style in which Essayists and Reviewers are to be dealt with[r]. Some respect-

---

[r] It should perhaps be stated that the edition of "Essays and Reviews" which I have employed is *the Third* (1860.)

able persons, I doubt not, will think my treatment of them harsh and uncharitable. I invite them to consider that we do not expect blasphemy from Ministers of the Gospel,—irreligion from the teachers of youth, —infidelity from the Professor's chair: nor are we called upon to tolerate it either. I have the misfortune to concur entirely with the verdict pronounced by the Bishop of Exeter on the subject of 'Essays and Reviews.' Let those who feel little jealousy for GOD's honour measure out in grains their censure of a volume, the confessed tendency of which is to sap the foundation of Faith, and to introduce irreligion with a flood-tide. Such shall not, at all events, be *my* method. Private regard, if it is to weigh largely with him who stands up for GOD's Truth, should first have weighed a little with those by whom it has been most grievously outraged. It may suit these Authors to wrap up their shameful meaning in a cloud of words; but their Reviewer avails himself of that Christian liberty to which they themselves so systematically lay claim, mercilessly to uncover their baseness, and uncompromisingly to denounce it. If I may declare my mind freely, punctilious courtesy in dealing with such opinions, becomes a species of treason against Him after whose Name we are called, and whom we profess to serve. Seven men may combine to handle the things of GOD, it seems, in the most outrageous manner; while *themselves* are to be the objects of consideration, tenderness, respect! I cannot see their title to any consideration at all.

It will be found, it is hoped, that when these writers have the courage to descend to argument, *there* I have gladly met them on their own ground, and sought to refute them: but *to reason* is no part of their plan. Unsupported dicta on every subject on which they treat: doubts promiscuously insinuated, but never once openly and honestly maintained: cool assumptions of intellectual superiority for themselves and their infidel allies: contemptuous allusions to the names which the respectable part of mankind agrees to hold in honour: foul imputations against the honesty of the Clergy:—*this* is all their method! The favourite *cant* of these writers is, that no one should shrink from free discussion, or fear the results of Criticism. Why then do not they themselves criticize? Why do not *they* reason? Charity herself after weighing these Essays carefully has no alternative but to assume that the Authors either have not the courage, or that they lack the ability, to descend to a free discussion, and risk all on a stand-up fight. A kind of guerilla warfare: half a dozen arrows, and a hasty retreat: *such* is their mode of attack! But this method, though it may occasion annoyance, is quite unworthy of an honest inquirer, and never can be decisive of anything. It is the cowardly expedient of men who shrink from scrutiny, and dread exposure. Nothing so easy, for example, as to repeat the old commonplace about "irreconcileable discrepancies" in the "Synoptical Gospels:" but why, instead, are we not told, *which these irreconcileable discrepancies are?* For my own part, I freely renew in this place the challenge I gave in my IIIrd Sermon[a]. Let any one of these Gentlemen publicly and definitely lay his

[a] pp. 72-3.

finger on one or more of these contradictory statements in the Gospels, during term-time; and within a week I hereby undertake publicly to refute him in the Divinity School of this University : and our peers shall be our judges.

Gentlemen who come abroad in the fashion above described, have no right to complain if they encounter rough usage on the road. When Critics are clamorous for the "free handling" of Divine Truth, they must not be surprised to find themselves freely handled too. If free discussion is to be the order of the day, then let there be free discussion of " Essays and Reviews," *as well as of* THE BIBLE. Six Clergymen of the Church of England who enter upon a crusade against the Faith of the Church of England must not be astonished if they are looked upon in the light of immoral characters, and treated as such. Accordingly, I have handled *them* just as freely as *they* have handled the Prophets, Apostles, and Evangelists of CHRIST.

I cannot therefore pretend to offer anything in extenuation of the style in which I have examined the statements of these Essayists and Reviewers. Perfectly sensible as I am of the gracefulness of highly courteous language in controversial writing, I will not so far violate my own conviction of what is right as to bandy compliments on such an occasion as *this*. This is no literary misunderstanding, or I could have been amicable enough : no private or personal matter, or I could have flung it from me with unconcern. No other than an attempt to destroy Man's dearest hopes, is this infamous book : no other than an insult, the grossest imaginable, offered to the Majesty of Heaven; an attack, the more foul because it is so insidious, against the Everlasting Gospel of JESUS CHRIST. In such a cause I will *not* so far give in to the smooth fashion of a supple and indifferent age, as to pay these seven writers a single compliment which they will care to accept. The most foolish composition of the seven is Dr. Temple's; the most mischievous is Professor Jowett's: but the germ of the last Essay is contained in the first; the foolishness of the first Essay is abundantly shared by the last: while the evidence of correspondence of sentiment between the two writers is unmistakable. The most unphilosophical Essay, (where *all* are unphilosophical,) is Professor Powell's: the most insolent, Dr. Williams': the most immoral, Mr. Wilson's: the most shallow, Mr. Goodwin's; the most irrelevant, Mr. Pattison's. Not one of these writers shews himself capable of recognizing the true logical result of his own opinions: of drawing from his own premisses their one inevitable issue. Not one of them has had the manliness to *speak out*, and to *say plainly* what he means. They seem to deny the Divinity of CHRIST, and the Personality of the HOLY GHOST: but how reluctant is a reader to believe that they really *mean* it! Quite inevitable is it that these clerical critics must choose between two alternatives. Either they hold opinions which make it impossible that they should retain Orders in the Church of England, and yet be honest men; or they have expressed themselves with such culpable inaccuracy and ambiguity, as shews that they are altogether incompetent to handle the Science of Theology.—Gladly would one give them the benefit of a third alternative: but I see not that any remains.

If it should be thought strange that one thinking so meanly of 'Essays and Reviews,' should have produced a yet larger volume in reply to them, it must suffice to point out that the refutation of a fallacy is almost of necessity the ampler writing.—Or again, if it be remarked that by far the largest part of what I have written is directed against the hundred pages of Professor Jowett, the explanation is still obvious. For not only does that concluding Essay of his bring to a terribly practical issue the speculative doubts and difficulties which had been started by all his predecessors; (namely, doubts as to (1) the relation in which the Bible stands to Man;—(2) the nature of Prophecy;—(3) the reality of Miracles;—(4) the worth of Creeds and formularies;—(5) the authenticity of Genesis;—(6) the basis on which Revelation is by the Church of England supposed to rest;)—by proposing that we should henceforth regard the Bible as a book *no otherwise inspired than Sophocles and Plato:* —not only does Professor Jowett's essay discharge this fatal office; but his style is somewhat peculiar; and what he says, cannot always be effectually disposed of by a few words. Let me explain.

There is a certain form of fallacy of statement in which this Gentleman's writings abound, which calls aloud for notice and signal reprobation. He has a marvellous aptitude, (one would fain hope through some intellectual infirmity,) of connecting together in the same sentence two or three clauses; one or two of which shall be true as Heaven, while the other is false as Hell. The reply to such a sentence is impossible, without many words,—far more than Mr. Jowett's sentences commonly deserve.—Sometimes he strings together several heads of thought; of which enumeration the kindest thing which can be said is that it betrays an utter want of intellectual perspective. To unravel even a part of this tangled web so as to expose its argumentative worthlessness, soon fills a page. .... But there is another kind of fallacy which the same gentleman wields with immense effect, and in the use of which he is a great master; which, because it was absolutely impossible to handle it fitly in the proper place, shall be briefly adverted to, here. I proceed to describe it not without indignation; for I am profoundly struck by the intellectual perversity, not to say the moral obliquity, which has so entirely made this vile instrument its own.

The fallacy then is of this nature. When Professor Jowett would put forth something especially deserving of reprehension,—some sentiment or opinion which he either knows, or ought to know, that the whole Church will resent with unqualified abhorrence,—he assumes a plaintive manner, and puts himself into an interesting attitude; sometimes even folds his hands, as if in prayer. He then begins by (1) throwing out a remark of real beauty, and so conciliating for himself an indulgent hearing; or (2) he goes off on some Moral question, and so defeats attention; or (3) he delivers himself of some undeniable truth, and so disarms censure; or (4) he says something of an entirely equivocal kind, and so leaves his reader at fault. Candour, of course, gives him the benefit of the doubt.

It is not till the sentence is well advanced, or till it is examined by the fatal light of its context, that one is shewn what the ambiguous writer really was intending. A cloven foot appears at last; but it is instantly withdrawn, with a shuffle; and you experience a scowl or a sneer, as the case may be, for your extreme unkindness in inquiring whether it was not a cloven foot you saw?..... Meanwhile, the learned Professor has gone off *in alia omnia*, with a look of earnestness which challenges respect, and a vagueness of diction which at once discourages pursuit and defeats inquiry. The fish invariably ends by disappearing in a cloud of his own ink.

It shall suffice to have said thus much. These pages must now be suffered to go forth; not without a hearty aspiration that a blessing may attend them from Him *sine Quo nihil est validum, nihil sanctum;* and that what was intended for the strength and help of those who want helping and strengthening, (I am thinking particularly of what has been offered on the subject of Inspiration,) may not prove misleading or perplexing to any.

Oriel, June 24*th,* 1861.

CONTENTS.

DEDICATION.

PREFACE. I. Some account of the present Volume.
II. Growth of irreligious Opinion.
III. 'Essayists and Reviewers' to be as 'freely-handled' as the Prophets, Evangelists, and Apostles of CHRIST.

TABLE OF CONTENTS.

PRELIMINARY REMARKS ON "ESSAYS AND REVIEWS."   PAGE
   I. Examination of the contribution of Rev. F. Temple, D.D.   ii
  II. . . . Rev. Rowland Williams, D.D. .   xxx
 III. . . . Rev. Professor Baden Powell, M.A.   xlvi
 IV. . . . Rev. H. B. Wilson, M.A. . .   lxiv
  V. . . . C. W. Goodwin, M.A. . . .   lxxxvi
 VI. . . . Rev. Mark Pattison, B.D. . .   cxii
VII. . . . Rev. Professor Jowett, M.A. . .   cxxxix

  In what sense Mr. Jowett's fundamental principle, (that "Scripture is to be interpreted like any other book,") may be cheerfully accepted   cxl

  Mr. Jowett's main assertion that "Scripture has one and only one true meaning," shewn to be founded on his assumption that the Bible is *uninspired*,— "like any other book"   cxlii

  1. Eight Characteristics of the Bible enumerated, which shew that it is *unlike* "any other book" . .   cl

  But the distinctive characteristic of the Bible, is, that *it professes to be the work of the* HOLY GHOST .   clx

  Mr. Jowett's syllogism corrected, in consequence . .   clxii

  2. Mr. Jowett's proposal accepted, that we should "Interpret Scripture from itself." Notion of *Interpretation* obtained from the volume of *Inspiration* .   clxii

  3. In addition to the testimony of Scripture, we have to consider the testimony of Antiquity . . .   clxix

  Remarks on primitive Patristic Interpretation . .   clxx

  This part of the subject misunderstood by Mr. Jowett .   clxxiii

Remarks on primitive Tradition.—The Creeds, the records of Primitive Christianity clxxvii
This part of the subject also misunderstood by Mr. Jowett . clxxix
4. Examination of some of Mr. Jowett's reasons for rejecting that method of Interpretation which has been (α) Established by our Lord; (β) Employed by His Apostles; (γ) Universally adopted by the primitive Church; and (δ) Accepted by the most learned and judicious of modern Commentators . . . clxxxvi
The peroration of Mr. Jowett's Essay examined and commented on ccvi
Retrospect of the entire subject ccxvi
Conclusion ccxxvii

SERMON I.

St. John vi. 68. *Lord, to whom shall we go? Thou hast the words of Eternal Life.*

THE STUDY OF THE BIBLE RECOMMENDED; AND A METHOD OF STUDYING IT DESCRIBED.

The Gospel, as a written message, meets with the same reception at the hands of the World now, as in the days of the Son of Man 1
Some points of analogy between the Written and the Incarnate Word 2
Difficulties and seeming contradictions in the Gospel . . 3
Unattractive aspect.—Union of the Human and Divine . . 4
The Bible is generally little read.—Its preciousness . . 6
The age unlearned as well as unfaithful 7
Want of preparation for the Ministry.—The question of preparation narrowed to the duty of studying the Bible . . 8
Conditions of successful Study:—a fixed time for reading the Bible, and a fixed quantity to be read 9
Vigilance, and independent inquiry 10
Consecutive reading.—The first chapter of Genesis . . . 11
Nothing to be skipped.—Result of such a method . . 12
The Bible is to be read, not in the same manner, but with at least the same attention, as a merely human work . . 13
A caution 14
Men not competent to make their own Religion out of the Bible 16
The advantages of such a study of the Bible as has been here recommended, explained 17

SERMON II.

HEBREWS xi. 3. *Through Faith, we understand that the worlds were framed by the Word of GOD.*

NATURAL SCIENCE AND THEOLOGICAL SCIENCE.

	PAGE
Special act of Faith assigned to ourselves in Hebrews xi.	23
The first Chapter of Genesis considered: Verse 1	24
Province of Geology	26
The Work of the First Day	28
——————— Second and the Third Day	29
——————— Fourth and the Fifth Day	30
——————— Sixth Day	31
The Mosaic History of the Creation true	33
Objections considered	34
Speech ascribed to GOD	35
Adam's knowledge	36
The first pair.—The days of Creation real days	37
Objections of pretenders to Natural Science	39
The plea that the Bible is not a scientific book	40
The historical truth of the Bible insisted upon	44
Natural Science not undervalued	46
The term "Science" not to be opposed to "Theology"	47
Theology the Queen of Sciences	48

SERMON III.

2 TIM. iii. 16. *All Scripture is given by inspiration of GOD.*

INSPIRATION OF SCRIPTURE. — GOSPEL DIFFICULTIES. — THE WORD OF GOD INFALLIBLE.—OTHER SCIENCES SUBORDINATE TO THEOLOGICAL SCIENCE.

	PAGE
The meaning of 2 Tim. iii. 16.	53
St. Paul nowhere disclaims Inspiration	54
Holy Scripture is attributed in Scripture to the HOLY GHOST	56
Forms of unbelief concerning Inspiration	57
Impertinence of the modern way of speaking of the Evangelists	60
Supposed inaccuracies, slips of memory, misstatements	61
The Gospels not *four* but *One*	62
A principle laid down for the reconcilement of all Gospel difficulties	63

CONTENTS.

	PAGE
Illustration from a supposed case of testimony	64
Computation of the hours in St. John's Gospel	66
The accounts of the blind man restored to sight at Jericho, harmonized	67
Characteristics of an Inspired narrative	68
The mention of "Jeremy the prophet," and of Cyrenius, considered	70
Faultlessness of the Gospel	72
Absurdity of the common allegations against it	73
The absolute Infallibility of Scripture maintained	74
Every syllable of Holy Scripture inspired	75
The nature of Inspiration illustrated	76
Theology, the noblest of the Sciences	79
Insubordination in these last days of Physical Science	80
The infidel spirit of the Age, protested against	81
Theological Science can never be called upon to give way before Physical Science	83
Relations of Morals to Theology	84
Conscience and the Moral Sense have been informed afresh by Revelation	87

SERMON IV.

St. John xvii. 17. *Thy Word is Truth.*

THE PLENARY INSPIRATION OF EVERY PART OF THE BIBLE, VINDICATED AND EXPLAINED.—NATURE OF INSPIRATION.— THE TEXT OF SCRIPTURE.

	PAGE
Cavils against the Bible	92
Absolute infallibility of every 'jot' and every 'tittle' of Holy Scripture	94
The popular view of Inspiration stated	95
No middle state between Inspiration and non-inspiration	96
The popular theory applied and tested	96
A different view of the nature and office of Inspiration stated	100
Inspiration still the same, however diverse the subject-matter	102
What is meant by 'a Prophet'	104
The message still God's, whatever its nature may be	106
Note of Inspiration in the Historical Books of the Bible	108
The Title on the Cross	109
Remonstrance	110

CONTENTS. xxxv

	PAGE
Theories of Inspiration to be rejected	115
Remarks on the nature of Inspiration	116
Proof that men generally hold that *the words* of Scripture are inspired	117
Absolute irrelevancy of objections drawn from *the state of the Text* of Scripture	118
The Substance of Scripture inseparable from the Form	120
Antichristian spirit of the age	121
The Study of Scripture in a childlike spirit recommended	122

SUPPLEMENT TO SERMON IV.

	PAGE
A favourite view of Inspiration stated	126
Vagueness of this theory	127
The theory practically tested, and found unmanageable	128
Further examination of the theory	132
Our SAVIOUR's reasoning as difficult as that of St. Paul	134

SERMON V.

ST. MATTHEW iv. 4. *It is written, Man shall not live by bread alone, but by every word that proceedeth out of the mouth of GOD.*

INTERPRETATION OF HOLY SCRIPTURE.—INSPIRED INTERPRETATION.—THE BIBLE IS NOT TO BE INTERPRETED LIKE ANY OTHER BOOK.—GOD, (NOT MAN,) THE REAL AUTHOR OF THE BIBLE.

	PAGE
Interpretation described	140
Three sources of Interpretation compared	141
Eusebius on "the Captain of the LORD's Host"	143
The principle must be ascertained, on which Inspiration is to be conducted	144
How this is to be done	145
This question may not be needlessly encumbered with difficulties	147
The HOLY SPIRIT's method of Interpretation must be the *true* method	148
Specimens of Inspired Interpretation	149
The very narrative of Scripture mysterious	152
Divine exposition of the history of Melchizedek	152
Further proofs of the mysterious texture of Holy Scripture	156
Moses wrote concerning CHRIST	157

Two propositions established by the foregoing inquiry: (1) That the Bible is *not to be interpreted like any other book:* (2) That *the meaning of Scripture is not always only one* . 160
Scripture to be interpreted literally 160
The story of Joseph and Potiphar's wife remarked upon . 162
The Bible is the Word of God 163
Bishop Butler on Inspiration 165
Unbelief remonstrated with from the analogy of Nature and of Providence 168
How the inspired writers may be supposed to have understood what they delivered 171
The question of Interpretation not be argued on *à priori* grounds 173
Interpretation would be hopeless, but that the fountain of Inspiration is *one* 174
An apology for these Sermons 177
Exhortation to transmit the Faith 180

SERMON VI.

ROMANS x. 6—9. *But the Righteousness which is of Faith speaketh on this wise,—'Say not in thine heart, Who shall ascend into Heaven?' (that is, to bring* CHRIST *down from above:) or, 'Who shall descend into the deep?' (that is, to bring up* CHRIST *again from the dead.) But what saith it? 'The word is nigh thee, even in thy mouth, and in thine heart:' that is, the word of Faith, which we preach; that if thou shalt confess with thy mouth the* LORD JESUS, *and shalt believe in thine heart that* GOD *hath raised Him from the dead, thou shalt be saved.*

THE DOCTRINE OF ARBITRARY SCRIPTURAL ACCOMMODATION CONSIDERED.

Many insidious methods of denying the Inspiration of Scripture 184
The most subtle method of all, characterized . . . 185
The term "Accommodation" not in itself objectionable . . 187
Arbitrary Accommodation explained 188
Reasons for rejecting this theory 189
Learned research proves that the theory is gratuitous . . 190
St. Paul's exposition of a passage in Deuteronomy xxx, (Rom. x. 6 to 9,) proposed for examination 191
License of Inspired quotation 194
How the phenomenon is to be regarded 195
St. Paul's exposition examined by the light of unassisted Reason 198

	PAGE
Shewn not to be an instance of arbitrary Accommodation, but of genuine Interpretation	211
The success or failure of such inquiries, unimportant	212
No "Accommodation" when an inspired writer quotes Scripture	213
Remarks on Inspired Reasoning	215

SERMON VII.

ST. MARK xii. 24. *Do ye not therefore err, because ye know not the Scriptures, neither the power of GOD.*

THE MARVELS OF HOLY SCRIPTURE,—MORAL AND PHYSICAL.— JAEL'S DEED DEFENDED.—MIRACLES VINDICATED.

	PAGE
Sadduceeism of the day	221
The Moral and Physical Marvels of Scripture proposed for consideration	222
Moral Marvels:—Jael.—How her story is to be read	223
History of Jael. Her conduct explained and defended	224
Jacob,—the Canaanites,—Abraham,—David	230
Physical Marvels:—The greatest of those in the Old Testament are witnessed to in the New	232
Design of the quotations in Holy Scripture	234
Dr. Arnold and the Book of Daniel	235
Miracles are not to be called violations, &c. of Nature	237
Law in relation to GOD	238
An objectionable Theory of Miracles exposed	239
Bishop Butler on Miracles	240
Miracles may be pared down, but cannot be explained away	242
"Ideology" applied to the explanation of Miracles	243
Ideology explained and exposed	245
The Resurrection of CHRIST the foundation-truth of Christianity	248
False and true Charity	250
A parting Exhortation	252

APPENDIX.

	PAGE
A *Bishop Horsley on the double sense of Prophecy*	257
B *Bishop Pearson on Theological Science*	258
C *The Bible an instrument of Man's probation*	260
D *St. Stephen's statement in Acts vii. 15, 16, explained*	261

		PAGE
E	*The simplest view of Inspiration the truest and the best*	265
F	*The written and the Incarnate Word*	267
G	*The volume of the Old Testament Scriptures, indivisible*	268
I	*Remarks on Theories of Inspiration.—The 'Human Element'*	269
J	*How the Inspired Authors of the New Testament handle the writings of the Inspired Authors of the Old*	271
K	*Bishop Bull on Deuteronomy* xxx.	273
L	*Opinions of commentators concerning Accommodation*	277

Preliminary Remarks.

PRELIMINARY REMARKS

ON A VOLUME ENTITLED

"ESSAYS AND REVIEWS:"

ADDRESSED TO THE

UNDERGRADUATE MEMBERS OF ORIEL COLLEGE.

MY Friends,—I have determined to address to yourselves the present remarks; their subject, a volume which has recently obtained such a degree of notoriety that it is almost superfluous even to specify it by name.

With unfeigned reluctance do I mix myself up in this strife; but the course of events, when I first took up my pen, left me almost without an alternative. Far more reluctant should I be to seem to make yourselves the arbiters of Theological controversy. But in truth nothing is further from my present intention. As a plain matter of fact, you are called upon weekly, at St. Mary's, to listen to Sermons which indicate plainly enough the troubled state of the religious atmosphere; and which, of late, (too frequently alas!) have inevitably assumed a controversial aspect. The Sermons here published, (which form the constructive part of the present volume,) were preached expressly with an eye to *your* advantage, and were intended to warn you against (what I deemed) a very serious danger. It is only natural therefore that I should desire to address to yourselves the present remarks likewise. *You* are, naturally, objects of special solicitude to myself in this place,—you, with whom I live as among friends, and for not a few of whom I entertain a sincere affection. And in addressing you, I am not by any means inviting you to exercise your own theological judgment; for *that* would indeed be an absurd proceeding. I am simply seeking to instruct you, and to guide you with mine.

The case of " Essays and Reviews" is, in fact, altogether exceptional,—whether the respectability of its authors, the wickedness of its contents, or the reception which it has met with, is considered. That volume embodies the infidel spirit of the present day. Turn where you will, you encounter some criticism upon it. No advertizing column but contains repeated mention of its name. To ignore so flagrant a scandal to the Church, is quite impossible. I have thought it better, therefore, to encounter the danger in this straightforward way; and I proceed, without further preamble, to remark briefly on each of the Seven " Essays and Reviews," in order.

I. The feeblest essay in the volume is the first. It is not without grave concern that I transcribe the name of its amiable, and (in every relation of private life) truly excellent author,—" FREDERICK TEMPLE, D.D., Chaplain in Ordinary to the Queen; Head Master of Rugby School; Chaplain to the Earl of Denbigh." Under the imposing title of "THE EDUCATION OF THE WORLD," we are presented with a worthless allegory, which has all the faults of a schoolboy's theme, (incorrect grammar included;) and not one of the excellencies which ought to characterize the product of a ripened understanding,—the work of a Doctor of Divinity in the English Church[*].

Dr. Temple's opening speculations are at once unintelligible, irrelevant, and untrue. But they are immaterial; and serve only to lug in, (not to introduce,) the assumption that the "power, whereby the present ever gathers into itself the results of the past, transforms the human race into a colossal man whose life reaches from the Creation to the day of Judgment. The successive generations of men are days in this man's life. The discoveries and inventions which characterize the different epochs of the world's history are his works. The creeds and doctrines, the opinions and principles of the successive ages, are his thoughts." [Alas, that the Creeds and Doctrines of the Church should be spoken of by a Professor of Divinity as the "thoughts" of men!] "The state of society at different times are (*sic*) his manners.

[*] I abstain from enumerating Dr. Temple's mistakes,—for such things do not belong to the essence of a composition. And yet I must remark that it is hardly creditable in a Doctor of Divinity to write as he does. "In *all* (!) the doctrinal disputes of the fourth and fifth centuries, the decisive voice came from Rome. Every controversy was finally settled by her opinion, because she alone possessed *the art of framing formulas*," &c. (p. 16.) Would the learned writer favour us with *a single warrant* for this assertion? ... At p. 9, Dr. Temple mistakes for Micah's, words spoken 700 years before by Balaam. At p. 10, he says that "Prayer, as a regular and necessary part of worship, first appears in the later books of the Old Testament."—His account of the papacy is contained in the following words:—"Law was the lesson which Rome was intended to teach the world. Hence (?) the Bishop of Rome soon became the Head of the Church. Rome was in fact the centre of the traditions which had once governed the world; and their spirit still remained; and the Roman Church developed into the papacy simply because a head was wanted (!), and no better one could be found."—p. 16. At p. 10 we have a truly puerile misconception of the meaning of 1 Cor. xv. 56, &c., &c.

He grows in knowledge, in self-control, in visible size, just as we do. And his education is in the same way and for the same reason precisely similar to ours. All this is no figure, but only a compendious statement of a very comprehensive fact." (p. 3.) "We may then," (he repeats,) "rightly speak of a childhood, a youth, and a manhood of the world." (p. 4.) And the process of this development of the colossal man, "corresponds, stage by stage, with the process by which the infant is trained for youth, and the youth for manhood. This training has three stages. In childhood, we are subject to positive rules which we cannot understand, but are bound implicitly to obey. In youth we are subject to the influence of example, and soon break loose from all rules, unless illustrated and enforced by the higher teaching which example imparts. In manhood we are comparatively free from external restraints, and if we are to learn, must be our own instructors. First comes the Law, then the Son of Man, then the Gift of the Spirit. The world was once a child under tutors and governors until the time appointed by the Father. Then, when the fit season had arrived, the Example to which all ages should turn was sent to teach men what they ought to be. Then the human race was left to itself, to be guided by the teaching of the Spirit within." (p. 5.)—So very weak an analogy, (where everything is assumed, and nothing proved,) singular to relate, is drawn out into distressing tenuity through no less than 49 pages.

The ANSWER to all this is sufficiently obvious, as well as sufficiently damaging; and need not be delayed for a minute.

That the Human Race has made considerable progress in Knowledge, from first to last,—is a mere truism. That, in the civilized world, one generation is the heir of the generations which went before it, is what no one requires to be told. Thus the discovery of the compass, of printing, and of the steam-engine, have been epochs in human knowledge from which a start was made by all civilized nations, without retrogression. But such facts supply no warrant for transforming the whole Human Race into one Colossal Man; do not constitute any reason whatever why the 6000 years of recorded time should be divided into three periods corresponding with the Infancy, Boyhood, and Manhood of an Individual.

To this theory, however, Dr. Temple even ostentatiously commits himself. It is the purpose of his entire Essay, to establish the fanciful analogy already indicated,—which is proclaimed to be "no figure" but a "fact." (p. 3.) But an educated man of ordinary intelligence, on reaching p. 7, (where the writer first discloses his view,) summons the known facts of History to his recollection; and before he proceeds any further, reasons with himself somewhat as follows:—

The Human Race had inhabited the Earth's surface for upwards of sixteen hundred years, when it was destroyed by the waters of the Flood. After that, the descendants of Noah peopled the earth's surface; a transaction of which the sole authentic record is to be found in the xth chapter of the Book of Genesis. Egypt first emerged into importance,—as history and monuments conspire to prove; having had a peculiar language and literature, Arts and Sciences, anterior to the period of the Exodus, viz. B.C. 1491. Meanwhile, the chart of History directs our attention to four great Empires: the Assyrian Empire, which was swallowed up by the Persian; and the Persian, which was merged in the Grecian Empire. The Roman Empire came last. [How *Law* can be considered to be the characteristic of all or any part of this period, I am at a loss to discover. Neither do I see any indication of puling Infancy here.] These four great Empires of the world had run their course when our SAVIOUR CHRIST was born. GOD sent His own Eternal SON into the world; and lo, a change passed over the whole fabric of the world's polity. The old forms of social life became, as it were, dissolved; or rather, a new spirit had been breathed into them all. A new era had commenced ; and a new principle henceforth animated mankind. That peculiar system of Divine Laws which for 1500 years had separated the Hebrew race from all the nations of the earth,—the Mosaic Law which had hitherto been the inheritance of a single family, isolated in Canaan,—was explained and expanded by its Divine Author. The ancient promises to Abraham and his posterity were declared in their application to be co-extensive with the whole race of Mankind by faith embracing them. Henceforth, the kingdoms of the world were proclaimed the kingdoms of CHRIST, and *Mankind became for the first time subject to a written LAW.* The Laws of CHRIST's Kingdom, the doctrines of CHRIST's Church, henceforth become supreme. Thus, when a Christian Sovereign is crowned, the Bible is solemnly placed in his hands; and it is required of him that he promise, on his oath, " to the utmost of his power, *to maintain the Laws of* GOD." " When you see this Orb set under this Cross," (says the Archbishop, on delivering those insignia of Royalty,) "remember that the whole World is subject to the power and empire of CHRIST our Redeemer .... so that no man can reign happily, who .... directs not all his actions *according to His Laws.*" ... No further change in the order of things is anywhere intimated. The Faith hath been ἅπαξ,—once and for ever,—delivered to the Saints. Forsaken, it may be: by many, (alas!) *it will be* forsaken before the consummation of all things: but it will not itself cease. Heaven and Earth shall pass away; but CHRIST'S Word, never. Not one jot nor one tittle of *the Law* shall fail. ... Such, in brief outline, is the World's true history,—past, present, future. Does it correspond with Dr. Temple's account? That may be very soon seen. He calls the human race a Colossal Man; and says that it passes through three stages,—Infancy, Boyhood, Manhood: and that during those three stages, it is governed by three corresponding principles,—Law, Example, Conscience. How does Dr. Temple establish the first?

The Jews, (he says,) were subject to Law from the period of the Exode to the coming of CHRIST.—We listen to the statement of a familiar fact without surprise: but we are inclined to express some stronger feeling than surprise when we discover that this is *the whole* of the proof concerning the infancy of the Colossal Man! Does this writer then mean to tell us that the Jews were all Mankind? If they were *not* the Colossal Man,—if, instead of being the whole Human Race, they were one of the most inconsiderable and least known of the nations,—an isolated family, in fact, inhabiting Canaan,—what becomes of the analogy? We really pause for an answer. ... Such a theory might have been expected, and would have been excusable if it had proceeded from a Sunday-school-boy of fifteen, —who had read the Bible indeed, but who was unacquainted with any book besides; and so, had jumped to the conclusion that the Jews were "the World." But Dr. Temple is a Schoolmaster, and therefore must surely know better. If he is fanciful enough to regard Mankind as a Colossal Man; and unphilosophical enough to consider that History is capable of being divided into three periods,—corresponding with Infancy, Boyhood, and Manhood; and forgetful enough of the facts of the case to assume that mankind was subject to Law *until* the coming of CHRIST, thenceforward to be emancipated therefrom :—yet Dr. Temple ought not to be so unreasonable as to pretend that Canaan was coextensive with the World,—the descendants of Abraham with the posterity of Noah! This amiable writer is inexcusable for excluding from the corporate entity of the Human Race the four great Empires of the world, (to say nothing of primæval Egypt and mysterious India;) and for the sake of elaborating a worthless allegory, identifying the least of all people with the Colossal Man, who, (according to his own account of the matter,) represents the aggregate of all the nations.

Once more. The Mosaic Law was not given till B.C. 1491. But the world was then upwards of 2500 years old. Far more than one-third, therefore, of recorded time had already elapsed. How does it happen that the theory under consideration gives no account of those 2500 years; or rather, does not begin to be applicable, until they have rolled away?

Other inconveniences await this silly speculation. Thus, the Colossal Man, (who was *under Law* from B.C. 1491 to the Christian æra,) proves to have been a marvellously precocious Infant. He wrote the Song of Moses *in the year of his birth.* Nay, he built pyramids,—had a Literature, Arts, and Sciences,—*ages before he was born!* ... While yet an infant, he sang with Homer, and carved with Phidias, and philosophized with Aristotle,—as none have ever sung, or carved, or philosophized since. Times and fashions have altered, truly; but these three men are still *our* Masters in Philosophy, in Sculpture, and in Song. Awkward fact, that the colossal Infant should have lisped in a tongue which for copiousness of diction, and subtlety of expression, absolutely remains to this hour without a rival in the world!

Again. At this writer's dogmatic bidding, we force ourselves to think of Mankind as a Colossal Man, who has already gone through three ages,—Infancy, Boyhood, and Manhood. *Old Age is therefore to come next.* When, (if it is a fair question,) may it be expected that the sad period of senile decrepitude will set in? What proof, in the mean time, is there, (we venture to ask,) that this period of decay has not begun already? Or does Dr. Temple perhaps imagine that the world is moving in cycles, (to adopt the grotesque speculation of his own first pages); and that after having run through the curriculum of Infancy, Boyhood, and Manhood, the Colossal Man, (escaping, for some unexplained reason, the penalty of Old Age,) is to grow young again,—shake his rattle and cut his teeth afresh? There is a childish vivaciousness, a juvenile recklessness, a skittish impatience of restraint, in this amiable author's speculations, which powerfully corroborate such a view of the case.

"The Childhood of the World was over when our Lord appeared on earth," (p. 20.) says Dr. Temple. But when at last he is compelled to introduce to our notice his Colossal Child (p. 9, *bottom*.) now developed into a Colossal Youth, he is painfully sensible that the

Law and the Prophets, (his schoolmasters,) (p. 8.) have not done their work quite so well as was to have been desired and expected. Some apology is necessary. (p. 13, *bottom*.) Two great results however he claims for their discipline:—"a settled national belief in the unity and spirituality of GOD, and an acknowledgement of the paramount importance of chastity as a point of morals." (p. 11.) Not however that the Law or the Prophets had taught them even *this*. (p. 10, *top*.) "It was in the Captivity, far from the temple and the sacrifices of the temple, that the Jewish people first learned that the spiritual part of worship could be separated from the ceremonial; and that of the two the spiritual was far the higher." (p. 10.) At Babylon also the Jews first distinctly learned the doctrine of the immortality of the soul. (p. 19.)—The Law, to be sure, had emphatically said,—"Hear, O Israel, the LORD thy GOD is *one GOD*[b]." The prophets, to be sure, had protested,—"Behold, to obey is better than sacrifice[c]." The Law and the Prophets, to be sure, are full of intimations that "mercy and not sacrifice[d]" is acceptable to the GOD of Heaven, and that GOD's Saints well understood the Doctrine[e]; as well as that a belief in the soul's immortality was a part of the instruction of the Jewish people. But what is all this to one who has an allegory to establish? . . .

The facts of the case, in the meantime, sorely perplex the truth-loving writer. "For it is undeniable that, in the time of our LORD, the Sadducees had lost

[b] Deut. vi. 4.
[c] 1 Sam. xv. 22, where see the places in the margin.
[d] Hos. vi. 6, quoted by our LORD, St. Matth. ix. 13: xii. 7.
[e] Consider Ps. xxvi. 6: l. 13, 14: li. 16, 17: cxvi. 15: cxix. 108: cxli. 2, &c.

all depth of spiritual feeling, whilst the Pharisees had succeeded in converting the Mosaic system into a mischievous idolatry of forms." (p. 10.) "In short, the Jewish nation had lost very much when John the Baptist came." (p. 11.) The hopelessly corrupt moral state of the youthful Colossus, described with such sickening force and power by the great Apostle in the first chapter of the Epistle to the Romans, cannot have occurred to Dr. Temple's remembrance, for he says nothing about it. Certain withering denunciations of "a wicked and adulterous generation[f];"— of "adulterers and adulteresses[g];"—"serpents," a "generation of vipers," which should hardly "escape the damnation of Hell[h];"—ought to have reached him with a reproachful echo; but he is silent about them all. Still less would it have suited the amiable allegorizer to state that *just midway* in the educational process, his Colossal Youth, "as if" the sins of Samaria and of Sodom " were a very little thing," "*was corrupted more than they in all his ways.* As I live, saith the LORD GOD," (apostrophizing Dr. Temple's Colossal Youth, in allusion to his character and conduct in the middle of his infant career,) "*Sodom thy sister hath not done as thou hast done: . . . neither hath Samaria committed half thy sins; but thou hast multiplied thine abominations more than they.* . . . Bear thine own shame for thy sins that thou hast committed *more abominable than they.* They are more righteous than thou[1]!" "Ah sinful nation, laden with iniquity, a seed of evildoers, children that are corrupters! . . . From the sole

---

[f] St. Matth. xvi. 4: xii. 39. Compare St. Mark viii. 38.
[g] St. James iv. 4.   [h] St. Matth. xxiii. 33.
[1] Ezek. xvi. 47—52.

of the foot even unto the head,"—[these words, remember, are addressed to the Colossal Infant just *midway* in his career; and Heaven and Earth are called upon to give ear, "for the LORD hath spoken!" ... From the sole to the crown,] "there is no soundness in it; but wounds, and bruises, and putrifying sores. ... Your hands are full of blood[k]!" ... About all this hideous retrospect of what was going on at school, Dr. Temple is silent.

In like manner, the great fact that our REDEEMER came to republish His own two primæval ordinances, —the spiritual observance of the Sabbath and the sanctity of Marriage,—is quietly ignored. A youth utterly degraded by sensuality[l], and blinded by unbelief[m], is a terrible picture truly. Dr. Temple therefore boldly gives the lie direct to History, sacred and profane; and insists that " side by side with freedom from idolatry, *there had grown up in the Jewish mind a chaster morality than was to be found elsewhere in the world:*" (p. 12 :) that " *in chastity the Hebrews stood alone;* and this virtue, which had grown up with them from their earliest days (!!!) *was still in the vigour of fresh life when they were commissioned to give the Gospel to the nations.*" (p. 13.)

[k] Is. i. 4, 6, 15.
[l] St. John viii. 9. "I cannot but speak my mind," (says Josephus, after taking a survey of the extreme wickedness of his countrymen, in connexion with the horrors of the siege of Jerusalem,) "and it is this: I suppose that if the Romans had delayed to come against these sinners, either the earth would have swallowed them up; or the city would have been swept away by another Flood; or it would have been consumed, like a second Sodom, by fire from Heaven."
[m] S. John xii. 38—40. "*They have blinded* their eyes," &c. (See the place in the LXX. :) sc. ὁ λαὸς οὗτος.

Behold the Colossal Child therefore, now grown into a Colossal "Youth too old for discipline." (p. 20, *bottom*.) "The tutors and governors have done their work;" (p. 20;) and he is now to go through a distinct process of training. Three tutors are now brought in to give the finishing touches to the youth's education, and to inaugurate his new career. Rome, Greece, and Asia,—which for some unexplained reason never become (according to Dr. Temple) any part of the Colossal Man *at all*,—now come in; "Rome to discipline the human will; Greece, the reason and taste; Asia, the spiritual imagination." (p. 19.) The Law and the Prophets had disciplined the Colossal Child's conscience,—with what success we have seen. At all events, Moses and Isaiah are for infants: we have passed the age for such helps as *they* could supply. In a word,—"The childhood of the world was over when our LORD appeared on earth." (p. 20.) It was "just the meeting-point of the Child and the Man; the brief interval which separates restraint from liberty." (p. 22.) "It was time that the second teacher of the Human Race should begin his labours. The second teacher is EXAMPLE:" (p. 20:) and "the period of youth in the history of the world, when the human race was, as it were, put under the teaching of example, corresponds, of course, to the meeting point of the Law and the Gospel. The second stage therefore in the education of man was the presence of our LORD upon earth." (p. 24.)

Let not this stage of Dr. Temple's allegory suffer by being stated in any language besides his own. "The world" had been a Colossal Child for 1490 years. It was to be a Youth for almost 100. "The whole period from the closing of the Old Testament to the close of the New was the period of the world's youth,—the age of examples: and our LORD's presence was not the only influence of that kind which has acted upon the human race. "Three companions were appointed by Providence to give their society to this creature whom GOD was educating, Greece, Rome, and the Early Church." (p. 26.) Behold then, our Blessed Redeemer with His "three companions." (I reproduce this blasphemous speculation with shame and sorrow.) What kind of Example *He* was, Dr. Temple omits to inform us. But Greece was "the brilliant social companion;"—Rome, "the bold and clever leader;"—the Early Church was "the earnest, heavenly-minded friend." (p. 26.) We are warned therefore against supposing that "our LORD's presence was *the only influence of that kind*," (i.e. example,) appointed by Providence for the creature whom GOD was educating. In a word: "The world was now grown old enough to be taught by seeing the lives of Saints, *better than by hearing the words of Prophets.*" (pp. 28-9.)

We come now to the conclusion of the allegory; and Dr. Temple shall again speak for himself. "The age of reflection begins. From the storehouse of his youthful experience the Man begins to draw the principles of his life. The spirit or conscience comes to full strength and assumes the throne intended for him in the soul. As an accredited judge, invested with full powers, he sits in the tribunal of our inner kingdom, decides upon the past, and legislates upon the future without appeal except to himself. He decides not by what is beautiful, or noble, or soul-inspiring, but by what is right. Gradually he frames his code of laws, revising, adding, abrogating, as a wider and deeper experience gives him clearer light. He is the third great teacher and the last." (p. 31.)

And now, it will reasonably be asked,—May not the head-master of Rugby write a weak and foolish Essay on a subject which he evidently does not understand, without incurring so much not only of public ridicule, but of public obloquy also? If his own sixth-form boys do not laugh at him, need the Church feel aggrieved at what he has written? Where is the special *irreligion* in all this?

I answer,—The offence is of the very gravest character; and in the course of what follows, it will appear with sufficient plainness wherein it consists. For the moment,—singly considered,—it is my painful duty to condemn Dr. Temple's Essay on the following grounds.

Whereas the Church inculcates the paramount necessity of *an external authoritative Law* to guide all her members;—Creeds to define the foundation of their Faith,—a Catechism to teach them the necessary elements of Christian Doctrine,—the several forms of Prayer contained in the Prayer Book to instruct them further in Religion, as well as to prescribe their exact mode of worshipping ALMIGHTY GOD: whereas too the Church requires of her ministers subscription to Articles "for the avoiding of Diversities of Opinions, and for the establishing of Consent concerning true Religion;"—above all, since all Christian men alike are taught to acknowledge the external guidance of the Divine Law itself contained in Holy Scripture,—and every Minister of the Church of England is further called upon to admit the authority of that Divine Law as it is by the Church systematized, explained, upheld, enforced:—notwithstanding all this, Dr. Temple, who has solemnly taken the vows of a minister of the Church of England, and writes after his name that he is *Sacræ Theologiæ Professor*, in his present Essay more than insinuates, he openly teaches that Man " draws *the principles of his life*," (not from Revelation, but) "*from* the storehouse of *experience:*" that we live in an age when " the spirit or conscience having come to full strength, assumes the throne intended for him in the soul." This "spirit or conscience" " legislates *without appeal except to himself*." " He is the third great teacher and the last." (p. 31.) The world, in the days of its youth, could not " walk by reason and conscience alone :" (p. 21:) but it is not so with us, in these, the days of the world's manhood. " The spiritual power within us . . . must be the rightful monarch of our lives." (p. 14.) *We*, (he says,) " walk by reason and conscience *alone*." (p. 21.)

Now this is none other than a deliberate dethroning of God; and a setting up of Self in His place. " A revelation speaking from without and not from within, is an external Law, and not a spirit,"—(p. 36,) says Dr. Temple. But I answer,—A revelation speaking from within, and not from without, is *no revelation at all*. " The thought of building a tower high enough to escape God's wrath, could enter into no man's dreams," (p. 7,) says Dr. Temple in the beginning of his Essay, in derision of the Old World. But he has carried out into act the very self-same thought, himself; and his " dreams " occupy the foremost place in 'Essays and Reviews.' He teaches, openly, that henceforth Man must learn by " *obedience to the rules of his own mind*." (p. 34.) He is express in declaring that " an external law " is for the age which is past. (pp. 34-5.) Ours is " an internal law ;" " which bids us yield,"—not to the revealed Will of GOD, "but,—to the majesty of truth and justice; *a law which is not imposed upon us by another power, but by our own enlightened will.*" (p. 35.) In this, the last stage of the Colossal Man's progress, Dr. Temple gives him four avenues of learning: (1) Experience, (2) Reflection, (3) Mistakes, (4) Contradiction. By withholding from this enumeration *the Revealed Will of GOD,* and *the known sanctions of the Divine Law,* he *thrusts out* GOD from every part of his scheme; denies that He is even one of the present teachers of the Human Race,—explaining that the time has even gone by when CHRIST could teach by example [n],—"for the faculty of Faith

---

[n] "Had the revelation of CHRIST been delayed till now, assuredly it would have been hard for us to recognize His Divinity.... We, of course, have in our turn counterbalancing advantages. (!) If we have lost that freshness of faith which would be the first (*sic*) to say to a poor carpenter,—Thou art the CHRIST, the SON of the living GOD,—yet we possess in the greater cultivation of our religious understanding, that which perhaps we ought not to be willing to give in exchange (!) .... They had not the same clearness of understanding as we; the same recognition that it is GOD and not the Devil who rules the World; the same power of discrimination between different kinds of truth. ... Had our LORD come later, He would have come to mankind already beginning to stiffen into the fixedness of maturity. ... The truth of His Divine Nature would not have been recognized." (pp. 24-5.)—Is this meant for bitter satire on the age we live in; or for disparagement of the Incarnate WORD? ... But in the face of such anticipations, the keenest satire of all is contained in the author's claim to a "religious understanding, cultivated" to a degree unknown to the best ages of the Church; as well as to surpassing "clearness of understanding," and "powers of discrimination." Lamentable in *any* quarter, how deplorable is such conceit in one who shews himself *unacquainted with the first principles of Theological Science;* and who puts forth an Essay on the Education of the World, which would have been discreditable to an advanced school-boy!·

has turned inwards, and cannot now accept any outer manifestations of the truth of GOD°." (p. 24.)—By this Essay, Dr. Temple comes forward as the open abettor of the most boundless scepticism. Whether or no his statements be such as Ecclesiastical Courts take cognizance of, is to me a matter of profound unimportance. In the estimation of the whole Church, it can be entitled to but one sentence. "We use the Bible," (he tells us,) "not to override, but to evoke the voice of conscience." (p. 44.) "The current is all one way,—it evidently points to the identification of the Bible with the voice of conscience. The Bible, in fact, is hindered by its form from exercising a despotism (!) over the human spirit; if it could do that, it would become an outer law at once." (p. 45.) Even if men "could appeal to a revelation from Heaven, they would still be under the Law (!!!); for a Revelation speaking from without, and not from within, is an external Law, and not a Spirit." (p. 36.) "The principle of private judgment puts conscience between

---

° Quite ineffectual, at the very close of this unhappy composition, as a set off to the compacted and often repeated asseverations of his earlier pages, is the amiable author's plaintive plea for "even the perverted use of the Bible;" adding,—"And meanwhile, how utterly impossible it would be in the manhood of the world to imagine any other instructor of mankind!" (p. 47.) It is one of the favourite devices of these seven writers, side by side with their most objectionable statements, to insert isolated passages of admitted truth,—and occasionally even of considerable beauty: which however are *utterly meaningless* and out of place where they stand; and (like the sentence above written,) powerless to undo the circumstantial wickedness of what went before. I repeat, that the words above-written are meaningless *where they stand:* for if Dr. Temple really means that it is "*utterly impossible in the manhood of the world to IMAGINE any other instructor of mankind*" than *THE BIBLE*,—what becomes of his Essay?

us and the Bible; making conscience the supreme interpreter, whom it may be a duty to enlighten, but whom it can never be a duty to disobey." (*Ibid.*)—Even those who look upon the observance of Sunday "as enjoined by an absolutely binding decree," are reproached as "thus at once putting themselves under a law." (p. 44.) .... Dr. Temple has written an Essay which he calls "an argument," and for which he claims "a drift." (p. 31.) *That* argument is neither more nor less than a direct assault on the Faith of Christian men; and carried out to its lawful results, *can* lead to nothing but open Infidelity;—which makes it a very solemn consideration that the author, (whose private worth is known to all,) should be a teacher of the youth of Christian England. *That* drift I deplore and condemn; and no considerations of private friendship, no sincere regard for the writer's private worth, shall deter me from recording my deliberate conviction that it is wholly incompatible with his Ordination vows.

I forbear to dive into the depth of irreligion and unbelief implied in what is contained from p. 37 to p. 40, and other parts of the present Essay: but I cannot abstain from asking why does this author,—who, in all the intercourse of private life, is so manly a character,—fall into the *un*manly trick of his brother-Essayists, of insinuating what they dare not openly avow? The great master of this cloudy shuffling art is Mr. Jowett. Even where he and his associates in "free handling," are express and definite in their statements, yet, as their rule is prudently to abstain from adducing a single example of their meaning, it is only by their disingenuous reticence that they escape punishment or exposure. Thus, Dr. Temple speaks of "many of the doctrinal statements of the early Church" being "plainly unfitted for permanent use;" (p. 41;) but he prudently abstains from explaining *which* of those "doctrinal statements" he means. He goes on to remark:— "In fact, the Church of the Fathers claimed to do what not even the Apostles had claimed,—namely, not only to teach the Truth, but to clothe it in logical statements .... for all succeeding time." He is evidently alluding to "the forms in which the first ages of the Church defined the Truth;" [i.e. to the Creeds;] of which he says, we "yet *refuse to be bound by them*." (p. 44.) He goes on,—"It belongs to a later epoch to see 'the law within the law' which absorbs such statements *into something higher than themselves*." (p. 41.) But the writer of that sentence ought to have had the manliness to explain *what* that "higher something" *is*.

Dr. Temple's estimate of the corruptions of the Papacy is of a piece with the rest of what I must be excused for calling a most unworthy performance. "Purgatory," &c. (he says) "was in fact, neither more nor less than *the old schoolmaster come back* to bring some new scholars to Christ." (p. 42.) (Is the Romish fable of Purgatory then to be put on the same footing as the Divine Revelation to Moses on Sinai?) It follows,—"When the work was done, men began to discover that the Law was no longer necessary." (*Ibid.*) (Is it thus that the head-master of Rugby accounts for, and explains the Reformation?) "The time was come when it was fit to trust to the conscience *as the supreme guide*." (*Ibid.*) "At the Reformation, it might have seemed at first as if the study of theology were about to return. But in reality an entirely new lesson commenced,—the lesson of toleration. Toleration is the very opposite of dogmatism." (p. 43.) "Its tendency is to modify the early dogmatism by substituting the spirit for the letter, and practical religion for precise definitions of truth." (*Ibid.*) "The mature mind of our race is beginning to modify and soften the hardness and severity of the principles which its early manhood had elevated into immutable statements of truth. Men are beginning to take a wider view than they did. Physical science, researches into history, a more thorough knowledge of the world they inhabit, have enlarged our philosophy beyond the limits which bounded that of the Church of the Fathers. And all these have an influence, whether we will or no, on our determinations of religious truth. There are found to be more things in heaven and earth than were dreamt of in patristic theology. GOD's creation is a new book to be read by the side of His revelation, and to be interpreted as coming from Him. We can acknowledge the great value of the forms in which the first ages of the Church defined the truth, and yet refuse to be bound by them." (p. 43-4.) ... Who so unacquainted with the method of a certain school as not to understand the fatal meaning of generalities, false and foul as these?

It may occur to some persons to inquire whether St. Paul, in a well-known place, does not affirm, (somewhat as it is affirmed in this Essay,) that "the heir, as long as he is a child, ... is under tutors and governors until the time appointed of the father?" And that, "Even so we, when we were children, were in bondage under the elements of the world: but when the fulness of time was come, God sent forth His Son .... to redeem them that were under the Law, that we might receive the adoption of sons?" Does not St. Paul also go on to reproach men for "turning again to the weak and beggarly elements, whereunto they desired to be again in bondage?" saying, "ye observe[p] days, and months, and times, and years[q]." It is quite true that St. Paul says all this: and I would fain believe that a puerile misconception of the Apostle's meaning has betrayed the misguided author of the present Essay into a notion that he enjoys a species of Divine sanction for what he has written concerning "the Education of the World." I may add that St. Paul also declares, (in the same Epistle,) that "the Law was our *pædagogus* to bring us to Christ. ... But after faith is come, we are no longer under a *pædagogus*[r]." He further adds an exhortation to the Galatians, (for it is still *them* whom he is addressing,) — "Stand fast therefore in the liberty wherewith Christ hath made us free, and be not entangled again with the yoke of bondage[s]."—St. John moreover, in many places, insists upon the spiritual powers and privileges of believers, in a very remarkable manner,—the same St. John, the same 'Apostle of Love,' who says of a certain Doctrine which 'Essayists and Reviewers' write as if they disbelieved,— "If there come any unto you, and bring not this doctrine, receive him not into your house, neither bid him God speed: for he that biddeth him God speed is partaker of his evil deeds[t]."

But it does not require much knowledge of Divinity

---

[p] παρα τηρεῖσθε: i.e. "ye misobserve," "keep *in a wrong way*."
[q] Gal. iv. 1—10.   [r] Gal. iii. 24, 25.   [s] Gal. v. 1.
[t] 2 St. John v. 10, 11.

to make a man aware that St. Paul's meaning and intention is as widely removed from Dr. Temple's, as Truth is removed from falsehood: or rather, that the Apostle is flatly against him. St. Paul is not bent on explaining what has been *the Education of the World*, but on pointing out in what relation *the Gospel of Christ stands to the Law of Moses.* He is reproving men who, having been converted to Christianity, were for lapsing into Judaism. Certain of the Circumcision had been striving, in St. Paul's absence, to bring his Galatian converts under the bondage of the Levitical Law; assuring them that the Gospel would avail them nothing unless they were circumcised and obedient to the Jewish ritual. Hence the Apostle's vehemence, and the peculiar form which his instruction assumes.

The Christian dispensation, (the scheme of Man's Justification by Faith in Christ,) is the fulfilment, (St. Paul says,) of the covenant which God once solemnly made with Abraham. The Mosaic Law, (which was not given till 430 years after the time of Abraham,) is powerless to cancel that earlier covenant of Faith. What was the use of the Law, then? some one may ask. It was a supplementary, parenthetical, superadded thing, which came in, as it were, accidentally, for certain assignable purposes. But now that the original covenant of Faith has at length found fulfilment in the person of Christ, it were monstrous (argues the Apostle) to revert to Judaism: which was a species of prison-house where we suffered bondage until Messiah came to set us free. We were *as prisoners*, says the Apostle. We were also *as children*,—(who, anciently, from the age of six to fourteen, used to be consigned by their father to the care of a slave called a 'pædagogus;' who was neither qualified nor allowed to teach them anything; but whose office it was *to conduct them to school.*) So *brought to the School of* CHRIST, where learning comes *by Faith*, (such is his argument,) let men beware how they revert to the carnal ordinances of the Jewish Law.

How different a view of our true state is thus discovered, from that which Dr. Temple describes! A glorious liberty is *in reserve* for us indeed[u]: a precious freedom is ours already. But it bears no resemblance whatever to that *lawlessness* (ἀνομία) with which Dr. Temple seems to be enamoured. It is the correlation of *slavery*, not of obedience. It implies emancipation from the *Levitical* Law, not from the sanctions, however strict, of the *Christian Church*. The Doctrines of CHRIST's kingdom are the Christian's crown and joy. *His* "service is perfect freedom," and imparts to life all its sweetness.—Not only, therefore, (according to St. Paul's view of the matter,) were men *not* released from school at "the meeting point of the Law and the Gospel," (p. 24,) but they only *began* to go to School *then*[v] *!*

How different a view of the Education of the World does the HOLY SPIRIT,—does our LORD Himself—furnish, from that which Dr. Temple here advocates! ... Fallen, in the person of Adam, and made subject to the penalty of eternal death, behold Mankind from

[u] Rom. viii. 21.

[v] It is presumed that the article in the *Dict. of Antiquities* will be held unexceptionable authority as to the office of the παιδαγωγός. —"Rex filio pædagogum constituit, et singulis diebus ad eum invisit, interrogans eum: Num comedit filius meus? *num in scholam abiit? num ex scholâ rediit?*"—Wetstein, in loc.—So Plato *Lysis*, p. 118.

the very first taught to believe that they should be ultimately redeemed by One born of woman. Under the image of a son who remained in his father's house, the favoured descendants of Abraham are set before us: while the rest of the world is pourtrayed in the person of another son, who goes into a far country, and there wastes his substance with riotous living. *Not* when grown into a colossal "youth too old for discipline," (p. 20, *bottom*,) but in the day of his dire necessity, and when he begins to be sensible of his utter need, behold the heathen nations, (in the person of the poor prodigal,) arising, and going to their true Father, and in the fulness of their misery asking for a hired servant's place in the household. Behold too God's mercies in CHRIST set forth by "the first robe," (*that* robe of innocence which when Adam lost he knew that he was naked!) and the ring, and the shoes, and the fatted calf! Lastly, in the embrace which the Father, (while yet the offending but repentant son is a long way off,) *runs* to bestow,—behold *how* God loved the World!

But Dr. Temple may say,—*My* parable relates to one person: that which you have quoted pourtrays two, and thus all parallelism is lost. (In other words, *our Lord's picture* of "*the Education of the World*" *is altogether unlike Dr. Temple's !*)—Take, however, a parable which ought to suit exactly; for in it mankind are exhibited in the person of "a certain man."

This individual is represented as one who, as he travels, is by thieves stripped, wounded, and left half dead. Such then, by nature, is the state of the human race! Priest and Levite, who "look on him," but "pass by on the other side," set forth the Education of the World (!) until CHRIST came. A certain

Samaritan, who has compassion on the naked and wounded wretch, goes to him, binds up his wounds, pours in oil and wine, sets him on his own beast, brings him to the inn, and takes care of him:—*this* one is CHRIST. The stranger's pence, and his promise to repay at his second coming what shall have been over-expended,—set forth, I suppose, *that* ministration of CHRIST's Word and Sacraments which Dr. Temple exercises .... Let me dismiss the subject by remarking that I find no countenance given by Holy Scripture to Dr. Temple's monstrous notions concerning the Infancy, the Youth, and the Manhood of the Colossal Man.

Our SAVIOUR CHRIST is indeed set before us in Scripture as our great Exemplar[x]; and St. Paul calls upon us to be followers, or rather imitators, ($\mu\iota\mu\eta\tau\alpha\acute{\iota}$), of himself; even as *he* was of CHRIST[y]. But this walking by example, did not supersede the walking by precept; neither was it to endure, (GOD forbid!) (as Dr. Temple emphatically says it was), (pp. 26: 28-9,) only for about a hundred years: still less was "Example," (the second Teacher of the Human Race,) straightway to find itself supplanted by "the Spirit or Conscience" of Man, — "the third great Teacher, and the last." What need to say that until His Second Coming to judge the world, we shall have *no* Teacher but CHRIST,—*no* other way proposed to us to walk in, but that which the Gospel discloses?

Neither is it true that the world has been old enough, for the last 1800 years, to be taught by "*see-*

---

[x] 1 St. Peter ii. 21. Comp. St. James v. 10.

[y] 1 Cor. xi. 1: iv. 16. Phil. iii. 17. 2 Thess. iii. 9. Heb. xiii. 7, &c.

ing the lives of Saints," (a sentiment worthy of the weakest of Romanists!) "*better than by hearing the words of Prophets.*" (pp. 28-9.) The Church of CHRIST will for ever listen to the blessed accents of that "goodly fellowship," until she beholds Him by whose Spirit they spake[z], coming again to judgment. True that the object with which she will all along *inform* her children, will ever be that they may become *conformed* to the model of her Divine LORD. But "sound doctrine[a],"—embodied in a "form of sound words[b],"—constitutes that παρακαταθήκη, or "deposit," which is her proudest inheritance and her greatest treasure[c]: and impatience of it is a note of evil men, and of a season at which Prophecy points her awful finger[d].

..... "Lawlessness," (ἀνομία,) is discoursed of by the SPIRIT with a mysterious earnestness which it seems to me impossible to survey without mingled awe and terror lest one may become oneself involved in the threatened condemnation. I allude of course especially to what St. Paul says in his second Epistle to the Thessalonians; the language of which, to be understood, must be studied in the original[e].

Conscience has her office, doubtless; and a most important one it is. Conscience is the very candle of the LORD within us. But, (as I have elsewhere shewn,) it were base treason to speak of conscience as Essayists and Reviewers speak of it. With *them*, it is indeed impossible to argue. They must first with-

[z] 1 St. Pet. i. 11.
[a] 1 Tim. i. 10: iv. 6. Tit. i. 9: ii. 1. Comp. 2 St. John v. 10. [b] 2 Tim. i. 13.
[c] 2 Tim. i. 13, 14: ii. 2. Also 1 Tim. vi. 20. On both places, Dr. Wordsworth's *Notes* may be consulted with advantage.
[d] 2 Tim. iv. 3. [e] 2 Thess. ii. 7, 8, &c.

draw from the cause which they have betrayed; cease to profess the teaching which they disbelieve; resign their commission in a Church to whose Doctrine and Discipline they openly proclaim themselves to be opposed. I will not argue *with them*, while they presume to write B.D. and D.D. after their names,—hold Chaplaincies,—preside over Schools and Colleges,—profess to lecture in Divinity,—officiate at the altars of the Church of England,—by virtue of their sacred office, *and by virtue of that only*, are instructors of youth. They *cannot*, (if they are in the full enjoyment of their faculties,) they *cannot* imagine, for a moment, that, as honest men, they can remain where they are! They *must* either recal their words or resign their stations!

But speaking to others, it will abundantly suffice to point out that such principles as the present Essay advocates are incompatible with the profession of Christianity in *any* country, and in *any* age. If the spirit or conscience of Man is to legislate "*without appeal except to himself;*" (p. 31;) if men are to "*refuse to be bound*" (p. 44.) by the Creeds of the Church; if the very Bible is not to be looked upon as "*an outer law:*" (p. 45:)—how is sentence *ever* to be pronounced with authority? how are men to know *what* they have to believe? how are we to enjoy the guidance of any "outer law" *at all?* I do not ask these questions as a clergyman; neither am I addressing those exclusively who have been admitted to the Christian priesthood. Common sense, ordinary piety, natural reverence, seem to cry out, and ask,—If *the Church* have no "authority in controversies of Faith[f];" if *the three Creeds* ought not "thoroughly to be received and

[f] Art. XX.

believed[g];" if *the Bible* is not "an outer Law;"—*where is Authority in things Divine to be sought for? What can be worthy of credit? Where* are we to look for external guidance on this side the grave? ... Surely, surely, common sense is outraged when she hears it insisted that the written Bible is a Revelation speaking NOT "from without," but "from within!" (pp. 36 and 45.) Surely it must be admitted that it were mere atheism to pretend that Man's "spirit or conscience, *without appeal except to himself,*" shall henceforth be the governing principle of Mankind!

Let me in conclusion do this writer an act of justice, (for which he will not perhaps altogether thank me,) even while with shame and sorrow I now dismiss his Essay. Unpardonable as he is for having written thus; and *wholly* without excuse for having suffered *nine editions* of his blasphemous allegory to go forth to the world without apology, explanation, or retractation of any kind,—although he labours under a weight of competent censure without a parallel, I believe, in the annals of the English Church[h]: notwithstanding all this, I am bound to say that if the unbelievers of this generation think they have an ally in *the man*, Frederick Temple,—they are very much mistaken. That so pure a heart, and earnest a spirit, will never work itself free of its present bondage,—I should be sorry indeed to think. (But O the mischief which the head-master of Rugby School will have done in the meantime!) His misfortune (or rather fault) it has been, that he has really never studied Divinity;

---

[g] Art. VIII.

[h] I allude especially to the terrible castigation he has individually received at the hands of the Bishop of Exeter. See *the Times*, of March 4th, 1861.

nor, in fact, *knows anything at all about it*,—as a volume of his, lately published, sufficiently shews. Apart from his opinions (!), he is a thoroughly amiable man; and—(with the same proviso!)—an excellent schoolmaster; but when he ventures upon the province of Theology, he shews himself something infinitely worse than *a very bad Divine.*

II. On turning the first page of the review which follows, " by ROWLAND WILLIAMS, D.D. Vice-Principal and Professor of Hebrew, St. David's College, Lampeter; Vicar of Broad Chalke, Wilts,"—we are made sensible that we are in company of a writer considerably in advance of Dr. Temple, though altogether of the same school. In fact, if Dr. Williams had not been Vice-Principal of a Theological College, and a Doctor of Divinity, one would have supposed him to be a complete infidel,—who found it convenient to vent his own unbelief in a highly laudatory review of the principles of the late Baron Bunsen. Hear him:—" When Bunsen asks 'How long shall we bear this fiction of an external Revelation,'—that is, of one violating the heart and conscience, instead of expressing itself through them;—or when he says, 'All this is delusion for those who believe it; but what is it in the mouths of those who teach it?'—Or when he exclaims, 'Oh the fools! who, if they do see the imminent perils of this age, think to ward them off by narrow-minded persecution'!—and when he repeats, 'Is it not time, in truth, to withdraw the veil from our misery? to tear off the mask from hypocrisy, and destroy that sham which is undermining all real ground under our feet? to point out the dangers which surround, nay, threaten already to engulf us?"—there will be some who think his language too vehement for good taste. Others will think burning words needed by the disease of our time. These will not quarrel on points of taste with a man who in our darkest perplexity has reared again the banner of Truth, and uttered thoughts which gave courage to the weak and sight to the blind. If Protestant Europe is to escape those shadows of the twelfth century which with ominous recurrence are closing around us, to Baron Bunsen will belong a foremost place among the champions of light and right." (pp. 92-3.)

But even the Prussian infidel is not advanced enough for the Vicar of Broad Chalke. Bunsen, it seems, was weak enough to believe that the prophet Jonah was a real personage. This evokes the following singular burst of critical indignation from the Reverend author of the present Essay :—"It provokes a smile on serious topics,"—(a kind of impropriety which the Vice-Principal of Lampeter will not commit except under protest and with an apology!)—"to observe the zeal with which our critic vindicates the personality of Jonah, and the originality of his hymn, (the latter being generally thought doubtful), while he proceeds to explain that the narrative of our book in which the hymn is imbedded, contains a late legend founded on misconception. One can imagine the cheers which the opening of such an essay might evoke in some of our circles, changing into indignation (!) as the distinguished foreigner developed his views. After this he might speak more gently of mythical theories." (p. 77.)

For the most part, however, the Vicar of Broad Chalke is able to cite the opinions of Bunsen with admiration and approval. They are both agreed that the Deluge "was but a prolonged play of the forces of fire and water rendering the primæval regions of North Asia uninhabitable, and urging the nations to new abodes." (Of what nature this "*prolonged play*" was, is however left unexplained : while "*the forces of fire and water* rendering *primæval regions* uninhabitable," and "*urging* nations to new abodes," has altogether a Herodotean sound.) "We learn approximately its antiquity, and infer limitation in its range from finding it recorded in the traditions of Iran and Palestine, (or of Japheth and Shem), but unknown to the Egyptians and Mongolians." (p. 56.) (A delightful method truly of attaining historical precision in a matter of this nature !) .... "In the *half ideal, half traditional* notices of the beginnings of our race compiled in Genesis, we are bid notice the combination of documents and the recurrence of barely consistent Genealogies." (*Ibid.*) Praise is at hand for " the firmness with which Bunsen relegates the long lives of the first patriarchs to the domain of legend, or of symbolical cycle." (p. 57.) "The historical portion begins with Abraham." (*Ibid.*)—After this admission, it is instructive to observe how the learned writer deals with the narrative. The Exode was "a struggle conducted by human means." (p. 59.) "Thus, as the pestilence of the Book of Kings becomes in Chronicles the more visible angel, so the avenger who slew the firstborn may have been the Bedouin host, (!) akin nearly to Jethro, and more remotely to Israel." (*Ibid.*) (It is really hardly worth stopping to point out that by 'Kings' the Reverend writer means 'the second Book of Samuel:' and to remind the reader that *the Angel is mentioned as ex-*

pressly in Samuel as in Chronicles[1]. Also, to ask what 'the Bedouin host' could have been doing *in Egypt* previous to the Exode?) "The passage of the Red Sea may be interpreted with the latitude of poetry." (*Ibid.*) "Moses would gladly have founded a free religious society, . . . but the rudeness or hardness of his people's heart compelled him to a sacerdotal system and formal tablets of stone." (p. 62.) Nay, Abraham's intended sacrifice of Isaac was an act of obedience to "the fierce ritual of Syria, with the awe of a Divine voice:" (p. 61:) while the Divine command, in conformity with which Abraham spared to slay his son, is resolved into an allegory. "He trusted that the FATHER, whose voice from Heaven he heard at heart, was better pleased with mercy than with sacrifice, and this trust was his righteousness." (p. 61.) Dr. Williams straightway shews us how *we* may tread in the steps of faithful Abraham. The perpetual response of our hearts, (he says,) to principles of Reason and Right of our own tracing, is a truer sign of faith than deference to a supposed external authority. (p. 61.) . . . . According to this writer, therefore, Genesis and Exodus are pure fable!

The whole of Scripture, in the hands of this Doctor of Divinity, undergoes corresponding treatment. They who "twist Prophecy into harmony with the details

---

[1] "And when the Angel stretched out his hand upon Jerusalem to destroy it, the LORD . . . said to the Angel that destroyed the people," &c. "And the Angel of the LORD was by the threshing-place of Araunah the Jebusite."—2 Sam. xxiv. 16.
"The Angel of the LORD stood by the threshing-floor of Ornan the Jebusite. And David lifted up his eyes, and saw the Angel of the LORD stand between the Earth and the Heaven, having a drawn sword in his hand stretched out over Jerusalem."—1 Chron. xxi. 15, 16.

of Gospel history, fall into inextricable contradictions." (pp. 64-5.) "The Book of Isaiah, as composed of elements of different eras," can only be accepted with a "modified theory of authorship and of prediction." (p. 68.) In the prophecy of Zechariah are "three distinct styles and aspects of affairs." (*Ibid.*) "The cursing Psalms," (! ! !) he informs us, were not "evangelically inspired;" (p. 63;) and yet we are constrained to remember that the cixth Psalm (specially alluded to) is evangelically interpreted by St. Peter[k]. The true translation of Psalm xxii. 17, (learnedly discussed, long since, by Bishop Pearson,) is not "they pierced My hands and My feet,"—but "like a lion;" (notwithstanding that Pearson has shewn that the substitution of *vau* for *yod* in this place is one of the eighteen instances where the Scribes have tampered with the text[l]; and notwithstanding that this modern corruption of the Hebrew, as every one must see, makes the place almost nonsense[m].)—Is. vii. 14 does not refer to the miraculous birth of CHRIST, (p. 69,) (although St. Matthew is express in his assertion that it *does*.) There is, it seems, an elder and a later Isaiah. (p. 71.) The famous liiird chapter does not refer to CHRIST; but either to Jeremiah or to "the collective Israel,"—(p. 73,) (although it is at least seven times quoted, and expressly applied to our SAVIOUR, in the New Testament[n].) Daniel, we are

[k] Acts i. 20.

[l] *On the Creed*, Art. iv. p. 244, *notes* (*u*) and (*x*).

[m] "It would take no great space," (says Dr. Pusey,) "to shew that the rendering 'as a lion,' is unmeaning, without authority, against authority; while the rendering 'they pierced' is borne out alike by authority and language."

[n] Ver. 1,—St. John xii. 38. Rom. x. 16. Ver. 4,—St. Matth.

assured, belongs to different ages; and it is "certain, beyond fair doubt . . . that those portions of the book, supposed to be specially predictive, are . . a history of past occurrences." (p. 69.) That "the book contains no predictions, except by analogy and type, can hardly be gainsaid." (pp. 76-7.) . . . . (If any of *us* had dogmatized as to Truth as these men do as to error, (remarks Dr. Pusey,) what scorn we should be held up to!) . . . . The Reverend author insolently adds,—" It is time for divines to recognize these things, since with their opportunities of study, the current error is as discreditable to them, as for the well-meaning crowd, who are taught to identify it with their creed, it is a matter of grave compassion." (p. 77.) " When so vast an induction on the destructive side has been gone through, it avails little that some passages may be doubtful; one perhaps in Zechariah, and one in Isaiah, capable of being made directly Messianic; and a chapter possibly in Deuteronomy foreshadowing the final fall of Jerusalem. Even these few cases, the remnant of so much confident rhetoric, tend to melt, if they are not already melted, in the crucible of searching enquiry." (pp. 69-70.) . . . . . Our Doctor of Divinity, having reduced the prophecies "*capable of being made*" Messianic, to *two*,—breaks out into a strain of refined banter which is altogether his own, and which we presume is intended to stand in the place of argument. "If our German, [viz. Bunsen,] had ignored all that the masters of philology have proved on these subjects, his countrymen would have raised a storm of ridicule, at which he must have drowned himself in the Neckar." (p. 70.) A catastrophe so fatal to

viii. 17. Ver. 4 to 11,—1 St. Pet. ii. 24, 25. Ver. 7 and 8,—Acts viii. 32. Ver. 12,—St. Mark xv. 28. St. Luke xxii. 37.

the cause of true Religion and sound learning may well point a paragraph ! .... But we must write gravely.

The absolute worthlessness of unsupported dicta such as these, ought to be apparent to all. It is useless to reason with a madman. We desiderate nothing so much as "searching enquiry," (p. 69,) but we are presented instead with something worse than random assertion. If the writer would state a single case, with its evidence,—we should know how to deal with him. We should examine his arguments seriatim; and either refute them, or admit their validity. From such "free handling," the cause of sacred Truth can never suffer. But when, in place of argument and evidence, we have merely bluster,—what is to be said? Pity and disregard are the only reply we can bestow; or our answers must be as brief as the calumny which provokes them. "How," (asks the Regius Professor of Hebrew,) "can such an undigested heap of errors receive a systematic answer in brief space, or in any one treatise or volume?"

"If any sincere Christian now asks, is not then our SAVIOUR spoken of in Isaiah; let him open his New Testament, and ask therewith John the Baptist, whether he was Elias? If he finds the Baptist answering *I am not*, yet our LORD testifies that in spirit and power this was Elias; a little reflexion will shew how the historical representation in Isaiah liii. is of some suffering prophet or remnant, yet the truth and patience, the grief and triumph, have their highest fulfilment in Him who said, 'FATHER, not My will but Thine.'" (p. 74.) I have transcribed this passage to illustrate the miserable sophistry of the author. It is foretold by Malachi that before the great and terrible day of the LORD, Elijah is to come back to

Earth°. John Baptist came in his "spirit and power^p," but was not Elijah himself. How does it follow from this that Isaiah may have prophesied merely of *qualities* and not of a person? The only logical inference from his words would surely be, that Elijah is yet to come^q!—Dr. Williams adds,—"We must not distort the prophets to prove the Divine WORD incarnate, and then from the Incarnation reason back to the sense of prophecy." (p. 74.) *Was* not then the Divine WORD incarnate?

The theory of one who writes like an open unbeliever concerning Divine things is really not worth developing: and yet, as I am examining an Essay which seems to be entirely built upon such a theory, it may be desirable, in this instance, that the deformity of the writer should be uncovered: especially since Dr. Williams writes such very dark English, that, until some of his sentences are translated, they are barely intelligible.

Anticipating that his doctrines may "alarm those who think that, apart from *Omniscience belonging to the Jews*, (!) the proper conclusion of reason is Atheism;"—(in other words, that the rejection of a belief in *the inspiration of Prophecy* will eventually conduct a man to the rejection of GOD Himself;) the Reverend writer declares that "it is not inconsistent with the idea that ALMIGHTY GOD has been pleased to educate men and nations, employing imagination no less than conscience, and suffering His lessons to play freely within the limits of humanity and its shortcomings." (p. 77.) (In other words, that what Scrip-

° Mal. iv. 5.   ^p St. Luke i. 17.
^q As the Fathers generally teach. See Brown's *Ordo Sæclorum*, pp. 702-3, &c., &c.

ture emphatically declares, and what men have for thousands of years believed to be inspired predictions of future events, are none other than the effusions of a lively imagination, or the suggestions of a well-informed conscience.) "The prophetical disquisitions," (p. 77,) therefore, are subject to error of every imaginable description; and possess no higher attributes than belong to any ordinary human work by "a master's hand." (p. 77.) "The Sacred Writers acknowledge themselves men of like passions with ourselves, and we are promised illumination from the Spirit which dwelt in them." (p. 78.) We may not think of the Sacred Writers as "passionless machines, and call Luther and Milton 'uninspired.'" (*Ibid.*) "The great result is to vindicate the work of the Eternal Spirit; that abiding influence which underlies all others, and in which converge all images of old time and means of grace now: temple, Scripture, finger, and Hand of GOD; and again, preaching, sacraments, waters which comfort, and flame which burns." (p. 78.) It follows,—"If such a Spirit did not dwell in the Church, the Bible would not be inspired, for *the Bible is*, before all things, *the written voice of the congregation.*" (p. 78.) Offended Reason, (for Piety has no place here,) has not time to reclaim against so preposterous a statement; for it follows immediately,—"Bold as such a theory of Inspiration (!) may sound, it was the earliest creed of the Church, and it is the only one to which the facts of Scripture answer." (p. 78.) . . . What reply *can* be offered to such an outrageous statement, but flat contradiction? What more effectual refutation of such a 'theory' (?) concerning Scripture, than simply to state it?

Let this miserable but conceited man yet further map out the nature of his own delusion respecting Prophecy. He applauds the wisdom of one who "accepts freely the belief of scholars, and yet does not despair of Hebrew Prophecy as a witness to the Kingdom of God:" (p. 70:) (that is, of one who, like Bunsen, altogether disbelieves in prophecy *as prophecy*, and yet is bent on finding something of an Evangelical character in the prophetic writings.) "The way of doing so left open to him, was to shew pervading the Prophets those deep truths which lie at the heart of Christianity, and to trace the growth of such ideas, the belief in a righteous GOD, and the nearness of Man to GOD, the power of prayer, and the victory of self-sacrificing patience, ever expanding in men's hearts, until the fulness of time came, and the ideal of the Divine thought was fulfilled in the Son of Man." (p. 70.) In other words, CHRIST was nothing more than the fullest development and impersonation of the best thoughts and feelings of the (so-called) prophets! He "fulfilled in His own person the highest aspiration of Hebrew seers and of mankind, thereby lifting the ancient words, so to speak, into a new and higher power; and therefore was recognized as having eminently the unction of a prophet whose words die not,—of a priest in a temple not made with hands,—and of a king in the realm of thought, delivering his people from a bondage of moral evil, worse than Egypt or Babylon." (pp. 74-5.) "A notion of *foresight by vision of particulars,* or a kind of clairvoyance," (p. 70,)—(such is this Doctor of Divinity's notion of the gift of prophecy!)—he deems inadmissible. "*Literal prognostication,*" (p. 65,) is his abhorrence. He would eliminate the Messianic passages altogether. (pp. 65-6.) That Prophecy was miraculous, was a dream of the Fathers. (p. 66.) Even the notion that Prophecy is "a natural gift, consistent with fallibility," (p. 70,) Dr. Williams rejects as an unwarrantable addition to the "moral and metaphysical basis of Prophecy." (p. 70.) Bunsen was for admitting that addition. "One would wish," (says the Vicar of Broad Chalke,) "*he might have intended only the power of seeing the ideal in the actual*, or of tracing the Divine Government in the movements of men. He seems to mean *more than presentiment or sagacity:* and this element in his system requires proof." (pp. 70-1.) . . . This, from a Doctor of Divinity! a Professor of Hebrew! the Vice-Principal of a Theological College! a shepherd of souls!

We are left to infer that "the Fall of Adam represents ideally the circumscription of our spirits in limits of flesh and time:" (p. 88:) that CHRIST is "the moral Saviour of mankind;" (p. 80;) and that Salvation from evil is to be attained by the conformity of our souls to a "*religious idea*" which was "brought to perfection" in CHRIST. (p. 80.) This "religious idea" "is the thought of the Eternal." (*Ibid.*) In other words, "Salvation from evil" is "through sharing the SAVIOUR's Spirit." (p. 87.)—We are further left to infer that "Justification by faith means the peace of mind, or sense of Divine approval, which comes of trust in a righteous GOD:" (p. 80:) that "Regeneration is a correspondent giving of insight, or an awakening of forces of the soul: Resurrection, a spiritual quickening: Salvation, our deliverance, not from the life-giving GOD, but from evil and darkness." (p. 81.) . . . And this from a Clergyman who has just subscribed, "willingly and *ex animo*," the three

Articles in the 36th Canon! ... After such specimens of Divinity, we are scarcely surprised to find that the fires of Hell (γέεννα) "may serve as images of distracted remorse:" (p. 81:) that "Heaven is not a place[r], so much as a fulfilment of the love of GOD." (pp. 81-2.) The very Incarnation, (which he calls "the embodiment of the Eternal Mind,") (p. 82.) is spoken of as if it were a myth. "It becomes with our author *as purely spiritual* as it was with St. Paul. The Son of David by birth is the SON of GOD *by the spirit of holiness.* What is flesh, is born of flesh; and what is spirit, is born of Spirit." (p. 82.) Rom. i. 1—3 is quoted in support of this, which I cannot but regard as blasphemy: for if it does not mean that our SAVIOUR was not, in a true and literal sense, the SON of GOD at all, it is hard to see *what* it can mean.—As for the following account of the mystery of the Blessed Trinity, it shall only be said that it sounds like a denial of the Catholic doctrine altogether. "Being, becoming, and animating; or substance, thinking, and conscious life, are expressions of a Triad which may be also represented as will, wisdom, and love; as light, radiance, and warmth; as fountain, stream, and united flow; as mind, thought, and consciousness; as person, word, and life; as FATHER, SON, and SPIRIT." (p. 88.)

The *nebulous* is a striking peculiarity of the style of the Vicar of Broad Chalke[s]. He informs us that "in virtue of the identity of Thought with Being the primitive Trinity represented neither three originant principles nor three transient phases, but three eternal subsistencies in one Divine Mind. ... The Divine Consciousness or Wisdom, consubstantial with the

---

[r] And yet,—"I go to prepare *a place* for you!"—St. John xiv. 2.
[s] See, for example, p. 60, (*lower half,*) p. 62, (*middle,*) &c.

Eternal Will, becoming personal in the Son of Man, is the express image of the FATHER; and JESUS actually, but also Mankind ideally, is the SON of GOD." (pp. 88-9.) Since this has "almost a Brahmanical sound" (p. 89.) even to the Vicar of Broad Chalke, we are content to pass it by in mute astonishment. He proceeds: "Both spiritual affection and metaphysical reasoning forbid us to confine Revelations like those of CHRIST to the first half century of our era; but shew at least affinities of our faith existing in men's minds, anterior to Christianity, and renewed with deep echo from living hearts in many a generation." (p. 82.) Was our SAVIOUR then a fabulous personage,—a virtuous principle,—and not a Man?... "Again. We find the evidences of our canonical books and of the patristic authors nearest to them, are sufficient to prove illustration in outward act of principles perpetually true, but not adequate to guarantee narratives inherently incredible or precepts evidently wrong." (pp. 82-3.) Are then the sacred "narratives" "inherently incredible?" or the Divine "precepts" "evidently wrong?"—These are, we presume, among the "traditional fictions about our Canon" (p. 83.) at which the Theological Professor sneers. "Hence we are obliged to assume in ourselves a verifying faculty,"—(p. 83,) and so, Dr. Williams and Dr. Temple shake hands[t]. An instance of the exercise of this faculty is immediately subjoined. "The verse 'And no man hath ascended up to Heaven, but he that came down,' is intelligible as a free comment near the end of the first century; but has no meaning in our LORD's mouth at a time when the Ascension had not been heard of." (p. 84.)—"The Apocalypse"

---

[t] Comp. p. 45.

in like manner, to "cease to be a riddle," must be "taken as a series of poetical visions which represent the outpouring of the vials of wrath upon the City where our LORD was slain." (p. 84.) . . . (Is it possible that a Minister of the Gospel of CHRIST can speak thus concerning the Divine record?) . . . "The second of the Petrine Epistles, having alike external and internal evidence against its genuineness, is necessarily surrendered as a whole." (p. 84.) (Can a man solemnly sign the vith Article, and yet so write?)—"A philosophical view [of the doctrine of the Trinity] recommends itself as easiest to believe." (p. 87.) The "view" expressed in the Athanasian Creed is we presume that which is stigmatized as "one felt to be so irrational, that it calls in the aid of terror." (p. 87.) The Reverend writer does not *name* the Athanasian Creed, indeed. It is not the general fashion of Essayists and Reviewers,—from Dr. Temple to Professor Jowett,—to speak plainly. But common sense asks, —If Dr. Williams does *not* allude to the Creed in question, what *does* he allude to? And common honesty adds,—How is such an allusion to that formula consistent with subscription to Art. viii.?

The Sacrament of Baptism, (he says,) has "degenerated into a magical form," (p. 86,) since it has "become twisted into a false analogy with circumcision,"—(twisted, at all events, by St. Paul[u]!)—and it is merely an "Augustinian notion" that "a curse is inherited by Infants."—How, one humbly asks, does the Reverend writer reconcile it to his conscience not only to have signed the ixth Article, but to employ the Baptismal Service, and to teach the little ones of the flock their Catechism?

[u] Col. ii. 11, 12. Rom. ii. 29. Phil. iii. 3, &c.

On reaching the last page of the present Essay, one is irresistibly led to remark that if a single word could convey an adequate notion of the author's manner, that word would be *Insolence*. When Dr. Williams would express difference of opinion, he has recourse to violence and bluster: when he would patronize, he is sure to make himself unspeakably offensive. But he seldom agrees with anybody, even with disciples of the same school with himself,—as Messrs. Bunsen and Arnold, Coleridge and Francis Newman. Professor Mansel is "a mere gladiator hitting in the dark," whose "blows fall heaviest on what it was his duty to defend." (p. 67.) Dr. Pusey receives a menacing intimation of what his Commentary must *not* be. Davison's reasoning labours under the inconvenient defect of an unproved minor premiss. (p. 66.) The majestic memory of Bp. Pearson is insulted by this vulgar man, and the fairness of his citations are impeached. (p. 72.)—Bp. Butler is declared to have turned aside from an unwelcome idea (!), literature not being his strong point (!) (p. 65.)—Justin, (p. 64,) —Augustine, (p. 65,)—Jerome, (pp. 65, 71,)—Anselm, (p. 67,)—all come in for a share of the Vice-Principal of Lampeter's contempt. Even the Apologist of *Essays and Reviews* is constrained to admit that "anything more" *un*becoming "than some of Dr. Williams's remarks we have never read, in writings professing to be written seriously[v]."

But faults of mind and manner, however gross, do but disqualify a writer for being the associate of men of taste and good breeding; and blemishes of style are, at least, venial. Not so easily to be excused is the deplorable spectacle of a Minister of the Gospel,

[v] *Edinburgh Review*, (Ap. 1861,) p. 429.

a Doctor of Divinity and Vice-Principal of a Theological College, lending all his critical powers, (which yet seem to be of the most indifferent description,) in order to undermine the authority of God's Word. He has been asked,—"Do you unfeignedly believe all the Canonical Scriptures of the Old and New Testament?" and he has answered,—"I do believe them." He has been asked, "Will you be ready, with all diligence, to banish and drive away all erroneous and strange doctrines contrary to God's Word?" and he has made reply,—"I will, the LORD being my helper." He has solemnly declared his trust that he was "*inwardly moved by the HOLY GHOST to take upon himself this office and ministration.*"—Yet this is the man who explains away Miracles, denies Prophecy, and idealizes Scripture; the man who disparages the formulæ he uses daily, mutilates the Canon, and evacuates the most solemn doctrines of the Church!

I have now said as much as I think necessary concerning Dr. Williams's Essay. The entire refutation of such a tissue of groundless assertions and unfounded statements, and unscholarlike criticisms, and unphilosophical views,—would fill many volumes. It is to be feared also that, to *him*, the result would not be convincing after all. To have stated in brief outline, as I have already done, the leading positions to which he commits himself, ought to suffice. The mere exhibition of such principles (?) ought to be their own abundant refutation. ... God give the unhappy author repentance of his errors!—And will not men believe that in the pages of the present Essay is to be seen the lawful development, and inevitable result of the opinions advocated *in every other part* of the present volume? I perceive scarcely any *essential* difference between the views of any of these seven writers. All are moving along the same fatal road; and are simply at different stages of the journey. But they conduct themselves wondrous differently in their progress, certainly; Dr. Williams being immeasurably the most offensive of the seven,—the only one who, besides seeming blasphemous, can truly be called *vulgar*.

III. The third Essay in the present volume is by "the Rev. Baden Powell, M.A., F.R.S., Savilian Professor of Geometry in the University of Oxford," —a gentleman with whose labours I shall deal briefly and gently for two reasons. His assertions admit of summary refutation; and he has already, (alas!) passed beyond the limit of earthly Criticism. I desire to add concerning him, that in the private relations of life he was a friendly and amiable person.

The solemn circumstance already adverted to, would have kept me silent altogether. When a writer is no longer able to defend himself, it is ungenerous to attack him: and at a time when he knows far more wonders than are dreamed of by any one on the Earth's surface, it seems unbecoming to stand reasoning over his grave about an "antecedent probability." But I am addressing not the dead, but the living,—to whom, in the pages of 'Essays and Reviews,' Professor Powell "being dead yet speaketh."

He entitles his contribution,—"On the Study of the Evidences of Christianity:" but, as often happens with performances of the like nature, the title of his Essay gives a wrong notion of its contents. It ought to have been called "The Validity of THE EVIDENCE FROM MIRACLES considered," or rather "denied."

There is nothing new in the present attack on the Miracles of Scripture. The author disposes of them by a single assertion. "What is alleged," (he says,) "is a case of the supernatural. *But no testimony can reach to the supernatural.*" (p. 107.) The inference is obvious.—Again: "an event may be so incredible intrinsically as to *set aside any degree of testimony.*" (p. 106.) Such an event he declares a Miracle to be; and explains that "from the nature of our antecedent convictions, the probability of *some* kind of mistake or deception *somewhere,* though we know not *where,* is greater than the probability of the event really happening in *the way,* and from *the causes* assigned." (pp. 106-7.) This merely amounts to asserting that the antecedent improbability of Miracles is so great as to make them incredible. The writer does not attempt to establish this point. "The present discussion," (he says,) "is not intended to be of a controversial kind; it is purely contemplative and theoretical." (p. 100.) And yet, he *cannot* suppose that the Universal Church will surrender its convictions and reverse its deliberate judgment, at the merely "contemplative and theoretical" suggestions of an individual, however respectable he may happen to be. Against his mere assertion, we claim a right to set the result of Bp. Butler's careful investigation of the same subject:—"*That there certainly is no such presumption against Miracles, as to render them in any wise incredible:* that, on the contrary, our being able to discern reasons for them, gives a positive credibility to the history of them, in cases where those reasons hold: and that it is by no means certain that there is any peculiar presumption at all, from analogy, even in the lowest degree, against Miracles, as distinguished from other extraordinary phenomena[x]."

[x] *Analogy,* P. II. ch. ii., *ad fin.*

Professor Powell's objection against Miracles is, in fact, practically that of the infidel Hume; who asserted "that no testimony for any kind of Miracle can ever possibly amount to a probability, much less to a proof." He argued that Miracles, being contrary to general experience, are incapable of proof. He maintained also, (with Spinoza,) that Miracles, being contrary to the established laws of Nature, imply, in the very character of them, a palpable contradiction. This latter position seems to be identical with that adopted by Professor Powell.

In a certain place, this author finds fault with "the too frequent assumption . . . of the part of the . . . . *Advocate*, when the character to be sustained should be rather that of the unbiassed *Judge*." (p. 95.) But what are we to think of the judicial fairness of one who is not only Advocate and Judge in his own cause; but who even turns the Witnesses out of Court; and will listen to no evidence,—on the plea that it *cannot* be trustworthy; or at least, that it *shall* be unavailing?—" I express myself with caution," (says Bp. Butler, with reference to arguments against the credibility of Revelation,) "lest I should be mistaken to vilify Reason; which is indeed the only faculty we have wherewith to judge concerning anything, even Revelation itself: or be misunderstood to assert that a supposed revelation cannot be proved false, from internal characters. For it may contain clear immoralities, or contradictions; and either of these would prove it false. Nor will I take upon me to affirm, that nothing else can possibly render any supposed revelation incredible. Yet still the observation is, I think, true beyond doubt; that *objections against*

Christianity, as distinguished from objections against its evidence, are frivolous[y]."

That a certain occurrence or phenomenon "is due to supernatural causes," Professor Powell maintains is "entirely dependent on the previous belief and assumptions of the parties." (p. 107.) He forgets that he grounds his own denial of the possibility of a Miracle, on nothing stronger than "the nature of" his own "antecedent convictions." Thus, the question becomes merely a personal one between Mr. Baden Powell and the Apostles of CHRIST. The reasonableness of the "antecedent convictions" in the one case have to be set against the reasonableness of the "antecedent convictions" in the other. Either party, (according to this view,) has its own "previous belief and assumptions;" which, in the one case, are known to have produced conviction; in the other, they are unhappily found to have resulted in a rejection of Miracles. But then it happens, unfortunately, that in the case of the Apostles and others, conviction of the truth of our LORD's Miracles was based on *knowledge*, and *experience of a matter of fact:* in the case of Professor Powell, disbelief is founded on certain "antecedent convictions" only: namely, "the inconceivableness of imagined interruptions of natural Order, or supposed suspensions of the Laws of matter." (p. 110.) He is never tired of repeating that "in an age of physical research like the present, all highly cultivated minds and duly advanced intellects (!) have imbibed, more or less, the lessons of the Inductive Philosophy; and have, at least in some measure, learned to appreciate the grand foundation conception of universal Law:" (p. 133:) that "the entire range

[y] *Analogy*, P. II. ch. iii., *ad init.*

of the Inductive Philosophy is at once based upon, and in every instance tends to confirm, by immense accumulation of evidence, the grand truth of the universal Order and constancy of natural causes, as a primary law of belief; so strongly entertained and fixed in the mind of every truly inductive inquirer, that he cannot even conceive the possibility of its failure." (p. 109.)

I gladly avail myself of a page from the writings of a thoughtful writer of our own, who, half a century ago, reviewed the very errors which are being so industriously reproduced among ourselves at this day,—certainly not with more ability than of old:—"Let us examine a little farther into the weight of the argument derived from the supposed immutability of the Laws of Nature. It has constantly been the theme of modern Unbelievers, that the course of Nature is fixed, eternal, unalterable; and that nothing which is supposed to violate it can possibly take place. Now, we may readily allow, that the course of Nature is unalterable by *human* power; nay, even by the power of any *created* being whatsoever. But the question is,—Are these Laws unalterable *by Him who made them?* Proof of this is requisite, before the argument from the immutability of the Laws of Nature can have the least force. We may safely assert, however, that proof of this is absolutely impossible.—'Facts,' it may be said, 'daily passing before us, warrant us in *supposing* its laws to be unchangeable.' Perhaps so. But if a thousand or more facts have occurred, since the Creation of the World, in which those Laws appear to have been over-ruled, or suspended, is such a conclusion *then* warrantable? Even if there had never been a single instance of a Miracle recorded, since the

Creation; yet the conclusion would not be just or logical, that no such thing is possible. But with such a multiplicity of instances to the contrary as are already on record, it is no better than a shameless assertion, in direct opposition to the evidence of men's senses and experience. Nay, more; the argument is *atheistical.* For, either GOD made and ordained these Laws of Nature; and may, consequently, at His pleasure, unmake or suspend them: or else, these laws are self-framed, and Nature is independent of the GOD of Nature; which is saying, in other words, that the material Universe is not governed by any Supreme Intelligence.

"This latter opinion appears, indeed, to be the tenet of all who resort to arguments of this kind, in opposition to the credibility of Miracles. Thus it is said, [by Hume,] that every effect must have a cause; and that, therefore, a Miracle must have a cause in *Nature;* otherwise, it cannot be effected.—But, is not the *Will of* GOD, without any other agency, or predisposing cause, sufficient for the purpose? When GOD created the World out of nothing, what pre-existing cause was there, except His own omnipotent Will to produce the effect? Why then is not the same Will sufficient to work Miracles?

"'But,' says another Sophist, [Spinoza,]—'GOD is the Author of the Laws of Nature; so that whatever opposes those Laws, is necessarily *repugnant to the Divine nature:* if, therefore, we believe that GOD may act in a manner contrary to those laws, we, in effect, believe that He may do what is contrary to *His own nature;* which is absurd and impossible.'

"The reasoning turns upon the supposition that GOD is actuated by an absolute *necessity* of His Nature, and not by his *Will:* or, rather, that He hath neither Will, nor Intellect. Otherwise, it were easy to perceive, that in suspending the operation of His own Laws, GOD cannot be charged with doing anything contradictory to *His own* nature; since He may justly be supposed to have as good reasons for *departing* from those Laws, as for *framing* them: and as we know not why He framed them in such a manner, and no otherwise; so He may have the best and wisest reasons for the suspension of them, which is not for us to call in question. To speak of the Supreme Being as actuated by a kind of physical necessity, and not by His *Will*, is to confound the GOD of Nature with Nature itself; which is the very essence of Atheism, and never can be reconciled with any just notions of the Deity, as a Being of intellectual and moral perfections[z]."

It is by no means inconceivable, therefore, that the great Cause of Creation, and first Author of Law should interfere at any given time in the established Order of Nature. Moreover, it is irrational, on sufficient testimony, to disbelieve that He has sometimes so interposed. To deny that this is conceivable, is to make GOD inferior to His own decree; to pronounce it incredible that the Lawgiver should be superior to His own Laws. "The universal subordination of causation," (p. 134,) we as freely admit as the Professor himself: but then we contend that *everything else* must be subordinate to the *First great Cause of all*. Worse than unphilosophical is it to argue as the Professor presumes to do, concerning the MOST HIGH; but unphilosophical in the strictest sense it is. For it is to reason about Him, (the finite concerning the

[z] Van Mildert's *Historical View of the Rise and Progress of Infidelity*, &c. Serm. xxi., (ed. 1806,) vol. ii. pp. 313-17.

Infinite!) as if we understood Him; we, who can barely decipher a little part of His works! A few more remarks on this subject will be found in my viith Sermon.

We are anxious to know if the whole of the case is really before us. A few more extracts from Professor Powell's Essay seem necessary to do full justice to his view of the matter:—" All moral evidence must essentially have respect to the parties to be convinced. 'Signs' might be adapted peculiarly *to the state of moral or intellectual progress of one age*, or one class of persons, and not be suited to that of others.... And it is to the entire difference in the ideas, prepossessions, modes, and grounds of belief in those times, that we may trace the reason why Miracles, which would be incredible *now*, were not so in the age, and under the circumstances, in which they are stated to have occurred." (p. 117.) ... "An evidential appeal which in a long past age was convincing, as made to *the state of knowledge in that age*[a], might have not only no effect, but even an injurious tendency, if urged in the present, and referring to what is at variance with existing scientific conceptions; just as the arguments of the present age would have been unintelligible to a former."

"In a period of advanced physical knowledge, the reference to what was believed in past times, if at variance with principles now acknowledged, could afford little ground of appeal: in fact, would damage the argument rather than assist it." (p. 126.)

"It becomes imperatively necessary, that such views should be suggested as may be really suitable to

---

[a] "Columbus' prediction of the eclipse to the native islanders, was as true an argument to them as if the event had really been supernatural." p. 115.

better informed minds, and may meet the increasing demands of an age pretending at least to greater enlightenment." (p. 126.)

There is nothing in the additional suggestions thus thrown out which in reality affects the question at issue. Certain antecedent considerations were before insisted on, which (it was said) "must be paramount to all attestation." (p. 107.) These have been disposed of. The writer now tells us that he does not question "the *honesty* or *veracity* of the testimony, or the reality of the *impressions* on the minds of the witnesses." (p. 106.) It remains to inquire therefore to what natural causes, events which were once thought miraculous, may reasonably be referred; since the so-called Miracles of the imperfectly-informed age of our LORD and His Apostles will not endure the scrutiny of the present age of scientific enlightenment.

But this, unless it be a proposal to open the whole question afresh,—to examine *the Miracles themselves*,—to consider them one by one,—to inquire into their exact nature,—and to investigate their attendant circumstances,—is unmeaning. For we cannot, as reasonable men, dismiss a vast body of august events, differing so considerably one from another, with a vague innuendo that there was probably "some kind of mistake or deception somewhere, though we do not know where:" (p. 106:) a hint that natural events may have been regarded as supernatural by an unscientific age, (which I believe was Schleiermacher's view:) and so forth. The two miraculous Draughts of fishes,—the Stater found in the fish's mouth,—the stilling of the Storm,—might perhaps, by a little rhetorical sophistry, in unscrupulous hands, be so disposed of. But the *Creative Power* displayed on the two occasions of a miraculous feeding of thousands,—the giving of sight to a man born blind,—the calling of Lazarus out of the grave where he had been for four days buried; —these are transactions which resist every attempt of the enemy to explain away, as unscientific misconceptions. They may be powerless to produce conviction in some *now*, as they were powerless to produce conviction in some *then:* but they cannot be set aside by an insinuation. There could not have been any mistake when the Five Thousand were fed with five loaves, and twelve baskets full were gathered up; or when the Four Thousand were fed with seven loaves, and fragments enough to fill seven baskets remained over[b]. There was no room for deception in the case of the man born blind; for *that* case immediately underwent a judicial scrutiny[c]. Lazarus bound hand and foot with grave-clothes required that the bystanders should "loose him and let him go[d]:" but from that moment, neither supposed scientific necessity, nor antecedent considerations, nor the ordinary course of Nature, nor any other creature, will avail to bind him any more!

This may suffice on the subject of Professor Powell's Essay. On the great question itself, I have said something in my Seventh Sermon, to which the reader is requested to refer.—The performance now under consideration abounds in incorrect statements, while it revives not a few exploded objections; but I have considered the only points in it which are material.

Thus the author assumes " that, unlike the *essential Doctrines* of Christianity, 'the same yesterday, to-

[b] St. Mark viii. 19, 20.   [c] St. John ix.   [d] St. John xi. 44.

day, and for ever,' these *external accessories*, [Miracles, for example,] constitute a subject which of necessity is perpetually taking somewhat at least of a new form, with the successive phases of opinion and knowledge." (p. 94.) But, (waiving for the moment the impossibility of severing the Doctrines of the Gospel from the miraculous evidence that our LORD was a Teacher sent from Heaven[e], it requires no ability to perceive that although "opinion" should alter daily, and "knowledge" increase ever so much, yet, events professing to be miraculous, being plain *matters of fact*, are to-day exactly what and where they were many centuries ago. Physical Science may pretend (with Paulus) to explain them on natural principles, truly; and while she does so, the world is sure to give her a patient, even an indulgent hearing. But then she must let it be known *what* she proposes to explain, and *how* she proposes to explain it. She must be so indulgent also, as to listen while we, in turn, shew her *on what* grounds we find it impossible to accept her Theory. "The inevitable progress of research," (says this author,) "must, within a longer or shorter period, unravel *all that seems most marvellous;* and what is at present least understood will become as familiarly known to the Science of the future, as those points which a few centuries ago, were involved in equal obscurity, but are now thoroughly understood." (p. 109.) Such a vaticination as regards Miracles, is, to say the least, premature; and until it can appeal to incipient accomplishment, it must be regarded

---

[e] Consider St. John iii. 2, (referring to ii. 23 and iv. 45.) So ix. 16: x. 21 and 38: xiv. 10, 11. Also xv. 24; and consider St. Luke vii. 16: also 21, 22: St. Matth. xii. 22, 23: St. John vii. 31: xii. 17—19.

as nugatory also. I am not aware, that as yet one single Miracle has been struck off the list; yet Miracles have now been before the world a long time, and they have not wanted enemies either.

To begin Divinity with a discussion of the "Evidences," we do indeed hold to be a beginning *at the wrong end*. At the same time, all of Professor Powell's opening remarks, in which he insinuates that the Church would bar, or would stifle discussion concerning the evidences of Religion, are obviously untrue. No scrutiny of Christian Miracles, however rigid, is stopped by the admonition that such narratives " ought to be held sacred, and exempt from the unhallowed criticism of human Reason." (p. 110.) We do not, by any means, " treat all objections as profane, and discard exceptions unanswered as shocking and immoral." (p. 100.) Neither does the Church think herself "omniscient and infallible;" (p. 96;) though she holds Omniscience to be an attribute of GOD; and Infallibility, of the Bible. But she deprecates in the strongest manner vague insinuations and unsupported doubts of the reality of her LORD's Miracles, sown broad-cast over the land; and she is at a loss to understand how the " difficulties" of any, can be in this manner "removed;" (p. 96;) except by a process analogous to that which would cure a malady by taking away the life of the patient. We are not in fact at all disposed to admit that " Miracles, which in the estimation of a former age were among the chief *supports* of Christianity, are at present among the main *difficulties*, and hindrances to its acceptance," (p. 140,)—although Professor Powell and Dr. Temple say so.

This Essay in fact is full of incorrect, or objectionable statements. Thus Professor Powell asserts that since " evidential arguments are avowedly addressed to the intellect, it is especially preposterous to shift the ground, and charge the rejection of them on *moral motives.*" (p. 100.) And yet it is worthy of notice that our LORD Himself assures us that the reception of Truth depends on our moral, rather than on our intellectual condition. "How can ye believe," (He said to the Jews,) "which receive honour one of another, and seek not the honour that cometh from GOD only'?"

This writer reasons also with singular laxity and inaccuracy. After quoting the dictum that "on a certain amount of testimony we might believe any statement, however improbable," (pp. 140-1,) he scornfully adds ;—" So that if a number of respectable witnesses were to concur in asseverating that on a certain occasion they had seen two and two make five, we should be bound to believe them !" (p. 141.) Does he fail to perceive, (1) that mathematical truths do not come within the province of probable reasoning, and (2) are not dependent on testimony ? . . . . Again, " The case of the *antecedent* argument of Miracles

---

' St. John v. 44. Comp. vii. 17 : viii. 12. St. Matth. v. 8. Ps. xix. 8 : cxix. 100. Also, Ecclus. i. 26 : xxi. 11.—" There is," (says an excellent living writer,) " scarcely any doctrine or precept of our SAVIOUR more distinctly and strongly stated, than that the capacity for judging of, and for believing the Truths of Christianity, depends upon Moral Goodness, and the practice of Virtue."—Let us hear our own Hooker on this subject :—" We find by experience that although Faith be an intellectual habit of the mind, and have her seat in the understanding, yet an evil moral disposition obstinately wedded to the love of darkness dampeth the very light of heavenly illumination, and permitteth not the Mind to see what doth shine before it."—*Eccl. Pol.*, B. v. c. lxiii. § 2.

is very clear, however little some are inclined to perceive it. In Nature and from Nature, by Science and by Reason, *we neither have nor can possibly have any evidence of a Deity working by Miracles;*—for that, we must go out of Nature, and beyond Science." (pp. 141-2.) Very true. We must go *to Scripture.* We must have recourse to testimony. This is precisely what we are maintaining. . . . . But,—" Testimony, after all, is but a second-hand assurance; it is but a blind guide; testimony can avail nothing against Reason." (p. 141.) True. But this, if it is intended as an argument against the reasonableness of admitting the truth of Miracles, is a mere *petitio principii.* . . . . Again. "It is not the *mere fact* but the *cause* or *explanation* of it, which is the point at issue." (p. 141.) Admitting then, as the learned author here does, that when CHRIST said "Lazarus, come forth," "he that was dead," (though he had been buried four days,) "came forth, bound hand and foot with grave-clothes[g];"—admitting these "facts," I say,—what other "cause," or "explanation" does the reverend gentleman propose to assign but the supernatural power of the Divine Speaker?

Far graver exception, however, must be taken against certain parts of Professor Powell's labours, which betray an animus fatally indicative of the tendency of such Essays and Reviews as these. Witness his assertion that "it is now acknowledged that 'Creation' is only another name for our ignorance of the mode of production;" (p. 139;) and that a recent work on the Origin of Species "substantiates on undeniable grounds the very principle so long de-

---

[g] St. John xi. 44.

nounced by the first naturalists,—*the origination of new Species by natural causes;*" (p. 139;) and that the said work "must soon bring about an entire revolution of opinion in favour of the grand principle of the *self-evolving powers of Nature.*" (p. 139.)

One object of the present Essay is to insist that since Miracles belong to the world of matter, "we must recognize the due claims of Science to decide" upon them. We are reminded that "beyond the domain of physical causation and the possible conceptions of *intellect* or *knowledge*, there lies open the boundless region of spiritual things, which is the sole dominion of Faith:" (p. 127:) and that "Advancing knowledge, while it asserts the dominion of Science in physical things, confirms that of Faith in spiritual." (p. 127.) It is proposed that "we thus neither impugn the generalizations of Philosophy, nor allow them to invade the dominion of Faith; and admit that what is not a subject for a problem, may hold its place in a Creed." (p. 127.)

But the fatal consequences of this plausible fallacy become apparent the instant we turn the leaf, and read that "the more knowledge advances, the more it has been, and will be acknowledged, that Christianity, as a real religion, must be viewed apart from connexion with physical things." (p. 128.) That "the first dissociation of the spiritual from the physical was rendered necessary by the palpable contradictions disclosed by astronomical discovery with the letter of Scripture. Another still wider and more material step has been effected by the discoveries of Geology. More recently, the antiquity of the Human Race, and the development of Species, and *the rejection of the idea of 'Creation'* (!) have caused new advances in the same direction." (p. 129.) . . . . From this it is evident, not only that the object of Science in thus taking the Miracles of Scripture into her own keeping, is (like an unnatural step-dame) to slay them; but that downright Atheism is to be the attitude in which men are expected to survey that "boundless region of spiritual things" which is yet proclaimed to be "the sole dominion of Faith!"

Faith, on the other hand, does not object to the constant visits of Science to any part of *her* treasure. She does but insist that all discussion shall be conducted *according to the rules of right Reason.* Vague insinuations about "a progressing Age," (p. 131,)—"new modes of speculation," (p. 130,)—"the advance of Opinion," (p. 131,)—and so forth, are as little to the purpose, *apart from specific objections,* as sneers at "the one-sided dogmas of an obsolete school, coupled with awful denunciations of heterodoxy on all who refuse to listen to them," (p. 131,) are unsuited to the gravity of the occasion. Faith insists moreover that a divorce between the miraculous parts of Scripture, and the context wherein they stand, is simply impossible. The unbeliever who boldly says, "I disbelieve the Bible,"—however much we may deplore his blindness and pity his misery,—is yet intelligible in his unbelief. But the man who proposes to believe *the narrative* of the Exode of Israel from Egypt, (for instance,) apart from the supernatural character of the events which are related to have attended it; who believes *the history* of the Gospels, (holding the Evangelists to have been veracious writers,) yet rejects the Divine nature of the Miracles which the Gospels relate; and proposes, after eliminating from the historical narrative everything which claims to be miraculous, to make what remains of that historical narrative, the strength and stay of his soul in life and in death:— *that* man we boldly affirm to be one who cannot have studied the Bible with that ordinary attention which would entitle him to dogmatize concerning its contents: or else, whose logical faculty must be so hopelessly defective that discussions of this class are evidently not his proper province.

Finally, we are presented in this Essay with the same offensive assumption of intellectual superiority on the part of the writer, which disfigures the entire volume. "It becomes *imperatively necessary* that views should be suggested really suitable *to better informed minds.*" (p. 126.) "Points which may be seen to involve the greatest difficulty to *more profound inquirers*, are often such as do not occasion the least perplexity to *ordinary minds*, but are allowed to pass without hesitation." (p. 125.) (And this, from one of those "profound inquirers," one of "those who have reflected most deeply," (p. 126,) who yet cannot get beyond a resuscitation of Hume and Spinoza's exploded objections to the truth of Miracles!)—Butler's unanswerable arguments, (for the allusion is evidently to *him*,) are spoken of as "a few trite and commonplace generalities as to the moral government of the World and the belief in the Divine Omnipotence; or as to the validity of human testimony; or the limits of human experience." (p. 133.) And yet the author is for ever informing us that his hostility to Miracles "is essentially built upon those *grander conceptions* of the order of Nature, those comprehensive primary elements of all physical knowledge, those ultimate ideas of universal causation, which can only be familiar to *those thoroughly versed in cosmical philosophy in its widest sense.*" (p. 133.) "All *highly cultivated minds, and duly advanced intellects,*" are supposed to find their exponent in Professor Baden Powell. All other thinkers have "*minds of a less comprehensive capacity,*" "accustomed to reason on *more contracted views.*" (p. 133. See also p. 131, *top.*) Is this the modesty of real Science? the language of a true Philosopher and Divine?

Finally, after all that has gone before we are not much astonished, but we *are* considerably shocked, to read as follows:—"The Divine Omnipotence is entirely an inference *from the language of the Bible,* adopted *on the assumption* of a belief in Revelation. That 'with God nothing is impossible' is the very declaration of Scripture; yet on this, the whole belief in Miracles is built [h]." Now, it happens that 'the whole belief in Miracles' is built on nothing of the kind: but the point is immaterial. By no means immaterial, however, is the intimation that the Divine attribute of Omnipotence is a mere inference from the language of Revelation,—the very belief in which is also a mere "assumption." If *belief in Holy Scripture* is to be treated as *an assumption,*—without at all complaining of the unreasonableness of one who so speaks, —we yet desire that he would say it very plainly; and let us know at least *with whom* we have to do, and *what* we are expected to prove. We do not complain, if any one calls upon us to shew that a belief in the Bible cannot be called an assumption; but it makes us very sad: and when the challenge comes from a Minister of the Church, we are unable to forbear the remark that there is something altogether

[h] P. 113. The italics are in the original.

immoral[1] in the entire proceeding. On the other hand, to find ourselves involved in an argument on questions of Divinity with one *who believes nothing*, is in a manner absurd; and provokes a feeling of resentment as well as of pity. . . . What need to add that life is not long enough for such processes of proof? "He that cometh unto God *must believe that He is!*" We cannot be for ever laying the foundation. The building must begin, at last, to grow. And when it *has* grown up, and is compact as well as beautiful, it *cannot* be necessary to pull it all down again once or twice in every century in order to ascertain whether the strong foundations be still there!

IV. The next performance is mainly directed against faith in the Church, as a society of Divine origin. "The Rev. HENRY BRISTOW WILSON, B.D., Vicar of Great Staughton, Hunts," claims that a National Church shall be regarded as a purely secular Institution,—the spontaneous development of the State. "If all priests and ministers of religion could at one moment be swept from the face of the Earth, they would soon be reproduced[k]." The Church is concerned with Ethics, not with Divinity. It should therefore be "free from dogmatic tests, and similar intellectual bondage:" (p. 168:) hampered by no traditional Doctrines; pledged to no Creeds: but, on the contrary, should be subject to periodical doctrinal

---

[1] See the *Quarterly Review*, (on Prof. Baden Powell's "Order of Nature,")—for Oct. 1859, (No. 212,) pp. 420-3.

[k] p. 169.—"Priests have neither been, as some would represent, a set of deliberate conspirators against the free thoughts of mankind; nor, on the other hand," &c. *Ibid.*—How partial becomes the judgment, when we have to discuss the merits of our own order!

re-adjustments. " Doctrinal limitations " (i. e. the Creeds) " are not essential to " the Church. " Upon larger knowledge of Christian history, upon a more thorough acquaintance with the mental constitution of man, upon an understanding of the obstacles they present to a true Catholicity (!), they may be cast off." (p. 167.) "In order to the possibility of recruiting any national Ministry from the whole of the nation, ... no needless intellectual or speculative obstacles should be interposed." (p. 196. So at p. 198.)

To all this, the answer is very obvious. Viewed as an historical fact, the Church is *not* of human origin. The Church *is* a Divine Institution. That a Priest of the Church, charged with a cure of souls, should desire her annihilation,—the reversal of the facts of her past History,—her reconstruction on an unheard-of basis, without even Creeds as terms of communion with her,—and so forth; all this may suggest some very painful doubts as *to the objector's honesty* in continuing to employ the formularies of that Church, and in professing to teach her doctrines;—but it can hardly be supposed to have any effect whatever on the question at issue.

Foreseeing this, Mr. Wilson begins by asserting,— (for to insinuate is not for so advanced a disciple of " the negative Theology,") (p. 151,)—" the fact of a very wide-spread alienation, both of educated and uneducated persons, from the Christianity which is ordinarily presented in our Churches and Chapels." (p. 150.) " A self-satisfied Sacerdotalism, confident in a supernaturally transmitted illumination," may amuse itself in trying to " keep peace within the walls of emptied Churches:" (p. 150:) but the day for " traditional Christianity" (p. 149.) has gone by.

We may no longer ignore "a great extent of dissatisfaction on the part of the Clergy at some portion, at least, of formularies of the Church of England,"—especially at the use of "one unhappy creed." (p. 150.) There has been "a spontaneous recoil" from some of the old doctrines: a distrust of the old arguments: and a misgiving concerning Scripture itself. "In the presence of difficulties of this kind, ... it is vain to seek to check open discussion." (p. 151.)

Why then does not this man proceed openly to discuss? is the obvious rejoinder. Instead of vaguely hinting that either the Reason or the Moral sense is shocked by what people hear "in our Churches and Chapels,"—why has not this writer, first, the honesty to withdraw from the Ministry of the Church of England; and next, the courage to indicate the particular doctrines which offend? To say that "the ordinances of public worship and religious instruction provided for the people of England" are not "really adapted to the wants of their nature as it is," (p. 150,) is a very vague and unworthy style of urging an objection. Why does not the reverend writer explain *wherein* the Doctrine and Discipline of the English Church are not really adapted to the actual wants of Man's nature?

Let every unbeliever however be allowed to state his difficulties in his own way. Mr. Wilson's difficulties certainly take a very peculiar shape. The increased *Geographical* knowledge of the present generation has evidently disturbed his faith. "In our own boyhood, the World as known to the ancients was nearly all which was known to ourselves (!). We have recently become acquainted,—intimate,—with the teeming regions of the far East, and with empires, pagan or even atheistic, of which the origin runs far back beyond the historic records of Judæa or of the West, and which were more populous than all Christendom now is, for many ages before the Christian era." (p. 152.) Such a statement is soon made; but it ought to have been substantiated. I take the liberty of doubting its accuracy.

But granting even that the heathen world "for many ages before the Christian era" *was* more populous than all Christendom now is: — what then? This fact "*suggests questions* to those who on Sundays hear the reading and exposition of the Scriptures as they were expounded to our forefathers, and on Monday peruse the news of a World of which our forefathers little dreamed." (pp. 152-3.)—And pray, (we calmly inquire,) *Why* are the Scriptures to be read or expounded after a novel fashion, even though our geographical knowledge *has* made a considerable advance? To this, we are favoured with no answer. The "questions" suggested are, we presume, the same which are contained in the following sentence. " In what relation does the Gospel stand to these millions[m]? Is there any trace on the face of its records that it even contemplated their existence[n]? We are told, that to know and believe in JESUS CHRIST is in some sense necessary to Salvation. It has not been given to these. Are they,—will they be, hereafter,—the worse off for their ignorance?" (p. 153.) ... "As to the necessity of faith in a SAVIOUR to these peoples

[m] *Ans.* Clearly in the relation of a blessing which has by all means to be communicated to them.

[n] *Ans.* Certainly there is. Those which most obviously present themselves are such as the following :—St. Matth. ix. 37, 38 : xxviii. 19, 20. St. Luke xxiv. 47. Acts ii. 38, 39, &c.

when they could never have had it, no one, upon reflection, can believe in any such thing. Doubtless they will be equitably dealt with." (p. 153.)

These last seven words, (which scarcely seem of a piece with the rest of the sentence,) we confess have always seemed a sufficient answer to the badly-expressed speculative difficulty which immediately precedes; a difficulty, be it observed, which does not depend *at all* on the popular advancement of Geographical knowledge; for it was urged with the self-same force anciently, as now; and was met by Bp. Butler, almost in the self-same words[o], upwards of a hundred years ago. But Mr. Wilson to our surprise and sorrow proceeds:—" We cannot be content to wrap this question up and leave it for a mystery, as to what shall become of those myriads upon myriads of non-Christian races. First, if our traditions tell us, that they are involved in the curse and perdition of Adam, and may justly be punished hereafter individually for his transgression, not having been extricated from it by saving faith,—we are disposed to think that our traditions cannot herein fairly declare to us the words and inferences from Scripture; but if on examination it should turn out that they have,—we must say, that the authors of the Scriptural books have, in those matters, represented to us their own inadequate conceptions, and not the mind of the SPIRIT of GOD." (pp. 153-4.)

I forbear to dwell upon the grievous spectacle with which we are thus presented. Here is a Clergyman of the Church of England deliberately proposing the following dilemma:—Either the Prayer Book is incorrect in its most important doctrinal inferences from

[o] *Analogy*, P. II. c. vi.

Holy Scripture; or else, the Authors of Holy Scripture itself are incorrect in their statements. The morality of one who declares that he finds himself placed between the horns of this dilemma, and yet retains his office as a public teacher in the Church of England,—it is painful to contemplate. But this is only *ad hominem.* The Reverend writer's difficulty remains.

And it seems sufficient to reply:—It is not *we* who "wrap up the question," but God. As a mystery we find it; and as a mystery, we not only "can," but *must* be content to "leave it." Further, it is not "*our traditions,*" but Holy Scripture itself which tells us that "by one man Sin entered into the World, and Death by Sin; and so Death passed upon all men, for that all have sinned[p]:"—that "in Adam all died[q]:"—that "we were by nature the children of wrath, even as others[r]:" and the like. Scripture, on the other hand, as unequivocally assures us that God is good, or rather that He is very Goodness. We are convinced, (in Mr. Wilson's words,) "that all shall be equitably dealt with according to their opportunities." (p. 154.) Moreover, *he* would be a rash Divine who should venture to adopt the opinion so strenuously disclaimed by Bp. Butler, "that none can have the benefit of the general Redemption, but such as have the advantage of being made acquainted with it in the present life[s]."

.... How, in the meantime, speculative difficulties concerning the hereafter of the unevangelized Heathen are affected by the fact that our population now "peruse the news of a World of which our forefathers little dreamed," (pp. 152-3,)—it is hard to see. Equally

---

[p] Rom. v. 12.   [q] 1 Cor. xv. 22.   [r] Eph. ii. 3.
[s] *Analogy,* P. II. c. v. note (d).

unable am I also to understand how the discovery that a larger number of persons are the subjects of this speculative difficulty than used once to be supposed, can constitute any reason why Scripture should not still be read and expounded on Sunday "as it used to be expounded to our forefathers."

We have been so particular, because whenever any of these writers condescend to be argumentative, *we are eager to bear them company*. No wish at all have we, in the abstract, to stifle inquiry; no objection whatever have we to the principle of free discussion. And yet, as a clergyman, I cannot discuss such questions as these with a *Minister of the Church of England*, except under protest. I deny that these are in any sense open questions. To dispute concerning them,—εἰ μὴ θέσιν διαφυλάττων,—one of the disputants must first, at least, resign his commission. It is simply dishonest in a man to hold a commission in the Church of England, under solemn vows, and yet to deny her doctrines. An Officer in the Army who should pursue a similar line of action, would be dismissed the Service,—or worse.—Under protest, then, we follow the Rev. H. B. Wilson, B.D.

Next come three other specimens "of the modern questionings of traditional Christianity," "whereby observers are rendered dissatisfied with old modes of speaking:" (p. 156:) viz. (1) St. Paul "speaks of the Gospel 'which was preached to every nation (*sic*) under heaven,' when it has never yet been preached to the half[t]." (2) "Then, again, it has often been appealed to as an evidence of the supernatural origin of Christianity, and as an instance of supernatural assistance vouchsafed to it in the first centuries, that

[t] Col. i. 23.—p. 155.

it so soon overspread the world:" (p. 155:) whereas "it requires no learning to be aware that neither then nor subsequently have the Christians amounted to a fourth part of the people of the Earth." (*Ibid.*) (3) So again, "it has been customary to argue that, *à priori*, a supernatural Revelation was to be expected at the time when JESUS CHRIST was manifested upon the Earth, by reason of the exhaustion of all natural or unassisted human efforts for the amelioration of mankind;" (pp. 155-6;) whereas "our recently enlarged Ethnographical information shews such an argument to be altogether inapplicable to the case." "It would be more like the realities of things, as we can now behold them, to say that the Christian Revelation was given to the Western World, because it deserved it better and was more prepared for it than the East." (p. 156.)—The remedy for the first of these difficulties (says Mr. Wilson,) is, "candidly to acknowledge that the words of the New Testament which speak of the preaching of the Gospel to the whole world, were limited to the understanding of the times when they were spoken." The suggestions of our own moral instincts are rather to be followed, "than the express declarations of Scripture writers, who had no such knowledge as is given to ourselves of the amplitude of the World." (p. 157.)

For my own part, I see not how Mr. Wilson's proposed remedy meets the case; unless he means to say that in the time of St. Paul the Gospel had been literally preached to the whole World *as far as the World was then known*. If not, it is clear that recourse must be had to some other expedient. Instead then of the "candid acknowledgment" required of *us* by the learned writer, may we be allowed to suggest to *him* the more prosaic expedient (1st) of making sure that he quotes Scripture accurately; and (2nd) that he understands it? ... It happens that St. Paul does not use the words "*every nation under heaven*," as Mr. Wilson inadvertently supposes. The Apostle's phrase, πάσῃ τῇ κτίσει, in Colossians i. 23, (as in St. Mark xvi. 15), means 'to the whole Creation,' or 'every creature;' (the article is doubtful;) in other words, he announces the universality of the Gospel, as contrasted with the Law; and he explains that it had been preached *to the Heathen* as well as to the Jews. Our increased knowledge therefore has nothing whatever to do with the question; and the supposed difficulty disappears. The two which remain, being (according to the same writer,) merely incorrect inferences of Biblical critics, need not, it is presumed, be regarded as insurmountable either.

Following Mr. Wilson through his successive vagaries of religious (?) thought, we come upon a succession of strange statements; the object of which seems to be to cast a slur on *Doctrine* generally.— The doctrine of Justification by faith "is not met with ∴ ... in the Apostolic writings, *except those of St. Paul*." (p. 160.) [A minute exception truly!].—" Then, on the other hand, it is maintained by a large body of Theologians, as by the learned Jesuit Petavius and many others, that the doctrine afterwards developed into the Nicene and Athanasian, is not to be found explicitly in the earliest fathers, nor even in Scripture, although provable by it." (p. 160.) [Would it not have been fair, however, to state what appears to have been the design of Petavius therein[n]? and should it not have been added that our own Bishop Bull in his immortal " Defensio Fidei Nicænæ" established the very reverse " out of the writings of the Catholic Doctors

[n] See Nelson's *Life of Bp. Bull*, p. 245.

who flourished within the first three centuries of the Christian Church[x]?"] "The nearer we come to the original sources of the History, the less definite do we find the statements of Doctrines, and even of the facts from which the Doctrines were afterwards inferred." (p. 160.) "In the patristic writings, theoretics assume continually an increasingly disproportionate value. Even within the compass of our New Testament, there is to be found already a wonderful contrast between the words of our LORD and such a discourse as the Epistle to the Hebrews." (pp. 160-1.) [What a curious discovery, by the way, that an argumentative Epistle should differ in style from an historical Gospel!] "Our LORD's Discourses," (continues this writer,) "have almost all of them a direct *Moral* bearing." (p. 161.) [The case of St. John's Gospel immediately recurs to our memory. And it seems to have occurred to Mr. Wilson's also. He says:—] "This character of His words is certainly more obvious in the first three Gospels than in the fourth; and the remarkable unison of those Gospels, when they recite the LORD's words, notwithstanding their discrepancies in some matters of fact, compels us to think, that *they embody more exact traditions of what He actually said than the fourth does.*" (p. 161.) [In other words, the authenticity of St. John's Gospel[y] is

---

[x] See Nelson's *Life of Bp. Bull*, p. 242.

[y] "The horizon which his view embraced was *much narrower* than St. Paul's,"—who had enlarged his mind by foreign travel. (p. 168.)

In a note, we are informed that "at any rate his Gospel cannot, by external evidence, be attached to the person (!) of St. John as its author." "Many persons," (it is added,) "shrink from a *bonâ fide* examination of the 'Gospel question,' because they imagine, that unless the four Gospels are received as . . . entirely the composition of the persons whose names they bear, and without any admixture

to be suspected rather than the worthlessness of the speculations of the Vicar of Great Staughton!]

The object of three pages which follow (pp. 162-5.) seems to be to shew that in the Apostolic Age, Immorality of life was more severely dealt with, even than erroneousness of Doctrine. Except because the writer is eager to depreciate the value of orthodoxy of belief, and to cast a slur on doctrinal standards generally,—it is hard to see why he should write thus. Let him be reminded however that our SAVIOUR makes Faith itself a *moral*, not an *intellectual* habit[a]; and, (if it be not an uncivil remark,) what but an *immoral* spectacle does a Clergyman present who openly inculcates distrust of these very Doctrines which he has in the most solemn manner pledged himself to uphold and maintain?

And thus we come back to the theme originally proposed. "A national Church," we are informed, "need not, historically speaking, be Christian (!); nor, if it be Christian, need it be tied down to particular forms which have been prevalent at certain times in Christendom (!). That which is essential to a National Church is, that it should undertake to assist the spiritual progress of the nation and of the individuals of which it is composed, in their several states and stages. Not even a Christian Church

---

of legendary matter or embellishment in their narratives, the only alternative is to suppose a fraudulent design in those who did compose them." (p. 161.) . . . . May one who has *not* shrunk from 'the Gospel question' be permitted to regret that the Reverend writer has not specified the charges which he thus vaguely brings against the Gospels? *What*, pray, is the legendary matter; and *which* are the embellishments?

In the same page we read of "the first, or genuine, epistle of St. Peter." Is not his *second* epistle genuine, then?

[a] See above, p. lviii.

should expect all those who are brought under its influence to be, as a matter of fact, of one and the same standard; but should endeavour to raise each according to his capacities, and should give no occasion for a reaction against itself, nor provoke the individualist element into separation." (p. 173.) Of what sort the Ministers of such a "chartered libertine" are to prove, may be anticipated. "Thought and speech, which are free among all other classes," must be free also " among those who hold the office of leaders and teachers of the rest in the highest things." The Ministers of the Church ought not "to be bound to cover up, but to open; and having, it is presumed, possession of the key of knowledge, ought not to stand at the door with it, permitting no one to enter unless by force. A National Church may also find itself in this position, which, perhaps, is our own." (p. 174.)— What a charming picture of the duties and the method of that class to which the Vicar of Great Staughton himself belongs! . . . The writer proceeds to set an example of that freedom of inquiry which he vindicates as the privilege of his Order; and without which he is apprehensive of being left isolated between "the fanatical religionist," (p. 174,) (i. e. the man who believes the truths he teaches,) and "the negative theologian," (i. e. those who, "impatient of old fetters, follow free thought heedlessly wherever it may lead them." (*Ibid.*) "The freedom of opinion[a]," (he says,)

---

[a] "Pleas for 'liberty of conscience' and 'freedom of opinion,'" (as an excellent writer has recently pointed out,) "can have neither place nor pretext, while there is liberty, for all who choose, to decline joining the Church of England; *and freedom, for all who choose, to leave her.*"—Rev. C. Forster's 'Spinoza Redivivus,' (1861,) p. 6.

"which belongs to the English citizen should be conceded to the English Churchman; and the freedom which is already practically enjoyed by the members of the congregation, cannot without injustice be denied to its ministers." (p. 180.) Let us see how the Reverend Gentleman exercises the license which he claims:—

The phrase "Word of God," (he says,) is unauthorized and begs the question. The epithet "Canonical" "may mean either books ruled and determined by the Church, or regulation books; and the employment of it in the Article hesitates between these two significations." (p. 175.) The declaration of the sixth Article simply implies "the Word of God is contained in Scripture; whence it does not follow that it is co-extensive with it." (p. 176.) "Under the terms of the Sixth Article one may accept literally, or allegorically, or as parable, or poetry, or legend, the story of a serpent-tempter, of an ass speaking with man's voice, of an arresting the earth's motion, of a reversal of its motion[b], of waters standing in a solid heap, of witches, and a variety of apparitions. So under the terms of the Sixth Article, every one is free in judgment as to the primeval institution of the Sabbath, the universality of the Deluge, the confusion of tongues, the corporeal taking up of Elijah into Heaven, the nature of Angels, the reality of demoniacal possession, the personality of Satan, and the miraculous particulars of many events." (p. 177.) "Good men," we are assured; (the Inspired Writers being the good men

[b] In what part of the Bible, (one begs respectfully to inquire,) is one called upon to "accept the story of an arresting of the Earth's motion, or of a reversal of its motion?" ... Would it not be as well to be truthful in one's references to the Bible?

intended;) "may err in facts, be weak in memory, mingle imaginations with memory, be feeble in inferences, confound illustration with argument, be varying in judgment and opinion." (p. 179.) [A "free handling" this, of the work of the HOLY GHOST, truly! .... It would, I suppose, be deemed very unreasonable to wish that a catalogue of facts misstated,—of slips of memory,—of imaginary details,—of feeble inferences,—of instances of logical confusion,—and so forth, had been subjoined by the Reverend writer. I will only observe concerning his method that such "frank criticism of Scripture" (p. 174.) as this, is dogmatism of the most disreputable kind: insinuating what it does not state; assuming what it ought to prove; asserting in the general what it may be defied to substantiate in particular.] It follows,—"But the spirit of absolute Truth cannot err or contradict Himself; if He speak immediately, even in small things, accessories, or accidents." (p. 179.) To this we entirely agree. Where then are the "errors?" and where the "contradictions?"

We cannot "suppose Him to suggest contradictory accounts:" [not *contradictory*, of course; because contradictories cannot both be true:] "or accounts only to be reconciled in the way of hypothesis and conjecture."—(*Ibid.*) *Why* not[c]?

"To suppose a supernatural influence to cause the record of that which can only issue in a puzzle, is to lower indefinitely our conception of the Divine dealings in respect of a special Revelation." (*Ibid.*)— *Why* more of a lowering puzzle in GOD's Word than in GOD's Works[d]?

Mr. Wilson proceeds:—"It may be attributed to

[c] See below, p. 68.   [d] See Butler's *Analogy*, P. II. c. iii.

the defect of our understandings, that we should be *unable altogether to reconcile the aspects* of the SAVIOUR as presented to us in the first three Gospels, and in the writings of St. Paul and St. John. At any rate, there were current in the primitive Church very distinct Christologies."—(*Ibid.*) Queer language this for a plain man! *I*, for my own part, have never yet discovered the difficulty which is here hinted at; but which has been prudently left unexplained.

It follows:—"But neither to any defect in our capacities, nor to any reasonable presumption of a hidden wise design, nor to any partial spiritual endowments in the narrators, can we attribute the difficulty, if not impossibility, of reconciling the genealogies of St. Matthew and St. Luke; or the chronology of the Holy Week; or the accounts of the Resurrection: nor to any mystery in the subject-matter can be referred the uncertainty in which the New Testament writings leave us, as to the descent of JESUS CHRIST according to the flesh, whether by His mother He were of the tribe of Judah or of the tribe of Levi."—(pp. 179-180.) I, for my part, can declare that I have found the reconcilement in the three subjects first alluded to, as complete as could be either expected or desired. The last part of the sentence discovers nothing so much as the writer's ignorance of the subject on which he presumes to dogmatize.

Presently, we read,—"It may be worth while to consider how far a liberty of opinion is conceded by our existing Laws, Civil and Ecclesiastical."—(p. 180.) "As far as *opinion privately entertained is concerned*, the liberty of the English Clergyman appears already to be complete. For no Ecclesiastical person can be obliged to answer interrogations as to his opinions; nor be troubled for that which he has not actually expressed; nor be made responsible for inferences which other people may draw from his expressions." (*Ibid.*) — Surely such language needs only to be cited to awaken indignation in every honest bosom! "With most men educated, not in the schools of Jesuitism, but in the sound and honest moral training of an English Education, the mere entering on the record such a plea as this, must destroy the whole case. If the position of the religious instructor is to be maintained only by his holding one thing as true, and teaching another thing as to be received,—in the name of the GOD of Truth, either let all teaching cease, or let the fraudulent instructor abdicate willingly his office, before the moral indignation of an as yet uncorrupted people thrust him ignominiously from his abused seat [e]!"

The remarks just quoted serve to introduce a series of views on subscription to the Articles, which, if they were presented to me without any intimation of the quarter from which they proceed, I should not have hesitated to denounce as simply dishonest [f]. . . .

[e] *Quarterly Review*, Jan. 1861, p. 275.

[f] Take a few as a specimen:—"A great restraint is supposed to be imposed upon the Clergy by reason of their subscription to the Thirty-nine Articles. Yet it is more difficult than might be expected, to define what is the extent of the legal obligation of those who sign them; and in this case, the strictly legal obligation is the measure of the moral one. Subscription may be thought even to be *inoperative upon the conscience* by reason of its vagueness. For the act of subscription is enjoined, but its effect or meaning nowhere plainly laid down; and it does not seem to amount to more than an acceptance of the Articles of the Church as the formal law to which the subscriber is *in some sense* subject. What that subjection amounts to, must be gathered elsewhere; for it does not appear on

The Statute 13 Eliz. c. 12, is next discussed with the same unhappy licentiousness; and the declaration that "the meshes are too open for modern refinements." (p. 185.) . . . . I desire not to speak with undue severity of a fellow-creature: but I protest that I cannot read the Review under consideration without a profound conviction that, (speaking for myself,) I have to do with one whom in the common concerns of life I would not trust. The aptitude here displayed [g] for playing tricks with plain language, is calculated to sap the foundations of human intercourse, and to destroy confidence. If plain words may mean anything, or may mean nothing,—then, farewell to all good faith in the intercourse of daily life. If Articles "for the avoiding of Diversities of Opinions, and for the establishing of Consent touching true Religion [h],"— such Articles especially as the IInd., "Of the WORD or SON of GOD, which was made very Man;" and the Vth., "Of the HOLY GHOST," (which the Rev. Mr. Wilson calls "humanifying of the Divine Word," and "the Divine Personalities,") (p. 186,)—may be signed by one who, even in signing, resolves to "*pass by the side of them*," (p. 186, line 6,)—then is it better at once to admit that no Logic can be supposed to be available with such a writer; that he places himself outside the reach of fair argumentation; and must not be astonished if he shall find himself regarded by his peers simply in the light of an untrustworthy and impracticable person.

The last stage of all in this deplorable paper is an

the face of the subscription itself."—(p. 181. See down to page 185.) Can equivocation such as this be read without a sense of humiliation and shame, as well as of disgust and abhorrence?

[g] p. 180 to p. 190. [h] Heading of the XXXIX Articles.

application to Holy Scripture itself of the tricks which the Vicar of Great Staughton has already played, so much to his own satisfaction, with the Articles. "We may say that the value of the historical parts of the Bible may consist, rather in their significance, in the ideas which they awaken, than in the scenes themselves which they depict." (p. 199.) To a plain English understanding, (unperplexed with the dreams of Strauss, and other unbelievers of the same stamp,) such a statement conveys scarcely an intelligible notion. But we are not left long in doubt.

"The application of Ideology to the interpretation of Scripture, to the doctrines of Christianity, to the formularies of the Church, may undoubtedly be carried to an excess; may be pushed so far as to leave in the sacred records no historical residue whatever. .... An example of the critical Ideology carried to excess, is that of Strauss; which resolves into an ideal *the whole of the historical and doctrinal person of* JESUS. .... But it by no means follows, because Strauss has substituted a mere shadow for the JESUS of the Evangelists, that there are not traits in the scriptural person of Jesus, which are better explained by referring them to an ideal than an historical origin: and without falling into fanciful exegetics, there are parts of Scripture more usefully interpreted ideologically than in any other manner,—as for instance, *the history of the Temptation of* JESUS *by Satan, and accounts of demoniacal possessions.*" (pp. 200—201.) "Some may consider the descent of all Mankind from Adam and Eve as an undoubted historical fact; others may rather perceive in that relation a form of narrative into which in early ages tradition would easily throw itself spontaneously. .... *Among a particular people, this historical representation became the concrete expression of a great moral truth,*—of the brotherhood of all human beings. . . . . The force, grandeur, and reality of these ideas are not a whit impaired in the abstract, nor indeed the truth of the concrete history (!) as their representation, even though mankind should have been placed upon the earth *in many pairs at once,* or in *distinct centres of creation.* For the brotherhood of men really depends," &c., &c. (p. 201.) "Let us suppose one to be uncertain whether our LORD were born of the house and lineage of David, or *of the tribe of Levi;* and even to be driven to conclude that the genealogies of Him have *little historic value;* nevertheless, in idea, JESUS is both Son of David and Son of Aaron, both Prince of Peace, and High Priest of our profession; as He is, under another idea, though not literally, 'without father and without mother.' And He is none the less Son of David, Priest Aaronical, or Royal Priest Melchizedecan, in idea and spiritually, even if it be unproved whether He were any of them *in historic fact.*—In like manner it need not trouble us, if in consistency, we should have to suppose both an ideal origin, and to apply an ideal meaning, to the birth in the city of David, (!) and to other circumstances of the Infancy. (!) So again, the Incarnification of the divine Immanuel remains, although the angelic appearances which herald it in the narratives of the Evangelists may be of ideal origin, according to the conceptions of former days." (pp. 202-3.) "And," lastly,—"*liberty must be left to all as to the extent in which they apply this principle!*" (p. 201.)

To such dreamy nonsense, what "Answer" *can* we return[1]? Such speculations would be a fair subject

---

[1] The reader is referred to some remarks on Ideology towards the close of Sermon VII., p. 243 to p. 251.

for ridicule and merriment, if the subject were not so unspeakably solemn,—the issues so vast, and terribly momentous. We find ourselves introduced into a new world,—of which the denizens talk like madmen, and in a jargon of their own. And yet, that jargon is no sooner understood, than the true character of our new companions becomes painfully evident[k]. . . . He who believes the plain words of Holy Writ, finds himself called "the literalist." He who resolves Scripture into a dream, and the LORD who redeemed him into "a mere shadow," (p. 200) is dignified with the title of "an idealist." "Neither" (we are assured) "should condemn the other. They are fed with the same truths; the literalist unconsciously, the idealist with reflection. Neither can justly say of the other that he undervalues the Sacred Writings, or that he holds them as inspired less properly than himself." (p. 200.) "The ideologian," (who is the same person as the

---

[k] " Unhappily, together with his *inauguration of Multitudinism*, Constantine also inaugurated a principle essentially at variance with it, the principle of *doctrinal limitation*." (p. 166.) . . . "The opportunity of reverting to the freedom of the Apostolic, and immediately succeeding periods, was finally lost for many ages by the sanction given by Constantine to the decisions of Nicæa." (*Ibid.*) " At all events, a principle at variance with a true Multitudinism was then recognised." (*Ibid.*)

How does it happen, by the way, that one writing B.D. after his name, however bitter his animosity against the Nicene Creed may be, is not aware that Creeds are co-eval with Christianity? Thus we find the Creed of Carthage in the works of Cyprian, (A.D. 225,) and Tertullian, (A.D. 210, 203): that of Lyons in the works of Irenæus, (A.D. 180.) [see Heurtley's *Harmonia Symbolica*, pp. 7-20.] We recognize fragments of the Creed in Ignatius, (A.D. 90.) We hear St. Paul himself saying—ὑποτύπωσιν ἔχε ὑγιαινόντων λόγων, ὧν (i.e. *the words* themselves!) παρ' ἐμοῦ ἤκουσας . . . . τὴν καλὴν παρακαταθήκην φύλαξον—2 Tim. i. 13, 14. A few more words on this subject will be found in the notice of Mr. Jowett's Essay.

"idealist;" for the gentleman, at this place, changes his name;) "is evidently in possession of a principle which will enable him to stand in charitable relation to persons of very different opinions from his own." (p. 202.) "Relations which may repose on doubtful grounds as matter of history, and, as history, be incapable of being ascertained or verified, may yet be equally suggestive of true ideas with facts absolutely certain. The spiritual significance is the same of the Transfiguration, of opening blind eyes, of causing the tongue of the stammerer to speak plainly, of feeding multitudes with bread in the wilderness, of cleansing leprosy; whatever links may be deficient in the traditional records of particular events." (*Ibid.*) .... I will but modestly inquire,—What would be said of *us*, if *we* were so to expound Holy Scripture *in defence of Christianity* ?

But it is time to dismiss this tissue of worthless as well as most mischievous writing;—even to exhibit which, in the words of its misguided author, ought to be its own sufficient exposure. Do men really expect us to "answer" such groundless assertions, and vague speculations as those which go before? A Faith without Creeds: a Clergy without authority or fixed opinions: a Bible without historical truth:— how can such things, for a moment, be supposed to be[1]? What

[1] It is really impossible to argue with a man who informs us that "*previous to the time of the divided Kingdom*, the Jewish History presents little which is thoroughly reliable:" (p. 170:)—that "the greater probability seems on the side of the supposition, that the Priesthood, with its distinct offices and charge, was constituted by Royalty, and that *the higher pretensions of the priests were not advanced till the reign of Josiah:*" (*Ibid.*:)—that, "The negative Theologian" demands "some positive elements in Christianity, on grounds more sure to him than *the assumption of an objective 'faith*

answer do we render to the sick man who sees unsubstantial goblins on the solid tapestried wall; and mistakes for shadowy apparitions of the night, the forms of flesh and blood which are ministering to his life's necessities? If the Temptation, and the Transfiguration, and the Miracles of CHRIST be not true history, but ideological allegories,—then why not His Nativity and His Crucifixion,—His Death and His Burial,—His Resurrection and His Ascension into Heaven likewise? "*Liberty*" (we have been expressly told,) "*must be left to all, as to the extent in which they apply the principle.*" (p. 201.)—*Where* then is Ideology to begin,—or rather, where is ideology to end? "Why then is Strauss to be blamed for using that universal liberty, and '*resolving into an ideal the whole of the historical and doctrinal person of* JESUS?' Why is Strauss' resolution 'an excess?' or where and by what authority, short of his extreme view, would Mr. Wilson himself stop? or at what point of the process? and by what right could he, consistently with his own canon, call on any other speculator, to stay the ideologizing process [m]?"

"Discrepancies in narratives, scientific difficulties, defects in evidence, do not disturb the ideologist as they do the literalist." (p. 203.) No, truly. *Nothing* troubles him; simply because he *believes nothing!*

---

once *delivered to the saints*,' which he cannot identify with the Creed of any Church as yet known to him:" (pp. 174-5:)—a man who can remark concerning the Bible, that,—"Those who are able to do so, ought to lead the less educated to distinguish between the different kinds of words which it contains, between *the dark patches of human passion and error which form a partial crust upon it,* and the bright centre of spiritual truth within." (p. 177.)

[m] *Quarterly Review*, (Jan. 1851,) No. 217, p. 259.

The very Sacraments of the Gospel are not secure from his unhallowed touch. "The same principle" (?) is declared to be "capable of application" to them also. "Within these concrete conceptions there lie hid the truer ideas of the virtual presence of the LORD JESUS everywhere that He is preached, remembered, and represented." (p. 204.) . . . Do we ever deal thus with any other book of History? And yet, on what possible principle is the Bible to be thus trifled with, and Thucydides to be spared?—I protest, if the historical personages of either Testament may be resolved at will into abstract qualities, and the historical transactions of either Testament may be supposed to represent ideas and notions only,—then, I see not why the Vicar of Great Staughton himself may not prove to be a mythical personage also. Why need Henry Bristow Wilson, B.D.,—who, (as "literalists" say,) in 1841 was one of the 'Four Tutors' who procured the condemnation of Tract No. 90, on the ground that it 'evaded rather than explained the Thirty-nine Articles;' and who, in 1861 writes that "Subscription to the Articles may be thought *even inoperative upon the conscience* by reason of its vagueness;" (p. 181.)— why need this author be supposed to be a man *at all?* Why should he not be interpreted "ideologically;" and resolved into the principle of disgraceful Inconsistency of conduct, and "variation of opinion at different periods of life?"

V. In the present crusade against the Bible and the Faith of Christian men, the task of destroying confidence in the first chapter of Genesis has been undertaken by MR. C. W. GOODWIN, M.A. He requires us to "regard it as the speculation of some

Hebrew Descartes or Newton, promulgated in all good faith as the best and most probable account that could be then given of GOD's Universe." (p. 252.)

Mr. Goodwin remarks with scorn, that "we are asked to believe that a vision of Creation was presented to him by Divine power, for the purpose of enabling him to inform the world of what he had seen; which vision inevitably led him to give a description which has misled the world for centuries, and in which the truth can now only with difficulty be recognized." (p. 247.) He puts "pen to paper," therefore, (he says,) in order to induce the world to a "frank recognition of the erroneous views of nature which the Bible contains." (p. 211.) The importance of the inquiry, he vindicates in the following modest terms:—"Physical Science goes on unconcernedly pursuing its own paths. Theology, (the Science whose object is the dealing of GOD with Man as a moral being,) *maintains but a shivering existence, shouldered and jostled by the sturdy growths of modern thought,* and *bemoaning itself* for the hostility it encounters." (p. 211.)—A few remarks at once suggest themselves.

I cannot help thinking that if any person of ordinary intelligence, unacquainted with the Bible, were to be left to obtain his notion of its contents from "Essays and Reviews," infidel publications generally, and (*absit invidia verbo!*) from not a few of the Sermons which have been preached and printed in either University of late years, — the notion so obtained would be singularly at variance with the known facts of the case. Would not a man infallibly carry away an impression that the Bible is a book abounding in statements concerning matters of Physical Science which are flatly contradicted by the ascertained phenomena of Nature? Would he not be led to expect that it contained every here and there a theoretical Excursus on certain Astronomical or Physiological subjects? and to anticipate, above all, an occasional chapter on Geology? Great would be his astonishment, surely, at finding that *one single chapter* comprises nearly the whole of the statements which modern philosophy finds so very hateful; and *that* chapter, the first chapter in the Bibleⁿ.

But the surprise would grow considerably when the conditions of the problem came to be a little more fully stated. Has then the actual history of the World's Creation been ascertained from some other independent and infallible source? No! Are Geologists as yet so much as agreed even about a theory of the Creation? No! Can it be proved that any part of the Mosaic account is false? Certainly not! Then why all this hostile dogmatism?—To witness the violence of the partisans of Geological discovery, and the arrogance of their pretensions, one would suppose that some Divine Creed of theirs had been impugned: that a revelation had been made to *them* from Heaven, which the profane and unbelieving world was reluc-

---

ⁿ A writer in the *Saturday Review*, (April 6, 1861,) in an admirable Article on the importance of retaining the office of 'Dean' in its integrity, (instead of suicidally merging it in the office of 'Bishop,') speaks of there being "no English Commentary on the New Testament brought up to the level of modern Theological Science." [As if "the level" had been rising of late!] "Butler and Paley are still our text-books on the Evidences; and we are defending *old beliefs* behind wooden walls *against the rifled cannon and iron broadsides of modern Philosophy.*"—p. 337. What a strange misapprehension of the entire question,—of the relation of Theological to Physical Science,—does such a sentence betray!

tant to accept. Whereas, these are Christian men, impatient, as it seems, to tear the first leaf out of their Bible: or rather, to throw discredit on the entire volume, by establishing the untrustworthiness of the earliest page!

One single additional consideration completes the strangeness of the picture. If our account of the Six Days of Creation were a sybilline leaf of unknown origin, it would not be unreasonable to treat its revelations as little worth. But since the author of it is confessedly Moses,—the great Hebrew prophet, who lived from B.C. 1571 to 1451, who enjoyed the vision of the Most High; nay, who conversed with GOD face to face, was with Him in the Mount for thrice forty days, and received from Him the whole details of the Sacred Law;—since this first chapter of Genesis is known to have formed a part of the Church's unbroken heritage from that time onward, and therefore must be acknowledged to be an integral part of the volume of Scripture which, (as our LORD says,) οὐ δύναται λυθῆναι,—" cannot be broken, diluted, loosened, explained away;" — since, further, this account of Creation is observed to occur in the most conspicuous place of the most conspicuous of those books which are designated by an Apostle by the epithet θεόπνευστος, or, "given by inspiration," "filled with the breath," or "Spirit of GOD;" and when it is considered that our SAVIOUR and His Apostles refer to the primæval history contained in the first two chapters about thirty times[o]:—when, (I say,) all this is duly weighed, surely too strong a *primâ facie* case has been made out on behalf of the first chapter of Genesis,

[o] See below, p. 235.

that its authority should be imperilled by the random statements of every fresh individual who sees fit to master the elements of Geology; and on the strength of that qualification presumes to sit in judgment on the Hebrew Scriptures,—of which, confessedly, he does not understand so much as the alphabet!

It is even amusing to see how vain a little mind can become of a little knowledge. Mr. Goodwin remarks,—"The school-books of the present day, while they teach the child that the Earth moves, yet assure him that it is a little less than six thousand years old, and that it was made in six days." (p. 210.) (I am puzzled to reconcile this statement with the author's declaration that "no well-instructed person now doubts the great antiquity of the Earth any more than its motion." (*Ibid.*) Would it not have been fairer to have *named* at least *one* of the school-books which perpetuate so wicked a heresy?) "On the other hand, Geologists of all religious creeds are agreed that the Earth has existed for an immense series of years,—to be counted by millions rather than by thousands; and that indubitably more than six days elapsed from its first Creation to the appearance of Man upon its surface. By this broad discrepancy between old and new doctrine is the modern mind startled, as were the men of the sixteenth century when told that the earth moved." (p. 210.)

But begging pardon of our philosopher, if all he means is that more than six days elapsed between the Creation of "Heaven and Earth," (noticed in ver. 1,) and the Creation of Man, (spoke of from ver. 26 to 28,) —he means to say mighty little; and need not fear to encounter contradiction from any "well-instructed person." True, that an ignorant man could not have suspected anything of the kind from reading the first chapter of Genesis: but this is surely nobody's fault but his own. An ignorant man might in like manner be of opinion that the Sun and Moon are the two largest objects in creation; and there is not a word in this same chapter calculated to undeceive him. Again, he might think that the Sun rises and sets; and the common language of the Observatory would confirm him hopelessly in his mistake. All this however is no one's fault but his own. The ancient Fathers of the Church, behind-hand as they were in Physical Science, yet knew enough to anticipate "the hypothesis of the Geologist; and two of the Christian Fathers, Augustine and Theodoret, are referred to as having actually held that a wide interval elapsed between the first act of Creation, mentioned in the Mosaic account, and the commencement of the Six Days' work." (p. 231.) Mr. Goodwin therefore has got no further, so far, than Augustine and Theodoret got, 1400 years since, without the aid of Geology.

But we must hasten on. The business of the Essayist, as we have said, is to undermine our confidence in the Bible, by exposing the ignorance of the author of the first chapter. "Modern theologians," (he remarks, with unaffected displeasure,) "have directed their attention to the possibility of reconciling the Mosaic narrative with those geological facts which are admitted to be beyond dispute." (p. 210.)—And pray, (we modestly ask,) is not such a proceeding obvious? A "frank recognition of the erroneous views of Nature which the Bible contains," (p. 211,) we shall be prepared to yield when those "erroneous views" have been demonstrated to exist,—*but not till then.* Mr. Goodwin must really remember that although, in *his* opinion, the "Mosaic Cosmogony," (for so he phrases it,) is "not an authentic utterance of Divine knowledge, but a human utterance," (p. 253,) the World thinks differently. The learned and wise and good of all ages, including the present, are happily agreed that the first chapter of Genesis is *part of the Word of God*.

After what is evidently intended to be a showy sketch of the past history of our planet,—"we pass" (says Mr. Goodwin) "to the account of the Creation contained in the Hebrew record. And it must be observed that in reality two distinct accounts are given us in the book of Genesis; one, being comprised in the first chapter and the first three verses of the second; the other, commencing at the fourth verse of the second chapter and continuing till the end. This is so philologically certain that it were useless to ignore it." (p. 217.) Really we read such statements with a kind of astonishment which almost swallows up sorrow. Do they arise, (to quote Mr. Goodwin's own language,) "from our modern habits of thought, and from the modesty of assertion which the spirit of true science has taught us?" (p. 252.) Convinced that *my* unsupported denial would have no more weight than Mr. Goodwin's ought to have, I have referred the dictum just quoted to the highest Hebrew authority available, and have been assured that it is utterly without foundation.

After such experience of Mr. Goodwin's *philological* "certainties," what amount of attention does he expect his dicta to command in a Science which, starting from "a region of uncertainty, where Philosophy is reduced to mere guesses and possibilities, and pronounces nothing definite," (p. 213,) has to travel through "a prolonged period, beginning and ending we know not when;" (p. 214;) reaches another period, "the duration of which no one presumes to define;" (*Ibid.;*) and again another, during which "nothing can be asserted positively:" (p. 215:) after which comes "a kind of artificial break?" (*Ibid.*)

For my own part, I freely confess that Mr. Goodwin's final admission that "the advent of Man may be considered as inaugurating a new and distinct epoch, *that* in which we now are, and during the whole of which the physical conditions of existence cannot have been very materially different from what they are now;" (p. 216;) and that "thus much is clear, that Man's existence on Earth is brief, compared with the ages during which unreasoning creatures were the sole possessors of the globe:" (p. 217:)—these statements, I say, contain as much as one desires to see admitted. For really, since the fossil Flora, and the various races of animated creatures which Geologists have classified with so much industry and skill, confessedly belong to a period of immemorial antiquity; and, *with very rare exceptions indeed*, represent *extinct species*,—I, as an interpreter of Scripture, am not at all concerned with them. Moses asserts nothing at all about them, one way or the other. What Revelation says, is, that nearly 6000 years ago, after a mighty catastrophe,—unexplained alike in its cause, its nature, and its duration,—the Creator of the Universe instituted upon the surface of this Earth of ours that order of things which has continued ever since; and which is observed at this instant to prevail: that He was pleased to parcel out His transcendent operations, and to spread them over Six Days; and that He ceased from the work of Creation on the Seventh

Day. All extant species, whether of the vegetable or the animal Kingdom, including Man himself, belong to the week in question. And this statement, as it has never yet been found untrue, so am I unable to anticipate by what possible evidence it can ever be set aside as false.

In my IInd Sermon, I have ventured to review the Mosaic record sufficiently in detail, to render it superfluous that I should retrace any portion of it here. The reader is requested to read at least so much of what has been offered as is contained from p. 28 to p. 32. My business at present is with Mr. Goodwin.

And *in limine* I have to remind him that he has really no right first to give, in his own words, his own notion of the history of Creation; and then to insist on making *the Revelation* of the same transaction ridiculous by giving *it* also in words of his own, which become in effect a weak parody of the original. What is there in Genesis about "*the air or wind* fluttering over the waters of the deep?" (p. 219.) Is this meant for the august announcement that "the SPIRIT of GOD moved upon the face of the waters?" —"On the third day, ... we wish to call attention to the fact that trees and plants destined for food are those which are particularly singled out as the earliest productions of the earth." (p. 220.) The reverse is the fact; as a glance at Gen. i. 11. will shew.—"The formation of the stars" on the fourth day, "is mentioned in the most cursory manner." (p. 221.) But *who* is not aware that "the formation of the stars" is *nowhere mentioned in this chapter at all?*

"Light and the measurement of time," (proceeds

Mr. Goodwin,) "are represented as existing before the manifestation of the Sun." (p. 219.) Half of this statement is true; the other half is false. The former idea, he adds, is "repugnant to our modern knowledge." (p. 219.) Is then Mr. Goodwin really so weak as to imagine that our Sun is the sole source of Light in Creation? Whence then the light of the so-called fixed Stars? But I shall be told that Mr. Goodwin speaks of *our* system only, and of our Earth in particular. Then pray, whence that glory[p] which on a certain night on a mountain in Galilee, caused the face of our REDEEMER to shine as the Sun[q] and His raiment to emit a dazzling lustre[r]? "We may boldly affirm," (he says,) "that those for whom [Gen. i. 3—5] was penned could have taken it in no other sense than that light existed before and independently of the sun." (p. 219.) We may indeed. And I as boldly affirm that I take the passage in that sense *myself:* moreover that I hold the statement which Mr. Goodwin treats so scornfully, to be the very truth which, in the deep counsels of GOD, this passage *was designed* to convey to mankind; even that "the King of Kings, and LORD of Lords, who only hath immortality, *dwelleth in the Light which no man can approach unto*[s]."

[p] As the excellent Townson observed long since,—"The brightness of countenance and raiment which dazzled and overcame the sight of His Apostles when He was Transfigured on the Mount, was to Him but *a ray of that glory in which He dwelt before the Worlds were made.*"—Sermon on "The manner of our SAVIOUR'S Teaching,"—*Works,* vol. i. p. 282.

[q] St. Matth. xvii. 2.   [r] St. Mark ix. 3.

[s] 1 Tim. vi. 15, 16.—If it be more philosophical to suppose that the Light which shone upon the earth during the first three days proceeded from the Sun, (the orb of which remained invisible,) and not from any extraneous independent source,—I have no objection

"The work of the second day of Creation is to erect the vault of Heaven (Heb. *Rakia;* Gr. στερέωμα; Lat. *Firmamentum,*) which is represented as supporting an ocean of water above it. The waters are said to be divided, so that some are below, and some above the vault. . . . No quibbling about the derivation of the word *Rakia,* which is literally ' something beaten out,' can affect the explicit description of the Mosaic writer contained in the words ' the waters that are

whatever to such a supposition,—or indeed to any other which suffers the inspired record to remain intact. I am by no means clear however that Philosophy (begging her pardon,) does not entirely mistake her office, when she pretends to explain the first chapter of Genesis. Hence, her constrained language, and unnatural manner, when she desires to be respectful,—her inconsequential remarks and perpetual blunders when she rather prefers to be irreligious. She is simply out of her element, and is discoursing of what *she does not understand.*—Theology, dealing with a physical problem by the method of Theological Science; and Philosophy, applying to a chapter in the Bible the physical method,—are alike at fault, and alike ridiculous. This truth, however obvious, does not seem to be generally understood.

But, (to return to the first three days of Creation,)—since the Author of Revelation seems to design that I should understand that Sun, Moon, and Stars not only did not come to view until the fourth day,—but also that they were not re-invested with their immemorial function and office until then,—I find no difficulty, *remembering with whom I have to do,* even *with Him who sowed the vault of Heaven so thick with stars,* each one of which may be not a sun but *a system*[t];—when, I say, I attend to the emphatic nature of the inspired record, on the one hand, and to GOD'S Omnipotence on the other,—I have no difficulty in supposing that He embraced the Sun in a veil, for just so long a period as it seemed Him good, and when He willed that it should re-appear, that He withdrew the veil again. The *name* for the operation just now alluded to belongs to the province of Philosophy. Divinity is all the while thinking about something infinitely better and higher.

[t] Herschel.

above the firmament,' or avail to shew that he was aware that the sky is but transparent space." (pp. 219, 220.) "The allotted receptacle [of Sun and Moon] was not made until the Second Day, nor were they set in it until the fourth." (p. 221.) Surely I cannot be the only reader to whom the impertinence of this is as offensive, as its shallowness is ridiculous! In spite of Mr. Goodwin's uplifted finger, and menacing cry,—"No quibbling!" I proceed with my inquiry.

For first; Why does Mr. Goodwin parody the words of Inspiration? The account as given by Moses is,—"And GOD said, Let there be a firmament in the midst of the waters, and let it divide the waters from the waters [t]." But surely, to make the "open firmament of Heaven" in which every winged fowl may fly [u], is not "*to erect the vault of Heaven*,"— "*a permanent solid vault*,"—"*supporting an ocean of water!*"

The Hebrew word here used to denote "firmament," on which Mr. Goodwin's indictment turns, ("*rakia*,") is derived from a verb which means to "beat." Now, what is beaten, or hammered out, while (if it be a metal) it acquires *extension*, acquires also *solidity*. The Septuagint translators seem to have fastened upon the latter notion, and accordingly represented it by στερέωμα; for which, the earliest Latin translators of the Old Testament coined an equivalent,—*firmamentum*. But that Moses by the word "*rakia*" intended rather to denote the *expanse* overhead, than to predicate *solidity* for the sky, I suspect will be readily admitted by all. True that in the poetical book of Job, we read that the sky is "strong, as a molten looking-glass [x]:" but then we meet more frequently

[t] Gen. i. 6.   [u] Ibid. 20.   [x] Job xxxvii. 18.

with passages of a different tendency. God is said to "*stretch out* the heavens *like a curtain*[y]," "and *spread them out as a tent* to dwell in[z]:" to "bind up the waters in His thick clouds[a]," and "*in a garment*[b]," &c., &c.[c] It is only needful to look out the word in the dictionary of Gesenius to see that *spreading out*, (as of thin plates of metal by a hammer,) is the *only* notion which properly belongs to the word. Accordingly, the earliest modern Latin translation from the Hebrew, (that of Pagninus,) renders the word *expansio*. And so the word has stood for centuries in the margin of our English Bible.

The actual *fact* of the case,—the *truth* concerning the physical phenomenon alluded to,—comes in, and surely may be allowed to have some little weight. Since expansion *is* a real attribute of the atmosphere which divides the waters above from the waters below, —and solidity is *not*,—it seems to me only fair, seeing that the force of the expression is thought doubtful, to assign to it the meaning which is open to fewest objections.

But "the Hebrews," (says Mr. Goodwin,) "understood the sky, firmament, or heaven to be a permanent solid vault, as it appears to the ordinary observer." This, he adds, is "evident enough from various expressions made use of concerning it. It is said to have pillars[d], foundations[e], doors[f], and windows[g],"— (p. 220.) Now, I really do not think Mr. Goodwin's inference by any means so "evident" as he asserts.

[y] Ps. civ. 2.   [z] Is. xl. 22.   [a] Job xxvi. 8.   [b] Prov. xxx. 4.
[c] See also Job ix. 8.   Even in Job xxxvii. 18, the sky is said to be "*spread out.*" So Is. xlv. 12, &c.
[d] Job xxvi. 11.   [e] 2 Sam. xxii. 8.
[f] Ps. lxxviii. 23.   [g] Gen. vii. 11.

If Heaven has "pillars" in the poetical book of Job, so has the Earth [h]. The "foundations" spoken of in 2 Sam. xxii. 8, seem rather to belong to *Earth* than to Heaven,—as a reference to the parallel place in Ps. xviii. 7 will shew [i]. Is Mr. Goodwin so little of a poet, as to be staggered by the phrase "windows of Heaven," when it occurs in the figurative language of an ancient people, and in a poetical book [k]?

For the foregoing reasons, I distrust Mr. Goodwin's inference that "the Hebrews understood the sky to be a solid vault, furnished with pillars, foundations, doors, and windows." But whether they did, or did not, it is to be hoped that he is enough of a logician to perceive that the popular notions of God's ancient people on this subject, are not the thing in question. The only FACT we have to do with is clearly *this*,—that *Moses has in this place employed the word "rakia:"* and the only QUESTION which can be moved about it, is (as evidently) the following,—whether he was, or was not, to blame *in employing that word;* for as to *the meaning which he, individually, attached to the phenomenon* of which "*rakia*" is the name, it cannot be pretended that any one living knows anything at all about the matter. A Greek, Latin, or French astronomer who should speak of Heaven, would not therefore be assumed to mean that it is *hollow;* although κοῖλον, '*cœlum*,' '*ciel*,' etymologically imply no less.

Now I contend that Moses employed the word "*rakia*" with exactly the same propriety, neither more nor less, as when a Divine now-a-days employs the English word "firmament." It does not follow

---

[h] Job ix. 6. Ps. lxxv. 3. See Blomfield's Glossary to Prom. Vinct. v. 357.   [i] Comp. Is. xxiv. 18.
[k] See Is. xxiv. 18 and Mal. iii. 10.

that the man who speaks of "the spacious firmament on high," is under so considerable a delusion as to suspect that the firmament is *a firm thing;* nor does it follow that Moses thought that "*rakia*" was *a solid* substance either,—even if *solidity* was the prevailing etymological notion in the word, and even if the Hebrews were no better philosophers than Mr. Goodwin would have us believe. The Essayist's objection is therefore worthless. GOD was content that Moses should employ the ordinary language of his day,—accommodate himself to the forms of speech then prevalent,—coin no new words. What is there unreasonable in the circumstance? What possible ground does it furnish for a supposition that the *etymological* force of the word,—or even that the popular physical theory of which that word may, or may not, have once been the connotation,—denoted *the sense in which Moses employed it?* Is it to be supposed that when a physician speaks of a "*jovial* temperament," he insinuates his approval of an exploded system of medicine? Do astronomers maintain that the Sun has *a disk*, or the Earth *an axis?* that the former *leaves its place* in the heavens when it suffers 'eclipse¹?' or that the latter has a superior *latitude*, from East to West? To give the most familiar instance of all,—Do scientific men believe that the sun *rises*, and *sets?*—And yet all *say* that it does, until this hour! ... Why is Moses to be judged by a less favourable standard than anybody else, — than Shakspeare, than Hooker, even than Mr. Goodwin? The first, in an exquisite passage, bids Jessica,—

<blockquote>
"Look how the floor of heav'n
Is thick inlayed with patens of bright gold."
</blockquote>

---

[1] ἐκλείπειν τὴν ἕδραν. (Herod.) See Copleston's *Remains*, p. 107.

Did Shakspeare expect his beautiful language would be tortured into a shape which would convict him of talking nonsense?—But this is poetry. Then take Hooker's prose:—

"If the frame of that heavenly arch erected over our heads should loosen and dissolve itself; ... if the Moon should wander from her beaten way [m]," &c.

Did Hooker suppose that heaven is "an arch," which could be "loosened and dissolved?" or that "the way" of the moon is "beaten?"—But this is a highly poetical passage, written three centuries ago.—Let an unexceptionable witness then be called; and so, let the question be brought to definite issue. *I*, for my part, am quite content that it shall be *the philosopher in person*. The present Essayist shall be heard discoursing about Creation, and shall be convicted out of his own mouth. Mr. Goodwin begins his paper by a kind of cosmogony of his own, which he prefaces with the following apology:—"It will be necessary for our purpose to go over the oft-trodden ground, which must be done with rapid steps. Nor let the reader object to be reminded of some of the most elementary facts of his knowledge. The human race has been ages in arriving at conclusions now familiar to every child." (p. 212.) After this preamble, he begins his "elementary facts," as follows:—

"This Earth, apparently so still and stedfast, lying in majestic repose beneath the ætherial vault,"—(p. 212.)

But we remonstrate immediately. "The ætherial *vault!*" Do you then understand the sky, firmament, or heaven to be "a permanent solid vault, as it appears to the ordinary observer?" (p. 220.)

[m] *Eccl. Pol.* I. iii. § 2.

"The Sun which seems to leap up each morning from the east, and traversing the skyey bridge,"— (p. 212.)

"The *skyey bridge!*" And pray in what part of the universe do you discover a "skyey bridge?" Is not *this* calculated "to convey to ordinary apprehensions an impression at variance with facts?" (p. 231.)

"The Moon which occupies a position in the visible heavens only second to the Sun, and far beyond that of every other celestial body in conspicuousness,"— (p. 212.)

Nay, but really Mr. Philosopher, while you remind us "of some of the most elementary facts of our knowledge," (p. 212,) you write (except in the matter of the "leaping Sun" and the "skyey bridge,")—*exactly as Moses does* in the first chapter of Genesis! What else does that great Prophet say but that "the Moon occupies a position in the visible heavens only second to the Sun, and far beyond that of every other celestial body in conspicuousness?" (p. 212.)

Enough, it is presumed, has been offered in reply to Mr. Goodwin, and his notions of "Mosaic Cosmogony." He writes with the flippancy of a youth in his teens, who having just mastered the elements of natural science, is impatient to acquaint the world with his achievement. His powers of dogmatism are unbounded; but he betrays his ignorance at every step. The Divine decree, "Let us make Man in Our image, after Our likeness"," he explains by remarking that "the Pentateuch abounds in passages shewing that the Hebrews contemplated the Divine being in the visible form of a man." (!!!) (p. 221.) A foot-note contains the following oracular dictum,—"See par-

" Gen. i. 26.

ticularly the narrative in Genesis xviii." What *can* be said to such an ignoramus as this? Hear him dogmatizing in another subject-matter:—" The common arrangement of the Bible in chapters is of comparatively modern origin, and is admitted on all hands to have no authority or philological worth whatever. In many cases the division is most preposterous." (p. 222.) That the division of chapters is occasionally infelicitous, is true: but is Mr. Goodwin weak enough to think that he could divide them better? The division into chapters and verses again is *not* so modern as Mr. Goodwin fancies. Dr. M'Caul, (in a pamphlet on the Translation of the Bible,) shews reason for suspecting that some of the divisions of the Old Testament Scriptures are as old as the time of Ezra.

To return, and for the last time, to Mr. Goodwin's Essay.—His object is, (with how much of success I have already sufficiently shewn,) (1) To fasten the charge of absurdity and ignorance on the ancient Prophet who is confessedly the author of the Book of Genesis: (2) To prove that a literal interpretation of Gen. i., "will not bear a moment's serious discussion." (p. 230.) I look through his pages in vain for the wished-for proof. He has many strong assertions. He puts them forth with not a little insolence. But he proves nothing! At p. 226, however, I read as follows:—" Dr. Buckland appears to assume that when it is said that the Heaven and the Earth were created in the beginning, it is to be understood that they were created in their present form and state of completeness, the heaven raised above the earth as we see it, or seem to see it now." (pp. 226-7.)

But Dr. Buckland "appears to assume" nothing of the kind. His words are,—" The first verse of Genesis seems explicitly to assert the creation of *the Universe:* the Heaven, including the sidereal systems,—and the Earth, ... the subsequent scene of the operations of the six days about to be described." (pp. 224-5.)

"This," continues Mr. Goodwin, "is the fallacy of his argument." (p. 227.)

But if this is "*the* fallacy of his argument," we have already seen that it is a fallacy which rests not with Dr. Buckland, but with Mr. Goodwin. He proceeds :—

"The circumstantial description of the framing of the Heaven out of the waters proves that the words 'Heaven and Earth,' in the first verse, must be taken proleptically."—(p. 227.)

But we may as well stop the torrent of long words, by simply pointing out that "the heavens," (*hash-amaim,*) spoken of in Gen. i. 1, are quite distinct from "the firmament," (*rakia,*) spoken of in ver. 6. The word is altogether different, and the sense is evidently altogether different also; although Mr. Goodwin seeks to identify the two[o]. And further, we take leave to

---

[o] "The difficulty," he says, (alluding to Gen. i. 1,) "lies in this, that the heaven is distinctly said to have been formed ... on the second day." (p. 226.) But this is the language of a man determined that there *shall* be a difficulty. "The Heavens and the Earth" clearly denote, (in the simple phraseology of a primitive age,) the sum of all created things; the great transaction which Nehemiah has so strikingly expounded :—" Heaven, *the Heaven of Heavens, with all their host,*—the Earth and all things that are therein;" including " the sea, with all that is therein." (Neh. ix. 6.) Whereas " the firmament" of ver. 6, (which God called " Heaven" in ver. 8,) can only indicate the blue vault immediately overhead, wherein fowls fly. (ver. 20.) If this be *not* the meaning of Gen. i. 1, one

remind our modern philosopher that *no* "circumstantial description of the framing of the heaven out of the waters," is to be found either in ver. 6, or elsewhere. And this must suffice.

The entire subject shall be dismissed with a very few remarks.—Mr. Goodwin delights in pointing out the incorrectness of "the sense in which the Mosaic narrative was taken by those who first heard it:" (p. 223 :) and in asserting "that this meaning is *primâ facie* one wholly adverse to the present astronomical and geological views of the Universe." (p. 223.) But we take leave to remind this would-be philosopher that "the idea which entered into the minds of those to whom the account was first given," (p. 230,) is not the question with which we have to do when we are invited to a "frank recognition of the erroneous views of Nature which the Bible contains." (p. 211.) "It is manifest,"—(in this I cordially agree with Mr. Goodwin,)—"that the whole account is given from a different point of view from that which we now unavoidably take:" (p. 223 :) and, (I beg leave to add,) *that* point of view is *somewhere in Heaven*,—not here on Earth! The "Mosaic Cosmogony," as Mr. Goodwin phrases it, (fond, like all other smatterers in Science, of long words,) is *a Revelation:* and the same HOLY GHOST who gave it, speaking by the mouth of St. John, not obscurely intimates that it is mystical, like the rest of Holy Scripture,—that is, that it was fashioned not without a reference to the Gospel [p].

half of the phrase is "proleptical,"—the other half not: for the creation of Earth is nowhere recorded, if not in ver. 1.... But surely it is a waste of words to discuss such "difficulties" as these.

[p] Consider especially Heb. iv. 9 and 10; and consider, (besides Exod. xx. 11,) Deut. v. 15. See also Col. ii. 17.

But we are touching on a high subject now, of which Mr. Goodwin does not understand so much as the Grammar. *He* is thinking of the structure of the globe: *we* are thinking of the structure *of the Bible.* But to return to Earth, we inform the Essayist that it is simply unphilosophical, even absurd, for him to insist on what *shall* be implied by certain words employed by Moses,—(of which he judges by their etymology;) and further to assume what erroneous physical theories those words must have been connected with, by his countrymen, and so forth; and straightway to hold up the greatest of the ancient prophets to ridicule, as if those notions and those theories were all *his!*

"After all," (as Dr. Buckland remarked, long since,) "it should be recollected that the question is not respecting the correctness of the Mosaic narrative, but of our interpretation of it:" (p. 231:)—"a proposition," (proceeds Mr. Goodwin,) "which can hardly be sufficiently reprobated." But I make no question which of these two writers is most entitled to reprobation. For the view which will be found advocated in Sermon II., (which is substantially Dr. Buckland's,) (p. 24 to p. 32,) it shall but be said that it recommends itself to our acceptance by the strong fact that it takes *no* liberty with the sacred narrative, whatever; and receives the Revelation of GOD in all its strangeness, (which it *cannot* be a great mistake to do;) without trying to reconcile it with supposed discoveries, (wherein we *may* fail altogether.) I defy anybody to shew that it is *impossible* that GOD may have disposed of the actual order of the Universe, as in the first chapter of Genesis He is related to have done; and *probability* can clearly have no place in such a speculation. I would only just remind the thoughtful student of Scripture, and indeed of Nature also, that the singular *analogy* which Geologists think they discover between successive periods of Creation, and the Mosaic record of the first Six Days, is no difficulty to those who hesitate to identify those Days with the irregular Periods of indefinite extent. Rather was it to have been expected, I think, that such an analogy would be found to subsist between His past and His present working, when, 6,000 years ago, God arranged the actual system of things in Six Days.—Neither need we feel perplexed if Hugh Miller was right in the conclusion at which, he says, he had been "compelled to arrive;" viz. that "not a few" of the extant species of animals "enjoyed life in their present haunts" "for many long ages ere Man was ushered into being;" "and that for thousands of years anterior to even *their* appearance many of the existing molluscs lived in our seas." (p. 229.) I find it nowhere asserted *by Moses* that the severance was so complete, and decisively marked, between previous cycles of Creation and *that* cycle which culminated in the creation of Man, that no single species of the præ-Adamic period was reproduced by the Omnipotent, to serve as a connecting link, as it were, between the Old world and the New,—an identifying note of the Intelligence which was equally at work on this last, as on all those former occasions. On the other hand, I *do* find it asserted *by Geologists* that between the successive præ-Adamic cycles such connecting links are discoverable; and this fact makes me behold in the circumstance supposed fatal to the view here advocated, the strongest possible confirmation of its accuracy. At the same time, it is admitted that in every department of animated and vegetable life, the severance between the last (or Mosaic) cycle of Creation, and all those cycles which preceded it, is *very broadly marked* ᵖ.

Mr. Goodwin's method contrasts sadly with that of the several writers he adduces,—whether Naturalists or Divines. Those men, believing in the truth of GOD's Word, have piously endeavoured, (with whatever success,) to shew that the discoveries of Geology are not inconsistent with the revelations of Genesis. But he, with singular bad taste, (to use no stronger language,) makes no secret of the animosity with which he regards the inspired record; and even finds "the spectacle of able, and we doubt not conscientious writers engaging in attempting the impossible, —painful and humiliating." He says, "they evidently do not breathe freely over their work; but shuffle and stumble over their difficulties in a piteous manner." (p. 250.) He asserts dogmatically that "the interpretation proposed by Buckland to be given to the Mosaic description, will not bear a moment's serious discussion:" (p. 230:) while Hugh Miller "proposes to give an entirely mythical or enigmatical sense to the Mosaic narrative." (p. 236.) He is clamorous that we should admit the teaching of Scripture to be "to some extent erroneous." (p. 251.) He "recognizes in it, not an authentic utterance of Divine Knowledge, but a human utterance." (p. 253.) "Why

---

ᵖ "There have been found within the area of these islands upwards of 15,000 species of once living things, *every one differing specifically from those of the present Creation*. Agassiz states that, with the exception of one small fossil fish, (discovered in the claystones of Greenland,) *he has not found any creature of this class, in all the Geological strata, identical with any fish now living.*" (Pattison's *The Earth and the World*, p. 27.)

should we hesitate," (he asks,) " to recognize the fallibility of the Hebrew writers?" (p. 251.)

With one general reflexion, I pass on to the next Essay.—The Works of GOD, the more severely they have been questioned, have hitherto been considered to bear a more and more decisive testimony to the Wisdom and the Goodness of their Author. The animal and the vegetable kingdoms have been made Man's instructors for ages past; and ever since the microscope has revealed so many unsuspected wonders, the argument from contrivance and design, Creative Power and infinite Wisdom, has been pressed with increasing cogency. The Heavens, from the beginning, have been felt to "declare the glory of GOD." One department only of Nature, alone, has all along remained unexplored. Singular to relate, the Records of Creation, (as the phenomena of Geology may I suppose be properly called,)—though the most obvious phenomena of all,—have been throughout neglected. It was not till the other day that they were invited to give up their weighty secrets; and lo, they have confessed them, willingly and at once. The study of Geology does but date from yesterday; and already it aspires to the rank of a glorious Science. Evidence has been at once furnished that our Earth has been the scene of successive cycles of Creation; and the crust of the globe we inhabit is found to contain evidence of a degree of antiquity which altogether defies conjecture. The truth is, that Man, standing on a globe where his deepest excavations bear the same relation to the diameter which the scratch of a pin invisible to the naked eye, bears to an ordinary globe;—learns that his powers of interrogating Nature break down marvellous soon: yet Nature is observed to keep from him no secrets which he has the ability to ask her to give up.

In the meantime, the attitude assumed by certain pretenders to Physical Science at these discoveries, cannot fail to strike any thoughtful person as extraordinary. Those witnesses of God's work in Creation, which have been dumb for ages only because no man ever thought of interrogating them, are now regarded in the light of depositaries of a mighty secret; which, because God knew that it would be fatal to the credit of His written Word, He had bribed them to keep back, as long as, by shuffling and equivocation, they found concealment practicable. It seems to be fancied, however, that *that* fatal secret the determination of Man has wrung from their unwilling lips, at last; and lo, on confronting God with these witnesses, He is convicted even by His own creatures of having spoken falsely in His Word[q].—Such, I say, is the tone as-

[q] I allude to such passages as the following,—all of which are to be found in Mr. Goodwin's Essay :—

"We are asked to believe that a vision of creation was presented to him (Moses) by Divine power, for the purpose of enabling him to inform the world of what he had seen; which vision inevitably led him to give a description which has misled the world for centuries, and in which the truth can now only with difficulty be recognized." (p. 247.) "The theories [of Hugh Miller and of Dr. Buckland] assume that appearances only, not facts, are described; and that, in riddles which would never have been suspected to be such, had we not arrived at the truth from other sources." (p. 249.) "For ages, this simple view of Creation satisfied the wants of man, and formed a sufficient basis of theological teaching :" but "modern research now shews it to be physically untenable." (p. 253.)

"The writer asserts solemnly and unhesitatingly that for which he must have known that he had no authority." But this was only because "the early speculator was harassed by no such scruples" as "arise from our modern habits of thought, and from the modesty of assertion (!) which the spirit of true science has taught us."

sumed of late by a certain school of pretenders to Physical Science.

What need to declare that to the well-informed eye of Faith,—(and surely Faith is here the perfection of Reason! for *Faith*, remember, is the correlative not of *Reason*, but of *Sight;*)—the phenomenon presented is of a widely different character. Faith, or rather Reason, looks upon God's Works *as a kind of complement of His Word.* He who gave the one, gave the other also. Moreover, He knew that He had given it. So far from ministering to unbelief, or even furnishing grounds for perplexity, the record of His Works was intended, according to His gracious design, to supply what was lacking to our knowledge in the record of His Word. . . . "Behold My footprints, (He seems to say,) across the long tract of the ages! I could not give you this evidence in My written Word. The record would have been out of place, and out of time. It would have been unintelligible also. But what I knew would be inexpedient in the page of Revelation, I have given you abundantly in the page of Nature. I have spared your globe from combustion, which would have effaced those footprints, —in order that the characters might be plainly decipherable to the end of Time. . . . . O fools and blind, to have occupied a world so brimful of wonders for wellnigh 6000 years, and only now to have begun to open your eyes to the structure of the earth whereon ye live, and move, and have your being! Yea, and the thousandth part of the natural wonders by which ye are surrounded has not been so much as dreamed of,

---

He therefore "asserted as facts what he knew in reality only as probabilities. . . . He had seized one great truth. . . . With regard to details, observation failed him."—(pp. 252-3.)

by any of you, yet! .... O learn to be the humbler, the more ye know; and when ye gaze along the mighty vista of departed ages, and scan the traces of what I was doing before I created Man,—multiply that problem by the stars which are scattered in number numberless over all the vault of Heaven; and learn to confess that it behoves the creature of an hour to bow his head at the discovery of his own littleness and blindness; and that his words concerning the Ancient of Days had need to be at once very wary, and very few!"

VI. By far the ablest of these seven Essays is from the pen of the "REV. MARK PATTISON, B.D., Rector of Lincoln College, Oxford." It purports to be an Essay on the "TENDENCIES OF RELIGIOUS THOUGHT IN ENGLAND, 1688—1750;" but it can hardly be said to correspond with that description. In the concluding paragraph, the learned writer gives to his work a different name. It is declared to be "*The past History of the Theory of Belief in the Church of England*[r]." But neither the title at the head, nor the title at the tail of the Essay, gives any adequate notion of the Author's purpose.

Had we met with this production, isolated, in the pages of a Review, we should have probably passed it by as the work of a clever man, who, after amusing himself to some extent with the Theological literature of the last century, had desired to preserve some record of his reading; and had here thrown his random jottings into connected form. There is a racy freshness in a few of Mr. Pattison's sketches, (as in his account of Bentley's controversy with Collins[s],) which forcibly

[r] p. 329. [s] pp. 307-309.

suggests the image of an artist whose pencil cannot rest amid scenery which stimulates his imagination. To be candid, we are inclined to suspect that, in the first instance, something of this sort was in reality all that the learned author had in view. But we are reluctantly precluded from putting so friendly a construction on these seventy-six pages. Not only does Mr. Pattison's Essay stand between Mr. Goodwin's open endeavour to destroy confidence in the writings of Moses, and Professor Jowett's laborious insinuations that the Bible is only an ordinary book; but it claims a common purpose and intention with both those writers. Mr. Pattison's avowed object is "to illustrate the advantage derivable to the cause of religious and moral truth, from a free handling, in a becoming spirit, of subjects peculiarly liable to suffer by the repetition of conventional language, and from traditional methods of treatment[t]." We proceed therefore to examine his labours by the aid of the clue which he has himself supplied. For when nine editions of a book appear in quick succession, prefaced by a description of the spirit in which "*it is hoped that the volume will be received,*"—it seems a pity that the author should not be judged by the standard of his own choosing.

We are surprised then to find how slightly Mr. Pattison's Essay fulfils its avowed purpose. The learned author does not, in fact, *directly* "handle" the class of subjects referred to, *at all:* or if he does, it is achieved in a couple of pages. And yet it is not difficult to point out the part which his Essay performs in the general scheme of this guilty volume. With whatever absence of "concert or comparison" the

[t] Notice prefixed to *Essays and Reviews*.

authors may have severally written, the fatal effect of their combined endeavours is not more apparent than the part sustained by each Essay singly in promoting it.

While Mr. Goodwin demolishes the Law, and Dr. Williams disbelieves the Prophets; while Professor Powell denies the truth of Miracles, and Professor Jowett evacuates the authority of Holy Scripture altogether;—while Dr. Temple substitutes the inner light of Conscience for an external Revelation; and Mr. Wilson teaches men how they may turn the substance of Holy Scripture into a shadow, evade the plain force of language, and play fast and loose with those safeguards which it has been ever thought that words supply;—Mr. Pattison, reviewing the last century and a half of our own Theological history, labours hard to produce an impression that, *here* also "all is vanity and vexation of spirit." He calls off our attention from the Bible, and bids us contemplate the unlovely aspect of the English "religious world" from the Revolution of 1688 down to the publication of the 'Tracts for the Times,' in 1833[u]. "Be content for a while, (he seems to say,) to disregard the prize; and observe the combatants instead. Listen to the historian of moral and religious progress," while he depicts "decay of religion, licentiousness of morals, public corruption, profaneness of language, a day of rebuke and blasphemy." Come attend to me; and I will draw the likeness of "an age destitute of depth or earnestness; an age whose poetry was without romance, whose philosophy was without insight, and whose public men were without character; an age of 'light without love,' whose 'very merits were of the

[u] p. 255.

earth, earthy.'" (p. 254.) "If we would understand our own position in the Church, and that of the Church in the age; if we would hold any clue through the maze of religious pretension which surrounds us; we cannot neglect those immediate agencies in the production of the present, which had their origin towards the beginning of the eighteenth century." (p. 256.) Let us then "trace the descent of religious thought, and the practical working of the religious ideas," (p. 255,) through some of the phases they have more recently assumed. You shall see the Apostles tried on a charge "of giving false witness in the case of the Resurrection of JESUS;" (p. 303;) and pronounced "not guilty," by one whose "name once commanded universal homage among us;" but who now, (!) with South (!!) and Barrow, (!!!) "excites perhaps only a smile of pity." (p. 265.) You shall be shewn Bentley in his attack on Collins the freethinker, enjoying "rare sport,"—"rat-hunting in an old rick;" and "laying about him in high glee, braining an authority at every blow." (p. 308.) "Coarse, arrogant, and abusive, with all Bentley's worst faults of style and temper, this masterly critique is decisive." (p. 307.) And yet, you are not to rejoice! "The 'Discourse of Freethinking' was a small tract published in 1713 by Anthony Collins, a gentleman whose high personal character and general respectability seemed to give a weight to his words, which assuredly they do not carry of themselves." (p. 307.) [Why, the man ought to have been an Essayist and Reviewer!] . . . "By 'freethinking'" he does but "mean liberty of thought, —the right of bringing all received opinions whatsoever to the touchstone of reason:" (p. 307:) [a liberty which has evidently disappeared from English Literature: a right which no man dares any longer exercise under pain of excommunication!] " Collins was not a sharper, and would have disdained practices to which Bentley stooped for the sake of a professorship." (p. 310.) [O high-minded Collins!] "The dirt endeavoured to be thrown on Collins will cleave to the hand that throws it." (p. 309.) [O dirty Bentley!] And though "Collins's mistakes, mistranslations, misconceptions, and distortions are so monstrous, that it is difficult for us now, forgetful how low classical learning had sunk, to believe that they *are* mistakes, and not wilful errors," (p. 308,)—yet " Addison, the pride of Oxford, had done no better. In his 'Essay on the Evidences of Christianity,' Addison 'assigns as grounds for his religious belief, stories as absurd as that of the Cock-lane ghost, and forgeries as rank as Ireland's 'Vortigern;' puts faith in the lie about the thundering legion; is convinced that Tiberius moved the Senate to admit JESUS among the gods; and pronounces the letter of Agbarus, King of Edessa, to be a record of great authority.'" (p. 307, quoting Macaulay's *Essays*.) All this and much more you shall see. Remember that it is the history of your immediate forefathers which you will be contemplating,—the morality of the professors of religion during the last century,—" the past history of the theory of Belief in the Church of England!" (p. 329.)

The curtain falls; and now, pray how do you like it? I invite you, in conclusion, to "take the religious literature of the present day, as a whole; and endeavour to make out clearly on what basis Revelation is supposed by it to rest; whether on Authority, on the Inward Light, on Reason, on self-evidencing Scripture, or on the combination of the four, or some of them, and in what proportions." (p. 329.) .... After this, you are at liberty to proceed to read 'Jowett on Inspiration,'—with what appetite you may!

Such is the impression which Mr. Pattison's Essay is calculated to leave behind. That he had no wicked intention in writing it, no one who knows him could for an instant suppose: but *the effect* of what he has done is certainly to set his reader adrift on a dreary sea of doubt. Discomfort and dissatisfaction, confusion and dismay, are the prevailing sentiments with which a religious mind, unfortified with learning, will rise from the perusal of the present Essay: while the irreligious man will study it with a sneer of ill-concealed satisfaction. The marks of Mr. Pattison's own better knowledge, (sufficiently evident to the quick eye of one who is aware of the writer's high theological attainments;)—the indications of a truer individual judgment, (discoverable throughout by one who *knows* the author's private worth, and is himself happily in possession of the clue by which to escape from this tangled labyrinth:)—*these* escape the common reader. To *him*, all is dreary doubt.

I must perforce deal with Mr. Pattison's labours in a very summary manner. The chief complaint I have to make against him is that he has altogether omitted what, to you and to me, is the *most* important feature of the century which he professes to describe, —namely, the vast amount of lofty Churchmanship, the unbroken Catholic tradition, which, with no small amount of general short-coming, is to be traced throughout the eighteenth century. To insinuate that the return to Catholic principles *began* with the publication of the 'Tracts for the Times,' (p. 259,) in 1833, is simply to insinuate what is *not true.* But Mr. Pattison does more than 'insinuate.' He states it openly. "In constructing *Catenæ Patrum*," (he says,) "the Anglican closes his list with Waterland or Brett, and leaps at once to 1833." (p. 255.)—Now, since Waterland *died* in 1740 and Brett in 1743, it is clear that, (according to Mr. Pattison,) a hundred years and upwards have to be cleared *per saltum:* during which the lamp of Religion in these kingdoms had gone fairly out. But how stands the truth? At least *four* "Catenæ Patrum" are given in the "Tracts for the Times [x];" *not one* of which is closed with Waterland or Brett. On the contrary, in the two former Catenæ (beginning with Jewel and Hooker) the names of these supposed 'ultimi Romanorum' occur little more than *half way!* ... "Les faits," therefore, (as usual with 'Essayists and Reviewers,')—"*les faits sont contraires.*"—It would be enough to cite Bethell's 'General View of the Doctrine of Regeneration in Baptism,' which appeared in 1822; and Hugh James Rose's 'Discourses on the Commission and Duties of the Clergy,' which were preached in 1826. But the case against Mr. Pattison, as I shall presently show, is abundantly stronger.

In short, to exclude from sight, as this author so laboriously endeavours to do, the Catholic element of the last century and the early part of the present, is extremely unfair. There had *never failed* in the Church of England a succession of illustrious men, who transmitted the Divine fire unimpaired, down to yesterday. Quenched in some places, the flame burned up brightly and beautifully in others. As for the 'Tracts for the Times,' they speedily assumed

[x] Nos. 74, 76, 78, 81.

a party character: and by the time that ninety-seven of them had appeared, the series was discontinued by the desire of the Diocesan,—who was yet the friend of its authors. The Tracts do not all, by any means, represent Anglican (i.e. Catholic) Theology. They were written by a very few men; while the greatest of those who had materially promoted the Catholic movement out of which they sprang, (*not* which they *occasioned*,) were dissatisfied with them; would not write in them; kept aloof; and foresaw and foretold what would be the issue of such teaching[y]. And yet, 'Tracts for the Times' did more good than evil, I suppose, on the whole.

The truth is, that in every age, (and the last century forms no exception to the rule,) the history of the Church on Earth has been *a warfare*. Mr. Pattison says contemptuously,—" The current phrases of ' the bulwarks of our faith,' ' dangerous to Christianity,' are but instances of the habitual position in which we assume ourselves to stand. Even more philosophic minds cannot get rid of the idea that Theology is polemical." (p. 301.) And pray, whom have we to thank, but such writers as Mr. Pattison, that it is so? I am one of the many who at this hour are (unwillingly) neglecting *constructive* tasks in order to be *destructive* with Mr. Pattison and his colleagues! So long as Infidelity abounds, our service *must* be a warfare. 'The Prince of Peace' foretold as much, when He prophesied to His Disciples that it would be found that He had " brought on earth, a sword." As much was typically adumbrated, I suspect, (begging Mr. Jowett's pardon,) when, at the rebuilding of the walls of the Holy City, " they which builded on the wall, and they that bare

[y] I allude particularly to the late Hugh James Rose, B.D.

burdens, with those that laded, every one with one of his hands wrought in the work, and *with the other hand held a weapon.* For the builders, every one had his sword girded by his side, and so builded ⁿ." May I not add that the unique position which the Church of England has occupied, ever since her great Reformation in respect both of Doctrine and of Discipline three centuries ago,—is of a nature which must inevitably subject her to constant storms? An object of envy to 'Protestant Europe,'—and of hatred to Rome;—exposed to the hostility of the State, (which would trample her under foot, if it dared,) — and viewed with ill-concealed animosity by Dissenters of every class; — admitting into her Ministry men of very diverse views,—and restraining them by scarcely any discipline;—allowing perfect freedom, aye, licentiousness of discussion,—and tolerating the expression of almost any opinions,—*except those of Essayists and Reviewers:*—how shall the Church of England fail to adopt 'the bulwarks of the faith' for one of her current phrases? how not, many a time, deem 'dangerous to Christianity' the speculations of her sons? .... Nay, polemics *must* prevail; if only because, in a certain place, the Divine Speaker already quoted foretells the partial, (if not *the entire,*) obscuration even of true Doctrine, in that pathetic exclamation of His,—"When the Son of Man cometh, shall He find the faith upon the Earth ᵃ?" .... In the face of all this, it is to confuse and mystify the ordinary reader to draw such a picture of the last century as Mr. Pattison has drawn here. As dismal a view might be easily taken of the first, of the second, of the third, of the fourth, of the fifth century. What Mr. New-

ⁿ Neh. iv. 17, 18.   ᵃ St. Luke xviii. 8.

man once designated as "ancient, holy, and happy times," might very easily indeed be so exhibited as to seem times of confusion and discord, blasphemy and rebuke. A discouraging picture might be drawn, (I suppose,) of every age of the Church's history. But in, and by itself, it would never be quite a *true* picture. For to the eye of Faith there is ever to be descried, amid the hurly-burly of the storm, the Ark of CHRIST's Church floating peacefully over the troubled waters, and making steadily for that Heavenly haven "where it would be." .... Yes, there is ever some blessed trace discoverable, that this Life of ours is watched over by One whose Name is Love; whether we con the chequered page of History, Ecclesiastical or Civil; or summon to our aid the story of our own narrow experience. From the fierce and fiery opposition, Good is ever found to have resulted; and *that* Good was *abiding*. Out of the weary conflict ever has issued Peace ; and *that* Peace was of the kind which 'passeth all understanding;' a Peace which the world cannot give,—no, nor take away. There are abundant traces that in all that has happened to the Church of CHRIST, from first to last, there has been a purpose and a plan! .... No one knows this better than Mr. Pattison. No man in Oxford could have drawn out what I have been saying into a convincing reality, better than he, had he yielded to the instincts of a good heart, and directed his fine abilities to their lawful scope.

The character of the last dismal century, Mr. Pattison has drawn with sufficient vividness: but that century armed the Church, (as we shall be presently reminded,) on the side of the "Evidences of Religion;" and if it taught her the insufficiency of such a method, the eighteenth century did its work. Above all, *it produced Bishop Butler.*—The previous century, (the seventeenth,) witnessed the supremacy of fanaticism. It saw the monarchy laid prostrate, and the Church trampled under foot, and the use of the Liturgy prohibited by Act of Parliament. The "Sufferings of the Clergy" fill a folio volume. But this was the century which produced our great Caroline Divines! From Bp. Andrewes to Bp. Pearson,—*what* a galaxy of names! Moreover, on the side of the Romish controversy, the seventeenth century supplied the Church's armoury for ever,—Stillingfleet, who died in the year 1699, in a manner closing the strife.—The sixteenth century witnessed the Reformation of Religion, with all its inevitably attendant evils; an unsettled faith,—gross public and private injustice,—an illiterate parochial clergy:—yet how goodly a body of sound Divinity did the controversies of that age call forth! The same century witnessed the rise of Puritanism; but then, it produced Richard Hooker!—What was the character of the century which immediately preceded the Reformation,—the fifteenth? .... A tangled web of good and evil has been the Church's history from the very first. The counterpart of what we read of in Eusebius and Socrates is to be witnessed among ourselves at the present day, and will doubtless be witnessed to the end! But then, in days of deepest discouragement, faithful men have never been found wanting to the English Church, (no, nor GOD helping her, ever *will!*) who, like the late Hugh James Rose, "when hearts were failing, bade us stir up the gift that was in us, and betake ourselves to our true Mother." Meanwile, such names as George Herbert and Nicholas Farrar, Ken and Nelson, Leighton and

Bishop Wilson, shine through the gloom like a constellation of quiet stars; to which the pilgrim lifts his weary eye, and *feels* that he is looking up to Heaven!

When the spirit of the Age comes into collision with the spirit of the Gospel, the result is sometimes (as in the earliest centuries,) portentous;—sometimes, (as in the last,) simply deplorable and grievous. The battle which seems to be at present waging is of a different nature. Physical Science has undertaken the perilous task of hardening herself against the GOD of Nature. We shall probably see this unnatural strife prolonged for many years to come;—to be succeeded by some fresh form of irreligion. Somewhat thus, I apprehend, will it be to the end: and the men of every age will in those conflicts find their best probation; and it will still be the office of the Creator, in this way to separate the Light from the Darkness, —until the dawn of the everlasting Morning!

It is not proposed to enter into the Rationalism of the last century, therefore; or to inquire into the causes of the barren lifeless shape into which Theology then, for the most part, threw itself. I have never made that department of Ecclesiastical History my study: and *who* does not turn away from what is joyless and dreary, to greener meadows, and more fertile fields? It shall only be remarked that when the *Credibility* of Religion is the thing generally denied, *Evidences* will of necessity be the form which much of the Theological writing of the Day will assume. Let it not be imagined for an instant that one is the apologist of what Mr. Pattison has characterized as "an age of Light without Love." (p. 254.) But I insist that the theological picture of the last century is incomplete, until attention has been called to the many redeeming features which it presents, and which are all of a re-assuring kind.

Thus, in the department of sacred scholarship, *who* can forget that our learned John Mill, in 1707, gave to the world that famous edition of the New Testament which bears his name, after thirty years of patient toil? Who can forget our obligations in Hebrew, to Kennicott? (1718—1783.) Humphrey Hody's great work on the Text, and older Versions of Holy Scripture, was published in 1705. — Bingham's immortal 'Origines' began to appear in 1708; and William Cave lived till 1714.

In the same connexion should be mentioned Bp. Gibson, who died in 1748, and Humphrey Prideaux, whose 'Connexion' is dated 1715. Pococke died on the eve of the commencement of the last century (1691); but so great a name casts a bright beam through the darkness which Mr. Pattison describes so forcibly. Archbishop Wake died in 1737. Warton, the author of 'Anglia Sacra,' died at the age of 35 in 1695.

Survey next the field of Divinity, properly so called; and in the face of Mr. Pattison's rash statement that " we have no classical Theology since 1660," (p. 265,) take notice that Bp. Bull, one of the greatest Divines which the Church of CHRIST ever bred, did not begin to write until 1669, and lived to the year 1709. This was the man, remember, who received the thanks of the whole Gallican Church for his 'Judicium Ecclesiæ Catholicæ,' (i. e. his learned assertion of our SAVIOUR's Godhead[b];)—the man whose writings would have won him the reverence and affection of Athanasius and

---

[b] See Nelson's *Life of Bull*, p. 329, &c.

Augustine and Basil, had he lived in their day; for he had a mind like theirs. Bp. Pearson did not die till 1686. Bp. Beveridge wrote till his death in 1707. Fell, the learned editor of Cyprian, died in 1686: Stillingfleet lived till 1699. Wall's History of Infant Baptism appeared in 1705. Wheatly, who led the way in liturgical inquiry, was alive till 1742; and Bp. Patrick was a prolific writer till his death in 1707. May we not also claim the excellent and learned Grabe as altogether one of ourselves?

Such names do not require special comment. They are their own best eulogium, and present a high title to their country's gratitude. The name of Prebendary Lowth, (the author of an excellent commentary on the prophets,) reminds us that there was living till 1732 one who fully appreciated the calling of an Interpreter of God's Word [c]. Bishop Lowth his son, in his great work, (1753,) recovered the forgotten principle of Hebrew poetry. To convince ourselves what a spirit existed in some quarters, (notwithstanding the general spread of the very opinions which 'Essayists and Reviewers' have been so industriously reproducing in our own day,) it is only necessary to transcribe the title-page of S. Parker's excellent 'Bibliotheca Biblica,' a Commentary on the Pentateuch, 1720—1735; 'gathered out of the genuine writings of Fathers, Ecclesiastical Historians, and Acts of Councils down to the year of our Lord 451, being that of the fourth General Council; and lower, as occasion may require.'—That learned man designed to achieve a Commentary on the whole Bible on the same laborious plan; but his labours and his life, (at the age of 50,) were brought to an end in 1730.—Dr. Water-

[c] See his admirable Preface.

land, born in 1683, and Dr. Jackson, born in 1686,— two great names!—died respectively in 1740 and 1763.—In 1778, appeared Dr. Townson's admirable 'Discourses on the Gospels.' The author lived till 1792. Pious Bp. Horne (1730—1792) has left the best evidence of his ability as a Divine in the Introduction to his Commentary on the Psalms. Jones of Nayland is found to have lived till 1800. Bp. Horsley, a great champion of orthodoxy of belief, as well as an excellent commentator, critic, and Sermon writer, lived till 1806. Not seven years have elapsed since there was to be seen among ourselves a venerable Divine, who was declared in 1838, by the chief promoter of the 'Tracts for the Times,' to have "been reserved to report to a forgetful generation what was the Theology of their Fathers [d]." Martin Joseph Routh, died in 1854, after completing a century of years. In 1832 appeared his 'Scriptorum Ecclesiasticorum Opuscula.' His 'Reliquæ Sacræ' had appeared in 1814. The work was undertaken so far back as 1788. The last volume appeared in 1848, and concluded with a *Catena* of authorities on the great question which was denied by the unbelievers of the last century, and *is* denied by the 'Essayists and Reviewers' of this [e]. Here then was one who had borne steady witness in the Church of England to what is her genuine Catholic teaching from a period dating long before the birth of any one who was concerned with the 'Tracts for the Times.'

---

[d] Newman's dedication of his 'Lectures on Romanism and popular Protestantism.'

[e] See the 'Monitum' prefixed to Dr. Routh's *Testimonia De Auctoritate S. Scripturæ Ante-Nicæna.*—*Reliqq. Sacræ*, vol. v. p. 335.

More ancient names present themselves as furnishing exceptions to Mr. Pattison's dreary sentence. From Abp. Potter and Leslie, down to Abp. Laurence and Van Mildert,—how many might yet be specified! We have not hitherto mentioned Abp. Leighton, who died in 1684: Hickes, Johnson, and Brett, who survived respectively till 1715, 1725, and 1743: the truly apostolic Wilson, Bishop of Sodor and Man (1663—1755,)—a name, by the way, which deserves far more distinct and emphatic notice than can here be bestowed upon it; and Nelson, the pious author of 'Fasts and Festivals,' who died in 1715. We had good Iz. Walton, till 1683, and holy Ken till 1711. Richard Hele, author of 'Select Offices,' (which appeared in 1717,) is a name not forgotten in Heaven certainly, though little known on Earth; while Kettlewell and Scandret begin a Catena of which good Bishop Jolly would be only one of the later links. Meanwhile, the reader is requested to take notice that there were many other excellent Divines of the period under consideration, (as Long and Horbery;) men who made no great figure indeed, but who were evidently persons of great piety and sound judgment; while their learning puts that of 'Essayists and Reviewers' altogether to the blush.

But I have reserved for the last, a truly noble name,—which Mr. Pattison, (with singular bad taste, to say no worse,) mentions only to disparage. I. allude to Dr. Joseph Butler, Bishop of Durham; whose 'Analogy of Religion, Natural and Revealed, to the Constitution and Course of Nature,'—remains, at the end of a century, unanswerable as an Apology,—unrivalled as a text-book,—unexhausted as a mine of suggestive thought. It may be convenient for an

'Essayist and Reviewer' to declare that "the merit of the Analogy lies in its want of originality." (p. 286.) There was not much originality perhaps in the remark that an apple falls to the ground. Whatever the faults of the Analogy, that work, under GOD, *saved the Church.* However "depressing to the soul" (p. 293.) of Mr. Pattison, it is nevertheless a book which will invigorate Faith, and brighten Hope, and comfort Charity herself,—long after the spot where he and I shall sleep has been forgotten: long after our very names will be hard to find.

Let me turn from this illustrious individual, to one whose very name is perhaps unknown. One loves to think that there are at all times plenty of good men, who are doing GOD's work in the world, in quiet corners; but whose names do not perhaps rise to the surface and emerge into notice, throughout the whole of a long life. Conversely, how many must there be, the blessing of whose example and influence has extended down from the surface, (where perhaps it was acknowledged and appreciated by all,) until it made itself felt by the humblest units of a lowly country parish!... The obscure village of Finmere, (in Oxfordshire,) was so happy as to enjoy for its Rector, from 1734 to 1771, the Rev. Thomas Long, M.A.,— "a man," (says the Register,) "of the most exemplary piety and charity." He presented to the church twelve acres of land, "charging it with a yearly payment of fifteen shillings to the Clerk, *as a recompense to him for attending on the Fasts and Festivals;* and ordering sixpence to be deducted from the payment, for each time the Clerk failed to attend on those days,—unless let by sickness." About ten years ago, there was found in the hands of a labouring man at Finmere, a solitary copy of a printed "Lecture," by this individual, "addressed to the young persons" of the village, (1762,) which begins as follows:—"I have usually, once every three years, gone through a course of Lectures upon the Catechism; but considering my age and great infirmities, it is not very probable I should continue this practice any longer. I am willing therefore, as a small monument of my care and affection for you, to print the last of these Lectures," &c. .... What heart so dull as not to admit that men like this, (and there were *many* of them!) are quite good enough to redeem an age from indiscriminate opprobrium and unmitigated contempt?

Shall we omit, after this enumeration, to notice the singular fact that *Discipline* still lingered on,—even the discipline of *public penance,*—until within the memory of aged persons yet living? Merchants in the city of London wore mourning during Lent, within the present century. It is only within the last thirty years that formulæ expressive of reliance on the Divine blessing have been expunged from bills-of-lading, and similar printed documents. In the beginning of the period discoursed of by Mr. Pattison, (viz. in the year 1714,) the excellent Robert Nelson, in "An Address to Persons of Quality and Estate," proposed as objects for the generosity of the affluent, such institutions as the following:—"the creating of Charity Schools,"—of "Parochial Libraries in the meanly endowed Cures throughout England,"—of "a superior School for training up Schoolmasters and Schoolmistresses,"—and of "Colleges or Seminaries for the Candidates of Holy Orders." He suggested that there should be "Houses of Hospitality for entertaining Strangers;" "Suffragan Bishops, both at home and in the Western Plantations;" "Colleges for receiving Converts from Popery." Some of Nelson's suggestions read like vaticinations. He points out the need of Ladies' Colleges,—of a Hospital for Incurables,—of Ragged Schools, (for what else is a school "for the distressed children called the *Black-guard?*"),—and of Houses of Mercy for the reception of penitent fallen women.—Is it right to speak of a century which could freely contemplate such works as these and carry into execution many of them[1], without some allusion to the leaven which was at work beneath the dry crust of Society? the living Catholic energy which neither the average dulness of the pulpit could quench, nor the lifeless morality which had been popularly substituted for Divinity could destroy?

We are abundantly prepared therefore for Mr. Pattison's admission that "public opinion was throughout on the side of the defenders of Christianity:" (p. 313:) —that, "however a loose kind of Deism might be the tone of fashionable circles, it is clear that distinct disbelief of Christianity was by no means the general state of the public mind. The leaders of the Low-Church and Whig party were quite aware of this. Notwithstanding the universal complaints of the High-Church party of the prevalence of infidelity, it is obvious that this mode of thinking was confined to a very small section of society." (p. 313.)

And surely it should not escape us that the peculiar form which unbelief assumed during the period under discussion, resulted in a benefit to the Church. "The eighteenth century," (says our author,) "enforced the

[1] "In 1781, the first Sunday School was established in England by Robert Raikes, a publisher and bookseller in Gloucester."—National Society's *Circular.*

truths of Natural Morality with a solidity of argument and variety of proof which they have not received since the Stoical epoch, if then." (p. 296.) "The career of the Evidential School, its success and its failure, has enriched the history of Doctrine," not indeed "with a complete refutation of that method as an instrument of theological investigation," (p. 297,) (witness the immortal 'Analogy' of Bishop Butler!) —but, certainly with very precious experience. That age has bequeathed to the Church a vast body of controversial writing which she could ill afford to part with at the present day.

So far, we have little to complain of in Mr. Pattison's Essay, except on the side of omission. *But for the fatal circumstance of the company in which the learned writer comes abroad, and the avowed purpose with which he is found there*, a charitable construction might have been put upon most of the present performance. The following sentences, on the other hand, are *not* excusable.

"In the present day when a godless orthodoxy threatens, as in the fifteenth century, to extinguish religious thought (!) altogether, and nothing is allowed in the Church of England but the formulæ of past thinkings, which have long lost all sense of any kind, (!) it may seem out of season to be bringing forward a misapplication of common-sense in a bygone age." (p. 297.)

The "orthodoxy" of the fifteenth century is something new to us. So is the prospect "in the present day," of an "extinction of religious thought,"—the result of "godless orthodoxy." The fault, or the misfortune of the Church of England then, is, that she retains "*the formulæ of past thinkings, which have long lost all sense of any kind.*" (p. 297.) If this does not mean the English *Book of Common Prayer*, what *does* it mean? And if it *means* the English Prayer-Book, how can Mr. Pattison retain his commission in the Church of England, and exclusively employ a Book which he presumes so to characterize?

But this is *ad hominem*. The learned writer proceeds:—" There are times and circumstances when religious ideas will be greatly benefited by being submitted to the rough and ready tests by which busy men try what comes in their way; by being made to stand their trial, and be fully canvassed, *coram populo*. As Poetry is not for the critics, so Religion is not for the Theologians." (p. 297.)

No doubt. But does Mr. Pattison then really mean to tell us that the proper tribunal before which the Creeds, (for example,) of the Catholic Church,—our Communion and Baptismal offices,—the structure of our Calendar, and so forth,— should " *stand their trial,* and be *freely canvassed,*" is, " *coram populo?*" A " rough and ready test," this, of Truth, I grant; aye, a *very* " rough " one. But was it ever,—can it ever be,—a *fair* test? Let us hear Mr. Pattison out, on the subject of Religion:—

" When it is stiffened into phrases, and these phrases are declared to be objects of reverence but not of intelligence, it is on the way to become *a useless encumbrance; the rubbish of the past; blocking the road.* Theology then retires into the position it occupies in the Church of Rome at present, an unmeaning frostwork of dogma, out of all relation to the actual history of Man." (pp. 297-8.)

It cannot be necessary to discuss such sentiments. With Mr. Pattison personally, I *will not* condescend to discuss them,—until he has divested himself of that "useless encumbrance," and ceased to employ daily "that rubbish of the past," which yet the two letters he subjoins to his name indicate, in the most solemn manner, his reverence for; and which alone make him *Reverendus*.

But speaking to others,—speaking to *you*, my friends,—let me point out that "the tendencies of *irreligious* thought in England, 1860-1861," are *indeed* in a direction where the Prayer-Book is found to be *effectually* "blocking up the road." (pp. 297-8.) Mr. Pattison is simply dreaming,—haunted by the phantoms of his own brain, and talking the language of the den,—when he complains that "the Philosophy, now petrified into tradition, may once have been a vital Faith; but now that" it is "withdrawn from public life," has ceased to be a "social influence." (p. 298.) And when he would exalt the last century at the expence of the present, (pp. 298-9,) he shews nothing so much as the morbid state of his own imagination,—the disordered condition of his own mind. He has blinded himself; and he will not or he cannot see in the healthier tone of our popular Divinity,—in the increased attention to the study of Holy Scripture,—in the impulse which Liturgical inquiries have received since Wheatly's useful volume appeared;—or again, in the immense number of Schools and Churches which have been recently built,—in the marvellous change for the better which has come over the Clergy of the Church of England within the present century,—in the vast development of our Colonial Episcopate within the last few years,—in the rapid increase of Institutions connected more or less directly with the Church,—and I will add, in the conspicuous loyalty of the nation;—a practical refutation of his own injurious insinuations; a blessed earnest that GOD has *not* forsaken us; and that we shall *yet* be a blessing to the World! The people of England, I am persuaded, are in the main very sincerely attached to their Prayer-Book. To them, it is not "a useless encumbrance, the rubbish of the past, blocking the road." Nay, there is a "rough and ready test" of what is the current temper of the age in things religious, to which I appeal with infinite satisfaction. I mean, *the general burst of execration with which* "*Essays and Reviews*" *have been received,* from one end of the kingdom to the other. *The censure of all the Bishops,* and of *both Houses of Convocation;* re-echoed, as it has been, through *all ranks of the community,* is a great fact;—a fact which I cordially recommend to Mr. Pattison's attention, when he would philosophize on the religious tendencies of his countrymen.

The age we live in, (Heaven knows!) has many drawbacks. *What* age of the Church has *not* had them? The fatal disposition which prevails to relax all the ancient safeguards,—the desire to tamper yet further with the Law of Marriage, and to desecrate the Christian Sabbath,—these are grievous features of the times; which may well occasion alarm and create perplexity. But nothing of the kind should ever make us despond; much less despair. There is One above "who is over all, GOD blessed for ever." Shall we not rather seek to employ these advantages which we have, with a single heart, a single eye to GOD's glory; and leave the issue, with a generous confidence, to *Him?* .... It was thus that the great philosophic Divine of the last century comforted himself, amid darker days than *we* shall ever experience.

"As different ages have been distinguished by different sorts of particular errors and vices, the deplorable distinction of ours," (he said,) "is an avowed scorn of Religion in some, and a growing disregard to it in the generality." "It is impossible for me, my brethren,"—(Butler is still addressing the clergy of his Diocese, 1751,)—"to forbear lamenting with you the general decay of Religion in this nation; which is now observed by every one, and has been for some time the complaint of all serious persons. The influence of it is more and more wearing out of the minds of men;" while "the number of those who profess themselves unbelievers, increases, and with their number their zeal. Zeal, it is natural to ask,—for what? Why truly *for* nothing, but *against* everything that is sacred and good among us[g]." And yet, in days dark as those, Piety could suggest that "no Christian should possibly despair;" and Faith could assign as the reason of this blessed confidence,—"*For He who hath all power in Heaven and Earth, hath promised that He will be with us to the end of the world.*"

It is time to dismiss Mr. Pattison's Essay. In doing so, I will not waste my time and yours by carping at the many errors of detail into which he has (not inexcusably) fallen. These are the accidents,—not the essence of his paper. The root of bitterness with the Author is, clearly enough, *the Theory of Religious Belief in the Church of England.* His concluding words shew this plainly. The sting of the Essay is in the tail :—

"In the Catholic theory the feebleness of Reason is met half-way, and made good by the authority of the Church. When the Protestants threw off this autho-

[g] *Primary Charge*, at the end of his *Sermons*.

rity, they did not assign to Reason what they took from the Church, but to Scripture. Calvin did not shrink from saying that Scripture 'shone sufficiently by its own light.' As long as this could be kept to, the Protestant theory of belief was whole and sound. At least it was as sound as the Catholic. In both, Reason, aided by spiritual illumination, performs the subordinate function of recognising the supreme authority of the Church, and of the Bible, respectively. Time, learned controversy, and abatement of zeal, drove the Protestants generally from the hardy but irrational assertion of Calvin. Every foot of ground that Scripture lost was gained by one or other of the three substitutes: Church-authority, the Spirit, or Reason. Church-authority was essayed by the Laudian divines, but was soon found untenable, for on that footing it was found impossible to justify the Reformation and the breach with Rome." [O shame!] "The SPIRIT then came into favour along with Independency. But it was still more quickly discovered that on such a basis only discord and disunion could be reared. There remained to be tried Common Reason, carefully distinguished from recondite learning, and not based on metaphysical assumptions. To apply this instrument to the contents of Revelation was the occupation of the early half of the eighteenth century; with what success has been seen. In the latter part of the century the same Common Reason was applied to the external evidences. But here the method fails in a first requisite,—universality; for even the shallowest array of historical proof requires some book-learning to apprehend."—(pp. 328-9.)

Now all this is discreditable to Mr. Pattison as a Philosopher and as a Divine. *When* did Protestant

England "throw off the authority" of the Church?—What are *Calvin's* opinions to *her*?—How does 'Independency,' 'Rationalism,' or any other unsound principle, affect *us?* Look at our Prayer-Book. Is it not the same which it was from the beginning? The Sarum Use, reformed and revised, has been our unbroken heritage as Christian men, from the first. Essentially remodelled in the days of Edward VI., the recension of our "Laudian Divines" is, (by God's great mercy!) still ours. What other teaching but that of *the Book of Common Prayer*, is, to this hour, the authoritative teaching of the Church of England? Why insinuate there has been vicissitude of Theory, where notoriously there has been none? Why imply that the storms which periodically sweep over the citadel of our Zion are effectual to remove the old foundations and to substitute new? What but a hollow heartless Scepticism *can* be the result of such an abominable passage as the foregoing?

"Whoever will take the religious literature of the present day as a whole, and endeavour to make out clearly on what basis Revelation is supposed by it to rest, whether on Authority, on the Inward Light, on Reason, on self-evidencing Scripture, or on the combination of the four, or some of them, and in what proportions; would probably find that he had undertaken a perplexing but not altogether profitless inquiry."—(p. 329.) And so the Essay ends.

With a short comment on the proposed problem, I also shall conclude.

No one but a fool would set about the task which Mr. Pattison here proposes. The current "religious literature *of the day*" cannot be supposed, for an instant, to be an adequate exponent of the mind of the Church of England,—or of any other Church. Revelation rests, at this hour, on exactly the same basis on which it has always rested, and on which it will rest, to the end of time; let the age be faithful, or faithless,—learned or unlearned,—rationalizing or scientific,—sceptical or superstitious,—or whatever else you will. And if I am asked to explain myself, I would humbly say,—(always submitting my own statements in such a matter to the judgment of the Bishops and Doctors of the Church of England,)—that we receive the Bible on the authority of *the Church*. The Church teaches us by the concurrent voices of many Fathers, Doctors, Saints, how to interpret the Bible; and convinces us that the three Creeds which she delivers to us as her own independent tradition, may be proved thereby; being in entire conformity with Holy Scripture, though not originally deduced from it. "Self-evidencing" is hardly a correct epithet to bestow upon Scripture. And yet, from the evidence which the New Testament supplies to the Old, and from the interpretation which it puts upon its teaching, we should not despair of proving the Truth of Revelation, to one who had neither darkened the inward Light, nor perverted his Reason.

In truth, however, it is idle thus to speculate. We have been born into the world during the nineteenth Century, whether we wish it or not. We have been nourished, (GOD be thanked!) in the bosom of the Christian Church, whether we would or no. The glory of the Gospel has informed our natural reason, and we cannot undo the blessed process, strive we as much as we will. The "inward Light," (as we call it,) is the lingering twilight of the Day of Creation, in the case of the heathen,—the reflected ray of the noontide of the Gospel, even in the case of the modern unbeliever.

We cannot escape from these conditions of our being, although we may affect to ignore them, or pretend to turn our eyes the other way. *No* help however is to be rejected. *No* faculty of the soul need be denied the privilege of assisting to convince the doubting heart. The inward Light may not be disparagingly spoken of: for what if it should prove to be a ray sent down from the Father of Lights, to illumine the dark places of the soul? The aid of Reason is not to be excluded; for what is Faith but the highest dictate of the Reason? Faith, (let us ever remember,) being opposed not to *Reason*, but to *Sight!* ... And who for a moment supposes that we disparage the office of Reason, because we speak of the authority of the Church, in controversies of Faith? We simply proclaim the Church to be the appointed witness and keeper of Holy Writ; and when we are invited "*to make out clearly* on what basis Revelation is supposed to rest," (p. 329,) we point,—where else *should* we point?— unhesitatingly to *her* unwavering witness from the beginning.

VII. The Essay which brings up the rear in this very guilty volume is from the pen of the "REV. BENJAMIN JOWETT, M.A., [Fellow and Tutor of Balliol College, and] Regius Professor of Greek in the University of Oxford,"—"a gentleman whose high personal character and general respectability seem to give a weight to his words, which assuredly they do not carry of themselves[h]." His performance is entitled "ON THE INTERPRETATION OF SCRIPTURE:" being, in reality, nothing else but a laborious *denial of its Inspiration*.

[h] Rev. M. Pattison, in *Essays and Reviews*, p. 307.

Mr. Jowett's quarrel is with the whole body of Commentators on the Bible,—ancient and modern; with the whole Church Catholic. He cannot endure the claim of that Book, (like its Divine object and Author,) to "a Name which is above every other Name." That Plato and Sophocles should be capable of but one method of Interpretation, and *that* the literal,—while the Bible lays claim to a yet profounder meaning,—so distresses the Regius Professor of Greek, that he has appropriated to himself almost a quarter of the present volume, in order that he may cast laborious and systematic ridicule on the very supposition. Some parts of his method I propose presently to submit to *exactly the same "free handling" which he has himself applied to* THE WORD OF GOD. In the meantime, since it is my intention not only to demonstrate the worthlessness of the structure which Mr. Jowett has with so much perverse industry here built up, by an examination of some parts of it in detail, but also to pull down as much of the fabric as I am able within a small compass,—(the construction of something which it is hoped will prove more durable, being to be found in my IIIrd and IVth, Vth and VIth Sermons,)—I proceed at once to inspect the foundation-stone of his edifice; and briefly to demonstrate its absolute insecurity.

1. Mr. Jowett's fundamental principle is expressed in the following brief precept: "*Interpret the Scripture like any other book.*" (p. 377.) To this favourite tune, (although he plays many intricate variations on it,) he invariably reverts in the end[1]. On this preliminary postulate therefore, which, at first sight, to a candid

---

[1] pp. 338, 375, 420 top line, 428, &c.

mind, seems fair enough, I proceed to remark as follows:—

Mr. Jowett's formula may be cheerfully and entirely accepted,—*apart from the sinister glosses which he immediately proceeds to put upon it.* By all means "Interpret the Scripture like any other book." Let us see to what result this principle will conduct us. As for the formula itself, I take the liberty to assume that it *ought to mean* somewhat as follows:—"Approach the volume of Holy Scripture with the same candour, and in the same unprejudiced spirit with which you would approach any other famous book of high antiquity. Study it with at least the same attention. Give at least equal heed to all its statements. Acquaint yourself at least as industriously with its method, and with its principle; employing and applying either, with at least equal fidelity, in its interpretation. Above all, beware of playing tricks with its plain language. Beware of suppressing any part of the evidence which it supplies as to its own meaning. Be truthful, and unprejudiced, and honest, and consistent, and logical, and exact throughout, in your work of Interpretation. 'INTERPRET SCRIPTURE LIKE ANY OTHER BOOK.'"

Now, (not to be tedious,) if *this* were Mr. Jowett's principle, all further discussion would be at an end. The general question of the right method of interpreting the Bible would be easily settled; but it would be hopelessly settled—*against the Regius Professor of Greek.* As I have briefly shewn, (from p. 144 to p. 160 of the present volume,) our LORD and His Apostles openly and repeatedly claim for Scripture that very depth of meaning, that very extent of signification, which Mr. Jowett so strenuously maintains that it does *not* possess.—This great fact, he prudently takes no notice of. He simply ignores it. Either he has overlooked it, through inadvertency: or he has omitted it, as not perceiving its force and bearing on the question: or he has disingenuously kept it back. He must choose between these three suppositions. If he has overlooked the fact on which I lay so much stress,—he is a careless and incompetent reader. If he has failed to see its force and bearing on the question,—he is a weak and illogical thinker. If he has deliberately suppressed it, knowing its fatal power,—he is simply a dishonest man. To prevent offence, I may as well state freely that my entire conviction is that he is simply a weak and illogical person. My warrant for this opinion is especially the very sad performance of his now under consideration.

It is clear however that the paraphrase above hazarded does *not* express Mr. Jowett's principle. "Interpret the Bible like any other book," means with him something else. And what it *does* mean, the Reverend author does not suffer us to doubt. He shews that his meaning is, *Interpret the Bible like any other book*, FOR *it is like any other book*. I proceed to shew that this *is* Mr. Jowett's meaning.

It becomes necessary however at once to introduce to the reader's notice the main inference which, (as already hinted,) flows from Mr. Jowett's favourite position. "*Interpret* Scripture like any other book," —he says. His business is with *the Interpretation* of "the Jewish and Christian Scriptures;" and he begins by eagerly assuring us,—and is strenuous in all that follows to make us believe,—(but simply on *à priori* grounds!)—that "the true glory and note of Divinity in these, is *not* that they have hidden, mysterious, or double meanings; but *a simple and universal one*, which is beyond them and will survive them." (p. 332.) "Is it admitted," (he asks, at the end of many pages,) "that *the Scripture has one and only one* true meaning?" (p. 368.)

Let us hear what reasons the Reverend author of this seventh Essay is able to produce in support of his favourite opinion. He approaches the subject from a respectful distance:—

(i) "It is a strange, though familiar fact,"—(such are the opening words of his Essay,)—"that great differences of opinion exist respecting the Interpretation of Scripture." (p. 330.)—'Familiar,' the fact is, certainly; but why 'strange?' A Book of many ages,—of immense antiquity,—of most varied character,—treating of the unseen world,—purporting to be a mysterious composition,—and by all Christian men believed to have GOD for its true Author: a book which has come into collision with every form of human error, and has triumphed gloriously over every form of human opposition:—*how* can it be thought 'strange' that the interpretation of such a book should have provoked "great differences of opinion?" ... Surely none but the weakest of thinkers, unless committed to the assumption that *the Bible is like any other book*, could ever have penned such a silly remark.

(ii) "We do not at once see *the absurdity* of the same words having many senses, or free our minds from *the illusion* that the Apostle or Evangelist must have written with a reference to the creeds or controversies or circumstances of other times. Let it be considered, then, that this extreme variety of interpretation *is found to exist in the case of no other book, but of the Scriptures only.*" (p. 334.)

But the "phenomenon" which Mr. Jowett represents as "so extraordinary that it requires an effort of thought to appreciate it," (*Ibid.,*) does not seem at all extraordinary to any one who does not begin by *assuming* that the Bible is "like any other book."—If *the Bible be inspired,*—then all is plain!

(iii) "Who would write a bulky treatise about the method to be pursued in interpreting Plato or Sophocles?"—asks Mr. Jowett. (p. 378.)—No one but a fool!—is the obvious reply. Plato and Sophocles are ordinary books; and therefore *are to be interpreted* like any other book. The Bible not so, as we shall see by and by. Again,—

(iv) "Each writer, each successive age, has characteristics of its own, as strongly marked, or more strongly, than those which are found in the authors or periods of classical Literature. These differences are not to be lost in *the idea of a Spirit from whom they proceed, or by which they were overruled.* And therefore, illustration of one part of Scripture by another should be confined to writings of the same age and the same authors, except where the writings of different ages or persons offer obvious similarities. It may be said, further, that illustration should be chiefly derived, not only from the same author, *but from the same writing, or from one of the same period of his life.* For example, the comparison of St. John and the 'synoptic' Gospels, or of the Gospel of St. John with the Revelation of St. John, will tend *rather to confuse than to elucidate the meaning of either.*" (pp. 382-3.)—But really, in reply, it ought to suffice to point out that the result of the Church's experience for 1800 years has been the very opposite of the Professor's. "*The idea of a* SPIRIT *from whom they proceeded*," is, to the thoughtful part of mankind, *the only intelligible clue* to the several books of Holy Scripture, from Genesis to Revelation! Hence "the marginal references to the English Bible," (to which Mr. Jowett devotes a depreciatory half page,) so far from being the dangerous or useless apparatus which he represents, we hold to be an instrument of paramount importance for eliciting the true meaning of Holy Writ.—In a word, he is reasoning about the Bible on *the assumption* that the Bible is *like any other book.*

(v) "To attribute to St. Paul or the Twelve the abstract notion of Christian Truth which afterwards sprang up in the Catholic Church ... is the same error as to attribute to Homer the ideas of Thales or Heraclitus, or to Thales the more developed principles of Aristotle and Plato." (p. 354.)—*Not if St. Paul and the Twelve were inspired.*

(vi) He bids us remark, with tedious emphasis, that although the same philological and historical difficulties which occur in Holy Scripture are found in profane writings, yet "the meaning of classical authors is known with comparative certainty; and the interpretation of them seems to rest on a scientific basis. ... *Even the Vedas and the Zendavesta*, though beset by obscurities of language probably greater than are found in any portion of the Bible, are interpreted, at least by European scholars, according to fixed rules, and beginning to be clearly understood." (p. 335.)

But at the end of several weak sentences, through which the preceding fallacy is elongated into distressing tenuity, *who* does not exclaim,—The supposed "scientific" basis on which the interpretation of books in general rests, is simply this; (a) that being *merely human*, and (β) *not professing* to have any other than their obvious literal meaning,—they are all interpreted in the obvious ordinary way!

For (a),—If any book were even *suspected* to be Divine, the manner of interpreting it would of course be different. Not that the "basis" of such Interpretation would therefore cease to be "scientific!" Take the only known instance of such a Book. The Bible has been suspected (!) for 1800 years to be inspired. How has it fared with the Bible?

The Science of Biblical Interpretation is one of the noblest and best understood in the world. It has been professed and practised in every country of Christendom. The great Masters of this Science have been such men as Hilary of Poictiers, Basil and the two Gregories in Asia Minor, Epiphanius in Cyprus, Ambrose at Milan, John Chrysostom at Antioch, Jerome in Palestine, Augustine in Africa, Athanasius and Cyril at Alexandria. The names descend in an unbroken stream from the first four centuries of our æra down to the age of Andrewes, and Bull, and Pearson, and Mill. These men all interpret Scripture in one and the same way. Their principles are the same throughout. They were all Professors of *the same Sacred Science*.

But (β),—If a book even *professes* to have a hidden meaning, it is interpreted by a special set of canons. Thus Dante's great poem[1] may not be read as Hume's History of England is read.—To proceed, however.

---

[1] See all this very ably and interestingly explained in an article reprinted from the 'Christian Remembrancer' (Jan. 1861,) *On certain Characteristics of Holy Scripture*, by the Rev. J. G. Cazenove, p. 11, &c.

(vii) Sophocles is perhaps the most subtle of the ancient Greek poets. "Several schools of critics have commented on his works. To the Englishman he has presented one meaning, to the Frenchman another, to the German a third; the interpretations have also differed with the philosophical systems which the interpreters espoused. To one the same words have appeared to bear a moral, to another a symbolical meaning; a third is determined wholly by the authority of old commentators; while there is a disposition to condemn the scholar who seeks to interpret Sophocles from himself only and with reference to the ideas and beliefs of the age in which he lived. And the error of such an one is attributed not only to some intellectual but even to a moral obliquity (!) which prevents his seeing the true meaning." (p. 336.)

It has fared with Sophocles therefore, (according to Mr. Jowett,) *in all respects as it has fared with the Bible.* "It would be tedious," (he justly remarks,) "to follow the absurdity which has been supposed into details. By such methods," Sophocles or Plato might "be made to mean anything." (p. 336.)

But who does not perceive that the obvious way to escape from the supposed difficulty, is to remember that *neither Sophocles nor Plato was inspired !* .... Mr. Jowett's difficulty is occasioned by his assumption that *the Bible stands on the same level as Plato and Sophocles.*

(viii) Again,—"If it is not held to be a thing impossible that there should be agreement in the meaning of *Plato and Sophocles*, neither is it to be regarded as absurd, that there should be a like agreement in the interpretation of *Scripture*." (p. 426.)—The whole force of this argument clearly consisting in the strictly equal claims of these books to Inspiration.—Elsewhere, Mr. Jowett expresses the same thing more unequivocally:—The old "explanations of Scripture," (he says,) "are no longer tenable. They belong to a way of thinking and speaking which was once diffused over the world, but has now passed away." Having quietly *assumed* all this, the Reverend writer proceeds:—"And what we give up as a general principle, we shall find it impossible to maintain partially; *e.g.* in the types of the Mosaic Law, and the double meanings of Prophecy, at least *in any sense in which it is not equally applicable to all deep and suggestive writings.*" (p. 419.)

(ix) "Still one other supposition has to be introduced, which will appear, perhaps, *more extravagant than any which have preceded*. Conceive then that these modes of interpreting Sophocles (!) had existed for ages; that great institutions and interests had become interwoven with them; and in some degree even the honour of Nations and Churches;—is it too much to say that, in such a case, they would be changed with difficulty, and that they would continue to be maintained long after critics and philosophers had seen that they were indefensible?" (pp. 336-7.)

I suppose we may at once allow Mr. Jowett most of what he asks. We may freely grant that if the Tragedies of Sophocles *had* exercised the same wondrous dominion over the world which the Books of the Bible have exercised:—if Œdipus and Jocasta and Creon; if Theseus and Dejanira and Hercules; if Ajax, Ulysses and Minerva;—*had* done for the world what Enoch and Noah;—what Abraham, Isaac, and Jacob;—what Joseph, and Joshua, and Hannah, and Samuel, and David;—what Elijah and Elisha;

what Isaiah and Jeremiah, Ezekiel and Daniel, and the rest;—what St. Peter, and St. John, and St. Paul;—what the Blessed Virgin and her name-sakes, have done:—In a word: had Homer's gods and heroes altogether changed the face of society, and revolutionized the world; *so that "great institutions and interests had become interwoven with them, and in some degree even the honour of Nations and Churches;"* (p. 336;) —if, I repeat, all this *had* really and actually taken place;—*great* "difficulty" would, no doubt, (as Mr. Jowett profoundly suggests,) be experienced, at the end of 2000 years, in getting rid of them.

But since it unfortunately happens that *they have done nothing of the kind*, we do not seem to be called upon to follow the Regius Professor of Greek into the supposed consequences of what he admits to be an "extravagant supposition;" and which we humbly think is an excessively foolish one also.

When, however, the Reverend Author of this speculation establishes it as *a parallel with what has taken place with regard to the Word of God*, we tell him plainly that his insinuation that "critics and philosophers are maintaining the present mode of interpreting Scripture *long after they have seen that it is indefensible*,"—is a piece of impertinence which seems to require a public apology. A man may retain Orders in the Church of England, if he pleases, while yet he repudiates her doctrines: may declare that he subscribes her Articles *ex animo*, and yet seem openly to deny them. But he has no right whatever to impute corresponding baseness to others. The charge should be either plainly made out, or openly retracted[1].

[1] Nor is this a mere slip of Mr. Jowett's pen. At p. 372, he states that "a majority of the Clergy throughout the world,"—

By such considerations then does Professor Jowett attempt to shew that we ought to "interpret Scripture like any other book." The gist of his observations, in every case, is one and the same,—namely, from *à priori* considerations to insinuate that *the Bible is not essentially unlike any other book.*

Now, quite apart from its Inspiration,—which is, obviously, THE one essential respect wherein the Bible is wholly unlike every other book in the world; (inasmuch as, if it is inspired, it differs from every other book *in kind;* stands among Books as the Incarnate WORD stood among Men,—*quite alone ;* notwithstanding that He spoke their language, shared their wants, and accommodated Himself to their manners ;)—*apart,* I say, *from the fact of its Inspiration,* it is not difficult to point out several particulars in which the Bible is *utterly unlike any other Book which is known to exist;* and therefore to suggest an *à priori* reason why *neither should it be interpreted* like any other book.

1. The Bible then contains in all (66 − 9 =) 57 distinct writings,—the work of perhaps upwards of forty different Authors[m]. Yet, for upwards of fifteen centuries those many writings have been all collected

(with whom he associates the "instincts of many laymen, perhaps also individual interest,")—are in favour of "*withholding the Truth.*" But, he adds, (with the indignant emphasis of Virtue when she is reproaching Vice,)—" a higher expediency pleads that 'honesty is the best policy,' and that truth alone ' makes free !' "—How would such insolence be treated in the common intercourse of daily life?—(I will not pause to remark on Mr. Jowett's wanton abuse of the Divine saying recorded in St. John viii. 32,—repeated at p. 351.)

[m] I suppose that there may have been many inspired Psalmists ; and that perhaps the book of Judges was not all by one hand. With reference to the two books of Samuel, Kings and Chronicles, see 1 Chron. xxix. 29, 30. 2 Chron. ix. 29 : xi. 2 : xii. 15, 5, 7 : xiii. 22.

into one volume: and, for a large portion of that interval, on the writings so collected the Church Universal has agreed in bestowing the name of *the Book*,—κατ' ἐξοχήν,—THE BIBLE.

2. The Bible is divided into two parts, which are severed by an interval of upwards of four centuries. On these two great divisions of the Bible, respectively, has been bestowed the title of the Old and the New Covenant. And, what is remarkable,—*The same phenomena which are observable in respect of the whole Bible, are observable in respect of either of its parts.* Thus,

(α) The several writings of which the Old Testament is composed,—(39−3=) 36 in all[n], are by many different hands: those of the New Testament, in like manner,—(27−6=) 21 in all, are by eight different authors.

(β) Those many writings of the Old Testament are found to have been collected into a single volume about four hundred years before the Christian æra; when they were denominated by a common name, ἡ γραφή,—" *The Scripture*[o];" and the supreme authority of the writings so collected together, was axiomatic[p]. One arguing with His Hebrew countrymen was able to appeal to a place in the Psalms, and to remind them parenthetically that " the Scripture *cannot be broken*[q],"—that is, might not be gainsaid,

[n] By the Jews themselves they were reckoned as 22.

[o] "It is remarkable that the word Γραφή, which means simply *Writing*, is reserved and appropriated in the New Testament (where it occurs fifty times) to the *Sacred* writings, i.e. to the *Holy Scriptures;* and marks the separation of the *Scriptures* from all " common books," indeed from *all other writings* in the world."—Wordsworth 'On Inspiration,'—p. 85.

[p] St. Luke xvi. 17.

[q] οὐ δύναται λυθῆναι ἡ γραφή,—St. John x. 35.

doubted, explained away, or set aside.—Precisely similar phenomena are observable in respect of the writings of the New Testament.

(γ) Although the books of the Old Covenant are scattered at intervals over the long period of upwards of a thousand years, the writers of the later books are observed to quote the earlier ones, as if by a peculiar secret sympathy: now, incorporating long passages,— now, simply adapting one or two sentences,—now, blending allusive references. For some proof of this assertion, (as far as I am able to produce it at a moment's notice,) the reader is referred to the foot of the page[r].

The self-same phenomenon is observable with regard to the New Testament Scriptures. Although all the books were written within so short a space as about fifty years, the later writers quote the earlier ones to a surprising extent. In the Gospels, the Gospels

[r] e. g. (i) *Long passages :*—
Judges i. 11—15 quotes Joshua xv. 15—19.—2 Sam. xxii. quotes Ps. xviii.—1 Chron. xvi. quotes Ps. xcvi., and Ps. cv.—2 Kings xix. quotes Is. xxxvii.—2 Kings xx. quotes Is. xxxviii., xxxix.

(ii) *One or two sentences :*—
Numb. xiv. 18 quotes Exod. xxxvi. 6, 7.—Ps. lxviii. 1 quotes Numb. x. 35.—Ps. lxviii. 7, 8 quotes Judges v. 4, 5.—Ps. cxviii. 14 quotes Exod. xv. 2.—Prov. xxx. 5 quotes Ps. xviii. 30.—Joel ii. 13 quotes Jonah iv. 2.—Isaiah xii. 2 quotes Exod. xv. 2.—Isaiah xiii. 6 quotes Joel i. 15.—Isaiah li. 6 quotes Ps. cii. 25-7.—Isaiah lii. 10 quotes Ps. xcviii. 2, 3.—Micah iv. 1, 2, 3 quotes Isaiah ii. 2, 3, 4.—Nahum i. 15 quotes Isaiah lii. 7.—Zeph. iii. 19 quotes Micah iv. 6.—Habakkuk ii. 14 quotes Isaiah xi. 9.—Jeremiah x. 13 : li. 16 quotes Ps. cxxxv. 7.—Jeremiah xlviii. quotes Isaiah xv. 16.—Jeremiah xxvi. 18 quotes Micah iii. 12.—1 Chron. xxix. 15 quotes Ps. xxxix. 12.

(iii) *Allusive references.*—(This would involve a prolonged reference to the Hebrew Scriptures, which would be even out of place here.)

are quoted times without number. In the Epistles, the Gospels are cited, or referred to, upwards of sixty times. The Epistles contain many references to the Epistles.—The phenomenon thus alluded to will also be found insisted upon in a later part of the present volume[s].

"The fact, I believe, on close examination, will be found to stand thus:—The Holy Bible abounds in quotations, even more perhaps than most other books; but they are introduced in a way which is peculiar to Revelation, and its own. When a Prophet or Apostle mentions one of his own holy brethren, as when Ezekiel names Daniel, or Daniel Jeremiah; when St. Peter speaks of St. Paul, or St. Paul of St. Peter, or of St. Luke the Physician; *when they mention them, they do not quote them; and when they quote them, they do not mention them*[t]."

(δ) The later writer in the Old Testament who quotes some earlier portion of narrative is often observed to supply independent information, — entering into minute details and particulars which are not to be found in the earlier record.—Now, "with the same Almighty SPIRIT for their guide, what was it to be expected that the historians of our Blessed LORD would do? What, but the very thing which they have done? that they would walk in the path, which the holy Prophets of old had marked out? that they would often tread full in each other's steps; often relate the same miracle, or discourse, or parts of it, in the words of the same prior writer; sometimes com-

[s] See pp. 234-5.
[t] Rev. Ralph Churton's Sermon "On the Quotations in the Old Testament," (1807,) published in Townson's *Works*, vol. i. p. cxxxiv.,—where see the interesting note.

press, sometimes expand; always shew to the diligent inquirer, that they did not derive their information, even of facts which they relate in another's words, from him whom they copy, but wrote with antecedent plenitude of knowledge and truth in themselves; without staying to inform us whether what they deliver is told for the first time, or has its place already in authentic history[u]."

(ε) It may be worth remarking that though *the Inspiration* of no part of either Testament has ever been doubted in the Church, there do exist doubts as to *the Authorship* of more than one of the Books of the Old Testament; and *one* Book in the New, (the Epistle to the Hebrews,) has been suspected by some orthodox writers *not* to have been from the pen of St. Paul, but to have been the work of some other inspired and Apostolic writer.

(ζ) History, Didactic matter, and Prophecy, — is found to be the subject of either Testament.

(η) In the New Testament, as in the Old, we are presented with the singular phenomenon of more than one Book being in a manner *copied* from another,— yet with the addition of much independent original matter. It is superfluous to name Samuel, Kings, and Chronicles, on one side,—and the Gospels on the other. To the Gospels may be added the Second Epistle of St. Peter and the Epistle of St. Jude.

(θ) Lastly, the same *modest* use of the Supernatural is to be found in either Testament.—In both, the writers are observed to pass without effort, and as it were unconsciously, from revelations of the most stupendous character, to statements of the simplest and

---

[u] Rev. Ralph Churton's Sermon, quoted in note (t), pp. cxliv-v.

most ordinary kind˟.—In both, there is the same prominence given to individual characters ʸ; the same occasional minuteness of detail where it might have been least expected ᶻ.

3. But by far the most remarkable phenomenon remains to be noticed; namely, the immense number of quotations, (so far more numerous than is commonly suspected,)—extending in length from a single word to nearly a hundred and fifty ᵃ,—together with allusive references, literally without number, which are found in the New Testament Scriptures; *the writings of the elder Covenant being in every instance, exclusively* ᵇ, *the source of those quotations,—the object of those allusions.*

4. When the nature of these quotations, references, and allusions is examined with care, several extraordinary phenomena present themselves, which it seems impossible to consider without the deepest interest, surprise, and admiration. Thus,—(i.) The New Testament writers, on repeated occasions, display *independent knowledge* of the Old Testament History to which they make reference ᶜ. The following instances occur to my memory:—All the later links

---

˟ E. g. Gen. xxviii. 11, 12: xxxii. 1—3. Exod. xxiv. 10.—St. Luke xxii. 43—45. St. Matth. xxvii. 52, 53. St. Jude ver. 9.

ʸ E. g. Jacob, Joseph, David.—St. Paul, St. Peter, St. John.

ᶻ E. g. Gen. viii. 9: xxxvii. 15—17: xlviii. 17, 18. Exod. ii. 6.—St. Luke viii. 55. St. John xiii. 4, 5: xxi.

ᵃ E. g. in Heb. viii. 8—12, where Jer. xxxi. 31—36 is quoted. See Acts ii. 17—21, where Joel ii. 28—32 is quoted.

ᵇ It is supposed that the three well-known references to profane writers, (Acts xvii. 28. 1 Cor. xv. 33. Tit. i. 12, [concerning which see Jerome, *Opp.* i. 424: vii. 471,])—the place in St. Matthew, (xxvii. 9,)—and St. James iv. 5,—are scarcely exceptions to the statement in the text.

ᶜ See above,—(δ).

in our LORD's Genealogy [d]; the second Cainan [e]: Salmon's marriage with Rahab [f]: the burial-place of the twelve Patriarchs [g]: the age of Moses in Exod. ii. 11 [h]: that in the days of Elijah the heaven was shut up for three years *and six months* [i]: that it was *the Devil* who tempted Eve [k]: the contest for the dead body of Moses [l]: the names of Pharaoh's magicians [m]: how Abraham reasoned with himself when he prepared to offer up his son Isaac [n]: the golden censer, mentioned in Heb. ix. 4: Abraham's purchase of Sychem [o]; and a few other things [p].

(ii.) The same New Testament writers are observed to handle the Old Testament Scriptures with an air of singular authority, and to exercise an extraordinary license of quotation; inverting clauses,—paraphrasing statements,—abridging or expanding;—and always without apology or explanation;—as if they were conscious that they were dealing with *their own*.

(iii.) Most astonishing of all, obviously, as well as most important, is *the purpose* for which the Evangelists and Apostles of our LORD make their appeal to the Old Testament Scriptures; invariably in order *to establish some part of the Christian Revelation.* "Every thoughtful student of the Holy Scriptures has been struck with the circumstance which I now allude to:

---

[d] Only given by St. Matthew and St. Luke.   [e] Only found in St. Luke iii. 36.   [f] Only found in St. Matth. i. 5.   [g] Only found in Acts vii. 16.   [h] Only found in Acts vii. 23.

[i] St. James v. 17,—mentioned also by our LORD, St. Luke iv. 25; who informs us that Jonah *was a sign* to the Ninevites. This is only revealed in St. Luke xi. 30.

[k] 2 Cor. xi. 3.   [l] St. Jude ver. 9.   [m] 2 Tim. iii. 8.

[n] See Heb. xi. 19. Consider Rom. iv. 19.   [o] Acts vii. 16.

[p] Compare Exod. ii. 2, 3 with Acts vii. 20. Consider Rev. ii. 14: also Heb. xii. 21: also Heb. ix. 19, &c.

the freedom, namely, with which the inspired Writers of the New Testament appeal back to the Old; and see in it, as its one proper theme, the Christian subject. They find themselves in that place, at length, to which former intimations had pointed, and recognize the connexion which they themselves have with their ancient forerunners q." .... It is as if for four hundred years and upwards, a mighty mystery,—described in many a dark place of Prophecy, exhibited by many a perplexing type, foreshadowed by many a Divine narrative,—had waited for solution. The world is big with expectation. The long-expected time at last arrives. Up springs the Sun of Righteousness in the Heavens; and lo, the cryptic characters of the Law flash at once into glory, and the dark Oracles of ancient days yield up their wondrous meanings! "GOD, who at sundry times and in divers manners spake in time past unto the Fathers by the Prophets,"—in these last days speaks "unto us by His SON:" and lo, a chorus of Apostolic voices is heard bearing witness to the Advent of "the Desire of all nations!" .... Such is the relation which the New Testament bears to the Old: such the true nature of the many quotations from the earlier Scriptures, which are found in the later half of the One inspired Volume.

5. And thus we are led naturally to notice the extraordinary connexion which subsists between the two Testaments. "For what is the Law," (asks Justin, A.D. 140,) "but the Gospel foretold? or what is the Gospel, but the Law fulfilled r?" "The contents

---

q *Sermons*, by the Rev. C. P. Eden, p. 185.

r Τί γάρ ἐστιν ὁ Νόμος; Εὐαγγέλιον προκατηγγελμένον· τί δὲ τὸ Εὐαγγέλιον; Νόμος πεπληρωμένος. Justin: *Quæst.* ci. p. 456.

of the Old and New Testament are the same," remarks Augustine: "*there* foreshadowed, *here* revealed: *there* prefigured, *here* made plain." "In the Old Testament there is a concealing of the New: in the New Testament there is a revealing of the Old [s]."— Mr. Jowett's inquiry,—"If we assume the New Testament as *a tradition running parallel with the Old*, may not the Roman Catholic assume with equal reason a tradition parallel with the New?" (p. 381.)—shews a truly childish misapprehension of the entire question. The New Testament is not a "parallel tradition" at all; but *a subsequent Revelation from Heaven*.

6. Now I might pursue these remarks much further: for it would be well worth while to exhibit what an extraordinary sameness of imagery, similarity of allusion, and unity of purpose, runs through the writings of either Covenant;—phenomena which can only be accounted for in one way. This subject will be found dwelt upon elsewhere; and to what has been already delivered, I must be content here to refer the reader [t].

(Mr. Jowett himself has been struck by the phenomenon thus alluded to: but after hinting at "some natural association" as having suggested the language of the Prophets, he proceeds: "We are not therefore justified in supposing any hidden connexion in the prophecies where [the prophetic symbols] occur. *Neither is there any other ground for assuming design of*

---

[s] Eadem sunt in Vetere et Novo: ibi obumbrata, hic revelata; ibi præfigurata, hic manifesta. (Augustine: *Quæst.* xxxiii., in Num. § 1. m. iii. p. 541.)—In Veteri Testamento est occultatio Novi: in Novo Testamento est manifestatio Veteris. (*Id. De Catechiz. Rudibus*, § 8.—See also Quæst. lxxiii. in Exod.)

[t] See below, from the foot of p. 174 to the beginning of p. 176.

any other kind in Scripture; any more than in Plato or Homer." (p. 381.) .... And thus our philosopher, assuming at the outset that the Bible is an uninspired book, is for ever coming back to the lie with which he set out. But to proceed.)

7. Still better worthy of notice, in this connexion, is the singular fact (which will also be found adverted to in another place [u],) that the Old and New Testaments alike profess to be a History of *Earthly* events from a *Heavenly* point of view. The writers of either Covenant claim to know *what God did*[x]; how characters and events appeared *in His sight*[y]: they profess to find themselves in a familiar, and altogether extraordinary relation with the unseen world[z]. Thus, Moses begins the Bible with an august account of the great Six Days,—when God was alone in Creation; the unwitnessed Agent, and Author of all things:— while St. John the Divine, concluding the inspired Canon, relates that he was "in the Spirit on the Lord's Day;" and heard behind him "a great Voice, as of a trumpet, saying, I am Alpha and Omega, the first and the last[a]." .... "The general design of Scripture," (says Bishop Butler,) "may be said to be, to give us an account of the World, in this one single view,—*as God's World: by which it appears essentially distinguished from all other books, as far as I have found, except such as are copied from it*[b]."

8. And *yet* the grand external characteristic feature of the Bible remains unnoticed! The one distinctive feature of the Bible, is *this*,—that the four-fold Gospel,

---

[u] Below, p. 108. The reader is requested to refer to the place.

[x] E. g. Gen. xi. 5—8: xviii. 17—21. [y] E. g. Gen. vi. 6. 2 Sam. xi. 27. [z] E. g. 2 Kings xix. 35. St. Matth. xxviii. 2, 3.

[a] Rev. i. 10, 11. [b] *Analogy*, P. II. ch. vii.

as a matter of fact, exhibits to us, the WORD "made flesh:" and, (O marvel of marvels!) suffers us to hear His voice, and look upon His form, and observe His actions. It does more. The New Testament professes to be, and is, the complement of the Old. The promise of CHRIST, solemnly, and repeatedly,—"at sundry times and divers manners,"—given in the one, is fulfilled in the other. Henceforth they are no more twain, for they have been by GOD Himself joined together; and the subject of both is none other than our SAVIOUR, JESUS CHRIST.

Enough surely has been already adduced to warrant a reasonable man in refusing to accept Professor Jowett's repeated asseveration that the Bible is "to be interpreted like any other book." A Book which proves on examination to be so *wholly unlike every other book,*—so entirely *sui generis,*—may surely well create an *à priori* suspicion that it is not to be interpreted either, after any ordinary fashion. But the grand consideration of all is *still* behind! The *one* circumstance which effectually refutes the view of the Reverend Professor, remains yet to be specified; namely, that THE BIBLE PROFESSES TO BE INSPIRED BY THE HOLY SPIRIT. The HOLY GHOST is again and again declared *to speak* therein, διά, "*by the instrumentality,*" "*by the mouth,*" of Man. In other words, GOD, *not Man, professes to be the Author of the Bible!*

That the Bible *does* set up for itself such a claim, will be found established at p. 53 to p. 57 of the present volume. Professor Jowett's assurance that "for any of the higher or supernatural views of Inspiration, *there is no foundation in the Gospels or Epistles,*" (p. 345,)—must therefore be regarded as an extraordinary, or rather as an unpardonable oversight on his part. One would have thought that a single saying, like that in Acts iii. 18 and 21, would have occurred to his memory, and been sufficient to refute him. Other places will be found quoted at p. cxcvii.

Very much is it to be feared however that the same gentleman has overlooked a consideration of at least equal importance; namely, the inevitable *inference* from the discovery that the origin of the Bible is Divine. He informs us that,—" It will be a further assistance (!) in the consideration of this subject, to observe that the Interpretation of Scripture has *nothing to do with any opinion respecting its origin.*" (p. 350.) "The *meaning* of Scripture," (he proceeds,) "is one thing: the *Inspiration* of Scripture is another."—True. But when we find the Reverend Author insisting, again and again, that " it may be laid down that Scripture has *one* meaning,—*the meaning which it had to the mind of the Prophet or Evangelist who first uttered, or wrote it,*" (p. 378,)—we are constrained to remind him that, " To say that the Scriptures, and the things contained in them, can have no other or farther meaning than those persons thought or had, who first recited or wrote them; is evidently saying, *that those persons were the original, proper, and sole authors of those books,* i. e. THAT THEY ARE NOT INSPIRED[c]." So that, in point of fact, *the origin* of Holy Scripture, so far from being a consideration of no importance, (as Mr. Jowett supposes,) proves to be a consideration of the most vital importance of all. And *the Interpretation* of Scripture, so far from having "*nothing to do* with any opinion respecting its origin," is affected by it most materially, or rather depends upon it altogether!

[c] Butler's *Analogy*, P. II. ch. vii.

On a review of all that goes before, it will, I think, appear plain to any person of sound understanding, that Professor Jowett's *à priori* views respecting the Interpretation of Holy Scripture will not stand the test of exact reason. To suggest as he has done that the Bible is to be interpreted like any other book, on the plea that it *is* like any other book, is to build upon a false foundation. His syllogism is the following:—

If the Bible is a book like any other book, the Bible is to be interpreted like any other book.

The Bible is a book like any other book.

Therefore,—

But it has been shewn that the learned Professor's minor premiss is false. It has been proved that the Bible is NOT a book like any other book.

Nay, I claim to have done *more*. I claim to have established the contradictory minor premiss. The syllogism therefore will henceforth stand as follows:—

If the Bible can be shewn to be a book like no other book, but entirely *sui generis*, and claiming to be the work of Inspiration,—then is it reasonable to expect that it will have to be interpreted like no other book, but entirely after a fashion of its own.

But the Bible *can* be shewn to be a book like no other book; entirely *sui generis;* and claiming to be the work of Inspiration.

Therefore,—

2. It remains however, now, to advance an important step.—Mr. Jowett, in a certain place, adopts a principle, the soundness of which I am able, happily, entirely to admit. "Interpret Scripture from itself,—like any other book about which we know almost nothing except what is derived from its pages." (p. 382.)

"*Non nisi ex Scripturâ Scripturam interpretari potes.*" (p. 384.)

Scarcely has he made this important admission however, and enunciated his golden Canon of interpretation, when he hastens to nullify it. His very next words are,—"The meaning of the Canon is only this,—'That we cannot understand Scripture without becoming familiar (!) with it.'"

But, (begging the learned writer's pardon,) so far from *that* being the whole of the meaning of the Canon, his gloss happens exactly to miss the only important point. The plain meaning of the words,— "Only out of the Scriptures can you explain the Scriptures,"—is obviously rather this:—'That in order *to interpret* the Bible, our aim must be *to ascertain how the Bible interprets itself.*' In other words, —'Scripture must be made *its own Interpreter.*' More simply yet, in the Professor's own words, (from which, *more suo*, he has imperceptibly glided away,)—"*Interpret Scripture from itself.*" (p. 382.) .... How then does Scripture interpret Scripture? *That* is the only question! for the answer to this question must be held to be decisive as to the other great question which Mr. Jowett raises in the present Essay,— namely, How are *we* to interpret Scripture?

Now this whole Inquiry has been conducted elsewhere; and will be found to extend from p. 144 to p. 160 of the present volume. It has been there established, by a sufficiently large induction of examples, that *the Bible is to be interpreted as no other book is, or can be interpreted*; and for the plain reason, that *the inspired Writers themselves,* (our LORD Himself at their head!) *interpret it after an altogether extraordinary fashion.* Mr. Jowett's statement at p. 339 that "the mystical interpretation of Scripture originated in the Alexandrian age," is simply false.

And in the course of this proof, (necessarily involved in it, in fact,) it has been incidentally shewn that the sense of Scripture is not, by any means, invariably *one ;* and *that* sense the most obvious to those who wrote, heard, or read it. It has been fully shewn that the office of the Interpreter is *not*, by any means, (as Mr. Jowett imagines,) "to recover the meaning of the words *as they first struck on the ears, or flashed before the eyes of those who heard or read them.*" (p. 338.) The Reverend writer's repeated assertion that "we have no reason to attribute to the Prophet or Evangelist any second or hidden sense different from that which appears on the surface," (p. 380,) has been fully, and as it is hoped effectually refuted.

And here I might lay down my pen. For since, at the end of 74 pages, the Professor thus delivers himself, (in a kind of imitation of St. Paul's language[d],)—"Of what has been said, this is the sum,—'That Scripture, *like other books*, has *one* meaning, which has to be gathered from itself .... *without regard to à priori notions about its nature and origin:*" that, "It is to be interpreted *like other books*, with attention to the prevailing state of civilization and knowledge," and so forth; (p. 404;)—it must suffice to say that, having established the very opposite conclusion, I claim to have effectually answered his Essay; because I have overthrown what he admits to be "the sum" of it. Let me be permitted however—before I proceed to review some other parts of his performance,—in the briefest manner, not so much to recapitulate, as to exhibit 'the sum' of what has been hitherto de-

[d] Heb. viii. 1.

livered on the other side; in somewhat different language, and as it were from a different point of view.

We are presented then, in the New Testament Scriptures, with the august spectacle of the Ancient of Days holding the entire volume of the Old Testament Scriptures in His Hands, *and interpreting it of Himself.* He, whose Life and Death are set forth in the Gospel;—whose Church's early fortunes are set forth historically in the Acts, while its future prospects are shadowed prophetically in the Apocalypse;—whose Doctrines, lastly, are explained in the twenty-one Epistles of St. Paul and St. Peter, St. James and St. John and St. Jude:—He, the Incarnate WORD, who was "in the beginning;" who "was with GOD," and who "was GOD:"—that same Almighty One, I repeat, is exhibited to us in the Gospel, repeatedly, holding the Volume of the Old Testament Scriptures in His Hands, and *explaining it of Himself.* "*To day is this Scripture fulfilled* in your ears[e],"—was the solemn introductory sentence with which, in the Synagogue of Nazareth, (after closing the Book and giving it again to the Minister,) He prefaced His Sermon from the lxist chapter of Isaiah.—" Had ye believed Moses, ye would have believed Me: *for he wrote of Me*[f]."—"'O fools, and slow of heart to believe all that the Prophets have spoken! Ought not CHRIST to have suffered these things, and to enter into His glory?' And *beginning at Moses, and all the Prophets, He expounded to them in all the Scriptures the things concerning Himself*[g]."— "These are the words which I spake unto you, that all things must be fulfilled *which are written in the*

[e] St. Luke iv. 21. [f] St. John v. 46.
[g] St. Luke xxiv. 27.

Law of Moses, and in the Prophets, and in the Psalms, concerning Me[h]."

"CHRIST was before Moses. The Gospel was not made for the Law; but the Law was made for the Gospel. The Gospel is not based on the Law, but the Law is a shadow of the Gospel. In order to believe the Bible, we must look upward; and fix our eyes on JESUS CHRIST, sitting in Heavenly Glory, holding both Testaments in His Hand; sealing both Testaments with His seal; and delivering both Testaments as Divine Oracles, to the World. We must receive the *written Word* from the Hands of the INCARNATE WORD[i]."

This august spectacle, let it be clearly stated,—(1) Establishes, beyond all power of contradiction, the intimate connexion which subsists between the Old and the New Testament; as well as the altogether unique relation which the one bears to the other:—(2) Invests either Testament with a degree of sacred importance and majestic grandeur which altogether makes the Bible *unlike* "*any other book:*"—(3) Proves that the Bible is to be interpreted as no other book ever was, or ever can be interpreted:—(4) Demonstrates that it has *more than a single meaning:*—and lastly, (5) Convincingly shews that *GOD, and not Man, is its true Author*.

It will of course be asked,—Then does Mr. Jowett take no notice at all of this vast and complicated problem? How does he treat of the relation between the Old Testament and the New? ... He despatches the entire subject in the following passage:—"The question," (he says,) "runs up into a more general one,

[h] St. Luke xxiv. 44.
[i] Dr. Wordsworth (Occasional Sermon 54,) *On the Inspiration of the Old Testament*, (1859.)—p. 70.

'the relation between the Old and New Testaments.' For the Old Testament *will receive a different meaning accordingly as it is explained from itself*, or *from the New.*" (Very different certainly!) "In the first case, —a careful and conscientious study of each one for itself is all that is required." (That is to say, it will not be explained at all!) "In the second case,— *the types and ceremonies of the Law, perhaps the very facts and persons of the history*, WILL BE ASSUMED (!) to be predestined or made after a pattern corresponding to the things that were to be in the latter days." (p. 370.) (And why not "*will be found* to be replete with Christian meaning,— full of lofty spiritual significancy?"—the *proved* marvellousness of their texture, the *revealed* mysteriousness of their purpose, being an effectual refutation of all Mr. Jowett's *à priori* notions!)

"And this question," (he proceeds,) "stirs up another question respecting the Interpretation of the Old Testament in the New. Is such Interpretation to be regarded as the meaning of the original text, or *an accommodation of it to the thoughts of other times?*" (Nay, but Reverend and learned Sir: "nothing so plain," as you justly observe, "that it may not be explained away;" (p. 359;) yet we cannot consent to have the sense of plain words thus clouded over at your mere bidding. It is now *our* turn to declare that the Interpreter's "object is to read Scripture *like any other book*, with a real interest and not merely a conventional one." It is now *we* who "want to be able to open our eyes, and see things as they truly are." (p. 338.) We simply petition for leave to "*interpret Scripture like any other book, by the same rules of evidence and the same canons of criticism.*" (p. 375.)

And if this freedom be but conceded to us, there will be found to be no imaginable reason why the Interpretation of the Old Testament in the New,—(CHRIST Himself being the Majestic Speaker! our present edification and everlasting welfare being His gracious purpose!)—should not be strictly "regarded as *the meaning of the original text.*" ... But let us hear the Professor out:—)

"Our object," (he says, and with this he dismisses the problem!)—"Our object is not to attempt here the determination of these questions; but to point out that they must be determined before any real progress can be made, or any agreement arrived at in the Interpretation of Scripture." (p. 370.) ... They must indeed. But can it be right in this slovenly, slippery style to shirk a discussion on the issue of which the whole question may be said to turn? especially on the part of one who scruples not to prejudge that issue, and straightway to apply it, (in a manner fatal to the Truth,) throughout all his hundred pages. Mr. Jowett's method is ever to *assume* what he ought to *prove*, and then either to be plaintive, or to sneer. "It is a *heathenish or Rabbinical fancy:*"—"Such complexity would place the Scriptures *below human compositions* in general; for it would deprive them of the ordinary intelligibleness of human language" (p. 382):—&c.

"Is the Interpretation of the Old Testament in the New to be regarded as the *meaning of the original text;* or an *accommodation of it to the thoughts of other times?*" (p. 370.) This is Mr. Jowett's question; the question which it is "*not his object* to attempt to determine;" but which I, on the contrary, have made it *my* object to discuss in my VIth Sermon,—p. 183 to p. 220. Without troubling the reader however now to wade through those many pages, let me at least explain to him in a few words what Mr. Jowett's question really amounts to: namely this,—Do the Apostles and Evangelists, does our Blessed LORD Himself, when He professes to explain the mysterious significancy of the Old Testament,—*invariably*,—*in every instance*,—*misrepresent* "*the meaning of the original text?*" And the answer to this question I am content to await from any candid person of plain unsophisticated understanding. Is it credible, concerning the Divine expositions found in St. Matth. xxii. 31, 32,—xxii. 43-5,—xii. 39, 40,—xi. 10,—St. John viii. 17, 18,—i. 52,—vi. 31, &c.,—x. 34-5:—the Apostolic interpretations found in 1 Cor. ix. 9—11,— x. 1—6,—xv. 20,—Heb. ii. 5—9,—vii. 1—10,—Gal. iv. 21—31:—is it conceivable, I ask, that *not one* of all these places should exhibit the actual '*meaning of the original text?*' And yet, (as Mr. Jowett himself is forced to admit,)—"If we attribute to the details of the Mosaical ritual a reference to the New Testament, or suppose the passage of the Red Sea to be regarded not merely as a figure of Baptism, but as a preordained type;—*the principle is conceded!*" (p. 369.) "A little more or a little less of the method does not make the difference." (*Ibid.*) In a word,—in such case, Mr. Jowett's Essay falls to the ground!... To proceed however.

3. The case of Interpretation has not yet been fully set before the reader. Hitherto, we have merely traced the problem back to the fountain-head, and dealt with it simply as *a Scriptural question*. We have shewn what light is thrown upon *Interpretation* by the volume of *Inspiration*. The subject has been treated in the same way in the Vth and VIth of my

Sermons. But it will not be improper, in this place, —it is even indispensable,—to develope the problem a little more fully; and to explain that it is of much larger extent.

Now, there is a family resemblance in the method of all ancient expositions of Holy Scripture which vindicates for them, however remotely, a common origin. There is a resemblance in the general way of handling the Inspired Word which can only be satisfactorily explained by supposing that the remote type of all was the oral teaching of the Apostles themselves. In truth, is it credible that the early Christians would have been so forgetful of the discourses of the men who had seen the LORD, that no trace of it,—no tradition of so much as *the manner* of it,—should have lingered on for a hundred years after the death of the last of the Apostles; down to the time when Origen, for example, was a young man? .... It cannot possibly be!

(i.) "The things which thou hast heard of me among many witnesses," (writes the great Apostle to his son Timothy,) "the same commit thou to faithful men, who shall be able to teach others also [k]." Provision is thus made by the aged Saint,—*in the last of his Epistles*,—for the transmission of his inspired teaching[1] to a second and a third generation. Now the words just quoted were written about the year 65, at which time Timothy was a young man. Unless we suppose that ALMIGHTY GOD curtailed the lives of the chief depositaries of His Word, Timothy will have lived on till A.D. 100; so that "faithful men" who died in the middle of the next century might have been trained and taught by him for many

---

[k] 2 Tim. ii. 2.   [1] See the middle of p. cxcvii.

years. It follows, that the "faithful men" last spoken of will have been "able to teach others also," whose writings (if they wrote at all) would range from A.D. 190 to A.D. 210. Now, just such a writer is Hippolytus,—who is known to have been taught by that "faithful man" Irenæus[m],—to whom, as it happens, the deposit was "committed" by Polycarp, —who stood to St. John in the self-same relation as Timothy to St. Paul!

(ii.) Our SAVIOUR is repeatedly declared to have interpreted the Old Testament to His Disciples. For instance, to the two going to Emmaus, "beginning at Moses and all the Prophets, *He interpreted to them in all the Scriptures the things concerning Himself*[n]." Moreover, before He left the world, He solemnly promised His Apostles that the HOLY GHOST, whom the FATHER should send in His Name, "should *teach them all things*, and *bring to their remembrance all things which He had spoken to them*[o]." Shall we believe that the Treasury of *Divine Inspiration* thus opened by CHRIST Himself was straightway closed up by its human guardians, and at once forgotten? Shall we not rather believe that Cleopas and his companion, (for instance,) forthwith repeated their LORD's words to every member of the Apostolic body, and to others also; that they were questioned again and again by

---

[m] Photius, p. 195, ed. Bekker.—"Eos simul jungendos censui,— Polycarpum, Irenæum, Hippolytum; cum Hippolytus discipulus Irenæi fuisset, Irenæusque Polycarpum, Joannis Apostoli discipulum, audivisset."—Routh, Preface to *Opuscula*, p. x.

[n] St. Luke xxiv. 27.

[o] St. John xiv. 26. The fulfilment of this promise repeatedly occurs: as in St. John ii. 17, 22: xii. 16: xiii. 7: St. Luke xxiv. 8. Consider St. John xx. 9.

adoring listeners, even to their extremest age; aye, and that they taxed their memories to the utmost in order to recal every little word, every particular of our SAVIOUR's Divine utterance? It must be so! And the echo, the remote echo of that exposition, depend upon it! descended to a second, aye and to a third generation; yea, and has come down, faintly, and feebly it may be, but yet essentially and truly, even to ourselves!

(iii.) And yet,—(for we would not willingly incur the charge of being fanciful in so solemn and important a matter,)—the great fact to be borne in mind, (and it is the great fact which nothing can ever set aside or weaken,) is, that for the first century at least of our æra, there existed within the Christian Church *the gift of Prophecy;* that is, of *Inspired Interpretation*[p]. The minds of the Apostles, CHRIST Himself "opened, *to understand the Scriptures*[q]." Can it be any matter of surprise that men so enlightened, when they had been miraculously endowed with the gift of tongues[r], and scattered over the face of the ancient civilized World, should have disseminated the same principles of Catholic Interpretation, as well as the same elements of Saving Truth? When this miraculous *gift* ceased, its *results* did not also come to an end. The fountain dried up, but the streams which it had sent forth yet "made glad the City of GOD." And by what possible logic can the teaching of the early Church be severed from its source? It cannot be supposed for an instant that such a severance ever took place. The teaching of the Apostolic age was the immediate parent of the teaching of the earliest

[p] 1 Cor. xii., xiii., xiv., &c.   [q] St. Luke xxiv. 45.
[r] Acts ii. 4—21.

of the Fathers,—in whose Schools it is matter of history that those Patristic writers with whom we are most familiar, studied and became famous. Accordingly, we discover a method of Interpreting Holy Scripture strictly resembling that employed by our SAVIOUR and His Apostles, *in all the earliest Patristic writings.* As documents increase, the evidence is multiplied; and at the end of two or three centuries after the death of St. John the Evangelist, voices are heard from Jerusalem and other parts of Palestine; from Antioch and from other parts of Syria; from the Eastern and the Western extremities of North Africa; from many regions of Asia Minor; from Constantinople and from Greece; from Rome, from Milan, and from other parts of Italy; from Cyprus and from Gaul;—all singing in unison; all singing the same heavenly song! . . . In what way but one is so extraordinary a phenomenon to be accounted for? Are we to believe that there was a general conspiracy of the East and the West, the North and the South, to interpret Holy Scripture in a certain way; and that way, the wrong way?

Enough has been said, it is thought, to shew that many of Mr. Jowett's remarks about the value of Patristic evidence are either futile or incorrect; or that they betray an entire misapprehension of the whole question, not to say a thorough want of appreciation of the claims of Antiquity. We do not yield to the 'Essayist and Reviewer' in veneration for the Inspired page; and trust that enough has been said to shew it. Our eye, when we read Scripture, (like his,) "is fixed on the form of One like the Son of Man; or of the Prophet who was girded with a garment of camel's hair; or of the Apostle who had a thorn in the flesh." (p. 338.)

We are only unlike Mr. Jowett we fear in *this*,—that *we* believe *ex animo* that the first-named was the Eternal Son, "equal to the FATHER," and "of one substance with the FATHER^s:" and further that St. Paul's fourteen Epistles are all *inspired writings,* in an entirely different sense from the Dialogues of Plato or the Tragedies of Sophocles. It follows, that however riveted our mental gaze may be on the awful forms which come before us in Holy Scripture,—as often as we con *the inspired record of the actions and of the sayings of those men,* we are constrained many a time to look upward, and to exclaim with the Psalmist, "Thy thoughts are very deep[t]!" And often if asked, "Understandest thou what thou readest?"—we must still answer with the Ethiopian, "How can I, except some man should guide me[u]?"

(iv.) To assume however that our defective knowledge "cannot be supplied by *the conjectures* of Fathers or Divines," (p. 338,) is in some sort to beg the question at issue. To say of the student of Scripture that "the history of Christendom, and all the after-thoughts of Theology, *are nothing to him:*" (p. 338:) that "he has to imagine himself a disciple of CHRIST or Paul, and *to disengage himself from all that follows:*" (*Ibid.:*) is not the language of modesty, but of inordinate conceit. In Mr. Jowett it is in fact something infinitely worse; for he shews that his object thereby is to "obtain an unembarrassed opportunity

---

[s] See Mr. Jowett's Essay, p. 354.   [t] Ps. xcii. 5.

[u] Acts viii. 30, 31.—"'Revela,' inquit David, 'oculos meos, et considerabo mirabilia de Lege Tuâ.' Si tantus Propheta tenebras ignorantiæ confitetur, quâ nos putas parvulos, et pene lactantes, inscitiæ nocte circumdari? Hoc autem velamen non solum in facie Moysi, sed et in Evangelistis et in Apostolis positum est."—Hieronymus, *Ep.* lviii. vol. i. p. 323.

of applying all the resources of a so-called criticism to discredit and destroy the written record itself[x]."

"True indeed it is, that more than any other subject of human knowledge, Biblical criticism has hung (*sic.*) to the past;" (p. 340;) but the reason is also obvious. It is because, in the words of great Bishop Pearson, "Philosophia quotidie *progressu*, Theologia nisi *regressu* non crescit[y]." "O ye who are devoting yourselves to the Divine Science of Theology," (he exclaims,) "and whose cheeks grow pale over the study of Holy Scripture above all; ye who either fill the venerable office of the Priesthood or intend it, and are hereafter to undertake the awful cure of souls:—rid yourselves of that itch of the present age, the love of novelty. Make it your business to inquire for that which was from the beginning. Resort for counsel to the fountain-head. Have recourse to Antiquity. Return to the holy Fathers. Look back to the primitive Church. In the words of the Prophet,—'*Ask for the old paths*[z].'"

When therefore Mr. Jowett classes together "the early Fathers, the Roman Catholic mystical writers, the Swiss and German Reformers, and the Nonconformist Divines," (p. 377,)—he either shews a most lamentable want of intellectual perspective, or a most perverse understanding. So jumbled into one confused heap, it may not be altogether untrue to say of Commentators generally, that "the words of Scripture suggest to them *their own thoughts or feelings*." (p. 377.) But when it is straightway added, "There is nothing in such a view derogatory to *the Saints and Doctors of former ages*," (*Ibid.*,) we are constrained, (for the reasons

---

[x] Dr. Moberly, as before, pp. liii.-iv.
[y] *Minor Works*, vol. ii. p. 10.   [z] *Ibid.* p. 6.

already before the reader,) to remonstrate against so misleading and deceitful a way of putting the case. Mr. Jowett desires to be understood not to depreciate " the genius or learning of famous men of old," when he remarks " that *Aquinas or Bernard did not shake themselves free from the mystical method of the Patristic times.*" (*Ibid.*) But with singular obtuseness, or with pitiful disingenuousness, he does his best by such words to shut out from view the real question at issue, — namely, *the exegetical value of Patristic Antiquity.* For the Church of England, when she appeals, (as she repeatedly does,) to " the Ancient Fathers," does not by any means intend such names as the Abbot of Clairvaux, who flourished in the middle of the twelfth century; or Thomas of Aquinum, who lived later into the thirteenth. It is the spirit of *the ante-Nicene age* which she defers to; the Fathers of *the first four or five centuries* to whose opinion she gives reverent attention; as her formularies abundantly shew. Whether therefore Aquinas and Bernard were or were not able to " shake themselves free from the mystical method *of the Patristic times*," matters very little. The point to be observed is that *the Writers of the Patristic times*, as a matter of fact, " did not shake themselves *free from the mystical method of*" CHRIST and *His Apostles!*

Very far am I from denying that " any one who, instead of burying himself in the pages of the commentators, would learn the Sacred Writings by heart, and paraphrase them in English, will probably make a nearer approach to their true meaning than he would gather from any Commentary." Quite certain is it that " the true use of Interpretation is to get rid of interpretation, and leave us alone in company with the author." (p. 384.) But this is quite a distinct and different matter, as every person of unsophisticated understanding must perceive at once. The same thing will be found stated by myself, in a subsequent part of the present volume, at considerable length [a]; the qualifying condition having been introduced at p. 16. The truth is, a man can no more divest himself of the conditions of thought habitual to one familiar with his Prayer-Book, than he can withdraw himself from the atmosphere of light in which he moves. *Not* the abuse of Commentators on Holy Scripture, but *the principle on which Holy Scripture itself is to be interpreted*,—is the real question at issue: the fundamental question which underlies this, being of course the vital one,—namely, *Is the Bible an inspired book, or not?*

Apart from what has been already urged concerning "the torrent of *Patristic* Interpretation [b]" which flows down not so much from the fountain-head of Scripture, (wherein so many specimens of *Inspired* Interpretation are preserved,) as from the fontal source of all Wisdom and Knowledge,—even the lips of the Incarnate WORD Himself;—apart from this, a very important Historical circumstance calls for notice in this place.

How did Christianity originate? how did it first establish a footing in the world? "The answer is, By the preaching of living men, who said they were commissioned by GOD to proclaim it. *That* was the origin and first establishment of Christianity. There is indeed a vague and unreasoning notion prevalent that Christianity was *taken from the New Testament*. The notion is historically untrue. Christianity was widely extended through the civilized world before the New Testament was written; and its several books were

[a] See Serm. I. pp. 10-11, 13, &c.   [b] See below, p. 142.

successively addressed to various bodies of Christian believers; to bodies, that is, who already possessed the faith of CHRIST in its integrity. When, indeed, GOD ceased to inspire persons to write these books, and when they were all collected together into what we call the New Testament, the existing Faith of the Church, derived from oral teaching, was tested by comparison with this Inspired Record. And it henceforth became the standing law of the Church that nothing should be received as necessary to Salvation, which could not stand that test. But still, though thus tested, (every article being proved by the New Testament,) Christianity is not taken from it; *for it existed before it.*

"What, then, was the Christianity which was thus established? Have we any record of it as it existed before the New Testament became the sole authoritative standard? I answer, we have. The Creeds of the Christian Church are the record of it. That is precisely what they purport to be: not documents taken from the New Testament, but documents transmitting to us the Faith as it was held from the beginning; the Faith as it was preached by inspired men, before the inspired men put forth any writings; the Faith once for all delivered to the Saints. Accordingly you will find that our Church in her viiith Article does not ground her affirmation that the Creeds ought to be 'thoroughly received and believed,' on the fact that they *were taken* from the New Testament, (which they were *not;*) but on the fact that '*they may be proved by most certain warrants of Holy Scripture.*'"

It follows therefore from what has been said, that even if bad men could succeed in destroying the authority of the Bible as the Word of GOD, all could not be up with Christianity. There would *still* remain to be dealt with the Faith as it exists in the world; the Faith held from the beginning; the Faith once delivered to the Saints. None of the assaults on Holy Scripture can touch *that;* for it traces itself to an independent origin. The evil work, therefore, would have to be begun all over again. The special doctrines which are impugned in 'Essays and Reviews' do not stand or fall with the Inspiration or Interpretation of Scripture; but are stereotyped in the Faith of Christendom. "The Fall of Man, Original Sin, the Atonement, the Divinity of CHRIST, the Trinity, all have their place in the Faith held from the beginning. They are imbedded in the Creeds, and in that general scheme of Doctrine which circles round the Creeds, and is involved in them. Nay, curiously enough,—or rather I should say providentially,—the very point against which the attacks of this book are principally directed, namely the Inspiration of the Old Testament, is in express terms asserted there:—*the* HOLY GHOST *'spake by the Prophets*[c].'"

It remains to shew the bearing of these remarks on Mr. Jowett's Essay.—With infinite perseverance, he dwells upon "the nude Scripture, the merest letter of the Sacred Volume, as if in it and in it alone, resided the entire Revelation of CHRIST, and all possible means of judging what that Revelation consists of: whereas this is very far indeed from being the

[c] From a Sermon by the Rev. F. Woodward, quoted below, at p. 249.—In illustration of the learned writer's concluding remark, take this from the Creed of Lyons, contained in Irenæus (A.D. 180),— Καὶ εἰς Πνεῦμα Ἅγιον, τὸ διὰ τῶν Προφητῶν κεκηρυχὸς τὰς οἰκονομίας, καὶ τὰς ἐλεύσεις. In the Creed of Constantinople, we read, Τὸ Πνεῦμα τὸ Ἅγιον . . . τὸ λαλῆσαν διὰ τῶν Προφητῶν.

case. Every single Book of the New Testament was written, as we have seen, to persons *already in possession of Christian Truth*. It is quite erroneous therefore, historically and notoriously erroneous, to suppose either that the Divine Institution of the Church, or that its Doctrines, were literally founded upon the written words of Holy Scripture; or that they can impart no illustration nor help in the Interpretation of those written words. . . . . The complete possession of the saving Truth belonged to the Christian Church not by degrees, nor in lapse of time, but from the first. Of that saving truth, thus taught and thus possessed, *the Apostles' Creed*, growing up as it did on every side of Christendom as the faithful record of the uniform oral teaching of the Apostles, is the true and precious historical monument[d]; and I ven-

---

[d] The Creed of Lyons begins by describing itself as that which ἡ μὲν Ἐκκλησία, καίπερ καθ' ὅλης τῆς οἰκουμένης ἕως περάτων τῆς γῆς διεσπαρμένη, παρὰ δὲ τῶν Ἀποστόλων καὶ τῶν ἐκείνων μαθητῶν παραλαβοῦσα, κ.τ.λ. Most refreshing of all, however, are the concluding words of that Creed: so comfortable are they that I *cannot* deny myself the consolation of transcribing them here, where indeed they are very much *ad rem* :—

Τοῦτο τὸ κήρυγμα παρειληφυῖα, καὶ ταύτην τὴν πίστιν, ὡς προέφαμεν, ἡ ἐκκλησία, καίπερ ἐν ὅλῳ τῷ κόσμῳ διεσπαρμένη, ἐπιμελῶς φυλάσσει, ὡς ἕνα οἶκον οἰκοῦσα· καὶ ὁμοίως πιστεύει τούτοις, ὡς μίαν ψυχὴν καὶ τὴν αὐτὴν ἔχουσα καρδίαν· καὶ συμφώνως ταῦτα κηρύσσει, καὶ διδάσκει, καὶ παραδίδωσιν, ὡς ἐν στόμα κεκτημένη· Καὶ γὰρ αἱ κατὰ τὸν κόσμον διάλεκτοι ἀνόμοιαι, ἀλλ' ἡ δύναμις τῆς παραδόσεως μία καὶ ἡ αὐτή. Καὶ οὔτε αἱ ἐν Γερμανίαις ἱδρυμέναι ἐκκλησίαι ἄλλως πεπιστεύκασιν, ἢ ἄλλως παραδιδόασιν, οὔτε ἐν ταῖς Ἰβηρίαις, οὔτε ἐν Κελτοῖς, οὔτε κατὰ τὰς ἀνατολὰς, οὔτε ἐν Αἰγύπτῳ, οὔτε ἐν Λιβύῃ, οὔτε αἱ κατὰ μέσα τοῦ κόσμου ἱδρυμέναι. Ἀλλ' ὥσπερ ὁ ἥλιος, τὸ κτίσμα τοῦ Θεοῦ, ἐν ὅλῳ τῷ κόσμῳ εἷς καὶ ὁ αὐτός, οὕτω καὶ τὸ κήρυγμα τῆς ἀληθείας πανταχῇ φαίνει, καὶ φωτίζει πάντας ἀνθρώπους τοὺς βουλομένους εἰς ἐπίγνωσιν ἀληθείας ἐλθεῖν. Καὶ οὔτε ὁ πάνυ δυνατὸς ἐν λόγῳ τῶν ἐν ταῖς ἐκκλησίαις προεστώτων ἕτερα τούτων ἐρεῖ, (οὐδεὶς γὰρ ὑπὲρ τὸν διδάσκαλον,) οὔτε ὁ ἀσθενὴς ἐν τῷ λόγῳ ἐλαττώσει τὴν παράδοσιν.

ture to say that if any person claims to reject the Apostles' Creed as an auxiliary, a great and invaluable auxiliary, in interpreting the writings of the Apostles, he shews himself to be very wanting indeed in appreciation of the comparative value of Historical Evidence, and of the true principles of Historical Philosophy.—And not the Apostles' Creed only; but the whole history and tradition of the universal Church,—needing, no doubt, skill and discretion in its application,—supply, when applied with requisite skill and discretion, very valuable and real aid in interpreting Holy Scripture[e]."

When therefore Mr. Jowett speaks contemptuously of "the attempt to adapt the truths of Scripture to the doctrines of the Creeds," (p. 353,) the kindest thing which can be said is that he writes like an ignorant, or at least an unlearned man. "The Creeds" (he says) "are acknowledged to be a part of Christianity .... Yet it does not follow that they should be pressed into the service of the Interpreter." Why not? we ask. "The *growth of ideas*," (he replies,) "in the interval which separated the first century from the fourth or sixth makes it *impossible* to apply the language of the one to the explanation of the other. Between Scripture and the Nicene or Athanasian Creeds, *a world of the understanding comes in;* and mankind are no longer at the same point as when the whole of Christianity was contained in the words 'Believe on the LORD JESUS CHRIST and thou mayest be saved;' when the Gospel centred in the attach-

---

Μιᾶς γὰρ καὶ τῆς αὐτῆς πίστεως οὔσης, οὔτε ὁ πολὺ περὶ αὐτῆς δυνάμενος εἰπεῖν ἐπλεόνασεν, οὔτε ὁ τὸ ὀλίγον ἠλαττόνησε.—See Heurtley's *Harmonia Symbolica*, p. 9.

[e] Abridged from Dr. Moberly, as before, pp. lii.-v.

ment to a living and recently departed friend and Lord." (p. 353.)

But there is a fallacy or a falsity at every step of this argument. For *when* did the Gospel ever "centre in attachment?" or *when* was "the whole of Christianity contained" in one short sentence? Supposing too that "a world of the understanding" *does* come in between the first century and the sixth; how does it follow that it is "impossible" to apply the language of the Creeds to the interpretation of Holy Scripture? Explain to me how that "world of understanding" affects *the Nicene* Creed? Even in the case of that most precious Creed called the Athanasian,—why need we *assume* that "the growth of ideas" has been a spurious growth? What if it should prove, on the contrary, that the development has been that of the plant from the seed[f]? Above all, why talk of "the fourth *or* sixth century,"—as if the Creeds were not essentially much older; nay, *co-eval with Christianity itself?* .... Such writing shews nothing so much as a confused mind,—a weak, ill-informed, and illogical thinker.

Indeed Mr. Jowett seems to be altogether in the dark on the subject of the Creeds: for he speaks of them as "the result of three or four centuries of reflection and controversy," (p. 353,)—which is by no means true of all of them; nor, except in a certain sense, of any. But when he inquires,—"If the occurrence of the phraseology of the Nicene age in a verse of the Epistles would detect the spuriousness

---

[f] Καὶ ὅνπερ τρόπον ὁ τοῦ σινάπεως σπόρος, ἐν μικρῷ κόκκῳ, πολλοὺς περιέχει τοὺς κλάδους, οὕτω καὶ ἡ Πίστις αὕτη, ἐν ὀλίγοις ῥήμασι, πᾶσαν τὴν ἐν τῇ Παλαιᾷ καὶ Καινῇ τῆς εὐσεβείας γνῶσιν ἐγκεκόλπισται.—Cyril. Hieros. Cat. v. § 12,—quoted by Heurtley.

of the verse in which it was found,—how can the Nicene *or Athanasian Creed* be a suitable instrument for the interpretation of Scripture?" (p. 354.)—he simply asks a fool's question. The cases are not only not parallel, but there is not even any analogy between them. Let us hear him a little further :—

"Absorbed as St. Paul was in the person of Christ, ... he does not speak of Him as 'equal to the Father,' or ' of one substance with the Father[g].' Much of the language of the Epistles, (passages for example such as Romans i. 2: Philippians ii. 6,) would lose their meaning if distributed in alternate clauses between our LORD's Humanity and Divinity[h]. Still greater difficulties would be introduced into the Gospels by the attempt to identify them with the Creeds[i]. We should have to suppose that He was and was not tempted[k]; that when He prayed to His Father He prayed also to Himself[l]; that He knew and did not know ' of that hour' of which He as well as the angels were ignorant[m]. How could He have said 'My God, My God, why hast Thou forsaken

[g] *Answer.* He certainly does not employ *the identical language* of the Nicene Council, or of the (so called) Athanasian Creed. But what then ?

[h] *Ans.* Passages of the Epistles " distributed in alternate clauses between our LORD's Humanity and Divinity," begging Mr. Jowett's pardon, is nonsense. But *no* passage in St. Paul's Epistles which relates to the Humanity, or to the Divinity of CHRIST, could be said to " lose its meaning" by being unlocked by its own proper clue : or, if the statement be complex, by being distributed under two heads.

[i] *Ans.* But not, I suppose, *to reconcile* them ? Why use inaccurate language on so solemn a subject ?

[k] *Ans.* Doubtless we have to suppose this !

[l] *Ans.* Not so. For " there is one Person of the FATHER, and another of the SON."

[m] *Ans.* Doubtless we have to suppose this !

Me?' or 'Father, if it be possible let this cup pass from Me.' How could He have doubted whether 'when the Son of Man cometh He shall find faith upon the earth[n]?' These simple and touching words," (p. 355,)—pah!

Now if what precedes means anything at all,—(I am by no means certain however that it does!)—it means that the writer does not believe in the Divinity of our LORD JESUS CHRIST. Unless the sentence which is without a reference to the foot of the page be not a denial of the fundamental Doctrine of the Faith[o],—I do not understand it. But look at *all* which precedes; and then say if those are the remarks of a man entitled to dogmatize "On the Interpretation of Scripture."

.... If Mr. Jowett really means that the Creeds *cannot be reconciled with the Bible*,—how can he himself subscribe to the VIIIth Article? If he means nothing of the kind,—why does he write in such a weak, cloudy, illogical way?

But the whole of the case has not even yet been stated. Down from the remote period of which we have been hitherto speaking,—the age of primitive Creeds, and œcumenical Councils, and ancient Fathers,—in every country of the civilized world to which the Gospel has spread,—the loftiest Intellect, the profoundest Learning, the sincerest Piety, have invariably endorsed the ancient and original method of interpretation. I am not implying that such corroboration was in any sense *required;* but the circumstance that it has been *obtained*, at least deserves attention. Modes of thought are dependent on times and countries. There is a fashion in all things. Great ad-

---

[n] *Ans.* But He did *not* doubt!

[o] 1 St. John iv. 2, 3.—2 St. John ver. 7.

vances in Science,—grand epochs in civilization,—vicissitudes of opinion,—difference of institutions, national traditions, and the like,—might be supposed to have wrought a permanent change even in this department of Sacred Science. But it is not so. The storm has raged from one quarter or other of the heavens, but has ever spent its violence in vain. Still has the Church Catholic retained her own unbroken tradition. To keep to the history of that Church to which we, by GOD's mercy, belong :—The constant appeal, at the time of our own great Reformation, was to the Fathers of the first four centuries. Ever since, the temper and spirit of our Commentators has been to revert to the same standard, to reproduce the same teaching. The most powerful minds and the most holy spirits,—English Divines of the deepest thought and largest reading, — let me add, of the soundest judgment and severest discrimination,—have, in every age, down to the present, gratefully accepted not only the method, but even the very details of primitive Patristic Interpretation. But "the acceptance of a hundred generations and the growing authority arising from it,"—like "the institutions based upon such ancient writings, and the history into which they have entwined themselves indissolubly for many centuries,"—all conspire to "constitute a perpetually increasing and strengthening [p]" body of evidence on the subject of Sacred Interpretation.

Now, to oppose (1) to the learning, and piety, and wisdom, of every age of the English Church,—(2) to the unbroken testimony of the Church Universal,—(3) to the torrent of Patristic Antiquity,—(4) to the decision of early Councils, and (5) the 'still small

[p] Dr. Moberly, as before, p. xlvii.

voice' of primitive Creeds,—yet more, (6) to the constant practice of the Apostles,—and, above all, (7) to the indisputable method of our Divine LORD Himself;—to oppose to all this mighty accumulation of evidence, the simple *à priori* convictions of—Mr. Jowett! savours so strongly of the ridiculous, that it really seems superfluous to linger over the antithesis for a single moment.

4. Our task might now be looked upon as completed.—It only remains, in justice to the gentleman whose method we have been considering, to ascertain by what considerations he is induced to reject that method of Interpretation which, as we have seen, enjoys such overwhelming sanction.

(i) In opposition to what goes before, then, he throws out a suggestion, that "nothing would be more likely to restore a natural feeling on this subject than a History of the Interpretation of Scripture. It would take us back to the beginning; it would present in one view the causes which have darkened the meaning of words in the course of ages." (p. 338-9.) "Such a work would enable us to separate the elements of Doctrine and Tradition with which the meaning of Scripture is encumbered in our own day." (p. 339.)

Let us here be well understood with our author. The advantage of a good "History of Interpretation" would indeed be incalculably great. But Mr. Jowett, (like most other writers of his class,) *assumes* the point he has to *prove*, when he insinuates that the result of such a contribution to our Theological Literature would be to show that all the world has been in error for 1700 years, and that he alone is right. That 'erring fancy' has *often* been at work in the fields of sacred criticism,—*who* ever doubted? That there have been epochs of Interpretation, — different Schools, — and varying tastes, in the long course of so many centuries of mingled light and darkness, learning and barbarism;—what need to declare? A faithful history of Interpretation would of course establish these facts on a sure foundation.

But the Reverend Author forgets his Logic when he goes on from these undoubted generalities to imply that all has been confusion and utter uncertainty until now. Above all, common regard for the facts of the case ought to have preserved him from putting forth so monstrous a falsehood as the following:—"*Among German Commentators* there is for the first time in the history of the world, an approach to agreement and certainty." (p. 340.)

Let us however,—passing by the many crooked remarks and unsound inferences with which the Reverend writer, (*more suo*,) delights to perplex a plain question ᵖ,—invite him to abide by the test which he himself proposes. For 1700 years, (he says,) the Interpretation of Scripture has been obscured and encumbered by successive Schools of Interpretation. The Interpreter's concern (he says) is *with the Bible*

ᵖ E.g. "We should observe how the popular explanations of Prophecy, as in heathen (Thucyd. ii. 54,) so also in Christian times, had adapted themselves to the circumstances of mankind." (The Reverend writer can *never for a moment* divest himself of his theory that Thucydides and the Bible stand on the same footing!) "We might remark that in our own country, and in the present generation especially, the interpretation of Scripture had assumed an apologetic character, as though making an effort to defend itself against some supposed inroad of Science and Criticism." (p. 340.) .... Just as if any other attitude was *possible* when one has to do with 'Essayists and Reviewers!'

itself. "The simple words of that book he tries to preserve absolutely pure from the refinements of later times. . . . The greater part of his learning is a knowledge of the text itself." [He is evidently the very man who *sweeps the house to discover the pearl of great price.* (p. 414.)] "He has no delight in the voluminous literature which has overgrown it. He has no theory of Interpretation. A few rules guarding against common errors are enough for him. . . . . He wants to be able to open his eyes, and see or imagine things as they truly are." (p. 338.) [How crooked by the way is all this! "He has no *theory* of Interpretation[q]?" Why, no; for the best of all reasons. He *denies Inspiration altogether!* His "theory" is that *the Bible is an uninspired Book!* . . . . How peculiar too, and how plaintive is the "want" of the supposed Interpreter, "*to be able to open his eyes;*"—glued up, as they no doubt are, by the superstitious tendencies of the nineteenth century, and the tyranny of an intolerant age!]

But we may perhaps state the matter more intelligibly and simply, thus:—In order to ascertain the *true* principle of Scriptural Interpretation, let us,—divesting ourselves of the complicated and voluminous lore of 1700 years,—*resort to the Bible itself.* Let us go for our views to the fountain-head; and abide by what we shall discover *there.*

A fairer proposal (as I think) never was made. It exactly describes the method which I have humbly endeavoured myself to pursue in the ensuing Sermons. The inquiry will be found elaborated from p. 141 to

[q] One would imagine that the Essayist and his critic were entirely agreed. See below, p. 74,—"I refuse to accept any *theory* whatsoever." And p. 115,—"*Theory* I have none."

p. 160 of the present volume; and the result is to be read on the last-named page, in the following words: —" that it may be regarded as a fundamental rule, that the Bible *is not to be interpreted like a common book.* This I gather infallibly from the plain fact, that *the inspired writers themselves* habitually interpret it *as no other book either is, or can be interpreted.*—Next, I assert without fear of contradiction that inspired Interpretation, whatever varieties of method it may exhibit, is yet uniform and unequivocal in this one result; namely, that it proves Holy Scripture to be of far deeper significancy than at first sight appears. By no imaginable artifice of Rhetoric or sophistry of evasion,—by no possible vehemence of denial or plausibility of counter assertion,—can it be rendered probable that Scripture has invariably one only meaning; and *that* meaning, the most obvious and easy."

Now, the reader is requested to observe that what precedes is *the direct contradictory* of the position which Mr. Jowett has written his Essay in order to establish. And thus we keep for ever coming back to his πρῶτον ψεῦδος,—the fundamental falsity which underlies the whole of what he has written.

(ii) But although we have eagerly resorted to Scripture itself in order to ascertain *on what principle* Scripture ought to be interpreted, we cannot for a moment allow some of the sophistries which which the Reverend Author has encumbered the question, to escape without castigation. He may not first court an appeal to the School of Apostolical Interpretation; and then, before the result of that appeal has been ascertained, go off in praise of the illumination of the present age; and claim to represent the Theological mind of Europe in his own person. "Educated persons," (he has the impertinence to assert,) "are *beginning to ask* (!), not what Scripture may be *made* to mean, but what it *does*. And it is no exaggeration to say that he who in the present state of knowledge will confine himself to *the plain meaning of words*, and the study of their context, may know more of the original spirit and intention of the authors of the New Testament *than all the controversial writers of former ages put together.*" (pp. 340-1.) This might be tolerated perhaps, in the self-constituted oracle of a Mechanics' Institute; but as proceeding from a Divinity Lecturer in one of the first Colleges in Oxford, I hesitate not to declare that such an opinion is simply disgraceful.

Very much of a piece with this, in point of flippancy,—(though barely consistent with his frequent assertions that the entire subject is hemmed in by grave difficulties,)—are the Regius Professor of Greek's remarks on the value of learning as a help to the Interpretation of Holy Writ. "*Learning obscures* as well as illustrates." (p. 337.)—"There seem to be reasons for doubting whether any *considerable light* can be thrown on the New Testament from inquiry into *the language.*" (p. 393.)—"Minute corrections of tenses or particles are *no good.*" (p. 393.)—"Discussions respecting the chronology of St. Paul's life and his second imprisonment; or about the identity of James, the brother of the LORD; or, in another department, *respecting the use of the Greek article,—have gone far beyond the line of utility.*" (p. 393.) "The minuteness of the study of Greek in our own day has also a tendency *to introduce into the text associations* which are not really found there." (p. 391.)—Lastly, he complains of "the error of interpreting every particle, as though it were a link in the argument; instead of being, as is often the case, *an excrescence of style.*" (p. 391.)

So then, in brief, the Fathers are in a conspiracy to mislead: Creeds and Councils encumber the sense: Modern Commentators are not to be trusted: the comparison of Scripture with Scripture, except it be "of the same age and the same authors," "will tend rather to confuse than to elucidate:" (p. 383:) "Learning obscures," and an accurate appreciation of the meaning of the text is " no good !"—" When *the meaning of Greek words* is once known[r], the young student has almost

---

[r] Had the following passage occurred sooner to my recollection, it should have been sooner inserted:—"Are we to conduct the Interpretation of Holy Scripture as we would that of any other writing? We are and we are not. *So far as* THE WORDS *are concerned, the mere words of Scripture* have the same office with those of all language written or spoken in sincerity." They must be studied "by the same means and the same rules which would guide us to the meaning of any other work; by a knowledge of the languages in which the books were written, the Hebrew, the Chaldee, the Greek, and of those other languages, as the Syriac and Arabic, which may illustrate them; and of all the ordinary rules of Grammar and Criticism, and the peculiar information respecting times and circumstances, history and customs,—all the resources, in a word, of the Interpretation of any work of any kind. *The Grammatical and Historical interpretation of profane or sacred writings is the same.* . . . " All Scripture," meanwhile, "is *given by Inspiration of* GOD:" and this at once introduces several important differences; which whoever neglects may yet, with whatsoever advantages of learning and talent, fail to discover the real meaning of the Word of GOD."—From Dr. Hawkins (Provost of Oriel) 's *Inaugural Lecture* as Dean Ireland's Professor, delivered in 1847,—pp. 29-30.

It is but fair to Mr. Jowett to add that, *in terms*, he has very nearly (not quite) said the self-same thing himself, at p. 337, (upper half the page.) But it is the peculiar method of this most slippery writer, or most illogical thinker, occasionally to grant almost all that heart can desire, as far as *words* go; but straightway to deny, or

all the real materials which are possessed by the greatest Biblical scholar, in the book itself." (p. 384.) In a word, (as Dr. Moberly has had the manliness to remark,)—" It simply comes to this: A little Greek, (not too much,) and a strong self-relying imagination, and you may interpret Holy Scripture as well as— Mr. Jowett!" (p. lxii.) . . . Benighted himself, the unhappy author of this Essay is so apprehensive lest a ray of light from Heaven shall break in upon one of his disciples,—even sideways, as it were, from the margin of the Bible,—that he carefully prohibits " the indiscriminate use of parallel passages" as " useless and uncritical." . . . Yet may one not *with discrimination* refer to the margin?—Better not! " No good!" (p. 393.) replies the Oracle. " Even the critical use of parallel passages is *not without danger.*" (p. 383.) . . . O shame! And all this from a College Tutor and Lecturer on Divinity! *this* from one entrusted with the care of educating young men! *this* from a Regius Professor of Greek^s!

---

evacuate, or explain away, *the thing* which those words ought to signify.—Thus, at p. 337, he volunteers the remark that " No one who has a Christian feeling would place Classical on a level with Sacred Literature;" and at p. 377, he observes that, " There are many respects in which Scripture is unlike any other book." And yet, (as I have shown, p. cxliii. to p. cl.,) Mr. Jowett *puts* the Bible on a level with Sophocles and Plato; and argues throughout as if Scripture were in *no* essential respect unlike any other book!

* " Had this writer reminded us that the New Testament Greek is a Greek of different age from that of the classical writers; had he simply warned us that we must not press our Attic Greek scholarship too far, but study the Alexandrian Greek of the Septuagint, Philo, &c. in order to ascertain the exact meaning of the words and phrases of the writers of the New Testament;—still more, if, as the result of such study on his own part, he had offered us some well-digested observations on the use of tenses, articles, or particles in

Mr. Jowett congratulates himself that "Biblical criticism has made two great steps onward,—at the time of the Reformation, and *in our own day.*" But his notion is amply refuted by the known facts of the case: for when he adds,— "The diffusion of a critical spirit in History and Literature is affecting the criticism of the Bible in our own day in a manner not unlike the burst of intellectual life in the fifteenth or sixteenth centuries;" (p. 340;) he clearly requires to be reminded that the success of the Divinity of the Reformation was owing to the grand appeal then made to *the Patristic writings.*

So far then as any of ourselves are resorting to *those* sources of information, there may be a faint resemblance *in kind* between the spirit which animates us, and that which wrought so nobly in the Fathers of our spiritual freedom,—Cranmer and Ridley and the other learned and holy men who revised our Offices. But if "*German* Commentators" and *their* method be supposed to be the ideals to which the age is tending, *then* the Theology of the middle of the nineteenth century stands in marked *contrast* to what prevailed in the middle of the sixteenth; and *our* spirit is *the very reverse of theirs.*—But I hasten on.

(iii) "The uncertainty which prevails in the Interpretation of Scripture," Mr. Jowett proposes to get rid of,—(this is in fact the aim of his entire Essay,)— the sacred writings;—he would have done some service. But this talk about 'excessive attention to the article,' and 'particles being often mere excrescences of style,' is of no effect except to expose the writer to ridicule. It sounds as if he had been accustomed to lay down the law to an admiring audience of 'clever young men,' and had forgotten that there were still 'men in Denmark' who understood Greek."—*Some Remarks on Essays and Reviews,* prefixed to Dr. Moberly's 'Sermons on the Beatitudes.' (1861.) pp. lxii.-iii.

by denying that there are in Scripture any deeper meanings to interpret. In the meantime, by every device in his power, he seeks from *à priori* considerations, (as we have seen,) to shew that no such meanings can exist. We allow ourselves to be biassed, to a singular extent, he says, "by certain previous suppositions with which we come to the perusal of Scripture." (p. 342.) *But* for this, "no one would interpret Scripture as many do." (*Ibid.*) Let us ascertain then what these erroneous "suppositions" are.

(*a*) "The failure of a prophecy is never admitted, in spite of Scripture and of history, (Jer. xxxvi. 30. Isaiah xxiii. Amos vii. 10—17.)" (p. 343.)

Now this can only mean two things: viz. first, that a Divine Prophecy is *not* an infallible utterance: and secondly, that the three places quoted from the Old Testament are *proofs* of the fallibility of Prophecy; proofs which ought to overcome prejudice, and persuade men to renounce their "previous supposition" that Prophecy is *in*fallible.

Certainly the charge is a grave one. For if *Prophecy* is untrue, then what becomes of Inspiration?

And yet, how stands the case? The writer seems to have expected "that no one would refer to the passages that he has bracketed, or that all would be too ignorant to know the utter groundlessness of his assumption. If there are, in the whole Scripture, two past prophecies which were signally and remarkably fulfilled, they are the first two which he has selected as instances to be dropped down, without a remark, of the failure of Scripture prophecies! And as to the third passage, surely it implies an 'incuria' which might be deemed 'crassa' to have asserted that it contained an instance of the non-fulfilment of Prophecy: for it implies that Mr. Jowett has read the verses to which he refers with so little attention as not to have discovered that the prediction which failed of its fulfilment was *no utterance of Amos*, but was *the message of Amaziah, the priest of Bethel*, in which he falsely attributes to Amos *words he had not spoken!* ... Surely such slips as these are as discreditable to a scholar as a Divine¹!"

And this, from a gentleman who has the impertinence to remind us oracularly, that "he who would understand the nature of Prophecy in the Old Testament, should have *the courage to examine how far its details were minutely fulfilled!*" (p. 347.) Are we then to infer that Mr. Jowett's courage failed him when he came to Amos vii. 10—17?

(β) "The mention of a name later than the supposed age of the prophet is not allowed, as in other writings, to be taken in evidence of the date. (Isaiah xlv. 1.)" (p. 343.)

But what is the meaning of this complaint when applied to Isaiah's well known prophecy concerning Cyrus? In the words of the excellent critic last quoted,—" We know not that we could point to such an instance as this in the writings of any other author of credit. Of course, Mr. Jowett knows as well as we do the distinction between History and Prophecy; and that the mention in any document of the name of one who was unborn at the time fixed as the date of the writing, would be at once a complete *disproof* of its accuracy as a history of the past, and a *proof* of its accuracy as a prediction of the future. Of course he also remembers that the point he has *to prove* is that this passage is History and not Predic-

¹ *Quarterly Review*, No. 217, p. 298.

tion; and his mode of proving is this; *he assumes that it is a history of the past,*—advancing as a charge against the believers of Revelation, that they do not, (as they would in any other History,) reject the genuineness of the passage because it embalms a future name in a past history! ... This audacious, (for we cannot use a weaker word,) *assumption* of what he has *to prove,* pervades his Essay[x]."

And thus, into whatever department of speculation we follow this writer, the tortuous path is still found to conduct us back to the same underlying fallacious *assumption,*—viz. that *the Bible is like any other Book;* in other words, is *not inspired.*

(γ) Persons in Mr. Jowett's position, "find themselves met by *a sort of presupposition that* ' God *speaks not as Man speaks.*' "—(p. 343.)

"A sort of presupposition," indeed! .... Does the Reverend gentleman really expect that we will stoop so low as argue *this* point also with him? It shall suffice to have branded him with his own words.

"The suspicion of Deism, or perhaps of Atheism, awaits inquiry. By such fears, a good man (!) refuses to be influenced: a philosophical mind (!) is apt to cast them aside with too much bitterness. It is better to close the book, than to read it under conditions of thought which are imposed from without." (p. 343.)

Well surely, the proximity to Balliol College of the scene of Cranmer and Ridley's martyrdom, must have turned the brain of the Regius Professor of Greek!—Let him be well assured however that not rational "Inquiry," but irrational *assumption;* not the modest cogitations of "a philosophical mind," but the *arrogant dreams of a weak and confused intellect,* are what have

[x] *Quarterly Review,* No. 217, pp. 265-6.

excited such general indignation of late, among "good men," from one end of the Kingdom to the other. Nor could anything probably of equal pretensions be readily appealed to, which is nevertheless more truly unphilosophical, fallacious, and foolish, than the Essay now under consideration.

(iv) Subsequently, (p. 344,) Mr. Jowett professes to grapple with the phenomenon of Inspiration. His method is instructive. He begins by inadvertently advancing a direct untruth: for he asserts that for none "of the higher or supernatural views of Inspiration is there *any foundation* in the Gospels or Epistles." (p. 345.)—Had he then forgotten St. Paul's statements in Gal. i. 1, 11—17 : ii. 2, 7—9. 1 Cor. xv. 3. Ephes. iii. 3, &c., &c. ? But I have established the contradictory of the Professor's position in the ensuing Sermons, p. 53 to p. 57, to which the reader must be referred.—This done, he proceeds to assert that,

(*a*) Inspiration does not preserve a writer from inaccuracy. And the charge is substantiated by the following ridiculous enumeration : — " One [Evangelist] supposes the original dwelling-place of our LORD's Parents to have been Bethlehem[y], another Nazareth[z]." (This from a Lecturer on Divinity ! Does Mr. Jowett then suppose that his readers have never opened the Gospels, and do not know better ? Why, *both* his statements are simply *false !*)—" They trace His genealogy in different ways." (Yes. In two. And why not *in twenty ?* Is Mr. Jowett not aware that a genealogy may be differently traced through different ancestors ?)—" One mentions the thieves blaspheming : another has preserved to after

[y] St. Matth. ii. 1, 22.   [z] St. Luke ii. 41.

ages the record of the penitent thief:" (And why should he not?)—"They appear to differ about the day and hour of the Crucifixion." (Yes, *they appear to differ: but they do not differ!*)—"The narrative of the woman who anointed our LORD's feet with ointment is told in all four, each narrative having more or less considerable variations." (There is no conceivable reason why this should *not* have been as Mr. Jowett relates; but, as a matter of fact, we have here another of this Gentleman's private *blunders*,—shewing what an uncritical reader he must be, of that book concerning which he presumes to dogmatize so freely.)—"These are a few instances of the differences which arose in the traditions of the earliest ages respecting the history of our LORD." (Nay, but this is to beg the whole question!) — " He who wishes to investigate the character of the sacred writings *should not be afraid* to make a catalogue of them all, with the view of estimating their cumulative weight." (p. 346.) (Truly, it would be well for Mr. Jowett if he had as little to fear from such "investigations" as the Evangelists!)

"In the same way, he who would understand the nature of Prophecy in the Old Testament, should have the courage to examine how far its details were minutely fulfilled. *The absence of such a fulfilment* may further lead him to discover that he took the letter for the spirit in expecting it." (p. 347.) But really this is again simply to beg the whole question. Unbecoming in any writer, how absurd also is such a sentence from the pen of one who, (as we have lately seen,) no sooner descends to particulars than he makes himself ridiculous by betraying his own excessive ignorance.... "The letter for the spirit," also! which is one of the 'cant' expressions of Mr. Jowett and his accomplices in 'free handling,'—based evidently on a misconception of the meaning of 2 Cor. iii. 6. The contrast recurs at pp. 36, 357, 375, 425, &c., &c.

(β) Still bent on shewing that Inspiration does not secure Scripture from blots and blemishes, Mr. Jowett proceeds as follows. (I must present him to the reader, for a short space, *in extenso;* since by no other expedient can the complicated fallacies of his very intricate and perverse method be exposed.)

"Inspiration is a fact which we infer from the study of Scripture,—not of one portion only, but of the whole." (p. 347.) (Now even *this* is not a correct way of stating the case. Still, because the words *may* bear an honourable sense, we pass on.)—"Obviously then, it embraces writings of very different kinds,— the book of Esther, for example, or the Song of Solomon, as well as the Gospel of St. John." (That *the volume* of Inspiration is of this complex character, and that *it* embraces writings so diverse, is beyond dispute.)—"It is reconcileable with the mixed good and evil of the characters of the Old Testament, which nevertheless does not exclude them from the favour of God." (*Why* the Inspiration of a writer should not be 'reconcileable' with *any* amount of wickedness in the persons about whom he writes,—I am quite at a loss to perceive. Neither do I see why "the mixed good and evil" of certain "characters of the Old Testament," (or of the New either,) should "exclude them from the favour of God." What else becomes of your hope, and mine, of Eternal Life?)—"Inspiration is also reconcileable," (he proceeds,)—"with the attribution to the Divine Being of *actions at variance with that higher revelation which He has given of Himself in the Gospel.*"   (Is this meant as an insult to "the Divine Being?" or simply as a slur on Revelation? Either way, we reject the charge with indignation [a].) —"It is not inconsistent with imperfect or opposite aspects of the Truth, as in the Book of Job or Ecclesiastes:" (Nothing which comes from GOD should be called "imperfect:" but why *different* aspects of the Truth should not be brought out, by different writers, as by St. Paul and by James,—it is hard to see.)—"With variations of fact in the Gospels, or the Books of Kings and Chronicles:" (We do not admit that Inspiration is consistent with "variations of *fact;*" but with *different versions* of the same incident, it is confessedly compatible.)—"With inaccuracies of language in the Epistles of St. Paul." (With *grammatical inelegancies*, no doubt; but not with *logical inaccuracies*.)—"For these are all found in Scripture:" (This statement, by the way, should have been substantiated by at least as many references as there are heads in the indictment,)—"neither is there any reason why they should not be; except a general impression that Scripture ought to have been written in a way different from what it has." (Just as if Mankind for 1800 years had been the victims of an *à priori* conception as to *how* Holy Scripture *ought to have been* written!) —"A principle of progressive revelation admits them all; and this is already contained in the words of our SAVIOUR, 'Moses because of the hardness of your hearts;' or even in the Old Testament, 'Henceforth there shall be no more this proverb in the house of Israel?'" (O if Catholic writers were to expound Holy Scripture with the license of *these* gentlemen! .... That the scheme of Revelation has been progressive, is

[a] See Sermon VII., pp. 222—232.

a Theological truism. What that has to do with the question in hand, I see not.)—"For what is progressive is necessarily imperfect in its earlier stages:" ("Imperfect" in what sense?)—"and *even erring* to those who come after." (No, not in *that* sense imperfect, certainly!).... "There is no more reason why *imperfect narratives* should be excluded from Scripture than imperfect grammar; no more ground for expecting that the New Testament would be logical or Aristotelian in form, than that it would be written in Attic Greek." (Now *why* this cloudy shuffling about "imperfect narratives,"—instead of saying *what you mean*, like a man! Further,—Is Mr. Jowett so weak as not to perceive that there is *no force whatever* in his supposed parallel? The Discourses of the Incarnate Son, for instance, are certainly anything but "Aristotelian in form." His dialect,—(Angels bowed to catch it, I nothing doubt!)—was that of the despised Galilee. But need *the teaching it conveyed* have *therefore* been "imperfect?" Why may not the least perfect *Greek* be the vehicle for the more perfect *Doctrine?* What connexion is there between the casket and the jewel which it encloses?)

(γ) The Reverend writer promises us help, from "another consideration which has been neglected by writers on this subject." (The announcement makes us attentive.)—"It is this,—that any true Doctrine of Inspiration must conform to all well-ascertained facts of History or of Science." (We scarcely see the drift of this ill-worded proposition; but are disposed to assent.)—"The same fact cannot be true and untrue," (Who ever supposed that it could?) — "any more than the same words can have two opposite meanings." (But why glide at once into a gross falsity? Are there not plenty of words and speeches, of the kind called 'equivocal' or 'ambiguous,' which are of this nature? I am content to refer this writer to *his own pages,* for the abundant refutation of his own assertion. No man in the world knows better than Mr. Jowett that "*the same words can have two opposite meanings.*") "The same fact cannot be true in Religion, when seen by the light of Faith; and untrue in Science, when looked at through the medium of evidence or experiment." (Why not? For example,—'He maketh His Sun to rise.' 'If God so clothe the grass of the field.' 'God said, Let there be light.' Who sees not that the view which Faith and which Physical Science respectively take of the same phenomenon, may essentially differ?)—"It is ridiculous to suppose that the Sun goes round the Earth in the same sense in which the Earth goes round the Sun;" (Very ridiculous.) — "or that the world appears to have existed, but has not existed, during the vast epochs of which Geology speaks to us." (Leave out the words, "appears to have," and this also is undeniable.)—"But if so, there is no need of elaborate reconcilements of Revelation and Science." (How does that follow? If what is thought to be Divinely revealed, and what is thought to be scientifically ascertained, seem to be conflicting truths,—why should not an effort be made to reconcile them?) "They reconcile themselves the moment any scientific truth is distinctly ascertained." (Yes: by the Human simply trying to thrust the Divine out of doors!)— "As the idea of Nature enlarges, the idea of Revelation also enlarges:" (I deny that there is any such intimate connexion as this author supposes between Physical Science and Divinity,)—"it was a temporary misunderstanding which severed them." (But *when* were Nature and Revelation ever for an instant "severed?")—"And as the knowledge of Nature which is possessed by the few is communicated in its leading features at least, to the many, they will receive it with a higher conception of the ways of GOD to Man. It may hereafter appear as natural to the majority of Mankind to see the Providence of GOD in the order of the world, as it once was to appeal to interruptions of it." (p. 349.) (As if an increased *knowledge of Nature* were the condition of Theological enlightenment! .... I presume that the latter clause,— so hazy and the reverse of obvious in its meaning!— is intended to convey the sentiment which Mr. Baden Powell expresses as follows:—"The inevitable progress of research must, within a longer or shorter period, unravel *all that seems most marvellous;* and what is at present least understood will become as familiarly known to the Science of the future, as those points which a few centuries ago were involved in equal obscurity, but now are thoroughly understood[b].")

(δ) We are next informed "that there are a class of scientific facts with which popular opinions on Theology often conflict. .... Such especially are the facts relating to the formation of the Earth and the beginnings of the Human Race." (p. 349.) (And pray, what "*facts*" are these, relative to the "beginnings of the Human Race," which conflict with Scripture?) .... "Almost all intelligent persons are agreed that the earth has existed for myriads of ages:" (Which is perfectly true.)—"The best informed are of opinion that the history of nations extends back *some thousand*

[b] *Essays and Reviews*, p. 109.

years before the Mosaic Chronology." (Which is decidedly false.)—" Recent discoveries in Geology *may perhaps* open a further vista of existence for the human species; while *it is possible, and may one day be known*, that Mankind spread not from one but from many centres over the globe; or, (as others say,) that the supply of links which are at present wanting in the chain of animal life *may lead* to new conclusions respecting the origin of Man." (A cool way, this, of anticipating that something which '*may*,'—(or *may not!*)—be discovered hereafter, will demonstrate that the beginning of the Bible is all a fable!)—"Now," (proceeds our author,) "let it be granted that" "*the proof* of some of these facts, especially of those last-mentioned, *is wanting;* still it is a false policy to set up Inspiration or Revelation *in opposition to them*, a principle which can have *no influence on them*, and should be kept rather out of their way." (Considerate man!) "The Sciences of Geology and comparative Philology are steadily gaining ground. Many of the guesses of twenty years ago have been certainties; and the guesses of to-day may hereafter become so. Shall we peril Religion (!) on the possibility of their untruth? on such a cast to stake the life of Man, implies not only a recklessness of facts (!), but a misunderstanding of the nature of the Gospel. If it is fortunate for Science, it is perhaps more fortunate for Christian Truth, that the admission of Galileo's discovery has for ever settled the principle of the relations between them."—(pp. 349-50.) . . . .

Now, what a curious picture of a perverse and crooked mind does such a sentence exhibit! Divine Revelation can "*have no influence*," of course, on facts of *any* kind, (including facts in Physical Science,) when once those facts have been well ascertained. But, *in the entire absence of such facts*, why should we refuse to listen to the *well ascertained Revelation of* G<small>OD</small>? Nothing is more emphatic, for example, than the Divine declaration that the whole Human family is derived from a single pair; and the origin of Man is plainly set down in Genesis. Why then oppose to this, the confessedly *undiscovered* fact that " mankind spread from many centres;" and the purely speculative possibility that, hereafter, a certain theory "*may lead* to new conclusions respecting the origin of Man?" —As for "Religion" being "perilled on the possibility" of the truth or untruth of the Sciences of Geology and comparative Philology;—we really would submit that G<small>OD</small> *may be safely left to take care of His own;* and that "peril," there is,—there *can* be,— *none!*

And then, the maudlin tenderness of an "Essayist and Reviewer" (of all persons in the world!) for "*the life of Man,*"—meaning thereby his Christian hope, and Faith in the R<small>EDEEMER</small>! . . . As if, (first,) Man's "*Life*" were *in any sense* endangered, by our upholding the honour and authority of the Bible! And (secondly,) as if the age had shewn itself in the least degree impatient of scientific investigation! And (thirdly,) as if Religion depended, or could be made to depend, on Physical phenomena, or on the progress of Natural Science, *at all!* . . . . I scruple not to say that arguments like these impress me with the meanest opinion of Mr. Jowett's intellectual powers: while they prove to demonstration that he does not in the least understand the subject on which he yet writes with such feeble vehemence.

But I may not proceed any further, or my pages

will equal in extent those of the gentleman already named. Indeed, to follow that most confused of thinkers, and crooked of disputants, through all his perverse pages; to expose his habitual paltry evasive dodging,—his shifting equivocations,—his misapplications of Scripture,—his unworthy insinuations,—his plaintive puerilities of thought and sentiment;—would require a thick volume.—If Mr. Jowett does not deny the Personality of the HOLY GHOST, he ought to be thoroughly ashamed of himself for penning sentences which can lead to no other inference. For he ought to know that when men talk of words "*receiving a more exact meaning than they will truly bear;*" and of what "is *spoken in a figure* being construed with the severity of a logical statement, while *passages of an opposite tenour are overlooked or set aside:*"—(p. 360.) men mean to repudiate the doctrine which those words are thought to convey; not to imply their acceptance of it.—So again, if Mr. Jowett holds the doctrine of Original Sin, he ought to be heartily ashamed of himself for having insinuated that it depends "on *two figurative expressions of St. Paul to which there is no parallel in any other part of Scripture.*" (p. 361.)—Nor, however moderate his attainments as a teacher of Divinity, ought he to be capable of putting forth such a notorious misstatement as that the doctrine of Infant Baptism *rests upon a verse in the Acts* (xvi. 33,)—which verse has really *nothing whatever to do with the question*[e]. (p. 360.)

Professor Jowett shuts up his Essay with a passage which, for a certain amount of tender pathos in the sentiment, has been often quoted, and sometimes admired. He says:—

[e] See Dr. Moberly, (as before,) p. lv.—lx.

"The suspicion or difficulty which attends critical inquiries is no reason for doubting their value. The Scripture nowhere leads us to suppose that the circumstance of all men speaking well of us is any ground for supposing that we are acceptable in the sight of God. And there is no reason why the condemnation of others should be witnessed to by our own conscience. Perhaps it may be true that, owing to the jealousy or fear of some, the reticence of others, the terrorism of a few, we may not always find it easy to regard these subjects with calmness and judgment. But, on the other hand, these accidental circumstances have nothing to do with the question at issue; they cannot have the slightest influence on the meaning of words, or on the truth of facts. . . .

"Lastly, there is some nobler idea of truth than is supplied by the opinion of mankind in general, or the voice of parties in a Church. Every one, whether a student of Theology or not, has need to make war against his prejudices no less than against his passions; and, in the religious teacher, the first is even more necessary than the last. . . . . He who takes the prevailing opinions of Christians and decks them out in their gayest colours,—who reflects the better mind of the world to itself—is likely to be its favourite teacher. In that ministry of the Gospel, even when assuming forms repulsive to persons of education (!), no doubt the good is far greater than the error or harm. But there is also a deeper work which is not dependent on the opinions of men, in which many elements combine, some alien to Religion, or accidentally at variance with it. That work can hardly expect to win much popular favour, so far as it runs counter to the feelings of religious parties. But he who bears a part in it may feel a confidence, which no popular caresses or religious sympathy could inspire, that he has by a Divine help been enabled to plant his foot somewhere beyond the waves of Time. He may depart hence before the natural term, worn out with intellectual toil; regarded with suspicion by many of his contemporaries; yet not without a sure hope that the love of Truth, which men of saintly lives often seem to slight, is, nevertheless, accepted before GOD."— (pp. 432-3.)

My respect for a fellow-man induces me to offer a few remarks on all this.

Let me be permitted then to declare that I am as incapable as any one who ever breathed the air of this lower world, of making light of the sentiments of true genius. I can respond with my whole heart to the passion-stricken cry of one who, when "regarded with suspicion by many of his contemporaries," is observed to hail his fellows with confidence, across the gulph of Time; and as it were implore them, after many days, to do him right. Nay, were I to behold a man of splendid, but misguided powers, elaborating from GOD's Word a plausible system of his own, whereby to bring back the Golden Age to suffering Humanity; and insisting that he beheld in the common revelations of the SPIRIT, the unsuspected outlines of such a form of polity as Man never dreamed of,—(nor, it may be, Angels either;)—I should experience a kind of generous sympathy with this bright-eyed enthusiast; even while I proceeded to test his wild dream by what I believed to be the standard of right Reason. Then, as the specious fabric was seen suddenly to collapse and melt away, should I not, with affectionate sorrow, secretly mourn that such brilliant parts had not been enlisted on the side of Truth? and feel as if I could have been content to go about for life maimed in body, or hopelessly impoverished in estate, if so great a disaster could but have been prevented as the loss of one who ought to have been a standard-bearer in Israel?

Once more. Although the cold shade of unbelief has never for an instant, (thank God!) darkened my spirit; so that one may not be very apt to sympathize with men who walk about hampered with a doubt; yet, were one to know, (as one has often known,—*too often, alas!*) that the arrow was rankling in a friend's heart,—who by consequence shunned the society of his fellows, and walked in moody abstraction,—looking as if life had lost its charm, and as if nothing on the earth's surface were any longer to him a joy;— would one not be the first to go after such a sufferer; and seek whether a firm hand and steady eye might not avail to extract the poisoned shaft? If that might not be, at least by daily acts of unaltered kindness, and the ways which brotherly sympathy suggests, *who* would not strive to recover such an one? If all other arts proved unavailing, it would remain for a man with the ordinary instincts of humanity, in silence and sorrow at least, to look on, while the solitary doubter was paying the bitter penalty,— doubtless, of his sin.

But how widely different,—rather, how utterly dissimilar,—is the phenomenon before us! Here is a singularly confused and shallow thinker oppressed with the vastness of his discovery, that the Bible— *has nothing in it!* Here is a Clergyman of the Church of England, and a Lecturer in Divinity, whose difficulty is how he shall convince the world that the Bible is—*like any other book!* Here is the sceptical fellow of a College, conspiring with six others, to produce a volume of which Germany itself, (having changed its mind,) would already be ashamed! ... Mr. Jowett is enthusiastic for *a negation!* Without belief himself, he cannot rest because Christendom has, on the whole, a good deal of belief remaining! If he may but *unsettle somebody's mind,*—his Essay will have achieved its purpose, and its author will not have lived in vain! ... Sublime privilege for "the only man in the University of Oxford who" is said to "exercise a moral and spiritual influence at all corresponding to that which was once wielded by John Henry Newman[d]!"

I shall be thought a very profane person, I dare say, by the friends and apologists of Mr. Jowett, if I avow that the passage with which he concludes his Essay, instead of sounding in my ears like the plaintive death-song of departing Genius, sounds to me like nothing so much as the piteous whine of a schoolboy who knows that he *deserves* chastisement, and perceives that he is about to experience his deserts. System, or Theory, the Reverend Gentleman has none to propose. Views, except negative ones, Mr. Jowett is altogether guiltless of. Can anybody in his senses suppose that a man "has, by a Divine help (!), been enabled to plant his foot *somewhere beyond the waves of Time,*" (p. 433,) who doubts everything, and believes nothing? Can any one of sane mind dream that posterity will come to the rescue of a man who, when he is asked for his story, rejoins, (with a well-known needy mechanic,) that he has "none to tell, Sir?" *What* then is posterity to vindicate? *What* has the Regius Professor of Greek written so many

[d] *Edinburgh Review*, (April, 1861,) p. 476.

weak pages to prove? Just nothing! If Mr. Jowett's Essay could enforce the message it carries, the result would simply be that the world would become *dis*believers in the Inspiration of the Bible: they would *dis*believe that Scripture has any sense but that which lies on the surface: they would therefore *dis*believe the Prophets and Evangelists and Apostles of CHRIST: they would *dis*believe the words of our LORD JESUS CHRIST Himself!... Has Mr. Jowett, then, grown grey under the laborious process of arriving at this series of negations? When he anticipates "departing hence before the natural term," does he mean that he is "*worn out with the intellectual toil*" of propounding *nothing!* and that he expects the sympathy and gratitude of posterity for what he has propounded?

But this is not all. Instead of coming abroad, (if come abroad he must,) in that garb of humility which befits doubt,—that self-distrust which becomes one whose fault, or whose misfortune it is, that he simply cannot believe,—Mr. Jowett assumes throughout, the insolent air of intellectual superiority; the tone of one at whose bidding Theology must absolutely 'keep moving.' A truncheon and a number on his collar, alone seem wanting. The menacing voice, and authoritative air, are certainly not away,—as I proceed to show.

"It may be observed that a change in some of the prevailing modes of Interpretation, is not so much a matter of expediency as *of necessity*. The original meaning of Scripture *is beginning to be understood*." (p. 418.)

"Criticism has *far more power* than it formerly had. It has spread itself over ancient, and even modern history.... *Whether Scripture can be made an exception to other ancient writings,* now that the nature of both is more understood; whether . . . *the views of the last century will hold out,*—these are questions respecting which" (p. 420.) it is hard to judge.

"It has to be considered whether the intellectual forms under which Christianity has been described, may not also be *in a state of transition.*" (p. 420.)

"Now, as *the Interpretation of Scripture is receiving another character*, it seems that distinctions of Theology which were in great measure based on old Interpretations, are *beginning to fade away.*" . . . "There are other signs that times are changing, and we are changing too." (p. 421.)

"These reflections bring us back to the question with which we began,—*What effect will the critical Interpretation of Scripture have on Theology?*" (p. 422.)

Again:—"As the time has come when it is no longer possible to ignore the results of criticism, it is of importance that Christianity should be seen to be in harmony with them." (p. 374.) (The sentences which immediately follow shall be exhibited in distinct paragraphs, in order that they may separately enjoy admiration. Each is a gem or a curiosity in its way.)

"That objections to some received views *should be valid*, and yet that they should be always held up as *the objections of Infidels,*—is a mischief to the Christian cause."

"It is a mischief that critical observations which any intelligent man can make for himself (!), should be ascribed to Atheism or Unbelief."

"It would be a strange and almost incredible thing that the Gospel, which at first made war only on the vices of mankind, should now be *opposed* to one of the highest and rarest of human virtues,—*the love of Truth.*"

"And that in the present day the great object of Christianity should be, not to change the lives of men, but to prevent them from changing their opinions; *that* would be a singular inversion of the purposes for which CHRIST came into the world."

We are really constrained to pause for a moment, and to inquire what this last sentence means. Are not "the lives of men" mainly *dependent* on "their opinions?" Why then contrast the two? And *which* of our "opinions" does Mr. Jowett desire to see changed? Would he have us resign our belief in the Atonement? reject the Divinity of CHRIST? deny the Personality of the HOLY GHOST? put the Bible on a level with Sophocles and Plato? ridicule the idea of Inspiration?... How would it be a "singular inversion of the purposes of CHRIST's Coming," that Christianity should "prevent" mankind from "changing" such "opinions" as *these?*

"The Christian religion is in a false position when *all the tendencies of knowledge are opposed to it.*" (*All the tendencies of knowledge, then, are opposed to the Christian Religion!*)

"Such a position cannot be long maintained, or can only end in the withdrawal of the educated classes from the influences of Religion." (So we are to look for "*the withdrawal of the educated classes from the influences of Religion*[c]!")

---

[c] The Rev. H. B. Wilson says,—"If those who distinguish themselves in Science and Literature cannot, in a scientific and literary age, be effectually and cordially attached to the Church of their nation, they must sooner or later be driven into a position of hostility to it." (p. 198.) This is one of the many notes, if not of "concert and comparison," at least of *intense sympathy* between the Essayists and Reviewers.

After anticipating "religious dissolution," because of "the progress of ideas, (!) with which Christian teachers seem to be ill at ease," (!) Mr. Jowett, (who we presume is speaking of himself,) says, "Time was when the Gospel was before the Age:" (The Gospel is therefore now *behind* the age!)—"when the difficulties of Christianity were difficulties of, the heart only:" (When was that?)—"and *the highest minds* found in its truths not only the rule of their lives, but a wellspring of intellectual delight." (All this then has *ceased to be the case!* "The highest minds" being of course represented by—Mr. Jowett!)

"Is it to be held a thing impossible that the Christian Religion, instead of shrinking into itself, (!) may again *embrace the thoughts of men upon the earth?*" (that is to say, "embrace the thoughts" of—Mr. Jowett!)—"Or is it true that *since the Reformation 'all intellect has gone the other way?'*"

"But for the faith that the Gospel might win again the minds of *intellectual men,*" (such men as Mr. Jowett?)—"it would be better to leave Religion to itself, instead of attempting to draw them together." (p. 376.)

Now this kind of language, in daily life, would be called sheer impertinence; and the person who could talk so before educated gentlemen would probably receive an intimation that he was making himself offensive. He would certainly be looked upon as a weak and conceited person. I really am unable to see why things should be *written and printed* which no one would presume *to say!* . . . Encircled by a little atmosphere of fog of his own creating, Mr. Jowett is evidently under the delusion that his own confused vision and misty language are the result of the giddy eminence to which, (leaving his fellow-mortals far behind him,) he has contrived, all alone, to soar. He anticipates the complaint of some unhappy disciple, that he " experiences a sort of shrinking or dizziness at the prospect which is opening before him :" whereupon Mr. Jowett invites the "highly educated young man," (p. 373,) to consider " that he may possibly not be the person who is called upon to pursue such inquiries." Who are they *for*, then? " No man should busy himself with them who has not clearness of mind enough to see things as they are." (p. 430.) The clearness of mind, for example, which belongs to Mr. Jowett!

True enough it is that had such airs been assumed by such an one as Richard Hooker, who achieved the first four books of his ' Laws of Ecclesiastical Polity' before he was 40 ; and dying in his 46th year, proved himself to be the greatest genius of his age :—had language like Mr. Jowett's been found on the lips of Joseph Butler, who when he was 44 produced his immortal 'Analagy,' and at the age of 26 delivered his famous Rolls 'Sermons :'—had Bishop Bull been betrayed into the language of self-complacency when, at the age of 35, he made himself famous by his ' Harmonia Apostolica :'—the proceeding would have been intelligible, however much one might have lamented such an exhibition of weakness. . . . But when the speaker proves to be one of the very shallowest of thinkers, and most confused of reasoners ; — a man who, although grey-headed, has done nothing whatever for Literature, sacred or profane ;—nor indeed is known out of Oxford except for having been thought to deny the Doctrine of the Atonement ;—a man who dogmatizes in a Science of which he clearly does not know so much as the very alphabet; and presumes to dispute about a Bible which he has evidently not read with the attention which is due even to a first-rate uninspired book;—*then*, one's displeasure and impatience assume the form of indignation and disgust. The Divine who, purposing to prove that Holy Scripture is in kind like any other book, does so *by inveighing against those who treat it differently;* and indeed, on every occasion, *assumes as proved* the thing he has *to prove*[f]*:*—is obviously the very man to vaunt the privileges of the intellect. The student of the Bible who mistakes the utterance of a lying prophet for the language of Amos, and then boldly charges the lie upon the inspired author of a book of Canonical Scripture;—is of course a proper person to discuss the Prophetic Canon. The gentleman who flatters himself that he has been *sweeping the house* to find *the pearl of great price*, (p. 414,) is a very pretty person, truly, to lecture about the Gospel! . . . I forbear reproaching Mr. Jowett with his *invariable* misapplications or misapprehensions of the meaning of Scripture: his false glosses, and truly preposterous specimens of exegesis[g]. I am content to take leave of him, while he is flattering himself that he has "*found the pearl of great price, after sweeping the house:*" (p. 414 :) and under that melancholy delusion, I fear he must be left,—holding the broom in his hands.

On a review of these Seven Essays, few things strike one more forcibly than the utterly untenable ground occupied by their authors. They are " in a position

[f] *Quarterly Review*, No. 217, p. 266.
[g] See at pp. 351, 352, 357, 358, 361, 365, 367, 413, &c.

in which it is impossible to remain. The theory of Mr. Jowett and his fellows is as false to philosophy as to the Church of England. More may be true, or less; but to attempt to halt where they would stop is a simple absurdity [h]."

To exactness of method or System, their work can hardly pretend; and yet they *have* a system,—which has only not been rounded into symmetry, by the singular circumstance that these seven writers "have written in entire independence of one another, and without concert or comparison." They *avow a common purpose,* however; for they "hope" that their joint labours "will be received as an attempt to illustrate," (whatever *that* may mean,) "the advantage derivable to the cause of Religion and Moral Truth" from what they have here attempted; and which they justly characterize as *"free handling."* Putting oneself in their position, it is easy to imagine the sorrow and concern,—the *horror* rather,—with which a good man, when the first edition of 'Essays and Reviews' made its appearance, would have discovered the kind of complicity into which he had been inadvertently betrayed; and how eagerly he would have withdrawn from a literary partnership which had resulted so disastrously. At the end of nine large editions, however, the corporate responsibility of each individual author has become fully established; and besides the many proofs of sympathy between the several authors which these pages contain [i], it is no longer doubtful

---

[h] *Quarterly Review*, as before, p. 282.

[i] Take a few instances:—Mr. Wilson and Mr. Jowett speak of the Gospels as more or less accurately embodying a common *tradition*, pp. 161 and 346.—Dr. Temple and Mr. Jowett propose the heart and conscience, as *the overruling principle*, pp. 42-5, and 410:—

that the sentiments of the work are to be quoted without reference to the individual writers. It would be unfair to assume that not one of these seven men has had the manliness to avow that his own individual convictions are opposed to those of his fellows. We are compelled to regard their joint labours as *one* production. It is the *corporate efficacy* of the several contributions which constitutes the chief criminality of the volume. It is to the respectability and weight of the *conjoined* names of its authors, and to their *combined* efforts, that 'Essays and Reviews' are indebted for all their power.

What then is the system, or theory, or view, advocated by these seven Authors?—They are all agreed that we are "placed evidently at an epoch when

and insist that the Bible is "a Spirit, not a Letter," pp. 36 and 357, 375, 425.—Dr. Temple and Dr. Williams regard the Bible as *the voice of conscience*, pp. 45 and 78:—look for *a verifying faculty* in the individual, pp. 45 and 83:—dwell on the "interpolations" in Scripture, pp. 47 and 78.—Mr. Wilson and Mr. Jowett insist on the meaning which Scripture had *to those who first heard it*, as its true meaning, pp. 219, 223, 230, 232, and 338, 378:—on the necessity of *reconciling Intellectual men to Scripture*, pp. 198 and 374. —Professor Powell and Mr. Jowett are of one mind as to Miracles, pp. 109 and 349.—Dr. Temple and Mr. Jowett delight in the same image of the Colossal Man, pp. 1—49 and 331, 387, 422.—Dr. Williams and Mr. Jowett coincide in their estimate of the German Commentators, pp. 67 and 340.—Dr. Temple and Dr. Williams are of one mind as to the past training of our Race, pp. 1—49, and 51. They are generally agreed as to the untrustworthiness of Genesis, and of the Scripture generally, the hopeless contradictions between the Evangelists, &c., &c. They hold the same language about our having outlived the Faith, ('Traditional Christianity,' as it is called;) the impossibility of freedom of thought; the necessity of providing some new Religious system; the effete nature of Creeds and formularies of Belief; the advance in Natural Science as likely to prove fatal to Theology, &c., &c.

Humanity finds itself under new conditions, to form some definite conception to ourselves of the way in which Christianity is henceforward to act upon the world which is our own." (p. 158.) To do this, we must emerge from our "narrow chamber of Doctrinal and Ecclesiastical prepossessions." (*Ibid.*) Accordingly, we find insinuated " a very wide-spread alienation, both in educated and uneducated persons, from the Christianity which is ordinarily presented in our Churches and Chapels." (p. 150.) There has been "a spontaneous recoil." (p. 151.) We cannot "resist the tide of civilization on which we are borne." (p. 412.) "The time has come when it is no longer possible to ignore the results of criticism." It is therefore " of importance that Christianity should be seen to be in harmony with them." (p. 374.) " The arguments of our genuine critics, with the convictions of our most learned clergy" (p. 66) are all opposed to the actual teaching of the Church. Meantime, " the Christian Religion is in a false position when all the tendencies of knowledge are opposed to it." (p. 374.) "Time was when the Gospel was before the age: . . . when the highest minds found in its truths not only the rule of their lives, but a well-spring of intellectual delight. Is it to be held a thing impossible that the Christian Religion may again embrace the thoughts of men upon the earth?" (pp. 374-5.)

In the mean time, THE BIBLE is a stubborn fact in the way of the new Religion. Nay, the English *Book of Common Prayer* is a great hindrance; for those "formulæ of past thinkings, have long lost all sense of any kind;" (p. 297;) so that the Prayer-book " is on the way to become a useless encumbrance, the rubbish of the past, blocking the road." (*Ibid.*) But the

Prayer-book confessedly stands on a different footing from the Bible. The Bible erects itself hopelessly in the way of "the negative religion." (p. 151.) O those many prophecies, which for 4000 long years sustained the faith of God's chosen people, and at last found fulfilment in the person of Christ, or in the circumstances which attended the establishment of His Kingdom! O that glorious retinue of types and shadows which heralded Messiah's approach! ... And then,—O the miraculous evidence which attested to the reality of His Divinity[k]! O the confirmation, (to those who needed it,) when He walked the water, and stilled the storm, and cast out devils by His word, and by one strong cry broke the gates of Death, and caused Lazarus to "Come forth!" ... O the solemn *independent* testimony borne by Creeds, from the very birthday of Christianity,—(whether planted in Syria or in Asia Minor, in Africa or in Italy, in Greece or in Gaul; "in Germany or in Spain, among the Celts or in the far East, in Egypt or in Libya, or in the middle regions of the globe[l].") Lastly,—O the adoring voice of the whole Church Catholic throughout the world, for many a succeeding century,—translating, expounding, defining, explaining, defending to the death! ... How shall all this formidable mass of evidence possibly be set aside?

It is plain that Prophecy must be evacuated of its meaning; or rather, must be denied entirely: and to do this, falls to the share of the vulgar and violent Vice-Principal of Lampeter College. Disprove he cannot; so he sneers and rails and blusters instead. Prophecy, he calls "omniscience;" "a notion of fore-

---

[k] See St. John iii. 2 : v. 36 : x. 25, 37-8 : xiv. 11 : xv. 24 : St. Luke vii. 20-22, &c., &c.

[l] Creed of Lyons, A.D. 180; see above, p. clxxx., note.

sight by vision of particulars;" (p. 70;) "a kind of clairvoyance," (p. 70,) and "literal prognostication." (p. 65.) Mr. Jowett (as we have lately seen [m],) lends plaintive help: but indeed Dr. Williams does not lack supporters.

To deny the truth of Miracles falls to the lot of the Savilian Professor of Astronomy. His method has the merit of extreme simplicity: for it is based on the ground that, in the writer's opinion, Miracles are impossible,—which of course must be held to be decisive of the question.

The battle against the Inspiration of the Word of GOD is reserved for the Regius Professor of Greek; who requires for his purpose twice the space of any of his fellows. *His* method is also of the simplest kind, when divested of its many encumbrances. He simply *assumes it as proved* that the Bible is a book not essentially different from Sophocles and Plato. In other words he *assumes* that the Bible is not inspired; and reproaches, pities, or sneers at every one who is not of his opinion.

In the meantime, What *is* Prophecy? What *are* Miracles? Of what sort *is* that Bible which has imposed upon mankind so grossly, and so long? They are *facts*, and must be explained. What *are* they? Prophecy, then, is "only *the power of seeing the ideal in the actual*, or of tracing the Divine Government in the movements of men." (p. 70.) As for Miracles, "their evidential force is wholly *relative* to the apprehensions of the parties addressed. . . . Columbus' prediction of the Eclipse to the native islanders," (p. 115,) is advanced as an illustration of the nature of the argument from Miracles. By whatever method

[m] pp. cxciv.-v.

the Bible has attained its present footing in the world, it is a book which has been hitherto misunderstood; and it must plainly be dealt with after a new fashion. Our Lord's Incarnation, Temptation, Death and Burial, Resurrection and Ascension into Heaven,—all His Miracles, in short, will be best interpreted *Ideologically;* in other words, by a principle "which resolves into an ideal the whole of the historical and doctrinal person of JESUS." (p. 200.) So interpreted, "the Gospel may win again the minds of intellectual men;" (p. 376;) but it will find it no easy matter. There is in fact "a higher wisdom" than the Gospel, "which is known to those who are perfect,"—"*that* reconcilement," namely, "of Faith and Knowledge which may be termed Christian Philosophy." (p. 413.)

The great object, in short, is to bring about "a reconciliation" (p. 375,) between "the minds of intellectual men" (p. 376,) and Christianity. Such a reconciliation is to be regarded as a "restoration of belief." (p. 375.) And it is to be effected by "taking away some of the external supports, because they are not needed and do harm: also because they interfere with the meaning." (p. 375.)—Those "external supports" are (1) a belief in the Inspiration of the Bible;—(2) the writings of the Fathers and Doctors of the Church;—(3) Creeds and the decisions of Councils;—(4) the works of Anglican Divines;—(5) Learning; (p. 337;)—(6) a profound acquaintance with the Greek language; (p. 393;)—(7) a minute knowledge of Greek Grammar; (p. 391;)—(8) the Doctrine of the Greek Article;—(9) the free use of the parallel passages. . . . The Bible, when interpreted by any self-relying young man who knows a little Greek, and attends to the meaning *of words*,—will be seen in all the freshness of its early beauty, like an old picture which has been recently cleaned. "A new interest" will be excited by this new Bible, which will "make for itself a new kind of authority." By being thus literally interpreted, it will be transformed into "a spirit." Then, (but not before) the Bible will enjoy the sublime satisfaction of keeping pace with the Age. It may so, even yet, "embrace the thoughts of men upon the earth."

But what kind of thing will this Bible be? The beginning of Genesis, (pp. 207—253,) is to be rejected because it "is not an authentic utterance of Divine knowledge, but a human utterance, which it has pleased Providence to use in a special way for the education of mankind." (p. 253.) We are invited to "a frank recognition of the *erroneous views of Nature* which the Bible contains." (p. 211.) Thus, *all* miraculous transactions will have to be explained away. The volume of Prophecy will have to be regarded as a volume of History. The very History will have to be read with distrust. Like other records, it is subject to the conditions of "knowledge which existed in an early stage of the world." (p. 411.) It does not even begin to be authentic, until B.C. 1900; or rather, until B.C. 900[n]. What remains is to be looked upon as "the continuous witness in all ages of the higher things in the heart of man," (p. 375,)—(whatever that may happen to mean.) The Gospel is to be looked upon as "a life of CHRIST in the soul, instead of a theory of CHRIST which is in a book, or written down," (p. 423.) "The lessons of Scripture, when disengaged from theological formulas, have a nearer way to the hearts of the poor." (p. 424.) Even "in

[n] See pp. 57 and 170.

Missions to the heathen, Scripture is to be treated as the expression of universal truths, rather than of the tenets of particular men and Churches." (p. 423.) It is anticipated that this " would remove many obstacles to the reception of Christianity." (*Ibid.*) " It is not the Book of Scripture which we should seek to give the heathen ;" " but the truth of the Book ; the mind of Christ and His Apostles, in which all lesser details and differences should be lost and absorbed ;" " the purer light or element of Religion, of which Christianity is the expression." (p. 427.) . . . . Such is the ghostly phantom, by the aid of which the Heathen are to become evangelized !

But this historical Bible is not to be regarded as the rule of a man's life, or indeed as an external Law at all. (pp. 36, 45.) " We walk now by Reason and Conscience *alone.*" (p. 21.) The Bible is to be identified " with the voice of Conscience," (p. 45,)—which it has " to evoke, not to override." (p. 44.) " The principle of private judgment . . . makes Conscience the supreme interpreter." (p. 45.) Ours is " a law which is *not imposed upon us by another power*, but *by our own enlightened will:*" (p. 35 :) for the "Spirit, or Conscience" " legislates" henceforth " *without appeal except to himself.*" (p. 31.)

Having thus disposed of " Traditional Christianity," (p. 156,) it is not obscurely hinted that something quite different is to be substituted in its place. And first, next to " a frank appeal to Reason, and a frank criticism of Scripture," (p. 174,) the nature and " office of the Church is to be properly understood." (p. 194.)

The Church then is a spontaneous development of the State, as " part of its own organization," (p. 195,)

—a purely secular Institution. The State will "develop itself into a Church" by "throwing its elements, or the best of them, into another mould; and constituting out of them a Society, which is in it, though in some sense not of it (?),—which is another (?), yet the same." (p. 194.) The nation must provide, from time to time, that the teaching of one age does "not traditionally harden, so as to become an exclusive barrier in a subsequent one; and so the moral growth of those who are committed to the hands of the Church be checked." (*Ibid.*) The Church is founded, therefore, not upon "the possession of a supernaturally communicated speculation (!) concerning GOD," but "upon *the manifestation of a Divine Life in Man.*" "Speculative doctrines should be left to *philosophical schools*. A national Church must be concerned with the *ethical development* of its members." (p. 195.) It should be "free from dogmatic tests, and similar intellectual bondage;" (p. 168;) hampered by no Doctrines, pledged to no Creeds. These may be retained indeed; but "*we refuse to be bound by them.*" (p. 44.) The Subscription of the Clergy to the Articles should also be abolished: for "no promise can reach fluctuations of opinion, and personal conviction." (!!!) *Open* heretical teaching may, to be sure, be dealt with by the Law; but the Law "should not require any act which appears to signify 'I think.'" (p. 189.) Witness "the reluctance of the stronger minds to enter an Order in which their intellects may not have *free play*." (p. 190.) . . . Such then is the Negative Religion! Such is the new faith which Doctors Temple and Williams, Professors Powell and Jowett, Messieurs Wilson, Goodwin, and Pattison, have deliberately combined to offer to the acceptance of the World!

It is high time to conclude. I cannot lay down my pen however until I have re-echoed the sentiments of one with whom I heartily agree. I allude to Dr. Moberly; who professes that he is "struck almost more with what seems to him the hardheartedness, and exceeding unkindness of this book, than with its unsoundness. Have the writers," (he asks,) "considered how far the suggesting of innumerable doubts,—doubts unargued and unproved,—will check honest devotion, and embolden timid sin? *For whom* do they intend this book? Is it written for the mass of general readers? Is it designed for students at the Universities? Do they suppose that this multitude of random suggestions will be carefully wrought out by these readers, and be rejected if unsound; so as to leave their faith and devotion untarnished? . . . Have they reflected how many souls for whom CHRIST died may be slain in their weakness by *their* self-styled strength?"

"Suppose, for a moment, that the Holy Scriptures *are* (p. 177,) the Word of the Spirit of GOD,—that the Miracles, (cf. p. 109,) including the Resurrection of CHRIST, are actual objective facts, which have really happened,—that the Doctrines of the Church are true, (p. 195,) and the Creeds (p. 355,) the authoritative expositions of them,—and that men are to reach Salvation through faith in CHRIST, Virgin-born, according to the Scriptures, and making atonement (cf. p. 87,) for their sins upon the Cross. ON THIS SUPPOSITION, —*Is not the publication of this book an act of real hostility to GOD'S Truth; and one which endangers the Faith and Salvation of Men?* And is this hostility less real, or the danger diminished, because the writers are, all but one, Clergymen, some of them Tutors and Schoolmasters; because they wear the dress, and use the language of friends, and threaten us with bitter opposition if we do not regard them as such"?"

With this I lay down my pen. My last words shall be simple and affectionate, addressed solely to yourselves.

I trace these concluding lines,—(of a work which, but for *you*, would never have been undertaken,)—in a *quite* empty College; and in the room where we have so often and so happily met on Sunday evenings. Can you wonder if, at the conclusion of what has proved rather a heavy task, (so *hateful* to me is controversy,) my thoughts revert with affectionate solicitude to yourselves, already scattered in all directions; and to those evenings which more, I think, than any other thing, have gilded my College life? ... In thus sending you a written farewell, and praying from my soul that God may bless and keep you all, I cannot suppress the earnest entreaty that you would remember the best words of counsel which may have at any time fallen from my lips: that you would persevere in the daily study of the pure Book of Life; and that you would read it, *not* as feeling yourselves called upon to sit in judgment on its adorable contents; but rather, as men who are permitted to draw near; and invited *to listen*, and *to learn*, and *to live*. And so farewell! ... "Watch ye, stand fast in the Faith,"—nay, take it in the original, which is far better:—Γρηγορεῖτε, στήκετε ἐν τῇ πίστει, ἀνδρί-

" *Some Remarks, &c.*, pp. xxiii.—xxv.

ζεσθε, κραταιοῦσθε. πάντα ὑμῶν ἐν ἀγάπῃ γινέσθω. Ἡ χάρις τοῦ Κυρίου Ἰησοῦ Χριστοῦ μεθ' ὑμῶν. ἡ ἀγάπη μου μετὰ πάντων ὑμῶν.

Your friend,
J. W. B.

Oriel,
June 22nd, 1861.

Seven Sermons.

SUBJECTS OF THE SERMONS.

(For a detailed account of the Contents of these Sermons, the Reader is referred to the beginning of the Volume.)

I.—THE STUDY OF THE BIBLE RECOMMENDED; AND A METHOD OF STUDYING IT DESCRIBED . . . . p. 1

II.—NATURAL SCIENCE AND THEOLOGICAL SCIENCE p. 23

III.—INSPIRATION OF SCRIPTURE.—GOSPEL DIFFICULTIES. —THE WORD OF GOD INFALLIBLE.—OTHER SCIENCES SUBORDINATE TO THEOLOGICAL SCIENCE . . p. 53

IV.—THE PLENARY INSPIRATION OF EVERY PART OF THE BIBLE, VINDICATED AND EXPLAINED.—NATURE OF INSPIRATION.—THE TEXT OF SCRIPTURE . . p. 91

V.—INTERPRETATION OF HOLY SCRIPTURE.—INSPIRED INTERPRETATION.—THE BIBLE IS NOT TO BE INTERPRETED LIKE ANY OTHER BOOK.—GOD, (NOT MAN,) THE REAL AUTHOR OF THE BIBLE . . . . p. 139

VI.—THE DOCTRINE OF ARBITRARY SCRIPTURAL ACCOMMODATION CONSIDERED . . . . p. 183

VII.—THE MARVELS OF HOLY SCRIPTURE, MORAL AND PHYSICAL. — JAEL'S DEED DEFENDED. — MIRACLES VINDICATED . . . . p. 221

PRÆVENERUNT OCULI MEI AD TE DILUCULO, UT MEDITARER ELOQUIA TUA.

QUAM DULCIA FAUCIBUS MEIS ELOQUIA TUA: SUPER MEL ORI MEO.

LUCERNA PEDIBUS MEIS VERBUM TUUM, ET LUMEN SEMITIS MEIS.

Οι ΚΑΛΩΣ ΠΟΙΕΙΤΕ ΠΡΟΣΕΧΟΝΤΕΣ, ΩΣ ΛΥΧΝΩι ΦΑΙΝΟΝΤΙ ΕΝ ΑΥΧΜΗΡΩι ΤΟΠΩι, ΕΩΣ ΟΥ ΗΜΕΡΑ ΔΙΑΥΓΑΣΗι, ΚΑΙ ΦΩΣΦΟΡΟΣ ΑΝΑΤΕΙΛΗι ΕΝ ΤΑΙΣ ΚΑΡΔΙΑΙΣ ΥΜΩΝ.

Domine Deus meus, ... sint castæ deliciæ meæ Scripturæ Tuæ. Nec fallar in eis, nec fallam ex eis.—Augustinus, *Confessiones*, lib. xi. c. ii. § 3.

The Book of this Law we are neither able nor worthy to look into. That little thereof which we darkly apprehend we admire: the rest with religious ignorance we humbly and meekly adore.— Hooker, *Eccl. Pol.*, B. I. ch. ii. § 5.

SERMON I.[a]

THE STUDY OF THE BIBLE RECOMMENDED; AND A METHOD OF STUDYING IT DESCRIBED.

St. John vi. 68.

Lord, to whom shall we go? Thou hast the words of Eternal Life.

IT was probably in that synagogue which the faithful Centurion built at Capernaum[b] that our SAVIOUR had been discoursing. At the end of His discourse, it is related that "many of His Disciples went back, and walked no more with Him." Thereupon, He asked the Twelve, "Will ye also go away?" the very form of His inquiry (Μὴ καὶ ὑμεῖς) implying the answer which the Divine Speaker expected and desired. And to this challenge of Love to Faith, St. Peter replied, not only on behalf of his fellow-Apostles, but on behalf of all faithful men to the end of time:— "LORD, to *whom* shall we go? *Thou* hast the words of Eternal Life!"

You perceive that St. Peter's confession takes a peculiar form,—resting the impossibility of unfaithfulness in the Apostles on the gracious discourse of Him to whom they had been listening. "A hard saying," and unpalatable, it had proved to many; but to his own taste it had seemed "sweeter than honey and the

---

[a] Preached in Christ-Church Cathedral, Oct. 21st, 1860.

[b] τὴν συναγωγήν,—from which it would appear that there was but *one*. See Bishop Middleton on St. Luke vii. 5.

B

honeycomb." So that while, to those others, it had been an occasion of going back, and walking with CHRIST no more,—to himself it had been a reason why he could never, as he felt, be persuaded to forsake CHRIST. Nay, it was to himself, (and, as he boldly assumed, to his fellow-Apostles,) a sufficient evidence that the Speaker was none other than the SON of GOD. "And we believe, and are sure, that Thou art the CHRIST, the SON of the living GOD!"

Here then, surely, a very solemn picture is set before us. The same message proves, in the case of some, the savour of death unto death: in the case of others, of life unto life. It is an image of what is still taking place in the world. The Gospel, whether veiled in the Old Testament, or unveiled in the New, is confessedly "a hard saying:"—to some, their very crown and joy; to others, only an occasion of distress and downfall. It was so, when proclaimed not by the tongue of men and of angels, but by the lips "full of grace and truth" of the Incarnate WORD Himself: and it is so still. The temper of mankind is still the same as it was of old, and the instrument of man's trial is still the same.

Of the written Gospel, many of the self-same things are said in Scripture which are said of Him by whom that Gospel was preached. Thus, it is proclaimed to be "the power of GOD to salvation[c]." It is described as "a discerner of the thoughts and intents of the heart[d]." It is declared to be eternal,—a thing which "shall never pass away[e]." "In the last day," it is prophesied that the words which CHRIST has spoken "shall judge" men[f]. The very Name by

[c] Rom. i. 16. [d] Heb. iv. 12. [e] St. Matth. xxiv. 35, &c.
[f] St. John xii. 48.

which St. John designates the Eternal Son, in the forefront of his Gospel[g], is the appellation by which the Gospel is emphatically known.—But even more remarkable are the analogies which subsist between the written record of our Lord's Life and Teaching, and the actual person of our Lord. And proposing, as I now do, to say a few earnest words to the younger men in recommendation of a more punctual, methodical, as well as attentive study of the Bible, than, I am persuaded, is practised by one young man in a thousand,—it may not prove unavailing in awakening attention, if I advert, in passing, to some of the circumstances whereby an even balance, (so to speak,) is established between the opportunities of the men of this generation, and of those who were blessed with the oral teaching of the Son of Man.

1. Thus, if the record has its difficulties, and its seeming contradictions, so had *He*. It did not appear that "Jesus *of Nazareth*" was born, (according to the prophet Micah's prediction,) at *Bethlehem*[h]. His title perplexed even Nathanael[i].—He was called the son of *Joseph*, even *by the Blessed Virgin*[k]. How then could He be the Son of God? And how was the famous prophecy of Isaiah fulfilled in Him[l]?—He grew up in a lowly estate. Once He is called "the carpenter[m]." How then could He be of the Royal House of David? And so, in many other respects, did He, in His own person, present the self-same class of difficulties to the world's eye which His Gospel presents to ours:—"the sixteenth of Tiberius,"—the two genealogies,—"Cyrenius,"—"the days of Abiathar,"—"Jeremy the prophet,"—and so on.

[g] St. John i. 1, &c. [h] Ibid. vii. 40—43. [i] Ibid. i. 45, 46.
[k] St. Luke ii. 48. [l] Is. vii. 14. [m] St. Mark vi. 3.

2. Somewhat less obvious, but not less true, is the unattractive aspect, at first sight, of the Gospel. Verily there is, until we become intimately acquainted with it, "no beauty that we should desire" it.—The style, (full of interest, to those who have tried to understand it a little,) is not, I suppose, what critics would call altogether a good style.—The Greek is not what learned men call *pure*.—Many a word, (brimfull of meaning to those who will give to the words of the Gospel their best care,) reminds one, that neither did *He* speak what, in the capital of Jewry, was accounted a classical idiom. He employed the accent of the despised Galilee.—The very reasoning, (until you give it your heart's homage and best attention,) often seems to be either inconsequential, or to contain a fallacy. Certain words of our Lord have been even *cited* as fallacious by a celebrated Divine whose writings we are all familiar with[n]. Now, *His* words were disregarded, cavilled at, made light of, in just the same manner.

3. Most surprising of all is the analogy observable between the union of the Divine and the human element in the Gospels,—and the strictly parallel union, as it seems, of the two natures, the Divine and the Human, in the person of our Lord.—As *He* was perfect and faultless, so do we deem *it* infallible also, without spot or blemish of any kind. We reject as monstrous any 'theory of Inspiration,' (as it is called,) which imputes blunders to the work of the Holy Ghost.—As, further, we claim for our Lord's recorded human actions mysterious significancy, so do we seem warranted in looking for a mysterious pur-

[n] Our Lord's words in St. John viii. 47 are so cited by Archbishop Whately in the Appendix of his Logic.—(App. II. No. 12, p. 418.)

pose, a divine meaning, in every expression of the written Word.—Lastly, although we may, nay we must, admit such a Divine and such a human element, we must altogether deny the possibility of separating the one from the other. We cannot separate Scripture into human and Divine. Like the Incarnate WORD, the Gospel is at once both human *and* Divine, yet one and indivisible. And the method of its inspiration is as great a difficulty in its way, and as much beyond our ken, as the nature of the union of the Godhead and the Manhood in the one person of CHRIST.

For whatever reason, and whether you please to accept the foregoing remarks or not, it is a plain fact that the Gospel is now in the world, fulfilling the same office towards mankind, which our Saviour CHRIST Himself fulfilled, and experiencing the same treatment at the hands of men in return. It is leavening society indeed, and remodelling the world, even while it is practically overlooked by politicians or experiencing evil treatment from them. It wins its way silently and secretly, yet surely; and it works miracles here and there. Moreover, it divides opinion; separating, as it will for ever separate, the light from the darkness[o]. It is slighted, and overlooked, and neglected by some; even while, by others, it is embraced with joy unspeakable. 'The humble and meek' adore it; even while, by the proud and rebellious, it is after a most strange fashion cavilled at, called in question, and denied. We specify *the Gospel*, instinctively, as that part of the Inspired Word which chiefly concerns ourselves, as Christian men; but the entire deposit shares the same fate. I do not think I am delivering a paradox when I say

[o] Consider all such places as St. John xi. 45, 46.

that the Bible is generally very little read. That the amount of *study* commonly bestowed upon it bears no proportion whatever to its transcendent importance and paramount value, shall not be any paradox at all; but a mere truism.

For I entreat you to consider, (trite and obvious as it may sound,) *What* have we, in the whole wide world, which may be put in competition with that Book which contains God's revelation of Himself to man? In its early portions, how does it go back to the very birthday of Time, and discourse of things which were done in the grey of that early morning! How mysterious is the record,—so methodical, so particular, so unique; preserving the very words which were syllabled in Paradise, and describing transactions which no one but the Holy Ghost is competent to declare! Come lower down, and *where* will you find more beautiful narratives,—still fresh at the end of three and four thousand years,—than those stories of Patriarchs, Judges, Kings, which wrap up divinest teaching in all their ordinary details: where every word is weighed in a heavenly balance, fraught with a divine purpose, and intended for some glorious issue: where the very characters are adumbrations of personages far greater than themselves; and where the course of events is made to preach to us, at this distant day, of the things which concern our peace! Is it a light thing again to know in what terms Isaiah, and the rest of "the goodly fellowship," when they opened their lips to speak in that remote age, foretold of the coming of the Son of Man?... But all seems to grow pale before the Everlasting Gospel, and the other writings of the New Testament. Surely we have become too familiar with the providence which has preserved to us the very words of the four Evangelists, if we can bend our thoughts in the direction of the Gospel without a throb of joy and wonder not to be described, at having so great a treasure placed within our easy reach. Can it indeed be, that I may listen while the disciple whom JESUS loved is discoursing of the miracles, and recalling the sayings of his LORD? May I hear St. Peter himself address the early Church,—or know the precise words of the message which St. Jude sent to the first believers,— or be shown the Epistle which the LORD's cousin addressed "to the Twelve Tribes scattered abroad"? How does it happen that the Book is not for ever in our hands which comes to us with such claims to our undivided homage?

But, on the contrary, it has become the fashion in certain quarters, on every imaginable pretext, to call in question the credibility of the Bible. It seems to be the taste of the age to invent hazy difficulties and dim objections to its statements. Inspiration, under a miserable attempt to explain it, is openly explained away. And the theory, however crude and preposterous, is tolerated: at least it escapes castigation. It cannot fail but that the unlearned and thoughtless ones of this generation will be growing up in a notion that these are open questions after all, and that "Truth" is but a name,—not a thing worth contending, aye *dying* for, if need be! The reason is but too obvious. It must be, partly, because we do not in reality prize the deposit nearly so much as we suppose. Partly, because of the indifferentism which is everywhere so prevalent. Partly too because, notwithstanding our intellectual activity, we are not a really learned body. And partly, it must be confessed, the reason is, because Theology has become so nearly a prostrate study with us, and because men really able to do battle for the Truth are somewhat hard to find. Nor is there any reasonable prospect of improvement either; for those who go forth from this place into the Ministry, go with such slender preparation, that it would be truer to say that they go with none at all.

Now, it would be a mere waste of time, to inveigh for half an hour against the indifferentism, or the spurious liberality, of the age: and it would be a most unbecoming proceeding, (not to say a highly distasteful one,) from this place to be suggesting remedies for an evil which already lies very near the heart of every serious man among us; and which, if discussed at all, must be discussed elsewhere. To say the truth, while the neglect of Theology, and the low ebb of Theological attainments in our Clergy, is generally recognized, the remedy for the evil is by no means so clear. From this subject, then, I pass at once: and I shall content myself with the far humbler task, of urging upon the younger men present,—those especially who are destined for the Ministry,—one act of preparation, one duty, about which, at all events, there cannot be any difference of opinion: I mean the duty of applying themselves, *now*, to the patient study of the Bible.

The thing is soon said; but the hint requires expanding a little, in order that it may become of any practical use.—By the "study of the Bible," I do not mean a chapter occasionally read with care: nor even a chapter regularly conned over at night; when a convivial meeting has blunted the edge of observation, or severe study has exhausted the powers of the brain.

The *devotional* use of a portion of Holy Scripture is quite a distinct affair. Still less would the practice satisfy me of following the lessons in the College Chapel: and this for reasons so obvious that I will not stop to point them out. Nor even is the reading of the Bible in College Lecture, the thing I mean; for reasons also which any acute person will readily ascertain for himself. None of these methods of acquainting yourselves with the contents of the Bible come up to the thing I contemplate, although each is good in its way; and of course I am not speaking in disparagement of any.

No. The thing I would so strenuously urge upon you, is, — that, during your undergraduate period, you should read the whole Bible consecutively through, from one end to the other, *by* yourself and *for* yourself, with consummate method, care, and attention. The fundamental conditions of such a study of the Bible, in order to make it of any real use, are these:—

1. First, that you should deliberately apportion to this solemn duty the best and freshest and quietest half-hour in the whole day; and then, that you should determine, let what will go undone, never to abridge *that* half-hour. You may sometimes be enabled to afford a little *more* time to the chapter: but you will find it quite fatal ever to devote a shorter period to it. And half an hour, if you employ it in right good earnest, at present, must be thought enough.

2. Next, (except on Sundays and in Vacation, when you may safely double your daily task and your daily time,) be persuaded to read each day exactly one chapter. On no account attempt to go reading on; but rather spend the moments which remain over,

(they *cannot* be many !) in reviewing that day's portion; or referring to some of the places indicated in the margin; or glancing over yesterday's chapter.

The effect of building up your Bible knowledge in this manner, bit by bit, is what you would not anticipate. The whole acquires a solidity and compactness not to be attained by any other method. You will find at the end of many days, not only that the structure has attained to symmetry and beauty,—but that the disposition of its several parts, in some respects, has become intelligible also: while, (what is not of least importance,) the foundation on which all the superstructure rests, proves wondrous secure and strong.

3. Then, while you read,—safe from the risk of interruption, (as I began by supposing,) and with every faculty intent on your task,—try, as much as possible, to go over the words as if they were new to you; and watch them, one by one, so that nothing may by any possibility escape your notice. Do not slumber over a single word. Nothing can be unimportant when it is the HOLY GHOST who speaketh. It is an excellent practice to mark the expressions which strike you; for it is a method of preserving the memory of what is sure else soon to pass away.

4. And next, be persuaded to read without extraneous helps of any kind; except, of course, such help as a map, or the margin of your Bible, supplies. Pray avoid Commentaries and notes. First, you cannot afford time for them: and secondly, if you could, they would be as likely to mislead you as not. But the real reason why you are so strenuously advised to avoid them, is, because they will do more to nullify your reading, than anything which could be imagined.

Your object is to obtain an insight into Holy Scripture, by acquiring the habit of reading it with intelligence and care: *not* to be saved trouble, and to be shown what *other persons* have thought about it.

5. But then, though you are entreated not to have recourse to the notes of others, you are as strongly advised to make brief memoranda of your own: and the briefer the better. Construct *your own* table of the Patriarchs,—*your own* analysis of the Law,—*your own* descent of the Kings,—*your own* enumeration of the Miracles. A pedigree full of faults, made by yourself, will do you more good than the most accurate table drawn up by another: but if you are at all attentive and clever, *it will not be* full of faults.—*You* will perhaps make the parables 56 instead of 30 : you will have gained 26 by your honest industry. Nay, keep a record of your difficulties, if you please ; or of anything which strikes you, and which you would be sorry to forget. But, as a rule, it is well to write little, and to give your time and thought to the record before you.

6. Above all, is it indispensable that your reading of the Bible should be strictly consecutive ; and on no account may any one pretend to begin such a study of that book as I am here recommending, except at *the first Chapter of Genesis*. It is a great mistake, (though one of the commonest of all,) for a man to imagine that he knows the beginning of the Bible pretty well. I say it advisedly, that it would be easy to write down twelve interesting questions on that first chapter, of which none of the younger men present would be able to answer three,—and yet, they should all be questions of such a sort that a labouring man's child with an

open Bible would be able infallibly to answer them every one.

7. It will follow from what has been offered, that you are invited to read every book in the Bible in the order in which it actually stands,—never, of course, skipping a chapter; much less a Book. In every mere catalogue of names, be resolved to find edification. Feel persuaded that details, seemingly the driest, are full of GOD. Remember that the difference between every syllable of Scripture and all other books in the world is, not a difference of *degree*, but of *kind*. All books but one, are *human:* that one book is *Divine!*

Now, you will perceive that the kind of study of the Bible here recommended, is somewhat different from what is commonly pursued. I contemplate the continued exercise of a most curious and prying, as well as a most vigilant and observing eye. *No* difficulty is to be neglected; *no* peculiarity of expression is to be disregarded; *no* minute detail is to be overlooked. The hint let fall in an earlier chapter is to be compared with a hint let fall in the later place. Do they tally or not? and what follows? The chronological details spontaneously evolved by the narrative, are to be unerringly discovered by the student *for himself*. The course of every journey is to be attentively noted. Things omitted are to be spied out as carefully as things set down; and whatever can possibly be gathered in the way of necessary inference, is to be industriously ascertained. The imagination is not to slumber either, because no pains are taken by the sacred writer to move the feelings or melt the heart.

How *soon* will any one who takes the trouble to

read the Bible after this fashion, be struck with a hundred things which he never knew before,—indeed, which are not commonly known! How will he be for ever eliciting unsuspected facts,—detecting undreamed of coincidences, but which are as important as they are true,—accumulating materials of value quite inestimable for future study in Divine things! However unpromising a certain collection of references may be, he is careful to extend it,—convinced, like a wise householder, that there will come an use for it after many days. His whole aim is to *master thoroughly* the record which he has undertaken to study.

Let me not be misunderstood if it is added that the Bible should be read,—I do not say *in the same manner*,—that is, in the same temper and spirit,—but at least *with the same attention*, as is bestowed upon a merely human work. In truth, it should be read with much more attention. But *that* diligence which a student commonly bestows on a difficult moral treatise, or an obscure drama, or a perplexed history,— analyzing it, comparing passage with passage, and learning a great deal of it by heart,—I am quite at a loss to understand why a student of the Bible should be a stranger to.—" I do much condemn," (says Lord Bacon), " I do much condemn that Interpretation of the Scripture which is only after the manner as men use to interpret a profane book." So do I. Scripture is to be approached and handled in quite a different spirit from a common history. The mind, the heart rather, must bow down before its revelations, in the most suppliant fashion imaginable. The book should ever be approached with prayer:—" LORD, open Thou mine eyes that I may see the wondrous things of Thy Law!" The very printed pages should be handled with reverence, in consideration of the message they contain. But what I am saying is, that none of the methods which diligence and zeal have ever invented to secure a complete mastery of the contents of any merely *human* performance, may be overlooked by a student of *the Bible*.

To what has gone before I will add one caution, and will trouble you with one only. It would be easy to multiply cautions: but I am talking to highly intelligent men; and there is only one rock which I am really fearful of your running against.

It was the advice of a great and good man, (to his clergy, I suspect,) that they should read the Bible *with a special object:* and an excellent recent writer has repeated the same advice; namely that men should "read with a view to some particular inquiry, with purpose to clear up some peculiar question of interest, which," (says he,) "you may create for yourselves[q]." I entreat *you* to do nothing of the kind. Whatever advantages may result to an advanced student from adopting this practice, to *you* it *must* be fraught with unmingled evil. You will be tempted to overrate the importance of everything you discover which suits your present purpose: you will disregard all that looks in a different direction: you will be disappointed if you meet with nothing *ad rem:* you will get a habit of slurring over many chapters, many whole books of the Bible. A very little reflection will convince you that it *must* be as I say. *Who*, for example, could be expected to find delight and edification in the calendar of the Deluge, who had determined to read Genesis with a view to discovering what knowledge existed in the patriarchal age of a future life? No. Your wisdom

[q] Blunt's *Duties of a Parish Priest*,—p. 81.

will be to divest your minds, as much as possible, of *any* preconceived notion as to what the Bible contains, or was intended to teach you. You should wish to find there nothing so much as the authentic evidence of *what* Divine Wisdom hath seen fit to communicate to man. Read it therefore, if you are wise, with unaffected curiosity: settling down upon every flower, in order to find out, if you can, *where* the honey *is:* clinging to it rather, *until you have found* the honey. Say to yourself,—" It cannot be that all these details of months and days should be given in vain[r]. I *must* find out the reason of it." And, at last, you will find,— what you will find.—" Very strange," (you will learn to say to yourself,) " that the history of nearly 1600 years should be curdled into one short chapter[s]; and yet that three verses of the Bible should be devoted to the history of a man's losing his way in a field, and then finding it again[t]!" The subject may be worth thinking about. You are perhaps naturally disposed to take what you are pleased to call "a common sense view" of the meaning of Holy Scripture; and to interpret it after a very dry unlovely fashion of your own: to evacuate its deeper sayings, and to doubt the mysterious significancy of its historical details. You will speedily perceive, however, that the Apostles and Evangelists of CHRIST,—as many as were moved by the HOLY SPIRIT of GOD, and spoke not their own words but *His*,—that all these are against you: and the effect of this discovery on an honest and good heart, reading *not* in order to be confirmed in some preconceived opinion, but with a sincere desire of enlightenment in Divine things,—may be anticipated.

[r] Gen. vii. 4 to viii. 14.   [s] Ibid. v.
[t] Ibid. xxxvii. 15, 16, 17.

Bishop Horsley relates that by a yet simpler process he became disabused of a favourite fancy with which he set out,—namely, that prophecy must of necessity carry a single meaning^u.—The attitude of mind which I so strongly recommend you to assume, (and it depends on an act of the Will, whether you assume it or not,) is very exactly represented by the cry of the child Samuel,—" Speak LORD, for Thy servant heareth!"

It seems right, in the fewest words, to state what we *do*,—and what we do *not*,—expect to result from such a study of the Bible as this; in other words, to assign the office of unassisted Biblical study. I would not willingly have my meaning mistaken *here*.

It is not implied then, for a moment, that a man is either at liberty, or able, to gather his own Religion for himself out of the Bible. The very thought were monstrous. But it is a widely different thing for one of yourselves to read his Bible patiently, and humbly, and laboriously, through,—without prejudice or theory, —unmolested by critical notes, undistracted by human comments, uninfluenced by party views: — all this, I say, is a widely different thing from a man's inventing his own system of Divinity. Members of the Catholic Church,—born in a Christian country,— educated amid the choicest influences for good,—*you* are by no means so left to yourselves. The BOOK OF COMMON PRAYER is your sufficient safeguard. The framework of the Faith,—the conditions under which you may lawfully speculate about Divine mysteries,— are all prescribed for you: and within those limits you cannot well go wrong.

On the other hand, the outlines of *Moral Theology*,

---

^u See Appendix A.

(as it may be called), you are fully competent to detect for yourselves. GOD's strictness in punishing sin, as in the case of Moses [x];—the efficacy of repentance, as in the case of Ahab [y];—the sure answer to prayer, (to *forgotten* prayer, it may be!) as in the case of Zacharias [z];—the seemingly roundabout methods of GOD's providence, (as in the case of Abraham,) yet conducting inevitably to a blessed issue at the last;—the rewards of obedience [a];—the faithfulness of the Divine promises;—the boundless wealth of the Divine contrivance, which, on man's repentance, is able to convert even a curse into a blessing, as in the case of Levi [b];—the peace and joy surely in reserve for those who fear GOD, as in the case of Joseph;—the extent to which things seemingly trivial are noticed by the Ancient of Days, as every page of the Bible shows;—these, and a hundred points like these, not only a man *can* gather for himself out of the Book of GOD's Law, but no one else can do the work for him. He *must* discover all such matters for himself.

And need I point out, for a minute, the immense advantage with which a mind so stored with Divine knowledge will approach the Ministry; and finally take in hand the actual oversight of the flock? It is really not to be expressed. The Bishop's examination for Orders will become nothing but an agreeable exercise, instead of an object of dread. You are quite sure of a few approving words in *that* quarter. But, (what is a thousand times more important,) you your-

---

[x] Deut. iii. 25, 26.   [y] 1 Kings xxi. 27—29.
[z] St. Luke i. 13.   [a] Jerem. xxxv. 18, 19.
[b] Comp. Gen. xlix. 5—7, with Exod. xxxii. 26—28, (alluded to in Deut. xxxiii. 9,) and finally Numb. iii. 9 and 45, and Josh. xxi. 3—8.

self feel safe and strong. You begin to read some treatise on Divinity; and you find yourself in some degree competent to test the writer's statements, to endorse or to suspect his conclusions, because you are familiar with the Rule of Faith which he himself employed. It becomes your turn at last to instruct others,—from the pulpit for example; and instead of timid truisms, and vague generalities, you are able to draw a bold clear outline round almost any department of Christian doctrine. You can explain with authority.—You are not afraid to catechize before the congregation: for although your Theological attainments are but slender after all, yet, you know your Bible well; and even if an absurdly wrong answer is given you, you know how to single out from the hank the golden thread of Truth, and to display it before the eyes of men and Angels. And let me tell you, by way of ending the subject, we should hear less about dull sermons, and inattentive congregations, and badly filled churches,—as well as about the astounding ignorance of many among the upper classes, in Divine things,—if our younger Clergy knew the Bible a great deal better than they do.— Aye, and we should not have so many unsound remarks about Holy Scripture either,—so many mistaken views of doctrine,—so many crude remarks about Inspiration,—made *by persons who ought to know better.*

You will perceive that I am saying all this, (except the last few words,) *at* you, (the younger men present;) because in *you* I see many of the future Clergy of England. And I say it, because, (for the last time,) I do entreat you, one and all, to follow the advice I have been giving you; and to set about such a careful study of the Bible, *at once*. Do not put it off for a single day. Begin it tomorrow morning. You will then have mastered Genesis this term, finishing the last chapter on Sunday the 10th of December; and on Monday, the 11th, you will have to read the first chapter of Exodus. I am confident that you will remember *this* day and hour with gratitude to the end of your lives, if you will but make the experiment and persevere.

And just one word to those who aspire, (and all *should* aspire,) to University honours. You will not find what I have been recommending any hindrance to you at all. But even supposing you *do*, now and then, find the inexorable daily half-hour stand in the way of something else,—shall not the very thought of Him whose Voice you have deliberately resolved to hear daily at that fixed time, make you full amends? Shall you resolve to pluck so freely of the Tree of Knowledge, and yet begrudge the approach once a day to the *Tree of Life*, which grows in the midst of the Paradise of God? Shall ample time be found for works of fiction,—for the Review, and the Magazine, and the newspaper,—yet half an hour a day be deemed too much to be given to the Word of God? What? room for everything and everybody; yet still "no room in the Inn" for Christ! .... I have, (I speak honestly,) I have far too high an opinion of your instincts for good, to think it possible. You have plenty of faults,—(God knoweth!),—but I am very much deceived indeed if there be not a spirit stirring among the young men of this place, overflowing with promise; a real inclination, (obscured at times, but still very energetic,) for whatever things are pure, and lovely, and of good report.

Of course, it is implied by what goes before, that you will read *no* work *of Divinity* just at present. Be counselled, on no account, to read any. Above all, shun the partial, ill-digested pamphlet,—and the one-sided review,—and the controversial letter,—and the Essay which seems to have been written in order to prove nothing. Be content, for the next three years, to study no book of Divinity but the Bible.

And the study of *that* Book, I repeat, you will find no hindrance, no impediment, no burthen to you at all. On the contrary. It will render you a very singular service,—let your classical and logical studies be as severe as they will; (and they cannot well be too severe, too engrossing,—for this is your golden opportunity which never will, never *can*, come back again!) The undersong of "Siloa's brook that flows, fast by the oracle of GOD," will many a time soothe and refresh your else dry and weary spirit. What was begun as a task will soon come to be regarded as a privilege. *That* jealously-guarded half-hour will be found to be the one green spot in the whole day,—like Gideon's fleece, fresh with the dew of the early morning, when it is "dry upon all the earth beside." Your secret study of that Book of Books, I say, will render you a very singular service. The contrast between the Divine and Human method will strike you with ever-recurring power. Unlike every other History, the Bible removes the veil, and discovers the causes of things,—including the First Great Cause of all, who dwelleth in Light unapproachable, but who yet humbleth Himself to behold, and to controul, and to over-rule for good, the things which are done in Heaven and on Earth. And thus, it is not too much to say that the Bible, to one who reads its pages aright, is a certain clue to every other History,—as well as a perpetual commentary on every other Book. It informs the judgment, and cleanses the eye, throughout the whole department of Morals: and as for History, what is it all, but the evidence of GOD in the world,—" traces of *His* iron rod, or of *His* Shepherd's staff [c] ?"

Profoundly sensible am I, that these have been very unintellectual, and somewhat common-place remarks: but I would rather, a hundred times, be of use to the younger men present; I would rather, a hundred times, succeed in persuading one of *them*, to adopt that method of reading the Bible which I have been recommending;—than try to say something which might be thought fine and clever. . . . . Let me only, in conclusion, faithfully remind them, that the *true* office of the study of Divine things is not, by any means, that which, for obvious reasons, I have been rather dwelling and enlarging upon. It is *not* merely to inform the understanding, that Holy Scripture is to be read with such consummate attention, and studied with such exceeding care. It is *not* for the illustration of History, or in order that it may be made a test of the value of other systems of Morals. *Not*, by any means, in order to facilitate admission into Holy Orders, (for which only some of you are destined;)—or to render a man's pulpit-addresses attractive and agreeable;—or even to enable a parish priest to teach with confidence and authority; —is he entreated now to "prevent the night watches," if need be, that he may be occupied (like one of old time [d],) with GOD's Word. O no! It is,—in order

[c] The Rev. C. Marriott's *Sermons*,—vol. I. p. 441.
[d] Ps. cxix. 148.

that his inner life may be made conformable to that outer Law ᵉ: that his aims may be ennobled, and his motives purified, and his earthly hopes made consistent with the winning of an imperishable crown! It is in order that when he wavers between Right and Wrong, the unutterable Canon of GOD's *Law* may suggest itself to him as a constraining motive. Its aim, and purpose, and real function, is, that the fiery hour of temptation may find the Christian soldier armed with "the sword of the Spirit, which is the Word of GOD ᶠ:"—that the dark season of Adversity may find his soul anchored on the Rock of Ages,—which alone can prove his soul's sufficient strength and stay. . . . Of a truth, as Life goes on, Men will find the blessedness of their Hope; if they have not found it out already. Under every form of trial,—and under every strange vicissitude;—in sickness,—and in perplexity,—and in bereavement,—and in the hour of death;—"LORD,—to *whom* shall we go? Thou,—*Thou* hast the words of Eternal Life!"

ᵉ Not so *Essays and Reviews,* pp. 36 and 45.   ᶠ Eph. vi. 17.

SERMON II.[a]

NATURAL SCIENCE AND THEOLOGICAL SCIENCE.

HEBREWS xi. 3.

Through Faith, we understand that the worlds were framed by the Word of GOD.

ST. PAUL, in a famous and familiar chapter of his Epistle to the Hebrews, having declared "what Faith is," proceeds, (as the heading of the chapter expresses it), to note "the worthy fruits thereof in the Fathers of old time." The Book of Genesis was obviously in his hands, or in his heart, while he wrote: for he appeals to the transactions there recorded, in the very order, and often in the very words, of Moses. The HOLY GHOST, I say, directs our attention to what is contained in the ivth,—vth,—vith,—xiith,—xviith,—xxiind,—xxviith,—xlviiith,—and lth chapters of Genesis. But He begins with a yet earlier chapter. *He begins with the first.* Abel, — Enoch, — Noah, — Abraham, — Sarah, — Isaac, — Jacob,—Joseph;—these stand forward as samples of GOD's faithful ones. But with them, the HOLY GHOST proposes to associate *us*. Moreover, He gives *us* the place of honour. Before mentioning one of *their* acts of Faith, He mentions one of *ours*. We come first,—then they. And the particular field in which *we* shine out so conspicuously, — the special province

[a] Preached in Christ-Church Cathedral, Nov. 11th, 1860.

which is assigned to *us*,—that portion of the inspired Narrative wherein *you and I* are supposed to shew a degree of undoubting faith which entitles us to rank with those "Fathers of old time,"—is found to be *the first chapter of the Book of Genesis.* "Through Faith *we* understand that the worlds were framed by the Word of God." An honourable place, and an honourable function truly! I would to God that it might be as gratifying to every one of the congregation, as it is to the preacher, to discover that *this* is the special stand-point which has been reserved for him and for them.

Since, however, it is impossible to forget that we have sometimes seen heads, which are supposed to be very much indeed in advance of the age, shaken ominously at the very chapter which the text bequeaths and commends to the special acceptance of you and me,—I propose that, in the very briefest manner, we now review the contents of that chapter; in order that we may discover what is the special absurdity, or impossibility, or improbability, or by whatever other name the thing is to be called,—which makes it quite out of the question that you or I should undertake the act of Faith here assigned us.

I read then, that "In the beginning, God created the Heaven and the Earth:"—by which I understand, that, at some remote period,—which may or may not baffle human Arithmetic[b],—it was the plea-

---

[b] "The whole period, from the beginning of the primary fossiliferous strata to the present day, *must be great beyond calculation,* and only bear comparison with the astronomical cycles, as might naturally be expected; the earth being without doubt of the same antiquity with the other bodies of the solar system."—Mrs. Somerville's *Physical Geography.*

sure of God the Father, God the Son, God the Holy Ghost,—*three* Persons, coeternal and coequal,—*one* God,—out of nothing, to create the entire Universe. "All things that are in Heaven, and that are in Earth, visible and invisible, whether they be thrones, or dominions, or principalities, or powers: all things were created by Him[c];" and they were created out of nothing. The word in the original does not indeed necessarily imply as much: but since there is *no* word in Hebrew, (any more than there is in Greek, Latin, or English,) peculiarly expressive of the notion of creating out of nothing, it need not excite our surprise that Moses does not employ such a word to describe what God did "in the beginning."—*Then* it was, in the grey of that far distant morning I mean, that all those glittering orbs which sow the vault of Heaven with brightness and with beauty, flashed into sudden being. "Thou, even Thou, art Lord alone: Thou hast made Heaven, the Heaven of Heavens, *with all their host*[d]." Suns, the centres of systems, many of them so distant from this globe of ours, that sun and system scarce shew so bright as a single lesser star: suns, I say, with their marvellous equipage of attendant bodies,— *our* sun among the rest, with all those wandering fires which speed their unwearied courses round it: suns, and planets with their moons, bathed once and for ever in the fountain of that Light which God inhabited from all Eternity, then marshalled themselves in mysterious order, according to "the counsel of His will[e]:" yea, and with their furniture, unimagined and unimaginable, went careering through the untrodden realms of space, each on its several errand of glory, because of obedience to its Maker's sovereign

[c] Col. i. 16.   [d] Neh. ix. 6.   [e] Eph. i. 11.

Law[f]. "By the Word of the LORD," (as it is written,) "were the Heavens made; and all the hosts of them by the breath of His mouth[g]!"

Now, it is reserved to the geologist,—(Nature's High-priest!)—to guess at the condition of this Earth of ours throughout all the long period of unchronicled ages which immediately succeeded the birthday of Time. It is for *him* to guess at the successive changes which this globe of ours underwent; and the progressive cycles of Creation of which it was the theatre; and the many strange races of creatures which, one after another, moved upon its surface,—walking the dry, or inhabiting the moist. *He* shall guess; and *I* will sit at his feet and listen, with unfeigned gratitude, wonder, and delight, while he reports to me his guesses: (for the really great man is eager to assure me that they are no more.)—But when his tale of perplexity is ended, and the last 6,000 years of this world's History have to be discussed, the geologist's function is at an end. I bid him, in GOD's Name, be silent; for now it is GOD that speaketh. If any question be moved as to how *that actual system of things to which Man belongs*, began,—I bid him come down, and take the learner's place; for now *I* mean to assume his vacant chair. *This* time, there shall at least be no guess-work. GOD is now the Speaker: and what GOD revealeth unto *me*, *that* I promise faithfully to report to *him*.

There was a time, then,—and it was certainly less than 6,000 years ago,—when "the Earth was without form, and void; and darkness was upon the face of the deep." What catastrophe it was which had caused that the fountains of the abyss should be broken up,

[f] Hooker's *Eccl. Pol.*, B. I. c. iii. § 2. [g] Ps. xxxiii. 6.

and the solid Earth submerged, I am not concerned to explain:—nor how it had come to pass that from a world of seas and continents, it had become a watery ball, wrapped about with superincumbent vapour:—nor how the blessed sunlight had suffered dire eclipse;—so that the Earth revolved in a horror of great darkness. *My faith* however is not troubled,—nor even perplexed,—by the strangeness of these things. Shall I think it a mere matter of course that one little flaw in a pipe shall, in a second of time, transform the orderly well-compacted seats of a goodly Church to one unsightly mass of shapeless and disordered ruin[h]; and shall I pretend to stand aghast at the strangeness of a similar overthrow of this Earth's furniture at the mere fiat of the Most High? .... Behold, "He measureth the waters in the hollow of His Hand, and weigheth the mountains in scales[i]." What if the Creator of the earth and the sea shall bid them of a sudden change places? Think you that they would hesitate to obey Him? Or what if He "calleth for the waters of the Sea, and *poureth them out upon the face of the Earth*[j]?"—Then further, if I believe, (as I *do* believe,) that when the Jews crucified the LORD of Glory "there was darkness over all the land" from the sixth hour unto the ninth[k];—nay, that when "Moses stretched forth his hand toward Heaven, there was a thick darkness in all the land of Egypt," even darkness which might be felt, for three whole days[l]:—

[h] Alluding to a catastrophe which had recently occurred at St. Mary's Church, and which necessitated considerable repairs; in consequence of which, the first four of these Sermons were preached in the Cathedral.
[i] Is. xl. 12. [j] Amos v. 8 and ix. 6.
[k] St. Matth. xxvii. 45. [l] Exod. x. 21—23.

more than *that;* if I believe, (as I *do* believe,) the solemn prediction of my Lord, that at the consummation of all things, "The Sun shall be darkened, and the Moon shall not give her light, and the Stars shall fall from Heaven ᵐ:"—shall it move me to incredulity, if God tells me, that six thousand years ago it was His Divine pleasure that the same phenomenon should prevail for a season? Surely,—(I say to myself,)—surely this is He "which removeth the mountains, and they know not: which shaketh the Earth out of her place, and the pillars thereof tremble. *Which commandeth the Sun, and it riseth not; and sealeth up the Stars* ⁿ *!*"

1. But it was now God's pleasure to bring Beauty out of Chaos, and to establish a fresh order of things upon the surface of our Earth. And, as the first step thereto, "the Spirit of God moved upon the face of the waters." The Hebrew phrase implies no less than the tremulous brooding as of a bird,—causing the dreary waste to heave and swell with coming life. "And God said, Let there be Light. And there was Light." "He spake and it was done º." From Himself, who is "the true Light," (not from the Sun, which,—like the rest of the orbs of Heaven,—is but a lamp of His kindling);—from Himself, I say, a ray of Light went forth; and *that* is why He was pleased to praise it. Look through the chapter, and you will find that it is the only one of His creatures of which it is specially said that "God saw that it was good ᵖ." ...
Thus, one hemisphere was illumined,—whereby "God divided the light from the darkness;" and when the Earth had completed a single revolution, there had

---

ᵐ St. Matth. xxiv. 29.   ⁿ Job ix. 5—7.
º Ps. xxxiii. 9.   ᵖ Gen. i. 4.

been a Day and there had been a Night,—so named by the Word of God: "and the evening and the morning were the first Day[q]." ... Do you see any impossibility so far? I, certainly, see none. It does not seem to me absurd that "the Light of the world[r]," "dwelling in the light which no man can approach unto[s]," should cause "the light to shine out of darkness[t]." We shall perhaps come upon the absurdity by and by. Let us hasten forward.

2. "And God said, Let there be a firmament in the midst of the waters, and let it divide the waters from the waters." The Hebrew word (*an expansion*), and the context, shew plainly enough what is meant. The atmosphere was now created,—whereupon the watery particles either subsided into sea, or rose aloft in the form of clouds. "And the evening and the morning were the second Day,"—which is the only day of which it is not said that God saw that it was good.

3. "And God said, Let the waters under the Heaven be gathered together unto one place, and let the dry land appear." Then it was that these continents were upheaved,—other than those which had been continents before; and the sea sank into the cavities which had been ordained for its reception. *Then*, "God saw that it was good." The sentence of approval which had been withheld from the work of yesterday, because that work, (namely, of dividing the

---

[q] "Can any one sensible of the value of words suppose," (asks Mr. Goodwin,) "that nothing more is here described, or intended to be described, than *the partial clearing away of a fog?*" (*Essays and Reviews*, pp. 227-8.) No one,—we answer. But to the question, we venture to rejoin another. To *whom* does this philosopher suppose his pleasantry likely to prove injurious? Is he making Moses ridiculous, or—himself?

[r] St. John ix. 5, &c.   [s] 1 Tim. vi. 16.   [t] 2 Cor. iv. 6.

waters from the waters,) was incomplete,—is freely bestowed to-day. And it may have been to teach us that no incomplete work is "good," in God's sight.— Next, the Creator called into being every extant form of vegetable life. So that, instead of a world of waters, which was all that was to be seen yesterday,—not only cliffs, and mountains, and bays,—but green hills, and fertile valleys, and grassy meadows had come to view,—with lakes, and rivers, and fountains, and falls of water. Again it is written, concerning Earth's green furniture, "God saw that it was good." "And the evening and the morning were the third Day."

4. "And God said, Let there be Lights in the firmament of the Heaven to divide the day from the night: and let them be for signs, and for seasons, and for days, and for years." And so it was. Sun, moon, and stars, came to view[n]; and this globe of ours, no longer illumined, as, for three days, it had been, rejoiced in the sun's genial light by day,—and by night in the splendours of the paler planet. And thus was also gained an easy measure for marking time,—the succession of months and years, as well as of days. "And God saw that it was good." "And the evening and the morning were the fourth Day."

5. "And God said, Let the waters bring forth abundantly the moving creature that hath life." Thus the inhabitants of the sea and of the air were called into existence; and it was from the sea that God seems to have commanded that they should derive their being. He saw that it was good, and He blessed

[n] "Whether the writer regarded them as already existing, and only waiting to have a proper place assigned them, may be open to question." (*E. and R.*, p. 221.) We accept the alternative given us by Mr. Goodwin.

the fish and the winged fowl; "and the evening and the morning were the fifth Day."

6. It remained only to provide for the dry land its occupants; and the Earth was accordingly commanded to bring forth the living creature after his kind,—beast and cattle and creeping thing. Unlike that first Creation which was of all things out of nothing, the work of the six days was a creation of new things out of old.—To the Creation of Man, His crowning work, God is declared to have come with deliberation; as well as to have announced His purpose with significant solemnity of allusion. "Let us make Man in our image, after our likeness; and let them have dominion over the fish of the sea, and over the fowl of the air, and over the cattle." "And the Lord God formed Man of the dust of the ground, and breathed into his nostrils the breath of life; and Man became a living soul."—Transferred to the Garden of God's planting in Eden, to dress it and to keep it, (for inactivity is no part of bliss!)—and brought into solemn covenant with God,—to Adam, God brings the beasts of the field and the fowls of the air, of set purpose that God may "see *what he will call them:*" a wondrous tribute, truly, to the perfection of understanding in which Man had been created!... "And the Lord God caused a deep sleep to fall upon Adam, and he slept: and He took one of his ribs, and closed up the flesh instead thereof; and the rib which the Lord God had taken from man, made He a woman, and brought her unto the man. And Adam said, This is now bone of my bone, and flesh of my flesh: she shall be called woman, because she was taken out of man. Therefore shall a Man leave his Father and his Mother, and shall cleave unto his wife, and they shall be one flesh."...

Man's creation was the crowning wonder, to which all else had, in a manner, tended.... Truly when we think of him,—newly made in God's image,—surveying this world, yet fresh with the dew of its birth, and beautiful as it came from the Hands of its Maker,—it seems scarcely the language of poetry that then " the morning stars sang together and all the sons of God shouted for joy [v]."

I have preferred thus to complete the history of Man's Creation; which presents us with the primal institution of all,—that, namely, of Marriage.—" On the seventh Day, God rested from all His work which He had made; and blessed the seventh Day, and sanctified it; because that in it He had rested from all His work."—This then is the other great primæval institution; more ancient than the Fall,—the Law of the Sabbath;—which in the sacred record is brought into such august prominence. And never do we ponder over that record, without apprehension at what may be the possible results of relaxing the stringency of enactments which would seem to be, to our nature, as the very twin pillars of the Temple, —its establishment and its strength [x].

Now, on a review of all this wondrous History, I profess myself at a loss to see what special note of impracticability it presents that I should hesitate to embrace it, in the plain natural sense of the words, with both the arms of my heart. That it is not such an account of the manner of the Creation as you or I should have ourselves invented, or anticipated, or on questionable testimony have felt disposed to accept, —is very little to the purpose. Apart from Revelation, we could really have known nothing at all

[v] Job xxxviii. 7.   [x] Alluding to 1 Kings vii. 21.

about the works of the Days of the first Great Week. Ejaculations therefore concerning the strangeness of the record, and cavils at the phraseology in which it is propounded, are simply irrelevant.

There exists however a vague suspicion after all that the beginning of Genesis is a vision, or an allegory, or a parable,—or anything you please, except true History. It is hard to imagine *why*. If there be a book in the whole Bible which purports to be a plain historical narrative of actual events, *that* book is the book of Genesis. In nine-tenths of its details, it is as *human*, and as matter of fact, as any book of Biography or History that ever was penned. *Why* the first page of it is to be torn out, treated as a myth or an allegory, and in short explained away,—I am utterly at a loss to discover. There is no difference in the style. Long since has the theory that Genesis is composed of distinguishable fragments, been exploded[r]. There is no pretence for calling this first chapter poetry, and treating it by a distinct set of canons. It is a pure *Revelation*, I admit: but I have yet to learn why the revelation of things intelligible, where the method of speech is not such as to challenge a figurative interpretation, is not to be taken literally: unless indeed it has been discovered that a narrative must of necessity be fabulous if the transactions referred to are unusually remote and extraordinary. The events recorded are unique in their character,—true.

[r] The test of *Elohim* and *Jehovah* has been, by the Germans themselves, given up; "and for this plain reason,—that in many parts of Genesis, [e. g. ch. xxviii. 16—22: xxxi.: xxxix., &c.] it is utterly untenable; the names being so intermingled as to admit of no such division." See the Appendix (C) to the Rev. Henry John Rose's *Hulsean Lectures* for 1833,—p. 233.

But this happens from the very necessity of the case. The creation of a world, to the inhabitants of that world is an unique event.

But we are assured that some of the statements in this first chapter of Genesis are palpably untrue;—as when it is said that the Sun, Moon, and Stars were created on the fourth Day,—which, it is urged, is a physical impossibility: for what forces else sustained, and kept this world a sphere? The phenomena of Geology again prove to demonstration, it is said, that the structure of the earth is infinitely more ancient than the Mosaic record states: and also that there must have been Light, and sunshine too, at that remote epoch,—which fostered each various form of animal and vegetable life.—Further, we are assured that it is unphilosophical to speak of the creation of Light before the creation of the Sun.—Then, the simplicity of the language is objected to:—" the greater light to rule the day, and the lesser light to rule the night:"—" dividing the light from the darkness:"—" waters above the firmament:" and so forth. The very ascription of speech to GOD, gives offence.—Again, some raw conceit of the advanced state of the human intellect rejects with scorn the notion of Adam oracularly bestowing names on GOD's creatures. Finally, the creation of Eve, moulded by GOD from the side of the Protoplast, is declared to savour so plainly of the mythical, allegorical, or figurative; that the narrative must be allowed to be altogether unworthy of such wits as ours.

But we have seen that *the creation* of Sun, Moon, and Stars is *not* assigned to the fourth day—but to " *the beginning.*"—The antiquity of this Earth we affirm to be a circumstance left wholly untouched by the Mosaic record: or, if touched, it is rather confirmed; for, before beginning to describe the work of the first Day, Moses describes the state of "the Earth" by two Hebrew words of most rare occurrence[z], which denote that it had become waste and empty: while "the deep" is spoken of as being already in existence.—There is nothing at all unphilosophical in speaking of Light as existing apart from the Sun. Rather would it be unphilosophical to speak of the Sun as the source and centre of Light.—I see nothing more childish again in the mention of "the greater and the lesser light," than in the talk of "sun-rise" and "sun-set,"—which is to this hour the language of the Observatory.—As for attributing speech to GOD, I am content to remind you of Hooker's explanation of the design of Moses therein, throughout the present Chapter. "Was this only his intent," (he asks,) "to signify the infinite greatness of GOD's power by the easiness of His accomplishing such effects without travail, pain, or labour? Surely it seemeth that Moses had herein besides this a further purpose; namely, first to teach that GOD did not work as a necessary, but a voluntary agent, intending beforehand and decreeing with Himself that which did outwardly proceed from Him; secondly, to shew that GOD did then institute a Law natural to be observed by Creatures, and therefore according to the manner of laws, the institution thereof is described, as being established by solemn injunction. His commanding those things to be which are, and to be in such sort as they are, to keep that tenure and course which they do, importeth

---

[z] Besides in Gen. i. 2, the expression (*tohu bohu*) recurs in Jer. iv. 23 and Is. xxxiv. 11,—both times with clear reference to the earlier place. Jeremiah in fact *quotes* Genesis.

the establishment of Nature's Law. .... And as it cometh to pass in a kingdom rightly ordered, that after a Law is once published, it presently takes effect far and wide, all states framing themselves thereunto; even so let us think that it fareth in the natural course of the world. Since the time that GOD did first proclaim the edicts of His Law upon it, Heaven and Earth have hearkened unto His voice, and their labour hath been to do His will[a]."—"*He spake the word,* and they were made: He commanded and they were created. He hath made them fast for ever and ever. *He hath given them a law which shall not be broken*[b]."

Whether or no South overestimated Adam's knowledge, I will not pretend to decide: but I am *convinced* the truth lies more with him than with certain modern wits, when he says concerning our first Father:— "He came into the world a philosopher; which sufficiently appeared by his writing the nature of things upon their names ... His understanding could almost pierce into future contingents; his conjectures improving even to prophecy, or the certainties of prediction. Till his Fall, he was ignorant of nothing but sin ... There was then no struggling with memory, no straining for invention. His faculties were ready upon the first summons ... We may collect the excellency of the understanding *then*, by the glorious remainders of it now: and guess at the stateliness of the building by the magnificence of its ruins ... And certainly that *must* needs have been very glorious, the decays of which are so admirable. He that is comely when old and decrepit, surely was *very* beautiful when he was young! An Aristotle was but the rubbish

[a] *Eccl. Pol.*, B. I. c. iii. § 2.   [b] Ps. cxlviii. 5, 6.

of an Adam; and Athens but the rudiments of Paradise ᶜ."

And lastly, as for so much of the Divine narrative as concerns the Creation of the first human pair, I am content to remind you of a circumstance which in addressing believers ought to be of overwhelming weight: namely, that our SAVIOUR and His Apostles, again and again, refer to the narrative before us in a manner which precludes the notion of its being anything but severest History. Our SAVIOUR CHRIST even resyllables the words spoken by the Protoplast in Paradise; and therein finds a sanction for the indissoluble nature of the marriage bond ᵈ.

I take leave to add that even the respectful attempt to make Genesis accommodate itself to the supposed requirements of Geology, by boldly assuming that the days of Creation were each a thousand years long,—seems inadmissible. Even were such an hypothesis allowed, nothing would be gained: for *Geology* does not by any means require us to believe that after a thousand years of misty light, there came a thousand years of ocean deposit: and again, a thousand years of moist and dry, during which vegetable life alone prevailed: and then a thousand years of sun, moon, and stars. The very notion seems absurd ᵉ.—But,

---

ᶜ South's *Sermons*, (Serm. II.)

ᵈ See St. Matth. xix. 4 to 6,—where Gen. i. 27 as well as Gen. ii. 24, are quoted by our SAVIOUR.

ᵉ "Holding," (says Hugh Miller,) "that the *six* days of the Mosaic account were not natural days, but lengthened periods, I find myself called on, as a geologist, to account for but three out of the six. Of the period during which light was created; of the period during which a firmament was made to separate the waters from the waters; or of the period during which the two great lights of the earth, with the other heavenly bodies, became visible from

what is more to the purpose, such an interpretation seems to stultify the whole narrative. A *week* is described. *Days* are spoken of,—each made up of *an evening and a morning*. God's cessation from the work of Creation on the Seventh Day is emphatically adduced as the reason of the Fourth Commandment,— the mysterious precedent for *our* observance of one day of rest at the end of every six days of toil,— "*for* in six days" (it is declared,) "the LORD made Heaven and Earth'." You may not play tricks with language plain as this, and elongate a week until it shall more than embrace the span of all recorded Time.

Neither am I able to see what would be gained by proposing to prolong the Days of Creation indefinitely, so as to consider them as representing vast and unequal periods; (though I am far from presuming to speak of *any* pious conjecture with disrespect.) My inveterate objection to this scheme is again twofold. (1) The best-ascertained requirements of Geology are *not satisfied* by a *sixfold* division of phenomena corresponding with what is recorded in Genesis of the Six Days of Creation. (2) This method does even greater violence to the letter of the inspired narrative than the scheme of reconcilement last hinted at.

I dare not believe that what has been spoken will altogether meet the requirements of minds of a certain

---

the Earth's surface;—we need expect to find no record in the rocks."
—*Testimony*, &c., p. 134.—This is ingenious, and is piously meant. But the first three days remain to be accounted for *by somebody*, all the same. If the last three days represent "lengthened periods," so, I suppose, do the *first* three.

' Exod. xx. 11.

stamp. A gentleman, who certainly has the advantage of appearing in good company, has lately favoured the world with the information that the first chapter of Genesis is the uninspired speculation of a Hebrew astronomer, who was bent on giving "the best and most probable account that could be then given of God's universe[g]." The Hebrew writer asserts indeed "solemnly and unhesitatingly that for which he must have known that he had no authority[h];" but we need not therefore "attribute to him wilful misrepresentation, or consciousness of asserting that which he knew not to be true[i]." If this "early speculator" "asserted as facts what he knew in reality only as probabilities," it was because he was not harassed by the scruples which result "from our modern habits of thought, and from the modesty of assertion which the spirit of true science has taught us[j]." The history of this important discovery and of others of a similar nature, (which, by the way, are one and all announced with the same "modesty of assertion" as what goes before,) would appear to be this.—Natural science has lately woke up from her long slumber of well nigh sixty ages; and with that immodesty for which youth and inexperience have ever been proverbial, she is impatient to measure her crude theories against the sure revelation of God's Word. Where the two differ, she assumes that of course the inspired Oracles are wrong, and her own wild guesses right. She is even indecent in her eagerness to invalidate the testimony of that Book which has been the confidence and stay of God's Servants in all ages. On any evidence, or on none, she is prepared to hurl to the winds the

[g] *Essays and Reviews*, p. 252. [h] *Ibid.*
[i] *Id.* p. 253. [j] *Id.* p. 252.

august record of Creation. Inconveniently enough
for the enemies of God's Word, every advance in
Geological Science does but serve to corroborate the
record that the Creation *of Man* is not to be referred
to a remoter period than some six thousand years ago.
But of this important fact we hear but little. On the
other hand, no trumpet is thought loud enough to
bruit about *a suspicion* that Man may be a creature of
yet remoter date. Thus, fragments of burnt brick found
fifty feet below the surface of the banks of the Nile,
were hailed as establishing Man's existence in Egypt
more than 13,000 years; until it was unhappily remembered that *burnt* brick in Egypt belongs to the
period of the Roman dominion.—More recently, implements of chipped flint found, with some bones, in
a bed of gravel, have been eagerly appealed to as
a sufficient indication that the Creation of Man is to
be referred to a period at least 10,000 years more remote than is fixed by the Chronology of the Bible.
. . . Brick and flint! a precious fulcrum, truly, for
a theory which is to upset the World!

But I shall be told,—with that patronizing air of
conscious intellectual superiority which a certain class
of gentlemen habitually assume on such occasions,—
that I mistake the case completely: that no wish is
entertained in any quarter to invalidate the truth of
Revelation, or to shake Men's confidence in the Bible
as the Word of God: that it has been the way of
narrow-minded bigots in all ages, and is so in this,
to raise an outcry of the Bible being in danger, and
so to rouse the prejudices of mankind: that the error
lies in claiming for the Bible an office which it nowhere claims for itself, and which it was never meant
to fulfil: that the harmony between the Bible and

Nature is complete, but that it is not *such* a harmony as is sometimes imagined : that the Bible is not a scientific book, and was never meant to teach Natural Science : that it was designed to inculcate moral goodness, and is clearly full of unscientific statements, which it is the office of Science to correct; and, if need be, to remove. All this, and much beside, I shall be told. Such fallacious platitudes have been put forth by men who are neither Divines nor Philosophers, *ad nauseam*, within the last forty or fifty years.

Now, in reply, we have a few words to say. The profession of faithfulness we hail with pleasure : the imputation of imbecility we accept with unconcern. But when gentlemen tell us that the Bible was never meant to teach Science ; and that wherever its statements are opposed to the clear inductions of reason, they must give way ; and so forth : we take the liberty of retaliating their charge. We inform them that *they* really mistake the case entirely. When they go on to tell us that they believe in the truth of the Bible as sincerely as ourselves : that its harmonics are complete, but not such as we imagine ; and so forth ;— we venture to add that they really know not what they assert. In plain language, they talk nonsense. Of a simple unbeliever we know at least what to think. But what is to be thought of persons who disbelieve just whatever they dislike, and yet profess to be just as hearty believers as you or I ?

That the Mosaic record of Creation has been thought at variance with certain deductions of modern observation, is not surprising : seeing that the deductions of each fresh period have been at variance with the deductions of that which went before ; and seeing that the theory of one existing school is inconsistent with the theory of another.—That the Bible is not, in any sense, *a scientific treatise* again, is simply a truism: (who ever supposed that it was?). Moses writes "the history of the Human Race as regards Sin and Salvation: not a cosmical survey of all the successive phenomena of the globe[k]." Further, that he employs popular phraseology when speaking of natural phenomena, is a statement altogether undeniable. But such remarks are a gross fallacy, and a mere deceit, if it be meant that the statements in the Bible partake of the imperfection of knowledge incident to a rude and primitive state of society. To revive an old illustration,—Is a philosopher therefore a child, because, in addressing children, he uses language adapted to their age and capacity? GOD speaks in the First Chapter of Genesis,—*hath* spoken for three and thirty hundred years,—as unto children: but there is no risk therefore that in what He saith, He either hath deceived, or will deceive mankind.

You are never to forget the great fundamental position, that the Bible claims to be the Word of GOD; and that *GOD'S Word can never contradict* or *be contradicted by GOD'S works*. We therefore reject, *in limine*, all insinuations about the "unscientific" character of the Bible. A scientific man does not cease to be scientific because he does not choose always to express himself scientifically. Again. A man of universal Science does not forfeit his scientific reputation, if, in the course of a *moral* or *religious* argument, his allusions to *natural* phenomena are expressed in the ordinary language of mankind. Even so, Almighty GOD, "in whom are hid all the treasures of wisdom

---

[k] Pattison's *The Earth and the World*, p. 99.

and knowledge[1]," — speaking to us by the mouth of His holy Prophets, never, that I am aware, teaches them to speak a strictly scientific language, — *except when the Science of Theology is being discoursed of.* On other occasions, He suffers their language to be like yours or mine. " Sun, stand thou still upon Gibeon[m]:" — "The clouds drop down the dew[n]:" — "The wind bloweth where it listeth[o]." — Not so when *Theology* is the subject. *Then* the language becomes scientific. " Except a man be born of water and of the Spirit, he cannot enter into the Kingdom of God[p]:" — "Take, eat, This is My Body[q]:" — " Before Abraham was, I am[r]:" — " I and the FATHER are One[s]."

But there is this great difference between the cases supposed. A man of universal scientific attainment will be less strong in one subject than another: and in the course of his *Geological* allusions, if *Mechanical* Science be his forte, — in the course of his *Metaphysical* allusions, if *Mathematical* Science be his proper department, — he may easily err. Above all, the limits of the knowledge of unassisted Man must infallibly be those of the age in which he lives. But, with the Ancient of Days, it is not so. *He* at least *cannot* err. Nothing that man has ever discovered by laborious induction was not known to Him from the beginning: nothing that *He* hath ever commissioned His servants to deliver, will be found inconsistent with the anterior facts of History. " He that *made* the eye, shall *He* not see[t]?" The records of Creation then *cannot* be incorrect. The course of Man's history *must* be that

---

[1] Col. ii. 3.   [m] Josh. x. 12.   [n] Prov. iii. 20.
[o] St. John iii. 8.   [p] St. John iii. 5.
[q] St. Matth. xxvi. 26.   [r] St. John viii. 58.
[s] St. John x. 30.   [t] Ps. xciv. 9.

which, speaking by the mouth of His Prophets, GOD hath described.

"I never said the contrary," is the reply. "All I say is that you interpret the records of Creation wrongly: and that you are disposed to lay greater stress on the historical accuracy of the Bible than the narrative will bear."

O but, sir, whoever you may be who censure me thus, let me in all kindness warn you of the pit, at the very edge whereof you stand!

Far be it from such an one as the preacher to assume that he so apprehends the First Chapter of Genesis, that if an Angel were to turn interpreter, he might not convince me of more than one misapprehension in matters of detail. But of this, at least, I am *quite* certain; that when I find it recorded that GOD took counsel about Man's Creation: and made him in "His own image," and "breathed into his nostrils the breath of life," whereby man became "a living soul:" and further, when I find it stated that Adam bestowed names upon all creatures: and spake oracularly of his spouse:—I am *certain*, I say, when I read such things, that GOD intended me to believe that Man was created with a Godlike understanding, and with the perfect fruition of the primæval speech. Further, I boldly assert that he who could prove the contradictory, would make the Bible, even as a Theological Book, nothing worth, to you and me.

The same must be said of the Bible chronology. And here I will adopt the words of one who is justly entitled to be listened to in this place; and who must at least be allowed to be a competent judge of the matter, for he made Chronology his province. Mr. Clinton says:—"Those who imagine themselves at liberty to enlarge the time [which elapsed from the Creation to the Deluge, and from the Deluge to the Birth of Abraham,] to an indefinite amount,—mistake the nature of the question. The uncertainty here is not an uncertainty arising from want of testimony: (like that which occurs in the early chronology of Greece, and of many other countries; when the times are uncertain because no evidence is preserved.) . . . The uncertainty here is of a peculiar character, belonging to this particular case. The evidence exists, but in a double form; and we have to decide which is the authentic and genuine copy. But if the one is rejected, the other is established:" the difference between the two being exactly 1,250 years.—Men are free to *reject* the evidence, to be sure; but we defy them to *explain it away.* The chronological details of the Bible are as emphatically set down as anything can be; and,—(with the exception of a few particulars, chiefly in the Book of Kings, which are to the record what misprints are to a printed book,)—they are entirely consistent; and hang perfectly well together. Let us not be told, then, that we entertain groundless apprehensions for the authority of God's Word when we hear it proposed to refer the Creation of Man to a period of unheard-of antiquity. Destroy my confidence in the Bible as an historical record, and you destroy my confidence in it altogether; for by far the largest part of the Bible *is* an historical record. If the Creation of Man,—the longevity of the Patriarchs,—the account of the Deluge;—if *these* be not true histories, what is to be said of the lives of Abraham, of Jacob, of Joseph, of Moses, of Joshua, of David,—of our Saviour Christ Himself?

But there is a scornful spirit abroad which is not

content to allegorize the earlier pages of the Bible,—to scoff at the story of the Flood, to reject the outlines of Scripture Chronology;—but which would dispute the most emphatic details of Revelation itself. Consistent, this method is, at all events. Let it have the miserable praise which is so richly its due. To logical consistency, it may at least lay claim. It refuses to stop anywhere: as why should it stop? Faith is denied her office, because Reason fails to see the reasonableness of Faith: and accordingly, unbelief enters in with a flood-tide. Miracles, for example, are now to be classed, (we learn,) among "the difficulties" of Christianity[u]. It was to have been expected. (*Who foresees not what must be the fate of such "difficulties" as these?*) And will you tell me that you may reject the miraculous transactions recorded in the Old and New Testaments, and yet retain the narrative which contains them? That were indeed absurd! Will you then reject one miracle and retain another? Impossible! You can make no reservation, even in favour of the Incarnation of our LORD,—the most adorable of all miracles, as it is the very keystone of our Christian hope. Either, with the best and wisest of all ages, you must believe *the whole* of Holy Scripture; or, with the narrow-minded infidel, you must *dis*believe the whole. There is no middle course open to you.

Do we then undervalue the discoveries of Natural Science; or view with jealousy the progress she has of late been making? GOD forbid! With unfeigned joy we welcome her honest triumphs, as so many fresh evidences of the wisdom, the power, the goodness of GOD. "Thou, LORD, hast made me glad

[u] On this subject, the reader is referred to Serm. VII.

through Thy works[x]!" The very guesses of Geology are precious. What are they but noble endeavours to unfold a page anterior to the first page of the Bible; or rather, to discover what secrets are locked up in the first verse of it? But when, instead of being a faithful Servant, Natural Science affects the airs of an imperious Mistress,—what can she hope to incur at the hands of Theology, but displeasure and contempt? She forgets her proper place, and overlooks her lawful function. She prates about the laws of Nature in the presence of Him who, when He created the Universe, invented those very laws, and impressed them on His irrational creatures.—Does it never humble her to reflect that it was but yesterday she detected the fundamental Law of Gravitation? Does she never blush with shame to consider that for well nigh six thousand years men have been inquisitively walking this Earth's surface; and yet, that, one hundred years ago, the prevalent notions concerning fossil remains, and the Earth's structure, were such as now-a-days would be pronounced incredibly ridiculous and absurd?

To conclude. The very phraseology with which men have presumed to approach this entire question, is insolent and unphilosophical. The popular phraseology of the day, I say, hardly covers, so as to conceal, a lie. We constantly find SCIENCE and THEOLOGY opposed to one another: just as if Theology were *not* a Science! History forsooth, with all her inaccuracy of observation, is a Science: and Geology, with all her weak guesses, is a Science: and comparative Anatomy, with nothing but her laborious inductions to boast of, is a Science: but Theology,—which is based

[x] Ps. xcii. 4.

on the express revelation of the Eternal,—is some other thing! What do you mean to tell us that Theology is, but the very queen of Sciences? Would Aristotle have bestowed on Ethic the epithet ἀρχιτεκτονική, think you, had he known of that θεῖος λόγος, which his friend,—"not blind by choice, but destined not to see [y],"—felt after yet found not? that "more excellent way," which you and I, by GOD's great mercy, possess? Go to! For popular purposes, if you will, let the word "Science" stand for the knowledge of the phenomena of Nature; somewhat as, in this place, the word stands for the theory of Morals, and some of the phenomena of Mind: and so, let SCIENCE be contrasted with THEOLOGY, without offence taken, because none is intended. But let it never be forgotten that Theology is *the* great Science of all, —the only Science which really deserves the name. What have other sciences to boast of which Theology has not? Antiquity,—such as no other can, in any sense, lay claim to: a Literature,—which is absolutely without a rival: a Terminology,—which reflects the very image of all the ages: Professors,—of loftier wit, from the days of Athanasius and Augustine, down to the days of our own Hooker and Butler,— men of higher mark, intellectually and morally,— than adorn the annals of any other Science since the World began: above all things, a subject-matter, which is the grandest imagination can conceive; and a foundation, which has all the breadth, and length, and depth and height [z], which the Hands of GOD Himself could give it.

For subject-matter, what Science will you compare with this? All the others in the world will not bring

[y] Cowper.   [z] Eph. iii. 18.

a man to the knowledge of GOD and of CHRIST! They will not inform him of the will of GOD, although they may teach him to observe His Works. "The Heavens declare the glory of GOD,"—but, as Lord Bacon remarked long since, we do not read that they declare His will. Neither do the other sciences of necessity lead to any belief at all in the GOD of Revelation [a].

And, for that whereon they are built, what Science again will you compare with this? Let the pretender to Geological skill,—(I say not the true Geologist, for *he* never offends!)—let the conceited sciolist, I say, go dream a little longer over those implements of chipped flint which have called him into such noisy activity, —and discover, as he *will* discover, that the assumed inference from the gravel and the bones is fallacious after all [b].—Let the Historian go spell a little longer over that moth-eaten record of dynasties which never were, by means of which he proposes to set right the clock of Time [c]. Let the Naturalist walk round the stuffed or bleached wonders of his museum, and guess again [d]. Theological Science not so! *Her* evidence is sure, for her Rule is GOD's Word. No laborious Induction here,—fallacious because imperfect; imperfect because human: but a direct message from the presence-chamber of the LORD of Heaven and Earth, —decisive because inspired; infallible because Divine. The express Revelation of the Eternal is that whereon Theological Science builds her fabric of imperishable

[a] This paragraph is mostly copied from a Sermon (MS.) preached before the University by the late Professor Hussey, Oct. 12, 1856.

[b] Professor Phillips refers me to a paper by Mr. Prestwich in the *Proceedings of the Royal Society*, 1859, vol. x. No. 35, p. 58. Also in the *Transactions of the R. S.* for 1860, p. 308.

[c] I allude to the supposed disclosures of Egyptian monuments.

[d] I allude to a recent work on the Origin of Species.

Truth: *that* fabric which, while other modes change, shift, and at last become superseded, shines out,—yea, and to the very end of Time will shine out,—unconscious of decay, incapable of improvement, far, far beyond the reach of fashion: a thing unchanged, because in its very nature unchangeable [e]!

O sirs,—we are constrained to be brief in this place. The field must perforce be narrowed; and so, for this time, it must suffice to have warned you against the men who resort to the armoury of Natural Science for weapons wherewith to assail God's Truth. Regard them as the enemies of your peace; and learn to reject their specious, yet most inconsequential reasonings, with the scorn which is properly their due. Contempt and scorn God implanted in us, precisely that we might bestow them on reasonings worthless in their texture, and foul in their object, as these; which teach distrust of the earlier pages of God's Word, on the pretence that they are contradicted by the evidence of God's Works. Learn to abhor that spurious liberality which is liberal only with what is *not its own;* and which reminds one of nothing so much as the conduct of leprous persons who are said to be for ever seeking to communicate and extend their own unhappy taint to others. I allude to that sham liberality which under pretence of extending the common standing ground of Christian men, is in reality attenuating it until it proves incapable of bearing the weight of a single soul. There is room on the Rock for all; but it is only on the Rock that we are safe. To speak without a figure,—He who surrenders the first page of his Bible, surrenders all. He knows not

---

[e] The reader is requested to read what Bishop Pearson has most eloquently written on this subject. It will be found in the Appendix (B).

where to stop. Nay, you and I cannot in any way *afford* to surrender the beginning of Genesis; simply because upon the truth of what is there recorded depends the whole scheme of Man's salvation,—the need of that "second Man" which is "the LORD from Heaven[f]." It is not too much to say that the beginning of Genesis is the foundation on which all the rest of the Bible is built[g]. We may not go over to those who would mutilate the Book of Life, or evacuate any part of its message. It is they, on the contrary, who must come over to us.—Much has it been the fashion of these last days, (I cannot imagine why,) to vaunt the character and the Gospel of St. John, "the disciple of Love," as he is called; as if it were secretly thought that there is a latitudinarianism in Love which would wink at Doctrinal obliquity; whereas *St. John is the Evangelist of Dogma;* and if there be anything in the world which is *jealous*, that thing is *Love*. Indifference to Truth, and laxity of Belief, are the growing characteristics of the age. But you will find that St. John has about four or five times as much about TRUTH as all the other three Evangelists; while *the act* of Faith receives as frequent mention in his writings alone as in all the rest of the New Testament Canon put together[h].

Let me end, as the manner of preachers is, by gathering out of what has been spoken one brief practical consideration.—This whole visible frame of things wherein we play our part, is hastening to decay. Everything we behold,—ourselves included,—carries

[f] 1 Cor. xv. 47. [g] Ibid. xv. 22, &c.
[h] Πίστις *does not occur once* in St. John's Gospel: πιστεύω (which is found about thirty-five times, in all, in the first three Gospels,) occurs about *one hundred times*, in the Gospel of St. John alone.

with it the prophecy of its own speedy dissolution.—What, amid the wreck of worlds, will be our confidence? . . . It is an inquiry worth making, in these the days of health, and vigour, and security, and peace. O my soul, (learn to ask yourselves,)—O my soul, when the Heavens shall depart, and the Earth reel before the Second Advent of its Maker;—when the Sun puts on mourning, and the very powers of Heaven are shaken;—what shall be *our* confidence,—*our* hope,—in that tremendous day? Whither shall we betake ourselves, amid the overthrow of universal Nature, but to the sure mercies of Him who " in the beginning created the Heaven and the Earth?"—To those strong Hands, we intend, (GOD helping us!) with unswerving confidence to commend our fainting spirits[l]. . . . *Him*, then, in life let us learn to reverence, on whom in death we propose so implicitly to lean! And we only know Him in, and through, and by His WORD. Nor can we in any surer way shew Him reverence or dishonour, than by the manner in which we receive His message,—yea, by the spirit in which we unfold this, the first page of it,—where stands recorded that primæval act of Almighty power which is the ground of all our confidence,—the very warrant for our own security. . . . " Blessed" of a truth, in that day, will he be, "that hath the GOD of Jacob for his help, and whose hope is in the LORD his GOD:—*who made the Heaven and the Earth,—the Sea and all that therein is:—who keepeth His promise for ever*[k]*!*"

[l] St. Luke xxiii. 46, (quoting Ps. xxxi. 5:) words which are alluded to in 1 St. Pet. iv. 19.

[k] Ps. cxlvi. 5,—words quoted by the early Church of Jerusalem, Acts iv. 24.

SERMON III.[a]

INSPIRATION OF SCRIPTURE.—GOSPEL DIFFICULTIES.—
THE WORD OF GOD INFALLIBLE.—OTHER SCIENCES
SUBORDINATE TO THEOLOGICAL SCIENCE.

2 TIM. iii. 16.

All Scripture is given by inspiration of God.

BUT *that* is not exactly what St. Paul says. The Greek for *that*, would be πᾶσα Ἡ γραφή—not πᾶσα γραφή—θεόπνευστος. St. Paul does not say that *the whole* of Scripture, collectively, is inspired. More than *that:* what he says is, that *every writing*,—every *several book* of those ἱερὰ γράμματα, or Holy Scriptures, in which Timothy had been instructed from his childhood,—is inspired by GOD[b]. It *comes* to very nearly the same thing; but it is *not* quite the same thing. St. Paul is careful to remind us that every Book in the Bible is an inspired Book[c]. And

---

[a] Preached in Christ-Church Cathedral, 25th Nov. 1860.

[b] Πᾶσαι αἱ θεόπνευστοι γραφαί,—as it is worded in the Epistle sent by the Council of Antioch in the case of Paul of Samosata, A.D. 269. (Routh *Reliqq.* iii. 292.) See Middleton *on the Greek Article*, (Rose's ed.) *in loc.* And so, in effect, Wordsworth and Ellicott.—It is right to add that it has been contended that πᾶσα γραφή = "the whole of Scripture." See Lee *on Inspiration*, p. 263, (note.) So Athanasius seems to have taken it: Πᾶσα ἡ καθ' ἡμᾶς γραφή, παλαιά τε καὶ καινή, θεόπνευστός ἐστι. (*Ep. ad Marcell.* i. 982.)

[c] That θεόπνευστος is the predicate, seems sufficiently obvious. So Athanasius, in the passage above quoted. So Gregory of Nyssa: διὰ τοῦτο πᾶσα γραφὴ θεόπνευστος λέγεται, διὰ τὸ τῆς θείας ἐμπνεύσεως

this statement is not confined to one place.—Elsewhere, he calls his message "the Word of God;" and says that it had been received by the disciples not as the Word of Men, but as it is in truth, the Word of God [d].—Elsewhere, "Which things also we speak, not in the words which man's wisdom teacheth, but which the HOLY GHOST teacheth [e]:"—where, if I at all understand the Apostle, (and he speaks very plainly!) he says that *his words* were inspired by the HOLY GHOST.—Accordingly, St. Peter declares that the Epistles of his "beloved brother Paul" are part of the Holy Scriptures [f];—Divinely inspired, therefore, like all the rest.

But does not St. Paul himself in a certain place express a doubt—saying "*I think* that I have the Spirit of God [g]?" and does he not contrast his own sayings with the Divine sayings, ("not I but the

---

εἶναι διδασκαλίαν. (*Contr. Eunom.* Orat. VI. ii. 605.) Amphilochius, Bishop of Iconium, quotes the place in the same way.—Basil also, saying—Πᾶσα γραφὴ θεόπνευστος καὶ ὠφέλιμος, διὰ τοῦτο συγγραφεῖσα παρὰ τοῦ Πνεύματος, (*Hom. in Psalm.* I. i. 90,)—clearly adopts the construction assumed in the text.—Ambrose (*De Spir. Sancto*, lib. II. c. 16. ii. 688,) says,—"In Scriptura Divina, θεόπνευστος omnis ex hoc dicitur, quod Deus inspiret quæ locutus est Spiritus." (The above are from Lee *on Inspiration*, which see, pp. 260, 493, 599.)—Tertullian (quoted by Tisch.) says, "Legimus omnem Scripturam ædificationi habilem, divinitus inspirari."—A few modern scholars have suggested that θεόπν. may be an epithet, not a predicate. The *doctrine* will remain the same either way; for the meaning of the place can only be, "Every Scripture, *being* inspired, *is also* profitable," &c. This is Origen's view: but his criticism is not in point, inasmuch as he read the text differently, (omitting the καί.) Lee aptly compares the construction of, πᾶν κτίσμα Θεοῦ καλὸν, καὶ οὐδὲν ἀπόβλητον. (1 Tim. iv. 4.)

[d] 1 Thess. ii. 13.   [e] 1 Cor. ii. 13.
[f] 2 St. Pet. iii. 16,—where see Wordsworth.
[g] 1 Cor. vii. 40.

Lord ʰ"), clearly implying that his own were *not* Divine? and does he not say that he delivers certain things "by permission, and not of commandment ¹," whereby he seems to insinuate a gradation of authority in what he delivers?—No. Not one of these things does he do. He says, indeed, of a certain hint to married persons that he offers it "by way of *advice* to them not by way of *precept:*" but *giving advice to men* is a very different thing from *receiving permission* from God. Again, "Unto the married," (he says,) "I command, yet not I but the Lord,"—alluding to our Lord's words, as set down by St. Matthew, chap. xix. verse 6 ᵏ; which is simply an historical allusion to the Gospel.—So far from "*thinking*" he had the Spirit of God, (as if it were an open question whether he had it or not,) he says the very contrary. Δοκέω, in all such places, implies, not *doubt* but *certainty* ¹: (as when our Lord asks,—"Doth he thank that servant because he did the things commanded him? οὐ δοκῶ,"—I fancy not indeed ᵐ!) On St. Paul's lips, as every scholar knows, the phrase is not one of doubt, but one of indignant, or at least emphatic asseveration ⁿ.—A man had need be very sure he *understands* the record, (let me just remark in passing,) before he presumes to criticize it.

• "*The Spirit of Christ*" is said by St. Peter to have

ʰ 1 Cor. vii. 10.

¹ 1 Cor. vii. 6. (Τοῦτο δὲ λέγω κατὰ συγγνώμην, οὐ κατ' ἐπιταγήν.)

ᵏ St. Matth. xix. 6 (= St. Mark x. 9:) and the following places, —St. Matth. v. 32 : xix. 9 (=St. Mark x. 11, 12.): St. Luke xvi. 18.

¹ Montfaucon, *præf. ad Euseb. Comm. in Psalm.*, cap. x. See also Æsch. Prom. V. v. 289.

ᵐ St. Luke xvii. 9. So St. Mark x. 42. St. Luke viii. 18. St. John v. 39.

ⁿ Comp. 1 Cor. iv. 9: Gal. ii. 9: Heb. iv. 1.

been "*in the prophets*[o]:" and in another place he declares that they "*spake as they were moved by the* HOLY GHOST[p]." The HOLY GHOST accordingly is said to have spoken the xlist Psalm "by the mouth of David[q]." The xcvth Psalm is declared absolutely to be the utterance of the HOLY GHOST[r]. Once, the cxth Psalm is ascribed simply to GOD[s]; and once, to David speaking under the influence of *the* HOLY GHOST[t]. The iind Psalm is described as the language of GOD the FATHER "by the mouth of His Servant David[u]." "*Well spake the* HOLY GHOST *by Esaias the Prophet unto our Fathers*[x]," — was the exclamation of the Apostle Paul, quoting the 9th and 10th verses of his vith chapter. When Jeremiah speaks, the HOLY GHOST is declared, (not Jeremiah, *but the* HOLY GHOST) to witness unto us[y]. The assertion is express that it was "GOD" who, "*by the mouth of all His Prophets*," foretold the Death of CHRIST[z]: "*the* LORD GOD *of Israel*" who, "*by the mouth of His holy Prophets of old*," gave promise of CHRIST's coming[a]. "*The* HOLY GHOST *signified*"

[o] Τὸ ἐν αὐτοῖς Πνεῦμα Χριστοῦ.—1 St. Pet. i. 11.

[p] ὑπὸ Πνεύματος Ἁγίου φερόμενοι ἐλάλησαν οἱ ἅγιοι Θεοῦ ἄνθρωποι.— 2 St. Pet. i. 21. (*lit.* "impelled,"—like a ship before the wind.)

[q] προεῖπε τὸ Πνεῦμα τὸ Ἅγιον διὰ στόματος Δαβίδ.—Acts i. 16.

[r] καθὼς λέγει τὸ Πνεῦμα τὸ Ἅγιον.—Heb. iii. 7.

[s] ὑπὸ τοῦ Θεοῦ.—Heb. v. 10.

[t] Δαβὶδ εἶπεν ἐν τῷ Πνεύματι τῷ Ἁγίῳ.—St. Mark xii. 36.

[u] ὁ Θεὸς ὁ ποιήσας τὸν οὐρανὸν καὶ τὴν γῆν καὶ τὴν θάλασσαν καὶ πάντα τὰ ἐν αὐτοῖς, ὁ διὰ στόματος Δαβὶδ τοῦ παιδός σου εἰπών.—Acts iv. 24, 25.

[x] τὸ Πνεῦμα τὸ Ἅγιον ἐλάλησε διὰ Ἡσαΐου τοῦ προφήτου.—Acts xxviii. 25.

[y] μαρτυρεῖ δὲ ἡμῖν καὶ τὸ Πνεῦμα τὸ Ἅγιον—Heb. x. 15, quoting Jer. xxxi. 33, 34.

[z] ὁ δὲ Θεὸς . . . . προκατήγγειλε διὰ στόματος πάντων τῶν προφητῶν αὐτοῦ παθεῖν τὸν Χριστὸν.—Acts iii. 18.

[a] Κύριος ὁ Θεὸς τοῦ Ἰσραὴλ . . . . ἐλάλησε διὰ στόματος τῶν ἁγίων τῶν ἀπ' αἰῶνος προφητῶν αὐτοῦ.—St. Luke i. 68, 70.

what the Mosaic Law enjoined [b]. "It is not ye that speak, *but the* HOLY GHOST [c],"—was our SAVIOUR's word of promise and of consolation to the Twelve: and, on an earlier occasion,—"It is not ye that speak; but the SPIRIT of your Father, *which speaketh in you* [d]." And this promise became so famous, that St. Paul says the Corinthians challenged him to *prove* that CHRIST was speaking in him [e]. . . . But why multiply places? The use which our SAVIOUR makes in the New Testament of the words of the Old,—from the writings of Moses to the writings of Malachi,—would be simply nugatory unless those words were much more than human. And the record of the Apostle is express and emphatic:—"All Scripture—every Book of the Bible,—is given *by Inspiration of* GOD."—In the face of such testimony, by the way, we deem it not a little extraordinary to be assured (by an individual who has acquired considerable notoriety within the last few months) that "for any of the higher or supernatural views of Inspiration there is no foundation in the Gospels or Epistles [f]."

Strange to say, there is a marvellous indisposition in Man to admit the notion of such a heaven-sent message. Not to dispute with those who deny Inspiration altogether, (for that would be endless,) there are many,—and, we fear, a daily increasing number of persons,—who, admitting Inspiration in terms, yet so mutilate the notion of it, that their admission be-

[b] τοῦτο δηλοῦντος τοῦ Πνεύματος τοῦ Ἁγίου.—Heb. ix. 8.

[c] οὐ γάρ ἐστε ὑμεῖς οἱ λαλοῦντες, ἀλλὰ τὸ Πνεῦμα τὸ Ἅγιον.—St. Mark xiii. 11.

[d] οὐ γὰρ ὑμεῖς ἐστε οἱ λαλοῦντες, ἀλλὰ τὸ Πνεῦμα τοῦ Πατρὸς ὑμῶν τὸ λαλοῦν ἐν ὑμῖν.—St. Matth. x. 20.

[e] ἐπεὶ δοκιμὴν ζητεῖτε τοῦ ἐν ἐμοὶ λαλοῦντος Χριστοῦ.—2 Cor. xiii. 3.

[f] Rev. B. Jowett, in *E. and R.*,—p. 345. Yet see Acts iii. 18, 21.

comes a practical lie. "St. Paul was inspired, no doubt. So was Shakspeare." He who says this, intending no quibble, declares that in his belief St. Paul was *not inspired at all.*

But this is a monstrous case, with which I will not waste your time. Far more numerous are they, who, admitting that the Authors of the Bible were inspired in quite a different sense from Homer and Dante, are yet for modifying and qualifying this admission after so many strange and arbitrary fashions, that the residuum of their belief is really worth very little. One man has a mental reservation of exclusion in favour of the two Books of Chronicles, or the Book of Esther, or of Daniel.—Another, is content to eliminate from the Bible those passages which seem to him to run counter to the decrees of physical Science;—the History of the Six Days of Creation,—of the Flood,—of the destruction of Sodom,—and of Joshua's address to Sun and Moon.—Another regards it as self-evident that nothing is trustworthy which savours supremely of the marvellous;—as the Temptation of our first Parents,—the Manna in the Wilderness,—Balaam reproved by the dumb ass,—and the history of Jonah.—There are others who cannot tolerate the Miracles of the Old and the New Testament. The more timid, explain away as much of them as they dare. What remains, troubles them. The more logical sweep them away altogether. A miracle (they say) cannot be true because it implies a violation of the fixed and immutable laws of Nature.

And then,—(so strangely constituted are some men's minds,)—there are not a few persons who, without exactly denying the inspiration of the Bible in any of its more marvellous portions,—(for *that* would be an inconvenient proceeding,)—are yet content to regard much of it as a kind of inspired myth. This is a class of ally (?) with whom one really knows not how to deal. The man does not reason. He assumes his right to disbelieve, and yet will not allow that he is an unbeliever. The world is singularly indulgent toward persons of this unphilosophical, illogical, presumptuous class.

Now, I shall have something to say to all these different kinds of objectors, on some subsequent occasion. But I shall be rendering the younger men a far more important service if to-day I address my remarks to a different class of objectors altogether: *that* far larger body, I mean, who without at all desiring to impugn the Inspiration of God's Oracles, yet make no secret of their belief that the Bible is full of inaccuracies and misstatements. These men ascribe a truly liberal amount of human infirmity to the Authors of the several Books of the Bible;—slips of memory, misconceptions, imperfect intelligence, partial illumination, and so forth;—and, under one or other of those heads, include whatever they are themselves disposed to reject. The writers who come in for the largest share of this indulgence, are the Evangelists; because the Historians of our Lord's life, having happily left us four versions of the same story, and often three versions of the same transaction, the evidence whereby *they* may be convicted of error is in the hands of all. Truly, mankind has not been slow to avail itself of the opportunity. You will seldom hear a Gospel difficulty discussed, without a quiet assumption on the part of the Reverend gentleman that *he* knows all about the matter in question, but that the Evangelist did *not*. His usual method is, calmly to inform us that it is useless to look for strict consistency in matters of minute detail; that *general agreement* between the four Evangelists there does exist, and *that* ought to be enough. The inevitable inference from his manner of handling the Gospels, is, that if his actual thoughts could find candid expression, we should hear him address their blessed authors somewhat as follows:—" You are four highly respectable characters, no doubt; and you *mean* well. But it cannot be expected that persons of your condition in life should have described so many intricate transactions so minutely without making blunders. I do not say it unkindly. I often make blunders myself,— *I*, who have a "clearness of understanding," "a power of discrimination between different kinds of Truth[g]" unknown to the Apostolic Age !" . . . Of course the preacher does not *say* all this. He has too keen a sense of "the dignity of the pulpit." And so he puts it somewhat thus:—" While we are disposed to recognize substantial agreement, and general conformity in respect of details, among the synoptical witnesses, in their leading external outlines, we are yet constrained to withhold our unqualified acceptance of any theory of Inspiration which should claim for these compilers exemption from the oscitancy, and generally from the infirmities of humanity." . . . This sounds fine, you know; and is thought an ingenious way of wrapping up the charge which the Reverend preacher brings against the Evangelists;—of having, in plain terms,—*made blunders*.

It will be convenient that we should narrow the ground to this single issue: for the time is short. And in the remarks I am about to offer, I shall not

[g] Dr. Temple, in *Essays and Reviews*, p. 25.

imitate the example of those preachers who dress out an easy thought in a superfluity of inflated language, only in order that its deformity may escape detection. Be not surprised if I speak to you this morning in uncommonly plain English; for I am determined that the simplest person present shall understand at least what *I* mean. The dignity of the Blessed Evangelists, who walked with JESUS, and whom JESUS loved,—the dignity of that Gospel which I believe to be penetrated through and through with the Holy Spirit of GOD,—for *that*, I confess to a most unbounded jealousy. As for the "dignity of the pulpit,"—I hate the very phrase! It has been made too often the shield of impiety and the cloak of dulness.

To begin, then,—Is it, I would ask you, a reasonable anticipation that the narrative of one inspired by GOD would prove full of inconsistencies, misstatements, slips of memory:—or indeed, that it should contain *any* misstatements, *any* inaccuracies at 'all? What then is the difference between an inspired and an uninspired writing,—the Word of GOD and the Word of Man?

The answer which I shall receive, is obvious. As a matter of fact (it is replied) there *are* these inaccuracies: that is, the same transaction is described by two or more writers, and their accounts prove inconsistent. Thus, St. Matthew begins his account of the healing of the blind at Jericho, with the words,—"And as they were *going out* of Jericho:" but St. Luke, "While He was *drawing nigh* to Jericho."—There *are* these slips of memory; as when St. Matthew ascribes to "Jeremy the prophet" words which are found in the prophet Zechariah.—There *are* these misstatements, as where the Census of the Nativity is said to have taken place under the presidentship of Cyrenius.—And these are but samples of a mighty class of difficulties, (it is urged:)—the two Genealogies; the Call of the four Disciples; the healing of the Centurion's servant; the title on the Cross; the history of the Resurrection:—and again, "the sixteenth of Tiberius;" "the days of Abiathar;" with many others.—Let me then briefly discuss the three examples first cited,—which really came spontaneously. Each is the type of a class; and the answer to one is, in reality, applicable to all the rest. I humbly ask for your patience and attention; promising that I will abuse neither, though I must tax both.

The great fundamental truth to be first laid down, is *this*,—that the Gospels are not *four*—but *one*. The Ancients knew this very well. Εὐαγγελισταὶ μὲν τέσσαρες,—Εὐαγγέλιον δὲ ἕν—says Origen[h]: "the Gospel-*writers* are four,—but the *Gospel* is one." And the ancients recorded this mighty verity four times over on the first page of the Gospel, lest it should ever be forgotten; and there it stands to this day:—the Gospel,—the *one* Gospel κατὰ,—*according to*—St. Matthew,—*according to* St. Mark,—*according to* St. Luke,—*according to* St. John. Like that river which went out of Eden to water the Garden,—it was by the HOLY GHOST "parted, and became into four heads."—The Gospels therefore, (to call them by their common name,) are not to be regarded as four witnesses, or rather as four culprits, brought up on a charge of fraud. Rather are they Angelic voices singing in sweetest harmony, but after a method of Heavenly counterpoint which must be studied before it can be understood of Men.

[h] *Contra Marcion*, sect. I. p. 9.

And next,—There is one great principle, and one only, which needs to be borne in mind for the effectual reconciliation of *every discrepancy* which the four narratives present: namely, that you should approach them in exactly the same spirit in which you approach the statement of any man of honour of your acquaintance. Whether the Apostles of the LAMB,—men whom we believe to have been inspired by the Holy Spirit of the Everlasting GOD,—are not entitled to far higher respect, far higher consideration, at our hands,—I leave *you* to decide. As one whose joy and crown it has been to weigh every word in the Gospel in hair-scales, I am prepared to risk the issue. Be only as fair to the four Evangelists as you are to one another; and I am quite confident about the result.

I appeal to the experience of every thoughtful man among you who has at all given his mind to the subject of evidence, whether it be not the fact,—(1st) That when two or more persons are giving true versions of the same incident, their accounts will sometimes differ so considerably, that it will seem at first sight as if they could not possibly be reconciled: and yet (2ndly), That a single word of explanation, the discovery of one minute circumstance,—perfectly natural when we hear it stated, yet most unlikely and unlooked-for,—will often suffice to remove the difficulty which before seemed unsurmountable; and further, that when this has been done, the entire consistency of the several accounts becomes apparent; while the harmony which is established is often of the most beautiful nature. (3rdly) That when (for whatever reason) two or more versions of the same incident are *not* correct, no ingenuity can ever possibly reconcile them, *as they stand*. They lean apart in hopeless divergence. In other words, they *contradict* one another.

Now, these principles are fully admitted in daily life. If your friend comes to you with ever so improbable a tale, the last thing which enters into your mind is to disbelieve him. Is he in earnest? Yes, on his honour. Is he sure he is not mistaken? *That* very doubt of yours requires an apology: but your friend says,—"I am as sure as I am of my existence." "Give it me under your hand and seal then." Your friend begins to suspect your sanity; but the matter being of some importance, he complies. "It must be so then," you exclaim, "though I *cannot* understand it." . . . . I only wish that men would be as fair to the Evangelists as they are to their friends!

You are requested to observe,—for really you *must* admit,—that *any* possible solution of a difficulty, however *improbable* it may seem, any *possible* explanation of the story of a competent witness, is enough logically and morally to exempt that man from the imputation of an incorrect statement. The illustration which first presents itself may require an apology; but the dignity of the pulpit shall not outweigh the dignity of *His* Gospel after whose blessed Name this House is called[1]: and I can think of nothing as apposite as what follows.

It is a conceivable case, that, hereafter, three persons of known truthfulness should meet, in a Court of Justice at the Antipodes; where the entire difficulty should turn on a question of time. The case is conceivable, that the first should be heard to declare that at Oxford, on such a day, of such a year, he had seen

---

[1] See the first foot-note, p. 53.

such an one standing before Carfax Church while the clock *was striking one:*—that the second should declare that he also, on the same day of the same year, had seen the same person passing by St. Mary's, when the clock of *that* Church was also striking one:—that the third should stand up and assert,—" I also saw the same person on that same day, but it was on the steps *of the Cathedral* I met him; and I also remember hearing the clock at that moment strike one."—Now I can conceive that the result of such evidence would be adverted upon in some such way as the following: —" While we are disposed to recognize the substantial agreement, and general conformity in respect of details, among the synoptical witnesses, in their leading external outlines, we are yet constrained,"— and the rest of the impertinence we had before. Whereas you and I know perfectly that the three clocks in question were, till lately, *kept five minutes apart:* a sufficient interval, (I beg you to observe in passing,) for the individual in question to have been seen *by you* walking in an easterly direction; and *by me* due west; and by a third person, due east again. Highly improbable circumstances, I freely grant, every one of them; and yet, by the hypothesis, all perfectly *true!* Meantime, it is conceivable that Judge and jury would have the indecency openly to tax the three men I spoke of with inexactitude in their statements: and it is conceivable that those three honest men—(the *only* true men, it might be, in the Colony, after all,)—would carry to their grave the imputation of untruth. Here and there, a generous heart would be found to say to them,—*I* share not in the vulgar cry against you! *I* nothing doubt that it all fell out precisely as you assert. Either,

F

the clocks in Oxford went wrong that day;—or there had been some trick played with the clocks;—any how, *I* believe *you*, for I have evidence that you are marvellously exact in all your little statements; and you cannot have been mistaken in a plain matter like this. I have heard too that you are not the ordinary men you seem. . . . . The men make no answer. *They* care nothing for *your opinion*, and *my opinion*. The rashness of mankind may astonish the Angels perhaps; but the Apostles and Evangelists of CHRIST are already safe within the veil!

The difficulty supposed is not an imaginary one. St. John says that when Pilate sat in judgment on the LORD of Glory, "it was about the sixth hour[j]." But since St. Mark says that at the third hour they crucified Him[k],—the two statements seem inconsistent. The ancients,—(giants at interpretation, babes in criticism,)—*altered the text*. Peter, Bishop of Alexandria, A.D. 300, says that he had seen it in the very autograph of St. John[l]. A learned man of our own, however, a hundred years ago, ascertained that, in the Patriarchate of Ephesus, the hours were not computed after the Jewish method: but, (strange to say,) exactly *after our own English method*[m]. And yet, not so strange either; for the Gospel first came to us from there.—You see at a glance that all the four mentions of time of day in St. John[n], which used to occasion so much difficulty, become beautifully intelligible at once.

[j] St. John xix. 14.   [k] St. Mark xv. 25.
[l] The passage may be seen in John Bois' *Vet. Interpretis cum Bezâ aliisque recentioribus collatio*, (1655,) p. 333.
[m] See a Dissertation by Dr. Townson at the end of his admirable book on the Gospels.
[n] Viz. St. John i. 39: iv. 6, 52: xix. 14.

To come then to the three samples of difficulty propounded a moment ago. And first, for the blind men of Jericho.

I. The difficulty lies all on the surface. Listen to a plain tale.

Our SAVIOUR, attended by His Disciples and followed by a vast concourse of persons, had reached the outskirts of Jericho. A certain blind man was sitting by the roadside begging. He heard the noise of a passing crowd, and inquired what it meant? He was told that Jesus of Nazareth was passing by. He rose at once,—hastened down the main street through which, in due time, CHRIST perforce must come; joined another blind man, (named Bartimæus, —a well-known character, who, like himself, was accustomed to sit and beg by the road side;) and the two companions in suffering, having stationed themselves at the exit of Jericho, waited till the Great Physician should appear.

The crowd begins to approach; and the two blind men implore the Son of David to have pity on them. So importunate is their suit, that the foremost of the passers-by rebuke them. The men grow more urgent. Our SAVIOUR pauses, and orders that they shall be called. At this gracious summons, both draw near; the more remarkable applicant flinging his outer garment from him as he rises from his seat; but both, when they appear in our SAVIOUR's presence, making the same request. The Holy One, touched with compassion, laid His Hands upon their eyes, and grants their prayer: whereupon they both follow Him in the way.

Well, (you will ask,)—what then?—"What then?" I answer. *Then* there is no difficulty in the three accounts about which you spoke so unbecomingly a moment ago. Assume this plain, and not at all improbable version of the incident, to be true, and you will find that no difficulty remains whatever. Every recorded circumstance is accounted for, and fits in exactly with it. I wish there were time to enlarge on some of the details, and to make some remarks on the manner of the Evangelists in relating events: but there *is* no time. Besides,—without a huge copy of the Gospel open before us all, I could not hope to make my meaning understood.

For of course you are to believe that he who would understand the Gospel must first *study* it. You must ascertain, by some crucial test, confirmed by a large and careful induction, what the character of a narrative purporting to be inspired, *is*. You have no right first to assume exactly *what* Inspiration shall result in, and then to deny that there is Inspiration because you fail to discover your assumed result[o]. That were foolish.

I shall perhaps be thought to lay myself open to the rejoinder,—"Neither have *you* any right to assume that Inspiration will result in Infallibility." But the retort is without real point. I do but assert that, just as every man of honour claims to be believed until he has been convicted of a falsehood,—inspired Prophets, Evangelists, and Apostles have a right to our entire confidence in the scrupulous accuracy of every word they deliver, until it can be *shewn* that they have once made a mistake.

If you will take the trouble to compare any of the

[o] And yet, we hear it asserted that we cannot "suppose the Spirit of absolute Truth" "to suggest accounts *only to be reconciled in the way of hypothesis and conjecture.*"—*E. and R.*, p. 179.

cases,—in Genesis for example,—where a conversation is first set down, and then reported by one of the speakers,—you will find that it is deemed allowable to omit or to add clauses, even when the discourse is related in the first person [p]. Something before inserted, is withheld: or something before withheld, is inserted. No discourse was probably ever set down, word for word, as it was delivered. In sacred, as in profane writings, the exact *substance*, or rather, the real *purport*, of what was spoken, very reasonably stands for what was *actually* spoken. The difference is this;—that a narrative, by man abridged, *may* convey a wrong impression: whereas an inspired abridgement of any history soever *cannot* mislead.

Other characteristics of an inspired narrative,—the lesser Laws of the Divine Harmony, as they may be called,—will be discovered by the attentive reader. For example, that intervening circumstances are often passed over, without any notice taken of them whatever: while yet it is singular how often the Evangelist shews himself conscious of what he omits by some very minute allusion to it [q]. This must suffice however. It would require a whole sermon, a whole volume rather, to enumerate all the features of the Evangelical method.

[p] E.g. Gen. xxiv. 2—8, compared with ver. 37—41; and again, ver. 12—14, compared with ver. 42—44. Again, Gen. xlii. 10—13, compared with ver. 31, 32: and again, ver. 14—16, compared with ver. 33, 34. Again, Gen. xlii. 36—8, compared with xliv. 27—29, &c., &c., &c.

[q] Instances of this will be very familiar to every attentive student of the Gospels. Thus St. Matth. xxvi. 68 implies acquaintance with a minute circumstance which is stated in St. Luke xxii. 64:— St. Matth. x. 13 *implies* what is *expressed* in St. Luke x. 5, &c., &c., &c.

II. The next sample of difficulty will not occupy us long. St. Matthew is charged with a bad memory, because he ascribes to "Jeremy the prophet[r]" words which are said to be found in Zechariah.—Strange that men should be heard to differ about a plain matter of fact! *I* have never been able to find these words in Zechariah yet! . . . There are words *something like them*,—but not those very words, by any means,—in Zech. xi. 12. Why then is St. Matthew to be taxed with a bad memory? Are there not other prophecies quoted in the New Testament not to be found in the Old? Yes[s]. Is not the selfsame prophecy sometimes found in two different prophets,—as in Isaiah and Nahum? Yes[t]. Are not some prophetic passages *common to Jeremiah and Zechariah?* Yes[u]. The Jews even had a saying that the Spirit of the one was in the other. *Where* then remains a pretence for supposing that St. Matthew was troubled with a bad memory?

III. So, it is generally assumed that St. Luke made a mistake when he said that the census of the Nativity was made when Cyrenius was President of Syria,—because not Cyrenius but *Varus* is known to have been President about that time.—Now, there are three fair conjectures,—each of which is sufficient to meet this difficulty: but instead of developing them, I will simply remind you of a minute circumstance in Jewish story which shews how dangerous it is to press a general fact against a particular statement.—

---

[r] St. Matth. xxvii. 9.   [s] E.g. St. Jude ver. 14, 15.

[t] Is. lii. 7, and Nahum i. 15.—Is. ii. 2, 3, 4, and Micah iv. 1, 2, 3.—Micah iv. 6, and Zeph. iii. 19.—Is. xi. 9, and Hab. ii. 14.—Micah iii. 12, and Jer. xxvi. 18, &c., &c.

[u] E.g. Jer. xxiii. 5 and Zech. vi. 13.

In the year 4 B.C., Matthias was undeniably the Jewish High-priest. Now, if St. Luke, describing the events of a certain day in September, B.C. 4, had recorded that the High-priest's name was *Joseph*, you would have thought him guilty of a misstatement: but the error would have been all your own,—for it has been discovered that a person bearing that name held the office of High-priest for *one single day*,—namely, the 10th of Tisri. ... "A very unlikely circumstance!" you will exclaim. O yes,—*a very unlikely circumstance indeed:* but, you will have the kindness to observe that *that* is not exactly the point in question.

Why then are difficulties of this, or of any kind, permitted in the Gospel at all? it may be asked.— I answer,—that they may prove instruments of probation to you and to me. The sensualist has *his* trials; and the ambitious man, *his*. . The difficulties in Holy Scripture,—which are numerous, and diverse, and considerable,—are admirable tests of the moral, the spiritual, the intellectual temper of Man[x]. Experience shews moreover that some of the minutest discrepancies of all, if they be but of a character almost hopeless, are more potent to create perplexity in minds of a certain constitution, than the gravest doubts which ever burthened the soul of Speculation.

I have confined myself to one class of objections, for an obvious reason. Difficulties which arise out of the *matter* of Scripture, as it is emphatically embodied in quotations from the Old Testament made in the New, must be separately considered in one or more Sermons on *Interpretation*. I must be content to-day with repudiating, in the most unqualified way,

---

[x] See Appendix (C).

the notion that a mistake of *any kind whatever* is consistent with the texture of a narrative inspired by the Holy Spirit of God. The allusion in St. Stephen's speech to "the sepulchre that Abraham bought for a sum of money of the sons of Emmor, the son" (not *the father*, but *the son*) "of Sychem," is a good example of confusion apparently existing in an inspired speaker; but, in reality, only in the writings of those who have sat in judgment upon his words[y].

To keep to the case of the Evangelists,—I appeal to your sense of fairness, whether it be not reasonable to assume, that until those blessed writers have been convicted of *one* single inaccuracy of statement, their narratives ought to be accounted faultless, like Him whose Life they record;—like Him by whose Spirit they are inspired. I would to Heaven that men would have the decency to suspect themselves, and one another, rather than the Evangelists,—of mistake; or at least, before they venture publicly to impugn the Authors of the Everlasting Gospel, that they would be at the pains to weigh the evidence with the care *that* evidence deserves, but which I am *sure* that sermon-writers and essayists do not bestow. Let them spend the long summer days of many a Long Vacation— from early morning until twilight,—dissecting every syllable of the blessed pages; and then they will learn to adore instead of to cavil. They will deem them absolutely faultless, instead of daring to charge all their own pitiful misconceptions, and weak misapprehensions, and miserable blunders, upon *them*. —They will be inclined, rather, to challenge the world to establish one blot in what they love so well;

[y] See Appendix (D).

and would gladly stake all upon the issue of a conflict before a fair tribunal,—if submission might follow upon defeat.

As for mistakes of the paltry kind last noticed—(the days of Abiathar, the sixteenth of Tiberius, and so forth,)—I wonder the glaring absurdity of charging them against Evangelists, does not strike any modest man of sane mind. To suppose that St. Matthew quoted the wrong prophet, or that St. Luke did not know the regnal years of the reigning Emperor; that St. Stephen confused Abraham with Jacob, and Sychem with Hebron;—all this is really so *grossly* absurd, that I can hardly condescend to discuss the question. It is like maintaining that Sir Isaac Newton, after discovering the Law of Gravitation, and calculating the pathway of a planet, persisted in saying that two and two make five: or that Columbus, after discovering America, despaired of finding the way to his own door. It is simply ridiculous!—Admirable as a subject for men to exercise their wits upon,—as instruments of *cavil*, objections like these are about as formidable as a child's sword of lathe in the day of battle.

I hear some one say,—It seems to trouble *you* very much that inspired writers should be thought capable of making mistakes; but it does not trouble *me*.—Very likely not. It does not trouble *you*, perhaps, to see stone after stone, buttress after buttress, foundation after foundation, removed from the walls of Zion, until the whole structure trembles and totters, and is pronounced insecure. Your boasted unconcern is very little to the purpose, unless we may also know how dear to you the safety of Zion is. But if you make indignant answer,—(as would to Heaven you may!)—

that your care for GOD's honour, your jealousy for GOD's oracles, is every whit as great as our own,—*then* we tell you that, on *your* wretched premises, men more logical than yourself will make shipwreck of their peace, and endanger their very souls. There is no stopping,—no knowing where to stop,—in this downward course. Once admit the principle of fallibility into the inspired Word, and the whole becomes a bruised and rotten reed. If St. Paul a little, why not St. Paul much? If Moses in some places, why not in many? You will doubt our LORD's infallibility next! ... It might not trouble *you*, to find your own familiar friend telling you a lie, every now and then: but I trust this whole congregation will share the preacher's infirmity, while he confesses that it would trouble *him* so exceedingly that after one established falsehood, he would feel unable ever to trust that friend implicitly again.

Do you mean to say then, (I shall be asked,) that you maintain the theory of Verbal Inspiration?—I answer, I refuse to accept any *theory* whatsoever[z]. But I believe that the Bible is the Word of GOD— and I believe that GOD's Word must be absolutely infallible. I shall therefore believe the Bible to be absolutely infallible, — until I am convinced of the contrary. "*Theories of Inspiration,*" (as they are called,) are the growth of an unbelieving age: and it is enough to disgust any one with the term, to find how it has been understood in some quarters. A well-known living editor of the Gospel[a], says,—" According to the Verbal-Inspiration Theory, each Evangelist has recorded the exact words of the Inscription on the Cross;—not *the general sense,* but *the Inscription itself;*

[z] See Appendix (E). [a] The Rev. H. Alford, Dean of Canterbury.

—not a letter less nor more. This is absolutely necessary to the theory." The advocates of the theory (he proceeds) " may here find an *undoubted* example of the absurdity of their view. . . . Let us bear this in mind when the narrative of words spoken, or of events, differs in a similar manner."—It is certainly very kind of the learned writer thus to apprize us of the danger of accepting a theory, which, so explained, we certainly never heard of before, — and trust we may never hear of again.

But if, instead of the "Theory of Verbal Inspiration," I am asked whether I believe *the words* of the Bible to be inspired,—I answer, To be sure I do,— every one of them: and every syllable likewise. Do not *you?*—*Where*,—(if it be a fair question,)—Where do you, in your wisdom, stop? The *book*, you allow *is* inspired. How about the chapters? How about the verses? Do you stop at the verses, and not go on to the words? Or perhaps you enjoy a special tradition on this subject, and hold that Inspiration is a general, vague kind of thing,—here more, there less: strong, (to speak plainly,) where you make no objection to what is stated,—weak, when it runs counter to some fancy of your own.—O Sir, but this "general vague kind of thing" will not suffice to anchor the fainting soul upon, in the day of trouble, and in the hour of death! " Here *more*, there *less*," will not satisfy a parched and weary spirit, athirst for the water of Life, and craving the shadow of the great Rock. What security can *you* offer *me*, that the promise which has sustained me so long occurs in the "more," and not in the "less?" How am I to know that your Bible is *my* Bible: in other words, what proof is there that either of us possesses the Word of God,—the authentic utterance of God's Holy Spirit,—*at all?*

And do you not feel, that this "will o' the wisp" phantom of your brain, can prove no guide to either of us in the pilgrimage of life? Perceive you not that the unworthy spirit in which you approach the Book of God's Law must effectually prevent you from getting any wisdom from it? Why, the pages which you look so coldly and carnally at, are written within and without, and burn from end to end with unutterable meaning! While you are quarrelling about the title on the Cross, you are missing the common salvation! You keep us, Sunday after Sunday, disputing outside the gates of Paradise, instead of bidding us enter in, and eat of the delicious fruit! While *you* are persisting that there is no beauty in the garden, (because you choose to be deaf as well as blind,)—the shadows are lengthening out, and the glory is departing, and the angels are getting weary of harping upon their harps!

No, Sirs! The Bible (be persuaded) is the very utterance of the Eternal;—as much God's Word, as if high Heaven were open, and we heard God speaking to us with human voice. Every book of it, is inspired alike; and is inspired entirely. Inspiration is not a difference of degree, but of kind. The Apocryphal books are not one atom more inspired than Bacon's Essays. But the Bible, from the Alpha to the Omega of it, is filled to overflowing with the Holy Spirit of God: the Books of it, and the sentences of it, and the words of it, and the syllables of it,—aye, and the very letters of it. "Nihil in Scripturis est otiosum," (said the great Casaubon): "non dictio, non dictionis forma, non syllaba, non littera." .... The difficulty which attends quotations, I must explain another day. It is *not* a difficulty.—The seeming paradox of calling a pedigree inspired, is only seeming.—The *text* of Holy Scripture has nothing at all to do with the question. Is a dead poet responsible for the clumsiness of him who transcribes his copy, or for the carelessness of the apprentice in the printer's attic?—Least of all do we overlook the personality of the human writers, when we so speak. The styles of Daniel,—of St. John,—of St. Paul,—of St. James,—differ as much as the sounds emitted by organ pipes of wholly diverse construction. But those human instruments were fabricated, one and all, by the Hands of the same Divine Artist: and I have yet to learn that when the same man builds an organ, fills it with breath, and performs upon it a piece of his own composition with matchless skill,—I have yet to learn that any part of the honour, any part of the praise, any part of the glory of the performance is to be withheld from *him!* ... The illustration is at least as old as Christianity itself. Pray take it in the noble words of Hooker.—" They neither spoke nor wrote one word of their own: but uttered syllable by syllable as the Spirit put it into their mouths; no otherwise than the harp or the lute doth give a sound according to the discretion of his hands that holdeth and striketh it with skill. The difference is only this: an instrument, whether it be pipe or harp, maketh a distinction in the times and sounds, which distinction is well perceived of the hearer, the instrument itself understanding not what is piped or harped. The prophets and holy men of GOD not so. 'I opened my mouth,' saith Ezekiel, 'and GOD reached me a scroll, saying, Son of Man, cause thy belly to eat, and fill thy bowels with this I give thee. I ate it, and it was sweet in my mouth as honey,' saith the prophet [b]. Yea, sweeter, I am persuaded, than either honey or the honeycomb. For herein, they were not like harps or lutes, but they felt, they felt the power and strength of their own words. When they spake of our peace, every corner of their hearts was filled with joy. When they prophesied of mourning, lamentations, and woes, to fall upon us, they wept in the bitterness and indignation of spirit, the Arm of the LORD being mighty and strong upon them [c]."

To conclude. The first time I enjoyed this privilege, I urged the younger men to a diligent and painful daily study of the Bible. On the next occasion, opening the Bible at the first page, I attempted to define the provinces of Theological and of Physical Science. All that was then offered may be summed up in one brief formula:—*GOD'S works CANNOT contradict GOD'S Word.* I adverted to the method of would-be geologists, (a class all apart from the grave and learned few who give their days and nights to a truly noble branch of study,)—because from *them* the most malignant attacks have proceeded: and I took my stand on the first chapter of Genesis, because the enemies of GOD'S Truth have made that chapter their favourite point of attack. But my argument was not directed more against Geology than against any other of the physical Sciences. They are all alike the handmaids of *Theological* Science. Geology, however, singularly honoured by the Creator in that He hath bequeathed for her inspection so many marvels of primæval Time,—evidences of how He was working in this remote planet before the Creation of Man;—Geology,

[b] Ezek. iii. 2, 3.   [c] Hooker, *Serm.* v. § 4. (*Works*, vol. iii. p. 663.)

I say, it especially behoves to be humble: partly, because she is the youngest of all the sciences; and partly, because the weak guesses of her childhood are yet in the memory of us all. If indeed she would *inherit the Earth*, let her remember that she asks for the blessing which CHRIST hath promised to none but *the meek* [d].

We altogether repudiated, then, the contrast which is often implied between Theology and Science; as if Theology were *not* a Science, but some other thing. Theological Science we declared to be the noblest of the Sciences,—the very Queen and Mistress of them all. And yet, supreme as she is, she not only admits, but desires, and thankfully accepts the ministerial offices of the other Sciences; all of which, like dutiful servants in a household, have it in their power to render her most important acts of homage. Language, for example, carries the keys of the casket wherein she keeps her treasures; and for that reason Theology hath promoted Language to great honour. History, and Geography, and Chronology, have each had their respective tasks assigned them. It is for Astronomy to make answer if question be raised of the date of Paschal full Moon, or of Eclipse. Let the physiologist explain, if he can, Scriptural allusions to the vegetable and animal kingdoms. How precious are the guesses of Geology, as she tries to fathom the Ocean of unrecorded Time!—*Who* would desire the silence of the Professor of *any* department of physical Science? Morals also have their place and their function assigned them; and a thrice blessed place,—a most holy function is theirs! Why should not Moral Science have an office even in the Court of

[d] St. Matth. v. 5.

Theology? Was not Morality the Schoolmaster of the sons of Japheth, what time there was dew on the fleece only, but it was dry upon all the earth beside? What are Morals else but the echoes of the voice of GOD yet lingering in the Hall of Conscience, or rather in the Chambers of Memory? .... Her function therefore is to bear willing witness to the Goodness, the Wisdom, the Justice of the Eternal: and her place,—the loftiest which can be imagined for a creature,—is somewhere beneath the footstool of Almighty GOD.

But when, instead of the submissive manners of a well-ordered Court, symptoms of insolence and insubordination are witnessed on every side,—then, the least and humblest takes leave, (time, and place, and occasion serving,) to speak out fearlessly on behalf of that which he loves with an unworthy, but a most undivided heart.—When Language impugns those Oracles which she was hired to decypher,—and pretends to doubt the Inspiration of that Book of which, confessedly, she barely understands the Grammar:—when History and Chronology cry out that the annals of Theology are false, and her record of Time a fable; that the Deluge, for instance, is an old wives' story, and the economy of times and seasons a human fabrication:—when Astronomical and Mechanical Science strut up to the Throne whereon sits the Ancient of Days,—prate to *Him*, (the first Author of Law,) about the "supremacy of Law,"—and tell Him to His face that His miracles are things impossible:—when Physiology insinuates that Mankind cannot be descended from one primæval pair; and that the lives of the Patriarchs cannot be such as they are recorded to have been:—when the pretender to Natural Philosophy gravely assures us that we ought not to pray for fair weather, because the weather depends *not* upon "arbitrary changes in the will of God," *but* upon laws as fixed and certain "as the laws of gravitation[g],"—which, mark you, Sirs, is no longer a dry verbal speculation, but is nothing less than an invasion of that inner chamber where you or I have retired to pour out the fulness of an aching heart, in prayer that God would prolong, if it may be, the life of the dearest thing we have on earth; and rudely to bid us rise from our knees and be silent, for that the health of Man depends not on the will of God, but on fixed physiological laws:—lastly, when the pretender to Geological skill denies the authenticity of the First Chapter of Genesis; which is to deny the Inspiration of all the rest; and therefore of the whole Bible;—and thus to rob Life's weary pilgrim of that rod and staff concerning which he has many a time exclaimed,—" they *comfort* me!":—whenever, as now, such things are spoken and printed, —not in a corner, and by insignificant persons, and in ambiguous language,—but in plain English, by clergymen and scholars in authority, openly in the face of God's sun;—then it is high time, even for the humblest and least among you,—if no man of mark will speak up, and speak out, for God's Truth,—to deliver a plain message with that freedom which Englishmen hold to be a part of their birthright. It should breed no offence, I say, if the most unworthy of God's servants, here, before you all,—before these younger men especially, who have been drawn hither by the fame of your piety and your learning,—and

[g] Professor Kingsley's Sermon,—" *Why should we pray for fair Weather?*"

who have been entrusted to your guardianship through the precious years of early manhood, with a well-grounded confidence that you would give them to eat not only of the Tree of Knowledge, but also largely of the fruit of the Tree of Life:—in this Holy House too where he received his commission[h], and vowed before GOD and Man, that he would " be ready," (the LORD being his helper,) "with all faithful diligence to drive away all erroneous and strange doctrines contrary to GOD's Word:"—before *such* an audience, and in such a place, it must and *shall* be lawful for me solemnly to denounce as false and deadly,—full of nothing but pernicious consequence,—that system of practical Infidelity which enjoys such unhappy popularity at this hour; which, under the mask of Science, and under the specious name of Progress, is spreading like a fatal contagion through the length and breadth of the land; and which, if suffered to go unchastised and unchecked, will end by shaking both the Altar and the Throne! . . . . Look well to it, Sirs, if you care for the safety of the Ark of GOD. For my part,—like one of old time whose words I am not worthy to take upon my lips,—" I cannot hold my peace: because thou hast heard, O my soul, the sound of the trumpet, the alarm of war[i] !"

The case is not altered,—rather is it made worse,—if this hostility to GOD's Truth proceeds from persons bearing Orders in the English Church. ("O my soul, come not thou into their secret!") The case is not altered: for the requirements of Physical Science are still the plea; and *Divines*, in *no* sense, these men are, however unsuccessful they may prove in establishing their claim to the title of *philosophers* either. Nay,

[h] See at the foot of p. 53, note (a).   [i] Jer. iv. 19.

Sirs,—suffer one of yourselves to ask you, whether these disgraceful developments are not the lawful result of your own incredible system, of sending forth, year by year, men to be teachers and professors of Divinity,—to whom you have yet never imparted *any Theological training whatever*[j].

You are requested to observe, that not only cannot God's Works contradict God's Word,—simply because they are twin utterances of one and the same Divine Intelligence;—but also the deductions of Physical Science cannot possibly run counter to the decrees of Theology[k],—simply because they are respectively in a wholly diverse subject-matter. Had Theology even *once* delivered a Geological decree, or pretended even *once* to pronounce upon any Astronomical problem; then, indeed, there would be reason why her disciples should watch with alarm the rapid advance of Physical Science,—instead of hailing it, as they do, with wonder and delight. Then, indeed, we should be constrained to admit that the day might be coming when Theology would have to reconsider the platform whereon she stands; and possibly to "give way." But it is an undeniable fact that there exist *no* Theological dogmas on matters Geological,—no, *not one!* Theology cannot retreat from ground on which she

---

[j] The complaint is a very old one. See Pearson's *Minor Works*, vol. i. pp. 429-30.

[k] It becomes necessary to explain, that on the Sunday after the delivery of the foregoing Sermon, a Sermon was preached *directly contravening its teaching*. Next week, it became the present writer's duty to address the same auditory,—which will explain as much of what follows in the present Sermon, (including something at p. 79,) as may seem to require explanation. It was impossible to proceed with the argument, until what had been advanced of a directly opposite tendency had been thus disposed of.

has never set foot. She cannot retract, what she has never advanced, or recal the words which she has never spoken. The decrees of Theology are all confined to the Science of Theology,—and with *that* subject-matter, the other Sciences have simply *no concern*. Their office *there*, as I have again and again explained, is simply ministerial; and when they enter the presence chamber of the great King, they are bid not to draw too nigh. "Put off thy shoes from off thy feet; for the place whereon thou standest is holy ground!"

And how about Moral Science,—whom we beheld, a moment since, shrouded in her mantle, beneath the footstool of the ALMIGHTY;—afraid to look up into His awful Face,—and not presuming to speak, unless called upon to bear her solemn witness to what she learned of Him "in the beginning?"—Must we imagine *her* too rising from her lowly seat, and presuming to sit in judgment upon the Author of her Being? Are we to picture her arraigning the Goodness of Him who commanded Abraham to slay his son;—or the Justice of Him who sent Saul to destroy the Amalekites;—or the Mercy of Him who inspired certain of David's Psalms;—or the Wisdom of Him who made the everlasting Gospel the mysterious fourfold thing it is?—Then, were she to do so, we should perforce exclaim,—This judgment of thine cannot possibly be just! For the echo *must* resemble the voice which woke it! Other spirits must have been intruding here; and the unholy din of their voices must have drowned the clear, yet still and small utterance of ALMIGHTY GOD within thy breast!.....
In other words, if there *be* antagonism, Ethics,—not Theology, *but (that which calls itself) Moral Science*,—must instantly and hopelessly give way.

For doubtless, that inference of ours as to what had happened, would be a true inference.—It *will* be the fact, I fear, before the end of all things; for it seems to be implied,—(a more heart-sickening sentence in all Scripture, I know not!),—that when the Son of Man cometh, He will not find the Faith on the Earth[1]. And if not *the Faith* (τὴν πίστιν),—what then? *The Moral Sense?* Hardly! for where was the Moral Sense when she *let go* the Faith?—It *was* the fact, (if I read the record rightly,) eighteen centuries ago: for children had then forgotten their duty to their Parents; and the sanctity of Marriage was unknown; and (O prime note of a darkened conscience!) men not only *did* things worthy of Death, but " *had pleasure in them that did them.*" Read the first chapter of St. Paul's Epistle to the Romans, and say what was *then* the condition of the Moral Sense in man. Tell me, while your cheek is yet burning, whether you think Moral Science was *then* competent to sit in judgment on a Revelation sent from the GOD of Purity, until GOD's own SON had republished the sanctions of the Moral Law, and informed Man's conscience afresh! . . . No Sirs. We are told expressly, that "as they did not like to retain GOD in their knowledge, GOD gave them over to a reprobate mind,"—" gave them up unto vile affections." And why? Hear the Apostle! It was because "when they knew GOD, they glorified Him not as GOD; neither were thankful:"—hence, they were suffered to become vain in their imaginations, and, " *their foolish heart was darkened!*"—In other words, the candle of the LORD, the light of conscience within them, was well nigh *put out.*

This will explain the reason why, when "THE

[1] St. Luke xviii. 8.

Word was made flesh and dwelt among us," He so frequently delivered precepts,—yea, preached whole Sermons,—on what would now-a-days be called mere "Morality." He was *republishing the Moral Law*. He was graving afresh those letters which had been well-nigh worn out through tract of Time, and the wear and tear of Man's ungoverned lusts.—Hence, to this hour, when question is raised of Right and Wrong,—the appeal is made, by the common consent of Christian men, *not* to the inner consciousness of the creature, but to the Creator's external Revelation of His mind and will. Let abler men explain to us what we mean when we talk about Immutable Morality. I am by no means sure that I understand myself. Sure only am I that it will carry us a very little way. Aristotle would never have made the average moral sense of mankind his standard, had *he* known of a λόγος θεόπνευστος. The principles of Morality do indeed seem to be fixed and eternal;—ἀεί ποτε ζῇ ταῦτα:—but it is no longer true, οὐδεὶς οἶδεν ἐξ ὅτου 'φάνη. Ever since the Gospel came into the world, *general opinion* has ceased to be the standard of Truth: for the Bible has simply superseded it; and put forth a standard to which "general opinion" itself must bow. "*I* am the Way, *the Truth*, and the Life." So spake the Eternal Son while yet on Earth. And He foresaw that there would come a day when the world would still ask, with Pilate, "What is Truth?" Accordingly, we heard his solemn reply in this Morning's Second Lesson—"Thy Word,"—"Thy Word is Truth." ...

"God made two great lights," I grant you: but what I maintain is, that He made "*the greater Light* to rule *the Day*."

And therefore are we very bold to assert that it is all

too late for men *now* to vaunt the authority of the Moral Sense, as a thing to be set up against the fixed and immutable Revelation of God's mind and will. "The sufficiency of Natural Religion is a paradox of modern invention, and the boast of it comes with an ill grace, and under great suspicions, so late in the day of trial[m]." Aye, it comes all too late. Here in England, (God be praised!) the moral sense is indeed strong. Is it *as* strong, think you, among those continental nations which are under the spiritual yoke of Rome? Is it as strong among the Hindoos? Is it as strong among the savage inhabitants of central Australia? ... Perceive you not that if Moral Science speaks with a loud and clear voice in Christian lands, it is because there the Moral Sense has been in those lands informed afresh by Revelation? "That the principles of Natural Religion have come to be so far understood and admitted, may fairly be taken for one of the effects of the Gospel[n]." The echoes of the voice of God are now so distinct, only because God hath suffered His awful voice to be heard on earth again: and if among ourselves those echoes are the loudest and the clearest, is it not because among ourselves the Bible is read the most?

"The fact" (says the thoughtful writer already quoted,)—"the fact is not to be denied; the Religion of Nature *has* had the opportunity of rekindling her faded taper by the Gospel light,—whether furtively or unconsciously availed of. Let her not dissemble the obligation, and make a boast of the splendour, as though it were originally her own; or had always, in her hands, been sufficient for the illumination of the World."—"It is not to be imagined that men fail to

[m] Davison's *Discourses on Prophecy*,—p. 7.   [n] *Ibid.*

profit by the light that has been shed upon them, though they have not always the integrity to own the source from which it comes; or though they may turn their back upon it, whilst it fills the very atmosphere in which they move, with glory°."

I say, therefore, that it is *all too late* to vaunt the supremacy of Conscience as opposed to Revelation,—Moral as opposed to Theological Science. Moral Science owes all its renewed strength and vigour to

---

° Davison's *Discourses on Prophecy*,—p. 8.—The following passage is from Bp. Horsley's *Primary Charge to the Clergy of Rochester*, (1796,):—"The question in this case is not abstract,—what Reason *may have* the ability to do. The question is upon a matter of fact,—*what she did*. Were these things, in point of fact, man's own discovery?—The sacred history is explicit that they were not. And notwithstanding the many useful lessons of Morality we find in the writings of the heathen sages,—the many eloquent discourses upon providence, and the immortality of the soul,—the many subtile disquisitions upon the great questions of necessity and moral freedom, upon fate and chance,—I am persuaded, that had it not been for the early communications of the Creator with mankind, Man never would have raised the conceptions of his mind to the idea of a God; he never would have dreamt of the immaterial principle within himself; and he never would have formed any general notions of Right and Wrong in the abstract; he would have had no Religion, perhaps no Morality . . . . . The prudent dispensers of the Word will resort to Revelation for his first principles, as well as for more mysterious truths. He will not trust to philosophy for any discoveries. He will suffer philosophy to be nothing more than his assistant in the study of the inspired Word. She must herself be instructed by those lively oracles before she can be qualified to take part in the instruction of men. To lay the foundation of Revelation upon any previous discoveries of Reason, is in fact to make Reason the superior teacher. It is not improbable, that Idolatry itself had its first beginning in an early adoration of this phantom of Natural Religion,—the idol, in later ages, of impolitic metaphysical Divines."—*Charges*, pp. 50, 51.—Bp. Butler says the same thing, but more briefly, in his *Analogy*, P. II., c. ii.: also P. I., c. vi.

Theology. And so, were Moral Science to dare call in question, (as she sometimes *has* done, and may dare to do again!), the Morality of the Bible,—we should find her monstrous image nowhere so fitly as in that of the man whose withered hand Christ healed in the Synagogue,—if the same man had proved such a wretch, as straightway to lift up his arm with intention to smite his Benefactor and his God.

Physical Science therefore, (for the last time!)—*all* the other Sciences,—Moral Science not excepted,—are the handmaids of Theological Science: and Morality, to which we omitted before to assign an office, we have stationed somewhere beneath the footstool, which is before the Throne, of the Most High.—But this day's Sermon, — (and with these words I conclude, sorry to have felt obliged to detain you so long!) — *this* Day's Sermon has had for its object to remind you, that THE BIBLE is none other than *the voice of Him that sitteth upon the Throne!* Every Book of it,—every Chapter of it,—every Verse of it,—every word of it,—every syllable of it,—(*where* are we to *stop?*)—every letter of it—is the direct utterance of the Most High!—Πᾶσα γραφὴ θεόπνευστος. "Well spake the HOLY GHOST, by the mouth of" the many blessed Men who wrote it.—The Bible is none other than *the Word of God:* not some part of it, more, some part of it, less; but all alike, the utterance of Him who sitteth upon the Throne;—absolute,—faultless,—unerring,—supreme!

Ἐγὼ μὲν οὖν ἰῶτα ἓν ἢ μίαν κεραίαν οὐ πιστεύω κενὴν εἶναι θείων μαθημάτων.

   ORIGENES, Comment. in S. Matth. tom. xvi. c. 12. p. 734.

Ταῦτά μοι εἴρηται . . . πρὸς σύστασιν τοῦ μηδὲν μέχρι συλλαβῆς ἀργόν τι εἶναι τῶν θεοπνεύστων ῥημάτων.

   BASILIUS, in Hex. Hom. vi. c. 11. tom. i. p. 61 c.

Scripturæ quidem perfectæ sunt, quippe a VERBO DEI, et SPIRITU ejus dictæ.

   IRENÆUS, Contr. Hær. lib. ii. c. xxviii. 2.

Μηδεμία ὑπεναντίωσις ἢ ἀτοπία ἐν τοῖς θείοις λόγοις.

   METHODIUS, Tyrius Episcopus, ap. Routh Reliqq. t. v. p. 351.

Ἔστι γὰρ ἐν τοῖς τῶν Γραφῶν ῥήμασιν ὁ Κύριος.

   ATHANASIUS, ad Marcellinum.

Ὅσα ἡ θεία γραφὴ λέγει, τοῦ Πνεύματός εἰσι τοῦ Ἁγίου φωναί.

   GREGORIUS NYSSEN. Contr. Eunom. Orat. vi.

Cedamus igitur et consentiamus auctoritati Sanctæ Scripturæ, quæ nescit falli nec fallere.

   AUGUSTINUS, De Peccator. Merit. lib. i. c. 22.

SERMON IV.*

THE PLENARY INSPIRATION OF EVERY PART OF THE BIBLE, VINDICATED AND EXPLAINED.—NATURE OF INSPIRATION.—THE TEXT OF SCRIPTURE.

St. John xvii. 17:

Thy Word is Truth.

I THANKFULLY avail myself of the opportunity which, unexpected and unsolicited, so soon presents itself, to proceed with the subject which was engaging our attention when I last occupied this place.

Let me remind you of the nature of the present inquiry, and of the progress which we have already made.

Taking Holy Scripture for our subject, and urging, as best we knew how, its paramount claims on the daily attention of the younger men,—who at present are our hope and ornament; to be hereafter, as we confidently believe, our very crown and joy;—even while we held in our hands that volume which our Fathers were content to call the volume of Inspiration, we were constrained to recollect that its claim to be inspired has of late years been repeatedly called in question. It has even become the fashion to cavil at almost everything which the Bible contains. We are

* Preached in Christ-Church Cathedral, Dec. 9th, 1860.

grown so exceedingly wise, have made so many strange discoveries, and have become so clear-sighted, that the more advanced among us are kindly bent on disabusing the minds of their less gifted brethren of that most venerable delusion of all,—(for it is coeval with Christianity,)—that the Bible is in any special sense the Word of GOD. I do not say that Theologians talk thus. But pretenders to Natural Science, knowing nothing whatever of Divinity, and therefore intruding into a realm of which they do not understand so much as the language;—together with, (sad to relate!) men bearing a commission in the Church of CHRIST, (and who ought therefore to be building up, where they are seeking to destroy,)—are employing the powers which GOD has given them, in this direction. It becomes indispensable, in consequence, that we should say somewhat on behalf of those Oracles which have been so vigorously impugned; and it should not seem strange if we oppose to such destructive dogmatism, the most uncompromising severity of counter statement.

The objections which have been raised against the Bible, although they have been industriously gleaned from various quarters, will all be most effectually met, I am persuaded, by getting men to acquaint themselves with the contents of the deposit itself. And yet, inasmuch as it is the nature of doubts, when once injected into the mind, to fester and to spread; inasmuch also as the bold confidence of plausible assertion, especially when recommended by men of reputation, and set off with some ability and skill, is apt to impose on youth and inexperience;—we seem reduced to a kind of necessity, to examine; and, as far as the limits of a sermon will allow, to refute; the charges which have been so industriously brought forward against the Bible.

The favourite objections of the day come partly from without,—partly from within. The classification is not exact, but it may serve to assist the memory. One class of objections is, in a manner, destructive,— for it results in entire disbelief of the Bible:—the other class, suggesting imperfections, results in a low and disparaging estimate of its contents. When exception is taken against certain portions of Holy Scripture, on the ground of discoveries in Physical Science, —of the dictates of the Moral Sense,—of the supremacy of mechanical Laws,—and the like,—we consider that the supposed difficulties come *from without*. As much as we care to say on this class of objections has either been already offered, or must be reserved for a subsequent occasion [b].—When doubts are insinuated, arising out of the subject-matter of the Bible, we consider the difficulties to proceed *from within*. The apparent contradictions of the Evangelists, are of this nature. Supposed errors or misstatements, come under the same head. Very imperfectly, yet sufficiently for our immediate purpose, we have touched upon both subjects. Those portions of the Old Testament which savour in the highest degree of the marvellous, must be reserved for separate consideration [c]. To-day I propose to speak of another kind of objection; but which arises, like the others, out of the subject-matter of the Bible. Moreover, it is the kind of difficulty which most readily presents itself to any who listened with unwilling ears to my last discourse. Some here present may remember my repeated and unequivocal assertion that Holy Scripture is inspired from the Alpha

[b] See Sermon VII.   [c] Ibid.

to the Omega of it;—not some parts more, some parts less, but all equally, and all to overflowing;—that we hold it to be, not generally inspired, but particularly; that we see not how with logical consistency we can avoid believing the words as well as the sentences of it; the syllables as well as the words; the letters as well as the syllables; every "jot" and every "tittle" of it, (to use our Lord's expression,) to be divinely inspired:—and further, that until the contrary has been *proved*, we shall maintain that no misapprehension or misstatement, no error or blot of any kind, can possibly exist within its pages:—that we hold the Bible to be as much the Word of God, as if God spoke to us therein with human lips;—and that, as the very utterance of the Holy Ghost, we cannot *but* think that it must be absolute, faultless, unerring, supreme.

I. To this, it has been objected as follows:—

You cannot possibly mean what you say. You will not pretend to assert that the list of the Dukes of Edom [d], is as much inspired,—inspired in *the same sense*,—as the Gospel of St. John.—To which I make answer, that I believe one to be just as much inspired as the other: and before I leave off, I will endeavour to bring my hearers to the same opinion. In the meantime, it is only fair to the objector, to hear him out: to follow his guidance; and to see whither he would lead us. It will be quite competent for us *then* to retrace our steps; to point out "a more excellent way;" and to entreat him, with all a brother's earnestness, to reconsider the matter, and to follow *us*.

The objection may, I believe, be fairly stated as follows.—It is unreasonable to consider any part of

[d] Gen. xxxvi.

Holy Scripture inspired which the author was competent to write without the aid of Inspiration. Just as you would not multiply miracles needlessly, and ascribe to special Divine interference results which might be otherwise accounted for, so neither ought you to call in the aid of Inspiration where it may clearly be dispensed with. A genealogy,—a catalogue of names, whether of places or persons,—whatever may reasonably be suspected to have been an extract from public Archives;—nothing of this sort *need* you, nor indeed, properly speaking, *can* you, call "inspired." More than that. All mere narratives of ordinary transactions,—or indeed of transactions extraordinary;—whatever, in short, a writer, having first beheld it with his eyes, appears to have simply described with his pen, it is unreasonable to regard as the work of Inspiration. For it is plain to common sense,—(so at least I have heard it said,) that there is much, both in the Old and in the New Testament, the delivery of which required no other than the ordinary gifts of men:—actual observation, good memory, high intellect, clearness of statement, honesty of purpose. Look at the preface to St. Luke's Gospel. It seems only to convey that the author of it believed himself to be bringing out a superior edition of a narrative which had already been attempted by many. I would apply, (it is said,) to the whole of the Old Testament the same observations which I apply to the New. There are parts which evidently required nothing but opportunity of experience, or research, and the ordinary qualities of a trustworthy historian.—This then is the way the case is put. There is no intentional irreverence on the part of the objector: no conscious hostility to God's Truth. Very much the reverse.

But having once assumed that the catalogue of the Dukes of Edom is not to be regarded as an inspired document, he has logical consistency enough to perceive that he cannot exactly stop *there*. And so, he carries his speculations a little further. He tries to take (what he calls) a "common sense" view of the question. He says that he thinks it a dangerous proceeding on the part of the preacher to insist on the infallibility of Apostles and Evangelists. Meanwhile, I suspect that he is not by any means without a suspicion that he is on a platform beset with *far greater dangers,* himself. He has walked a little this way, and that way; and his "common sense" has shewn him that there is an ugly precipice on every side. Nay; he perceives that the ground trembles, and cracks, and shakes,—and even yawns beneath his feet.

For I request you to observe, that there is absolutely no middle state between Inspiration and non-inspiration. If a writing be inspired, it is Divine: if it be not inspired, it is human. It is absurd to shirk the alternative. *Some* parts of the Bible, it is allowed, *are* inspired; other parts, it is contended, are *not.* Let it be conceded then, for the moment, that the catalogue of the Dukes of Edom is *not* an inspired writing; and let it be ejected from the Bible accordingly. We must by strict parity of reasoning, eject the xth chapter of Genesis, which enumerates the descendants of Japheth, of Ham, and of Shem, with the countries which they severally occupied,—that truly venerable record and outline of the primæval settlement of the nations! The ten Patriarchs before, and the ten after Noah: the many enumerations contained in the Book of Numbers: much of the two Books of Chronicles: together with the Genealogies of our SAVIOUR as given by St. Matthew and St. Luke.

It is clear that the history of the Flood,—very much of it at least,—is of the same nature: a kind of calendar as it were, and record of dates.

But we may go on faster, and use the knife far more freely. Every thing in the Pentateuch of which Moses had been an eye or ear-witness, and which he set down from his own personal knowledge, may be eliminated from the Bible, as not inspired. According to the principle already enunciated by yourself, I call upon you to excise from the Book of GOD's LAW, Exodus, and Leviticus, and Numbers, and Deuteronomy: those passages only excepted which are prophetical,—as the xxxiiird of Deuteronomy. Joshua must go of course: for if the son of Nun did not write the Book which goes under his name,—(as the wise men in Germany say, or used to say, he did not [e],)—of course the narrative is not authentic; and if he *did*, *you* say that it ought not to be regarded as inspired. Judges and Ruth cannot hope to stand; for they are mere stories,—narratives of events which any contemporary author who enjoyed "actual observation, good memory, high intellect, clearness of statement, and honesty of purpose," was abundantly qualified—(according to *your* view of the matter)— to commit to writing. The Books of Samuel and of Kings cannot be claimed as the work of Inspiration, of course. Chronicles we have got rid of already. No imaginable plea can be invented for the Books of Ezra, of Nehemiah, and of Esther; those writings

[e] See the Hulsean Lectures for 1833, (*The Law of Moses viewed in connexion with the History and character of the Jews, with a defence of the Book of Joshua*, &c.) by Henry John Rose, B.D.

having evidently required nothing (to use your own phrase) but "opportunity of experience or research, and the ordinary qualities of a trustworthy historian." The prophetical books you spare; natural piety suggesting that since "Prophecy came not in old time by the will of man, but holy men of GOD spake as they were moved by the HOLY GHOST[f];"—the writings of Isaiah and the rest, must be retained as inspired. We expunge those portions only which are simply historical and moral; since to these, by the hypothesis, the spirit of Inspiration cannot be thought to have extended.

We come now to the New Testament; and two of the Gospels are found to be mutilated already, by the elimination of one chapter of St. Matthew and one of St. Luke. But on the principle that personal observation, a good memory, honesty of purpose, and so forth, are the only requirements necessary, we may proceed to carry forward the work of excision with spirit, so that we be but careful to use discernment. For example, we may begin with the Call of St. Matthew, and the Feast which he made to our LORD in his own house. *Who* so competent to relate this, as the Evangelist himself? Whenever, in short, the Twelve were present, St. Matthew, (as one of the Twelve,) may be assumed to have written from personal observation; and *that* portion of his narrative is to be rejected accordingly as uninspired.

It is painful to anticipate what will be the fate of St. John's Gospel, on this principle,—together with most of the Divine Discourses therein recorded. Not, to be sure, that we shall lose the conversation with Nicodemus, nor that with the woman of Samaria;

[f] 2 St. Peter i. 21.

because St. John was not present when either of those conversations took place: but all, from the xivth to the xviith chapter inclusive; as well as the discourse in the vith chapter, must of course be dismissed. The matter of these discourses, it will be urged,— (with more of logical consistency, alas! than of essential truth,)—might have been faithfully handed down by St. John without any extraordinary gift. He was bound to our LORD by more than ordinary affection. He was ever nearest to Him. Is it not conceivable, (we are asked,) that these two causes, aided by a retentive memory, would at least *enable* him to give us the record which he has given?

Quite superfluous must it be to state that the Acts of the Apostles, under the expurgatory process which now engages our attention, will cease to be regarded as an inspired Book; and therefore must be at once disconnected from the confessedly inspired portions of Holy Scripture.—St. Paul's Epistles, you say, on the contrary, are probably inspired, and therefore are probably to be spared..... And I really think we need go no further. If your own handling of Holy Scripture,—your own method, by yourself applied, —be not a *reductio ad absurdum*, I know of nothing in the world which is. ... Look only at that handful of mutilated pages in the hands of one who is supposed to be the impersonation of "common sense;" turn the tattered and mangled leaves over and over, which *you* are pleased to call the Volume of Inspiration; and get all the comfort and help out of it you can. But be not surprised to hear that you are exposing yourself to the ridicule of the sane part of Mankind,—even while haply you are acting a part which makes the Angels weep..... How much of the Bible will remain, when *Science*, (Physical, Moral, Historical,) has further done *her* work, I forbear now to inquire: but I shrewdly suspect that she will leave you very little beyond the back and the covers.

Let us not be told, (as we doubtless shall,) that the human parts of Scripture need not be *ejected* from the Canon because they are human: that they may be allowed to stand with the rest, although uninspired; and the like. About this, *we* at least are competent judges. We are now bent on discovering how much of Holy Scripture is *the Word of God;* and we refuse, for the moment, to regard as such, and to retain, a single passage which, being (as you say) uninspired, is simply *the word of Man.*

II. Let me now be permitted to lay before you a somewhat different view of the office of Inspiration. Since the illumination of Science, falsely so called, and the process of Common Sense, would seem to have resulted in the extinction of the deposit, I ask your patience while I try to shew, that common sense, informed by a somewhat loftier Theological Instinct, may give such an account of the matter as will enable us to preserve every word of the deposit entire.

You call my attention to the catalogue of the Dukes of Edom, and tell me that it required no supernatural aid to enable Moses to write it. How, may I ask, do you ascertain that fact? No specimens of the documentary evidence of the land of Seir in the days of Moses, are known now to exist on the earth's surface. You therefore know absolutely nothing whatever about the matter of which you speak so confidently.

But, that we may grapple with the question fairly, let us come down from an age concerning which neither of us knows anything beyond what the Bible teaches, to a period with which all are familiar, and to documents of which we know at least a little. It will suit your purpose far better that you should instance the two Genealogies of our LORD,—of which you also say that it is impossible to maintain that they exhibit the work of Inspiration in the same sense as when some lofty statement of Christian doctrine comes before us. Indeed, you deny that they are inspired at all. I, on my side, am willing to admit that it is quite possible,—even probable,—that the first and the third Evangelist had access to extant documents of which they respectively availed themselves, when they recorded our LORD's descent.

But, do you not perceive that the great underlying fallacy in all you have been saying, is your own wholly gratuitous assumption that you are a competent judge of what *did*,—what did *not*,—require supernatural aid to deliver? that whatever *seems* as if it might have been written without Inspiration, *was* therefore written without it?—I see so many practical inconveniences, or rather I see such glaring absurdity, resulting from the supposition that Inspiration goes and comes before an authentic document, that I am constrained to think that you are altogether mistaken in the office which you assign to Inspiration, —in the kind of notion which you seem to entertain concerning its nature.

An Evangelist, if you please, is inspired. It becomes necessary to introduce a genealogy. Following the Divine guidance, (the nature of which, neither you nor I know anything at all about,) he applies in a certain quarter, and obtains access to a certain document. Or he repairs to a well-known repository of public archives, and out of the whole collection he is guided to make choice of one particular writing. He proceeds to transcribe it,—omitting names (dropping three generations for instance,)—or inserting names (the second Cainan for example,)—or, if you please, neither omitting nor inserting anything. The document, (suppose,) requires no correction whatever. —Well but, this man was inspired a moment ago, in what he was writing; and no reason has been shewn why he should not be inspired still. He has adopted a document, by incorporating it into his narrative. By transcribing it, he has made it his own. I am at a loss to see that its claim to be an inspired writing, from that moment forward, is in any respect inferior to the rest of the narrative in which it stands.

You are requested to remember that when we call the Bible an inspired book, we mean nothing more than that the words of it are the very utterance of the HOLY SPIRIT;—that the Book is as much the Word of GOD as if high Heaven were open, and we heard GOD speaking to us with human voice. All I am contending for *now*, is, that this is at least as true of one part of the Gospel as of another: that if it be true of anything in the Gospel, it is at least *as* true of the Genealogy of CHRIST. The *subject-matter* indeed is different; but it is a mere confusion of thought to infer therefrom a different degree of *Inspiration*. Let me try and make this plainer by a few familiar illustrations.

1. When the Sovereign reads a speech from the Throne, does she speak the words of it in any *different sense* from the words of a speech which she has herself composed?—Nay, are words of investiture, mere

words of form and state, in any *less degree spoken*, than words of confidence, and private friendship?

2. Again. The substance of paper and the substance of gold, are widely different. And yet, when paper has been subjected to a certain process, and stamped with a certain impress, there is practically *no difference whatever* between the value of what was, a moment ago, absolutely worthless, and an ingot of the purest gold.

3. Consider how the case stands with a merely human author. An historian has occasion to introduce into his narrative the descent of a House, or the preamble of an Act, or any other lifeless thing. Does his responsibility cease when he comes to it, and recommence immediately afterwards? Is he not responsible just to the same extent for *that*, as for every other part of his story?

That he did not *compose it himself*, is certain: but *neither did he compose the sayings which he has recorded of great men.*—True also is it that the edification to be derived from the pedigree is not so great,—certainly, not so obvious,—as from certain of the events which he describes. But it is nevertheless henceforth an integral part of his history. He sought for it,— and he found it: he weighed it,—and he approved of it: he transcribed it,—and he interwove it into his narrative. In a word, he adopted; and by adopting, he *made it his own*. Henceforth, it will be quoted as authentic, because it is found to have satisfied *him*.

The utmost praise which can be accorded to any creature is, that it thoroughly fulfils the office whereunto GOD sends it. A genealogy is not intended to make men wise unto Salvation: the threats and promises of God's Law are not intended to acquaint men with the descent of David's Son. But because *their offices* are different, it does not follow that *their origin* shall not be the same! Is a shoe-latchet in any sense *less* an article manufactured by Man, than a watch? Is the Archangel Michael, burning with glory, and intent on some celestial enterprise, with twelve legions of glittering seraphs in his train;—is such a host as *that*, one atom more a creation of the ALMIGHTY than the handful of yellow leaves which flutter unheeded on the blast?

None of these figures present a strict parallel; and yet, successively, they seem to set forth different aspects of the same case, with sufficient vividness and truth. . . . So bent am I on conveying to your minds the strong sense of certainty, the clear definite view, which I cherish for myself on this subject, that I take leave to add yet another illustration.

4. If I commission a Servant to deliver a message,—is not the message which he delivers *mine?* If I give him words to deliver,—are not *the words* which he delivers *mine?* So obvious a proposition is no matter of opinion. You *cannot* deny it. Nor,—(to apply the illustration to the matter in hand,)—nor *do* you deny it, probably, so far as *Prophecy*, (in the popular sense of the term,) is concerned: but you begin to doubt, it seems, when any other function of the prophetic office is in question. "Any other function," I say; for, (as all men ought to be aware,) a prophet,—(*navē* in Hebrew, προφήτης in Greek,)—does not, by any means, of necessity imply one who describes *future* events. Πρό does not denote futurity of time, but vicariousness of office. The προ-φήτης is one who speaketh πρό, "on behalf of," "in the person of," GOD; whether

declaring things past,—(as when Moses describes the Creation of the World, the Fall of Man, the Patriarchal Age): things present,—(as when St. Luke, "having had perfect understanding of all things from the very first," writes of them "in order"): things future,—(as when David, and Isaiah, and the rest of the goodly fellowship, "testified beforehand the sufferings of CHRIST, and the glory that should follow[g].") This is no arbitrary statement, but a well-known fact, which modern unbelievers and ancient heathen writers have declared with sufficient plainness[h].

[g] 1 St. Peter i. 11.

[h] "With the idea of a Prophet," (says Gesenius in his Hebrew Lexicon, on the noun,) "there was this necessarily attached; that he spoke not his own words, but those which he had divinely received; (see Philo, t. iv. p. 116, ed. Pfeifferi,—προφήτης γὰρ ἴδιον μὲν οὐδὲν ἀποφθέγγεται, ἀλλότρια δὲ πάντα ὑπηχοῦντος ἑτέρου); and that he was the messenger of GOD, and the declarer of His will. This is clear from a passage of peculiar authority in this matter, (Ex. vii. 1,)—where GOD says to Moses,—'I have made thee a god to Pharaoh; and Aaron thy brother *shall be thy prophet.*'" ... Elsewhere, (speaking of the Hebrew verb, 'to prophesy,') Gesenius has the following remarkable statement :—"The *passive forms*, Niphal and Hithpael, are used in this verb; from the Divine Prophets having been *supposed to be moved rather by another's powers than their own.*" (Just as if the Oracles of GOD were not express on the subject! viz. "No prophecy ever came by the will of Man; but, [because they were] borne along (φερόμενοι) by the HOLY GHOST, spake those holy men of GOD."—2 St. Pet. i. 21.)

Προφήτης, in fact, means '*an interpreter*' rather than 'a prophet,' (for which, in our popular sense, the Greek is rather μάντις :) hence the use of the words προφήτης, προφητεύω, προφητεία in the New Testament, e.g. 1 Thess. v. 20. 1 Cor. xi. 4: xii. 10. Rom. xii. 6, (where see Wordsworth.) See also 1 Cor. xiv. 1, 3, 4, 5, &c.: in all which places, the προφήτης was what we should rather now call *a preacher*. But then, the expounding of GOD's Word is the special function of the preacher's office from which he takes this name.—The reader is referred to Blomfield's Glossary, *Agam.* v. 399, and to

So long then as the message which the Servant delivers is prophetic, you do not object to the notion that it is God's message; nay, that the words spoken are God's words. You begin to doubt, it seems, when a collection of genealogies, (as the two Books of Chronicles;) or when a story like that contained in the Book of Esther is concerned.

But what is this but very trifling, and mere childishness? The message *may* be mine, it seems, if it be of a lofty character: it may *not* be mine if it be of a homely, ordinary kind!—I send a message by my Servant, and he delivers it faithfully: but whether it *is* to be called my message, or is *not* to be called my message, is to depend entirely on the subject-matter! .... Thus, if a King, refusing to appear in person, should issue a reprieve to prisoners under sentence of Death, a proclamation of Peace or of War, an address to the representatives of the constitution, (Clergy, Lords, and Commons,) in parliament assembled,—the message would be *his*. But if, on the contrary, he were only to send a few homely words, the expression of some wish or intention which has nothing that seems particularly royal in it,—then, the message would *cease* to be his! .... I protest that as I am unable to see the reasonableness of such a method of regarding things human, so am I at a loss to understand why men should so regard things Divine.

5. This entire matter may be usefully illustrated by having recourse to an analogy which was established on a former occasion: namely, the analogy between

Liddell and Scott's *Lexicon;* (in both of which, some important references are given:) also to Trench's *Synonyms of the New Testament,* pp. 22—26.

the Written and *the Incarnate* Word[1]. That our LORD JESUS CHRIST is at once very GOD and very Man, we all fully admit; although *the manner* of the union of GODHEAD and Manhood in His one Person we confess ourselves quite unable to comprehend. Even so, that there is a human as well as a Divine element in Holy Scripture,—*who* so blind as to overlook? *who* so weak as to deny? And yet, to dissect out that human element,—*who* (but a fool) so rash as to attempt? .... To apply this to the matter before us. *Certain parts* of Holy Scripture you think, (for reasons to yourself best known,) are not to be looked upon as inspired in the same sense as the rest of the volume. Just as reasonably might you try to persuade me that our SAVIOUR was not *in the same sense* our SAVIOUR when He ate and drank at the Pharisees' board, as when He cast out devils and raised the dead. Was He not equally the Incarnate WORD at every stage of His earthly career; from the time that He was laid in the manger, until the instant when He expired upon the Cross? The degradation which He endured in Pilate's judgment-hall did not affect the reality of the great truth that the GODHEAD was indissolubly joined to the Manhood in His Person. He was not less very GOD as well as very Man when some one spat upon Him, than at His Transfiguration and at His Ascension into Heaven! ... Why then should the mean aspect and lowly office of certain parts of Scripture,— (genealogical details and the narrative of what we think ordinary occurrences,)—be supposed to disentitle those parts to the praise of being *as fully inspired as any thing in the whole compass of the Bible?*

---

[1] See above, pp. 2—5.—The reader will find an interesting passage based on this analogy, in the Appendix (F).

I may remind you, in passing, that the narrative of Scripture, even in its humblest, and (to all appearance) most human parts, has a perpetual note of Divinity set upon it. The historical portions are throughout interspersed with indications that the writer is beholding the transactions which he records, from a Divine, (not a human,) point of view. GOD is invariably, (sooner or later,) mentioned as the Agent; or there is some reference made to GOD; or to GOD's Word. As Butler expresses it,—"The general design of Scripture . . . . may be said to be, to give us an account of the world, in this one single view,—*as God's world:* by which it appears essentially distinguished from all other books, so far as I have found, except such as are copied from it [k]."

[k] *Analogy*, P. II. c. vii.—The same thing has been more fully expressed in a volume of Sermons which deserves to be far better known than it is:—"I suppose that if there is one portion of the Old Testament which a discriminator would set aside as less needing to be reckoned inspired than other parts, it is the Historical; the books which are strictly narrative. Now it may seem to have been providentially ordered, in the purpose of meeting this view, that these books are made to bear on them most peculiarly the stamp and the claim of Inspiration. For they do not profess to be so much the account of what Man did, as what GOD did in ruling men, and guiding human events. They are a history of a providential course of events, and, (which is the point,) as seen from the providential point of view. They are a history written not on Earth, but above the skies. Events are spoken of therefore in this view. A man's obduracy is recorded thus,—'GOD hardened his heart.' A king numbers his people; it is recorded as a thing suggested in the spiritual world. In fact, the historic volume of the Old Testament is a history of the secret springs of things; it is a narrative of things which none but GOD ALMIGHTY could know; not Man's Word therefore at all, but GOD's."—*Sermons*, by the Rev. C. P. Eden, pp. 153—155. Several other extracts from the same suggestive volume of a very excellent Divine, will be found in the Appendix.

I entreat you therefore to disabuse your minds of the very weak,—aye and very fatal,—notion that the catalogue of the Dukes of Edom is *less,* or *in any different sense,* inspired, from the rest of the narrative in which it stands. We may not multiply miracles needlessly, it is true; but neither may we deny the miraculous character of certain transactions, (as the two Draughts of Fishes,) which, apart from the recorded attendant circumstances, would not have been deemed miraculous.—In truth, however, Holy Scripture, in one sense, is a miracle from end to end; and if we may not multiply miracles needlessly, certainly we are not at liberty to dismiss the recorded details of a single miracle, as of no account.—Consider also, I entreat you, whether it is credible that Inspiration should be a thing of such a nature, that it comes and goes,—is here and is gone,—once and again in the course of a single page. What? does it vanish, like lightning, when the Evangelist's pen has to record the title on the Cross,—to re-appear the instant afterwards?

This allusion to the title on the Cross of our Blessed Lord, variously given by each of the four Evangelists, reminds me of the singular perversity of mankind when this subject of Inspiration is being treated of; and to this, I now particularly desire to invite your attention.—When a document is simply transcribed by the Evangelist, or may be *supposed* to have been merely transferred to his pages, men assert that so purely mechanical an act precludes the notion that Inspiration has had any share in the transaction. Be it so!—Behold now, four inspired writers exhibiting the brief title on our Lord's Cross with considerable verbal diversity; and you will hear the same critics open-mouthed against the Evangelists' claim to Inspiration, for exactly the opposite reason!—It is just so of places quoted from the Old Testament in the New. Faithful transcription, (we are told,) is in the power of all. What note of an inspired author have we here? But the places are *not* faithfully transcribed. On the contrary. They exhibit every possible degree of deflection from the original standard. And lo, the Apostles of CHRIST are thought not to have quite understood Greek,—to have mistaken the sense of the Hebrew,—and to have been the victims of a most capricious memory.—For the last time. Certain narrative portions of Holy Scripture, (it is assumed,) could have been written without the aid of Inspiration; and therefore it is unphilosophical, (we are told,) to assign to them a divine original. But the marvellous parts of Holy Scripture, which seem to claim a loftier original than man's unaided wit,—*these* you view with suspicion, or you deny!.... "Whereunto shall I liken the men of this generation?"

Before dismissing the subject, I must ask you to observe, that this arbitrary, irreverent method of approaching Holy Scripture, is absolutely fatal; and can result in nothing but general unbelief. It confessedly leaves the individual reader to decide what parts of the Bible he thinks could, what parts could not, have been written without Divine assistance;— a point on which I am bold to say that he is not competent even to form an opinion. In other words, it constitutes every man the judge of how much of the Bible he will retain,—how much he will reject. To put the case yet more plainly, it makes every man a GOD to himself, and the maker of his own Bible.— For, mark you, the exceptions taken against a genealogy, or a catalogue of names, are just as applicable to the account of our LORD's Discourses as given by St. John. Once convince me that the function of Inspiration ceases when a genealogy has to be set down,—because (say you) it requires no Inspiration to enable an Evangelist to copy *written* words;—and I shall have no difficulty in convincing myself that St. John's Gospel, from the xivth to the xviith chapters inclusive, is not inspired,—because I cannot *but* infer that then neither can it require Inspiration to enable an Evangelist to copy *spoken* words.—The original fallacy, I repeat,—the πρῶτον ψεῦδος,—consists in your supposing yourself a competent judge of the nature and office of Inspiration; concerning which, in reality, you know nothing. You can but reverently examine the phenomena of the Book of Inspiration; remembering that you have everything to learn.

The Bible, it cannot be too often repeated, too clearly borne in mind,—the Bible must stand or fall, —or rather, be received or rejected,—*as a whole.* A Divinity hath over-ruled it, that those many Books of which it is composed should come to be spoken of collectively as if they were one Book. As it was formerly called ἡ γραφή—"the Scripture,"—so is it happily called "the Bible"—(the Book)—*now.* "Moses —the Prophets—and the Psalms," was the recognized analysis of the volume of the Old Testament. The Gospels, the Epistles, and the Apocalypse, exhibits the sum of the contents of the New.—There is no disjoining the Law from the Gospel. There is no disconnecting one Book from its fellows. There is no eliminating one chapter from the rest. There is no taking exception against one set of passages, or supposing that Inspiration has anywhere forgotten her office, or discharged it imperfectly. All the Books of the Bible must stand or fall together. "Nothing can be put to it, nor anything taken from it[1]." It is a fabric hard as adamant; and the gates of Hell will assuredly never prevail against it. But remove in thought a single stone; and in thought, that goodly work of Lawgivers and Judges—Kings and Prophets—Evangelists and Apostles,—collapses into a shapeless and unmeaning ruin[m].

Nor may it occasion perplexity, or breed mistrust in any thoughtful mind to find this Book of GOD's Law so complex in its character,—so various in its contents,—so fruitful in its difficulties. Might it not, on the contrary, have been expected beforehand, that some analogy would have been recognizable between the general complexion of GOD's Works and of GOD's Word? While I behold the creatures of GOD so various,—their functions so marvellous,—their nature so little understood,—the very purpose of their creation so great a mystery;—shall I think it strange that *that* Book which is but another expression of GOD's Mind and Will, proves diverse in texture, and difficult of interpretation?—Shall I grow rebellious against the message, because the history of it is hid in the long night of ages; say rather, in the counsels of GOD's inscrutable will? or shall I be incredulous that it comes from Heaven, because I see the fingers of a Man's hand writing upon the plaister of the wall? or shall I despise those parts of it of which I cannot detect the medicinal value? As there are riddles in Nature, so are there riddles in Grace. Anomalies too, it may be, are discoverable in both worlds.

[1] Eccl. iii. 14. So Deut. iv. 2: xii. 32. Rev. xxii. 19.
[m] See the Appendix (G).

—Give me leave to add, that as the microscope reveals unsuspected wonders in the one, so does minute examination bring to light undreamed of perfections in the other also; unimagined proofs of divine wisdom, and skill. . . . . But beyond all things, there is perhaps this further thing which it behoves us to consider:—that the field of either is very vast; the subject-matter very complex: and as, in one, many Professors are needed,—(for the Animal kingdom and the Vegetable kingdom are realms apart: the analysis of substances, and the structure of the Earth demand the undivided attention of different minds;)—so does it fare with the other also. The languages of Scripture are in themselves a mighty study; and the collation of the Text is the portion of a long life. The Law of Moses would abundantly engross the time of one who should undertake to explain its depths; as the Gospel of JESUS CHRIST would assuredly fill to overflowing the soul of another who should desire to appreciate its perfections. The Prophetic writings are a distinct field of labour. The same may well be said of the Epistles of St. Paul. It would be easy to multiply departments;—for I have said nothing yet of Sacred History; and above all, of Sacred Exegesis. But enough has been stated to introduce the remark that considering how slenderly one man is able to labour in all these various provinces, it behoves each one of us to be humble; and certainly to be a vast deal more mistrustful of ourselves than some of us unhappily seem to be; especially when the errand on which we propose to come abroad is the assailing of the authenticity, or the morality, or the integrity, or the Inspiration, of any part of the Bible. Our own amazing ignorance, —our many infirmities,—our faculties limited on every side,—might well keep us humble in the presence of Him whose knowledge is infinite;—whose attributes are all perfections;—whose very Name is ALMIGHTY!— Shall we, on the contrary, presume to sit in judgment upon His Word, which claims to be none other than the authentic record of His Providence,—the Revelation of His very mind and will? . . . Truly, in this behalf, beyond all others, we seem to stand in need of the solemn warning: "Dangerous it were for the feeble brain of Man to wade far into the doings of the Most High: whom although to know be life, and joy to make mention of His Name; yet our soundest knowledge is to know that we know Him not as indeed He is, neither can know Him. And our safest eloquence concerning Him is our silence, when we confess without confession that His glory is inexplicable; His greatness above our capacity and reach. He is above, and we upon earth: therefore it behoveth our words to be wary and few[n]."

And this brings me naturally back to the subject of my first Sermon from this place; and enables me to conclude, as I began, with an earnest entreaty to the younger men present, that,—whatever their future destination in life may be,—but especially if the Ministry is to be their high privilege, (and the blessedness of *that* choice they can have no idea of, until they prove it by experience!);—an entreaty, I say, that they would *now* be assiduous, and earnest, and regular, and punctual, and devout, in their daily study of one chapter of the Bible.—And while you read the Bible, read it believing that you are reading an inspired Book:—not a Book inspired in parts only, but a Book inspired in *every* part:—not a Book unequally inspired,

[n] Hooker's *Eccl. Pol.*, B. I. c. ii. § 2.

but all inspired equally:—not a Book generally inspired,—the substance indeed given by the Spirit, but the words left to the option of the writers; but the words of it, as well as the matter of it, all—all given by GOD. As it is written,—" Man shall not live by bread alone, but by *every word that proceedeth out of the mouth of GOD.*"

I illustrated sufficiently, last time, in what way fulness of Inspiration is consistent with the expression of individual character: even while I availed myself of the ancient illustration that an inspired writer is like an instrument in the harper's hand[o]. I did not, of course, "intend thereby to affirm that the Writers of Holy Scripture were *constrained* to write, without any volition or consciousness on their part. ... ALMIGHTY GOD, while He *inspired* the Writers of Scripture, did not impair their moral and intellectual faculties, nor destroy their personal identity[p]." Let me not be told therefore that this is to advocate a mechanical theory of Interpretation. Theory I have none[q]. The Bible comes to me as the Word of GOD; and, *as the Word of GOD,* (the LORD being my helper!) I will receive it. I should as soon think of holding a theory of Providence and Freewill, as of holding a theory of Inspiration. I *believe* in Providence. I *know* that I am a free agent. And that is enough for me.—The case of Inspiration seems strictly parallel. I *believe* in the Divine origin of the Bible. I *see* that the writers of the several books wrote like men. . . .

[o] See above, p. 77.

[p] *The Inspiration of the Bible, five Lectures,* by Chr. Wordsworth, D.D. 1861,—p. 5.

[q] For some remarks on Theories of Inspiration, see the Appendix (H.)

That outer circle of causation, which, leaving each individual will entirely free, so controuls without coercing, so overrules without occasioning, the actions of men,—that all things shall work together for good in the end, and the great designs of God's Providence find free accomplishment;—all this, far, far transcends your and my powers of comprehension. It is as much beyond us as Heaven is higher than the Earth. And, in like manner, we must be content to own that Inspiration,—the analysis of which is so favourite a problem with this inquisitive age,—is far, far above us likewise. To St. Luke "it seemed good" to write a Gospel; and doubtless he held high communing on the subject,—which may, or may not, have sounded like ordinary human converse, — with St. Paul. St. Mark in like sort, beyond a question, enjoyed the help of St. Peter, while he wrote his Gospel. But St. Peter and St. Mark, and St. Paul and St. Luke, were all alike,—however unconsciously,—held by the Ancient of Days within the hollow of His palm; and, as Augustine says,—" Whatsoever He willed that *we* should read concerning His acts and sayings,—*that* He commissioned the Evangelists to write,—as though it had been *Himself* that wrote it[r]."—The guidance was remote, I grant you. The mechanism which moved the pens of those blessed writers was far above out of their sight; and complex beyond anything which the mind of man can imagine; (so that the publican lisped of "gold, and silver, and brass[s];"—and the companion of St. Peter, at Rome, wrote Latin

---

[r] "Quicquid Ille de Suis factis et dictis nos legere voluit, hoc scribendum illis tanquam Suis manibus imperavit."
[s] St. Matth. x. 9.

words in Greek letters[t];—and the Physician of Antioch withheld the statement that the woman who had spent all that she had in consulting many physicians, "*was nothing bettered, but rather grew worse*[u];"— and the beloved disciple perhaps indulged his own personal love while he recalled so largely the discourses of his LORD:)—but, for all that, the long sequence of cause and effect existed; and the other end of that golden chain which terminated in the man, and the pen, and the ink, and the paper,—the other end of it, I say, was held fast within the Hand of GOD. —The method of Inspiration is but another of the many thousand marvels which on every side surround me; one of the many things I cannot fully understand, much less pretend to explain. But I may at least believe it in silence, and adore[x].

And,—(forgive me for keeping you so long; but I *cannot* let you go until I have emptied my heart a little more on this great, and most concerning subject;)— mark you, Sirs, however reluctant some of you may be to admit that you agree with me, you *do* agree with me,—almost to a man. For, what mean your reasonings on Holy Scripture,—your sermons, and your dissertations, and your catechizings,—your formulæ of belief, and your definitions of Faith,—except you believe in a vast deal more than *the substance* of Holy Scripture? How can you pretend to expound a text, unless you hold *the words* of that text to be inspired? What inferences can you venture to draw from words, the Divinity of which you dare not affirm?

---

[t] E. g. κεντυρίων : σπεκουλάτωρ : ξέστης.

[u] Comp. St. Luke viii. 43, with St. Mark v. 26.

[x] The reader will be grateful for a beautiful and highly suggestive passage from Eden's *Sermons,* in the Appendix (I.)

O, to what endless, hopeless scepticism are you pointing the way! What a variety of most unanswerable questionings will you provoke! How can you hope ever to convince or convict, if you begin by acquainting your adversary that it is only for the substantial verity of Scripture that you claim Inspiration; the verbal details being quite a different matter! See you not that you put into his hands a weapon with which he will infallibly slay *yourself?* Did the Bishops and Doctors of the Church, when they met in solemn Council, — did *they* hold such a theory concerning Holy Scripture, think you, as that the matter of it alone is Divine,—the language human? More briefly, that *the words* of Scripture are *not inspired?* What then mean their weighty definitions of Doctrine;— God the Father, "Maker of Heaven and Earth,"— God the Son, "by whom all things were made:"— the Son, "Θεὸς ἐκ Θεοῦ,"—" being *of one substance* with the Father:"—" incarnate by the Holy Ghost of the Virgin Mary:"—who "descended into Hell"— "whose kingdom shall have no end:"—the Holy Ghost, "τὸ Κύριον καὶ τὸ ζωοποιόν," "who proceedeth from the Father and the Son?"—What means every article of that Creed to which you and I have given our unfeigned assent, and which Athanasius would have gladly subscribed to,—the most precious jewel in the Church's casket!—Nay, what means St. Paul's commentary on the history of Melchizedek, if the very words *omitted* from Holy Scripture are not a *Divine* omission?

You will perhaps be told hereafter, (I am speaking now to the younger men,) that quite fatal to this view of the question, is the state of the Text of Scripture: that no one can maintain that the words of Scripture are inspired, because no one can tell for certain what the words of Scripture *are;* or something to that effect. Now I will not stop to expose the falsity of this charge against the text of Scripture; (which is implied to be a very corrupt text, whereas, on the contrary, it is the best ascertained text of any ancient writing in the world.) Rather let me remind you, once and for ever, how to refute this silly sophism,—the transparent fallacy of which one would have thought unworthy of exposure before men of trained understandings; but that one hears it urged so often and so confidently. See you not that the state of the text of the Bible has no more to do with the Inspiration of the Bible, than the stains on yonder windows have to do with the light of GOD's Sun? Let me illustrate the matter,— (though it surely cannot need illustration!)—by supposing the question raised whether Livy did or did not write the history which goes under his name. *You*, (suppose,) are persuaded that he *did*,—*I*, that he did *not*. So far, we should both understand, and perhaps respect one another. But what if I were to go on to condemn your opinion as untenable, because of the corrupt state of Livy's *text?* Would you not reply that I mistook the question entirely: that *you* were speaking of the *authorship of the work*,—not about the *fate of the copies!* . . . Suppose, however, I were to contend that Livy may indeed have furnished the matter of his history, but that the form of expression must needs have been supplied by some one else; *still* on the same ground of the corrupt state of the historian's text. What would you think of me *then?*—a man who not only confounded two things utterly dissimilar,—(the authorship of a book, and the amount of care with which it had been transcribed and printed;)—but who was for distinguishing the mind of the writer from the expression of that mind; the *thoughts,* from the *words* which are essential to their transmission! A hopelessly illogical person, surely!

O no, Sirs! Banish the fancy at once and for ever from your minds. You cannot thus dissect Inspiration into substance and form. It is a mere delusion of these last days,—prated of from man to man, until respectable persons begin to give in to the fallacy; and persuade themselves that they themselves believe it. They hope thus to avoid the danger which is supposed to attach to hearty belief in the Bible as the very Word of God; as well as to secure for themselves a side-door, (so to speak,) by which to escape, whenever they are inconveniently hard pressed. How much more faithful, to leave God to take care of His own! How much more manly, to be prepared sometimes to confess ignorance! . . . As for *thoughts* being inspired, apart from the *words* which give them expression,—you might as well talk of a tune without notes, or a sum without figures. No such dream can abide the daylight for a moment. No such theory of Inspiration, (for a theory it *is,* and a most audacious one too!), is even intelligible. It is as illogical as it is worthless; and cannot be too sternly put down. The philosophical mind of Greece, (far better taught!), knew of only one word for both Reason and the expression of it. Lodged within the chambers of the brain, or put forth into living energy,—it was still, with them, the Λόγος.—I invite you, as the only intelligible view of the matter,—your only alternative, unless you resolve to run the risk of the most irrational rationalism,—to take this high view of Inspiration: to believe, concerning the Bible, that it is in the most literal sense imaginable, verily and indeed, *the Word* of GOD.

And do you,—(for I am still addressing myself to the younger men,)—learn to put away from your souls that vile indifferentism which is becoming the curse of this shallow and unlearned age. Be as forgiving as you please of indignities offered to yourselves; but do not be ashamed to be very jealous for the honour of the LORD of Hosts; and to resent any dishonour offered to Him, with a fiery indignation utterly unlike anything you could possibly feel for a personal wrong. Attend ever so little to the circumstance, and you will perceive that every form of fashionable impiety is one and the same vile thing in the essence of it: still Antichrist, disguise it how you will. We were reminded last Sunday that the sensualist, by following the gratification of his own unholy desires, in bold defiance of GOD's known Law, is in reality setting himself up in the place of GOD, and becoming a GOD unto himself[y]. The same is true of the Idolatry of Human Reason; and of Physical Science: as well as of that misinformed Moral Sense which finds in the Atonement of our LORD nothing but a stone of stumbling and a snare. It is true of Popish error also;—for what else is this but a setting up of the Human above the Divine,—(Tradition, the worship of the Blessed Virgin, the casuistry of the Confessional, and the like,)—and so, once more substituting the creature for the Creator?—What again is the fashionable intellectual sin of the day, but the self-same detestable offence, under quite a different disguise? The idea of Law,—(*that* old idea

[y] Alluding to a sermon preached by the Provost of Queen's.

which is declared to be only now emerging into supremacy in Science,)—takes the hideous shape of rebellion against its Maker; and pronounces, now Miracles, now Prophecy, now Inspiration itself, to be a thing impossible; or is content to insinuate that the disclosures of Revelation are at least untrue. What is this, I say, but another form of the self-same iniquity, —a setting up of the creature before the Creator who is blessed for evermore; a substitution of some created thing in the place of GOD!

The true antidote to all such forms of impiety, believe me, is not controversy of any sort; but the childlike study of the Bible, each one for himself,—not without prayer.—Humble must we be, as well as assiduous; for the powers of the mind as well as the affections of the heart should be prostrated before the Bible, or a man will derive little profit from his study of it. Humble, I repeat, for mysteries, (remember), are revealed unto the meek[z]; and the fear of the LORD is the beginning of Wisdom[a]; and he that would understand more than the Ancients must keep GOD's precepts[b]; and it is the commandments of the LORD which give light unto the eyes[c].—The dutiful student of the Bible is permitted to see the mist melt away from many a speculative difficulty; and is many a time reminded of that saying of his LORD,—"Do ye not therefore err, *because ye know not the Scriptures*, neither the power of GOD[d]?" . . . The humble and attentive reader of the Bible becomes impressed at last with a sense of its Divinity, analogous I suppose to the conviction of Eleven of the Apostles that the Man they walked with was none other than the SON

---

[z] Ecclus. iii. 19.   [a] Ps. cxi. 10.   Prov. ix. 10.
[b] Ps. cxix. 100.   [c] Ps. xix. 8.   [d] St. Mark xii. 24.

of God. *That* similarity of allusion,—*that* sameness of imagery,—*that* oneness of design,—*that* uniformity of sentiment,—*that* ever-recurring anticipation of the Gospel message;—*all* goes to produce a secret and sure conviction that every writer, under whatever variety of circumstances, had access to but one Treasury,—drew from but one and the same Well of living water. Marks of purpose, shewn in the choice or collocation of single words, often strike an attentive reader; which, singly, might be thought fortuitous; but which, collectively, can only be accounted for on a very different principle. The beautiful structure of the Gospels strikes him especially; and he could as soon believe that a song harmonized for four Angel voices had been the result of accident, as that the Evangelists had achieved their task without special aid, throughout, from Heaven. A lock of very complicated mechanism, which four keys of most peculiar structure will open simultaneously,—must have been as evidently made for them, as they for it.

It is almost treason, in truth, to the Majesty of Heaven to discuss the Bible on the low ground which I have been hitherto forced to occupy. It is quite monstrous, in the first University of the most favoured of Christian lands, that a man should be compelled thus to lift up his voice in defence of the very Inspiration of God's Word. O that Divine narrative, which is for ever rending aside the veil, and disclosing to us the counsels of the presence-chamber of the ALMIGHTY!—O those human characters, beset with all the infirmities of our fallen nature,—whose words and actions yet are shadows of things heavenly and eternal!—O that majestic retinue of types which, from the very birthday of recorded Time, heralded the approach of the King of Glory!—O that scarlet thread which runs through all the seemingly tangled web of Scripture, to terminate only in the cross of CHRIST!—How do the features of the Gospel struggle into sight through the veil of the Law! How do the holy and humble men of heart ever and anon break out into speech, as it were, before the time;—as if they felt the burden of silence too great to be endured! . . . . . Whence is it that we dare to handle the pages of GOD'S Book as if they were a common thing,—doubting, questioning, cavilling, disbelieving, denying? Why choose for ourselves the soldiers' part, who buffeted, reviled, smote, spat upon Him? . . . O my friends, far, far be all this from you and from me! Never imagine, because this day we have thus spoken, that such discussions are congenial to us; or that we deem them the proper theme for addresses from the pulpit; although the coincidence of this day's Collect seems, for once, to lend a kind of sanction to our present endeavours. Look through the whole range of patristic homilies, and you will not find *one* of the kind, with which, unhappily, our ears are grown so familiar in this place,—ingenious attempts to evacuate Holy Writ of its fulness, on the one hand;—or apologies of some sort for its Divinity and Inspiration, on the other. You will take, if you are wise, far, far higher ground, in your private study of its pages; remembering that "the most generous faith is invariably the truest;"—nor ever stoop so low as *we* have been this day doing. Waste not thy precious time in cavil about the structure of the casket which contains thy treasure; but unlock it once with the Key of Faith, and make thyself rich indeed.—Already, —(as we were last week reminded),—already the

Judge standeth at the door; and assuredly, thou and I, (to whom GOD hath entrusted so much!) shall have to render a very strict account of the use we have made of the Bible,—when we shall stand face to face with its undoubted Author. The season of the year reminds us, as with a trumpet, of that tremendous hour when the veil will be withdrawn from our eyes, —and the office of Faith will be ended,—and we shall be confronted with One who hath "a vesture dipped in blood, and whose Name is called THE WORD OF GOD." ... "*I* have heard of *Thee*," (we shall, every one of us, exclaim),—"I *have heard of Thee*, by the hearing of the ear; but *now*,—mine eye *seeth* Thee[e]!"

* Job xlii. 5.

SUPPLEMENT TO SERMON IV.

There is yet another view of the nature and office of Inspiration,—another 'Theory' as it would perhaps aspire to be called,—which limits *the extent* of the Divine help and guidance which the writers, confessedly inspired, may be supposed to have enjoyed. According to this view, it is admitted that Inspiration was, from first to last, a continuous influence; exerted equally throughout: but then, it has been suggested that perhaps *its office* was not to protect a Writer against a certain class of errors. The office of the Bible, (it is argued,) is to make men wise unto Salvation. It does not follow that Inspiration, because it guided a sacred writer so long as he wrote of Christian Doctrine, so as to make what he wrote unerringly true, should have protected him against slips of memory; preserved him from inaccuracies of statement; from inconclusive reasonings; from incorrect quotations; from mistaken inferences; from scientific errors.—This is what is said: and because this is a view of the question which is observed to recommend itself occasionally to candid, and even to reverential minds, it seems to deserve distinct and careful consideration.

But I must preface all I have to reply by remarking that "a Book cannot [properly] be said to be inspired, or to carry with it the authority of being God's Word, if only *portions* come from Him, and there exists no plain and infallible sign to indicate *which* those portions are; and if the same Writer may give us in one verse of the Bible a revelation from the MOST HIGH, and in the next verse a blunder of his own. How can we be certain, that the very texts, upon which we rest our doctrines and hopes, are not the *uninspired* portions? What can be the meaning or nature of an Inspiration to teach Truth, which does not guarantee its recipient from error?"—So far a living sceptical writer.

1. Now, the first thing which strikes one in this theory, is its extreme vagueness. We hardly know what we have to consider; for nothing is definitely stated. Neither are we informed how many of the phenomena of Inspiration, this view is intended to explain. Again, does the theory apply equally to the Old Testament and to the New? If it does apply equally to the Old Testament, (and I can see no possible reason why it should *not*,) then, I apprehend this theory will be found *practically* to run up into, and to identify itself with, that last described[a]. For a guidance *which has failed to guide*, has been no guidance at all; and since whole chapters of the Old Testament will occur to every one's memory which may be thought to have no connexion whatever with 'Christian Doctrine,'—to conduce wondrous little to the 'making men wise unto Salvation,'—it will follow that Inspiration is, according to this theory, in effect, of the nature already described,—namely, a quality which can never be predicated of any passage of Scripture with entire certainty. The larger part of the Old Testament in fact, by this theory, is exhibited in the light of a common book; having no pretension to be regarded as part of the Inspired Canon.

[a] See above, p. 95—99.

But if this theory simply shirks the question of the Old Testament, then, those who are inclined to accept it, are bound to explain why there should be one theory of Inspiration applicable to the Old Testament, and another for the New:—in which difficulty, I must candidly profess that I am not able to render any assistance at all. It is clearly not allowable to overlook the intimate connexion which subsists between the two great divisions of Holy Scripture; the habitual references of the Writers of the New Testament to the writers of the Old,—Moses, David, Isaiah, and the rest;—or rather, *to the utterance of the* HOLY GHOST, *speaking by the mouth of those writers.* Whatever may have been the Inspiration of the Authors of the New Testament must be assumed to have been that of the Authors of the Old Testament also.

2. But further,—(to confine our remarks to the Scriptures of the New Testament; which, it is manifest, the view under consideration specially contemplates;)—however plausible in the abstract a theory may sound, which would account for a Chronological difficulty,—the insertion of what seems to be a wrong name,—a quotation made with singular license,—an unscientific statement,—the apparent inconsistency of two or more accounts of one and the same transaction, in respect of lesser details,—a (supposed) inconclusive remark, or specimen of reasoning which seems to be fallacious;—on the supposition that it is not the office of Inspiration to enlighten the understanding on points like these, or to preserve the pen from error;—however plausible, I say, this theory, abstractedly considered, may appear;—it will be found that it will not bear the searching test of a practical application.

It would indeed be a great advantage to the cause

of Truth, and a great help to individual minds, as well as wonderfully promote the arriving at a sound conclusion in this perilous department of speculative Divinity,—if, instead of putting up with a vague theory, (like the present,) regardless of its logical bearings and necessary issues;—men would compel themselves to apply their view to the actual phenomena of Holy Scripture: to carry it out to its legitimate consequences, and steadily to contemplate the result. I venture to predict that the theory which we are now considering, when submitted to such a test, would be found not only inconvenient, but absolutely untenable. The inconsistency and absurdity which results from it, can, I think, easily be made to appear.

For if any one who is disposed to regard it with favour,—instead of idly, (as is the way with nine-tenths of mankind,) repeating the formula in terms more or less vague and indefinite; and straightway wincing, falling back on generalities, and in a word shirking the point, the instant it is proposed to bring the question to a definite issue;—if a favourer of the present theory I say, instead of so acting, would take up a copy of the New Testament, and proceed, with a pen in his hand, to *apply* the theory, by running his pen through the places, (and they *must* be capable of individual specification!), which he suspects of being external to the influence of Inspiration;—or, if you please, which he thinks have been penned without that Divine help which makes what is written infallible;—I venture to predict that such an one will speedily admit that his erasures are either so very few, or so very many, as to be fatal to the theory of which they are the expression.

If they be confined to " the fifteenth year of Tiberius[b]; to the names of the second Cainan[c], Cyrenius[d], Abiathar[e], 'Jeremy the prophet[f];' to "the sixth hour[g]," and so on;—no great inconvenience truly will result. But the instant you go a step further, the difficulty begins. Many of the quotations from the Old Testament may be made to correspond with the Hebrew, doubtless, without sensible inconvenience: but there are others which refuse the process. However, let it be supposed that all such indications of imperfect memory, or misapprehension of the sense of the Hebrew Scriptures, have been removed; and here and there, that an irrelevant clause in the reasoning has been lopped off, or an unscientific remark expunged.—After all this has been done, I venture to say that the result will be the reverse of satisfactory, even to the theorist himself. He will infallibly exclaim secretly,—I seem to have gained wondrous little by this corrective process. Was it worth while, in order to achieve *this*, to tamper with the Divine Oracles? The great body of Scripture remains after all, in all its strangeness, all its perplexing individuality. Meanwhile, piety and wisdom modestly suggest, — Is it reasonable to think that Evangelists and Apostles should have stumbled, like children, before dates, and names, and quotations from their own Scriptures? Surely if *this* be all that can be objected against the Bible, the very slenderness of the charge becomes its sufficient refutation! . . . . . . *The erasures are so few, in fact, that they refute the theory.*

But if, on the other hand, the pen be freely used, then the result will be fatal to the theory, *because it*

[b] St. Luke iii. 1.   [c] Ibid. iii. 36.   [d] Ibid. ii. 2.
[e] St. Mark ii. 26.   [f] St. Matth. xxvii. 9.   [g] St. John xix. 14.

will be fatal to the record. If an 'Essayist and Reviewer' were to reduce the Gospels to consistency, according to *his* view of consistency, the Gospels would scarcely be recognizable. If he were to reject from St. Paul's writings every instance of what *he* thinks fanciful exposition, illogical reasoning, inexact quotation, and mistaken inference; the result would be altogether unmanageable. For any one who attends to the matter will perceive that such things run into the very staple of the Apostle's argument; and therefore cannot be detached without destroying the whole. The householder's reason for not removing the tares, ("lest while ye gather up the tares ye root up also the wheat with them [h],") applies exactly. If St. Paul's exposition of Melchizedek be fanciful and untrustworthy, then does the proof of the superiority of our SAVIOUR's Priesthood over that of Aaron, fall to the ground. If his handling of the story of Sarah and Hagar be an uninspired allegory, then does his argumentation respecting the rejection of the Jews and the calling of the Gentiles disappear. If the furniture of the Temple, and the provisions of the Jewish ritual, were not dictated by the SPIRIT of GOD [i], then will the Epistle wherein it is found be reduced to proportions which make it meaningless. If Deuteronomy xxv. 4 has no reference to the Christian Ministry, then the entire context (in two of St. Paul's Epistles) must go at once [k]. . . . . It is useless to multiply such instances. Any one familiar with the writings of St. Paul will know the truth of what has been offered; and will admit that the erasures required by the theory before us will become so numerous as to

---

[h] St. Matth. xiii. 29. [i] Heb. ix. 8.
[k] 1 Cor. ix. 9 and 1 Tim. v. 18.

prove,—(to a devout mind at least, or indeed to any one of sense and candour,)—that the theory is altogether untenable.

It cannot escape observation, therefore, that however plausible this view of Inspiration may sound, as long as some few petty historical, chronological, and scientific inaccuracies are all that have to be accounted for;—the theory (unhappily) proves worthless when it comes to be practically applied; inasmuch as in the writings of St. Paul, for example, there is little or nothing of the kind just specified, to be condoned. Erroneous dates, unscientific statements, wrong names, and the like, form no part of the staple of the New Testament. Such instances may be counted on one's fingers; and are to be sufficiently explained to render any special theory of Inspiration in order to meet them, quite a gratuitous exercise of ingenuity.

3. On the other hand, if a wider class of phenomena is to be dealt with by this theory, the reader is requested to observe that we involve ourselves in a gross contradiction; for we forsake the very principle on which it pretends to be built. The theory set out by reminding us that " the office of the Bible is to make men wise unto Salvation,"— not to teach physical Science, nor to deal with facts in chronology and the like: and the plea was allowed. But the theory which was devised to account for one class of phenomena is now most unwarrantably applied to account for another. We have travelled into a widely different subject-matter,—namely, *Divinity proper!* Let it therefore be respectfully asked,—If the Inspiration which the Apostles enjoyed did not preserve them against unsound inferences in respect of *Holy Scripture;* and illogical, inconclusive argumentation in *things Divine;*

—pray, of what use was it? We have not been reviewing a set of *Geological* mistakes on the part of the great Apostle. To Physical Science, he has scarcely so much as a single allusion. He deals with *Christian Doctrine;* with *Divinity,* properly so called; and *with that only.* Pray, was not Inspiration a sufficient guide to him, *there?*

4. It is high time also to remind the reader that although the office of the Bible, confessedly, is " to make men wise unto Salvation," it does not by any means follow that *that* is its *only* office. In other words, we have no right to assume that we know all the possible ends for which the Bible was designed; and to lay it down, as if it were an ascertained fact, that it was *not* designed to enlighten men in matters of Chronology, History, and the like; seeing, on the one hand, that all the evidence we are able to adduce in support of such an opinion, does not establish so much as a faint presumption that any part of Scripture *is* uninspired; and seeing that, on the other, as a plain matter of fact, historical details constitute so large a part of the contents of the Bible; and that the sacred volume is *the sole depository* of the History and Chronology of the World for by far the largest portion of the interval since that World's Creation.

5. In passing, it may also be reasonably declared, that it is to take a very derogatory view of the result of the HOLY SPIRIT's influence, to suppose that imperfections and inaccuracies can freely abound,—nay, can exist at all,—in a Revelation which the same HOLY SPIRIT is believed to have inspired. They ought surely to be *demonstrated* to exist, before we are called upon to listen to the apologies which have been invented to account for their existence!

6. Let me also advert to a dilemma which seems hardly ever to obtain from a certain class of critics the attention it deserves. If a writing be not inspired, *it is of no absolute authority.* If a part of a writing be not inspired, that part is of no absolute authority. If a single word in the text of Holy Scripture be even uncertain,—(as, for example, whether we are to read ος or θεος in 1 Tim. iii. 16,)—*that word becomes without absolute authority.* We cannot venture to adduce it *in proof* of anything. Without therefore, in the remotest degree, desiring to discourage the application of a *true* theory of Inspiration to the phenomena of Holy Scripture, through fear of the necessary consequences,—may we not call attention to the manifest awkwardness of a theory which no one knows how to apply, and about the application of which no two men will ever be agreed?—the issue of the discussion being, in every case, neither more nor less than this,—whether the portion of Scripture under consideration is Human, and therefore *of no absolute authority;* or Divine, and therefore *infallible!*

7. A far more important consideration remains to be offered, and with this I shall conclude. Although, when St. Paul appears to reason inconclusively, some of us do not hesitate to refer the Apostle's (supposed) imperfect logic to his personal infirmity,—yet, common piety revolts against the proposal to apply the same solution to the same phenomenon when it is observed to occur in the Discourses of our Blessed Lord Himself. It seems to have been providentially ordained, however, that the discourses of CHRIST Himself should supply examples of every one of those difficulties which it is thought lawful to account for,—when an Apostle or an Evangelist is the speaker,

—on the hypothesis of partial, imperfect, or suspended Inspiration. Now, since *I*, at least, shall not be permitted to be either vague or general, I proceed to subjoin the proof of what has been thus advanced:—

α. The well-known difficulty about "the days of Abiathar," *is found in one of our Lord's discourses*[l]. Here then is a case of what, if an Evangelist or an Apostle had been the author of the statement, would have been called an historical inaccuracy.

β. However unworthy of scientific attention the Mosaic account of the descent of Mankind from a single pair may be deemed,—the universality of 'the Noachian Deluge,'—the destruction of the Cities of the plain,—the fate of Lot's wife,—Jonah in the fish's belly,—and so forth;—to all these (supposed) unscientific statements our Blessed Lord commits Himself unequivocally[m].

γ. When the Holy One inferred the Resurrection of the Dead from the words spoken to Moses "in the bush[n];"—when He proved that Christ is not the son of David, because "David in spirit calls Him 'Lord[o];'"—and when He shewed from a clause in the 6th verse of the lxxxiind Psalm, ("I said ye are gods,") that it was not unlawful for Himself to claim the title of Son of God[p];—I humbly think that the argumentation is of such a nature as would not produce conviction in captious minds cast in a modern mould[q]. I desire not

---

[l] St. Mark ii. 26.

[m] All will be found more fully insisted upon at the beginning of the VIIth Sermon.

[n] St. Luke xx. 37-8.

[o] St. Matth. xxii. 41-6.

[p] St. John x. 34-6.

[q] 'Essayists and Reviewers' would reply, that in the first instance, the supposed inference has no connexion with the premisses:—that

to dwell longer upon this subject; and only hope in what I have ventured to say concerning some of the recorded sayings of Him to whose creative Power and Goodness I am indebted for the exercise of my own reason,—I have not written amiss. But the point of what I am urging is, that I defy any one to bring a charge of faulty logic against passages in St. Paul's Epistles which might not, *with the same show of reason*, be brought against certain of our LORD's recorded sayings.

δ. When the Chief Priests and Scribes remonstrated with our LORD because of the children crying in the Temple; and asked Him,—" Hearest Thou what these say?" He replied,—" Yea, have ye never read, 'Out of the mouths of babes and sucklings Thou hast perfected praise [r] ?' " . . . Now, this quotation from the viiith Psalm is what an 'Essayist or Reviewer' would have pronounced irrelevant.

ε. It seems clear from Gen. ii. 24, that *Adam* was the author of the words, " Therefore shall a man leave his father and his mother," &c. And yet, our LORD (in St. Matth. xix. 4, 5,) as unmistakeably seems to make GOD the Speaker. An Evangelist or an Apostle would be thought here to have made a slip of memory.

ζ. In St. John viii. 47, the following words occur. " He that is of GOD heareth GOD's words: ye there-

---

in the second, (1) it has to be proved that the person intended in Psalm cx. is CHRIST; and (2) it does not follow, because David calls him "lord," that the person so spoken of is not his "son:"—that in the third instance, 'gods' is used in Psalm lxxxii. of *earthly* rulers; whereas, when our SAVIOUR called Himself " the SON of GOD," He claimed to be "*of one substance with the* FATHER,—GOD *of* GOD."

[r] St. Matth. xxi. 16.

fore hear them not, because ye are not of God." This passage (as already pointed out [s],) has been adduced by one who now occupies an Archiepiscopal throne, as containing a logical fallacy.

Many more examples might be adduced: but these will suffice. It is plain that when the like phenomena are observed in the writings of Apostles and Evangelists, we need not, in order to account for them, have recourse to any theory of partial or imperfect Inspiration; since nothing of the kind is supposed necessary when they occur in the Discourses of our Lord.—As much as I care to offer on the subject of *Inspired Reasoning* will be found in the course of the Sixth of these Sermons, where the Doctrine of 'Accommodation' is considered.

[s] See above, p. 4.

To say that the Scriptures, and the things contained in them, can have no other or farther meaning than those persons thought or had, who first recited or wrote them; is evidently saying, that those persons were the original, proper, and sole Authors of those Books, i.e. *that they are not inspired:* which is absurd, whilst the authority of those Books is under examination; i.e. till you have determined they are of no Divine authority at all. Till this be determined, it must in all reason be supposed, (not indeed that they have, for this is taking for granted that they are inspired; but) that they may have, some farther meaning than what the compilers saw or understood.

Bishop Butler, *Analogy*, P. ii. ch. vii.

As the Literal sense is, as it were, the main stream or river, so the Moral sense chiefly, and sometimes the Allegorical or Typical, are they whereof the Church hath most use: not that I wish men to be bold in allegories, or indulgent or light in allusions; but that I do much condemn that Interpretation of the Scripture *which is only after the manner as men use to interpret a profane book.*

Lord Bacon, *Advancement of Learning.*

The Book of this Law we are neither able nor worthy to open and look into. That little thereof which we darkly apprehend, we admire; the rest, with religious ignorance we humbly and meekly adore.

Hooker, *Eccl. Pol.*, B. i. c. ii. § 5.

Open Thou mine eyes that I may see the wondrous things of Thy Law!

ΟΥ ΛΟΓΟΣ ᾿ΑΝΘΡΩΠΩΝ, ᾿ΑΛΛΑ ΚΑΘΩΣ ᾿ΕΣΤΙΝ ᾿ΑΛΗΘΩΣ
ΛΟΓΟΣ ΘΕΟΥ.

SERMON V.[a]

INTERPRETATION OF HOLY SCRIPTURE.—INSPIRED INTERPRETATION.—THE BIBLE IS NOT TO BE INTERPRETED LIKE ANY OTHER BOOK.—GOD, (NOT MAN,) THE REAL AUTHOR OF THE BIBLE.

St. Matthew iv. 4.

It is written, Man shall not live by bread alone, but by every word that proceedeth out of the mouth of God.

IT is impossible to preserve exact method in Sermons like these, uncertain in number, and delivered at irregular intervals. It shall only be stated that, having already spoken at considerable length, of the Inspiration of Holy Scripture;—not, one part more, one part less, but every part equally inspired throughout; not general, (whatever the exact notion may be of a book *generally* inspired,) but particular, by which I mean that *every word* is none other than the utterance of the Holy Ghost[b]: having, moreover, explained the

---

[a] Preached at St. Mary-the-Virgin, on the Third Sunday in Lent, March 3rd, 1861.

[b] "It cannot be said that this, [viz. that *the Bible is the Word of God,*] is always remembered. It cannot be said that they who write respecting the Bible, even Christian writers who are looked up to, always appear to have been in that frame of mind while contemplating the statements of the Sacred Volume, which they, the same men, would have been in if they had been listening *for a voice out of a cloud;* a word reaching them which was simply, and in that sense, the Word of God. Yet the Sacred Volume comes to us with

reasonableness,—(the logical necessity, as it seems,)—of giving such an account of the Bible;—I propose to-day to proceed to the subject of INTERPRETATION. Really, it has become the fashion of a School of unbelief which has lately emerged into infamous notoriety, to deal with both these questions in so insolent a style of dogmatism, that the preacher is compelled to halt *in limine;* and to explain that he begs that no offence may be taken at the account which he has just given of the Bible; for that really he means no more than Bp. Pearson meant when he said that "*the Scripture phrase*" is "*the Language of the* HOLY GHOST[c]:"—that he desires to say no other thing than what *He* said, by whose Spirit, (as St. Peter declares[d],) the prophets prophesied;—the preacher, I say, wishes to explain that he desires to mean no other thing than our LORD JESUS CHRIST Himself meant, when He spoke of "*every word that proceedeth out of the mouth of* GOD."

I. INTERPRETATION, then, in the largest sense of the term, I take to denote the discovery of the method and meaning of Holy Scripture.—I exclude those critical labours which merely aim at establishing a correct text.—I exclude also the learning which merely investigates the grammatical force of single words. True, that even to translate is often to interpret; but this results only from the imperfection of language,—which can seldom represent the words of one idiom by the words of another, without at the

---

no less claims than as conveying such a message; and on every feature of it, it carries that claim. It professes to be this,—an account of what went on in the secret council-chamber of the MOST HIGH."—Eden's *Sermons,* pp. 150-1.

[c] *Exposition of the Creed,* Art. II. ("Our LORD,")—vol. i. p. 183.
[d] 1 St. Peter i. 11.

same time parting with the associations which belong to the old words, and importing those which are inseparable from the new.—Moreover, except occasionally, it is presumed that the lore of the Antiquary, Geographer, and so forth, does not aspire to the dignity of Interpretation.—To be brief,—whatever simply puts us on a level with ordinary hearers of ancient days; does no more than inform us what custom, locality, or date is intended by the sacred writer; (things which once were obvious, and which *ought not* to be any difficulty now;)—all this, I say, seems external to the province of Interpretation; the purpose of which is to discover *the method* and *the meaning* of Holy Writ. And I find that every extant specimen of this sacred Science is either (1) what God hath Himself revealed; or (2) what the Church hath with authority delivered; or (3) what individuals have thought themselves competent to declare.

Of these three authorities concerning the sense of Scripture, it is evident that the last-named is entitled to least notice. So unimportant indeed is it, as scarcely to be of any weight at all. What one individual asserts, on his own unsupported authority, another individual may, with as much or as little authority, deny; and *who* is to decide?

But the authority indicated in the second place, clearly challenges very different attention. When, for example, our own Hooker declares, concerning the 5th verse of the iiird chapter of St. John, that "of all the ancients *there is not one to be named* that ever did otherwise expound or allege this place than as implying external Baptism^e," we perceive at once that such consent, on the part of men in whose ears the echoes of the Apo-

^e *Eccl. Pol.*, B. v. c. lix. § 3.

stolic Age had not yet quite ceased to vibrate; and who were themselves professors of that Divine Science which takes cognizance of the subject-matter in hand:—such general consent of Antiquity, I say, on a point of Interpretation, must evidently be held to be decisive.

"Religio mihi est, eritque, contra torrentem omnium Patrum, Sanctas Scripturas interpretari; nisi quando me argumenta cogunt evidentissima,—quod nunquam eventurum credo [f]." So spake one who had read the Fathers with no common care, and who turned his reading to no common account. "I persuade myself," he says, "that you will learn the modesty of submitting your judgment to that of the Catholic Doctors, where they are found generally to concur in the interpretation of a text of Scripture, how absurd soever that interpretation may, at first appearance, seem to be. For upon a diligent search you will find, that *aliquid latet quod non patet*,—'there is a mystery in the bottom:' and that which at first view seemed even ridiculous, will afterwards appear to be a most certain truth [g]." "No man can oppose Catholic consent, but he will at last be found to oppose both the Divine Oracles and Sound Reason [h]."

---

[f] Bp. Bull, *Defensio Fid. Nic.* I. i. 9, (*Works*, vol. v. i. p. 22.)

[g] Disc. v. *The state of Man before the Fall.* Bull's Works, vol. ii. p. 99.

[h] "Deus novit cordis mei secreta: in dogmatis theologicis a novaturiendi prurigine (quam etiam supremi Judicis tribunal insiliens fidenter mihi tribuit theologiæ professor) adeo alienus sum, ut quæcunque catholicorum Patrum et veterum episcoporum consensu comprobata sunt, etiamsi meum ingeniolum ea non assequatur, tamen omni reverentia amplexurus sim. Nimirum non paucis experimentis monitus didiceram, cum adhuc juvenis Harmoniam scriberem, (quod mihi jam confirmata ætate persuasissimum est,) *neminem*

The distinction thus drawn between individual opinion and the collective voice of the Church, was far better understood anciently than at present. The interpretation of a Council, especially if œcumenical, was accounted decisive. Even the generally consentient voice of Doctors and Fathers, as far as it could be ascertained, was held to be of the same authoritative kind. An interesting illustration occurs. Than Eusebius, Bishop of Cæsarea, few Fathers of the fourth century were more learned in Holy Scripture. He, commenting upon "the Captain of the LORD's Host," mentioned in the vth chapter of the Book of Joshua, delivers it as his opinion that it was the same Personage who spoke to Moses 'in the Bush;' viz. the Eternal Son[1]. On which opinion, a learned man of the same age, in a scholion of singular beauty which has come down to us, remarks as follows:—"Aye, but the Church, O most holy Eusebius, holds a view on this subject altogether at variance with thine[k]."

---

catholico consensui repugnare posse, quin is (utcunque ipsi aliquantisper adblandiri videantur sacræ Scripturæ loca nonnulla perperam intellecta, et levicularum ratiuncularum phantasmata) *tandem et Divinis Oraculis et sanæ rationi repugnasse deprehendatur.*"—Bp. Bull's *Works*, vol. iv. p. 313.

[1] In days of unbelief, one is tempted to add a note even on a Theological truism like that in the text,—"Esto igitur, inquies; fuerit DEUS, qui in Veteri Testamento, sive per Angelum, sive sub angelicâ repræsentatione sanctis viris apparuit et locutus est; at quâ demum ratione adducti crediderunt doctores, fuisse DEI FILIUM? Respondeo: *Ratione, ni fallor, optimâ, quam ex traditione Apostolicâ edidicerant.*" — *Def. Fid. Nicæn.* I. i. 12. Bp. Bull's *Works*, vol. v. i. p. 27.

[k] Ἀλλ' ἡ ἐκκλησία, ὦ ἁγιώτατε Εὐσέβιε, ἑτέρως τὰ περὶ τούτου νομίζει καὶ οὐχ ὡς σύ. τὸν μὲν γὰρ ἐν τῇ βάτῳ φανέντα τῷ Μωϋσῇ θεολογεῖ· τὸν δὲ ἐν Ἱεριχῷ τῷ μετ' αὐτὸν ὀφθέντα, τὸν τῶν Ἑβραίων ἐπιστασίαν λαχόντα, μάχαιραν ἐσπασμένον, καὶ τῷ Ἰησοῦ λῦσαι προστάττοντα τὸ ὑπόδημα, τοῦτον

He goes on to allege reasons why the ἀρχιστράτηγος of Joshua must be held to have been not an *uncreated*, but a *created* Angel; the Archangel Michael, in fact. We will not now go into that matter. You are but requested to observe, how profoundly unimportant the opinion of a very learned individual was held to be, by one in whose ears the Patristic "torrent" was yet sounding; although Justin Martyr is known to have been of the same mind with Eusebius.—And thus much for individual views as to the meaning of Holy Scripture; as contrasted with the decisions of Councils and Fathers. To judge from the signs of the Age, we have exactly reversed the ancient estimate; and expect that more respect will be shewn to our own private fancies, than to a general consensus of Divines, ancient and modern. It seems to have been discovered that the supreme guide of Life is the individual conscience,—" without appeal—except to himself[1]!"

II. Before descending, however, to the *business* of Interpretation, there is clearly one preliminary question to be settled: namely, *the principle* on which Interpretation is to be conducted. And this is all that can be discussed to-day. To seek for that principle in the contradictory pages of solitary theorists, would of course be hopeless, as well as absurd. To elicit it from Patristic Commentaries, would obviously leave a door open for cavil. The ancient Fathers, (allowing

---

δέ γε τὸν ἀρχάγγελον ὑπείληφε Μιχαήλ, κ.τ.λ.—The entire passage may be seen in the best annotated editions of Eusebius, (lib. I. c. ii. § 17.) since that of Valesius, who first introduced it to notice. But to read it in a truly valuable context, reference should be made to Dr. Mill's *Christian Advocate's* publication for 1841, p. 92. The note alluded to has been reprinted in Dr. Lee's Discourses *On Inspiration*, p. 535.

[1] *Essays and Reviews*, p. 31.

that they often speak with consentient voice,) singly, were but fallible men,—however famous, as professors of Theological Science, they may have been. *This*, however, I venture to assume without any hesitation whatever,—that if, instead of either of these two ways of ascertaining how Holy Scripture ought to be handled, we can be so fortunate as to discover from the Inspired Writers themselves what *their* method was with respect to the Word of GOD,—in such case, I say, we shall be in a position of entire certainty[m]. We shall then have full warrant for disregarding the dicta of modern sciolists on this great subject;— however arrogant their dogmatism, however confident their unsupported asseverations.

I desire to be very clearly understood. My position is this. All Christian men allow that the Apostles and Evangelists of our LORD were inspired. Before such an audience as the present, I will not condescend even to *allude* to the absolute claim of our SAVIOUR CHRIST, who, as the Son of Man, enjoyed the gift of the Spirit without measure; who, as very GOD, "in the beginning created the Heaven and the Earth,"—(for, "In the beginning was THE WORD; and THE WORD was with GOD; and THE WORD was GOD. . . . All things were made by Him, and without Him was not anything made that was made[n]:")— I will not, I say, for every utterance of our SAVIOUR CHRIST pause even, to claim the entire reverence of our hearts,—the prostrate homage of our understandings. . . . Well then. If we *can* but discover what the mind and method of these several speakers and writers was, with regard to the Interpretation of Holy Scripture; on what principle, and with what senti-

[m] See Appendix (J).   [n] St. John i. 1—3.

ments, *they* handled the Book of God's Law; we shall have discovered the thing of which we are in search. For the *Author* of a book must perforce be allowed to be the best judge of the method and intention of that book:—the Holy Spirit *must* be allowed to be the best authority as to His own meaning!

Now this method,—(of which, as I will presently remind you, we possess a great many specimens,)—proves to be very extraordinary. It altogether establishes the fact that the Bible *is not to be interpreted* "*like any other book.*" That it *could* not be so interpreted, might have been confidently anticipated beforehand, from the very fact of its Divine origin°. What I mean,—Since, "by the mouth of David," the Holy Ghost is expressly declared by Christ and by St. Peter to have " spoken ;" and since the Psalms collectively are described by St. Paul as the utterance of the Holy Ghost; since Jeremiah's witness is said to be the witness of the Holy Ghost; and the Holy Ghost is actually said to have spoken by Isaiah; while the Spirit of Christ Himself, (St. Peter says,) dwelt in the Prophets:—in a word, since "holy men of God spake *as they were moved by* the Holy Ghost," and the provisions of the Mosaic Law are to the same Holy Ghost by St. Paul emphatically ascribed ᵖ;—stubborn *facts*, you are requested to observe, which Essayists may prudently suppress but which no Sophistry on earth can either evade or

---

° So Bp. Butler, in a passage which will be found below, at p. 165-6.—Very different is the judgment of Professor Jowett, who is of opinion that " it will be a further assistance in the consideration of this subject, to observe that *the Interpretation of Scripture has nothing to do with any opinion respecting its origin.*"—*Essays and Reviews*, p. 350.

ᵖ See above, pp. 55—57.

deny:—seeing, I say, that Holy Scripture is declared by inspired men to be the utterance of the Eternal GOD, it was to have been expected beforehand that its texture would bear witness to its Divine origin; and that, to interpret it "like any other book," would be to forget its extraordinary character. Interpret Sophocles and Plato, if you will, like any other book, for a very plain reason; but beware how you apply your purely human notions to the utterance of the Ancient of Days; for that utterance, enshrined in one particular volume, clearly makes that one volume essentially unlike any other volume in the world.

You are particularly requested to observe, further,—that singular pains have been taken to mystify this entire subject. It has been a favourite device to multiply difficulties,—real or imaginary,—and so, to create a miserable sense of the dangers which fairly hem the subject in,—in order to render more palatable a desperate escape from them all. Thus, we are told of the risks to which Grammatical nicety, and Rhetorical accommodation expose us; and again, the snares into which the Logical method may betray. Metaphysical aid, we are assured, mystifies; and even Learning, (would to Heaven we had a little more of it!) obscures the sense[q]. Might we just take the liberty of suggesting that the study of the exploded works of German unbelievers, (of which Germany herself, thank

---

[q] Professor Jowett in *Essays and Reviews*, pp. 393—402. He adds,—"Discussions respecting the use of the Greek article, have gone far beyond the line of utility. There seem to be reasons for doubting whether any considerable light can be thrown on the New Testament from inquiry into the language.... Minute corrections of tenses or particles are no good." (p. 393.) And this, from a Regius Professor of Greek!

God! is beginning to be ashamed,) on the part of men of very moderate intellectual powers, however wise in their own conceit; and with no previous Theological knowledge to guide them,—is another yet more fruitful avenue to error? ... Next, we are threatened with the manifold inconveniences which would ensue from the discovery that there is more than one sense in Holy Scripture,—(*that* one sense being assumed to be, *not* the sense intended by its Divine Author, but the sense which the first hearers may be supposed to have put upon it[r].) "If words may have more than one meaning," (it is not very logically argued,) "they may have *any* meaning[s]." We are told a great deal about "the growth of ideas;" and of human prejudices; and of "the disturbing influence of Theological terms."—But all this kind of thing, it will be perceived at once, is altogether foreign to the matter in hand. *Ought Scripture to be interpreted like any other book,—or not? That* is the real question! *Has Scripture only one meaning,* or *more? That* is the point in dispute! Above all, *What is the true principle of Scripture Interpretation? That* is the only thing we have to discover!

Now, as for *how* the principles of Divine Interpretation are to be discovered, it is undeniable that there can be no surer way than by discovering *what is the method of the* HOLY GHOST; by inquiring, what is the method of our SAVIOUR CHRIST, and of His Evangelists, and of His Apostles?

1. Surely it is needless to remind an audience like the present, *what* that method is! Turn the first page of St. Matthew's Gospel, and weigh well the three famous cases of Interpretation which there encounter

[r] See below, pp. 164-5.   *Essays and Reviews*, p. 372.

you[t]:—namely, the assurance that Hosea's words, "Out of Egypt have I called my son[u];"—that Jeremiah's declaration concerning the tears of Rachel[x];—and that the many prophetic utterances concerning "the Branch[y];"—found fulfilment, each, in CHRIST. The first,—when, at Jehovah's bidding, He was carried up out of Egypt into Palestine; the second,—when the bereaved mothers of Bethlehem wept for their murdered offspring; the third,—when CHRIST, being bred up in Nazareth, was called a "Nazarene,"—the root of which, etymologically, denotes "a branch."—But look further, and your surprise will increase at discovering how extraordinary the Divine method is. When our Saviour cast out evil spirits and healed the sick, St. Matthew declares that He fulfilled that prophecy of Isaiah, "Himself took our infirmities and bare our sicknesses[z];" the language of the prophet in fact being, "Surely He hath borne our *griefs* and carried our *sorrows*[a];" which, as far as the words go, is rather a different thing.

2. But it is St. Paul who affords us the largest induction of instances. When he would establish the right of the Clergy to have due provision made for them, he finds his warrant in a most unexpected place of Scripture. "Say I these things as a man? or saith not the Law the same also? For it is written in the Law of Moses, 'Thou shalt not muzzle the mouth of the ox that treadeth out the corn.' Doth GOD care for the oxen here alluded to[b]? ($\mu\grave{\eta}$ $\tau\hat{\omega}\nu$ $\beta o\hat{\omega}\nu$

---

[t] St. Matth. ii. 15: 17, 18: 23.   [u] Hos. xi. 1.
[x] Jer. xxxi. 15.   [y] e.g. Is. xi. 1. Also Zech. iii. 8: vi. 12. Jer. xxiii. 5 and xxxiii. 15.
[z] St. Matth. viii. 17.   [a] Is. liii. 4.
[b] For consider Exod. ix. 19, Jonah iv. 11, &c.

μέλει τῷ Θεῷ;) or saith He it altogether for our sakes? *For our sakes,* no doubt, this is written [c]." I remind you of the entire passage, because it is so very express.—Elsewhere, St. Paul adduces a few verses from the viiith Psalm, the primary and more obvious meaning of which appears to assert nothing more than the supremacy of Man's present nature over the inferior races of animals; ("all sheep and oxen, yea and all the beasts of the field [d].") The application of it, in a prophetic sense, to the supreme dominion of our Redeemer over all created beings in Heaven and Earth, is certainly not one which would naturally suggest itself to us; yet is it for this purpose, and this only, that St. Paul adduces it; and as confirmatory of the universal sovereignty of CHRIST, the place in question is three times quoted by the same Apostle [e].—Elsewhere, when he would warn persons who have been partakers of both Sacraments, of the danger of final rejection, he cites the example of the Fathers of Israel in the Wilderness. "The waters of the Red Sea were a wall unto them, on their right hand and on their left [f]," and the watery Cloud covered them

[c] 1 Cor. ix. 8—10, quoting Deut. xxv. 4. See also 1 Tim. v. 18.—"It seems providentially appointed that texts of the Old Testament should be called out into Christian meaning which are the very texts we might have dismissed into a transitory interest. 'Thou shalt not muzzle the ox that treadeth out the corn.' 'Humane provision!', modern observation might say. 'Is it for oxen GOD careth?' is an Apostle's interpretation of the same text; 'or saith He it altogether *for our sakes?*' . . . . It is a law, we find, prospectively set down for the Christian Church."—Eden's *Sermons,* p. 189.

[d] Ps. viii. 7.

[e] Heb. ii. 6—8. 1 Cor. xv. 25, and Eph. i. 22.—See Shuttleworth's *Paraphrase* of the first place cited, p. 394.

[f] Exod. xiv. 22, 29.

above; whereby it came to pass that "all our Fathers were under the Cloud, and all passed through the Sea; and were all therefore *baptized* unto Moses in the Cloud and in the Sea." Moreover, he declares that they " did all eat the same spiritual meat;" (alluding to the Manna;) "and did all drink the same spiritual drink: for they drank of that spiritual Rock that followed them: and *that Rock was* Christ[g]." .... Our Saviour's emphatic application to Himself (in the vith of St. John) of the Manna, "the bread which came down from Heaven,"—none can forget[h].

3. But St. Paul further largely interprets the ordinances of the Mosaic Law. Thus, the provision that the High-priest alone should enter, once a year, into the Holy of Holies, not without blood, he interprets as follows;—"the Holy Ghost this signifying,"— (" the *Holy Ghost this signifying !*)—that the way into the holiest of all was not yet made manifest, while as the first Tabernacle was yet standing[i]." He explains further that "Christ being come an High-Priest of good things to come, by a greater and more perfect Tabernacle, ... by His own Blood entered in once into the Holy Place, having obtained eternal Redemption for us[j]." — The Veil of the Temple, (he says,) typified Christ's flesh[k]; and St. Paul intimates that he could further have spoken particularly of the Golden Censer, and the Ark of the Covenant, and the Pot of Manna, and Aaron's rod, and the Tables of the Covenant, and the Cherubims of Glory[l].—Again, he says, that "the bodies of those beasts whose blood

[g] 1 Cor. x. 1—4.
[h] St. John vi. 32—58.
[i] Hebr. ix. 6—9.
[j] *Ibid.*, v. 11, 12.
[k] Διὰ τοῦ καταπετάσματος, τουτέστι τῆς σαρκὸς αὐτοῦ. Hebr. x. 20.
[l] Hebr. ix. 2—5.

is brought into the Sanctuary by the High Priest for Sin, are burned without the camp. Wherefore JESUS also, that He might sanctify the people with His own Blood, *suffered without the gate*[m]."—*Who* is not familiar with the same Apostle's declaration that the words of our father Adam relative to Marriage, are expressive of a great mystery, and set forth symbolically the union of CHRIST and His Church; "For we are members of His Body,—of His Flesh and of His Bones[n]?"—St. Peter is at least as remarkable in his Interpretations as St. Paul; for he says of the Ark "wherein eight souls were saved by water,"—"The like figure whereunto, even Baptism, doth also now save us[o]."

Now these samples of *Inspired Interpretation* would be abundantly sufficient for our present purpose. But before I proceed to make any use of them, it is right to draw attention to a phenomenon, even more extraordinary.

4. It is found then, that besides vindicating for the Scriptures of the Old Testament this unsuspected depth and fulness of prophetic and typical meaning, the very Narrative itself teems to overflowing with mysterious purpose. You have but to weigh well what the HOLY SPIRIT hath delivered concerning Abraham and Melchizedek, Hagar and Sarah,—to perceive that the texture of the Historical Narrative itself is of supernatural fabric. All are familiar with what I allude to; but I *must* remind you of it, in detail. The Apostle is bent on shewing the superiority of our SAVIOUR's Priesthood to that of Aaron. How does he proceed? He lays his finger, unhesi-

---

[m] Hebr. xiii. 11, 12.   [n] Eph. v. 30—32.
[o] Ὅτι καὶ ἡμᾶς ἀντίτυπον νῦν σώζει βάπτισμα. 1 St. Pet. iii. 21.

tatingly, on a verse in the cxth Psalm, ("Thou art a Priest for ever after the order of Melchizedek;")—declares with authority that it is CHRIST whom the prophet there alludes to,—or rather, whom GOD apostrophizes,—(for *that* is what St. Paul actually *says;* προσαγορευθεὶς ὑπὸ τοῦ Θεοῦ[p] : although David undeniably wrote the Psalm;)—and proceeds, without more ado, to draw out minutely the characteristics of our SAVIOUR's Priesthood, from the very brief narrative contained in the xivth Chapter of Genesis. Do but hear him!

The compound name "Melchi-zedek," being interpreted, denotes " King of Righteousness:" while " King of Salem" denotes " King of Peace." These titles, (it is implied,) are emphatically appropriate to CHRIST our King; to Him who " is our Righteousness," and the very " Prince of Peace." It happens that nothing is said in Genesis about the parentage of Melchizedek, nor about the family from which he sprang: not a word as to when he was born, or when he died. From this *silence* of Scripture, St. Paul collects the typical adumbration of One who, as very GOD, was *without* human parentage,—had *no* earthly lineage;—" was before all things," GOD from all eternity,—having *indeed* " neither beginning of days nor end of life."—Did not Abraham give to Melchizedek a tithe of the spoils? Consider then, (St. Paul says,) how great an one Melchizedek must have been! Nay, consider that the descendants of Levi are commanded to take tithe of their brethren, although all are sprung from Abraham alike; but here is one, altogether of a different family, taking tithes *of Abraham*,—aye and *blessing* Abraham too;—(δεδεκάτωκε,

[p] Hebr. v. 10.

εὐλόγηκε, "*hath* tithed," "*hath* blessed,"—the effect of the act *remaining* for ever in CHRIST typified by Melchizedek.)—This mysterious King of Salem and Priest of the Most High GOD not only tithes but blesses Abraham, who had received from ALMIGHTY GOD the promises, which included all blessedness, earthly and heavenly. Now, this implies Melchizedek's superiority,—for, of course, the less is blessed of the greater.—Men who receive tithe here below are mortal; but the very silence of Scripture respecting Melchizedek's death, symbolically teaches that HE whom Melchizedek typified, yet liveth.—And indeed, (so to speak,) the tribe of Levi who take tithes, *paid* tithes to Melchizedek in the person of their great progenitor; because Levi was as yet in the loins of his father Abraham when Melchizedek met him[q]. . . . I do not ask your pardon for thus leading you in detail over one unusually minute specimen of Divine Interpretation. I know well that there are many persons to whom the Divine method is highly distasteful; and who think their own method of Interpretation infinitely better. But, unfortunately for those persons, the question in hand is not a question of taste, but a dry *matter of fact*. We have to discover what is *the Divine method* of Interpretation, and no other thing. Its improbability and its inconvenience, —its difficulty, and its strangeness,—its seeming inconclusiveness, (apart from the authority on which it rests,) and its certain uniqueness, (notwithstanding the many injunctions we have met with that we must

---

[q] Hebr. vii. 1—10. The student in Divinity will find it well worth his while to inquire for a Latin Dissertation by the late learned Dr. W. H. Mill on this subject.

interpret the Bible like any other book[r],)—all these considerations are all together irrelevant, and beside the question. St. Paul himself admits that the Discourse now before us is πολὺς καὶ δυσερμήνευτος,— long and of difficult interpretation[s].—Some will perhaps be found to inquire how it happens that while so many remote points of analogy are adduced, so obviously typical a circumstance as Melchizedek's *bringing forth " bread and wine*[t]*"* obtains no notice from the Apostle? I answer,—For the same reason that Isaac is nowhere spoken of, nowhere so much as hinted at, in the Bible, as being a type of CHRIST. A blind man may see it. It requires no Revelation from Heaven to teach such things as *that !* But the typical foreshadowing of the superiority of our SAVIOUR's Priesthood over that of Aaron, in the story of Melchizedek, would infallibly have escaped mankind altogether, unless it had been thus specially revealed.

Some there may be so utterly wanting in Theological instinct, or so depraved of taste; so utterly unused to the study of GOD's Word, or so unobservant of the characteristic method of it,—as to imagine that there is something trifling in the specimens of Interpretation before us. I am only concerned to maintain that they are Divine. You may think what you please about them. They are the teaching of the HOLY GHOST. Nay, if unfortunately any persons here present should think themselves wiser than GOD, I would request them to observe that, singularly enough, GOD has connected with this very exposition a short address *to themselves.* It runs as follows:—" Concern-

---

[r] *Essays and Reviews*, pp. 338, 375, 377, 419-20, 426, 428, 429, &c. The advice is Professor Jowett's.

[s] Hebr. v. 11.   [t] Gen. xiv. 18.

ing Melchizedek, we have to deliver a long and difficult interpretation; difficult, however, *only because ye have become dull of hearing*ⁿ." ('The fault, you observe, is *yours*. Whereas GOD made your spiritual senses sharp and quick, you have blunted their edge, and are become stupid and obtuse. It follows:)—"For when, by reason of the length of time that ye have professed Christianity, ye ought to be Teachers,"—(pray mark *that!*),—"ye have need that some one should teach *you* the first Principles of the Oracles of GOD; and ye have become such as have need of milk, and not of solid food. For every one that useth milk, is without experience in the Word of Righteousness; for he is an infant. But solid food (στερεὰ τροφή) is for them that are of full age ᵛ." Where you are requested to observe that a specimen of Interpretation *you* think trifling, the HOLY GHOST calls "*solid food;*" and yourselves, who in your own conceit represent the World's Manhoodˣ, *He* calls νηπίους,—"*babes.*" .... This discrepancy of opinion strikes me as rather curious.

5. The time would fail, were we to enter as particularly into the Divine Interpretation elsewhere given of another story, apparently as little fraught with mystery as any in the Bible. *Who* would ever have imagined that the brief narrative of Hagar's dismissal from the house of Abraham at Sarah's instance, was the ἀλληγορία of so Divine a thing as St. Paul declares;—the two Mothers setting forth the two Covenants, (one, bearing children unto bondage,—the other, the free Mother of us all: Sinai symbolized by *that*, the heavenly Jerusalem by *this:*) and even Ish-

---

ⁿ Νωθροὶ γεγόνατε ταῖς ἀκοαῖς.—Hebr. v. 11.
ᵛ Hebr. v. 12—14.   ˣ Dr. Temple in *Essays and Reviews*.

mael's mockery not being without mysterious meaning?—Such however is the Divine Interpretation.—Elsewhere, when St. Paul desires to contrast the method of the Gospel with the method of the Law,—(*this*, glorious; *that*, with the same glorious features concealed;)—and also to illustrate the present unbelief of the Jewish nation;—the Apostle finds a prophetic emblem of their blindness in the veiled countenance of their great Lawgiver, as described in the xxxivth chapter of Exodus. The mystical intention of that veil, (he says,) was to symbolize the nation's inability to look steadfastly to the end of the dispensation, and to recognize MESSIAH. Nay, to this hour, while they read their Scriptures, that veil (he says) is upon their hearts. And yet, even as Moses, when he returned to GOD, is related to have taken off the veil from his face, so (St. Paul says) will it fare with the Jews, when *they* convert and turn themselves to CHRIST. The veil will be withdrawn[y].—Now, I gather from all this, and many a hint of the like kind,—that the whole of Scripture is of the same marvellous texture, the Old Testament and the New, alike,—whether we have the eyes to see it or not.

6. But I cannot dismiss the typical character of the Scripture narrative, until I have reminded you of one striking intimation of it which you might easily overlook. "O fools and slow of heart," was our LORD's reproof to Cleophas and his companion on the evening of the first Easter: "Ought not CHRIST

---

[y] 2 Cor. iii. 12—16.—Take notice that in allusion to the place, Exod. xxxiv. 34, (ἡνίκα δ' ἂν εἰσεπορεύετο Μωϋσῆς ἔναντι Κυρίου λαλεῖν αὐτῷ, περιῃρεῖτο τὸ κάλυμμα,) St. Paul says,—ἡνίκα δ' ἂν ἐπιστρέψῃ πρὸς Κύριον, περιαιρεῖται τὸ κάλυμμα. The expression is altered in order to bring out more clearly the allegorical meaning.

to have suffered these things, and to enter into His
Glory? And *beginning at Moses* and all the Prophets,
He expounded unto them in all the Scriptures the
things concerning Himself[z]." In like manner, St.
Paul at Rome expounded to the unbelieving Jews,
"persuading them concerning Jesus both *out of the
Law of Moses* and out of the Prophets, from morning
till evening[a]." The same thing is repeated elsewhere[b]: but the most express declaration is that of
our Lord Himself to the Jews:—" Had ye believed
Moses, ye would have believed Me; *for he wrote of
Me*[c]." Moses therefore *wrote concerning* Christ.
Christ Himself says so. But *where?* Shew me the
places in the Pentateuch which prove that Christ
was "to suffer these things" and then to "enter into
glory?" You cannot do it; unless indeed in Isaac's
Sacrifice you are content to find the adumbration of
the scene on Calvary. You cannot do it; unless in
Joseph's betrayal for twenty pieces of silver, (the deed
of another Judas!) and his letting down into the pit
without water, you recognize the image of the death
of One by the blood of whose Covenant the prisoners
of hope were set free[d]. You cannot do it; unless in
the same Joseph's exaltation to the supreme power of
Egypt, (when they "cried before him, Bow the
knee!") you behold Messiah's session at the Right
Hand of God. You cannot do it; unless you notice
how "Joseph, who was ordained to save his Brethren
from death, who would have slain *him*, did represent
the Son of God, who was slain by us and yet dying
saved us[e]." You cannot do it; unless in the Paschal

[z] St. Luke xxiv. 25—27.
[b] Acts xxvi. 22, 23.
[d] Zech. ix. 11, 12.
[a] Acts xxviii. 23.
[c] St. John v. 46, 47.
[e] Bp. Pearson.

Lamb, and the wave-sheaf, you discern things Heavenly, and of eternal moment. You cannot do it; unless you remember " that as, in order to consecrate the Harvest by offering to God the first-fruits of it, a sheaf was lifted up and waved; as well as a Lamb offered on that day by the priest to God; so Messiah, that immaculate Lamb which was to die, that Priest which dying was to offer up Himself to God, was upon the same day lifted up and raised from the dead; or rather shook and lifted up, and presented Himself to God, and so was accepted for us all; that so our dust might be sanctified, our corruption hallowed, our mortality consecrated to eternity." Many who hear me will perceive that I have been quoting from Bp. Pearson; and will be constrained to admit that Isaac and Joseph,—the wave-sheaf and the Paschal Lamb,—may well be types of Christ; and that, thus lightly touched, there can be little objection to tracing in such histories and provisions of the Law, the main outlines of the Life and Death and Resurrection of our Redeemer. But remember, we have handled wondrous little of the patriarchal History and of the Law; and that little, wondrous cursorily; more, as it seems to me, in the manner of children in a Sunday-school, than as Divines in the first University of Europe! ... Now, *St. Paul* entertained *his* audience " from morning until evening." Had he nothing to say about Paradise, think you, and the mysterious parallel between the first and second Adam? nothing to say about the Ark of Noah, and the waters of the Flood? What of the history of the patriarch Jacob, and of Joseph " at the second time made known to his brethren?" What of Moses, and the miracles of the Exode? What of the many minute provisions, (all of them, no doubt, significant!) of the Mosaic Law? What of Esau's posterity and Balaam's prophecies,—the Cloud and the Flame,—the Manna and the Quails,—the riven Rock and Jordan driven back? . . .

I have already said enough to feel at liberty to gather out of it all, the two chief propositions concerning Holy Scripture, which it is my business this morning to establish. And first, I assert that it may be regarded as a fundamental rule, that the Bible *is not to be interpreted like any other book*. This I gather infallibly from the plain fact, that *the inspired Writers themselves* habitually interpret it *as no other book either is, or can be interpreted*.

Next, I assert without fear of contradiction that inspired Interpretation, whatever varieties of method it may exhibit, is yet uniform and unequivocal in this one result; namely, that it proves Holy Scripture to be of far deeper significancy than at first sight appears [f]. By no imaginable artifice of Rhetoric or sophistry of evasion,—by no possible vehemence of denial or plausibility of counter assertion,—can it be rendered probable that Scripture has invariably one only meaning; and *that* meaning, the most obvious and easy to those who first heard or read it.

I would not be misunderstood by this audience, nor do I fear that I shall be. I am not denying (GOD forbid!) the literal sense of Scripture. Rather am I, above all, contending for it. We may *never* play tricks with the letter. Those Six Days of Creation, depend upon it, were *six days:* and the Tree of Life, and the Tree of Knowledge, and the Serpent, were the very things they are called,—and

[f] Consider St. John ii. 17, 22: xii. 16. St. Luke xxiv. 8, 45. Acts xi. 16.

no other things. So of every other part of the Bible. The Temptation of our LORD was as matter of fact a transaction as one of His walks by the sea of Galilee. *In what form* the Tempter came to Him, hath not been revealed. *After what fashion* the Prince of the power of the air contrived the dazzling panorama "in a moment of time[g]," I do not pretend to understand. The literal sense of what has been revealed, is, for all that, to be depended on. All is sincere History: *nothing* is ever allegory,—*nothing* may ever be evacuated or explained away! We have our LORD's own word for it. The speech in Paradise, and what happened at the time of the Flood; the fate of Lot's wife, and what befel the cities of the plain; the conduct of David (when he ate the shew-bread), and the visit to Solomon of the Queen of Sheba; the history of the widow of Sarepta, and of Naaman the Syrian: —all these stories of the Old Testament are by our LORD Himself appealed to as veritable History[h].

But I am proving that Scripture itself, literally understood, compels us to believe that *under* the letter of Scripture, (which *of course* is to be *interpreted* literally,) there lies a deeper and sometimes a far less obvious meaning; occasionally a meaning so improbable, (as men account improbability,) that, but for the finger of GOD pointing it out, we could never by possibility have discerned it; so extraordinary, that when it is shewn us, it needs an effort of the heart and of the mind to embrace it fully.

Cases of literal Interpretation are indeed of constant occurrence in Scripture; but the principle on

[g] 'Εν στιγμῇ χρόνου.—St. Luke iv. 5.
[h] St. Matth. xix. 5. St. Luke xvii. 27 and 32. St. Matth. xi. 23: xii. 4 and 42. St. Luke iv. 25—27.

which they depend is obvious, and common to all writings alike. I do not doubt, for a moment, that the history of Joseph and Potiphar's wife, (which we heard read this morning,) is a *bonâ fide* narrative,—*truer* and *more* authentic in details, than is to be found in any other book of History.—Neither do I doubt that the obvious teaching, (the *moral* Interpretation as it may be called,) of that incident, is the proper one: viz. that even for the most fiery of fleshly trials, GOD's grace is sufficient:—that Joseph's safety lay in refusing even to *be* with her, joined to his holy fear of sinning *against* GOD :—that lust is ever cruel, and will hunt for the precious life[1]:—finally, that the way of purity, though it may lead at first to sorrow, will infallibly conduct to blessedness at the last. Considerations like these, which are obvious and easy, are also unquestionably *true;* and especially precious, (*who* ever doubted it?) as helps to personal holiness. —But still, there may underlie this narrative, for aught I see to the contrary, a mystical signification. Potiphar's wife may, (as the best and wisest of ancient and modern Divines have thought,) symbolize the Power of Darkness; and Joseph, our Divine LORD. The garment Joseph left in the woman's hand, may represent that fleshly garment of which the true Joseph divested Himself,—(ἀπεκδυσάμενος as St. Paul speaks in a very remarkable place,)—the mortal body which Satan apprehended (his sole triumph!) and by which he was ensnared, when a greater than Joseph gat Him out from an adulterous world[k]. Joseph in the prison,

[1] Prov. vi. 26. Consider v. 9. Eccl. vii. 26. Gen. xxxix. 20. 2 Sam. xi. 15. St. Mark vi. 25.

[k] The learned reader,—(and the unlearned reader too, who will bear in mind that ἀπεκδυσάμενος, [in the E. V. 'having spoiled,']

and CHRIST in the grave: Joseph exalted, and CHRIST Ascended: Joseph at last feeding the families of the World, and CHRIST becoming the Bread of Life to all: —let it not occasion offence, Brethren, if I confess that, for aught I see to the contrary, some such hidden teaching as this, may underlie the plain historical narrative; and in no way interfere with a literal interpretation.

III. From the two foregoing negative positions, however, (which almost need an apology, such obvious truisms are they,) I eagerly pass on to something better and higher.

1. And first, I boldly declare that the clue to all that has been advanced concerning the marvellous method of Holy Writ is supplied by the single consideration that the Bible is *the Word of GOD*,—that Holy Scripture, from the Alpha to the Omega of it, is the language of the HOLY GHOST. Incomprehensible and unmanageable on any other hypothesis,—all the disclosures of inspired Interpretation, by the hearty reception of this one revealed truth, are rendered perfectly intelligible and clear. The HOLY SPIRIT may surely be assumed competent to interpret what the

certainly means 'having stripped off from himself,')—is invited to consider with attention those words of Col. ii. 15:—ἀπεκδυσάμενος τὰς ἀρχὰς καὶ τὰς ἐξουσίας, ἐδειγμάτισεν ἐν παρρησίᾳ, θριαμβεύσας αὐτοὺς [not αὐτάς, observe;] ἐν αὐτῷ [sc. τῷ σταυρῷ. See by all means Pearson *on the Creed*, Art. v. note (*l*): (ed. Burton, vol. ii. p. 217-8.) Cf. Eph. ii. 16. Consider St. Luke xi. 22.] To complete the teaching of the passage, the reader is invited to study also, in connexion with what goes before, 1 Cor. ii. 6—8; taking notice, that of ἄρχοντες τοῦ αἰῶνος τούτου are not, (as the marginal references suggest,) the powers of the visible, but of the *invisible* World. See St. John xii. 31: xiv. 30: xvi. 11, and Ephes. ii. 2: vi 12.—See Ignatius *Ep. ad Ephes.* c. xix., (with the notes in Jacobson's ed.) See also Dr. Mill *on the Temptation*, p. 165.

HOLY SPIRIT has already delivered! His disclosures therefore are beyond the reach of censure; however marvellous they may happen to be. But they are all a hopeless riddle to those who have blinded their eyes and hardened their hearts.

Thus, to advert for a moment to the prophetic character (as it may be called) of the historical parts of Scripture,—What is it which moves secret unbelief, and prompts a reference to the human devices of Allegory and Accommodation[1]? It is the profound conviction that no merely human narrative could be handled as St. Paul handles Genesis, except by indulging in rhetorical license, and giving to Fancy a very free rein. But disabuse your mind of this lurking suspicion, so derogatory to the honour of Him by whose Spirit the Bible is inspired,—cease to suspect that the narrative of Scripture is a merely human narrative,—and how different becomes the problem! Why should the HOLY GHOST have spoken less by the mouth of Moses, than by the mouth of David and Isaiah, Jeremiah and the rest of the prophets? But if *He* speaks in Genesis, then are the words of Genesis *His*;—and every word of the narrative "*proceedeth*" (as our LORD phrases it,) "*out of the mouth of GOD.*"

I am constrained to be thus express and emphatic, because it has been lately "*laid down that Scripture has one meaning;*—the meaning which it had to the mind of the Prophet or Evangelist who first uttered or wrote,—to the hearers or readers who first received it[m]." The original sense of Scripture, (says this writer,) is "the meaning of the words as they first struck on the ears, or flashed before the eyes, of those who

---

[1] See Sermon VI.
[m] Professor Jowett in *Essays and Reviews*, p. 378.

heard and read them ⁿ." Now, I will not pause to remark on the complicated fallacy involved in this. For (1), Why should a hearer's first impression of a speaker's meaning be assumed *to be* that speaker's meaning º ? And (2), Why may not Prophets and Evangelists have *intended* secondary meanings ᵖ ? But I do not dwell on this, for it does not touch the point. Let us hear the voice of one who adorned this place many years before the present controversy arose, and who has exactly anticipated the question now at issue. "Observe how this matter really is," says Bp. Butler. "If one knew a person to be *the sole Author* of a book; and were certainly assured, or satisfied to any degree, that one knew the whole of what he intended in it; one should be assured or satisfied to such degree, that one knew the whole meaning of that book: for *the meaning of a book is nothing but the meaning of the Author.* But if one knew a person to have compiled a Book out of memoirs *which he received from Another, of vastly superior knowledge in the subject of it;* especially if it were a Book full of great intricacies and difficulties; it would in no wise follow that one knew the whole meaning of the Book, from knowing the whole meaning of the compilers: for the original memoirs, (i.e. the Author of them,) might have, (and there would be no degree of presumption, in many cases, against supposing Him to have,) some farther meaning than the compiler saw. To say then, that the Scriptures, and the things contained in them, can have no other or farther meaning than those persons

---

ⁿ Professor Jowett in *Essays and Reviews*, p. 338.

º Consider St. John xii. 16: x. 6: xi. 13. St. Luke xviii. 34. St. Matth. xvi. 11, 12. St. John viii. 27, &c., &c.

ᵖ See St. John xi. 49—52: vi. 37—39.

thought or had, who first recited or wrote them; is evidently saying, *that those persons were the original, proper, and sole authors of those books,* i. e. THAT THEY ARE NOT INSPIRED: which is absurd, whilst the authority of these books is under examination; i.e. till you have determined they are of no divine authority at all. Till this be determined, it must in all reason be supposed,—not indeed that they *have*, (for this is taking for granted that they are inspired;) but,—that they *may* have, some farther meaning than what the compilers saw or understood ᵠ."—So far Bp. Butler.

2. Now, if GOD be in effect the Speaker, why need we hesitate to believe that He has so framed the stories, that they shall be throughout adumbrations of the things which concern our peace ʳ? Let some garment be shewn me of merely human manufacture, and however costly it may prove, I look for nothing in it beyond the known properties of any other earthly fabric. But give me the assurance that, on the contrary, it was woven by Divine hands, and fashioned in a Heavenly loom, and do I not straightway expect to find it a mystery and a marvel of Art? It is even so with the language of Holy Writ. It is all framed and fashioned after a Diviner model than men are able to imagine. It is instinct with sublimest meanings. It is penetrated, through and through, with the Spirit of the Most High GOD. It is of so celestial a texture, that, to the eye of the soundest Reason, informed by the purest Faith, it reveals, (when the

ᵠ *Analogy*, Part II. ch. vii.

ʳ Augustine, speak ng of the New Testament, says,—" Factum quidem est, et ita ut narratur, impletum; sed tamen etiam ipsa, quæ a DOMINO facta sunt, aliquid significantia erant,—quasi verba (si dici potest) visibilia, et aliquid significantia."—*Opp.*, tom. v. p. 421 F.

Spirit of its Divine Author shines upon it,) the glorious outlines of an imperishable Life!

3. The strong root of bitterness out of which springs unbelief in this supernatural character of the historical parts of the Bible, is an unworthy notion of GOD's Power. Because *human* histories are perforce barren and lifeless, it is assumed that the Book of GOD's Law must be a dead thing also. And then, the conceit of self-relying Reason glides in, (like a serpent,) and remonstrates as follows:—"Yea, can GOD have sanctioned a method of such subtlety and pliability as will make His own Scriptures mean *anything*[s]? Is it not rather, an exploded fashion, which the age has outgrown,—*that* fashion of supposing that there is sometimes a double sense in Prophecy, and that the Gospel is symbolized in the Law? Were then the worthies of the Old Testament puppets in GOD's Hands, acting parts?—now, typifying remote personages; now, exhibiting future transactions; now, symbolizing national events? Is it credible? Not so! Accept one of two alternatives, and never dream of a third. Believe either that the Evangelists, the Apostles, our SAVIOUR CHRIST Himself,—partaking of the ignorance of their age, and speaking according to the modes of thought then prevalent, were mistaken in their interpretations of Holy Scripture; or else, deny boldly that there are interpretations at all. Assume that they are mere allegory and accommodation! Something must be allowed for the backwardness of the Past;—and 'the time has come when it is no longer possible to ignore the results of criticism[t].' A change of method 'is not so much a matter of expediency as

---

[s] *Essays and Reviews*, pp. 368, 372.
[t] Professor Jowett in *Essays and Reviews*, p. 374.

of necessity. The original meaning of Scripture' is at last 'beginning to be understood ⁿ.' Be persuaded, and make it thy business to persuade others, that the Bible *is but a common Book!*"

4. To all of which, we make summary answer:—Passing by thy self-congratulation on the enlightenment of the age,—of which, except in certain departments of physical Science, *we* see *no* evidence;—the whole of thy argument concerning Holy Scripture amounts to this;—that it would be very distasteful *to thee*, to find that it contained any sense beyond that which lies on the surface. Types, intended by the Author of Scripture *to be* types: Prophecy with sometimes more than a single application: historical events foreshadowing remote transactions:—all these *thou* deniest, because *thou* dislikest. Observe, however, that while *thou* art urging thine own private opinion, *we* are dealing with a revealed *fact*. *Thou* talkest about a probability, but *we* are establishing a proof. "It is written" that Scripture *is* thus significant, *is* thus mysterious in its historical outlines. And thou canst not explain away one syllable, though thou shouldest deny "*every word that proceedeth out of the mouth of God.*"

5. Let us, however, examine the question merely by the light of unaided reason.—Consider then! If GOD made this world the particular kind of world which He is found to have made it, in order that it might in due time preach to mankind about Himself, and about His providence:—if He contrived beforehand the germination of seeds, the growth of plants, the analogies of animal life; all, evidently, in order that they might furnish illustrations of His teaching;

ⁿ Professor Jowett in *Essays and Reviews*, p. 418.

and that so, great Nature's self might prove one vast Parable in His Hands:—*why* may not the same GOD, by His Eternal Spirit, have so overruled the utterance of the human agents whom He employed to write the Bible, that their historical narratives, however little their authors meant or suspected it, should embody the outline of things heavenly; and, while they convey a true picture of actual events, should *also* after a most mysterious fashion, yield, in the Hands of His own informing Spirit, celestial Doctrine also?

6. For let me remind you,—The very actions of men,—the complicated transactions of our common lives,—are thus overruled by GOD'S Providence; and, without restraint, are so controlled that they shall subserve to the ulterior purposes of His will,—after a fashion which altogether defies analysis. Beyond this inner circle of comprehensible causation,—external to the immediate sphere of cause and effect which courts our daily scrutiny,—there is an outer circle, which rounds our lives; and (as I said) overrules all we do; fashioning, by virtue of a supreme fiat which is altogether beyond our comprehension, all our ends. *Why* then, I ask, may not the Bible be, what it purports to be,—the authentic record of transactions which the marvellous skill of Him who governeth all things in Heaven and Earth did so overrule, that they should become foreshadowings of chief transactions in the Kingdom of CHRIST? Shall prophecy, in the ordinary sense of the term, be admitted by all,—and yet *a prophetic transaction* be deemed impossible with GOD? If Isaiah may prophesy of one "red in His apparel," after "treading the winepress alone [x];" may describe Him as "despised and rejected of men;" "a Man of Sorrows

[x] Is. lxiii. 2, 3.

and acquainted with grief;" "wounded for our transgressions and bruised for our iniquities;" "brought as a lamb to the slaughter," and "making intercession for the transgressors;" and at last destined to find "His grave with the wicked, yet with the rich in His death ʸ :"—if this may be *in words* described minutely, and move no doubt; shall we close our eyes that we may not see,—or seeing shall we fail to recognize,—in the person of such an one as David, a divinely-intended type of MESSIAH? What! when he who was born in Bethlehem, overcomes the Philistine at the end of forty days, and takes from him the armour wherein he trusted;—when he,—a prophet, priest, and king,—is persecuted by his enemies, and betrayed by his own familiar friend; when *he* at last passes over the brook Kidron and ascends Olivet, sorrowing as he goes;—yea, when he utters words which our REDEEMER resyllables with *His* dying breath ᶻ;—wilt thou refuse to discern in the person of David, the lineaments of David's Son? and sneer at *us*, who herein have been better taught than thou; although thou hast no better reason to give for thy unbelief than that the view of Holy Scripture which the Church Catholic hath held in all ages, seems to thee a thing impossible?

7. Take once more, if thou wilt, the analogy of Nature; and thence infer what is *probable* concerning things Divine. Is it observed that *the works* of GOD are thus single in their office; or are they, on the contrary, manifold in their virtues and uses? Than the metal Iron, what substance more serviceable for every ordinary mechanical purpose of daily life? Yet, ask the physician which of the metals *he* could least

---

ʸ Is. liii.   ᶻ Comp. Ps. xxxi. 5 with St. Luke xxiii. 46.

afford to forego as an instrument of cure: and he will tell thee that *he* finds Iron the fullest of healing virtues also. Shall then plants and animals, yea, and the whole of the Animal Kingdom, be admitted to subserve to manifold, and at first sight unsuspected uses, —so that the wisest are ready to confess that the function of most remains to this hour a secret:—and shall we be reluctant to allow that *the Word of God*— "the Tree of Life," whereof "the leaves are for the healing of the nations,"—may also be thus various in its purpose; fraught with other teaching besides that which on its very surface meets the careless eye?

8. To speak without a figure,—It is not of course to be supposed that the inspired writers knew all the wondrous qualities of the message they delivered, or of the narrative they were divinely guided to indite. Altogether a distinct question *this;* although the two have been sometimes confused together[a]. Nay, Revelation itself comes in to help us here. St. Peter, in express words, declares that concerning the mystery of Redemption "the prophets *inquired and searched diligently;* ... searching what, or what manner of time the Spirit of CHRIST which was in them did signify, when it,"—(not *they,* observe, but *It*)—"testified beforehand the sufferings of CHRIST, and the glory that should follow." That "not unto themselves, but unto *us* they did minister,"—thus much, indeed, *was* revealed to them; but no more. The rest, to this hour, the very "Angels desire to look into!"

[a] By Professor Jowett for example. "The time will come when educated men will no more be able to believe that the words of Hos. xi. 1 *were intended by the prophet* to refer to the return of Joseph and Mary from Egypt, than," &c.—*E. and R.*, p. 418. *When* did "educated men" ever believe anything of the kind?

9. But between the words which a man delivers *being* full of Divine significancy, and *himself knowing* the full scope and purport of those words,—there is surely a mighty difference! When Caiaphas foretold the universal efficacy of Christ's Death, *who* less than Caiaphas suspected the far-reaching truth of the words which fell from his unholy lips? *He* knew nothing about the triumphs of the Cross; and yet he could prophesy very accurately concerning them. "This spake he not of himself," (says the Evangelist,) "but being high-priest that year, he prophesied that Jesus should die for that nation; and not for that nation only, but that also He should gather together in one the children of God that were scattered abroad[b]." ... It may safely be assumed that the sacred writers no more knew the force and power of their own words, than those Priests who lived and moved amid the shadows of the Mosaic Ritual were able to discern therein, the substance of things eternal in the Heavens. And yet we believe concerning those ritual types that "they were a concealed prophetic evidence, the force of which was made apparent by the presence of the Gospel[c]." I am prone to suspect that the burning vehemence of their own language must many a time have moved the Prophets of old to deepest astonishment; and that when there broke from them words of more than mortal power,—or images of unearthly grandeur,—or the outlines of a grief more than human; when they spake of a betrayal for thirty pieces of silver[d], of blows and spitting[e], and of pierced hands and feet[f]; of parted garments and lots cast upon

[b] St. John xi. 50. Comp. xviii. 14.
[c] Davison *on Prophecy*, p. 192.   [d] Zech. xi. 12, 13.
[e] Is. l. 6.   [f] Ps. xxii. 16. Zech. xiii. 13.

a vesture[g];—they must have felt, they must have felt the awfulness of the message they were commissioned to deliver; and longed, yea yearned unutterably to see and to hear the things which were reserved to be witnessed in the days of the Son of Man!

10. Enough, however, of all this. In reply to *à priori* objections, I have been content to argue the question as if the Bible were a newly-discovered Book without a history; whereas the consentient writings of all the Fathers and Doctors of every age, in every portion of the Christian Church, is an overwhelming *fact!* Rather have I reasoned as if the Bible were a book altogether silent concerning itself. But the plain truth, as I have fully shewn, is the very reverse. Scripture is *full* of interpretations of Scripture;—and the constant method of Scripture in such interpretations, is spiritual or mystical;—and this witness of Scripture is the strongest proof possible that the principle involved is correct. Meanwhile, the great underlying truth which I now desire, more than any other to bring before you, is this:—that it is the HOLY GHOST who, in the New Testament, interprets what the same HOLY GHOST had delivered in the Old. This, believe me, is the true key, the only intelligible solution, to all those difficulties respecting places of the Old Testament, whether interpreted, or only quoted, in the New, which have so exercised the ingenuity of learned men. We are always to remember, in a word, that the *true* Author of either Testament,—the *real* Author of every part of the Bible, is (not Man, but) GOD!

IV. Such then, (to conclude,) is *the Divine method of Interpretation.* We are not concerned now to

[g] Ps. xxii. 18.

classify, and sort it out under different heads. *To apply*, even to a small extent, the principles we have been labouring to establish, would not only lead us much too far, but would constrain us to travel out of our proper subject and prescribed province. Our purpose has only been, to vindicate the profundity, or rather *the fulness* of Holy Writ[h]; and to shew that under the obvious and literal meaning of the words, there lies concealed a more recondite, and a profounder sense: call that sense mystical, or spiritual, or Christian, or what you will. Unerringly to elicit that hidden sense is the sublime privilege of inspired Writers; and they do it by allusion, by quotation, by the importation of a short phrase[l], by the adoption of a single word[k],—to an extent which no one would suspect who had not carefully studied the subject. How that method of theirs is to be *applied by ourselves*, it is impossible, I repeat, for me even to hint at in a single discourse. But *this*, I will say; and with *this* I dismiss the subject;—that Interpretation would be a hopeless task, but for the solemn circumstance that the whole of the Bible is inspired by one and the self-same Spirit; so that one part may always be safely

---

[h] "Adoro Scripturæ plenitudinem."—Tertullian *adv. Hermog.*, c. 22.

[l] Comp. St. Matth. ii. 20, with the LXX Version of Exod. iv. 19: St. Matth. iii. 4, with the same version of 2 Kings i. 8: St. Matth. xxvi. 38 with Ps. xlii. 5. St. Luke i. 37, with Gen. xviii. 14,—i. 48, with 1 Sam. i. 11, and with Gen. xxx. 13,—i. 50, with Ps. ciii. 17. St. John i. 52, with Gen. xxviii. 12,—&c., &c.

[k] A few examples may prove suggestive to a thoughtful reader:— ἔξοδος, in St. Luke ix. 31 and in 1 St. Pet. i. 15:—ἀποκαταστήσει, in St. Matth. xvii. 11, (cf. Mal. iv. 5): σιτομέτριον, in St. Luke xii. 42, (cf. Gen. xlvii. 12): παράδεισος, in St. Luke xxiii. 43. The reference is of course always to the *Septuagint* version.

compared with any other part of it, you please. Nay, by no other method can you hope to understand the Bible, than by such a laborious comparison of its several parts. "Non nisi ex Scripturâ Scripturam potes interpretari." The more you study the Book, the more you will feel convinced that its many authors all resorted to one and the same Fountain of Inspiration. They all use the same imagery; they all speak the same language; they all mean the same thing. St. John the Divine, in the Book of Revelation, shuts up the Canon by reproducing the combined imagery of all the ancient prophets,—by declaring that the Song of Moses and of the LAMB is sung by the redeemed in Heaven,—by marvellous words about "the Tree of Life," which is "in the midst of the Paradise of GOD." The Inspired writers of either Testament all draw from the same Treasury, and therefore all say the same things. The Heavenly Jerusalem, (with her gates of pearl and streets of gold,) is the home of the spirit of each one of them[l]; JESUS CHRIST, and He Crucified, is the abiding theme of them all. And O, how their words do sometimes teem, and their phrases swell, almost to bursting, with their blessed argument[m]! You shall be troubled

[l] Ps. xlvi. 4: xlviii. 1, 8: lxxxvii. 3. Is. lii. 1: lx. 14. Ezek. xlviii. Ephes. ii. 19, 20. Phil. iii. 20. Gal. iv. 26. Hebr. xi. 10: xii. 22: xiii. 14. Rev. xxi. 2, 10: iii. 12, &c.

[m] "Scriptores θεόπνευστοι, de typo disserentes, divinius quiddam ex inopinato pati solent, et ad antitypum vehementiore Spiritus afflatu rapi et elevari. Assertionis hujusce veritas inde constat, quod verba quædam haud expectata sæpius inferant, quæ MESSIÆ vel solum vel aptius quam Illius typo congruant."—Spencer *De Legg. Hebr.*, vol. ii. p. 1035. Consider such places as Ps. ii. 6, 7: xli. 9, 10: xlv. 10, 11: lxi. 6: lxxii. 5, 7, 11, 16, 17: lxxxix. 29. Gen. xlix. 18. Is. lxi. 1, 2, 3. Zech. vi. 11, 12.

with only one example of what I mean. — Moses having described the interview between Melchizedek and Abraham, the mighty secret of MESSIAH's priesthood which therein lay enshrined was curtained all so close, that neither Angels nor Men could possibly discern it. Must it then remain a mystery for 2000 years? Not so! Midway between the day of Abraham and the day of CHRIST,—just midway,—David, speaking by the HOLY GHOST,—(of *that*, our LORD Himself assures us[n],)—David, I say, when a thousand years had rolled by, utters the cxth Psalm; and in the fulness of his prophetic fervour, the great secret bursts unexpectedly into light! A thousand years had passed since Abraham returned from 'the slaughter of the Kings.' It wanted yet a thousand years to the date of our SAVIOUR's Birth. And lo, midway, a voice is heard, shouting to Him across the gulf of Ages,—" *Thou* art a Priest for ever *after the order of Melchizedek!*"

"And let not Reason be alarmed. Her vocation is not gone. Yea rather, I know not if Human Intellect ever had a loftier problem presented to her than to follow out that deep Analogy which has been noticed above; and to learn, (if it may be called Reason's learning,) how to deal with Holy Scripture as Apostles and Evangelists deal with it. Let not Reason be alarmed. She is only asked to listen, and to discern the nature and laws of Sacred Study. She is asked but to discern the evidence which there is of her being in a world which she imperfectly understands. . . . . The student of the Bible is advised so to address himself to the study of that Book, so to deal with its language, as one should deal with THE WORD

[n] St. Mark xii. 36.

of God,—the measure of whose import is in the infinite, not in the finite World.—Surely, by these things the Lord tries the spirits of us all; tries other men by other means, but tries the intellectual man by the Word of God °, and watches him as he reads it; hardens the obdurate; blinds the self-blinded; but pours into the humble mind the riches of His divine Wisdom like showers into a valley; making it soft with the drops of rain and blessing the increase of it ᵖ."

V. Friends and brethren, it is not without reluctance that on a Sunday in Lent, when penitential thoughts should rather occupy us,—and in this place too, where the promotion of practical piety should rather be our aim,—I have so addressed you. But indeed, I seem to have no choice. It is idle crying "peace, peace," when there is *no* peace. If the Inspiration of Holy Scripture be a deceit, and the Divine meaning of Holy Scripture a superstition,—then, farewell to all our hopes in Life and in Death; farewell to peace in days of despondency and gloom. Our faith is gone, and our teaching becomes a hollow heartless thing. Since, under the name of freedom of discussion, unbounded licentiousness of speculation is openly the fashion of the age, we are constrained to give a reason for the hope which is in us; and to defend, without compromise or hesitation, that Bible, which is the great bulwark of the Faith. It shall not be said that we can condemn, but that we make no answer. It must be seen that we put forth in reply

---

° "And their manner of treating this subject when laid before them, shews what is in their heart, and is an exertion of it." Bp. Butler's *Analogy*, P. II. ch. vi.—See Appendix (C).

ᵖ Eden's *Sermons*, pp. 192-5.

the ancient Truths; and it will be felt that before the majesty of those ancient Truths, the arts of the enemy will prove weak and unavailing,—rather, will stand revealed in all their native deformity. If English Clergymen, coming abroad in the cast-off clothes of German unbelief[q], and decked out with the exploded sophisms of the last century, are to declare openly that the faith of our Fathers is already looked upon among ourselves as 'a kind of fossil of the Past,'—then is it high time that voices should be heard vindicating *that* ancient method of our Fathers; and boldly proclaiming that this imputation against the Clergy of England is a disreputable untruth. The Church of England, (GOD be praised!) hath *not* left her first love; hath *not* given up her ancient method; Christianity is *not* 'a difficulty to the highest minds.' The Christian Religion embraces, as much as ever it did, "the thought of men upon the Earth." "All the tendencies of Knowledge" are *not* "opposed to it." The Gospel is still immeasurably before the age. Intellect has not gone,—the loftiest order of well-trained intellects will never go,—the other way[r]. It is, on the contrary, none but a very shallow wit which errs. Had it confined its speculations to the cloister, or

---

[q] "With the exception of the still-imperfect science of Geology," (says Dr. Pusey,) "the Essays and Reviews contain nothing with which those acquainted with the writings of unbelievers in Germany have not been familiar these thirty years." Even the Apologist for the volume in question assures us that one who "had looked ever so cursorily through the works of Herder, Schleiermacher, Lücke, Neander, De Wette, Ewald, &c., would see that the greater part of the passages which have given so much cause for exultation or for offence in this volume, have their counterpart in those distinguished Theologians."—*Edinb. Rev.*, Ap. 1861, p. 480.

[r] Rev. B. Jowett in *Essays and Reviews*, pp. 374-5.

come abroad with sorrow and shame, we should have pitied in silence, and in silence also have lamented. But when it comes insultingly abroad, and sets up a claim to intellectual superiority even while it denies the most sacred truths;—*then* pity gives way before indignation and disgust. Crown the whole with the iniquity of imputing these views generally to the more thoughtful of the English Clergy[e],—and we are constrained openly to resent the grievous wrong. We declare it to be an unfounded calumny; a calumny which, in the name of the whole Church, I solemnly repel before GOD,—and His Holy Angels,—and *you!*

Vain, utterly vain,—worthless, utterly worthless,— must any superstructure of intellectual, moral, or religious training be, which is built up on the doctrine that the Bible is to be interpreted like any other Book; in other words, that the Bible *is* a common Book; in other words, that *Inspiration is a fable and a dream.* We have no fear whatever that *your* high instincts, (with all your faults!),—*your* English manliness,—will, to any extent be led astray, by sophistry worthless as that which we have been exposing. But we know you look to your appointed Teachers from this place, (as well you may,) for advice, and support, and encouragement, in your better aspirations;—and let *me*, at least, in plain language, warn you that novelties in Religion never *can* be true. "Philosophia," says the great Bishop Pearson speaking of Physical Science; "Philosophia quotidie *progressu:* Theologia nisi *regressu* non crescit[f]." "Ask

---

[e] Rev. B. Jowett in *Essays and Reviews*, pp. 372, (*bottom*,) 340, 374, &c.

[f] *Minor Works,* vol. ii. pp. 9-10.—"In Christianity, there can be no concerning truth which is not ancient; and *whatsoever is*

for the old paths!".. The faith, remember, was ἅπαξ,—*once for all*,—delivered to the Saints. There will be no new deposit. There can be no new doctrines. There has been no fresh Revelation,—no new principle of guidance vouchsafed to man. A new method of interpreting Scripture is *quite* impossible. And the true method,—the only *true* method—*must* be that which was adopted by our Saviour, by His Evangelists, and by His Apostles: a method which *they* taught to their first disciples, and which those early Bishops and Doctors handed on in turn to the generation which came after them. That method, by God's great goodness, has descended in an unbroken stream, even to ourselves; who have described it this morning, feebly indeed and unworthily,—yet, in the main, as it would have been described at *any* time, by *any* of the glorious company of the Apostles, the goodly fellowship of the Prophets, the noble army of Martyrs,—by any of the Doctors and Fathers of the Holy Church throughout the world! O let it be our great concern,—yours and mine,—to preserve with undiminished lustre the whole deposit of Heaven-descended teaching which is the Church's treasure! . . . . Like runners in a certain ancient race of which we all have read, let it be *our* pride and joy,—yours and mine,—to grasp the torch of Truth with a strong unwavering hand; to run joyously with it so long as the days of this earthly race shall last; and dying, to hand it on to another, who, with strength renewed like the eagle's, may again,—swiftly, steadily, exultingly,—run with it, till he fails! . . . *So*, when the Judge of quick and dead appeareth,—*so* let

truly new is certainly false."—Epistle Dedicatory prefixed to Pearson *on the Creed*, p. x.

Him find *you* occupied,—O young men, (many of you, my friends,) who are already the hope of half the English Church! So faithfully may *we*, Brethren and Fathers, one and all, be found employed, when *He* cometh,—whose answer to the Tempter is emphatically *the* text of the present solemn season, as well as a mighty voucher for the Divine origin, and sustaining efficacy of that Book concerning which I have been detaining you so long,—"It is written, Man shall not live by bread alone; but by every word that proceedeth out of the mouth of God!"

Ut verum fatear, semper existimavi, allusiones istas, (ad quas confugiunt quidam tanquam ad sacrum suæ ignorantiæ asylum,) plerumque nihil aliud esse, quam Sacræ Scripturæ abusiones manifestas.
Bishop Bull, *Harmonia Apostolica*, cap. xi. sect. 3.

There would be no need to scruple the term, if it were not meant to imply that this Accommodation was arbitrary on the part of the Evangelist; or that the mind of the Spirit that spoke by the Prophet does not most fully include this application.
Dr. W. H. Mill.

SERMON VI.[*]

THE DOCTRINE OF ARBITRARY SCRIPTURAL ACCOMMODATION CONSIDERED.

ROMANS x. 6—9.

*" But the Righteousness which is of Faith speaketh on this wise,
—' Say not in thine heart, Who shall ascend into Heaven?'
(that is, to bring* CHRIST *down from above:) or, ' Who shall
descend into the deep?' (that is, to bring up* CHRIST *again
from the dead.) But what saith it? ' The word is nigh thee,
even in thy mouth, and in thine heart:' that is, the word of
Faith, which we preach; that if thou shalt confess with thy
mouth the* LORD JESUS, *and shalt believe in thine heart that*
GOD *hath raised Him from the dead, thou shalt be saved."*

IT is quite marvellous in how many different ways different classes of professing Christians have contrived to nullify the value of their admission that the Bible is *inspired*. Some would distinguish the inspiration of the Historical Book from that of those which we call Prophetical. Others profess to lay their finger on what are *the proper subjects* of Inspiration, and what are not. Some are for a general superintending guidance which yet did not effectually guide; while others represent the sacred Writers as subject, in what they delivered, to the conditions of knowledge in the age where their lot was cast. The view of Inspiration which Scripture itself gives us,—namely, that GOD *is therein*

[*] Preached at St. Mary-the-Virgin, April 27, 1851.

speaking by human lips[b]*;* so that 'holy men of GOD' delivered themselves as they were 'impelled,' 'borne along,' or 'lifted up,' (φερόμενοι) *by the* HOLY GHOST[c]*;* —*this* plain account of the matter, I say, which converts 'all Scripture' into something '*breathed into by* GOD,' (θεόπνευστος,)[d]—men are singularly slow to acknowledge. The methods which they have devised in order to escape from so plain a revealed Truth, are 'Legion.'

Second to none of the enemies of Holy Writ, practically, are they who deny its depth and fulness. It is only another, and a more ingenious way, of denying the Inspiration of the Bible, to evacuate its more mysterious statements. Those who are for eluding the secondary intention of Prophecy, the obviously mystical teaching of Types, the allegorical character of many a sacred Narrative,—are no less dangerous enemies of GOD's Word than those who frame unworthy theories in order to dwarf Inspiration to the standard of their own conceptions of its nature and office. I say, it is only another way of denying the Inspiration of Scripture, to deny what is sometimes called its mystical, sometimes its typical, sometimes its allegorical sense. . . . . And thus,—what with the arbitrary decrees of our own unsupported opinion, or the self-sufficient exercise of our own supposed discernment; —what with our insolent mistrust; or our short-sighted folly and presumption; or, lastly, our coldness and deadness of heart, — our slender appetite for Divine things, which makes us yearn back after Earth, at the very open gate of Heaven;—in one way or other, I repeat, we contrive to evacuate our own

[b] See above, pp. 55-7.   [c] 2 St. Pet. i. 21.
[d] See above, pp. 53-4.

admission that the Bible is an inspired Book: we fasten discredit on its every page: we become profane men, like Esau: we despise our birthright.

But the most subtle enemy of all remains yet to be noticed. It is he, who,—finding the plain Word of GOD against him: finding himself refuted in his endeavour to fix one intention only on the words of the HOLY GHOST, and *that* intention, the most obvious and literal one; finding himself refuted even by the express revelation of the same HOLY GHOST, elsewhere delivered;—bends himself straightway to resist, and explain away, that later revelation of what was the earlier meaning. It is a marvellous thing but so it is, that the very man who contended so stoutly a moment ago for the literal meaning of Scripture, *now* refuses, and denies it. Anything but *that!* If he allows that St. Matthew, or St. Paul,—yea, or even our Blessed LORD Himself,—are to be *literally* understood; are severally to be taken to *mean* what they *say;*—then, Moses and David,—narrative, law, and psalm,—besides their literal meaning, have, at least *sometimes,*—and they *may* have *always,*—a mystical meaning also. *Under* the evident, palpable signification of the words, there lies concealed something grander, and deeper, and broader; high as Heaven,—deep as Hell.

And this supposition is so monstrous an one; seems so derogatory to their notions of the mind of GOD;—it is deemed so improbable a thing, that the words of Him, whose ways are not like Man's ways, should span the present and the future, at a grasp;—that He whose "thoughts are very deep," should, with language thereto corresponding, be setting forth CHRIST and His Redemption, while He tells of Patriarchs and

Lawgivers,—Judges and Kings,—priests and prophets of the LORD:—I say, it is deemed so incredible a thing that Moses should have written concerning CHRIST, (though our SAVIOUR CHRIST Himself declares that Moses did write concerning Him)ᵉ; or that the occasional expressions of the Prophets should really contain the far-reaching allusions which in the New Testament are assigned to them; that the men I speak of,—men of learning (sometimes), and of piety too,—will condescend to every imaginable artifice in order to escape the cogency of the Divine statement. St. Paul—was infected with the Hebrew method of interpretation. (It is of course *assumed* that this method was essentially erroneous! It is overlooked that our LORD had recourse to it, as well as St. Paul! It is either forgotten, or denied, that the HOLY GHOST, speaking by the mouth of St. Paul, acquiesced in every instance of such interpretation on the part of His chosen vessel!) .... As for St. Matthew, he addressed his Gospel to the Jews, and therefore reasoned as a Jew would. (St. Matthew's Gospel was not of course intended for the Christian Church! The blessed Evangelist was also deeply learned,—it is of course reasonable to suppose,—in the sacred hermeneutics of the Hebrew Schools!) .... The other Sacred Writers, it is pretended, all wrote according to the prejudices of the age in which they lived.—In all these cases, it is contended that *merely in the way of Accommodation*, is the language of the Old Testament cited in the New. What was said of one thing is transferred to quite another,—to suit the purpose of the later writer; to illustrate his reasoning, to adorn or to enforce his statements. .... And this

ᵉ See above, pp. 157—160.

brings me to a question of so much importance, that I pause to make a few remarks upon it. In the present discourse, it shall suffice to remark on the doctrine of *Scriptural* ACCOMMODATION; for which it is presumed that the text, (selected not without reference to the present Sacred Season,) affords ample scope, as well as supplies a fair occasion.

Now, it is not to the *term* "Accommodation," that we entertain any dislike; but to the *notion* which it seems intended to convey; and to the *principle* which we believe that it actually embodies. That the HOLY SPIRIT in the New Testament sometimes accommodates to His purpose a quotation in the Old,—is very often a mere matter of fact. In all those places, for instance, where St. Paul inverts the clauses of a place cited,—there is a manifest accommodation of Scripture, in the strictest sense of the word. When two, three, or more texts, widely disconnected in the Old Testament, are continuously exhibited in the New,— a species of accommodation has, of course, been employed. The same may be said when a change of construction is discoverable. Again, there is accommodation, of course, when narrative,—legal enactment,—or prophecy, is *so exhibited* that the point of its hidden teaching shall become apparent. Nay, in a certain sense of the word, there is "accommodation," as often as a prophecy, however plain, is applied to the historical event which it purports to foretel. The prophecy may be said,—(with no great propriety indeed, but still, intelligibly,)—to have been accommodated to its fulfilment.—Occasionally, a general promise is made particular,—as in Hebrews xiii. 6; and perhaps *this* might be called an accommodation of the text to the needs of an individual believer. Yet is it plain that in all these cases '*application*,' or '*adaptation*,' would be a better word.

But such ways of adducing Holy Scripture, we suspect, are not by any means what is *meant* by 'Accommodation;' and they do not certainly correspond with the notion which the term is calculated to convey. The place in the Old Covenant, seems, (from the term employed,) to have been forced, against its conscience, as it were, to bear witness in behalf of the New. It has been wrenched away from its natural bearing and intention; and made to accommodate itself,—and, on the part of the writer, quite arbitrarily, —to a purpose, with which it has, in reality, no manner of connexion. This, I say, is the notion which the term "Accommodation" seems to convey.

I am supposing, of course,—(as the opposite school is, of course, supposing,)—*not* an *illustration*,—which obviously *any* writer, whether ordinary or inspired, has a right to introduce at will; but a case where the cogency of the argument depends entirely on the place cited. A sudden and unforeseen requirement arose; —nothing entirely fit and applicable occurred to the memory: but by an arbitrary handling of the ancient Oracles of GOD,—(altogether illogical and inconclusive indeed, yet entitled to a certain measure of respectful consideration at our hands, and certainly having a strong claim on our indulgence,)—the later writer saw that he should be able to substantiate his position, or to strengthen his argument, or to prove his point. And he did not hesitate to do so. It is surprising that his hearers or his readers should have accepted his statements, and admitted his reasoning;—very! But they *did*. And it is for us, the heirs of the wisdom of all the ages, to detect the time-honoured fallacy and to expose it.—This, I say, is the notion which the term "Accommodation" seems calculated to convey; and it is to be feared, *does* very often represent.

And the introduction of this principle, as already explained, I cannot but regard as the most insidious device of all. It admits fully all that we have elsewhere laboured to establish. It freely grants that Apostles and Evangelists were inspired. But then, it denies that much of what they deliver in the way of interpretation of Scripture, is to be regarded as *real* interpretation. By a taste for Allegory; by Rhetorical license; on *any* principle, it seems, *but one*, is the Divine method to be accounted for; and the plain facts of the case to be obscured, or explained away.

Now - I *altogether reject* this principle of arbitrary "Accommodation." I hold it to be a mere dream and delusion. And I reject it on the following grounds:—

1. It is evidently a mere excuse for Human ignorance,—a transparent deceit. Men do not see how to explain, or account for, the apparent license of the Divine method; and so they have invented this method of escape. Most cordially do I subscribe to the opinion expressed by Bishop Bull, in his discussion of the very text which we are now about to consider:—
"Atque, ut verum fatear, semper existimavi, allusiones istas, (ad quas confugiunt quidam tanquam ad sacrum suæ ignorantiæ asylum,) plerumque aliud nihil esse, quam sacræ Scripturæ abusiones manifestas[f]."

2. The "theory of Accommodation," (as it is called,) is attended with this fatal inconvenience,—that, (like certain other expedients which have been invented to get over difficulties in Religion,) it altogether fails of its object. For even if we should grant, (for argu-

[f] *Harm. Apost.* Diss. Post., cap. xi. § 3.

ment's sake,) that *some* quotations from the Old Testament *can* be explained on this principle,—so long as there remain others which defy it altogether, nothing is gained by the proposed expedient. Thus, so long as attention is directed to certain of the places in St. Paul's writings already referred to[g], there is certainly *no absurdity* in adducing them as instances of Rhetorical license. But how can it be pretended that the text whereby St. Paul establishes, (on two distinct occasions,) the right of the Christian Ministry to a liberal maintenance,—with what propriety can it be thought that Deut. xxv. 4 lends itself to such a theory? Those words *seem*,—and, apart from Revelation, might without hesitation have been declared,—to have *nothing at all to do with the matter*[h]*!* To talk of the "accommodation" of words so eminently unaccommodating, is unreasonable, and even absurd.

3. But, allowing the advocates of this theory all they can possibly require, the result of their endeavours is but to make the Sacred writers ridiculous after all. For it attributes to them a method, which, if it be a *mere* exhibition of human fancy, often seems to be but a species of ingenious trifling,—scarcely entitled to serious attention at our hands. There is no alternative, in short, between certain of the expositions which we meet with, being Divine, — and therefore worthy of all acceptation; or Human, —and therefore entitled to no absolute deference whatever.

4. On the other hand, learned research has hitherto invariably tended to shew that the meaning claimed

---

[g] See above, pp. 152-7.

[h] Consider again the Divine exposition, (in 1 St. John v. 6,) of St. John xix. 34.

for Scripture by an Apostle or Evangelist, *does* actually exist there. Thus, it has been admirably demonstrated that the Evangelical meaning attributed by St. Matthew, (in the first chapters of his Gospel,) to certain places in the ancient Prophetical Scriptures of the Jewish people, derives nothing but corroboration from the inquiries of Piety and Learning[l]. . . . It is proposed on the present occasion, without pretending to bring to the question any such helps as these, to examine the portion of Holy Scripture already under our notice, with a view to ascertaining what light it will throw on the main question at issue. To this task, I now address myself.

St. Paul's words, from the 6th to the 9th verse (inclusive) of the xth chapter of his Epistle to the Romans, present probably, as fair an example as could be desired of what is sometimes called "Accommodation." To say the truth, I know not an instance of what, *in any uninspired writing*, I should have been myself more inclined to stigmatize as such. The Apostle begins an affectionate remonstrance with his countrymen by declaring that they " did not understand the Righteousness of GOD ;" (that is, the Divine method whereby GOD wills that we shall be made righteous, by faith *in* CHRIST*;*) but desired to set up ($\sigma\tau\hat{\eta}\sigma\alpha\iota$) a righteousness of their own, on the worthless foundation of their own Works[k]. "For," (he proceeds; with plain reference to *what* " the Righteousness of GOD" *is ;*)—" *For*

---

[l] See Dr. Mill's *Christian Advocate's* publication for 1844, *The Historical Character of the circumstances of our* LORD's *Nativity vindicated against some recent mythical interpreters,*—especially p. 402 to p. 434.

[k] Cf. Phil. iii. 7—9.

CHRIST is the end" (aim, or object,) " of the Law[1] to every one who hath faith" in CHRIST. St. Paul straightway proceeds, (as his manner is,) to establish this latter proposition. How does he do it? *"For,"* (he begins again,)—" Moses describes the nature of the righteousness which proceeds from the Law, when he declares [in Leviticus xviii. 5,] that ' *The man who hath done* the deeds commanded by the Law, shall live thereby.'—But concerning the Righteousness which proceeds from Faith,"—[it was called before, ' the Righteousness of GOD,']—" Moses writes as follows[m]: —' Say not in thine heart, Who shall ascend into Heaven? (that is, to bring CHRIST down:) or, Who shall descend into the deep? (that is, to bring CHRIST up from the dead.) But what saith it? The word is nigh thee, in thy mouth, and in thy heart: that is, the word of faith, which we preach: because if thou shalt confess with thy mouth the LORD JESUS, and shalt believe in thine heart that GOD raised Him from the dead, thou shalt be saved."

Here then is a quotation from the xxxth chapter of the Book of Deuteronomy,—a quotation introduced in the way of argument, in support of a proposition: the remarkable circumstance being, that St. Paul adduces the words of Moses with extraordinary license. For first, he omits as many of the Prophet's words as make little for his purpose, while he introduces a very remarkable alteration in some of the words which he

---

[1] Consider St. John vi. 46, and all similar places.

[m] On the words, Ἡ δὲ ἐκ πίστεως δικαιοσύνη οὕτω λέγει,—Theodoret remarks :—'Ἀντὶ τοῦ, περὶ δὲ τῆς ἐκ πίστεως δικαιοσύνης, οὕτως λέγει· οὐ γὰρ ἡ δικαιοσύνη ταῦτα λέγει, ἀλλὰ διὰ Μωσέως, ὁ τῶν ὅλων Θεὸς, περὶ τοῦ νόμου ταῦτα εἴρηκε· διδάσκων Ἰουδαίους ὡς δίχα πόνων τὴν τῶν πρακτέων διδασκαλίαν ἐδέξαντο.—Theodoret, *Cat.*, p. 374.

retains: amounting to a substitution of one sentence for another. And next, there is one single word, which he expands into an important phrase; and *that* merely to suit his own argument. But the strangest thing of all is the interpretation which he delivers of words, which as we have just seen, are partly his own,—partly, the words of Moses: by which interpretation, the most strikingly *Christian* character is fastened upon sayings pronounced by the ancient Lawgiver in the land of Moab, to the Jewish people.— We do further, for our own part, most freely admit, that the place,—as it stands in the Old Testament,— neither at first, nor at second sight, seems to have any such meaning as the Apostle assigns to it. I will remind you of the words in Deuteronomy, by reading the entire passage:—" This commandment which I command thee this day, . . . is not hidden from thee, neither is it far off. It is not in Heaven, that thou shouldest say, Who shall go up for us to Heaven, and bring it unto us, that we may hear it, and do it? Neither is it beyond the sea, that thou shouldest say, Who shall go over the sea for us, and bring it unto us, that we may hear it, and do it? But the word is very nigh unto thee, in thy mouth, and in thy heart, that thou mayest do it." . . . Now, I say, one of ourselves might read this passage in the Book of Deuteronomy over a hundred times, and never suspect that Moses, when he so wrote, was writing concerning faith in CHRIST: and yet we have the sure testimony of the HOLY SPIRIT to the fact that he *was*.—The inquiry, " Who shall ascend into Heaven?", signifies, we are told, " Who shall ascend,—*to bring down* CHRIST *from above?*"—And just so, the other clause, " Who shall descend into the deep?", is declared to be an incomplete expression: the full phrase being,—" Who shall descend,—*to bring up* Christ[n] *from the dead.*" . . . . Now we never desire to see a non-natural sense fastened on the Inspired Word. With Hooker, we "hold it for a most infallible rule in expositions of sacred Scripture, that, where a literal construction will stand, the furthest from the letter is commonly the worst." We contend therefore that whereas we have here the explicit assurance that Moses wrote of none other than Christ,—though his words do not bear upon them any evidence of the fact,—it is a mere trifling with holy things, to call the fact in question.

Here, however, we shall be reminded that the great Apostle,—though professing to quote,—confessedly argues in part from *his own* language, which is *not* the language of Moses. Moses says,—" Who shall go *over the sea* for us?" (τίς διαπεράσει ἡμῖν εἰς τὸ πέραν τῆς θαλάσσης;) And since the version of the LXX is what the Author of the Epistle to the Romans follows in this place, it is reasonable to expect that he would adhere to that version, or at least to the sense of that version, in the exhibition of so important a clause as the present. Whereas, instead of " Who shall go *over the sea,*" we find St. Paul writing, —" Who shall *go down into the deep?*" (Τίς καταβήσεται εἰς τὴν ἄβυσσον;)—language evidently highly suggestive of the mysterious transaction to which the same St. Paul says it contains a reference[o]; but certainly *not* the language of Moses. And we shall be

[n] Our E. V., following the translations since Cranmer's, here inserts the word "again,"—which is certainly not implied by the Greek.

[o] The expression is, of course, wholly dissimilar from that in Ps. cvii. 23,—οἱ καταβαίνοντες εἰς θάλασσαν ἐν πλοίοις, κ. τ. λ.

reminded that this is not merely phraseology rescued from vagueness, and made definite; but it is the actual substitution of one thought for another. This is what will be said; and if it be followed up by the assertion that here, therefore, we have a clear example of Scriptural Accommodation, it might seem, at first sight, impossible to deny the fact.

For our own parts, we are inclined to meet the present difficulty, and every similar one, in quite another spirit; and dispose of the objection, somewhat in the following way. The same GOD who gave us the Scriptures of the Old Testament, gave us the New Testament also. The Bible is *one*. He who inspired the Law, inspired the Gospel. The HOLY GHOST pleads with us in both alike.—Surely, therefore, He who spake of old time by the Prophets, may be allowed, when, in the last days, He speaks by the Apostles of CHRIST,—to explain His earlier meaning, if He will. Surely, He may tell the Israel of GOD,—if He pleases,—what He meant by the language He held of old time to Israel after the flesh! Yea, and if it seemeth good to Him to call in the wealth of His ancient treasury, in order to recoin it that He may the more enrich us thereby:—if it pleases Him to take His ancient speeches back again into His mouth, in order that He may syllable them anew,—making them sweeter than honey to our lips, yea, sweeter than honey and the honeycomb;—what is *Man* that he should reply against GOD? What should be our posture, at witnessing such a spectacle, but one of Adoration? What, our becoming language, but praise?

It is easy to anticipate the answer that will be made to all this. We shall be told that we are, in some sort, begging the question. The Bible is an Inspired Book, indeed: but *what is Inspiration?*—Moses wrote the Book called "Deuteronomy:" St. Paul wrote the Epistle to the Romans. And St. Paul,—quoting a passage out of the older record,—has substituted a sentiment of his own for a sentiment contained in the writings of Moses. He does the same thing in other places; and elsewhere, as here, he proceeds to reason upon the data he has so obtained. *This*, it will be said, is the phenomenon which we have to deal with.

But, we reply, it is manifest that he who so argues,—with all his apparent good sense, and fairness,—is entirely committed to a theory concerning Inspiration; and *that* a very unworthy one. The Bible comes to us as an Inspired Book; claiming to be the very Word of God. The Holy Church throughout all the World, doth acknowledge it to be so. Surely, therefore, it is for *us* to study its contents by the light of this previous fact.—But quite contrary is the method of our opponents. They treat the Bible as if it were an ordinary Book. They submit its contents to the same irreverent handling as they would the productions of a merely human intellect. They not only reason *about* its claims from its contents,—but they would even pronounce *upon* its claims, from the same evidence. They dare to sit in judgment upon it. Hence their lax notions on the subject of Inspiration. They first run riot among statements which are too hard for them; and when they have perplexed themselves with these, till the field is strewed with doubts, and the limits of unbelief and mistrust have become extended on every side,—Inspiration, like an ill-defined boundary-line on a map, is suffered faintly to hem in, and enclose the utmost verge of the unhappy domain. —Whereas, we maintain that a belief in the Bible, as an Inspired Book, should, at the outset, prescribe a limit to human speculations.

Let this belief encircle us exactly, and entirely; and define, at once, the area within which all our reasonings must be taught to marshal themselves, and to find their full development. In brief, our opponents meet our remonstrance by another; but, as we contend, an unreasonable one;—at least, as proceeding from men who, no less than ourselves, allow freely the Inspiration of Scripture. *We* say,—The Bible is the word of GOD. Fill your heart with this conviction, and then humbly address yourself to the study of its pages.—It is argued on the other side,—The pages of the Bible are full of perplexing statements. They evolve strange phenomena, interminably. Convince yourself of this; and then make up your mind, if you can, about the Inspiration of the Bible [p].... I shall

---

[p] I cannot forbear transcribing the following passage in an elaborate apology which has recently appeared for *Essays and Reviews*:—" Among the many proposals which are floating about for Essays and Counter-essays to vindicate the Doctrines supposed to be combated in this volume, let us be allowed to suggest this one:—' The Nature of Biblical Inspiration, as tested by a careful examination of the Septuagint Version with special reference to the sanction given to it by the Apostles, and to its variations, by way of addition or omission, from the revised Text of the Canonical Scriptures.' The conclusions of such an investigation would be worth a hundred eager declarations on one side or the other, and would be absolutely decisive of the chief questions at issue." (*Edinburgh Review*, April, 1861, p. 483.) .... Now I scruple not to affirm that a well-informed, and faithful student of the Scriptures would covet no better portion for himself than liberty to accept, in the most public manner possible, such a challenge as the foregoing.

have occasion, by and by, to explain more in detail the spirit in which the Divine Logic,—*Inspired reasoning* as it may be called,—is to be approached. For the moment, I am content to waive the question; and to be St. Paul's apologist, almost as if I had met with his words in an uninspired book.

Solemnly protesting, then, that the ground we have just occupied is the only *true* ground on which to take our stand; but withdrawing from it because we do not fear the appeal to unassisted Reason, even in matters of Faith,—so that the proper limits and conditions of inquiry be but observed;—we proceed to inquire whether,—apart from Revelation,—there be not good ground for believing that the words of the ancient Hebrew Lawgiver and Prophet contain and mean the very thing which the Christian Apostle *says* they do.—We change our language at this stage of the inquiry. We no longer assert, (as before we did,) that the HOLY GHOST speaking by the mouth of Moses, *must have meant*, what the same HOLY GHOST, speaking by the mouth of St. Paul, declares that He *did* mean. We are willing to study the sacred text solely by the light which grave criticism and patient learning have thrown upon it.—Our inquiry now, is this; —Although the words in Deuteronomy, read over attentively by ourselves, suggest no such Christian meaning as we find affixed to them in the Epistle to the Romans,—is there no reason, traditional or otherwise, for supposing that they *do* envelope that meaning; yea, so teem and swell with it, that the germ of the flower may be actually detected in the yet unopened bud? . . . . I proceed to this inquiry.

1. And first, it is obvious, to any one reading the xxixth and xxxth chapters of the last Book of Moses,

that they contain *another Covenant*, beside that of Horeb. This is expressly stated in the first verse of the xxixth chapter:—"These are the words of the Covenant which the LORD commanded Moses to make with the children of Israel in the land of Moab, *beside the Covenant which He made with them in Horeb*[q]." Not to stand too stiffly thereupon, however[r], let it be at least freely allowed that even if we choose to regard this chapter and the next as a *renewal* only of the Covenant made in Horeb, it is a *distinct* renewal;—both in respect of time and of place. Of time,—for whereas the Covenant of Sinai belongs to the *first* of the forty years of wandering, the Covenant of Moab belongs to the *last*. Of place,—for whereas the other was made at the furthest limit of the people's wanderings, *this* belongs to their nearest approach to Canaan.—And I confidently ask, After *such* an announcement, and at a moment like *that*,—the forty years of typical wandering ended, and the earthly type of the heavenly inheritance full in view, Jordan alone intercepting the vision of their Rest;—shall we wonder, if here and there a ray of coming glory shall be found to flash through the language of the dying patriarch? if some traces shall be discernible, even in the language of Moses, of the dayspring of the Gospel of CHRIST?

2. We find that it contains not a few sayings in support of such a presumption. The 10th verse opens the covenant, and in the following solemn language:

[q] See the valuable exposition of the text, by Bp. Bull, in the Appendix (K),—to which I am very largely indebted.

[r] Opposed to Bp. Bull in his opinion, on this matter, seem Ainsworth, Patrick, Parker (*Biblioth. Bibl.*), Cornelius à Lapide, the *Critici Sacri*, &c. I cannot but think that the truth is with the first-named Commentator.

—" Ye stand, this day, all of you, before the LORD your GOD: the Captains of your tribes, your Elders, and your officers, with all the men of Israel;—your little ones, your wives, and the stranger that is in thy camp,—from the hewer of thy wood, to the drawer of thy water." And what was the *intention* of this solemn standing before the LORD? Even—" that thou shouldest enter into Covenant with the LORD thy GOD, and enter into His oath, which the LORD thy GOD maketh with thee this day."—The purport of the Covenant thus to be made, was, that GOD might establish Israel that day for a people unto Himself, and that He might be unto them a GOD,—(an expression elsewhere appropriated by the Great Apostle to the Christian Church[s],)—as He had . . . sworn unto their Fathers, *to Abraham, to Isaac, and to Jacob*. So that we have here the renewal of the *Evangelical* Covenant made with Abraham, and renewed to Isaac and Jacob, —which is clearly distinguished in Scripture from the *Legal* Covenant, made with their children 430 years after; and which is declared ineffectual to disannul the earlier one, confirmed before by GOD, and pointing entirely to CHRIST[t]. That earlier Evangelical Cove-

---

[s] See 2 Cor. vi. 16, (quoting Lev. xxvi. 12), where see Wordsworth's note. Heb. viii. 6—13, especially ver. 10, (quoting Jer. xxxi. 33. Comp. Jer. xxiv. 7: xxx. 22: xxxi. 1: xxxii. 38.) Compare Rom. ix. 25, 26, (also 1 St. Pet. ii. 10,) with Hos. ii. 23: i. 10. See also Ezek. xi. 20: xiv. 11: xxxvi. 28: xxxvii. 27; and Zech. viii. 8: xiii. 9. Lastly, consider Rev. xxi. 3; where " the types of the itinerant Tabernacle in the Wilderness, the figurative ritual and festal joys of the Feast of Tabernacles, celebrated in the literal Jerusalem, are consummated in the Heavenly Jerusalem." (Wordsworth.) See also Rev. vii. 15, with the annotation of the same Commentator.

[t] προκεκυρωμένην . . . . εἰς Χριστόν. Gal. iii. 17.

nant then, it was, which was renewed in the land of Moab;—in the course of renewing which, the words of the text occur.

3. And that it was indeed the Evangelical, (not the Legal Covenant,) which is here spoken of, is abundantly confirmed by the subsequent language of the passage: for Moses proceeds,—"Neither with you only do I make this Covenant and this oath; but with him that standeth here this day with us before the LORD our GOD, and also *with him that is not here with us this day*ᵘ:" meaning, (as the ancient Targum expounds the place,) "*with every generation that shall rise up unto the world's end.*" It was the same Covenant, therefore, which is made with *ourselves;* "for the promise is unto" us, and to our "children, and to all that are afar off, even as many as the LORD our GOD shall call ˣ:" "*not* according to the Covenant which GOD made with the Fathers of Israel in the day that He took them by the hand to bring them out of the Land of Egyptʸ."

Yet more remarkably perhaps is this established by the language of the ensuing chapter: for GOD therein promises that *Circumcision of the heart* whereby men should be enabled to love the LORD their GOD with *all their heart* and with *all their soul.* Now this seems clearly to intimate not legal but Evangelical obedience,—the result of the free outpouring of the HOLY SPIRIT of GOD; of which, in the Law, (properly so called,) we find no promise whatever. Here then we discover another anticipation of something which belongs to the times of the Gospel.

And this Evangelical complexion is to be recognized

ᵘ Deut. xxix. 14, 15.   ˣ Acts ii. 39: Compare iii. 25.
ʸ Jer. xxxi. 32. Consider verses 33-4 quoted in Heb. x. 16, 17. See above, note (t).

in the entire contents of the xxixth and xxxth chapters. They contain no single mention of ceremonial rites or observances,—of which the Law is, for the most part, full. But free obedience and perfect love are inculcated as the condition of blessedness: while hearty repentance is made the sole condition of forgiveness of sin.

In connexion with this, I may call your attention to a curious coincidence,—if indeed it be not something more. On the sincere repentance of the people, it is promised "that then the LORD thy GOD will turn thy captivity;" which the Targum of Jonathan paraphrases,—"His WORD will receive with delight thy repentance:" while the Septuagint even more remarkably renders the words—"will heal thy sins;" that is,—"will be thy JESUS." Moses proceeds,—"and gather thee from all the nations whither the LORD thy GOD hath called thee." And what is this but one of the very places, if it be not *the very place*, to which St. John alludes when he declares that Caiaphas prophesied that JESUS should die for that nation; and not for that nation only; but that He should gather together in one, the children of GOD that were scattered abroad [z]?"

4. Nor is it, finally, a little remarkable that, by the general consent of the Hebrew Doctors, this xxxth chapter has ever been held to have reference to the times of MESSIAH. The restoration spoken, is referred by them to the restoration to be effected by CHRIST: while the promises it contains are connected with those prophetic intimations which clearly point to the days of the Gospel [a].

---

[z] St. John xi. 49—52.

[a] "Diligenter observandum est, ex consensu Hebræorum, caput

So much, then, for the evidence, *apart from Revelation*, which the general complexion of the place in Deuteronomy affords to the reasonableness of the meaning affixed to it by the voice of the later Scriptures. Before we proceed to examine a little in detail the words of the text, we may be surely allowed to remind ourselves of the Testimony which St. Paul bears to the Evangelical character of what is here delivered. He asserts, in the most direct and emphatic manner, that it is the Righteousness which is by Faith which here speaks[b]. He is contrasting the spirit of the Law, with that of the Gospel. He is setting the requirements of the one against those of the other. To exhibit the former,—he quotes from Leviticus. To enable us to judge of the latter,— he quotes this very place in Deuteronomy. Having shewn the justification under the Law,—which is by entire fulfilment of every enjoined work;—the Apostle describes the Righteousness of the Gospel,— which is by Faith in CHRIST. And he discovers its voice in the present chapter: nay, he calls our attention to its language; and, lest the intention of it should escape us, he proceeds to supply us, not only with an interpretation of it, but with a paraphrase as well.

Enough has been said, I trust, to render this proceeding on the part of the Apostle no matter of sur-

hoc ad regnum CHRISTI pertinere. Unde etiam Bachai dicit, hoc loco promissionem esse quod sub Rege MESSIAH omnibus qui de federe sunt, circumcisio cordis contingat, citans Joelem, ii. 28."— Fagius, (in the *Critici Sacri,*) on Deut. xxx. 11.

[b] "Apostolus dicit hoc esse verbum fidei, quod ad Novum Testamentum pertinet. Quæ ergo scripta sunt in libro legis hujus in figurâ dicta sunt, pertinentia ad Novum Testamentum."—Augustinus, in Nic. Lyra, *ad loc.*

prise. Let us see whether the particulars of his interpretation are altogether novel and unprecedented either.—The words of Moses which we have to consider, it will be remembered, are these:—The "commandment which I command thee this day, it is not hidden from thee, neither is it far off. It is not in Heaven, that thou shouldest say, Who shall go up for us to Heaven, and bring it unto us, that we may hear it and do it? Neither is it beyond the Sea, that thou shouldest say, Who shall go over the Sea for us, and bring it unto us, that we may hear it, and do it? But the word is very nigh unto thee, in thy mouth, and in thy heart, that thou mayest do it^e."

Now, that all this denotes something close at hand and easy,—in place of something supposed to be remote and difficult, — is obvious. The whole of the earlier part of it, St. Paul affirms to be tantamount to the following injunction,—"Say not in thine heart, Who shall ascend into Heaven, to bring CHRIST down; or who descend into the abyss, to bring CHRIST up from the dead." Concerning which words of caution, we have to remark that there seems to have been no intention whatever on the part of the Apostle, to warn *his readers* against requiring a renewed Revelation of CHRIST in the flesh, or a second Resurrection of the Eternal SON from the dead. He is illustrating the nature of Legal and Evangelical Righteousness, by the language of the Jewish Law. He contrasts the two, in their respective requirements; finding the voice of both in the writings of Moses: of the former,—in connexion with the covenant of Sinai; of the latter,—in connexion with the covenant which the LORD commanded Moses to make with the children

^e Deut. xxx. 11—14.

of Israel in the land of Moab, *besides* the former Covenant. With characteristic fire and earnestness, glancing, as usual, at every side of the question before him,—having, a little way back, explained himself, without explanation, when he inserted that remarkable parenthetical clause, τέλος γὰρ νόμου Χριστος[d], —" for *Christ* is the object of the Law;"—in order now to shew how thoroughly this is the case,—how full the Law is of *Him*, in whom alone it finds its perfect scope, end, and completion,—he explains that the very phrase "Who shall ascend up into Heaven?" pointed to nothing less than *the Incarnation* of Christ: that, "Who shall go over the Sea?" contained a wondrous far-sighted allusion,—(not the less real because unsuspected,)—even to *the Resurrection* of our Lord from death. So true is it, " that both in the Old and New Testament Everlasting Life is offered to Mankind by Christ, who is the only Mediator between God and Man, being both God and Man. Wherefore they are not to be heard, which feign that the old Fathers did look only for transitory promises[e]."

Moses then here warns the ancient people of God against an evil heart of unbelief. "Say not in thy heart, Who shall ascend up into Heaven?" for such words on the part of Man would imply disbelief in the doctrine that the Son of God should hereafter take upon Him human flesh. (Since "no man hath ascended up to Heaven, but He that came down from Heaven, even the Son of Man which is in Heaven[f].") "Neither say, Who shall descend into the deep?" for such words on human lips must imply disbelief in Messiah's Descent into Hell, and Resurrection from the Dead.—The mystery of Redemption might not

[d] Rom. x. 4.   [e] Art. vii.   [f] St. John iii. 13.

be impatiently demanded; but must be looked for in faith, until the fulness of time should come, and the whole mystery of godliness should be revealed to the wondering eyes of Men and Angels[g].

We shall perhaps be asked, whether it is credible that Moses can have had any conception that such a meaning as St. Paul here ascribes to his words, did really underlie them? To which we answer, first, that it is by no means incredible[h]. And next, that whether Moses knew the full meaning of the language he was commissioned to deliver, or not,—seems, (as already explained[i],) to be an entirely separate question: the only question before us, being, *whether his language contained that meaning*, or not.... To what extent the Prophets,—who, (we know,) studied their own prophecies[k],—were ever permitted to fathom their depth, is a mere matter of speculation[l]; delightful indeed, but in the present case quite irrelevant. In the meantime, we know for certain that *Moses prophesied of* CHRIST[m].

And next, if it be said that really this is only a proverbial expression,—a Hebrew phrase to denote something passing difficult, and hard of attainment:

---

[g] 1 Tim. iii. 16.

[h] The reader is invited to consider Acts ii. 24 to 31,—attending particularly to what St. Peter says in ver. 30-1. "Even without this key," (says Dr. M'Caul,) "the Rabbis interpreted Psalm xvi. of the Resurrection."

[i] See above, pp. 171-2.   [k] St. Pet. i. 11.

[l] "Though I think it clear that the Prophets did not understand the full meaning of their predictions; it is another question how far they thought they did, and in what sense they understood them."—Butler's *Analogy*, P. II. ch. vii.

[m] See Acts xxvi. 22, 23: xxviii. 23. St. John i. 46: v. 46. St. Luke xxiv. 27, &c.

—(as when, in the Book of Proverbs, it is asked,—
"Who hath ascended up into Heaven, or who hath
descended ⁿ?")—we answer, we see no ground whatever for supposing that in the place just quoted, it *is*
a proverb, and no more,—although from its use in
the Talmud, the expression would certainly appear to
have become, at last, proverbial °. *If* a proverb, however, it seems to have been a sacred one; nor can
any place be appealed to where it occurs, nearly of
the antiquity of *this*, in the writings of Moses. To
pretend therefore to explain away a certain mode of
expression, in the place where it *first* stands on record,
—and where it is declared to have a deep and mysterious meaning,—simply because, *subsequently*, it was
(to all appearance) used *without* any such pregnancy
of signification,—is, manifestly illogical.

Nay, there is good ground for presuming, that the
very place last quoted, contains a reference to the
Eternal SON: for Agur proceeds to ask,—"What is
His Name, and *what is His Son's Name*, if thou canst
tell ᵖ?" ... But the reference is far more obvious when

ⁿ Prov. xxx. 4.

° e.g. "Si quis dixerit mulieri, Si adscenderis in firmamentum,
aut descenderis in abyssum, eris mihi desponsata,—hæc conditio
frustranea est."—*Nasir* ix. 2, apud Wetstein, (in Rom. x. 6.)

ᵖ "The whole passage (Prov. xxx. 2—5,) may be thus paraphrased:—With my limited understanding I cannot attain the
knowledge of GOD; *for to know GOD, is to know Him who is
omnipresent, filling Heaven and Earth;* it is to know Him who
is omnipotent, ruling over the winds and the waters, the most
unstable of all elements; it is to know Him who created all things;
it is to know His Name, and the name of His SON. But this knowledge can be attained only by Revelation: and he that would attain
to it even from Revelation, must not pass over any one word as
insignificant, for every word is purified like silver: neither must

the same expressions occur in the Book of Baruch. "Who hath gone up into Heaven, and taken her, and brought her down from the clouds? Who hath gone over the sea, and found her[q]?" For *Wisdom* is there spoken of; and Wisdom, as we remember, is one of the names of CHRIST,—the name by which He is discoursed of, in the Book of Proverbs.

The uninspired evidence which completes the connexion of this place of Deuteronomy with the second Person in the Blessed Trinity, is the traditional interpretation assigned to it by the Hebrew Commentators. The Targum of Jerusalem expounds the latter clause as follows:—"Neither is the Law beyond the Great Sea, that thou shouldest say, O that we had one *like Jonas the prophet* that might go down to the bottom of the Great Sea, and bring it to us." So that the very Jewish Doctors themselves here become our instructors; and teach us that a greater than Jonas must be here,—even while they guide our eyes to that especial type of our SAVIOUR CHRIST in His Descent into Hell, and Rising again from the dead. I say, the very Jewish Doctors themselves here contribute their testimony; and yield a most unsuspicious witness to the inspired exegesis of the Apostle: for, "as Jonas was three days and three nights in the whale's belly,"—so, (they clearly mean to say), so should it be with the man whom Moses here indicateth: and so,—(these are the words of CHRIST Him-

---

he add to Revelation, or he will be sure to go astray."—From the Appendix (pp. 46-7) to a Sermon by Dr. M'Caul, on *The Eternal Sonship of the Messiah*, 1838. (Interesting and precious as this paraphrase is, I humbly suspect that the words *in italics* contain a vast deal more than the learned writer indicates.)

[q] Baruch iii. 29.

self),—so was "*the Son of Man* three days and three nights in the heart of the Earth[r]."

You will of course notice the facility with which the Jews themselves, interpreting their own Scriptures, have here exchanged the notions of going "*over* the sea,"—("*beyond* the sea," as it is in the Hebrew,)—and "*going down to the bottom*" of the sea. St. Paul seems, in this place, to have "accommodated" the words of Moses: but we cannot fail to perceive that the Hebrew text must cry aloud for such supposed "accommodation;" yea, cry aloud, even in the uncircumcised ears of the Jewish people; that their own Commentators, as if divinely guided by the good hand of GOD, should bear their own independent witness to the correctness of the Apostolic interpretation.

Nor may I fail to call your attention to the term employed by St. Paul to denote the Sea:—a term, surely divinely chosen. He had just before, (in the 6th and 7th verses,) employed the Version of the LXX: he was about to use it again in the 8th verse: but in this, (the 7th,) he departs from it. Instead of, —Τίς διαπέρασει ἡμῖν εἰς τὸ πέραν τῆς θαλάσσης; he writes,—Τίς καταβήσεται εἰς τὴν ἄβυσσον. The term ἄβυσσος,—which is applicable to the deep places of the Earth, *and* to the depth of the Sea, with equal propriety;—(being a more indifferent term even than our own expression "the deep");—affords a memorable example of the fulness and pregnancy of language on inspired lips. Adhering to the letter of the text he quotes, the Apostle, by changing *the word* expressive of that literal sense, embraces the whole spiritual breadth and fulness of the passage:—reminding us of Him, by the blood of whose covenant

[r] St. Matth. xii. 20.

were sent forth the prisoners of hope out of the pit *wherein is no water*ˢ,—even before he names Him; our Saviour Christ!

I must also remind you, that there are many expressions used by our Lord, or used concerning Him by His Apostles, which help to shew, that, to have come down from Heaven,—and to have been brought up from the deep of the Earth again,—may be regarded as the mysterious summary of the Saviour's Missionᵗ.—"No man hath *ascended up* to Heaven," (saith our Lord,) "but He that *came down* from Heavenᵘ." "I am the living Bread which *came down* from Heaven. . . . Doth this offend you? What and if ye shall see the Son of Man *ascend up* where He was beforeˣ?" In another place,—"I came forth from the Father and am come into the World: again I leave the World, and go to the Fatherʸ."—But the most remarkable place remains: "Now, that He *ascended*, what is it but that He also *descended first* into the lowest parts of the Earth? He that *descended*, is the same also that *ascended up* far above all Heavensᶻ." I say, this brief summary,—given by Christ Himself, or by those who had seen Him,—of the mystery of His manifestation in the flesh,—throws light on the language of the Hebrew lawgiver. It shews that the language of Moses to Israel, in the plains of Moab, fairly embraced the two great truths which Faith even now can but be exhorted to lay fast hold upon, and to appropriate:—"If thou shalt confess with thy mouth that Jesus is the Lord,"—that is, confess that the man Jesus is the uncreated, Incarnate

---

ˢ Zech. ix. 11.   ᵗ Consider Ps. cxxxix. 7. Amos ix. 2, 3.
ᵘ St. John iii. 13.   ˣ Ibid. vi. 33, 38, 51, 62.
ʸ Ibid. xvi. 28.   ᶻ Ephes. iv. 9, 10.

JEHOVAH; "and believe with thy heart that God raised Him up from the dead,—thou shalt be saved." .... Such is the form which the exhortation *now* assumes. More darkly, of old time,—(as was fitting,)—was the same thing spoken: and, because reference was then made to an event not yet accomplished, the impatience of Unbelief is there repressed,—rather than the ardour of Faith stimulated. "Say not in thy heart who shall ascend into Heaven? or, who shall go down into the deep place?" .... But shall we deal so faithlessly with the Divine Oracles of the Old Testament, as to deny them the deeper meaning assigned to them in the New, because they speak darkly? Let us, from a review of all that has been humbly offered,—let us at least admit that there is good independent ground for believing that when Moses spake of ascending into Heaven,—it was with reference to the future coming of CHRIST:—when he made mention of descending into the Deep,—the Resurrection of the SAVIOUR of the World was, in reality, the thing he spake of.—Let us allow that *here*, at least, there is nothing in the language of the New Testament, which, when studied by the light of unassisted Reason, does not appear to have been fully included, contemplated, intended by the language of the Old:—that the accommodation has not been arbitrary;—say rather, that *here* at least there has been *no accommodation at all!*

But I am impatient to leave this low rationalistic ground, and take my stand again, on the vantage ground of Faith. The position, I trust, has been established, that even in the case of words which seem least promising,—least likely to enfold the deeply mysterious meaning claimed for them by an

Apostle,—the result of patient inquiry and research is to shew that such a meaning really *does* exist there, to the fullest extent. We have discovered, from mere grounds of Reason, apart from Revelation, that what St. Paul has cited in this place from Deuteronomy, may very well contain all that he says it contains. But, were nothing of the kind discoverable;—were it a most hopeless endeavour to reconcile the meaning evolved by the inspired Apostle, with the text he professes to interpret,—the claims of the sacred exegesis would remain wholly unimpaired. We should still say that *this*, because it is an *inspired* Commentary, is entitled to our fullest acceptance. We have, anyhow, the HOLY SPIRIT interpreting Himself. He surely must be the best judge of His own Divine meaning. He does but enrich the Treasury of Truth, even by His apparent departures from the original Hebrew verity. Shall not the HOLY GHOST, the Comforter, be allowed to speak comfort to His people in whatever way seemeth best to Himself? Is it not lawful for Him to do what He will with His own? Is thine eye evil, because He is very good?

Yes, it cannot be too emphatically insisted on, that the success which may attend investigations of this nature, is not to be admitted for a moment as the measure of the soundness of the principle on which they proceed. The reasoning whereby Newton shewed that the diamond is a combustible substance would have been no whit invalidated had the diamond resisted to this hour every chemical attempt to reduce it to carbon. We do not,—(what need to say?)—we do not discourage the endeavour to enucleate the deep Christian significancy of passages for which Inspired writers claim such sublime meaning. Rather do we think that Human Reason could not find a worthier field for the employment of her powers[a], than this. But we are strenuous to insist that the full and sufficient, and only irrefragable proof that a mighty Christian meaning does actually underlie the unpromising utterance of one of GOD's ancient Saints, is,—*that an Inspired Writer declares it to exist there.*

There is no *accommodation* therefore, when an inspired writer adduces Scripture. Human language *will* sometimes require to be "accommodated:" Divine language, never! May not the HOLY SPIRIT lay His finger on whatever parts of His ancient utterance He sees fit? may He not invert clauses, and (in order to bring out His meaning better) even alter words? If He tells thee that the prophetic allusion of Isaiah to "our griefs" and "our sorrows" comprehends "our infirmities" and "our sicknesses" in its span[b],—is it for *thee* to discredit His assertion? If He is pleased to intimate that the providential arrangement whereby CHRIST, though born at Bethlehem, grew up at Nazareth,—had for its object the fulfilment of many a detached and seemingly disconnected prophecy[c],—shall the unexpectedness of His disclosure excite ridicule in such an one as thyself? When He tells thee that besides the immediate scope of certain well-known words of Hosea and of Jeremiah, there was the ulterior aim He indicates; if behind Israel after the flesh, He shews thee the Anointed SON[d],—if behind those captive Jews of the tribe of Benjamin whom Nebuzar-Adan led past their mother's grave on their way to Babylon, He points to the slaughtered infant of Bethlehem; assuring thee that when He spake by the

[a] See above, pp. 176-7.   [b] St. Matth. viii. 17.
[c] St. Matth. ii. 23. See above, p. 149.   [d] Ibid. ii. 15.

mouth of Jeremiah concerning the nearer event that remoter one was full before Him also; and that the solemn and affecting utterance of the Prophet was divinely intended by Himself to cover both*;—wilt thou, when He discourses to thee thus, presume to talk to Him of "*accommodation?*" Is it not enough for thee to have cavilled at the first page of the *Old* Testament on "scientific" grounds? Must thou, for Theological considerations, dispute the first page of the *New* Testament also?

Scripture then, whether in its Historical or its more obviously prophetic parts, has this depth of meaning for which I have been contending. We must perforce believe it, for it is a matter of express Revelation. We cannot pretend to deny the probability,—much less the possibility of it; for we really *can* know nothing of the matter except from an attentive study of Scripture itself. And the witness of Scripture, as we have seen, is ample, emphatic, and express.—Our LORD, being indignantly asked by the Jews if He heard what the children, crying in the Temple, said of Him, —made answer by quoting the 2nd verse of the viiith Psalm: "Yea, have ye never read, 'Out of the mouth of babes and sucklings Thou hast perfected praise'†?" —Pray was this "accommodation," or what was it? It was deemed a sufficient answer, at all events, by the Anointed JEHOVAH; whatever men may think! ... When the Sadducees, disbelieving in the Resurrection of the Body, assailed our LORD with a speculative difficulty, He told them that they erred because they did not understand the Scriptures. "Now that the dead *are* raised, even Moses shewed at the bush, when he calleth the LORD, the GOD of Abraham, and

* St. Matth. ii. 18. † Ibid. xxi. 16.

the GOD of Isaac, and the GOD of Jacob. For He is not a GOD of the dead, but of the living: for all live unto Him ᵍ." How, by the popular method,—how, by any of the new lights which have lately been let in on Holy Scripture,—was the Resurrection of the dead to have been proved by the words which the SECOND PERSON in the Trinity spake to Moses "in the Bush?" And yet we behold *that* same Divine Personage in the days of His humiliation, proposing from those words, uttered by Himself 1500 years before, to *establish* the doctrine in dispute! .... Only once more. "In the last day, that great day of the Feast [of Tabernacles,] JESUS stood and cried, saying, If any man thirst, let him come unto Me and drink. He that believeth on Me,—*as the Scripture hath said*, ' *Out of his belly shall flow rivers of living water* ʰ*!* ' "— But *where* does the Scripture say *that?* You will look a long while to find it. You will never find it at all if you adhere to the method which of late has been declared to be the method most in fashion. You will never even understand what our Blessed LORD *means*, unless you attend to the hint which immediately follows,—and which the Divine Author of the Gospel would not suffer us to be without,—namely, that, "This spake He of the SPIRIT, which they that believe on Him should receive:"—by which is meant, that as many of the Prophets as discoursed in dark phrase of that free outpouring of the SPIRIT which was to mark MESSIAH's Reign, did, *in effect*, say the thing which He here attributes to them.

Inspired Reasoning, wherever found, may fitly obtain a few words of distinct notice here; but I shall perhaps speak more becomingly, as well as prove more

ᵍ St. Luke xx. 37.   ʰ St. John vii. 37, 38.

intelligible, if,—(without further allusion to the sayings of that Almighty One "in whom are hid all the treasures of Wisdom and Knowledge[1];" sayings which it seems a species of impiety to approach except in adoration;)—I confine my remarks to the logical processes observable in the inspired writings of some of His servants, the Evangelists and Apostles of THE LAMB.

The difficulty which has been occasionally felt in respect of the argumentative parts of St. Paul's Epistles, is considerable, and may not be overlooked. His definitions, his inferences, his entire method of handling Scripture, gives offence to a certain class of minds. His reasoning seems inconsequential. There appears to be a want of logical order and consistency in much that he delivers. But,—can it require to be stated?—the fault is entirely our own. "The radical fallacy of any attempt to analyze the reasoning of Scripture by the ordinary Laws of Logic" requires to be pointed out. And the root of it all is our assumption that an inspired Apostle must perforce argue like any other uninspired man.

But, in the first place, it is to be recollected that he did not collect the meaning and bearing of the Old Testament Scriptures from induction, and study *only*. He was,—by the hypothesis,—*an inspired Writer*. The same HOLY SPIRIT who taught the authors of the Old Testament what to deliver, taught *him*, in turn, how to explain their words. By direct Revelation, he perceived the intention of a text, and at once bore witness to it. Thus St. Paul says of our LORD,—"He is not ashamed to call them brethren, saying,—'I will declare Thy Name unto My brethren, in the midst of

[1] Col. ii. 3.

the Church will I sing praise unto Thee.' And again, —'I will put my trust in Him.' And again,—'Behold I and the children which God hath given Me[k].'" Now, "the Apostles quoted such places as these from the Psalms and Isaiah, not as they were gathered by any certain reason, but as revealed to them by the HOLY SPIRIT, to be principally spoken of CHRIST. This understanding the mysteries of GOD in the Old Testament, being a special gift of the HOLY GHOST[l],—of the truth of which interpretations, the same SPIRIT, without any necessary demonstration thereof, bore witness also to their auditors and converts; and by miracles manifested the persons thus expounding them herein to be infallible[m]."

To quote the language of a thoughtful writer of more recent date,—"Inspired teaching,—explain it how we may,—seems comparatively indifferent to (what seems to us so peculiarly important) close logical connexion, and the intellectual symmetry of doctrines. . . . The necessity of confuting gainsayers, at times forced one of the greatest of CHRIST's inspired servants, St. Paul, to prosecute continuous argument; yet even with him, how abrupt are the transitions, how intricate the connexion, how much is conveyed *by assumptions such as Inspiration alone can make*, without any violation of the canons of reasoning,—FOR WITH IT ALONE ASSERTION IS ARGUMENT. . . . The same may be said of some passages of St. John, supposed to have been similarly occasioned. Inspiration has ever left to human Reason the filling up of its outlines, the

---

[k] Heb. ii. 12, 13; quoting Ps. xxi. 23 and Is. viii. 17.

[l] 1 Cor. xii., xiii., xiv.

[m] Pseudo-Fell's *Paraphrase and Annotations* on the New Testament, (Jacobson's ed.), *in loc.*

careful connexion of its more isolated truths. The two are, as the lightning of Heaven, brilliant, penetrating, far-flashing, abrupt, — compared with the feebler but *continuous* illumination of some earthly beacon[n]."

"In a train of inspired Reasoning," (as the same writer elsewhere remarks,) "each new premiss may have been supernaturally communicated; and thus, in point of fact, the inspired reasoner but connects the different threads of the Divine Counsels; exemplifies how 'deep answereth to deep' in the mysteries of Revelation; and presents, in one connected train of argument, those words of GOD which had been uttered 'at sundry times and in divers manners[o].'"

To conclude.—There is no such thing as inconsequential Reasoning to be met with in the writings of St. Paul[p];—no such thing as arbitrary Accommodation of the Old Testament Scriptures, in the New: —though not a few have thought it; and the language of many more writers, Papist as well as Protestant, is calculated to convey the same mischievous impression[q]. The hypothesis is as unworthy of ourselves,—with our boasted critical resources and many appliances of varied learning,—as it is derogatory to the Sacred Oracles to which it is applied. It is a deadly blow, aimed at the very Inspiration of Scripture itself; for it pretends to discover a human element only, where we have a right to expect a Divine one: an irresponsible *dictum*, when we listened for the voice of the SPIRIT; the hand of man, where we depended on finding the very Finger of GOD! We come to the

[n] Professor Archer Butler, quoted in Professor Lee's *Discourses on Inspiration*, pp. 415-6.   [o] *Ibid.*, p. 586.
[p] See above, pp. 132-7.   [q] See the Appendix, (L).

blessed pages, for Divinity, and we are put off with Rhetoric. We come for bread, and the critics we speak of offer us a stone.

I will not detain you any longer. No apology can be needed for the subject which has been engaging our attention[r]. Those who watch " the signs of the times" attentively, will bear me witness that *unbelief* is one fearful note of the coming age. The self-same principle, working in different classes of minds, produces results diametrically different: but it is still the same principle which is at work. Unbelief is no less the cause why so many have forsaken the Church of their Fathers, to run after the blasphemous fables and dangerous deceits of the Church of Rome,—than it is the parent of that shallow Rationalism which unhappily is now so popular among us. . . . Intimations of what is to be hereafter, may be every now and then detected. At intervals, hoarse sounds, from a distance, are known to smite upon the listening ear; signals of the coming danger,—sure harbingers of the approaching storm.—Holy Scripture is the stronghold against which the Enemy will make his assault, assuredly: nor can we employ ourselves better than by building one another up in reverence for its Inspired Oracles: opposing to the crafts of the Evil One the simplicity of a child-like faith; and resolutely refusing to see less than GOD, in GOD's Word!

This must be the preacher's apology for disputing where he would rather adore; for discussing the Revelations of Scripture, instead of *feeding* upon them; especially at this holy Season when the Apostle's ex-

[r] In the earlier part of the present Sermon many passages have been re-written. What follows stands exactly as it was preached in 1851.

hortation finds an echo in all our services: — the mouth, engaged in the constant confession that JESUS is the LORD,—the heart, filled with the thought of Him, who as at this time died for our sins, and rose again for our Justification.

GOD grant us grace,—at this and every other time, —so to put away the leaven of malice and wickedness, that we may always serve Him in pureness of living and truth: through the merits of the same His SON, JESUS CHRIST our LORD!

SERMON VII.[a]

THE MARVELS OF HOLY SCRIPTURE,—MORAL AND PHYSICAL.—JAEL'S DEED DEFENDED.— MIRACLES VINDICATED.

St. Mark xii. 24.

Do ye not therefore err, because ye know not the Scriptures, neither the power of God.

ON a certain occasion, the Son of Man was asked what was thought a hard question by those who, in His day, professed "the negative Theology[b]." There was a moral and there was physical marvel to be solved. Both difficulties were met by a single sentence. The Sadducean judgment had gone astray from the Truth, ($\pi\lambda\alpha\nu\tilde{\alpha}\sigma\theta\epsilon$ our Saviour said,) from a twofold cause: (1) The men did not understand those very Scriptures to which they appealed so confidently: and, (2) They had an unworthy notion of God's power. —There are plenty of Sadducees at the present day among ourselves. They are as fond as ever of finding difficulties in the self-same Scriptures. They are to be met, I am persuaded, exactly as of old; by shewing that their error is still the fruit of their ignorance of Scripture; the consequence of their unworthy conceptions of God. I propose to illustrate this on the present occasion. My subject, (one certainly not un-

---

[a] Preached at St. Mary-the-Virgin, Whit-Sunday, May 19th, 1861.
[b] Acts xxiii. 8. For the phrase in the text, see *Essays and Reviews*, p. 151. Also p. 174.

suited to the day,) is *the Marvels of Scripture*,—whether Moral or Physical. I would fain have discussed them apart; but I shall not have another opportunity. I must handle the whole subject therefore within the limits of a single Sermon: and by consequence I must be extremely brief.

Now, I venture to assume that whatever, from its extraordinary character, perplexes us in Scripture, is a difficulty only *to ourselves;* that moral Marvels and physical Miracles, alike, would cease to create any difficulty if we knew more about GOD. The Morality of the Life to come, I do believe will prove none other than the Morality of the life which now is; and so I presume that it may be their Divine Author's will, that the physical Laws of the Universe shall be eternal likewise. And yet, as no thoughtful man will probably be found to say that he thinks he knows as much about the nature of these last now, as he expects to know hereafter,—so it is to be presumed that a sublimer, and therefore a juster view of the relation in which the Creature stands to the CREATOR, will disclose to us much which, at present, we should be little prepared to admit, if it were speculatively presented to us, ("as in a glass, darkly,") respecting the Moral Government of GOD.

I. In the very fore-front, however, of what I have to say concerning those phenomena which are generally cited as the *Moral Marvels* of Holy Scripture, I must freely declare my opinion that nothing is wanted but that the whole of the *historical* evidence should be before us, in every case, in order that we might cease to look upon them as marvels at all. But so it is, that Scripture is severely brief: takes no pains to conciliate our good opinion: seems to care nothing either for our applause or our censure. Scripture, in short, has been made *an instrument of Man's probation*[b]. It is for *us* to search curiously into the record; to take an enlarged view of times and manners; and finally, in the exercise of a generous Faith, to decide whether the difficulty is such as ought to occasion us any real distress. I proceed, in this spirit, to consider, as briefly as possible, the history of Jael; simply because I have heard stronger things said against *her*, than against any of the Worthies of old time who are mentioned with distinct approbation in the Book of Life.

1. Now, if you choose to consider Jael as one who lured a weary and unsuspecting soldier into her tent,—shewed him hospitality,—and when he was asleep, murdered him in cold blood,—you certainly cannot help recoiling from the inspired decision that, "Blessed above women shall Jael the wife of Heber the Kenite be." But I take the liberty of saying that this is quite the wrong way to read her story. You must begin it from the other end.

God pronounces this woman blessed, and distinctly commends her for her deed. From this point you must start; remembering that *no action can be immoral which God praises.* The Divine sentence, instead of creating a difficulty, is, on the contrary, exactly the thing which removes it[c]. To weigh the story apart from this, (which is the prime consideration of all,) is like condemning the immorality of an executioner without caring to hear that he is but carrying out the

[b] See the Appendix (C).

[c] Should one not as readily acknowledge a hint which was gathered from the conversation of the thoughtful Vicar of Stanford-in-the-Vale, as if it had been derived from some of his published writings?

sentence of the Lawgiver. Furnished with the clue of GOD's approbation of Jael's deed, we retrace our steps, and reconsider the narrative. If all were still dark and hopeless, we might be sure that there are circumstances withheld, which if known would have made GOD's justice clear as the light. But, as a matter of fact, it generally happens that, when we "know the Scriptures," the difficulty in great measure disappears; and I am going to shew that it is so on the present occasion.

I find that when the people of GOD were on their way out of Egypt into Canaan, they were indebted to one family (the Kenites) for kindness and help [d]. The head of that family was Jethro, the father-in-law of Moses, high-priest of Midian, — in which land the LORD, from the burning bush, had commissioned the future Lawgiver of Israel to redeem His people from the bondage of Egypt. Jethro met them in the Arabian desert; became their guide [e] till they reached the promised Land; and with them entered the borders of their future possession. It was a covenant between the two races that they should share the goodness of JEHOVAH. Accordingly, the Kenites made their settlement amid the Royal tribe of Judah; and it is easy to foresee how close a bond would spring up between the alien family and their avowed protectors, when, to the memory of past dangers shared together, was superadded the consciousness of present blessings;— especially in an age when the law of hospitality was held most sacred. How strong the bond became, the sequel of the story convincingly shews [f].

[d] 1 Sam. xv. 6. [e] Numb. x. 29—32.
[f] A hint has here been taken from one of Dr. W. H. Mill's admirable *University Sermons*, pp. 239-40.

The children of Israel, at the end of a hundred and fifty years, find themselves cruelly oppressed by the most powerful of the Kings of the conquered but not extirpated race. GOD promises deliverance: and Deborah is raised up to organize the resistance against Jabin, "the captain of whose host was Sisera." Now, while Heber the Kenite is gone with the rest to the battle,—(for he had pitched his tent, remember, by Kedesh; and it was from Kedesh [g] that Deborah "sent and called Barak the son of Abinoam;")—while Heber, the husband, I say, is gone to the battle, and Jael the wife is left alone, distracted with anxiety, in the tent; —when, weak and unprotected woman as she is, she beholds the Captain of the hateful oppressor of GOD's people hastening to her tent, slumbering at her feet, and unexpectedly within her power:—will you pretend that *she*, a Midianitess, is to blame if she yields to the strong impulse which prompts her to compass the man's downfall, as speedily as she may? "There was peace between Jabin the King of Hazor and the house of Heber the Kenite [h]," you will remind me. True: (between *Jabin*,—not between *Sisera*, by the way:) without this, the whole incident would not have happened. Sisera presumed on the peaceful relations which existed between his lord and Heber; and supposed that the sympathy of one alien race for another was to outweigh every other consideration. Yet, how stood the case? Heber had thrown in his lot, irrevocably, with the people of GOD; while Jabin had already utterly violated the conditions of peace. For twenty weary years, had Jael and her family shared the hardships of that sacred line which Jabin had "mightily oppressed." All her life long [i], the

[g] Judges iv. 6.   [h] Ibid. iv. 17.   [i] Ibid. v. 6.

highways have been unoccupied; and travellers have had to walk through by-ways; and the villages have been deserted by their inhabitants. Archers have infested the very places of drawing water[k]. Meanwhile, a sure word has gone forth from the Prophetess who dwells under the palm-tree between Ramah and Bethel on Mount Ephraim[l], to the effect that God will give a mighty victory this day to His people[m]. Moreover, Deborah, (to whom the children of Israel go up for judgment,) has foretold that the Lord will "*sell Sisera into the hand of a woman*[n]." How can you marvel at the rest! . . . With a faith strong and undoubting as Rahab's, Jael,—weak woman as she is,—seizes the wooden tent-pin and the mallet, (the only weapons which are within her reach!); and, (somewhat as David afterwards employed a stone and a sling for the slaughter of the Philistine,) with these vile instruments, at one blow, she smites to the earth the enemy of God's people. . . . O, it was *not* because she was treacherous, or because she was cruel! Treachery and cruelty were not the vices to which a dweller in tents (and she a woman!) was prone, when a thirsty soldier begged a draught of water; and most assuredly, had she been either, she would not,—she *could* not, have won praise from God! (Witness God's wrath against David in the matter of Uriah, because *he* had no pity[o]; as well as dying Jacob's denunciations against Simeon and Levi because "instruments of cruelty" were "in their habitations[p].") O no! It was because she beheld in the slumbering captain at once the enemy of her own afflicted race,—and of God's oppressed people,—and above all of God Himself. *That*

[k] Judges v. 6, 7, 11.   [l] Ibid. iv. 4, 5.   [m] Ibid. v. 7.
[n] Ibid. v. 5 and 9.   [o] 1 Sam. xii.   [p] Gen. xlix. 5.

was why "she put her hand to the nail, and her right hand to the workman's hammer!" ... The fight, you are requested to remember, had been a tremendous fight; and the battle, as she thought, was yet raging. Reuben, and Dan, and Asher had kept aloof from the encounter;—the first, in his rich pasture-land east of the Jordan, abiding "among the sheepfolds, to hear the bleatings of the flocks;" the two others, intent on their maritime pursuits. Only some of Ephraim, Benjamin, and Manasseh [q], had been found willing to throw in their lot with the two northern tribes of Zebulun, and Naphtali,—who had "jeoparded their lives unto the death." And the battle which these had fought had been the LORD's; and as many as had taken part with them, were considered to have come "*to the help of the LORD.*" Such then was the quarrel which Jael had made her own; and such the spirit in which she had done her wild deed of unassisted prowess!

To appreciate her constancy and courage, you may not overlook how fearful were the odds against the cause she was espousing: on the oppressor's side, nine hundred chariots of iron; whereas, "was there a shield or spear seen among forty thousand in Israel?" It had been so terrific a day, that if the LORD had not been on their side,—if the stars in their courses had not fought for Israel,—how could Sisera have possibly been overcome? But the very river was employed to sweep the enemies of Israel away,—"that ancient river, the river Kishon!" ... Now I boldly ask you, if the Angel of the LORD may curse bitterly the inhabitants of Meroz, " because they came not to the help of the

[q] Comp. Judges v. 14, 17, with Numb. xxxii. 39, 40, and Josh. xiii. 31.—Consider Ps. lxxx. 2.

Lord,"—(pray mark that phrase; for it shews exactly in what light the conflict was regarded!)—"*to the help of the* Lord *against the mighty;*" shall we wonder if, by the Spirit of God, Deborah the prophetess proclaims " blessed above women in the tent" Jael the wife of Heber the Kenite to be.;—the undaunted one by whose right hand the captain of all that mighty host had been slain ? Find me another "*woman in the tent*" who may be compared with *her!* ... Or rather, (for *that* is the only question,) shall these words embolden us to impeach the morality of Holy Writ?... I am sure there is not one of you all who really thinks it. She was—was she not?—a courageous, a faithful, and (according to her light,) a strictly virtuous woman. She was content to risk *all*, " as seeing Him who is invisible:" and *to believe* that " they that be with us are more than they that be with them[r]." From the unmistakeable evidence of her uncompromising boldness in a good cause, her unwavering faith, her readiness to cast in her lot with the people of God,—no one but a hypocrite will turn away to criticize the details of her deed by the Gospel standard of Grace and Truth. " He asked for water, and she gave him milk." What would you have had her do? It is by no means certain that she foresaw the deed which was to follow, and which *cannot*, (from the nature of the case,) have been the result of a preconcerted plan. The impulse to terminate the tyranny of Canaan, and the sufferings of her adopted people, as well as to decide the fortune of that critical day, by slaying one whom she regarded as the enemy of God Himself, may have seized her while she stood in the door of the tent, —weighing Sisera's petition against Deborah's pro-

[r] 2 Kings vi. 16.

phecy. Be this as it may,—would you have had the woman connive at Sisera's escape,—the enemy of GOD's people, when GOD Himself had unexpectedly put him into her power?

It will assist us to understand this story, that we should bear in mind how it fared with Ahab, King of Israel, in the matter of Ben-hadad, King of Syria, as recorded in the xxth chapter of the First Book of Kings. "Thus saith the LORD," (was the Divine sentence,) "*Because thou hast let go out of thy hand a man whom I appointed to utter destruction*, therefore thy life shall go for his life, and thy people for his people[s]." It is quite evident that as the *enemy of GOD*, in the strictest sense, each fresh oppressor of Israel was regarded; and that, as the enemy of the LORD GOD of Israel, Sisera was summarily slain by the Kenite's wife.

Be so good as to remember also, that forgiveness of enemies is strictly a *Christian* duty. You have no right to expect to find the brightest jewels of the kingdom of Heaven glittering on the swarthy brow of an Arabian wife in the days of the Judges. "Grace and *Truth* came by JESUS CHRIST[t]." You cannot expect to find the wife of Heber the Kenite more truthful than Sarah, and Rebekah, and Rachel,—or even than Abraham, and Isaac, and Jacob, and David: neither should you be so unreasonable as to expect that the GOD of Truth will award praise and blame to His creatures by a higher standard of Morality than He has seen fit, at any given period, to allow. A perfectly enlightened conscience, no doubt, will never consent to lie. A Christian woman in Jael's place, ought not, of course, to be guilty of Jael's deed. But

[s] 1 Kings xx. 42. [t] St. John i. 17.

you are forgetting the time of the world in which *your* lot is thrown. I say nothing of the circumstances of terror under which *she* acted,—*she* was *forced* to act. How could she tell that Sisera would not awake ere she should strike the blow,—or at least before she could achieve his death? What if a company of Jabin's host should come up to the tent-door, the instant she had done the deed, and inquire after Sisera? Suppose the issue of that day's encounter should prove disastrous, what would be her own and Heber's fate? ... Feel a little for the poor wife,—for the lonely, helpless "woman in the tent,"—*not* entirely for the fierce soldier against whom you have heard the LORD's decree of death! ... O ye, who, living in the full blaze of Gospel light, in cold blood can reject the doctrine of the Atonement, and deny the LORD who bought you, and teach that the Bible is "like any other book;" who can make light of its Inspiration, and evacuate its Prophecy, and idealize its Miracles; who with your lips can profess the Church's doctrines, and with your pens can deny them;—go *ye* and prate of Morality, and Honesty, and Truth! *We* shall heed mighty little your opinion of Jael's conduct, and of the Divine Commendation which it met with. I believe that, instead of suspecting the morality of the Bible in this instance, there is hardly an honest Christian heart among us, but cries out, on the contrary,—"*So let all* Thine enemies perish, O LORD! But let them that love Him be as the sun when he goeth forth in his might."

2. There is no time to consider, as I fain would, any other story; that of Jacob for example. It is quite amazing to hear the presumptuous speeches concerning that great Saint, in which good men sometimes permit

themselves: as if the sum total of Jacob's history were *this:*—that he once obtained an ungenerous advantage over his Brother, and then shamefully deceived his blind and aged Father. Whereas those were the two great blots in an otherwise holy life! actions which were followed by severe, aye lifelong punishment.—But I must not enter on Jacob's history,—even to shew you that a careless reader overlooks certain circumstances which go a very long way indeed to excuse the actions just alluded to. I prefer reminding you that since, at Bethel, GOD blessed the exile's slumbers with a glorious vision, and most comfortable promise, on his first setting out for Haran; and again at Jabbok, as well as at Mahanaim, blessed him with a vision of Angels, and a renewal of the blessing, on his return; *from this point,* as before, it will be our wisdom to reason; and we shall reason backwards. Had Scripture been quite silent in all other respects, such proofs of the Divine approval ought to be enough to convince a believing heart that the only thing wanting must be fuller details,—more evidence,—in order to shew us that the Patriarch *deserved* the SPIRIT's praise. But in truth, in Jacob's case, the details are abundant and the evidence decisive.

3. Of all the other (so called) difficulties which occur to my memory,—as the extinction of the Canaanites, (who yet were *not* extinguished,)—the Sacrifice of Isaac, (who yet was *not* sacrificed,)—the life of David;—I have only to say that before you can pretend to have an opinion upon the subject you must be sure that you "know the Scriptures:" else, I make bold to say, you will inevitably err in your cogitations concerning them. Thus, men are heard to insinuate astonishment that the King who so basely compassed Uriah's

death should have been "a man after GOD's own heart:" whereas the Hebrew original, (as they would know, *if they knew the Scriptures*,) conveys nothing of the kind; while the murder of Uriah is found to have drawn down upon David unmitigated wrath and terrible punishment from the right Hand of Him who is of purer eyes than to behold iniquity.

II. Turn we now, briefly, to the physical Marvels which are described in the Bible; and chiefly those which occur in the Old Testament.

I am about to speak of Miracles in general; but it may be convenient to say a few words first about certain mighty transactions which eclipse, by their vastness or their strangeness, most isolated events. Thus, as the Nativity, Temptation, Transfiguration, Resurrection, Ascension, of our LORD, together with the Coming of the HOLY GHOST, eclipse in a manner the other Miracles of the New Testament,—so the Temptation of our first Parents, the Flood, the destruction of Sodom and the fate of Lot's wife, the burning bush, the Plagues which prepared the way for the Exode, the crossing of the Red Sea, the Manna, and the brazen Serpent; Balaam's ass, and the fate of the walls of Jericho; the history of Jonah, and of Daniel among the lions:—events like these stand out from the Old Testament narrative and challenge astonishment.

Of all these latter events, viewed as difficulties,— (for it is as difficulties *in the way of Revelation* that we are now expected to look on Miracles,)—you are requested to observe that they enjoy, one and all, the confirmation of *express citation in the New Testament*. I am saying that either St. Paul, or St. Peter, or St. James, or (above all) our Blessed LORD Himself, appeal to, or else explain, every one of these marvellous passages in Old Testament History. And this is the only remark I propose to offer concerning any of them. It will certainly prove unavailing to convince a certain class of persons of the historical reality of the Deluge, to find that our SAVIOUR, that St. Peter, and St. Paul, have all spoken of it as an actual event:— Men who are disposed to reject the story of the dumb ass speaking with man's voice, will not perhaps believe it one whit the more because they find it appealed to by St. Peter[u]:—and the Divine exposition offered by CHRIST Himself of Jonah, three days and three nights in the fish's belly, will not, it may be feared, reconcile others to an event which strikes them as being too improbable to be true. But *this*, at least, will infallibly result from the discovery:— men will perceive that they must positively make their election; and either accept the Bible as a whole, or else reject it as a whole; for that there is no middle course open to them. The New Testament stands committed irrevocably to the Old. Every Book of the Bible stands committed to all the other Books. Not only does our LORD quote the Canon in its collected form, and call it "the Law and the prophets,"—or simply ἡ γραφή, "the Scripture,"—and so set His seal upon it, as one undivided and indivisible roll of Inspiration; but He and His Apostles single out the very narratives which the imbecility of Man was most likely to stumble at, and employ them for such purposes, and in such a manner, that escape from them shall henceforth be altogether hopeless. To eliminate the marvels of Scripture, I say, is impossible; for a Divine Hand has been laid upon almost

[u] 2 St. Peter ii. 16.

every one of them. The subsequent references are not only most numerous, but they run into the very staple of the narrative,—and will not,—*cannot* be eradicated.

I question whether all students of the inspired page are aware of the extent to which what I have been saying holds true. Let me only invite you to investigate the structure of the Bible under this aspect, and you will be astonished at the result. For you will find that the system of tacit quotation and allusive reference is so perpetual, that it is as if the design had been that the fibres should be incapable of being disentangled any more. Balaam's story for example in the Book of Numbers, is found alluded to in Deuteronomy, in Joshua, in Micah, in Nehemiah; by St. Peter, by St. Jude, and by St. John in the Apocalypse[x].—The Exodus, with its attendant wonders, is alluded to in Joshua, and in Judges, and in Job, and in the Psalms; in Amos, and Isaiah, and Micah, and Hosea, and Jeremiah, and Daniel; in Kings, in Samuel, in Nehemiah; and in the New Testament repeatedly[y]. The Evangelists quote one another times without number. In the Epistles, the Gospels are quoted upwards of fifty times; and St. Peter quotes St. Paul again and again. It is a favourite device of

---

[x] Numb. xxii., xxiii., xxiv., xxv., xxxi. 8 and 16. Joshua xxiv. 9, 10: xiii. 22. Micah vi. 5. Nehem. xiii. 1, 2 (quoting Deut. xxiii. 3, 4.) 2 St. Peter ii. 14—16. St. Jude ver. 11. Rev. ii. 14.

[y] Exod. xiv. 19—31, &c. is thus referred to in Josh. ii. 10: iv. 23. Judges v. 4, 5. Job xxvi. 12. Ps. lxxiv. 13: cvi. 7—11: cxiv. 1—8: lxxvii. 14—20: lxvi. 6: lxxviii. 12—31. Amos ii. 10. Hos. xii. 13. Is. lxiii. 11—13: xliii. 16: li. 9, 10, 15. Micah vi. 4—5. Jer. ii. 6: xxxii. 20-1. Dan. ix. 15. 2 Sam. vii. 23. 2 Kings xvii. 7. Neh. ix. 9—21. Acts vii. 30—41. 1 Cor. x. 1—11. 2 Tim. iii. 8. Hebr. xi. 29. Rev. xv. 3.

these last days to hint at the allegorical character of the beginning of Genesis. But I find upwards of thirty references in the New Testament to the first two Chapters of Genesis[z]. Certain parts of Daniel have incurred suspicion,—for no better reason, as it seems, than because certain persons have found it hard to believe that Prophecy can be "an anticipation of History[a]." Now it is strange certainly to find

[z] Gen. i. 1, (Heb. xi. 3:) 3, (2 Cor. iv. 6:) 5, (1 Thess. v. 5:) 6, 9, (2 St. Pet. iii. 5:) 11, 12, (1 St. John iii. 9:) 14, (Phil. ii. 15: Rev. xxi. 11:) 24, (Acts x. 12: xi. 6:) 26, (St. James iii. 9:) 26, 27, (Col. iii. 10:) 27, (1 Cor. xi. 7: St. Matth. xix. 4: St. Mark x. 6:) 28, (Ps. viii. 6—8, commented on in Heb. ii. 5—9: 1 Cor. xv. 25: Eph. i. 22.)—Gen. ii. 2, (Heb. iv. 4, 10:) 7, (1 Cor. xv. 45, 47:) 9, (Rev. ii. 7: xxii. 2, 14, 19:) 18, (1 Cor. xi. 9:) 22, (1 Tim. ii. 13:) 23, (Eph. v. 30:) 24, (Eph. v. 31: St. Matth. xix. 5: St. Mark x. 7: 1 Cor. vi. 16:) &c.

[a] "It is a very misleading notion of Prophecy," says Dr. Arnold, —(a writer to whom, more than to any other person, I conceive that we are indebted for "Essays and Reviews;" *that* unhappy production being the lawful development and inevitable result of the late Head-master of Rugby's most unsound and mischievous religious teaching:)—"It is a very misleading notion of Prophecy, if we regard it as an anticipation of History." (*Sermons*, i. p. 375.) "I think that, with the exception of those prophecies which relate to our LORD, the object of Prophecy is rather to delineate principles and states of opinion which shall come, than external events. I grant that Daniel *seems to furnish an exception*." (*Life and Correspondence*, p. 59.) This was written in 1825. In 1840, we are informed:—"The latter chapters of Daniel, *if genuine, would be a clear exception to my Canon of Interpretation*. . . . But I have long thought that the greater part of the Book of Daniel is most certainly a very late work, of the time of the Maccabees; and the *pretended prophecy* about the Kings of Grecia and Persia, and of the North and South, is *mere history, like the poetical prophecies in Virgil and elsewhere*. . . . That there may be genuine fragments in it, is very likely." (*Ibid.*, p. 505.)—In other words, Dr. Arnold, rather than suppose "*my* Canon of Interpretation" (!) worthless,

a thing objected to for being what it is: and "Prophecy is nothing *but* the history of events before they come to pass,"—as Butler remarked long ago [b]. Waiving this, however, you are requested to observe that our SAVIOUR quotes from *those very parts of Daniel which have been objected to*. You cannot get rid of those parts of Daniel therefore. You are not to suppose that the Bible is like an old house, where a window may be darkened, or a door blocked up, according to the caprice of every fresh occupant. The terms on which men dwell there are that every part of the structure shall be inhabited; and that every part shall be retained in its integrity. What I am insisting upon is, that the sacred Writers plainly say, —We stand or we fall together. They reach forth their hands, and they hold one another fast. They rehearse comprehensive Genealogies,—they furnish a summary view of long histories,—they enumerate the various worthies of old time, and cite their deeds in order. They recognize one another's voices, and they interpret one another's thoughts, and they adopt one another's sayings. Verily the Bible is *not* "like any other Book!" The prophets and Apostles and Evangelists of either covenant reach out one to another; and lo, among them is seen the form of One like the SON of GOD. . . . How far it may be rational *to reject the Bible*, I will not now discuss: but it is demonstrable that a man cannot accept the Bible, and straightway propose to omit from it one jot or one tittle of its contents. As for abstracting from Scripture

is prepared to eject the Book of Daniel from the Inspired Canon. Any thing is "very likely," in short, except that GOD could foretell future events, and Dr. Arnold be in error! . . . Ἆρ' οὐχ ὕβρις τάδ';

[b] *Analogy*, P. II. ch. vii.

the marvels of Scripture, it is precisely for the protection and preservation of *them*, as I have been shewing, that the most curious and abundant provision has been made.

1. The miracles, properly so called, whether of the Old or New Testament, have lately been cavilled at with exceeding bitterness[c]. That they are sufficiently attested, is allowed[d]; the objection is a (so called) Philosophical one, and is briefly this,—that the Laws of Nature being fixed and immutable, it is contrary not only to experience, but also to reason, to suppose that they have ever been suspended, or violated, or interrupted. Events "contrary to the order of Nature,"—events which would introduce "disorder" into Creation,—are pronounced incredible.—This is a very old objection; but it has been lately revived. I will dispose of it as briefly as I can.

You are requested to observe then, that this difficulty,—(such as it is,)—is entirely occasioned by the terms in which it is stated. *Who* ever asserted that Miracles are "violations of natural causes[e]?" "suspensions of natural laws[f]?" Who ever said that the effect of Miracles is to "interrupt"—"violate"—"reverse,"—the Laws of Nature? Why assume "contrariety" and "disorder" in a κόσμος which seems to have had no experience of either?

[c] *Throughout* the volume entitled "Essays and Reviews;" while the third Essay is simply an affirmation of their *impossibility*.

[d] And yet, Bp. Butler says,—"The facts, both miraculous and natural, in Scripture, appear in all respects to stand upon the same foot of historical evidence:" .... "and though testimony is no proof of enthusiastic opinions, or of any opinions at all; yet, it is allowed, in all other cases, to be a proof of facts."—*Analogy*, P. II. ch. vii. (ed. 1833, pp. 285 and 293.)

[e] *Essays and Reviews*, p. 140.   [f] *Ibid*. p. 104.

But God is, I suppose, superior to His own Laws! He is not the creature of circumstances,—even of His own creating. Supreme is He in Creation,—albeit in a manner which baffles thought. He does not even suspend His Laws, perhaps, so much as fulfil them after a Diviner fashion;—somewhat as He was fulfilling the Mosaic Economy even while He seemed to be violating one or other of its sanctions. He does not reverse or disorder the fixed course of Nature, so much as rise above it, and shew Himself superior to it. He does not disturb anything, but our notions of His mode of acting. God coming suddenly to view in Nature, (which is an essential part of the notion of a miracle,) occasions perplexity, it is true; but only because we do not understand fully either Nature or God. "We know Him not as He is, neither indeed can know Him." While of Nature, we know nothing but a few Laws which we have discovered by a long and laborious induction of phenomena. In fact, this whole manner of speaking concerning the Creator of the Universe, with reference to the Laws which He is found to have prescribed to things natural, has, I suspect, some great foolishness in it: for, even if we do not so far dishonour God as to imagine that He is subject to Law, yet we seem to imply that we think ourselves capable of understanding the relation in which He stands to Law. Whereas, the very notion of Law may be utterly inapplicable to God,— who is not only its first Author, (as He is indeed the first Author of all things,) but the very source and *cause* of it also. So that what are Laws to ourselves may be not so much as Law at all to God; but, (if I may so speak,) something which depends on " the counsel of His will," and which, (considered as a restraining cause,) is to Him as if it were not. There can be no miracles with God[g]!

Briefly then:—That He who, (surely I may say *confessedly*,) is above Law, when He manifests Himself in the midst of Creation, should act in a manner which defies conception; and yet should disturb nothing, reverse nothing, violate nothing;—(except to be sure, possibly, certain preconceived notions of His rational creatures;)—in *this*, I say, there is surely nothing either incredible or absurd.

2. So much, to say the truth, seems to be admitted, by all but professed Atheists. But then, certain formulæ have been invented to bridge over the difficulty, which Miracles are supposed to occasion, which I cannot but think are just as objectionable as unbelief itself.

By way of saving the credit of "the Laws of the Universe," a kind of compromise has been discovered; to which I do not find that God has been made any party.

The idea of Law, which has been falsely declared to be only now "emerging into supremacy in Science[h]," seems to have usurped such a dominion over the minds of a few persons, superficially acquainted with Physical studies, that Miracles can be only tolerated on the supposition that they are "the exact fulfilment of much more extensive Laws than those we suppose to exist[i]." We are kindly assured that what we call a Miracle is not "an exception to those laws which

---

[g] There are some admirable observations on this subject in the 'Preliminary Essay' prefixed to Dean Trench's *Notes on the Miracles.*—See pp. 10, 12, 15, 60, &c.

[h] Dr. Temple.

[i] Mr. Babbage's *Bridgewater Treatise*, (2nd. Ed. 1838,) p. 92.

we know, but really the fulfilment of a wider Law which we did not know before[k]." Men are eager to remind us that this is the view of Bp. Butler[l], (whom every one, I observe, is fond of having for an ally.) Thus, a very recent writer says,—" What we call interferences may, (as Bp. Butler observed long ago,) be fulfilments of general laws not perfectly apprehended by us[m]."—But I cannot find that Bp. Butler anywhere says anything of the sort. What Butler says, is,—that we know nothing of the laws of storms and earthquakes,—tempers and geniuses;—yet we conclude, (but only from analogy,) that all these seemingly accidental things are the result of general laws. Now, (he proceeds,) since it is only " from our finding that the course of Nature, in some respects and so far, goes on by general laws, that we conclude this of the rest;"—it is credible " that God's miraculous interpositions may have been, all along, in like manner, *by general laws of wisdom.*" Butler says that it " may have been *by general laws,*" " that the affairs of the world, being permitted to go on *in their natural course* so far, should, just at such a point, have a new direction given them *by miraculous interposition.*" He does not say, you observe, that those " miraculous interpositions" are " the exact fulfilment of *much more extensive Laws* than those we suppose to exist;" (as if *a larger induction* were all that was needed, in order

---

[k] " *Why we should pray for Fair Weather:* being Remarks on Professor Kingsley's Sermon,"—by a Member of the University [of Cambridge,]—12mo. Cambridge, 1860, p. 8.

[l] "The view taken of Miracles in chapter viii., is the same as that contained in the work of Butler, on *the Analogy,*" &c.—Babbage (as above), p. 191.

[m] *Edinburgh Review,* for April 1861, p. 486.

to get rid of the obnoxious word "Miracle:")—not, that Miracles may be "fulfilments of general laws *not perfectly apprehended by us;*" (as if the only thing wanted, were an enlargement of the human formula, in order to bring a miraculous interposition within the definition of an extraordinary phenomenon.) Such notions belong altogether to the inventors of calculating machines; whose speculations, even concerning Divine things, clearly cannot soar above their instrument[n]. It is called the "argument from laws intermitting[o];" and evidently reduces a miracle to a phenomenon of periodical recurrence. The aloe, watched for ninety-nine years and observed to blossom in the hundredth, is (according to this view) an emblem of the constitution of Nature at last interrupted by a Miracle.

I will not waste your time further with this view of the subject, having exposed its fallacy. Station yourself, in thought, at the grave of Lazarus; and see him that was dead and had been four days buried,

---

[n] How exactly, in this instance, has Dr. Whewell's anticipation received fulfilment!;—"We may, with the greatest propriety, deny to the mechanical Philosophers and Mathematicians of recent times any authority with regard to their views of the administration of the Universe; we have no reason whatever to expect from their speculations any help, when we ascend to the first Cause and supreme Ruler of the Universe. But we might perhaps go further, and assert that *they are in some respects less likely than men employed in other pursuits, to make any clear advance towards such a subject of speculation.*"—(Whewell's *Bridgewater Treatise*, p. 334.)—Scarcely less acute is the remark which the late excellent Hugh James Rose has somewhere left on record, concerning the chapter wherein the preceding remark occurs,—That the world would not easily forgive Dr. Whewell for those two chapters on "Inductive" and "Deductive Habits."

[o] Babbage (as before), p. 92, (heading of ch. viii.)

come forth bound hand and foot with grave-clothes;—and then prate of any "general Laws," except those "OF WISDOM," to as many as you can get to listen to you. A "miraculous interposition," (as Butler phrases it,) has given a new direction to affairs which, so far, had been permitted to go in their natural course. That "general Laws" of inscrutable Wisdom determined such a "*miraculous interposition,*"—is a position which, so far from objecting to, I embrace with both the arms of my heart [p].

3. Another favourite recipe there is for escaping from the bondage of Miracles, which is so childish, that it would seem scarcely to deserve notice: but that it has been largely resorted to by writers of whom the world thinks highly. These men, in a word, try to *explain them away* where they can: where they cannot, they *pare them down* as much as they are able, or rather as much as they dare. Demoniacal possession? Symptoms like those described are known to accompany epilepsy. Manna? Something like it falls in the wilderness of Sinai to this hour. The Red Sea parted? Well, but a strong East wind blew all night. Stilling the storm, and healing Peter's wife's mother? Every storm is stilled if let alone; and a fever will burn out, often without occasioning death. The miraculous draught of fishes, and the stater in the fish's mouth? .... but you can readily supply a suggestion for yourselves.

Now, two remarks present themselves on this kind of handling, which may be worth stating. (1) Those who so speak forget that the Devils are related to have *conversed with* CHRIST[q]:—that the manna, (of which so

---

[p] See the *Analogy*, P. II. ch. iv. sect. iii.
[q] St. Mark i. 24. St. Luke iv. 34: viii. 28, 30—32, &c. &c.

many miraculous properties are related[r],) fed 600,000 men for forty years, *and then suddenly ceased*[s]:—that the waters of the Red Sea were *a wall to the children of Israel, on their right hand and on their left*[t]:—that when CHRIST said to the waves of the sea of Galilee "Peace, be still," "there was *a great calm*[u]:"—that Peter's wife's mother, cured of her fever, "rose and *ministered unto*," (that is "waited upon,") her Benefactor[x]. . . . It is worse than absurd to explain away *part* of a miracle, with a view to getting rid of the whole of it: as if the essence of the miracle were not sure to reside in the residuum,—in the very part which is left unaccounted for! (2) But above all, what place have such explanations in the recorded cases of feeding the multitudes, opening the eyes of one born blind, and raising the dead? While you leave the chiefest miracles of the Gospel untouched, you may not flatter yourself that you have got at the kernel of the matter; or indeed that the real question at issue has been touched by you, at all.

4. There remains to notice one subtle and most treacherous method of dealing with the marvels of Scripture,—(moral and physical alike,)—to which I desire in conclusion to direct your special attention; and which I would brand with burning words if I had them at command. I allude to what is called "IDEOLOGY,"—the plain English for which term is, *a denial of the historical reality of Scripture*. I will not waste time with inquiring whether this method is old or new. It is certainly much in fashion; and it

---

[r] Exod. xvi. 18—21: 22—24:—25—27: 31: 33-34. Add Wisdom xvi. 20-1.

[s] Exod. xvi. 35, and Josh. v. 12. [t] Exod. xiv. 22, 29.

[u] St. Matth. viii. 26. St. Mark iv. 39. [x] St. Matth. viii. 15.

is certainly finding advocates in high quarters. I therefore make no apology for introducing the monstrous thing to your notice. It requires, I should hope, only to be understood, to be rejected with unqualified indignation.

You and I, then, have been taught to believe that "the WORD was made flesh and dwelt among us," in the way St. Matthew and St. Luke describe: that our LORD was Baptized and Tempted of Satan; that He wrought Miracles,—casting out Devils, and even raising the Dead; that He was Transfigured on a mountain; that He was Crucified, died, and was buried; that He rose again the Third Day, ascended into Heaven, and at last, (as on this day,) sent down the PARACLETE to dwell with His Church for ever. All this, I say, you and I,—with the whole Church Catholic for 1800 years,—have been taught to believe as plain historical truths, mere matters of fact; past telling wonderful indeed, but yet as *historically true*, as that I am standing here and you are sitting yonder,—neither more nor less.

But you are to understand that we, and all mankind with us, have been under a very curious delusion on this head. We are assured that every one of these things, or at least that some of them, are only *ideologically* true: that *Historically*, they are false. In plain language, we are requested to believe that they never occurred at all. It is only a lively way of putting it,—no more!

You will inevitably suppose that I must be trifling with you: I therefore proceed to give you a sample of this kind of teaching. A living dignitary of our Church writes as follows concerning the Transfiguration of CHRIST. "It may be asked, of what kind was the vision which we here call the Transfiguration? Was it an effect produced within on the minds of the Apostles; or was it that an actual external change came for the time over the person of our LORD? We cannôt say." I give you this as the mildest form of the poison. Quite evident is it that the same suggestion is just as applicable to our LORD'S Birth, or to His Death; to His Temptation, or to His Resurrection. But to see whither all this *tends*, and what it really *means*, you must have recourse to the pages of a more advanced proficient in the Science of Ideology. He admits that its " application to the interpretation of Scripture, to the doctrines of Christianity, to the formularies of the Church, may undoubtedly be pushed so far as to leave in the sacred records *no historical residue whatever*. An example of the critical ideology carried to excess," (he says,) " *resolves into an ideal*" the whole of our LORD'S Life and Doctrine; and " *substitutes a mere shadow* for the JESUS of the Evangelists." But for all that, (says the writer I am quoting,) " there are traits in the Scriptural person of JESUS, which are better explained by referring them to an ideal than an historical origin: parts of Scripture are more usefully interpreted ideologically than in any other manner,—as for instance, the history of the Temptation by Satan, and accounts of Demoniacal possession." This writer, (who is a clergyman of the Church of England, and a Graduate in Divinity,) goes on to idealize the descent of Mankind from Adam and Eve, together with the chiefest marvels of the Old Testament: insisting that " the force, grandeur, and reality of these ideas are not a whit impaired," although we discredit and reject the history, *as* history. So, our SAVIOUR, (he says,) " is none the less the Son of David, in idea and spiritually, even if it be unproved whether He were so in historic fact." "The spiritual significance is still the same," (he says,) "of the Transfiguration, of opening blind eyes, of causing the tongue of the stammerer to speak plainly, of feeding multitudes with bread in the wilderness, of cleansing leprosy,—whatever links may be deficient in the traditional record of particular events."

"Whatever links may be deficient!" O that men would have the courage or the honesty to *say* what they *mean!* Why not say plainly, "*however untrustworthy we may account the narrative to be?*" And this writer cannot mean any other thing; for missing "links," assuredly, there are *none*.—In truth this method of wrapping up a monstrous abortion in "purple and fine linen," in order to make it look like "a proper child," is so much in vogue, that plain men are obliged first to *translate* a fallacy in order to understand it. Thus, a recent Apologist for the very writer I have been quoting,—after surrendering the beginning of Genesis as "parabolic," (that is, *not historically true*,) is yet so obliging as to contend that "there still remain events" in Scripture,—our LORD's Resurrection to wit,—"in which the garb of flesh,"—(pray mark the phraseology!)—"in which *the garb of flesh* seems to be so indispensable a vehicle for the spirit within, that we can hardly conceive how the one could have sustained itself in the world, unless it had been from the beginning allied to the other^y." In plain English, the writer is so candid as to admit that if the Resurrection of our LORD JESUS CHRIST from death be a mere fabrication,—in plain terms, a hoax practised upon the

---

[y] *Edinburgh Review*, (art. on 'Essays and Reviews,') April 1861, p. 487.

credulity of an unscientific age,—it is hard to understand how it can have *imposed* upon mankind so completely for the last eighteen hundred years.

I will not insult the understanding of those who hear me so grossly as to suppose that dreams like these, —(and really they are no more!)—require answer or refutation. Such desperate shifts to elude the meaning of plain words, as the whole theory of Ideology discloses, would be even ludicrous, if the subject-matter were not so very sacred and solemn. As in the case of certain acts of flagrant dishonesty which one sometimes reads of,—one cannot forbear exclaiming, The man must certainly have felt himself *very sore pressed indeed* to have been induced to resort to a step so utterly disgraceful to his character! . . . . Anyhow, since certain persons have adopted this course, I do but plead for consistency. Only let them be sure that they apply this precious method of Interpretation to the History of England, and to everything their friend tells them: and let them not feel surprised if the same kind of ideological handling is bestowed upon everything they tell their friend. Idealize away, and be sure you stick at nothing! *Why* be outdone in logical consistency by such an one as Strauss? Let men also make their election whether Scripture shall be a lie or not. And when they have made up their minds, let them, in the Name of GOD, instead of dealing in unmanly insinuations, and dark hints, and shuffling equivocations,—let them declare themselves plainly, that we may know at least *with whom* and *with what* we have to do. For while false Brethren are thus playing fast and loose with Revelation, they are trifling with the faith of thousands,— and imperilling other immortal souls besides their own.

But I shall be reminded that the subject-matter of daily life, and of the Everlasting Gospel, is very different: and that the marvellous character of certain events recorded in the Bible constrains us to relegate those events to a distinct region. A child's plea, which was effectually disposed of upwards of a century ago! What does it amount to but this,—that what is *supernatural,* or even highly extraordinary, must be also *untrue?* ... When, however, the argument is shifted, and is made an appeal *ad misericordiam:*—when I am entreated to remember that though *I* believe in the Resurrection of CHRIST from Death, the same event is a "stumbling block" to many; and that I am "bound to treat with tenderness those who prefer to lean on the other, and, as *they* think, *more secure foundation*ᶻ;" (viz. on the hypothesis that the Resurrection of the Son of Man is all a fable;)—I say, when I am so addressed, really, friends and Brethren, I am constrained to cry out that there is a limit beyond which Nature cannot endure; and that *that* limit has now been overstepped. Will men try to persuade us that *the idea* of our LORD's Resurrection is a more secure basis for the Church's faith than *the fact* of our LORD's Resurrection? Why, they might as well try to convince the world that a broken reed is a better support than an oaken staff;—or that a handful of waste paper is of more value than the titledeeds of an estate. How *can* a shadow,—how *can* what is confessedly an imagination,—be, in any sense, or for any body, a "secure foundation;" or indeed, *any foundation at all?* how, above all, can a fancy be a "*more* secure foundation" than *a fact?* .... Not

ᶻ *Edinburgh Review,* (art. on 'Essays and Reviews,') April 1861, p. 487.

only will I *not* treat men with tenderness who put forth such blasphemous folly,—(men who, in their rashness, their recklessness, their arrogance, shew no manner of tenderness or consideration for others!)—but I will hold them up to ridicule, to the very utmost of my power. Nay, I would make them objects of unqualified reprobation to all, if I could, as they deserve to be reprobated; for they are the worst enemies of the Gospel of CHRIST[a]. "If CHRIST be not risen, then is our preaching vain, *and your faith is vain also*[b]*!*" "The Apostle *rests the truth of the Christian Religion* on the fact that CHRIST was risen..... The whole system turns upon this central point; the several doctrines gather round it, they depend upon it, they grow out of it; so that without it, Christianity would have no coherence or meaning[c]."

You and I know very well "that nothing could more effectually shake the whole fabric of Revealed Religion, than thus converting its history into fable, and its realities into fiction. For if the narratives most usually selected for the purpose may thus be explained away; what part of the Sacred History will be secure against similar treatment? Nay, what doctrines, even those the most essential to Christianity, might not thus be undermined? For are not those doctrines

[a] I have softened the expression originally employed in this place, out of deference to the opinions of some wise and good men. But I do not think that St. John, (the Evangelist and Apostle *of Dogma,*) would have thought my language too strong: nor St. Paul either. Εἴ τις οὐ φιλεῖ,—

[b] 1 Cor. xv. 14.

[c] From a Sermon by the pious and learned chaplain to the English congregation at Rome, the Rev. F. B. Woodward,—*CHRIST risen the Foundation of the Faith,*—preached on Easter Day, 1861. (Rivingtons.)

dependent upon the *facts* recorded in Scripture for the evidence of their truth? Does not, for instance, the whole system of our Redemption presuppose the reality of the Fall as an historical fact? And do not the proofs of the Divine authority of the whole, rest upon the verification of its Prophecies and Miracles, as events which have actually taken place? Allegory thus misapplied is therefore worse than frivolous or useless; it strikes a deadly blow at the very vitals of the Christian Faith[d]." Away then with that very questionable form of liberality, which makes most free with *what belongs to God!* The truths of Revelation are yours and mine, I grant you: but only *so* yours and mine that, to our eternal blessedness, we embrace,—to our eternal loss, we let them slip! We add to them, or we take away from them, under peril of God's curse. . . . Away too with that mawkish sentimentality which can find no better object for its sympathy than the hardened blasphemer, and the confirmed sceptic! *My* sympathy shall be reserved for those who have never so offended, but are, on the contrary, full of precious promise;—for the young and as yet inexperienced;—for *you*, who will have the battle of Christ and His Church to fight, when *we* shall be mouldering in the grave. Let those who do not know me, deem me uncharitable if they will. I care not. The uncharitable man,—mark me, Brethren!—the truly uncharitable man, is he, who shews no consideration for weak and unstable souls; who does not regard the trials and perils of the young; who beguiles unsteady feet to the edge of the precipice, and there forsakes them; whose destructive

[d] Van Mildert's *Bampton Lectures* for 1814, ("An Inquiry into the general principles of Scripture-Interpretation,")—pp. 242-3.

method, (for constructiveness is no part of that man's philosophy!)—whose destructive method leaves the young without chart and compass,—aye, without moon or stars to sail by; who labours hard to communicate the taint of his own foul leprosy to those who were before unpolluted; who dims the eye, and deadens the ear, and defiles the thoughts, and darkens the hope of as many as have the misfortune to come in his way, and feels no pity!—Yes, yes! The man who sows his own vile doubts broadcast over two continents,—doing his very best to destroy the faith of those for whom CHRIST died,—he, *he* is the uncharitable man[e]! Not he who, forsaking the flowery fields of the Gospel, (whither he would far, far rather lead you!) and foregoing the free mountain air of imperishable Truth, for your sakes only keeps treading these dreary stifling paths of speculation;—a friend of yours, I mean, who with stammering eloquence, (the more's the pity!) clings thus to you, Sunday after Sunday,—imploring you, with all a brother's earnestness, not to venture where to venture is to die; and warning you against the men who have conspired against your *life;* —even while he labours hard to shew you what he *knows* to be "a more excellent way;" and implores you to come where CHRIST Himself hath promised that "ye shall find rest to your souls!"

This is all there is time for, to-day. Let me, in

[e] The reader is particularly requested to read what Dr. Moberly has said on this subject in *Some Remarks on 'Essays and Reviews,'* being the *Revised Preface to the Second Edition of 'Sermons on the Beatitudes,'*—p. xxii to p. xxv.—The *constructive* value of the 'Remarks' of that excellent Divine will long outlive the occasion which has called them forth. I allude particularly to the considerations which occur from p. xxxii to p. lxiii.

the fewest possible words, gather up what has been spoken into a practical shape.

Friends and brethren,—(I am still addressing the younger men present!)—Divinity is not debate; and Religion is not controversy; and Life is not long enough for perpetual disputings. "He that cometh unto GOD must believe that *He is.*" The heart dries up, and the affections wither away, and the soul faints, amid an atmosphere of cloudy doubts, and captious difficulties, and perverse disputations. You must rise above it, if you would discern the colours on the everlasting hills, and behold the beauty of the promised Land, and see objects as they really are. O put away from yourselves, (if any of you are so unhappy as to have acquired it,) a habit of mind which will effectually unfit you for profiting by what you read in Holy Scripture: and you, who are free from such dreadful bondage, beware lest, by the indulgence of some sin,—whether of the flesh or of the spirit,—you darken that spiritual eye by which alone spiritual things are to be discerned. It is like talking about colours to the blind, or about sounds to the deaf, to discuss with a certain class of persons the Inspiration, or the Interpretation, or the Marvels of Scripture. The Bible is, with them, *a common book,*— "to be *interpreted like any other book.*" Prophecy is denied, and Miracles are rejected or explained away, —on the plea that they are alike incredible. These men lay claim to intellectual gifts above their fellows; and know not that they are "wretched, and miserable, and poor, and blind, and naked." Rebels are they against the Most High; and find their exact image in those citizens who "sent a message after Him, saying, We will not have this Man to reign over us[1]." The gist of all they deliver, is *rebellion against God.*

But it is not so with yourselves, who have yet everything to learn in respect of Divine things. O beware lest it ever become your own dreadful case! Begin betimes to acquaint yourselves with the wealth of that celestial armoury which contains a weapon which must prove fatal to every foe; but which it depends *on yourselves* whether you shall have the skill to wield or not. Suffer not yourselves to be cheated of your birthright, the Bible, either by the novel fictions of unstable men, or by the exploded heresies of a bygone age, revived and recommended by living unbelievers. You, especially, who aspire to the Ministerial office, and are destined hereafter to undertake the cure of souls, O do you be doubly watchful! Give to the Bible the undivided homage of a childlike heart; and bow down before its revelations with a suppliant understanding also; and let no characteristic of its method by any means escape you. Notice how it is indeed all one long narrative, from end to end; and see therein God's provision that nothing shall be idealized, nothing explained away. Learn too that Man is thus called upon to look outward, and to sustain himself by an external Law; *not* to depend on the promptings of his own conscience, and so to become a god unto himself. The Bible, I repeat, is all severest history, from the Alpha to the Omega of it. But then, underneath the surface there are meanings high as Heaven, deep as Hell: and why? because *the true Author of it is not Man, but God!*

Let it quicken you in your desire to understand that Book out of which you will have hereafter to

[1] St. Luke xix. 14.

preach, reprove, rebuke, exhort[g],—sometimes to bethink yourselves of the flocks which already are expecting you; and among which GOD already sees your future going out and coming in; your faithful teaching, or (GOD forbid!) your betrayal of a most sacred trust. Acquaint yourselves in due time, by all means, with the scientific grounds on which the Bible is to be received as the Word of GOD: but of a truth, hereafter, you will forget to require that external testimony; for you will be convinced of its Divine origin, when you have become the adoring witnesses of its Divine power. Truly *that* must be from GOD which can so change the life and affect the heart; which can sustain the spirit under bereavement, and become the soul's satisfying portion under every form of adversity! It has already altered the aspect of the World; and it has still a mighty work to do in India, and in China, and in Africa, and in the Islands of the Sea.

Difficulties there are in Scripture, doubtless: but I should be far more perplexed by the absence of them, than I shall ever be by their presence. Nay, they are a chief source of joy to a rightly constituted mind; for they exercise the moral nature and the intellectual powers, in the noblest possible way. It is the office of the highest Intellect to know when to walk *by Faith*, and when *by sight:* and when, to "ask for the old paths." It needs a mind of no common order fully to recognize the distinctive difference between a system which comes from GOD; and one which has been elaborated by human Reason: the latter progressive,—the former incapable of progress; the one liable to change,—the other, unchangeable for ever. There are certain indelible characteristics of

[g] 2 Tim. iv. 2.

a Divine Revelation, I say, which it is the office of the keenest wit to detect and hold fast,—which it is a prime note of imbecility in a thoughtful man to overlook and let go. . . . . The Bible in truth, as one grows older,—(to me at least it seems so,)—becomes almost the only thing in the world really deserving of a man's attention. *Above* Reason, many things in it confessedly are: but *against* Reason, I do not know of *one*. Meantime, is it not a glorious anticipation for you and for me, that to understand those hard things fully may be hereafter a part of our chiefest bliss? There is but a step between us and death[h]; and assuredly when we wake up after His likeness, we shall be satisfied with it[i]! . . . Already "the shadows of the evening are stretched out[k]." Be patient, O my soul, "until the day break, and the shadows flee away[l]!"

[h] 1 Sam. xx. 3.
[k] Jer. vi. 4.
[i] Ps. xvii. 16.
[l] Song of S. ii. 17: iv. 6.

THY STATUTES HAVE BEEN MY SONGS IN THE HOUSE
OF MY PILGRIMAGE.

APPENDIX A.
(p. 16.)

[*Bishop Horsley on the double sense of Prophecy.*]

"I shall not wonder, if, to those who have not sifted this question to the bottom, (which few, I am persuaded, have done,) the evidence of a Providence, arising from prophecies of this sort[a], should appear to be very slender, or none at all. Nor shall I scruple to confess, that time was when I was myself in this opinion, and was therefore much inclined to join with those who think that every prophecy, were it rightly understood, would be found to carry a precise and single meaning; and that, wherever the double sense appears, it is because the one true sense hath not yet been detected. I said,—'Either the images of the prophetic style have constant and proper relations to the events of the world, as the words of common speech have proper and constant meanings, or they have not. If they have, then it seems no less difficult to conceive that many events should be shadowed under the images of one and the same prophecy, than that several likenesses should be expressed in a single portrait. But, if the prophetic images have no such appropriate relations to things, but that the same image may stand for many things, and various events be included in a single prediction, then it should seem that prophecy, thus indefinite in its meaning, can afford no proof of Providence: for it should seem possible, that a prophecy of this sort, by whatever principle the world were governed, whether by Providence, Nature, or Necessity, might owe a seeming completion to mere accident.' And since it were absurd to suppose that the Holy Spirit of God should frame prophecies by which the end of Prophecy might so ill be answered, it seemed a just and fair conclusion, that no prophecy of holy writ might carry a double meaning.

"Thus I reasoned, till a patient investigation of the subject brought me, by God's blessing, to a better mind. I stand clearly and unanswerably confuted, by the instance of Noah's prophecy concerning the family of Japheth; which hath actually received various accomplishments, in events of various kinds, in various ages of the world,—in the settlements of European and Tartarian conquerors in the Lower

---

[a] Gen. ix. 25-7.

Asia; in the settlements of European traders on the coasts of India; and in the early and plentiful conversion of the families of Japheth's stock to the faith of CHRIST. The application of the prophecy to any one of these events bears all the characteristics of a true interpretation,—consistence with the terms of the prophecy, consistence with the truth of history, consistence with the prophetic system. Every one of these events must therefore pass, with every believer, for a true completion."

BP. HORSLEY's *Sermons*, No. xvii. Vol. ii. pp. 73-4.

APPENDIX B.
(p. 50.)

[*Bishop Pearson on Theological Science.*]

"AD publicam Theologiæ professionem electus et constitutus sum; cujus cum præstantiam dignitatemque considero, incredibili quadam dulcedine perfundit mirificeque delectat; cum amplitudinem difficultatemque contemplor, perstringit oculos, percellit animum, abigit longe atque deterret.

"Cum Artes omnes Scientiæque Athenis diu floruissent, cum novam sedem Alexandriæ occuparent, cum ingenia Romana toto terrarum orbe personarent, etiam tum dixit CHRISTUS ad Apostolos, *Vos estis lux mundi.* Omnes aliæ Scientiæ, etiam cum maxime clarescerent, tenebris sunt involutæ, et quasi nocte quadam sepultæ. Tum sol oritur, tum primum lumine perfundimur, cum DEI cognitione illustramur; radii lucis non nisi de cœlo feriunt oculos; cætera, quæ artes aut scientiæ nominantur, non Athenæ sed noctuæ. Quid enim? nonne animis immortalibus præditi sumus, et ad æternitatem natis? Quæ autem Philosophiæ pars perpetuitatem spirat? Quid Astronomicis observationibus fiet, cum cœli ipsi colliquescent? Ubi se ostendet corporis humani peritus, et medicaminum scientia præclarus, cum *corruptio induet incorruptionem?* Quæ Musicæ, quæ Rhetoricæ vires, cum Angelorum choro et Archangelorum cœtibus insereremur? Si nihil animus præsentiret in posterum, e coævis sibi scientiis aliquid solatii carpere fas esset, secumque perituris delectari: sed in hoc tam exiguo vitæ curriculo, et tam brevi, quid est, tam cito periturum, quod impleret animum, in infinita sæculorum spatia duraturum? Sola Theologiæ principia, æternæ felicitatis certissima expectatione fœta, auræ divinæ particulam, cœlestis suæ originis consciam, et sempiternæ beatitudinis candidatum, satiare possunt.

"Cætera Scientiæ exiguum aliquid de mundi opifice delibant, norunt; hæc, aquilæ invecta pennis, cœli penetralia perrumpit, in ipsum Patrem luminum oculos intendit, et audaci veritate promittit, DEUM *nobis aliquando videndum sicut et nos videbimur.*

"Quantum igitur moli corporis [anima materiæ expers,] quantum operosæ conjecturæ divina visio, quantum brevi temporis spatio æternitas, quantum Parnasso Paradisus, tantum reliquis disciplinis Theologia præferenda est.

"Sed hanc severam rebus humanis necessitatem imposuit DEUS, ut quæ pulcherrima sunt, sint et difficillima. Si Sacrarum Literarum copiam, si studiorum theologicorum amplitudinem prospicias, crederes promissionem divinam, sicut Ecclesiæ, ita doctrinæ terminos nullos posuisse.

"Scriptura ipsa, quam copiosa, quam intellectu difficilis! historiæ quam intricatæ! prophetiæ quam obscuræ! præcepta quam multa! promissiones quam variæ! mysteria quam involuta! interpretes quam infiniti! Linguæ, quibus exarata est, et nobis, et toti orbi terrarum peregrinæ. Tres in titulo crucis consecratæ sunt; satis illæ erant, cum CHRISTUS moreretur; sed pluribus nobis opus est ut intelligatur. Latina parum subsidii præbet, originibus exclusa. Græcæ magna est utilitas, nec tamen illa, si pura, multum valet; nam aliam priorem semper aut reddit, aut imitatur. Hebræa satis per se obscura, nec plene intelligenda, sine suis conterraneis, Chaldaica, Arabica, Syriaca. Non est theologus, nisi qui et Mithridates!

"Jam hæc ipsa oracula Ecclesiæ DEI sunt commendata, ad illam a CHRISTO ipso amandamur; illa testis, illa columna veritatis. Nec est unius aut ævi, aut regionis, Ecclesia DEI: per totum terrarum orbem, quo disseminata, sequenda est; per Orientis vastissima spatia, per Occidentis regna diversissima: antiquissimorum Patrum sententiæ percipiendæ, quorum libri pene innumeri prodierunt, et nova tamen monumenta indies e tenebris eruuntur.

"Quid dicam Synodos, diversarum provinciarum fœtus? quid Concilia, e toto orbe coacta, et suprema auctoritate prædita? quid canonum decretorumque infinitam multitudinem? quorum sola notitia insignem scientiam professionemque constituit; et tamen Theologiæ nostræ quantula particula est?

"Quot hæreses in Ecclesia pullularunt, quarum nomina, natura, origines detegendæ: quæ schismata inconsutilem CHRISTI tunicam lacerarunt; quo furore excitata, quibus modis suppressa, quibus machinis sublata!

"Jam vero, scholasticorum quæstiones, quam innumera! Ad hæc omnia subtiliter disserenda, acute disputanda, graviter determinanda, quanta Philosophiæ, quanta Dialecticæ necessitas! quæ leges disputandi, quæ sophismatum strophæ detegendæ!

"Hæc sunt quæ me a professione deterrent, hæc quæ exclamare cogunt, τίς πρὸς ταῦτα ἱκανός;"

Bp. PEARSON's *Oratio Inauguralis*, 'Minor Works,' (ed. Churton,) vol. i. pp. 402-5.

APPENDIX C.
(p. 71.)

[*The Bible an instrument of Man's probation.*]

"MULTA enim *propter exercendas rationales mentes* figurata et obscure posita."—Aug. *De Unit. Eccl.* c. v.—"Obscuritates Divinarum Scripturarum quas *exercitationis nostræ causâ* DEUS esse voluit."—*Id. Ep. lix. ad Paulinum*, tom. ii. p. 117.

"The evidence of Religion not appearing obvious, may constitute one particular part of some men's trial, in the religious sense: as it gives scope, for a virtuous exercise, or vicious neglect of their understanding, in examining or not examining into that evidence. There seems no possible reason to be given, why we may not be in a state of moral probation, with regard to the exercise of our understanding upon the subject of Religion, as we are with regard to our behaviour in common affairs. The former is as much a thing within our power and choice as the latter."

* * * *

"Nor does there appear any absurdity in supposing, that the speculative difficulties, in which the evidence of Religion is involved, may make even the principal part of some persons' trial. For as the chief temptations of the generality of the world are the ordinary motives to injustice or unrestrained pleasure; or to live in the neglect of Religion from that frame of mind, which renders many persons almost without feeling as to any thing distant, or which is not the object of their senses: so there are other persons without this shallowness of temper, persons of a deeper sense as to what is invisible and future; who not only see, but have a general practical feeling, that what is to come will be present, and that things are not less real for their not being the objects of sense; and who, from their natural constitution of body and of temper, and from their external condition, may have small temptations to behave ill, small difficulty in behaving well, in the common course of life. Now when these latter persons have a distinct full conviction of the truth of Religion, without any possible doubts or difficulties, the practice of it is to them unavoidable, unless they will do a constant violence to their own minds; and religion is scarce any more a discipline to them, than it is to creatures in a state of perfection. Yet these persons may possibly stand in need of moral discipline and exercise in a higher degree, than they would have by such an easy practice of religion. Or it may be requisite for reasons unknown to us, that they should give some further manifestation what is their moral character, to the creation of GOD, than such a practice of it would be. Thus in the great variety of religious situations in which men are placed, what constitutes, what chiefly and peculiarly constitutes, the probation, in all senses, of some persons, may be the difficulties in which the evidence of religion is involved: and their principal and distinguished trial may be, how they will behave under and with respect to these difficulties."—BISHOP BUTLER's *Analogy*, P. II. ch. vi. (ed. 1833,) p. 266. and pp. 274-5.

Further on, (p. 277,) Butler has the following note:—
"Dan. xii. 10. See also Is. xxix. 13, 14: St. Matth. vi. 23, and xi. 25, and xiii. 11, 12. St. John iii. 19, and v. 44: 1 Cor. ii. 14, and 2 Cor. iv. 4: 2 Tim. iii. 13; and that affectionate as well as authoritative admonition, so very many times inculcated, 'He that hath ears to hear let him hear.' Grotius saw so strongly the thing intended in these and other passages of Scripture of the like sense, as to say, that the proof given us of Christianity was less than it might have been for this very purpose: 'Ut ita sermo Evangelii tanquam lapis esset Lydius ad quem ingenia sanabilia explorarentur.' (*De Verit. R. C.* lib. ii. towards the end.)"

APPENDIX D.

(p. 72.)

[*St. Stephen's Statement in Acts* vii. 15, 16, *explained.*]

IN a work like the present which purports to deal solely with the grander features of INSPIRATION and INTERPRETATION, it is clearly impossible to enter systematically into details of any kind. If, here and there, something like minuteness has been attempted[b], it has only been by way of sample of what one would fain have done,—of what one would fain do,—time and place and occasion serving. In the same spirit I will add a few remarks on the famous passage in Acts vii. 15, 16; for, confessedly, to a common eye it *seems* to contain several erroneous statements. The words, as they stand in our English Bible, are these:—

"So Jacob went down into Egypt, and died, he, and our Fathers; and were carried over into Sychem, and laid in the sepulchre that Abraham bought for a sum of money of the sons of Emmor *the father* of Sychem."

For obvious reasons, it will be convenient to have under our eyes, at the same time, the original of the passage:—

Κατέβη δὲ Ἰακὼβ εἰς Αἴγυπτον, καὶ ἐτελεύτησεν αὐτὸς καὶ οἱ πατέρες ἡμῶν· καὶ μετετέθησαν εἰς Συχὲμ, καὶ ἐτέθησαν ἐν τῷ μνήματι ᾧ ὠνήσατο Ἀβραὰμ τιμῆς ἀργυρίου, παρὰ τῶν υἱῶν Ἐμμὸρ τοῦ Συχέμ.

On this, Dr. Alford, Dean of Canterbury, delivers himself as follows:—

"There is certainly, and that not dependent upon any Rabbinical or Jewish views of the subject, an inaccuracy in Stephen's statement: for the burying-place was not at Sychem which Abraham bought, but at Hebron, and it was bought of Ephron the Hittite, as you will find in the 23rd of Genesis from the 7th to the 20th verses. It is not worth while for us now to read the account, but so it is: Abraham bought a field at Hebron of Ephron the Hittite. There is no mention at all made of its being for a burying-place. But it was Jacob who bought a field near Shechem 'of the children of Hamor, Shechem's father.' These two incidents, then, in this case are confused together. And again I say, if it is necessary to say it again, that there is no reason at all for us to be ashamed of such a statement—no reason for us to be afraid of it, or in any way staggered at it. It was not Stephen's purpose to give an accurate history of the children of Israel, but to derive results from that history, which remain irrefragable, whatever the details which he alleged."—*Homilies on the former part of the Acts of the Apostles*, by Henry Alford, B.D., Dean of Canterbury, London, 1858, p. 219.

A northern Professor, (Patrick Fairbairn, D.D., Principal

---

[b] As in the case of the healing of the two blind men at Jericho, (p. 67.): 'Jeremy the Prophet,' (p. 70.): the type of Melchizedek, (pp. 152-6.): a passage in Deut. xxx. (pp. 191-5.): the conduct of Jael, (pp. 223—230.): &c., &c.

and Professor of Divinity in the Free Church College, Glasgow,) also writes as follows:—

"Now, there can be no doubt, that viewing the matter critically and historically, there *are* inaccuracies in this statement; for we know from the records of Old Testament history, that Jacob's body was not laid in a sepulchre at Sychem, but in the cave of Machpelah at Hebron;—we know also that the field, which was bought of the sons of Emmor, or the children of Hamor (as they are called in Gen. xxxiii. 19), the father of Sichem, was bought, not by Abraham, but by Jacob."—*Hermeneutical Manual, or Introduction to the Exegetical Study of the Scriptures of the New Testament*, &c. Edinburgh, 1858, p. 101.

Now when it is considered that the speaker here was St. Stephen,—a man who is said to have been "full of the HOLY GHOST," so that "no one could resist the wisdom and the spirit by which he spake," (Acts vi. 3, 5, 8, 10.)—there is evidently the greatest *primâ facie* unreasonableness in so handling his words. But let the adverse criticism be submitted to the test of a searching analysis; and how transparently fallacious is it found to be!

First, we have to ascertain the *meaning* of the passage. And it is evident to every one having an ordinary acquaintance with Greek, that the words Ἐμμὸρ τοῦ Συχὲμ *cannot* mean "Emmor *the father* of Sychem." This is a mere mistranslation, as the invariable usage of the New Testament shews. The genitive denotes *dependent* relation. The Vulgate rightly supplies the word "filii;" and there can be no doubt whatever that what St. Stephen says, is, that Abraham bought the burial-place "of the sons of Emmor, *the son* of Sychem."

Next, it is evident that "our Fathers," (οἱ πατέρες ἡμῶν,) *exclusive of Jacob*, form the nominative to the verb "were carried over" (μετετέθησαν.) In English, the place ought to be exhibited as follows:—"he and our Fathers; and *they* were carried." But, in truth, the idiom of the original is so easy, to one familiar with the manner of the sacred writers[c]; and the historical fact so exceedingly obvious; that it must have been felt by St. Luke, in recording St. Stephen's words, that greater minuteness of statement was quite needless. Who remembers not the affecting details of where Jacob was

---

[c] The nominative has, in like manner, to be supplied in the following places:—Gen. xlviii. 10. Exod. iv. 26: xxxiv. 28. Deut. xxxi. 23. 2 Sam. xxiv. 1. 1 Kings xxii. 19. 2 Kings xix. 24, 25. Job xxxv. 15. Jer. xxxvi. 23. —St. Matth. xix. 5. St. Mark xv. 46. St. John viii. 44: xix. 5: xxi. 15—17. Acts xiii. 29. Eph. iv. 8. Col. ii. 14, &c., &c.

to be buried, as well as the circumstantial narrative of whither his sons conveyed his bones [d] ? *Who* remembers not also that the bones of Joseph, (and, as we learn from this place, the rest with him,) were carried up out of Egypt by the children of Israel, at the Exode [e] ?

Where then is the supposed difficulty? Moses relates (in Gen. xxiii.) that Abraham bought of Ephron the Hittite, the son of Zohar, the field and the cave of Machpelah: and says that Machpelah was before Mamre, otherwise called Kirjath-Arba, and Hebron. St. Stephen further relates that Abraham bought the sepulchre at Sychem in which the Twelve Patriarchs were eventually buried, of the sons of Emmor, (or Hamor.) May not the same man buy two estates?

True enough it is that Jacob, when he came from Padan Aram, "bought a parcel of a field" at "Shalem a city of Shechem," "at the hand of the children of Hamor, Shechem's father." But there is no pretence for saying that these last two transactions are identical, and have been here confused together: for the sellers, in the one case, were "the sons of Emmor, *the son* of Sychem;" and in the other, "the children of Hamor,"—*father of that Shechem whose tragic end is related in Gen.* xxxiv.: while the buyer was in the one case, Abraham; in the other case, Jacob. Not to be tedious however, let me in a few words, state what was the evident truth of the present History.

It is found that Jacob, in order to build an altar at Shechem with security, judged it expedient to purchase the field whereon it should stand. Who can doubt that the purchase was a measure of necessity also? If, at the present day, one desired to erect a church on some spot in India, where the value of land was fully ascertained [f], and where there were many inhabitants [g],—how would it be possible to set about the work, with the remotest purpose of retaining possession, unless one first *bought* the ground on which the structure was to stand? I infer that when Abraham first halted at Sichem [h], and built an altar there [i], (the Canaanite being then in the land,) *it is very likely* that *he* bought the ground also. But when St. Stephen informs me that the thing which *I* think only *probable,* was *a matter of fact;* am I, (with Dean Alford,) to hesitate about believing him? Abraham then, in the first instance, bought Sichem, Shechem, or Sychar; and there built an altar. To that same spot, long after, his grandson Jacob resorted. What wonder,

[d] Gen. xlix. 29—32; l. 5—13. Josh. xxiv. 32.
[f] Gen. xxiii. 15.
[h] Ibid. xiii. 7.
[i] Ibid. xiii. 7.
[e] Ibid l. 25. Exod. xiii. 19.
[g] Ibid. xxiii. 10 to 12, 18.

since the wells of Abraham were stopped during his absence, and had to be recovered by his son, (as related in Gen. xxvi. 17—22,)—what wonder, I say, if Jacob, on coming to Shechem after an interval of nearly 200 years, finds that he also must renew the purchase of the cherished possession? The importance of that locality, and the sacred interest attaching to it, has been explained in a *Plain Commentary on the Gospels*, on St. John iv. 1—6, and 41. See also a Sermon by the same author,—*One Soweth and another Reapeth.*

APPENDIX E.

(p. 74.)

[*The simplest view of Inspiration the truest and the best.*]

"I suppose all thoughtful persons will allow that intellectual licentiousness is the danger of this our intellectual age. For speculation indulges our pride. Faith is an inglorious thing; any one can believe, a cottager just as well as a philosopher: but not all can speculate. The privilege of an intellectually advanced person is that. And the more novel the view he offers, the more evident the proof it gives of an independent mind. Therefore the danger of a highly advanced state of society like our own, is Theory, as distinguished from Catholic Truth. And the most inviting field of theory, is that high subject, the intercourse which hath gone on between the Intellect above us, and our own; the communications which have been made from the Creator to His creatures. In a word, man is under a temptation to frame a theory of Inspiration; whether his attempts to frame one have been successful, is a matter of much interest to consider.

"I am going to offer a few plain remarks on what the Bible professes to be. I say, professes to be, because those whom I speak to will believe that what it professes to be, it is. I mean they will not suspect the writers of any dishonesty or ambitious pretence. But there may be some readers of the Bible, among persons whose profession is the exercise of the intellect, who are impatient at being left behind in the intellectual race; who, when continental critics are going on into theories of inspiration, do not like the imputation (so freely cast upon us by foreign writers) of being unequal to such things, of having no turn for philosophy. So they must have a theory, or go along with one; they must receive the Bible,—for they do receive it,—in some intellectual way; through some lens which they hold up; with a consciousness of some intellectual action in receiving it, something which not every one could practise, something beyond the mere simple apprehension of terms, and simple faith in embracing propositions.

"But in striking contrast with all such views and all such desires, stands the singular character of the sacred volume itself. It manifestly addresses itself to a mind in an attitude of much simplicity; to a mind coming to receive a theory, not to hold up one; coming to be shaped, not holding out a mould to shape a communication made. For it presents itself as a document containing a message from on high; as conveying the Word of God; nor can all that is ever said on the subject get beyond this plain account of its contents, 'the Word of God.' Nor need any one who desires to impress on his own mind and that of others the true character of the sacred page, try to do more than to remind himself that it professes to convey to him the Word of God."—*Sermons* by the Rev. C. P. Eden, pp. 148—150.

"What I desire to impress upon myself and those who hear me is this, that the words of God are always perfect, always complete; and that the feeling with which a poor cottager sits down to his Bible is the right one, and that the student hath the best hope of successful study who in attitude of mind is most likened to him."—*Ibid.*, p. 192.

"The conclusion, then, is this; that Faith hath not been wrong through these many years, in her simple acceptance of God's Word. To come round to simplicity, is what we have always had to do in the great questions of Divinity. There have been great questions; they have agitated the Church; but, as I said, to come round to simplicity hath ever been her work first or last. When in the fourth century men refined upon the doctrine of the Holy Trinity, and Arians and semi-Arians would be telling us *how* these things could be, the unity of God in three Persons; to come round to the simplicity of the Athanasian doctrine, and to disown the several explanatory statements which, offering to explain, explained away, was the Church's work. I am not sure that since the days of the Arian dispute, a more important question has arisen than that which seems likely to be ere long forcing itself upon us, of the Inspiration of Holy Writ. I freely permit myself to anticipate that the simplest possible view of the subject, that on which rich and poor may meet together, is the one to which we shall come round."—*Ibid.*, pp. 172-3.

APPENDIX F.

(p. 107.)

[*The written and the Incarnate Word.*]

"I suppose we all have learned from the language used by the Evangelist St. John, always to look on each of these two employments of the expression, (the WORD OF GOD,) with reference to the other; and to see in each, the other also. I shall not attempt to express more definitely this connexion; I only need to suppose that we all apprehend it as existing. But I shall claim from it thus much to my present purpose;—that as He whom the Evangelist saw riding in the heavenly pomp on high, and who was revealed to him as bearing this title, 'The Word of God[k],' was the same who rode as at this time into Jerusalem; in humiliation here, in glory there; here veiled, there in brightness unveiled:—I would now associate the two, and would regard that sacred volume which the poor cottager knows as the 'Word of God,' as placed under the same dispensation; as veiled here, reserved for Revelation hereafter. I say, as all the other circumstances of our condition are certainly to be regarded in this aspect, viz., as things waiting for development; so ordered by a Divine wisdom as that they shall sustain faith and instruct piety now, but shall shew themselves for what they are, (if ever to a created being, yet) only in a later stage than that to which they were given as its present religious provision: as other things, so the written page (I will assume) which speaks of GOD. I assume that in this world we are using sounds which mean more than we know. I assume that in our churches we are in the highest sense singing the songs of Sion, of the future and heavenly Sion. If Saints in Heaven shall sing (as we are told they shall) the song of Moses, then the song of Moses is already a song for Heaven; only *there* we shall know its meaning, or more of it than now we do. And the use which I make of the reflection is, to suggest (as I said) the frame of mind in which we should approach the consideration of the sacred page; such a frame of mind as that no future revelations of the import of that page shall have power to reproach us as having dishonoured it by our interpretations here, and having betrayed an inadequate feeling of what Inspiration was."—*Sermons*, by the Rev. C. P. Eden, pp. 180-2.

[k] Rev. xix. 13.

APPENDIX G.

(p. 112.)

[*The volume of the Old Testament Scriptures, indivisible.*]

"In regard of the Old Testament, it will be observed that the whole volume stands or falls altogether. In whatever sense we understand the falling or standing, the volume stands or falls together. Each page of it is committed to the credit of the rest, and the whole book or collection of books is committed to the credit of each page. For this plain reason, that the book as we have it, is the book which, being known in the Jewish Church as the volume of her authentic and sacred Scriptures, our blessed SAVIOUR accepted and referred to as such. By whatever marks the canonicity of the several books was in the first instance attested,—marks which were sufficient for GOD's purpose, and which did His work,—*there* is the volume. 'It is written,' said our SAVIOUR; that is, in a book which all His nation knew of, and understood to be inspired. The scrupulous care which the Jews shewed in preserving their sacred writings intact, is one of the most remarkable facts in history; it is a fact of which the Christian student can give perhaps the right account, seeing it to have been so ordered in the good providence of God, that we might have firm ground in calling the book, as we have it, the Word of GOD. The volume stands or falls then together; which we may with advantage bear in mind, because it makes an argument which is available for any portion of the volume, available for the whole; and no one can now say, 'You do not surely hold the genealogies in the books of Chronicles, to be inspired: Isaiah and the Psalms may be inspired; but do you mean the same of the long extracts from mere annals?' No man, I say, can take this freedom, until he can extract and remove those chapters from the book which our blessed SAVIOUR unquestionably referred to as the canonical Scriptures of the Church. If a verse stands, the Old Testament stands."—*Sermons*, by the Rev. C. P. Eden, pp. 152-3.

APPENDIX H.

(p. 115.)

(Some remarks had been partially prepared for insertion in this place, on Theories of Inspiration: but my volume has already been delayed too long, and has extended to a greater length than was originally contemplated. The paper in question is therefore reserved for the present.)

APPENDIX I.

(p. 117.)

[Remarks on Theories of Inspiration.—The 'Human Element.']

"It will be allowed by all persons accustomed to a calm and charitable view of Theological differences, that in those differences there is generally on each side some great truth wrongly held, because taken out of its due place, and wrongly set. Applying this topic to the subject before us, we are led to consider whether a mistake has not been made in bringing forward the Human Element of Inspiration, instead of permitting the eye to rest upon that which God presents to us,—the Divine. The Human Element no doubt is there; no doubt our Maker acts through our faculties in every respect; no doubt He is acting through laws when He seems to suspend laws; and even in Miracles, employs the powers of Nature instead of thwarting them; but then this is His machinery, which He has not explained to us. He presents Himself to us, acting sometimes supernaturally; i.e. in a way above nature as we understand nature. He made the Sun to stand still for Joshua; what refractive cloud came in and held the daylight that it should not go down is not made known to us; God said that it should stay, and it stayed; there was the miracle. To have set the Creation going two thousand years before in such a way and train that in that hour a cloud should rise to refract the sun's rays for a time, because in that hour the Lord's armies would need the interference, the prolonging of the daylight,—that was miracle enough. We say not that God interrupts His own laws; nay, rather we believe that He hath them always in smooth and orderly operation. Similarly of Inspiration; we know not the way in which God acts on human minds, the Spirit on the spirit; for He hath not told us. But, as I said in the beginning, in an age like the present, where analysis of process is the work of men's minds, the way in which man is feeling his strength in every direction, it is not very unnatural that the operations of this philosophy should have been carried beyond their due line; into the subject, namely, of the secret communication between the Divine Spirit, and the spirit and apprehensions of Men, i.e. the Work of Inspiration. To accept the Bible as the word of God, just as a cottager or a child in a village school accepts it, is an inglorious thing. He whose intellect is his instrument, that which he is to work with, wishes to feel his intellect operating on any subject which he has to meet. He feels a desire, in apprehending a thing as done, to have as part of his apprehension, a view of how it is done, more or less. ˙It is natural to him to take what he feels to be an intelligent view of a subject. In accepting the Bible therefore as the Word of God, he must have a view as to *how* it is the Word of God; the nature of the illapse which the Spirit from on high makes on the spirit and faculties of the man. In a word, he would get between the Creator, and man to whom the Creator speaks; and *there* would make his observations. But how little encouragement have we to do this in the Word of God! When God sent prophets to speak to men, to convey a message to them from their Maker, or when He tells Apostles to speak to us, doth He invite us to come within the veil with our philosophy, and examine? I shall offend the piety of those who hear me by pursuing the thought. But I cannot but think that something of this kind has been done by those who have presented us with theories of Inspiration, setting forth to us that which it cannot be shewn that God hath set forth to them, or to any one. Yes, they are right; our Creator makes use of our faculties; and when He hath given to one man faculties different from those given to another, faculties of whatever kind, of intellectual power or of moral temperament, He employs them all. Hath He a message of Love? He employs a St. John to utter it, and to prolong the delightful note. Hath He a message of freedom, that liberty wherewith Christ hath made us free? He hath a Paul ready to accept and to fulfil the congenial errand. But God speaks, not man; and they who would have us be dwelling on the Human Element, when God invites us to be lost in the Divine, are doing not well. Yes, God employs all our faculties: He hath made us different, as He made the flowers of the field different, and Christianity shews us why He hath so made us; because He hath a work for each of us to do,—a work which none else could do so well. Doubtless He employs all our faculties, doing violence to none. This doubtless is His glory, that He can bring about His results by the means which He Himself hath made. Who has not felt, in reading some sacred narrative, the history, e.g. of Joseph, that the wonderful part of it was this, how naturally all came about,—all by natural operation of human motives and man's free will? So in Inspiration. No doubt God's instruments which He hath made are enough for His work; no doubt He employs men as they are; not their tongues only, but their minds and spirits, acting on them and employing them as they are. Only in that great process, the point which I call attention to is this,—God speaks of it as divine, and fixes the thought of those who hear Him on the divine element: we, dropping our view on the human, are not wise. He shews us providence; He condescends to shew us His work: we do not well when we shew an interest rather in lower parts of the scheme, especially when in those we may so greatly err, having so little information."—*Sermons,* by the Rev. C. P. Eden, pp. 164—170.

APPENDIX J.

(p. 145.)

[*How the Inspired authors of the New Testament handle the writings of the Inspired authors of the Old.*]

"LET me repeat:—The question is, how we should address ourselves to the study of the sacred page? For example, how am I to regard, and how to deal with, the great diversities there are between the several sacred writers? For there is the greatest diversity of mind appearing between them. St. Paul is no more the same with St. John, than any two good men now are perfectly alike in their constitution of mind. Nay, the diversity seems especially great in the case of the sacred writers: as if to forbid us to adopt any theory which should ignore or neglect that diversity. It is striking. How shall I deal with these and like circumstances? ... Can it be suggested to me what a good and wise man would do in this matter?

"In answer; it can apparently be suggested; and through that which is the best and safest of arguments, the argument from analogy. For there has been a parallel case; the case of the *inspired writers of the New Testament dealing with the Scriptures of the Old.* To this parallel I now invite your attention. If we can observe how and upon what great principles, piety and wisdom, guided by Inspiration, dealt with the volume of the Holy Scriptures which were then its whole volume, namely the Old Testament; we have so far forth a parallel case to the case of Christians now. The first Christians looked back on the Old Testament as their sacred Scriptures. If we can discern how they regarded their sacred volume, and how they proceeded in interpreting it, we have a pattern to guide us in regard of the question, how we shall regard the sacred volume, and how proceed in the study and interpretation of it; they with the Bible that they had,—we with the Bible that we have, the completed volume.—In this point of view I cannot but regard it as most distinctly providential that there are introduced in the pages of the New Testament so many quotations from the pages of the Old. For they furnish us with an answer applicable in every age of the Church to the question, How shall piety and wisdom deal with a sacred volume; that volume being from the pen of many writers; but with this aggravated difficulty in the former case, that the writers there were widely separated from one another in point of time, were in contact therefore with most difficult forms of life and stages of society? How in approaching a volume so originated, did the New Testament writers regard and deal with its contents?"—*Sermons*, by the Rev. C. P. Eden, pp. 183-5.

"And it is impossible for us to imagine, — I say the thoughtful reader of the Holy Scriptures will find it impossible to imagine,—an Evangelist or Apostle, evoking out of its grave the Human Element of the ancient prophetic communications; disinterring it once more as if to gaze upon it. I am sure the impression left on the mind by the passages in the New Testament where the Old is referred to, is in accordance with what I say. In other words,—(for it is but in other words the same,)—these divinely instructed students,—these inspired readers of the sacred page,—are aware of that which they read, being inspired; GOD its author, and not Man. And they shew this consciousness, putting off their shoes from their feet, as if on holy ground. A divinely instructed mind, interprets a divinely indited Scripture; the Spirit His own interpreter; and we are taught,—not by man but by the Author of Inspiration,—how Inspiration is to be dealt with.—Let him who would deal aright with the sacred pages of the New Covenant, observe in due seriousness what instruction he may gain from the consideration now suggested to his thoughts. Let him learn from the sacred page, how to deal with the sacred page. And if he has observed these things; if he has seen how the writers of the New Testament, discern in lines and words of the Old Testament, that which speaks to *them*,—(for it speaks to CHRIST, and in Him to His Church, i.e. to them :) .... how these utterers of inspired sounds are found, when their words receive at length an authentic interpretation, to have been speaking of the Christian Church, its terms of Salvation, its spiritual gifts;—a reader of the Holy Scriptures practised in these observations will have learned in some measure *how* to approach the sacred volume; with a sense not only of its unfathomed depth, but also of its unity of scope; and a conscious interest rather in its universal truths,—its ever present truths,—than in those transitory imports which some of its pages can be shewn to have had, over and above their Evangelical meaning."—(*Ibid.*, pp. 186-9.)

APPENDIX K.

(p. 199.)

[*Bishop Bull on Deut.* xxx.]

"JAM hic etiam quæstionem unam et alteram solvendam exhibebimus.—Quæritur, *An nullum omnino extet in lege Mosis* SPIRITUS SANCTI *promissum?* Resp. Legem, si per eam intelligas pactum in monte Sinai factum, et mediatore Mose populo Israelitico datum, (quæ, ut modo diximus, est maxime propria ac genuina ipsius in Paulinis Epistolis notio atque acceptio,) nullum Spiritus Sancti promissum continere, manifestum est. Si, inquam, per eam intelligas pactum in Sinai factum; quia in hagiographis et Scriptis Propheticis, (quæ nomine legis et Veteris Test. laxius sumpto non raro veniunt,) de SPIRITU SANCTO, tum ex gratiâ Divinâ promisso, tum precibus hominum impetrato, passim legimus. Imo et in Mosaicis scriptis, licet non in ipso Mosaico fœdere, promissum (ni fallor) satis clarum de gratia SPIRITUS SANCTI Israelitis a DEO danda reperire est.

"Ejusmodi certe est illud Deut. xxx. 6: 'Circumcidet JEHOVA DEUS tuus animam tuam et animam seminis tui, ad diligendum Jehovam Deum tuum ex toto corde tuo,' &c. Etenim circumcisionem cordis, præsertim ejusmodi quâ ad DEUM toto corde diligendum homines præparentur, non sine magna SPIRITUS SANCTI vi atque efficacia fieri posse, apud omnes, qui a Pelagio diversum sentiunt, in confesso est. Sed hoc etiam ad Evangelicam Justitiam pertinebat, quam sub cortice externorum rituum et ceremoniarum latitantem primum Moses ipse, dein prophetæ alii, digito quasi commonstrarunt. Justitia enim Fidei, quæ in evangelio πεφανέρωται olim erat ὑπὸ τοῦ νόμου καὶ τῶν προφητῶν μαρτυρουμένη,—ut diserte affirmat Apostolus. (Rom. iii. 21.) Dixi autem, exerte hanc SPIRITUS SANCTI promissionem in ipso Mosaico fœdere non haberi. Addam aliquid amplius,—*partem eam fuisse Novi Testamenti,* ab ipso Mose promulgati. Nam fœdus cum Judæis sancitum, (Deut. xxix., *et seq.*, in quo hæc verba reperiuntur,) plane diversum fuisse a fœdere in monte Sinai facto, adeoque renovationem continuisse pacti cum Abrahamo initi, h. e. fœderis Evangelici tum temporis obscurius revelati,—multis argumentis demonstrari potest. (1°.) Diserte dicitur, (cap. xxix. 1.) verba, quæ ibidem sequuntur, fuisse ' verba fœderis quod DEUS præcepit Mosi, ut pangeret cum Israelitis, *præter fœdus illud, quod pepigerat cum illis in Chorebo.*' Qui renovationem tantum hic intelligunt fœderis in monte Sinai facti, nugas agunt, quin et textûs ipsius apertissimis verbis contradicunt. Neque enim verba fœderis in Sinai facti repetita ac renovata ullo sensu dici possunt verba fœderis, quod DEUS sancivit præter illud, quod in monte Sinai pepigerat. (2°.) Diserte dicitur, hoc fœdus idem prorsus fuisse cum eo, quod DEUS juramento sanciverat cum Israelitici populi majoribus, Abrahamo puta, Isaaco et Jacobo, (ejusdem cap. ver. 12, 13,)—quod fœdus ipsum Evangelicum fuit, obscurius revelatum, ipso apostolo Paulo interprete, Gal. iii. 16, 17. (3°.) Nonnulla hujus fœderis verba citat Paulus, ut verba fœderis Evangelici, quæ fidei justitiam manifesto præ se ferant. (Vide Rom. x. 6. *et seq.* Coll. Deut. xxx. 11, *et seq.*) *Haud me fugit esse nonnullos, qui statuunt, hæc Mosis verba ab Apostolo ad fidei justitiam per allusionem tantum accommodari :* sed fidem non faciunt, cum Paulus verba ista manifesto alleget ut ipsissima verba justitiæ fidei, h. e. fœderis Evangelici, in quo justitia ista revelatur. *Atque, ut verum fatear, semper existimavi, allusiones istas (ad quas confugiunt quidam tanquam ad sacrum suæ ignorantiæ asylum,) plerumque aliud nihil esse, quam sacræ Scripturæ abusiones manifestas.* Sed non necesse erat, hoc saltem in loco, ut tali κρησφυγέτῳ uterentur. Nam, (4°.) quæcunque in hoc fœdere continentur, in Evangelium mire quadrant. (i.) Quod ad præcepta attinet, præscribuntur hic ea tantum, quæ ad mores pertinent, et per se honesta sunt ; illorum rituum, qui, si verba spectes, pueriles videri possent, quorumque totum fœdus legale fere plenum est, nulla facta mentione. Addas, totam illam obedientiam, quæ hic requiritur, ad sincerum sedulumque studium Deo in omnibus obediendi referri. (Vid. cap. xxx., 10, 16, 20.) (ii.) Ad promissa quod spectat, plenam hic omnium peccatorum, etiam gravissi-

morum, remissionem post peractam pœnitentiam repromittit
DEUS; (cap. xxx., 1—4.) quæ gratia in fœdere legali nus-
piam concessa est, ut supra fusius ostendimus. Deinde,
gratia SPIRITUS SANCTI, qua corda hominum circumcidantur,
ut JEHOVAM diligant ex toto corde atque ex tota anima, hoc
in loco, de quo agimus, (nempe prædicti capitis ver 6.) clare
promittitur. Hui! quam procul ab usitata Mosaicorum
scriptorum vena!.... (5°.) Fœdus illud, de quo prædixit
Jeremias, (xxxi. 31. et seq.) fœdus esse Evangelicum, negavit
Christianus nemo; cum Divinus auctor Epistolæ ad Hebræos
idipsum expresse doceat, (viii. 8, et seq.) Jam quæ de pacto
isto prænuntiat propheta, omnia huic fœderi Moabitico ad
amussim respondent. Appellat suum fœdus Jeremias 'fœdus
novum; ab eo, quod cum majoribus populi Israelitici Ægypto
exeuntibus pepigerat DEUS, omnino diversum.' Idem etiam
de Moabitico fœdere dicit Moses. Causam reddit Jeremias
cur novum DEUS pactum, Sinaiticum aboliturus, molitus
fuerit; nempe, quod Israelitæ, præpotentiore gratia desti-
tuti, Sinaiticum illud irritum fecissent, præceptis ejusdem
non obtemperando, (ver. 32.) Eandem causam et Moses
manifesto designat; 'Nondum,' inquit, 'dederat vobis JE-
HOVA mentem ad cognoscendum, et oculos ad videndum, et
aures ad audiendum, usque ad diem hunc:' (Deut. xxix. 4.)
h. d. Pactum prius vobiscum pepigerat DEUS, in quo volunta-
tem suam præceptis, tum promissis tum minis, tum denique
miraculis omne genus satis superque communitis, vobis ipsis
patefecerat. Sed vidit fœdus illud parum vobis profuisse;
vidit vobis opus esse efficaciore adhuc gratia, qua nempe
corda vestra circumcidantur, &c. ideoque novum fœdus medi-
tatur, in quo gratiam illam efficacissimam vobis adstipula-
turus sit. Eandem autem cordis circumcisionem procul du-
bio designant verba Jeremiæ, v. 33, præd. cap.; 'Indam legem
meam menti eorum, et cordi eorum inscribam eam.' Porro
remissio ista omnium peccatorum, quæ pœnitentibus promittitur a Mose, (Deut. xxx. 1. et seq.) a Jeremiâ etiam clare
exprimitur prædicti cap. ver 34. 'Ero propitius iniquitatibus
eorum, et peccatorum ipsorum et transgressionum ipsorum
non recordabor amplius.' Denique Jeremias claritatem os-
tendit adeoque facilitatem præceptorum, quæ in novo suo
fœdere continebantur, ob quam Dei populo non opus esset
laboriosa disquisitione, aut exactiori disciplina, ut præcepta
istius fœderis cognoscerent implerentque, (Ejusdem capitis,
ver. 34.) Idem Mosen quoque voluisse manifestum erit, (si
verba ejus Deut. xxx. 11, et seq. cum iis, quæ Apostolus ad
eundem locum disserit Rom. x. 6, et seq. accuratius perpend-
eris.) Mihi certe clara videntur omnia. (6°.) Ac postremo,

ut res hæc tota extra omnem controversiæ aleam ponatur, *ipsi Hebræorum magistri ea, quæ Deut.* xxix. *et deinceps continentur, ad Messiæ tempus omnino referenda censuerunt.* Testem advoco fide dignissimum P. Fagium, qui (ad Deut. xxx. 11,) hæc annotat; 'Diligentur observandum est, ex consensu Hebræorum caput hoc ad regnum Christi pertinere. Unde etiam Bachai dicit, hoc loco promissionem esse, quod sub Rege Messiah omnibus, qui de fœdere sunt, circumcisio cordis contingat, citans Joelem, ii. 28.' Fagio consentit Grotius in ejusdem capitis ver. 6.

"In his ideo prolixius immorati sumus, tum, ut vel hinc manifestum fieret, omnia, quæ in Mosaicis scriptis continentur, ad fœdus Mosaicum, proprie sic dictum, nequaquam pertinere; adeoque quam vera ac prorsus necessaria sit distinctio Augustini, (de qua aliquoties jam dictum est,) legem veterem κυρίως sumptam ad solum pactum in monte Sinai factum restringentis; tum imprimis ut exinde etiam clare eluceret optima ac sapientissima DEI οἰκονομία, quam in dispensando gratiæ suæ fœdere usurpare visum ipsi fuerit. Pepigerat DEUS cum Abrahamo fœdus illud gratiosum multis ante latam legem annis; cui postea placuit ipsi superaddere pactum aliud, multis, iisque operosis, ritibus ac ceremoniis conflatum, quibus rudem et carnalem Abrahami posteritatem, recens ex Ægypto eductam, adeoque paganicis ritibus ac superstitionibus nimis addictam, in officio contineret, i.e. ab ethnicorum idololatrico cultu arceret. Quod optime expressit Tertullianus (adversus Marcion. 2.) his verbis: 'Sacrificiorum onera, et operationum et oblationum negotiosas scrupulositates nemo reprehendat, quasi DEUS talia proprie sibi desideraverit, qui tam manifeste exclamat, "Quo mihi multitudinem sacrificiorum vestrorum?" et, "Quis exquisivit ista de manibus vestris?" sed illam DEI industriam sentiat, qua populum pronum in idololatriam et transgressionem ejusmodi officiis religioni suæ voluit adstringere, quibus superstitio sæculi agebatur, ut ab ea avocaret illos, sibi jubens fieri quasi desideranti, ne simulacris faciendis delinqueret.' (Conf. Gal. iii. 19.) Sed prævidens sapientissimus DEUS, fore, ut hoc ipsius propositum populus obtusi pectoris non intelligeret, post latam istam carnalem legem, præcepit Mosi, ut Israelitis novum fœdus promulgaret, seu potius ut vetus illud, cum Abrahamo ante multos annos initum, (quod spiritualem imprimis justitiam exigebat, et gratia ac misericordia plenum erat,) renovaret: ut hinc tandem cognoscerent Judæi, pactum Abrahamiticum etiam post latam legem ritualem adhuc viguisse, adeoque pro fœdere habendum fuisse, cui unice salus ipsorum inniteretur. (Conf. Gal. iii. 17.) . . . . Quis hic cum

Apostolo non exclamet, 'Ω βάθος πλούτου καὶ σοφίας καὶ γνώσεως Θεοῦ! (Rom. xi. 33.) Sed hæc obiter, etsi haudquaquam frustra. Pergo."—From Bp. Bull's *Harmonia Apostolica*, cap. xi., sect. 3.—*Works*, vol. iii. pp. 197-201.

APPENDIX L.

(p. 218.)

[*Opinions of Commentators concerning Accommodation.*]

CORNELIUS à Lapide, on this place, writes as follows:—
"Licet Cajetanus, Adamus, Pererius, Toletus, putent Mosem ad litteram loqui de Christo et Christi justitiâ, referunt enim hæc ejus verba ad pœnitentiam, de qua eodem capite egerat Moses, ver. 1; (Pœnitentia enim et dilectio Dei, ac consequenter peccatorum venia, ipsaque justitia sine fide Christi haberi non potest;) tamen *longe planius est, ut non litteraliter, sed allegorice tantum alludat Apostolus ad Mosem. Moses enim ad litteram, sive in sensu litterati loquitur, non de Christo ejusque Evangelio, sed de lege data Judæis, ut patet cum intuenti.* Ita Chrysostomus, Theodoretus, Theophylactus, Œcumenius, Abulensis, Soto . . . . . . Hæc, inquam verba, Mosem ad suos Judæos literaliter loqui planè certum, evidens, et manifestum est; ita tamen ut eadem hæc ejus verba *allegorice Evangelio ejusque catechumenis et fidelibus optime conveniant.* Æque enim, imo magis, ad manum est omnibus jam Evangelium et fides Christi, quam olim fuerit lex Mosis: ita ut fidem hanc omnes facillime corde, id est mente, complecti: et ore proloqui, itaque justificari et salvari possint."

Our own learned Hammond writes as follows:—"The two phrases of 'going up into Heaven,' or 'descending into the deep,' are proverbial phrases to signify the doing or attempting to do some hard, impossible thing.... These phrases had been of old used by Moses in this sense, Deut. xxx. 12." [And then, the place follows.] "Which words being used by Moses to express the easiness and readiness of the way which the Jews had to know their duty and to perform it, are here by the Apostle *accommodated* to express the easiness of the Gospel condition, above that of the Mosaical Law."—So far Dr. Hammond; whose notion that there was any accommodation here, I altogether deny. As for his belief that the paraphrase in the Targum of Jerusalem, ["Utinam esset nobis aliquis Propheta, Jonæ similis, qui in profundum maris magni descenderet,"] is the "ground of St. Paul's application" of the place to the Death and Resurrection of Christ, I can but feel surprised to find such a view advocated by so learned a man, and so excellent a Divine. But it is not Hammond's way to write thus. In his "Practical Catechism," he often expounds similar Scripture, (e.g. St. Luke i. 72-5,) after a very lofty fashion.

Again:—"Hunc locum accommodavit ad causam suam B. Paulus, Rom. x. Nam cum proprie hic locus pertineat ad Decalogum, transfertur eleganter et erudite a Paulo ad fidem quæ os requirit ut promulgetur, et cor ut corde credamus."—Fagius, ad Deut. xxx. 11, apud *Criticos Sacros*.

Occasionally, however, we meet with a directly different gloss:—

"Locum hunc divinus Paulus divine de Evangelica prædicatione ac sermone fidei est interpretatus, tametsi sensum magis, ut æquum est, quam textum ad verbum expresserit; ut illius etiam alibi est mos. Satis enim fuit, atque adeo magis consentaneum viris Spiritu Dei plenis significare quid idem Spiritus in Scriptura intelligi vellet."—Clavius, ad Deut. xxx. 14, apud *Criticos Sacros*.

Concerning the general principle of Accommodation, (as explained above, p. 188,) the following passages present themselves as valuable.

"Men have suggested that these things were accommodations of the Sacred Writers; and that the New Testament Writers, in the interpretations they gave of passages in the Old, meant to say, that the texts *might* be applied in such way as they applied them. But the suggestors of this view can hardly have considered carefully those conversations of our Blessed SAVIOUR with His disciples going to Emmaus; and afterward in the evening of the same day, in which He distinctly reprehends them for their dulness of heart in not seeing in the pages of the Old Testament the predictions of His Death and of His Resurrection; though, of His Resurrection the intimations are, in those ancient Scriptures, to our view so scanty and obscure. He unfolds to them as they walk the reference of the Old Testament Scriptures to Himself. Then in a later interview He resumes the instruction and 'opens their understanding,' (it is said,) to discover the same; the relation of the Old Testament Scriptures (namely) to Himself.—He is a bold Commentator who having seen the Disciples thus instructed,—having witnessed this scene,—then, when he meets with these same Disciples' interpretations of the ancient Scriptures in relation to CHRIST, calls them 'Accommodations,' and gives them to a human original. But I ask leave to turn from this theory."— *Sermons* by the Rev. C. P. Eden, pp. 189—190.

"If we believe that the Apostles were inspired, then all idea of accommodation must be renounced ... The theory of Accommodation, i.e. of erroneous interpretation of the Scripture, cannot be thought of without imputing error to the SPIRIT of Truth and Holiness; or to Him who sent the SPIRIT to recal to the minds of the Apostles all things which He had said to them, and to guide them into all Truth."— From a Sermon by Dr. M'Caul, *The Hope of the Gospel the Hope of the Old Testament Saints*, (1854,)—p. 8.

ΔΙΑ ΤΟΝ ΛΟΓΟΝ ΤΟΥ ΘΕΟΥ.

A List of Books

RECENTLY PUBLISHED BY

JOHN HENRY AND JAMES PARKER,

OXFORD, AND 377, STRAND, LONDON.

NEW THEOLOGICAL WORKS.

REV. DR. MOBERLY.

SERMONS ON THE BEATITUDES, with others mostly preached before the University of Oxford; to which is added a Preface relating to the recent volume of "Essays and Reviews." By the Rev. GEORGE MOBERLY, D.C.L., Head Master of Winchester College. *Second Edition.* 8vo., price 10s. 6d.

The Preface separately, price 2s. *Vide* p. 6.

ARCHDEACON CHURTON.

A MEMOIR OF THE LATE JOSHUA WATSON, ESQ. By the Venerable Archdeacon CHURTON. 2 vols., post 8vo., with Portrait, 15s.

THE LATE REV. H. NEWLAND.

A NEW CATENA ON ST. PAUL'S EPISTLES.—A PRACTICAL AND EXEGETICAL COMMENTARY ON THE EPISTLES OF ST. PAUL: in which are exhibited the Results of the most learned Theological Criticisms, from the Age of the Early Fathers down to the Present Time. Edited by the late Rev. HENRY NEWLAND, M.A., Vicar of St. Mary Church, Devon, and Chaplain to the Bishop of Exeter. Vol. I., containing THE EPISTLE TO THE EPHESIANS. 8vo., 10s. 6d.

——— Vol. II., containing THE EPISTLE TO THE PHILIPPIANS. 8vo., cl., 7s. 6d.

REV. WILLIAM BRIGHT.

A HISTORY OF THE CHURCH, from the EDICT of MILAN, A.D. 313, to the COUNCIL of CHALCEDON, A.D. 451. By WILLIAM BRIGHT, M.A., Fellow of University College, Oxford; late Professor of Ecclesiastical History in the Scottish Church. Post 8vo., price 10s. 6d.

ARCHBISHOP LAUD.

LETTERS OF ARCHBISHOP LAUD, now first published from the Original MSS. Edited by the Rev. JAMES BLISS, M.A., Oriel College, Oxford, (Anglo-Catholic Library.) 8vo., price 13s. cloth.

REV. DR. SEWELL.

CHRISTIAN VESTIGES OF CREATION. By WILLIAM SEWELL, D.D., late Professor of Moral Philosophy in the University of Oxford. Post 8vo., cloth, price 4s. 6d.

REV. J. W. BURGON.

INSPIRATION AND INTERPRETATION. Seven Sermons preached before the University of Oxford; with an Introduction, being an answer to a Volume entitled "Essays and Reviews." By the Rev. JOHN W. BURGON, M.A., Fellow of Oriel College, and Select Preacher. 8vo.

[*In the Press.*

NEW THEOLOGICAL WORKS, (continued).

THE LORD BISHOP OF OXFORD.

THE ORDINATION SERVICE. ADDRESSES ON THE QUESTIONS TO THE CANDIDATES FOR ORDINATION. By the Right Rev. the LORD BISHOP OF OXFORD. *Third Edition.* Crown 8vo., cloth, 6s.

A CHARGE delivered at the Triennial Visitation of the Diocese, November, 1860. By SAMUEL, LORD BISHOP OF OXFORD, Lord High Almoner to Her Majesty the Queen, and Chancellor of the Order of the Garter. Published by request. 8vo., 1s. 6d.

MONTAGU BURROWS, M.A.

PASS AND CLASS. An Oxford Guide-Book through the Courses of *Literæ Humaniores*, Mathematics, Natural Science, and Law and Modern History. By MONTAGU BURROWS, M.A. *Second Edition, with some of the latest Examination Papers.* Fcap. 8vo., cloth, 5s.

REV. R. W. MORGAN.

ST. PAUL IN BRITAIN; or, THE ORIGIN OF BRITISH AS OPPOSED TO PAPAL CHRISTIANITY. By the Rev. R. W. MORGAN, Perpetual Curate of Tregynon, Montgomeryshire, Author of "Verities of the Church," "The Churches of England and Rome," "Christianity and Infidelity intellectually contrasted," &c. Crown 8vo., cloth, 4s.

REV. T. LATHBURY, M.A.

A HISTORY OF THE BOOK OF COMMON PRAYER, AND OTHER AUTHORIZED BOOKS, from the Reformation; and an Attempt to ascertain how the Rubrics, Canons, and Customs of the Church have been understood and observed from the same time: with an Account of the State of Religion in England from 1640 to 1660. By the Rev. THOMAS LATHBURY, M.A., Author of "A History of the Convocation," "The Nonjurors," &c. *Second Edition, with an Index.* 8vo., 10s. 6d.

REV. E. B. PUSEY, D.D.

THE MINOR PROPHETS; with a Commentary Explanatory and Practical, and Introductions to the Several Books. By the Rev. E. B. PUSEY, D.D., Regius Professor of Hebrew, and Canon of Christ Church. Part II. Joel, Introduction—Amos, chap. vi. ver. 6. 4to., sewed, price 5s.

THE COUNCILS OF THE CHURCH, from the Council of Jerusalem, A.D. 51, to the Council of Constantinople, A.D. 381; chiefly as to their Constitution, but also as to their Objects and History. By the Rev. E. B. PUSEY, D.D., Regius Professor of Hebrew; Canon of Christ Church; late Fellow of Oriel College. 8vo., 10s. 6d.

NINE SERMONS preached before the University of Oxford, and printed chiefly A.D. 1843—1855, now collected into one volume. By the Rev. E. B. PUSEY, D.D. 8vo., 9s.

PROFESSOR GOLDWIN SMITH.

THE FOUNDATION OF THE AMERICAN COLONIES. A Lecture delivered before the University of Oxford, June 12, 1860. By GOLDWIN SMITH, M.A., Regius Professor of Modern History. 8vo., price 1s.

THE STUDY OF HISTORY. Two Lectures delivered by GOLDWIN SMITH, M.A., Regius Professor of Modern History in the University of Oxford. 8vo., sewed, price 2s. 6d.

ON SOME SUPPOSED CONSEQUENCES OF THE DOCTRINE OF HISTORICAL PROGRESS. A Lecture delivered by GOLDWIN SMITH, M.A., Regius Professor of Modern History in the University of Oxford, April, 1861. 8vo., sewed, price 1s. 6d.

NEW ARCHÆOLOGICAL WORKS.

JOHN HENRY PARKER.

AN INTRODUCTION TO THE STUDY OF GOTHIC ARCHITECTURE. By JOHN HENRY PARKER, F.S.A. Second Edition, Revised and Enlarged, with 170 Illustrations, and a Glossarial Index. Fcap. 8vo., cloth lettered, price 5s.

EDITOR OF GLOSSARY.

SOME ACCOUNT OF DOMESTIC ARCHITECTURE IN ENGLAND, from Richard II. to Henry VIII. (or the Perpendicular style.) With Numerous Illustrations of Existing Remains from Original Drawings. By the EDITOR OF "THE GLOSSARY OF ARCHITECTURE." In 2 vols., 8vo., 1l. 10s.

Also,

VOL. I.—FROM WILLIAM I. TO EDWARD I. (or the Norman and Early English styles). 8vo., 21s.

VOL. II.—FROM EDWARD I. TO RICHARD II. (the Edwardian Period, or the Decorated Style). 8vo., 21s.

The work complete, with 400 *Engravings,* and a General Index, 4 vols. 8vo., price £3 12s.

REV. WILLIAM STUBBS.

THE TRACT "DE INVENTIONE SANCTÆ CRUCIS NOSTRÆ IN MONTE ACUTO ET DE DUCTIONE EJUSDEM APUD WALTHAM," now first printed from the Manuscript in the British Museum, with Introduction and Notes by WILLIAM STUBBS, M.A., Vicar of Navestock, late Fellow of Trinity College, Oxford. Royal 8vo., (only 100 copies printed), price 5s.; demy 8vo., 3s. 6d.

PROFESSOR WILLIS.

FACSIMILE OF THE SKETCH-BOOK OF WILARS DE HONECORT, an Architect of the Thirteenth Century. With Commentaries and Descriptions by MM. LASSUS and QUICHERAT. Translated and Edited, with many additional Articles and Notes, by the Rev. ROBERT WILLIS, M.A., F.R.S., Jacksonian Professor at Cambridge, &c. With 64 Facsimiles, 10 Illustration Plates, and 43 Woodcuts. Royal 4to., cloth, 2l. 10s.

The English letterpress separate, for the purchasers of the French edition, 4to., 15s.

RAYMOND BORDEAUX.

SPECIMENS OF MEDIEVAL IRONWORK. Serrurerie du Moyen-Age, par RAYMOND BORDEAUX. Forty Lithographic Plates, by G. Bouet, and numerous Woodcuts. Small 4to., cloth, 20s.

JOHN HEWITT.

ANCIENT ARMOUR AND WEAPONS IN EUROPE. By JOHN HEWITT, Member of the Archæological Institute of Great Britain. Vols. II. and III., comprising the Period from the Fourteenth to the Seventeenth Century, completing the work, 1l. 12s. Also Vol. I., from the Iron Period of the Northern Nations to the end of the Thirteenth Century, 18s. The work complete, 3 vols., 8vo., 2l. 10s.

M. VIOLLET-LE-DUC.

THE MILITARY ARCHITECTURE OF THE MIDDLE AGES, Translated from the French of M. VIOLLET-LE-DUC. By M. MACDERMOTT, Esq., Architect. With the 151 original French Engravings. Medium 8vo., cloth, price £1 1s.

OUR ENGLISH HOME: its Early History and Progress. With Notes on the Introduction of Domestic Inventions. *Second Edition.* Crown 8vo., price 5s.

"It contains the annals of our English civilization, and all about our progress in social and domestic matters, how we came to be the family and people which we are. All this forms a book as interesting as a novel, and our domestic history is written not only with great research, but also with much spirit and liveliness."—*Christian Remembrancer.*

NEW THEOLOGICAL WORKS, (continued).

REV. W. H. DAVEY.

ARTICULI ECCLESIÆ ANGLICANÆ; or, The Several Editions of the Articles of the Church of England, as agreed upon in Convocation, and set forth by Royal Authority, during the Reigns of King Edward VI. and Queen Elizabeth, arranged in one Comparative View. By WILLIAM HARRISON DAVEY, M.A., Vice-Principal of Cuddesdon Theological College, in the Diocese of Oxford. 8vo., cloth, price 2s. 6d.

OXFORD LENTEN SERMONS.

A SERIES OF SERMONS preached in Oxford during the Season of Lent, 1859. Fcap. 8vo., 5s.

THE DEAN OF FERNS.

THE LIFE AND CONTEMPORANEOUS CHURCH HISTORY OF ANTONIO DE DOMINIS, Archbishop of Spalatro, which included the Kingdoms of Dalmatia and Croatia; afterwards Dean of Windsor, Master of the Savoy, and Rector of West Ilsley in the Church of England, in the reign of James I. By HENRY NEWLAND, D.D., Dean of Ferns. 8vo., cloth lettered, 7s.

REV. P. FREEMAN.

THE PRINCIPLES OF DIVINE SERVICE. An Inquiry concerning the true manner of understanding and using the order for Morning and Evening Prayer, and for the Administration of the Holy Communion in the English Church. Vol. I. 8vo., cloth, 10s. 6d. Vol. II., Part I. containing THE HOLY EUCHARIST considered as a MYSTERY. 8vo., cloth, 6s.

REV. L. P. MERCIER.

CONSIDERATIONS RESPECTING A FUTURE STATE. By the Rev. LEWIS P. MERCIER, M.A., University College, Oxford. Fcap. 8vo., 4s.

REV. H. DOWNING.

SHORT NOTES ON THE ACTS OF THE APOSTLES, intended for the use of Teachers in Parish Schools, and other Readers of the English Version. By HENRY DOWNING, M.A., Incumbent of St. Mary's, Kingswinford. Fcap. 8vo., cloth, 2s.

REV. J. M. NEALE.

A HISTORY OF THE SO-CALLED JANSENIST CHURCH OF HOLLAND; with a Sketch of its Earlier Annals, and some Account of the Brothers of the Common Life. By the Rev. J. M. NEALE, M.A., Warden of Sackville College. 8vo., cloth, 10s. 6d.

REV. T. T. CARTER.

LIFE of JOHN ARMSTRONG, D.D., late Lord Bishop of Grahamstown. By the Rev. T. T. CARTER, M.A., Rector of Clewer. With an Introduction, by SAMUEL, LORD BISHOP OF OXFORD. Third Edition. Fcap. 8vo., with Portrait, cloth, 7s. 6d.

ST. ANSELM.

MEDITATIONS AND SELECT PRAYERS, by ST. ANSELM, formerly Archbishop of Canterbury. Edited by E. B. PUSEY, D.D. Fcap. 8vo., 5s.

CUR DEUS HOMO, or WHY GOD WAS MADE MAN; by ST. ANSELM. Second Edition. Fcap. 8vo., 2s. 6d.

PAROCHIAL SERMONS, by the Rev. HENRY W. BURROWS, B.D., Perpetual Curate of Christ Church, St. Pancras. Fcap. 8vo., cloth, 6s.
——————————— Second Series. Fcap. 8vo., cloth, 5s.

PARISH SERMONS. Second Series. By WILLIAM FRASER, B.C.L., Vicar of Alton, Staffordshire, and Domestic Chaplain to the Earl of Shrewsbury and Talbot. Fcap. 8vo., cloth, red edges, 3s.

THE WISDOM OF PIETY, AND OTHER SERMONS, addressed chiefly to Undergraduates. By the Rev. FREDERICK MEYRICK, M.A., Her Majesty's Inspector of Schools; Fellow of Trinity College; late Select Preacher before the University of Oxford, and Her Majesty's Preacher at Whitehall. Crown 8vo., 4s.

THE YEAR OF THE CHURCH. A Course of Sermons by the late Rev. RICHARD WEBSTER HUNTLEY, M.A., sometime Fellow of All Souls' College, Oxford; Rector of Boxwell-cum-Leighterton, Gloucestershire, and Vicar of Alberbury, Salop; and for eleven years Proctor in Convocation for the Clergy of the Diocese of Gloucester and Bristol: with a short Memoir by the Editor, the Rev. SIR GEORGE PREVOST, Bart., M.A. Fcap. 8vo., cloth lettered, 7s. 6d.

ARMSTRONG'S PAROCHIAL SERMONS. Parochial Sermons, by JOHN ARMSTRONG, D.D., late Lord Bishop of Grahamstown. A New Edition, Fcap. 8vo., cloth, 5s.

ARMSTRONG'S SERMONS FOR FASTS AND FESTIVALS. A new Edition. Fcap. 8vo., 5s.

PLAIN SERMONS ON THE BOOK OF COMMON PRAYER. By a Writer in the "Tracts for the Christian Seasons." Fcap. 8vo., cloth, 5s.

SHORT SERMONS FOR FAMILY READING. Ninety Short Sermons for Family Reading, following the course of the Christian Seasons. By the Author of "A Plain Commentary on the Gospels." 2 volumes, cloth, 8s.

CONCERNING CLERICAL POWERS AND DUTIES, "RELIGIOUS ENQUIRY," and **DAILY PRAYERS.** Nine Sermons preached at St. Mary Magdalene Church, Oxford, by the Rev. R. ST. JOHN TYRWHITT, M.A., Vicar of the Parish; late Student and Rhetoric Reader of Christ Church. Fcp., 2s. 6d.

SINGLE SERMONS.

The Lord Bishop of Oxford.
THE REVELATION OF GOD THE PROBATION OF MAN. Two Sermons preached before the University of Oxford, on Sunday, Jan. 27, and Sunday, Feb. 3, 1861. By SAMUEL, LORD BISHOP OF OXFORD. 8vo., in wrapper, price 1s. 6d.

Rev. William Basil Jones.
RELIGION AND MORALITY. A Sermon preached in the Church of St. Mary-the-Virgin, before the University of Oxford, on the Fifth Sunday in Lent, March 17, 1861. By WILLIAM BASIL JONES, M.A., Prebendary of St. David's; late Fellow and Tutor of University College. 8vo., price 1s.

Rev. C. A. Heurtley.
THE INSPIRATION OF HOLY SCRIPTURE. CONSTANCY IN PRAYER: Its Importance Considered with Especial Reference to the Temptations of a Student's Life. Two Sermons preached before the University of Oxford. By CHARLES A. HEURTLEY, D.D., Margaret Professor of Divinity, and Canon of Christ Church. 8vo., price 2s.

Rev. E. B. Pusey.
THE THOUGHT OF THE LOVE OF JESUS FOR US, THE REMEDY FOR SINS OF THE BODY. A Sermon preached to the Younger Members of the University, at St. Mary's Church, Oxford, on Friday Evening, March 1. By the Rev. E. B. PUSEY, D.D., Regius Professor of Hebrew, and Canon of Christ Church. 8vo., price 6d.

Rev. Osborne Gordon.
A SERMON preached in the Cathedral Church of Christ Church, on Easterday, 1861. By the Rev. O. GORDON, B.D., Censor of Christ Church. 8vo., 6d.

Rev. Edward H. Plumptre.
DANGERS PAST AND PRESENT. A Sermon preached before the University of Oxford, on Easter Tuesday, 1861. By EDWARD H. PLUMPTRE, M.A., Professor of Pastoral Theology and Chaplain of King's College, London. 8vo. 1s.

PAMPHLETS RECENTLY PUBLISHED ON "ESSAYS & REVIEWS."

Some Remarks on "Essays and Reviews:"

Being the Revised Preface to the Second Edition of "Sermons on the Beatitudes," by GEORGE MOBERLY, D.C.L., Head Master of Winchester College. 8vo., sewed, price 2s.

The Reviewers Reviewed and the Essayists Criticised:

An Analysis and Confutation of each of the Seven "Essays and Reviews." (Reprinted from the LITERARY CHURCHMAN.) 8vo., sewed, price 2s. 6d.

A Letter on the Inspiration of Holy Scripture,

Addressed to a Student. By WILLIAM SEWELL, D.D., Late Professor of Moral Philosophy in the University of Oxford. 8vo., sewed, price 3s.

No Antecedent Impossibility in Miracles.

Some Remarks on the Essay of the late Rev. BADEN POWELL, M.A., F.R.S., on "The Study of the Evidences of Christianity," in a Letter by a COUNTRY CLERGYMAN." 8vo., price 1s.

Evidence of Unsoundness in the Volume entitled "Essays and Reviews."

A Speech delivered in the Jerusalem Chamber, Feb. 26, 1861, on moving an Address from the Lower to the Upper House of Convocation respecting that Volume. By R. W. JELF, D.D., Proctor for the Chapter of Oxford, Canon of Christ Church, Principal of King's College, London. 8vo., price 1s.

Scriptural Interpretation.

The ESSAY of PROFESSOR JOWETT briefly Considered, in a Letter to the Rev. PROFESSOR STANLEY, D.D., Regius Professor of Ecclesiastical History; Canon of Christ Church. By ROBERT C. JENKINS, M.A., of Trinity College, Cambridge; Rector and Vicar of Lyminge. 8vo., price 1s.

By the same Author.

A Word on Inspiration.

Being a Second Letter on the ESSAY of PROFESSOR JOWETT, addressed to the Rev. PROFESSOR STANLEY, D.D. 8vo., price 6d.

A Letter on the "Essays and Reviews,"

By Dr. PUSEY. (Reprinted from "The Guardian.") 8vo., price 1d.

A Few Words of Apology for the late Professor Baden Powell's Essay

On the Study of the Evidences of Christianity contained in the volume entitled "Essays and Reviews." By a LAY GRADUATE. 8vo., price 1s.

Statements of Christian Doctrine and Practice,

Extracted from the Published Writings of the Rev. BENJAMIN JOWETT, M.A., Regius Professor of Greek in the University of Oxford. 8vo., price 2s.

"These extracts have been made from Professor Jowett's writings without his sanction and knowledge. As this practice has been largely adopted by those who have attacked or misrepresented his opinions, his friends have taken the liberty to place before the public a collection of passages which in most notices of his works have been withheld from view."

NEW DEVOTIONAL WORKS.

REV. E. MONRO.

PLAIN SERMONS ON THE BOOK OF COMMON PRAYER. By a Writer in the "Tracts for the Christian Seasons." Fcap. 8vo., cloth, 5s.

HISTORICAL AND PRACTICAL SERMONS ON THE SUFFERINGS AND RESURRECTION OF OUR LORD. By a Writer in the Tracts for the Christian Seasons. 2 vols., fcap. 8vo. cloth, 10s.

SERMONS ON NEW TESTAMENT CHARACTERS. By the Author of "Sermons on the Prayer-book," and "On the Sufferings and Resurrection of our Lord." Fcap. 8vo., 4s.

REV. G. ARDEN.

BREVIATES FROM HOLY SCRIPTURE, arranged for use by the Bed of Sickness. By the Rev. G. ARDEN, M.A., Rector of Winterborne-Came; Domestic Chaplain to the Right Hon. the Earl of Devon; Author of "A Manual of Catechetical Instruction." Fcap. 8vo. *Second Edition.* 2s.

THE CURE OF SOULS. By the Rev. G. ARDEN, M.A. Fcap. 8vo., 2s. 6d.

OXFORD SERIES OF DEVOTIONAL WORKS.

THE IMITATION OF CHRIST.
FOUR BOOKS. By Thomas A KEMPIS. A new Edition, revised, handsomely printed on tinted paper in fcap. 8vo., with Vignettes and red borders, cl., 5s.; antique calf, red edges, 10s. 6d.

LAUD'S DEVOTIONS.
THE PRIVATE DEVOTIONS of Dr. WILLIAM LAUD, Archbishop of Canterbury, and Martyr. A new and revised Edition, with Translations to the Latin Prayers, handsomely printed with Vignettes and red lines. Fcap. 8vo., antique cloth, 5s.

WILSON'S SACRA PRIVATA.
THE PRIVATE MEDITATIONS, DEVOTIONS, and PRAYERS of the Right Rev. T. WILSON, D.D., Lord Bishop of Sodor and Man. Now first printed entire. From the Original Manuscripts. Fcap. 8vo., 6s.

ANDREWES' DEVOTIONS.
DEVOTIONS. By the Right Rev. Father in God, LAUNCELOT ANDREWES, Translated from the Greek and Latin, and arranged anew. Fcap. 8vo., 5s.; morocco, 8s.; antique calf, red edges, 10s. 6d.

SPINCKES' DEVOTIONS.
TRUE CHURCH OF ENGLAND MAN'S COMPANION IN THE CLOSET; or, a complete Manual of Private Devotions, collected from the Writings of eminent Divines of the Church of England. Sixteenth Edition, corrected. Fcap. 8vo., floriated borders, cloth, antique, 4s.

The above set of 5 Volumes, in neat grained calf binding, £2 2s.

TAYLOR'S HOLY LIVING.
THE RULE AND EXERCISES OF HOLY LIVING. By BISHOP JEREMY TAYLOR. In which are described the means and instruments of obtaining every virtue, and the remedies against every vice. *In antique cloth binding,* 4s.

TAYLOR'S HOLY DYING.
THE RULE AND EXERCISES OF HOLY DYING. By BISHOP JEREMY TAYLOR. In which are described the means and instruments of preparing ourselves and others respectively for a blessed death, &c. *In antique cloth binding,* 4s.

WORKS OF THE

Standard English Divines,

AT THE FOLLOWING PRICES IN CLOTH.

ANDREWES' (BP.) COMPLETE WORKS. 11 vols. 8vo., £3 6s.

ANDREWES' (BP.) SERMONS. *Second Edition.* 5 vols., £1 15s.

BEVERIDGE'S (BP.) COMPLETE WORKS. 12 vols. 8vo., £4 4s.

BEVERIDGE'S (BP.) ENGLISH WORKS. 10 vols. 8vo., £3 10s. 6d.

BRAMHALL'S (ABP.) WORKS. 5 vols. 8vo., £1 15s.

BULL'S (BP.) HARMONY OF THE APOSTLES ST. PAUL AND ST. JAMES ON JUSTIFICATION. 2 vols., 10s.

BULL'S (BP.) DEFENCE OF THE NICENE CREED. 2 vols. 8vo., 10s.

BULL'S (BP.) JUDGMENT OF THE CATHOLIC CHURCH. 8vo., 5s.

COSIN'S (BP.) WORKS. 5 vols. 8vo., £1 10s.

HAMMOND'S PRACTICAL CATECHISM. 8vo., 5s.

HAMMOND'S MISCELLANEOUS WORKS. 8vo., 5s.

HAMMOND'S SERMONS. 2 Parts. 8vo., 10s.

HICKES'S TREATISES ON THE CHRISTIAN PRIESTHOOD. 3 vols. 8vo., 15s.

JOHNSON'S (JOHN) UNBLOODY SACRIFICE. 2 vols. 8vo., 10s.

JOHNSON'S (JOHN) ENGLISH CANONS. 2 vols. 8vo., 12s.

LAUD'S (ABP.) COMPLETE WORKS. 7 vols. 8vo., £3 3s.

TAYLOR'S (BP. JER.) WORKS (Eden's Ed.) 10 vols., £5 5s.

THORNDIKE'S (HERBERT) THEOLOGICAL WORKS. 10 vols. 8vo., £2 10s.

WILSON'S (BP.) WORKS. Vols. II. to VI., £2 12s. 6d.

Vol. I., containing the LIFE OF BISHOP WILSON, &c., by the Rev. JOHN KEBLE, M.A., *is in the press.*

CHURCH POETRY.

THE AUTHOR OF "THE CHRISTIAN YEAR."

THE CHRISTIAN YEAR. Thoughts in verse for the Sundays and Holydays throughout the Year. *Imperial Octavo*, with Illuminated Titles,—Cloth, 1*l.* 5s.; morocco, 1*l.* 11s. 6d.; best morocco, 2*l.* 2s. *Octavo Edition*,—Large type, cloth, 10s. 6d.; morocco by Hayday, 21s.; antique calf, 18s. *Foolscap Octavo Edition*,—Cloth, 7s. 6d.; morocco, 10s. 6d.; morocco by Hayday, 15s.; antique calf, 12s. 32*mo. Edition*,—Cloth, 3s. 6d.; morocco, plain, 5s.; morocco by Hayday, 7s. *Cheap Edition*,—Cloth, 1s. 6d.; bound, 2s.

LYRA INNOCENTIUM. Thoughts in Verse for Christian Children. *Foolscap Octavo Edition*,—Cloth, 7s. 6d.; morocco, plain, 10s. 6d.; morocco by Hayday, 15s.; antique calf, 12s. 18*mo. Edition*,—Cloth, 6s.; morocco, 8s. 6d. 32*mo. Edition*,—Cloth, 3s. 6d.; morocco, plain, 5s.; morocco by Hayday, 7s. *Cheap Edition*,—Cloth, 1s. 6d.; bound, 2s.

THE AUTHOR OF "THE CATHEDRAL."

THE CATHEDRAL. Foolscap 8vo., cloth, 7s. 6d.; 32mo., with Engravings, 4s. 6d.

THOUGHTS IN PAST YEARS. The Sixth Edition, with several new Poems, 32mo., cloth, 4s. 6d.

THE BAPTISTERY; or, The Way of Eternal Life. 32mo., cloth, 3s. 6d.

The above Three Volumes uniform, 32mo., neatly bound in morocco, 18s.

THE CHRISTIAN SCHOLAR. Foolscap 8vo., 10s. 6d.; 32mo., cloth, 4s. 6d.

THE SEVEN DAYS; or, The Old and New Creation. Second Edition, foolscap 8vo., 7s. 6d.

MORNING THOUGHTS. By a CLERGYMAN. Suggested by the Second Lessons for the Daily Morning Service throughout the year. 2 vols. foolscap 8vo., cloth, 5s. each.

THE CHILD'S CHRISTIAN YEAR. Hymns for every Sunday and Holyday throughout the year. Cheap Edition, 18mo., cloth, 1s.

COXE'S CHRISTIAN BALLADS. Foolscap 8vo., cloth, 3s. Also selected Poems in a packet, sewed, 1s.

FLORUM SACRA. By the Rev. G. HUNT SMYTTAN. Second Edition, 16mo., 1s.

A NEW SERIES OF TALES.

HISTORICAL TALES, illustrating the chief events in Ecclesiastical History, British and Foreign, adapted for General Reading, Parochial Libraries, &c. In Monthly Volumes, with a Frontispiece, price 1s.

The Series of Tales now announced will embrace the most important periods and transactions connected with the progress of the Church in ancient and modern times. They will be written by authors of acknowledged merit, in a popular style, upon sound Church principles, and with a single eye to the inculcation of a true estimate of the circumstances to which they relate, and the bearing of those circumstances upon the history of the Church. By this means it is hoped that many, who now regard Church history with indifference, will be led to the perusal of its singularly interesting and instructive episodes.

Each Tale, although forming a link of the entire Series, will be complete in itself, enabling persons to subscribe to portions only, or to purchase any single Tale separately.

Already published.

No. 1.—THE CAVE IN THE HILLS; or, Crecilius Viriāthus.
No. 2.—THE EXILES OF THE CEBENNA: a Journal written during the Decian Persecution, by Aurelianus Gratianus, Priest of the Church of Arles; and now done into English.
No. 3.—THE CHIEF'S DAUGHTER; or, The Settlers in Virginia.
No. 4.—THE LILY OF TIFLIS: a Sketch from Georgian Church History.
No. 5.—WILD SCENES AMONGST THE CELTS.
No. 6.—THE LAZAR-HOUSE OF LEROS: a Tale of the Eastern Church in the Seventeenth Century.
No. 7.—THE RIVALS: a Tale of the Anglo-Saxon Church.
No. 8.—THE CONVERT OF MASSACHUSETTS.
No. 9.—THE QUAY OF THE DIOSCURI: a Tale of Nicene Times.
No. 10.—THE BLACK DANES.
No. 11.—THE CONVERSION OF ST. VLADIMIR; or, The Martyrs of Kief. A Tale of the Early Russian Church.
No. 12.—THE SEA-TIGERS: a Tale of Mediæval Nestorianism.
No. 13.—THE CROSS IN SWEDEN; or, The Days of King Ingi the Good.
No. 14.—THE ALLELUIA BATTLE; or, Pelagianism in Britain.
No. 15.—THE BRIDE OF RAMCUTTAH: A Tale of the Jesuit Missions to the East Indies in the Sixteenth Century.
No. 16.—ALICE OF FOBBING; or, The Times of Jack Straw and Wat Tyler.
No. 17.—THE NORTHERN LIGHT: a Tale of Iceland and Greenland in the Eleventh Century.
No. 18.—AUBREY DE L'ORNE; or, The Times of St. Anselm.
No. 19.—LUCIA'S MARRIAGE; or, The Lions of Wady-Araba.
No. 20.—WOLFINGHAM; or, The Convict-Settler of Jervis Bay: a Tale of the Church in Australia.
No. 21.—THE FORSAKEN; or, The Times of St. Dunstan.
No. 22.—THE DOVE OF TABENNA.—THE RESCUE: A Tale of the Moorish Conquest of Spain.
No. 23.—LARACHE: a Tale of the Portuguese Church in the Sixteenth Century.
No. 24.—WALTER THE ARMOURER; or, The Interdict: a Tale of the Times of King John.
No. 25.—THE CATECHUMENS OF THE COROMANDEL COAST.
No. 26.—THE DAUGHTERS OF POLA. Family Letters relating to the Persecution of Diocletian, now first translated from an Istrian MS.

NEW WORKS OF FICTION.

ALICE LISLE: A Tale of Puritan Times. Fcap. 8vo., cloth, 4s.

THE SCHOLAR AND THE TROOPER; or, OXFORD DURING THE GREAT REBELLION. By the Rev. W. E. HEYGATE. *Second Edition.* Fcap. 8vo., cloth, 5s.

SOME YEARS AFTER: A Tale. Fcap. 8vo., cloth lettered, 7s.

ATHELINE; or, THE CASTLE BY THE SEA. A Tale. By LOUISA STEWART, Author of "Walks at Templecombe," "Floating away," &c. 2 vols., fcap. 8vo. 9s.

MIGNONETTE: A SKETCH. By the Author of "The Curate of Holy Cross." 2 vols., fcap., cloth, 10s.

STORM AND SUNSHINE; or, THE BOYHOOD OF HERBERT FALCONER. A Tale. By W. E. DICKSON, M.A., Author of "Our Workshop," &c. With Frontispiece, cloth, 2s.

AMY GRANT; or, THE ONE MOTIVE. A Tale designed principally for the Teachers of the Children of the Poor. *Second Edition.* Fcap. 8vo., cloth, 3s. 6d.

THE TWO HOMES. A Tale. By the Author of "Amy Grant." *Second Edition.* Fcap. 8vo., cloth, 2s. 6d.

DAWN AND TWILIGHT. A Tale. By the Author of "Amy Grant," "Two Homes," &c. 2 vols. fcap. 8vo., cloth, 7s.

KENNETH; or, THE REAR-GUARD OF THE GRAND ARMY. By the Author of the "Heir of Redclyffe," "Heartsease," &c., &c. *Third Edition.* Fcap. 8vo., with Illustrations, 5s.

TALES FOR THE YOUNG MEN AND WOMEN OF ENGLAND. A Series of Tales adapted for Lending Libraries, Book Hawkers, &c.

Fcap. 8vo., with Illustrations, strongly bound in coloured wrapper, 1s. each.

No. 1. Mother and Son.
No. 2. The Recruit. *A new Edition.*
No. 3. The Strike.
No. 4. James Bright, the Shopman.
No. 5. Jonas Clint.
No. 6. The Sisters.
No. 7. Caroline Elton; or, Vanity and Jealousy. } 1s.
No. 8. Servants' Influence.
No. 9. The Railway Accident.
No. 10. Wanted, a Wife.
No. 11. Irrevocable.
No. 12. The Tenants at Tinkers' End.
No. 13. Windycote Hall.
No. 14. False Honour.
No. 15. Old Jarvis's Will.
No. 16. The Two Cottages.
No. 17. Squitch.
No. 18. The Politician.
No. 19. Two to One.
No. 20. Hobson's Choice. 6d.
No. 21. Susan. 4d.
No. 22. Mary Thomas; or, Dissent at Evenly. } 4d.

"To make boys learn to read, and then to place no good books within their reach, is to give them an appetite, and leave nothing in the pantry save unwholesome and poisonous food which, depend upon it, they will eat rather than starve."—*Sir W. Scott.*

NEW PAROCHIAL BOOKS.

CATECHETICAL WORKS, Designed to aid the Clergy in Public Catechising. Uniform in size and type with the "Parochial Tracts."

Already published in this Series.

I. CATECHETICAL LESSONS on the Creed. 6d.
II. CATECHETICAL LESSONS on the Lord's Prayer. 6d.
III. CATECHETICAL LESSONS on the Ten Commandments. 6d.
IV. CATECHETICAL LESSONS on the Sacraments. 6d.
V. CATECHETICAL LESSONS on the Parables of the New Testament. Part I. Parables I.—XXI. 1s.
VI. PART II. PARABLES XXII.—XXXVII. 1s.
VII. CATECHETICAL NOTES on the Thirty-Nine Articles. 1s. 6d.

VIII. CATECHETICAL LESSONS on the Order for Morning and Evening Prayer, and the Litany. 1s.
IX. CATECHETICAL LESSONS on the Miracles of our Lord. Part I. Miracles I—XVII. 1s.
X. PART II. MIRACLES XVIII.—XXXVII. 1s.
XI. CATECHETICAL NOTES on the Saints' Days. 1s.
QUESTIONS ON THE COLLECTS, EPISTLES, AND GOSPELS, throughout the Year; edited by the Rev. T. L. CLAUGHTON, Vicar of Kidderminster. For the use of Teachers in Sunday-Schools. Two Parts, 18mo., cloth, each 2s. 6d.

COTTAGE PICTURES. Cottage Pictures from the Old Testament. Twenty-eight large Illustrations, coloured by hand. The set, folio, 7s. 6d.

COTTAGE PICTURES from the New Testament, (uniform with above). The set of 28, 7s. 6d.

SCRIPTURE PRINTS FOR PAROCHIAL USE. Printed in Sepia, with Ornamental Borders. Price One Penny each; or the set in an ornamental envelope, One Shilling.

1. The Nativity.
2. St. John Preaching.
3. The Baptism of Christ.
4. Jacob's Dream.
5. The Transfiguration.
6. The Good Shepherd.
7. The Tribute-Money.
8. The Preparation for the Cross.
9. The Crucifixion.
10. Leading to Crucifixion.
11. Healing the Sick.
12. The Return of the Prodigal.

Ninety thousand have already been sold of these prints. They are also kept mounted and varnished, 3d. each.

TALES AND ALLEGORIES reprinted from the "PENNY POST." Fcap. 8vo., with Illustrations.

THE CHILD OF THE TEMPLE. 1s.
THE HEART-STONE. 10d.
FAIRTON VILLAGE. 8d.
FOOTPRINTS IN THE WILDERNESS. 6d.
TALES OF AN OLD CHURCH. 4d.
MARGARET OF CONWAY. 4d.
MARY WILBRAM. 4d.

MARION. 4d.
MARY MERTON. 2d.
THE TWO WIDOWS. 2d.
LEFT BEHIND. 2d.

LITTLE TALES. 4d.
LITTLE ALLEGORIES. 2d.
LITTLE FABLES. 2d.

ANNALS OF ENGLAND. An Epitome of English History. From Cotemporary Writers, the Rolls of Parliament, and other Public Records. 3 vols. fcap. 8vo., with Illustrations, cloth, 15s. *Recommended by the Examiners in the School of Modern History at Oxford.*

    Vol. I. From the Roman Era to the deposition of Richard II. Cloth, 5s.
    Vol. II. From the Accession of the House of Lancaster to Charles I. Cloth, 5s.
    Vol. III. From the Commonwealth to the Death of Queen Anne. Cloth, 5s.

Each Volume is sold separately.

" The book strikes us as being most useful as a Handbook for teachers. It is just the sort of help for a tutor to have lying by him as a guide to his lecture. The main facts he will find marshalled in strict chronological order, and he will be assisted by references to the statute-book and the old chronicles. The 'ANNALS' will, in short, supply the dry bones of an historical lecture, which each teacher must clothe for himself with life and spirit. But the work will also be highly useful to students, especially for the purpose of refreshing the memory and getting details into order, after the perusal of more regular narratives. We trust to see it extensively employed in the Universities. At Oxford it may be especially serviceable. A reliable guide to the original authorities, and one which gives its proper prominence to the early history, may, if it falls into the hands of either students or teachers, do something to dispel the illusion that English history can be profitably studied by beginning at the momentary overthrow of English nationality, and that, after all the labours of Turner, Lingard, Palgrave, Kemble, Lappenberg, and Pauli, David Hume still remains the one correct, orthodox, and unapproachable text-book for its study."—*Saturday Review.*

THE ETHICS OF ARISTOTLE. With Notes by the Rev. W. E. JELF, B.D., Author of "A Greek Grammar," &c. 8vo., cloth, 12s.
    The Text separately, 5s.   The Notes separately, 7s. 6d.

SOPHOCLIS TRAGŒDIÆ, with Notes, adapted to the use of Schools and Universities. By THOMAS MITCHELL, M.A. 2 vols. 8vo., £1 8s.

The Plays may also be had separately, at 5s. each.

ŒDIPUS TYRANNUS.	AJAX.
ŒDIPUS COLONEUS.	TRACHINIÆ.
ELECTRA.	ANTIGONE.
PHILOCTETES.	

THUCYDIDES, with Notes, chiefly Historical and Geographical. By the late T. ARNOLD, D.D. With Indices by the Rev. R. P. G. TIDDEMAN. 8vo.
Complete, 3 volumes, 8vo., cloth lettered, £1 16s.

MADVIG'S LATIN GRAMMAR. A Latin Grammar for the Use of Schools. By Professor MADVIG, with additions by the Author. Translated by the Rev. G. F. WOODS, M.A. Uniform with JELF's "Greek Grammar." *Fourth Edition, with an Index of Authors,* 8vo., cloth, 12s.

    Competent authorities pronounce this work to be the very best Latin Grammar yet published in England. This new Edition contains an Index to the Authors quoted.

JELF'S GREEK GRAMMAR.—A Grammar of the Greek Language, chiefly from the text of Raphael Kühner. By WM. EDW. JELF, M.A., Student of Ch. Ch. 2 vols. 8vo. *Third Edition.* 1l. 10s.

    This Grammar is now in general use at Oxford, Cambridge, Dublin, and Durham; at Eton, King's College, London, and other public schools.

A MANUAL OF GREEK AND LATIN PROSE COMPOSITION, specially designed to illustrate the differences of Idiom between those Languages and the English. By E. R. HUMPHREYS, LL.D., late Head Master of Cheltenham Grammar-school. Crown 8vo., cloth, 3s. 6d.

LAWS OF THE GREEK ACCENTS. By JOHN GRIFFITHS, M.A. 16mo. *Fifth Edition. Price Sixpence.*

A NEW SERIES of the Greek and Latin Classics for the use of Schools.

"Mr. Parker is supplying a want long felt, in issuing a series of good classical texts, well edited, and in a cheap form. The expensiveness of our school-books is a crying evil, which cannot be too soon abated. It is absurd extravagance to put costly books into the hands of schoolboys, to be thumbed and torn to pieces, when cheaper ones would answer every useful purpose just as well. In this respect our neighbours on the Continent are far more rational than we are. We look with satisfaction upon Mr. Parker's efforts to bring about an amendment. Though we think it would have been better to announce the editor's name, we willingly bear testimony to the ability with which he has executed his task, and have much pleasure in recommending the Texts as suitable for school purposes."—*Athenæum.*

GREEK POETS.

	Paper.	Bound.
	s. d.	s. d.
Æschylus	2 6	3 0
Aristophanes. 2 vols.	5 0	6 0
Euripides. 3 vols.	5 0	6 6
Or the 6 Plays only	3 0	3 6
Sophocles	2 6	3 0
Homeri Ilias	3 0	3 6
——— Odyssea	2 6	3 0

GREEK PROSE WRITERS.

Aristotelis Ethica	1 6	2 0
Demosthenes de Corona, et Æschines in Ctesiphontem	1 6	2 0
Herodotus. 2 vols.	5 0	6 0
Thucydides. 2 vols.	4 0	5 0
Xenophontis Memorabilia	1 0	1 4
——————— Anabasis	1 6	2 0

LATIN POETS.

Horatius	1 6	2 0
Juvenalis et Persius	1 0	1 6
Lucanus	2 0	2 6
Lucretius	1 6	2 0
Phædrus	1 0	1 4
Virgilius	2 0	2 6

LATIN PROSE WRITERS.

Cæsar	2 0	2 6
Cicero De Officiis, de Senectute, et de Amicitia	1 6	2 0
Ciceronis Tusculanarum Disputationum Libri V.	1 6	2 0
Cornelius Nepos	1 0	1 4
Livius. 4 vols.	5 0	6 0
Sallustius	1 6	2 0
Tacitus. 2 vols.	4 0	5 0

NEW SERIES OF ENGLISH NOTES. 15

THE PLAYS OF SOPHOCLES, with English Notes by Members of the University of Oxford. Complete in 2 vols., cloth, 6s., or separately—

	s. d.		s. d.
Ajax (Text with Notes)	1 0	Antigone	1 0
Electra	1 0	Philoctetes	1 0
Œdipus Rex	1 0	Trachiniæ	1 0
Œdipus Coloneus	1 0		

THE PLAYS OF ÆSCHYLUS, with English Notes by Members of the University of Oxford. Complete in 2 vols., cloth, 7s. 6d.

Prometheus Vinctus (Text with Notes)	1 0	Agamemnon	1 0
		Choephoræ	1 0
Septem Contra Thebas	1 0	Eumenides	1 0
Persæ	1 0	Supplices	1 0

THE PLAYS OF EURIPIDES, with English Notes by Members of the University of Oxford. Complete in 2 vols., cloth, 6s. 6d.

Hecuba (Text with Notes)	1 0	Hippolytus	1 0
Medea	1 0	Phœnissæ	1 0
Orestes	1 0	Alcestis	1 0

"The notes contain sufficient information, without affording the pupil so much assistance as to supersede all exertion on his part."—*Athenæum*, Jan. 27, 1855.

"Be all this as it may, it is a real benefit to public schoolboys to be able to purchase any Greek Play they want for One Shilling. When we were introduced to Greek Plays, about forty years ago, we had put into our hands a portly 8vo. volume, containing Porson's four Plays, without one word of English in the shape of notes; and we have no doubt the book cost nearer twenty than ten shillings, and after all was nothing near so useful as these neat little copies at One Shilling each."—*Educational Times*.

The Text of SOPHOCLES separately. One vol., cloth, 3s.—The Notes, ditto, 3s.
The Text of ÆSCHYLUS separately. One vol., cloth, 3s.—The Notes, ditto, 3s. 6d.
The Text of EURIPIDES separately. One vol., cloth, 3s. 6d.—The Notes, ditto, 3s

Pocket Editions of the following have also been published with Short Notes.

DEMOSTHENES.

De Corona	2 0	Æschines in Ctesiphontem	2 0

VIRGIL.

The Bucolics	1 0	The Georgics	2 0

The First Three Books of the Æneid, 1s.

HORACE.

Odes and Epodes	2 0	Satires	1 0

Epistles and Ars Poetica, 1s.

SALLUST.

Jugurtha	1 6	Catiline	1 0

CORNELIUS NEPOS—Lives (with Short Notes)	1 6
PHÆDRUS—Fables (ditto)	1 0
HOMER—First Six Books of Iliad (ditto)	2 0
LIVY, Books XXI.—XXIV. (ditto). Cloth, 4s. 6d.; sewed,	4 0
CICERO, Orationes in Catilinam (ditto), 16mo., sd.,	1 0
———— Oratio pro Milone (ditto), 16mo., sewed,	1 0
CÆSAR, De Bello Gallico, Bks. I.—III. (ditto), 16mo., sd.,	1 6

In the Press.
Short Notes to CICERO DE SENECTUTE, and ARISTOPHANES' THE KNIGHTS.

THE LITERARY CHURCHMAN. A Journal devoted to the interest and advancement of Religious Literature.

THE LITERARY CHURCHMAN was established in order to extend to RELIGIOUS LITERATURE the advantages which General Literature already possessed in the *Athenæum, Literary Gazette, Critic,* and other similar journals. Previously, Religious Literature had been dependent for publicity on a few scattered notices in Newspapers or Religious Magazines; while the weekly issue of some twenty or thirty works, bearing more or less on Religious subjects, proved an importance sufficient to demand a journal distinctly set apart for the interests of that class of publications.

SUBSCRIPTIONS.

For the Year . . . 8s. 0d.	For Six Months . . 4s. 0d.
Ditto Free by post . . 10s. 0d.	Ditto Free by post . . 5s. 0d.

THE PENNY POST. A Church of England Illustrated Magazine, issued Monthly. Price One Penny.

That this Magazine is wanted, a circulation of 22,000 copies of each number testifies. It is *the only Penny Magazine* upholding sound Church principles. That it does good, and is appreciated, testimony whence it would be least expected, abundantly proves. But at the same time it must be borne in mind, that this is a small circulation for a Penny religious periodical. Those who differ, depend much upon their periodicals for inculcating doctrine hostile to the Church, and circulate thousands, where the Church of England, unfortunately, circulates only hundreds.

MONTHLY.—ONE PENNY.

Subscribers' names received by all Booksellers and Newsmen.

THE GENTLEMAN'S MAGAZINE.—The times, it is readily allowed, have greatly changed since *Sylvanus Urban* first solicited public attention, but it may be fairly doubted whether the tastes and habits of thought of the educated classes, to whom he addresses himself, have changed in a like degree. Hence he does not fear that History and Antiquities, in their widest sense, can ever become unpalatable to them, but, on the contrary, he is glad to mark an increased avidity in pursuing such studies. This is a state of things that he thinks he may claim a considerable share in bringing about, and the steady progress of which he is desirous of forwarding by all available means. He alludes to the growing appreciation of the Past, as the key to the understanding of the Present, and (in a sense) of the Future, as testified by the formation of Archæological and Literary Societies, which have already achieved much good, and may do still more; and as a means to that end, he devotes a portion of his pages every month, under the title of "ANTIQUARIAN AND LITERARY INTELLIGENCER," to a record of their progress.

It has ever been the desire of *Sylvanus Urban* to see his CORRESPONDENCE a leading feature in his pages, and he has the gratification of reckoning many of the most erudite men of the time as his fellow-workers, who have, through him, conveyed an invaluable amount of knowledge to the world. He invites those of the present day to imitate them. Another important feature has been, and will be, the OBITUARY, to the completeness of which he requests friends or relatives to contribute by communicating fitting notices of eminent persons daily removed by the hand of death from among us.

All Communications to be addressed to Mr. URBAN, 377, STRAND, W.C.

APPENDIX

A Brief Summary of
Inspiration and Interpretation

By Dean John William Burgon
1861

Summarized by
Pastor D. A. Waite, Th.D., Ph.D.

B.F.T. #2925

TABLE OF CONTENTS

SECTION   **PAGES**

I **Introductory Remarks** 1
   A. The Purpose of This Booklet 1
   B. Limitation of the Summary 2

II **The Preface** 3
   A. The General Problem. 3
      1. A System of Unbelief Must Be Answered 3
      2. A Conspiracy Against the Faith 3
   B. Details about *Essays and Reviews* 3
      1. Six Anglican Clergymen Made Light of their Profession. 3
      2. *Essays and Reviews* Had a Mix of Writers 4
      3. *Essays and Reviews* Was 433 Pages Long 4
   C. Dean Burgon's Assessment of *Essays and Reviews* 4
      1. The *Reviewers* Have Disbelief in the Word of God 4
      2. The *Reviewers* Have No Bible at All 4
      3. The *Reviewers* Wrote Blasphemy 5
      4. The *Reviewers* "Free-Handled" Divine Truth 5

III **"Preliminary Remarks on a volume entitled *ESSAYS AND REVIEWS* addressed to the undergraduate MEMBERS of ORIEL COLLEGE"** 6
   A. The Writers of the *Essays and Reviews* Listed 6
   B. Summary of *Essays and Reviews* in *The Preface* 6

IV **SERMON I: "The Study of the Bible Recommended; and a Method of Studying it Described"** 7
   A. Seven Rules for Bible Study 7
      1. Take a Half Hour Early Each Day For Bible Study. 7
      2. Read a Chapter a Day in the Bible. 7
      3. Go Over the Words as if They Were New to You. 7
      4. Avoid Commentaries, Maps, or Helps 8
      5. Make Brief Memoranda of Your Own. 8
      6. Read the Bible Consecutively from Genesis to Revelation. 8
      7. Read Every Book Without Skipping a Chapter. 8
   B. Proper Attitudes While Bible Reading 8
      1. Look for Things Not Known Before 8
      2. Begin With Prayer 8
      3. Find Honey in the Bible 9
      4. Have a Mind Like Samuel 9
   C. Suggestions and Goals for Pastors as a Result of Their Bible Reading 9

1. Bible Reading Will Cut Down on Boredom in the Congregation 9
2. Never Neglect Bible Reading even for a Day 9
3. Partake of the Tree of Life by Bible Reading 9
4. Don't Read Commentaries for Three Years at Least 10
5. Keep a Jealously-Guarded Half-Hour Daily 10
6. Bible Reading Is Vital 10
7. Bible Reading Arms Pastors with the Sword of the Spirit 10

V SERMON II: "Natural Science and Theological Science" 11
A. Genesis Must Be Accepted As Scientific. 11
  1. Suspicion of Genesis 11
  2. Creation Days of 1,000 Years Will Not Do. 11
  3. Creation Days Must Be Literal and Solar. 11
  4. Man's Creation No More Than some 6,000 years ago 12
  5. The Bible Contains Accurate Science 12
B. Proper Interpretation of the Bible is Essential 12
  1. The Bible Should not Be Allegorized 12
  2. Miracles Must Be Accepted, Not Reinterpreted 12
  3. Proper Interpretation of Genesis Is Especially Important 12

VI SERMON III: "Inspiration of Scripture--Gospel Difficulties--The Word of God Infallible--Other Sciences Subordinate to Theological Science" 13
A. Some Definitions Concerning the Inspiration of the Bible 13
  1. The Inspiration of Scripture Rightly Understood 13
  2. Verbal Inspiration 13
  3. Inspired Words 13
  4. The Bible Is Inspired Entirely 14
B. Biblical Inspiration Must Be Defended Properly 14
  1. It's Time to Speak Out for God's Truth 14
  2. The Safety of the Ark of God 14
  3. The Inerrancy of Every Letter of the Bible Must Be Defended ... 14

VII SERMON IV: "The Inspiration of Every Part of the Bible Vindicated and Explained--Nature of Inspiration--the Text of Scripture" 16
A. The Extent of Inspiration 16
  1. Scripture Inspired from the Alpha to the Omega of it 16
  2. No Middle Ground Between Inspiration and Non-Inspiration ... 16
  3. The Bible Is the Very Utterance of the Holy Spirit 16
B. Illustrations of the Bible's Inspiration 17
  1. The Bible Like the Speech of a Sovereign 17
  2. The Bible like a Servant Delivering a Message 17

C. The Bible Can Be Trusted In Even The Smallest Detail 17
      1. The Dukes of Edom Are as Inspired as much as any other
         Portion 17
      2. Inspiration Does not Come and Go 17
      3. The Bible Must Stand or Fall as a Whole 17
   D. A Proper Attitude in Dealing With the Bible Is Important 18
      1. Our Own Amazing Ignorance 18
      2. The Safest Eloquence of Silence 18
      3. Believe You Are Reading an Inspired Book 18
      4. The Method of Inspiration Cannot Be Fully Understood 18
   E. Other Important Quotations Defending Bible Inspiration 19
      1. How Can You Expound an Uninspired Text? 19
      2. The Bible Is the Best Ascertained Text of any Ancient Writing ... 19
      3. Thought Inspiration Versus Word Inspiration 19
      4. Resent Any Dishonour to the Lord 19
      5. A Childlike Study of the Bible Is an Antidote to Impiety 19
      6. Unlock the Bible Treasure with the Key of Faith 20
      7. The Bible Is the Sole Depository of History and Chronology 20
      8. An Uninspired Writing Has No Absolute Authority 20
      9. The Lord Jesus Christ Verified Many Old Testament Details 20

VIII SERMON V: "Interpretation of Holy Scripture--Inspired interpretation--the Bible Is not to be Interpreted Like any Other Book--God, (not man,) the Real Author of the Bible" 21
   A. The Bible Is a Unique Book 21
      1. It Is Unlike Any Other Volume in the World 21
      2. Bible Writers Interpret it as No Other Book 21
   B. Some Important Rules in Bible Interpretation 21
      1. Don't Deny the Literal Sense of Scripture 21
      2. Nothing is Ever Allegory or May Be Explained Away 22
      3. There Are Often Deeper Meanings of Scripture 22
   C. The Holy Spirit's Role in Bible Interpretation 22
      1. The Holy Spirit Is the True Author of Old and New Testaments .. 22
      2. The Whole Bible Is Inspired by the Holy Spirit 22
      3. The True Method of Interpretation 22
      4. Grasp the Torch of Truth and Run With It 23

IX SERMON VI: "The Doctrine of Arbitrary Scriptural Accommodation Considered" 24
   A. We Must Recognize That the Source of the Bible Was God
      Himself 24
      1. God Was Speaking With Human Lips 24
      2. The Holy Spirit's Meaning Must Be Accepted 24
      3. Arbitrary "Accommodation" of the Holy Spirit's Words Is

      Rejected 24
    4. The Same God Gave Old and New Testaments 25
  B. Some Special Considerations for Bible Interpretation 25
    1. Humbly Address Yourself to the Bible 25
    2. Remember that Divine Language Never Needs To Be "Accommodated" 25
    3. The Lord Jesus Christ Did Not "Accommodate" Psalm 9:2 25
    4. The Lord Jesus Christ Was Spoke to Moses in the Bush 25
    5. There Is No Arbitrary Accommodation of Old Testament in the New 26
    6. Unbelief Must Not Blur our Bible Interpretation 26

X SERMON VII: "The Marvels of Holy Scripture--Moral and Physical--Jael's Deed Defended--Miracles Vindicated" 27

  A. The Miracles Must Be Taken With the Entire Bible 27
    1. Accept the Bible as a Whole Or Reject It as a Whole 27
    2. There Are 30 New Testament References to the First Two Chapters of Genesis 27
    3. All Parts of the Bible Stand or Fall Together 27
  B. Miracles Must be Accepted As the Bible Gives Them and Not Doubted 28
    1. Miracles Should not Be Explained Away or Pared Down 28
    2. Miracles' Historical Reality Must not Be Denied by Ideology ... 28
    3. Miracles Are Historically True 28
    4. Miracles Are Historically True, Not Merely Ideologically True .. 28
    5. Denial of Bible Miracles Is Blasphemous Folly 28
  C. Dean Burgon's Final Words of Challenge 29
    1. Ministers Have a Battle for Christ to Fight 29
    2. Ministers Must Rise Above Perpetual Disputings 29
    3. Ministers Must Make Use of the Wealth of the Celestial Armoury 30
    4. Ministers Must Have a Desire to Understand the Bible 30
    5. Ministers Must Accept the Divine Origin and Power of the Bible 30
    6. Ministers Must Realize that the Bible Is the Only Thing that Deserves Man's Attention 30

Introducing the "Index of Words and Phrases 32
Index of Words and Phrases 33
About the Author 39
Order Blank Pages 40

A Brief Summary of *Inspiration and Interpretation*

BY DEAN JOHN WILLIAM BURGON

1861

Summarized by Pastor D. A. Waite, Th.D., Ph.D.
President of THE DEAN BURGON SOCIETY, and
Director of THE BIBLE FOR TODAY, INCORPORATED
900 Park Avenue, Collingswood, NJ 08108
Phone: 609-854-4452; FAX: 609-854-2464;
Orders: 1-800-JOHN 10:9; E-Mail: BFT@BibleForToday.org
www.BibleForToday.org

I
Introductory Remarks

A. The Purpose of this Booklet.

As the title indicates, it is the purpose and intention of this booklet to summarize some of the teachings and important arguments contained in Dean Burgon's excellent book, *Inspiration and Interpretation*. It is planned that the substance of this material will be given to the Dean Burgon Society's 21st Annual Conference, meeting at the Heritage Baptist University in Greenwood, Indiana, July, 1999. It is hoped that the reader will purchase and read *Inspiration and Interpretation* in its entirety. It is available as **B.F.T. #1220** for a GIFT of **$25.00** **+ $5.00** for shipping and handling. It is the new hardback edition published by the Dean Burgon Society.

There has been no attempt to give all of the arguments and excellent material contained in *Inspiration and Interpretation*. This "SUMMARY" has sought to set forth some of the more important themes and statements found in this well-written textbook on the subjects of the inspiration and the interpretation of the Scriptures. The reader of the entire book will find it to be a worthwhile document. It is hoped that some of the following quotations will whet the reader's appetite for more of the truths so skillfully propounded by Dean Burgon.

B. Limitation of the Summary

Though there will be some quotations from the Preface of *Inspiration and Interpretation*, there will be no references to what Dean Burgon calls: **"PRELIMINARY REMARKS on a Volume Entitled '*ESSAYS AND REVIEWS*:' Addressed to the Undergraduate Members of Oriel College."** This section is numbered with a second set of roman numeral pages (i-ccxxviii). In that section, Dean Burgon has devoted 228 pages to answer the apostasy contained in *Essays and Reviews*. Even though I have not quoted from it in this summary, it should be read by all in its entirety. This apologetical refutation of Biblical error shows the following important things about Dean Burgon: (1) He was not ashamed to refute apostate theology even though it was within his own church denomination. (2) He showed himself to be the champion of Biblical orthodoxy without apology. (3) He was not concerned about how many ministers of the Church of England he may have offended because of his careful and rational defense of the teachings of the Word of God.

II
The Preface

The **Preface** of this book introduces Dean Burgon's refutation of the *Essays and Reviews*. Before giving his undergraduate students at Oriel College, Oxford University, instruction on the inspiration and interpretation of the Bible, he warned them about a current 433-page book. This book was loaded with apostasy, heresy, and unbelief of all kinds.

A. The General Problem.

The thing which was uppermost in the mind of Dean Burgon was his belief in the centrality of Bible study. He wrote that there was, in his day, a
"prevalent *neglect of the noblest study of all,--the study of God's Word.*"
(Dean John William Burgon, *Inspiration and Interpretation*, p. viii)

1. A System of Unbelief Must Be Answered

Dean Burgon did not believe in remaining silent when Bible doctrine was being attacked. He wrote:
"*I determined at all events not to be a party to a craven silence; and denounced from the University pulpit with hearty indignation that whole system of unbelief, (if system it can be called,) which has been growing up for years among us; and which, I was and am convinced, must be openly met,--not silently ignored until the mischief becomes unmanageable: met, too, by building up men in THE TRUTH: above all, by giving Theological instruction to those who are destined to become Professors of Theological Science, and are about to undertake the cure of souls. . . . In this spirit, I asserted the opposite fundamental verities; and so, would have been content to dismiss the* 'Essays and Reviews' *from my thoughts for ever.*" (Dean John William Burgon, *Inspiration and Interpretation*, pp. ix-x)

2. A Conspiracy Against the Faith

The *Essays and Reviews* was a conspiracy against the faith of Scripture. Dean Burgon wrote:
"Here was a conspiracy *against the Faith. Seven Critics had* avowedly combined. . ." (Dean John William Burgon, *Inspiration and Interpretation*, p. x)
There were seven separate writers in these *Essays and Reviews*.

B. Details about *Essays and Reviews*

There are several details concerning the *Essays and Reviews* that are mentioned in this Preface.

1. Six Anglican Clergymen Made Light of their Profession.

Dean Burgon especially was upset that six out of the seven men writing in the

Essays and Reviews were members of the Church of England Clergy. He felt they had betrayed the Bible and their church. He outlined some of the doctrines these men questioned. He wrote:

> "Secondly,--'Essays and Reviews' attracted notice because six of its authors were Ministers of the Church of England. Here were six Clergymen openly making light of their sacred profession, and apparently worse than regardless of their Ordination vows. . . . [A reviewer stated]: 'there has been discarded the Word of God, the Creation, the Fall, the Redemption, Justification, Regeneration, and Salvation, Miracles, Inspiration, Prophecy, Heaven and Hell, Eternal punishment and a Day of Judgment, Creeds, Liturgies, and Articles, the truth of Jewish History and of Gospel narrative; a sense of doubt thrown over even the Incarnation, the Resurrection, and Ascension, the Divinity of the Second Person, and the personality of the Third.'" (Dean John William Burgon, *Inspiration and Interpretation*, p. xi)

2. *Essays and Reviews* Had a Mix of Writers.

Dean Burgon pointed out that the writers of the *Essays and Reviews* were from a variety of backgrounds. He wrote:

> "But here is a combination of Doctors of Divinity; Professors; Fellows, nay Heads of Colleges; Instructors of England's Youth; Teachers of Religion; Chaplains to Royal and noble personages!" (Dean John William Burgon, *Inspiration and Interpretation*, pp. xii-xiii)

3. *Essays and Reviews* Was 433 Pages Long

It was no easy task to reply to a book that had 433 pages in it and do it justice. This book was filled with fallacies and falsities. Dean Burgon's reply was 228 pages in length. He wrote:

> "To reply to a volume of 433 pages, each of which contains a fallacy or a falsity,--while some pages are packed full of both,--is a serious undertaking . . ." (Dean John William Burgon, *Inspiration and Interpretation*, p. xv)

C. Dean Burgon's Assessment of *Essays and Reviews*

Dean Burgon described his assessment of *Essays and Reviews* in a number of different ways.

1. The *Reviewers* Have Disbelief in the Word of God

The root problem with the *Essays and Reviews* was one of disbelief in the Word of God. He wrote:

> "At the root of the whole mischief of these last days lies disbelief in the Bible as the Word of God. This is the fundamental error." (Dean John William Burgon, *Inspiration and Interpretation*, p. xvii)

2. The *Reviewers* Have No Bible at All

In point of fact, the *Essay and Reviewers* have no Bible at all because they have denied its inspiration. The Dean wrote:

"Common Sense is able to see that an uninspired Bible is no Bible at all." (Dean John William Burgon, *Inspiration and Interpretation*, p. xix)

3. The *Reviewers* Wrote Blasphemy

Dean Burgon considered the *Essays and Reviews* to have contained "blasphemy," "irreligion," and "infidelity." He had a strong reaction against such. He wrote:

"Some respectable persons, I doubt not, will think my treatment of them harsh and uncharitable. I invite them to consider that we do not expect blasphemy from Ministers of the Gospel,--irreligion from the teachers of youth,--infidelity from the Professor's chair; nor are we called upon to tolerate it either. . . . Let those who feel little jealousy for God's honour measure out in grains their censure of a volume, the confessed tendency of which is to sap the foundation of Faith, and to introduce a flood-tide. Such shall not, at all events, be my method. . . . their Reviewer [meaning Dean Burgon] *avails himself of that Christian liberty to which they themselves so systematically lay claim, mercilessly to uncover their baseness, and uncompromisingly to denounce it. If I may declare my mind freely, punctilious courtesy in dealing with such opinions, becomes a species of treason against Him after whose Name we are called, and whom we profess to serve."* (Dean John William Burgon, *Inspiration and Interpretation*, p. xxiv)

4. The *Reviewers* "Free-Handled" Divine Truth

Since the *Reviewers* had "free-handled" God's Divine Truth, Dean Burgon felt obliged to "handle" them in like manner. He wrote:

"When Critics are clamorous for the 'free handling' of Divine Truth, they must not be surprised to find themselves freely handled too. . . . Accordingly, I have handled them just as freely as they have handled the Prophets, Apostles, and Evangelists of Christ. . . . This is no literary misunderstanding, or I could have been amicable enough: no private or personal matter, or I could have flung it from me with unconcern. No other than an attempt to destroy Man's dearest hopes, is this infamous book: no other than an insult, the grossest imaginable, offered to the Majesty of Heaven; an attack, the more foul because it is so insidious, against the Everlasting Gospel of Jesus Christ." (Dean John William Burgon, *Inspiration and Interpretation*, p. xxvi)

III

"Preliminary Remarks on a volume entitled ESSAYS AND REVIEWS addressed to the undergraduate MEMBERS of ORIEL COLLEGE"

As I said above in *The Preface*, I have not attempted to comment on the first 228 pages of Dean Burgon's *Inspiration and Interpretation*. Suffice it to say that Dean Burgon answered every heretical and false comment in the *Essays and Reviews* book of 433 pages in all. Of the seven writers in this unscriptural and heretical book, six of them were clergymen of the Church of England, Dean Burgon's own denomination. This section of the book shows that Dean Burgon was a defender of The Faith of the Bible, regardless of whether or not denial of that Faith arose within his own denomination. It shows his solid devotion to the Words of God, defending those Words with all the talent he possessed in putting words on the printed page.

A. The Writers of the *Essays and Reviews* Listed.

Though this Summary will lack comments on each of the sections of the *Essays and Reviews*, I think it is at least appropriate to list the names of the writers, giving the pages where Dean Burgon answered their false arguments. The following is a list of the men who wrote in the *Essays and Reviews*:

1. Dr. F. Temple, D.D. (pages ii-xxx)
2. Rev. Rowland Williams, D.D. (pages xxx-xlvi)
3. Rev. Professor Baden Powell, M.A. (pages xlvi-lxiv)
4. Rev. H. B. Wilson, M.A. (pages lxiv-lxxxvi)
5. C. W. Goodwin, M.A. (pages lxxxvi-cxii)
6. Rev. Mark Pattison, B.D. (pages cxii-cxxxix)
7. Rev. Professor Jowett, M.A. (pages cxxxix-ccxxvii) (Dean John William Burgon, *Inspiration and Interpretation,* pp. ii-ccxxvii)

B. Summary of *Essays and Reviews* in *The Preface*.

The reader is urged to read all 228 pages of Dean Burgon's masterful answer to the *Essays and Reviews*. As in his other books that the Dean Burgon Society has reprinted and published, Dean Burgon reveals his superb talent in refutation of false teaching. His other books are: *The Last Twelve Verses of Mark, The Revision Revised, The Traditional Text,* and *The Causes of Corruption of the Traditional Text.* He refused to put up with heresy and apostasy when it came to the clear and fundamental teachings and doctrines of the Word of God. His **Preface** is a good summary of this and should be studied carefully.

IV
SERMON I.
"The Study of the Bible Recommended; and a Method of Studying it Described"

Finally, after 228 pages of refutation of the *Essays and Reviews*, Dean Burgon begins his positive 279-page advice and counsel to the young men in his Oriel College at Oxford University concerning their preparation for the ministry. Sermon #1 is the first of seven that Dean Burgon presented in this formal series. It dealt with the most important topic for anyone--the study of the Bible. All seven of these sermons are soundly grounded on the inerrant, infallible Bible.

A. Seven Rules for Bible Study

Dean Burgon opened sermon #1 by suggesting seven rules to his ministerial students for the personal study of their Bibles. He wrote:

"The thing I would so strenuously urge upon you, is,--that, during your undergraduate period, you should read the whole Bible consecutively through, from one end to the other, by yourself and for yourself, with consummate method, care, and attention. The fundamental conditions of such a study of the Bible, in order to make it of any real use, are these:--
(Dean John William Burgon, *Inspiration and Interpretation*, p. 9)

1. Take a Half Hour Early Each Day For Bible Study.

"1. First, that you should deliberately apportion to this solemn duty the best and freshest and quietest half-hour in the whole day; and then, that you should determine, let what will go undone, never to abridge that half-hour. You may sometimes be enabled to afford a little more time to the chapter: but you will find it quite fatal ever to devote a shorter period to it."
(Dean John William Burgon, *Inspiration and Interpretation*, p. 9)

2. Read a Chapter a Day in the Bible.

"2. Next, (except on Sundays and in Vacation, when you may safely double your daily task and your daily time,) be persuaded to read each day exactly one chapter. . . ." (Dean John William Burgon, *Inspiration and Interpretation*, p. 9)

3. Go Over the Words as if They Were New to You.

"3. Then, while you read,--safe from the risk of interruption, (as I began by supposing,) and with every faculty intent on your task,--try, as much as possible, to go over the words as if they were new to you; . . . Nothing can be unimportant when it is the Holy Ghost who speaketh. It is an excellent practice to mark the expressions which strike you; for it is a

method of preserving the memory of what is sure else soon to pass away." (Dean John William Burgon, *Inspiration and Interpretation*, p. 10)

4. Avoid Commentaries, Maps, or Helps.

"4. And next, be persuaded to read without extraneous helps of any kind; except, of course, such help as a map, or the margin of your Bible, supplies. Pray avoid Commentaries and notes. First, you cannot afford time for them; and secondly, if you could, they would be as likely to mislead you as not. . . . they will do more to nullify your reading, than anything which could be imagined. Your object is to obtain an insight into Holy Scripture, . . . not to be saved trouble, and to be shown what other persons have thought about it." (Dean John William Burgon, *Inspiration and Interpretation*, pp. 10-11)

5. Make Brief Memoranda of Your Own.

"5. make brief memoranda of your own: and the briefer the better. Construct your own table of the Patriarchs, . . ." (Dean John William Burgon, *Inspiration and Interpretation*, p. 11)

6. Read the Bible Consecutively from Genesis to Revelation.

"6. Above all, is it indispensable that your reading of the Bible should be strictly consecutive; and on no account may any one pretend to begin such a study of that book as I am here recommending, except at the first Chapter of Genesis. . . ." (Dean John William Burgon, *Inspiration and Interpretation*, p. 11)

7. Read Every Book Without Skipping a Chapter.

"7. It will follow from what has been offered, that you are invited to read every book in the Bible in the order in which it actually stands,--never, of course, skipping a chapter; much less a Book. . . ." (Dean John William Burgon, *Inspiration and Interpretation*, p. 12)

B. Proper Attitudes While Bible Reading

Dean Burgon suggested some things when beginning daily Bible reading from Genesis to Revelation that pertain to a proper attitude. Here are a few helpful things concerning attitude that he mentioned.

1. Look for Things Not Known Before.

"How soon will any one who takes the trouble to read the Bible after this fashion, be struck with a hundred things which he never knew before,--indeed, which are not commonly known!" (Dean John William Burgon, *Inspiration and Interpretation*, pp. 12-13)

2. Begin With Prayer.

"The book should ever be approached with prayer:--'Lord, open Thou mine

3. Find Honey in the Bible.

"Read it therefore, if you are wise, with unaffected curiosity: settling down upon every flower, in order to find out, if you can, where the honey is: clinging to it rather, until you have found the honey." (Dean John William Burgon, *Inspiration and Interpretation*, p. 15)

4. Have a Mind Like Samuel.

"The attitude of mind which I so strongly recommend you to assume, (and it depends on an act of the Will, whether you assume it or not,) is very exactly represented by this cry of the child Samuel,--'Speak Lord, for Thy servant heareth!'" (Dean John William Burgon, *Inspiration and Interpretation*, p. 16)

C. Suggestions and Goals for Pastors as a Result of Their Bible Reading.

Dean Burgon offered a series of suggestions and goals for Pastors which should result from their daily Bible reading program.

1. Bible Reading Will Cut Down on Boredom in the Congregation.

"It becomes your turn at last to instruct others, . . . we should hear less about dull sermons, and inattentive congregations, and badly filled churches,--as well as about the astounding ignorance of many among the upper classes, in Divine things,--if our younger Clergy know the Bible a great deal better than they do.--Aye, and we should not have so many unsound remarks about Holy Scripture either,--so many mistaken views of doctrine,--so many crude remarks about Inspiration,--made by persons who ought to know better." (Dean John William Burgon, *Inspiration and Interpretation*, p. 18)

2. Never Neglect Bible Reading even for a Day.

"I do entreat you, one and all, to follow the advice I have been giving you; and to set about such a careful study of the Bible, at once. Do not put it off for a single day. Begin it tomorrow morning." (Dean John William Burgon, *Inspiration and Interpretation*, pp. 18-19)

3. Partake of the Tree of Life by Bible Reading.

"But even supposing you do, now and then, find the inexorable daily half-hour stand in the way of something else,-- . . . daily at that fixed time, make you full amends? Shall you resolve to pluck so freely of the Tree of Knowledge, and yet begrudge the approach once a day to the Tree of Life, which grows in the midst of the Paradise of God? What? room for

everything and everybody; yet still 'no room in the Inn' for Christ!" (Dean John William Burgon, *Inspiration and Interpretation*, p. 19)

4. Don't Read Commentaries for Three Years at Least.

". . . you will read no work of Divinity just at present. Be counselled, on no account, to read any. . . . Be content, for the next three years, to study no book of Divinity but the Bible." (Dean John William Burgon, *Inspiration and Interpretation*, p. 20)

5. Keep a Jealously-Guarded Half-Hour Daily.

"What was begun as a task will soon come to be regarded as a privilege. That jealously-guarded half-hour will be found to be the one green spot in the whole day,-- . . . Your secret study of that Book of Books, I say, will render you a very singular service." (Dean John William Burgon, *Inspiration and Interpretation*, p. 20)

6. Bible Reading Is Vital.

". . . but I would rather, a hundred times, be of use to the younger men present; I would rather, a hundred times, succeed in persuading one of them, to adopt that method of reading the Bible which I have been recommending;--than try to say something which might be thought fine and clever." (Dean John William Burgon, *Inspiration and Interpretation*, p. 21)

7. Bible Reading Arms Pastors with the Sword of the Spirit.

"It is not merely to inform the understanding, that Holy Scripture is to be read with such consummate attention, and studied with such exceeding care. . . . It is,--in order that his inner life may be made conformable to that outer Law: . . . Its aim, and purpose, and real function, is, that the fiery hour of temptation may find the Christian soldier armed with 'the sword of the Spirit, which is the Word of God:'--that the dark season of Adversity may find his soul anchored on the Rock of Ages,--which alone can prove his soul's sufficient strength and stay." (Dean John William Burgon, *Inspiration and Interpretation*, pp. 21-22)

V
SERMON II.
"Natural Science and Theological Science"

Sermon #2 by Dean Burgon to his ministerial students concerned the battles between "natural science" and "theological science." As there are many doubters of the scientific accuracy of the Bible today, so there were in Dean Burgon's day. He defended the accuracy of the Bible in all areas of science.

A. Genesis Must Be Accepted As Scientific.

The very first thing that must be established when so-called "science" comes up against Bible truth is that the Bible is absolutely and totally true--scientifically and in every other way. Dean Burgon nobly defended God's truth.

1. Suspicion of Genesis

"There exists however a vague suspicion after all that the beginning of Genesis is a vision, or an allegory, or a parable,--or anything you please, except true History. It is hard to imagine why. If there be a book in the whole Bible which purports to be a plain historical narrative of actual events, that *book is the book of Genesis. . . . Why the first page of it is to be torn out, treated as a myth or an allegory, and in short explained away,--I am utterly at a loss to discover."* (Dean John William Burgon, *Inspiration and Interpretation,* p. 33)

2. Creation Days of 1,000 Years Will Not Do.

"I take leave to add that even the respectful attempt to make Genesis accommodate itself to the supposed requirements of Geology, by boldly assuming that the days of Creation were such a thousand years long,--seems inadmissable." (Dean John William Burgon, *Inspiration and Interpretation,* p. 37)

3. Creation Days Must Be Literal and Solar.

"Days are spoken of,--each made up of an evening and a morning. . . 'for in six days' (it is declared,) 'the Lord made Heaven and Earth.' You may not play tricks with language plain as this, and elongate a week until it shall more than embrace the span of all recorded Time. Neither am I able to see what would be gained by proposing to prolong the Days of Creation indefinitely, so as to consider them as representing vast and unequal periods;" (Dean John William Burgon, *Inspiration and Interpretation,* p. 38)

4. Man's Creation No More Than some 6,000 years ago

"... the Creation of Man is not to be referred to a remoter period than some six thousand years ago.... fixed by the Chronology of the Bible." (Dean John William Burgon, *Inspiration and Interpretation*, p. 40)

5. The Bible Contains Accurate Science.

"But when gentlemen tell us that the Bible was never meant to teach Science; and that wherever its statements are opposed to the clear inductions of reason, they must give way; and so forth: we take the liberty of retaliating their charge." (Dean John William Burgon, *Inspiration and Interpretation*, p. 39)

B. Proper Interpretation of the Bible is Essential.

1. The Bible Should not Be Allegorized.

"But there is a scornful spirit abroad which is not content to allegorize the earlier pages of the Bible,--to scoff at the story of the Flood, to reject the outlines of Scripture Chronology;--but which would dispute the most emphatic details of Revelation itself." (Dean John William Burgon, *Inspiration and Interpretation*, pp. 45-46)

2. Miracles Must Be Accepted, Not Reinterpreted.

"Will you then reject one miracle and retain another? Impossible! You can make no reservation, even in favour of the Incarnation of our Lord,--the most adorable of all miracles, as it is the very keystone of our Christian hope. Either, with the best and wisest of all ages, you must believe the whole of Holy Scripture; or, with the narrow-minded infidel, you must disbelieve the whole. There is no middle course open to you." (Dean John William Burgon, *Inspiration and Interpretation*, p. 46)

3. Proper Interpretation of Genesis Is Especially Important.

"To speak without a figure,--He who surrenders the first page of his Bible, surrenders all. He knows not where to stop. Nay, you and I cannot in any way afford to surrender the beginning of Genesis; simply because upon the truth of what is there recorded depends the whole scheme of Man's salvation,--the need of that 'second Man' which is 'the Lord from Heaven.' It is not too much to say that the beginning of Genesis is the foundation on which all the rest of the Bible is built." (Dean John William Burgon, *Inspiration and Interpretation*, pp. 50-51)

VI
SERMON III.
"Inspiration of Scripture--Gospel Difficulties--The Word of God Infallible--Other Sciences Subordinate to Theological Science"

Sermon #3 by Dean Burgon to his ministerial students argued for the inspiration of the Bible in every part. He explained the nature of the Bible's plenary, verbal inspiration the its extent. Dean Burgon believed that all the Bible, all the books, all the chapters, all the verses, all the sentences, all the words, all the syllables, and all the letters were inspired by God.

A. Some Definitions Concerning the Inspiration of the Bible

1. The Inspiration of Scripture Rightly Understood

"2 Tim. iii.16. All Scripture is given by inspiration of God."
"But that *is not exactly what St. Paul says. The Greek for* that, *would be* ‛Η γραφή--not πᾶσα γραφή--θεόπνευστος. *St. Paul does not say that the whole of Scripture, collectively, is inspired. More than that: what he says is, that every writing,--every several book of these* ἱερὰ γράμματα, *or Holy Scriptures, in which Timothy had been instructed from his childhood,--is inspired by God. It comes to very nearly the same thing; but it is not quite the same thing. St. Paul is careful to remind us that every Book in the Bible is an inspired Book."* (Dean John William Burgon, *Inspiration and Interpretation,* p. 53)

2. Verbal Inspiration

"Do you mean to say then, (I shall be asked,) that you maintain the theory of Verbal Inspiration?--I answer, I refuse to accept any theory *whatsoever. But I believe that the Bible is the Word of God--and I believe that God's Word must be absolutely infallible. I shall therefore believe the Bible to be absolutely infallible,--until I am convinced of the contrary. Theories of Inspiration,' (as they are called,) are the growth of an unbelieving age; . . ."* (Dean John William Burgon, *Inspiration and Interpretation,* p. 74)

3. Inspired Words

"But if, instead of the 'Theory of Verbal Inspiration,' I am asked whether I

believe the words *of the Bible to be inspired,--I answer, To be sure I do,-- every one of them: and every syllable likewise. Do not you?--Where,--(if it be a fair question,)--Where do you, in your wisdom, stop? The book, you allow is inspired. How about the chapters? How about the verses? Do you stop at the verses, and not go on to the words?"* (Dean John William Burgon, *Inspiration and Interpretation*, p. 75)

4. The Bible Is Inspired Entirely.

"The Bible (be persuaded) is the very utterance of the Eternal;--as much God's Word, as if high Heaven were open, and we heard God speaking to us with human voice. Every book of it, is inspired alike; and is inspired entirely. Inspiration is not a difference of degree, but of kind. The Apocryphal books are not one atom more inspired than Bacon's Essays. But the Bible, from the Alpha to the Omega of it, is filled to overflowing with the Holy Spirit of God: the Books of it, and the sentences of it, and the words of it, and the syllables of it,--aye, and the very letters of it." (Dean John William Burgon, *Inspiration and Interpretation*, p. 76)

B. Biblical Inspiration Must Be Defended Properly.

Though the teachings of Biblical inspiration are clear to those who believe the Bible, they must be defended even today with as much conviction and skill as used by Dean Burgon in 1861.

1. It's Time to Speak Out for God's Truth.

". . . then it is high time, even for the humblest and least among you,--if no man of mark will speak up, and speak out, for God's Truth,--to deliver a plain message with that freedom which Englishmen hold to be a part of their birthright." (Dean John William Burgon, *Inspiration and Interpretation*, p. 81)

2. The Safety of the Ark of God

"Look well to it, Sirs, if you care for the safety of the Ark of God. For my part,--like one of old time whose words I am not worthy to take upon my lips,--'I cannot hold my peace: because thou hast heard, O my soul, the sound of the trumpet, the alarm of war!'" [Jeremiah 4:19] (Dean John William Burgon, *Inspiration and Interpretation*, p. 82)

3. The Inerrancy of Every Letter of the Bible Must Be Defended.

"--this Day's Sermon has had for its object to remind you, that THE BIBLE is none other than the voice of Him that sitteth upon the Throne! Every Book of it,--every Chapter of it,--every Verse of it,--every word of it,--every syllable of it,--(where are we to stop?)--every letter of it--is the direct utterance of the Most High!--Πᾶσα γραφή θεόπνευστος. 'Well spake the HOLY GHOST, by the mouth of' the many blessed Men who wrote it.--The

Bible is none other than the Word of God: *not some part of it, more, some part of it, less; but all alike, the utterance of Him who sitteth upon the Throne;--absolute,--faultless,--unerring,--supreme!"* (Dean John William Burgon, *Inspiration and Interpretation,* p. 89)

VII
SERMON IV.
"The Inspiration of Every Part of the Bible Vindicated and Explained--Nature of Inspiration--the Text of Scripture."

Sermon #4 by Dean Burgon to his ministerial students outlined his belief that the Bible was given by God and is verbally inspired from beginning to end. It is as if God Himself was speaking to us from His throne in heaven. There was no doubt in Dean Burgon's mind as to this important doctrine in the Bible.

A. The Extent of Inspiration.

1. Scripture Inspired from the Alpha to the Omega of it

"... *Holy Scripture is inspired from the Alpha to the Omega of it;--not some parts more, some parts less, but all equally, and all to overflowing;--that we hold it to be, not generally inspired, but particularly; that we see not how with logical consistency we can avoid believing the words as well as the sentences of it; the syllables as well as the words; the letters as well as the syllables; every 'jot' and every 'tittle' of it, (to use our Lord's expression,) to be divinely inspired:--and further, that until the contrary has been proved, we shall maintain that no misapprehension or misstatement, no error or blot of any kind, can possibly exist within its pages:--that we hold the Bible to be as much the Word of God, as if God spoke to us therein with human lips;--and that, as the very utterance of the HOLY GHOST, we cannot but think that it must be absolute, faultless, unerring, supreme.*" (Dean John William Burgon, *Inspiration and Interpretation*, pp. 93-94)

2. No Middle Ground Between Inspiration and Non-Inspiration

"*For I request you to observe, that there is absolutely no middle state between Inspiration and non-inspiration. If a writing be inspired, it is Divine: if it be not inspired, it is human.*" (Dean John William Burgon, *Inspiration and Interpretation*, p. 96)

3. The Bible Is the Very Utterance of the Holy Spirit

"*You are requested to remember that when we call the Bible an inspired book, we mean nothing more than that the words of it are the very utterance of the HOLY SPIRIT:--that the Book is as much the Word of God as if high Heaven were open, and we heard God speaking to us with human voice."* (Dean John William Burgon, *Inspiration and Interpretation*, p. 102)

B. Illustrations of the Bible's Inspiration.

1. The Bible Like the Speech of a Sovereign

"1. When the Sovereign reads a speech from the Throne, does she speak the words of it in any different sense from the words of a speech which she has herself composed?--Nay, . . ." (Dean John William Burgon, *Inspiration and Interpretation*, p. 102)

2. The Bible Like a Servant Delivering a Message

"4. If I commission a Servant to deliver a message,--is not the message which he delivers mine? *If I give him words to deliver,--are not* the words which he delivers mine? (Dean John William Burgon, *Inspiration and Interpretation*, p. 104)

C. The Bible Can Be Trusted In Even The Smallest Detail.

1. The Dukes of Edom Are as Inspired as much as any other Portion

"I entreat you therefore to disabuse your minds of the very weak,--aye and very fatal,--notion that the catalogue of the Dukes of Edom is less, *or in any different sense, inspired, from the rest of the narrative in which it stands."* (Dean John William Burgon, *Inspiration and Interpretation*, p. 109)

2. Inspiration Does not Come and Go

"Consider also, I entreat you, whether it is credible that Inspiration should be a thing of such a nature, that it comes and goes,--is there and is gone,-- once and again in the course of a single page. What? does it vanish, like lightning, when the Evangelist's pen has to record the title on the Cross,--to re-appear the instant afterwards?" (Dean John William Burgon, *Inspiration and Interpretation*, p. 109)

3. The Bible Must Stand or Fall as a Whole

"The Bible, it cannot be too much repeated, too clearly borne in mind,--the Bible must stand or fall,--or rather, he received or rejected,--as a whole. . . . All the Books of the Bible must stand or fall together." (Dean John William Burgon, *Inspiration and Interpretation*, pp. 111-12)

D. A Proper Attitude in Dealing With the Bible Is Important.

1. Our Own Amazing Ignorance

"Our own amazing ignorance--our many infirmities,--our faculties limited on every side,--might well keep us humble in the presence of Him whose knowledge is infinite,--whose attributes are all perfections:--whose very Name is Almighty!--Shall we, on the contrary, presume to sit in judgment upon His Word, which claims to be none other than the authentic record of His Providence,--the Revelation of His very mind and will?" (Dean John William Burgon, *Inspiration and Interpretation*, pp. 113-14)

2. The Safest Eloquence of Silence

"And our safest eloquence concerning Him is our silence, when we confess without confession that His glory is inexplicable; His greatness above our capacity and reach. He is above, and we upon earth: therefore it behoveth our words to be wary and few." (Dean John William Burgon, *Inspiration and Interpretation*, p. 114)

3. Believe You Are Reading an Inspired Book

"I say, that they would now be assiduous, and earnest, and regular, and peaceful, and devout, in their daily study of one chapter of the Bible.--And while you read the Bible, read it believing that you are reading an inspired Book:--not a Book inspired in parts only, but a Book inspired in every part:--not a Book unequally inspired, but all inspired equally;--not a Book generally inspired,--the substance indeed given by the Spirit, but the words left to the option of the writer; but the words of it, as well as the matter of it, all--all given by God. As it is written--'Man shall not live by bread alone, but by every word that proceedeth out of the mouth of God.'" (Dean John William Burgon, *Inspiration and Interpretation*, pp. 114-15)

4. The Method of Inspiration Cannot Be Fully Understood

"The method of Inspiration is but another of the many thousand marvels which on every side surround me; one of the many things I cannot fully understand, much less pretend to explain. But I may at least believe it in silence, and adore. And,--(forgive me for keeping you so long; but I cannot let you go until I have emptied my heart a little more on this great, and most concerning subject;)--. . ." (Dean John William Burgon, *Inspiration and Interpretation*, p. 117)

E. Other Important Quotations Defending Bible Inspiration

1. How Can You Expound an Uninspired Text?

"How can you pretend to expound a text, unless you hold the words of that text to be inspired? What inferences can you venture to draw from words, the Divinity of which you dare not affirm? O, to what endless, hopeless scepticism are you pointing the way! What a variety of most unanswerable questionings will you provoke! How can you hope ever to convince or convict, if you begin by acquainting your adversary that it is only for the substantial verity of Scripture that you claim Inspiration; the verbal details being quite a different matter!" (Dean John William Burgon, *Inspiration and Interpretation*, pp. 117-18)

2. The Bible Is the Best Ascertained Text of any Ancient Writing.

"Now I will not stop to expose the falsity of this charge against the text of Scripture; (which is implied to be a very corrupt text, whereas, on the contrary, it is the best ascertained text of any ancient writing in the world.) ... See you not that the state of the text of the Bible has no more to do with the Inspiration of the Bible, than the stains on yonder windows have to do with the light of God's Sun?" (Dean John William Burgon, *Inspiration and Interpretation*, p. 119)

3. Thought Inspiration Versus Word Inspiration

"As for thoughts being inspired, apart from words which give them expression--you might as well talk of a tune without notes, or a sum without figures." (Dean John William Burgon, *Inspiration and Interpretation*, p. 120)

4. Resent Any Dishonour to the Lord.

". . . but do not be ashamed to be very jealous for the honour of the Lord of Hosts; and to resent any dishonour offered to Him, with a fiery indignation utterly unlike anything you could possibly feel for a personal wrong." (Dean John William Burgon, *Inspiration and Interpretation*, p. 121)

5. A Childlike Study of the Bible Is an Antidote to Impiety

"The true antidote to all such forms of impiety, believe me, is not controversy of any sort; but the childlike study of the Bible, each one for himself,--not without prayer.--Humble must we be, as well as assiduous; for the powers of the mind as well as the affections of the heart should be

prostrated before the Bible . . ." (Dean John William Burgon, *Inspiration and Interpretation*, p. 122)

6. Unlock the Bible Treasure with the Key of Faith

"Waste not thy precious time in cavil about the structure of the casket which contains thy treasure; but unlock it once with the Key of Faith, and make thyself rich indeed.--Already,--(as we were last week reminded),--already the Judge standeth at the door; and assuredly, thou and I (to whom God hath entrusted so much!) shall have to render a very strict account of the use we have made of the Bible,--when we shall stand face to face with its undoubted Author." (Dean John William Burgon, *Inspiration and Interpretation*, pp. 124-25)

7. The Bible Is the Sole Depository of History and Chronology

". . . historical details constitute so large a part of the contents of the Bible; and that the sacred volume is the sole depository *of the History of the History and Chronology of the World for by far the largest portion of the interval since that World's Creation."* (Dean John William Burgon, *Inspiration and Interpretation*, p. 133)

8. An Uninspired Writing Has No Absolute Authority

"If a writing be not inspired, it is of no absolute authority. If a part of a writing be not inspired, that part is of no absolute authority. If a single word in the text of Holy Scripture be even uncertain,--(as for example, whether we are to read ΟΣ **or** ΘΕΟΣ *in 1 Tim. iii.16,)--that word becomes without absolute authority. We cannot venture to adduce it is proof of anything."* (Dean John William Burgon, *Inspiration and Interpretation*, p. 134)

9. The Lord Jesus Christ Verified Many Old Testament Details

"However unworthy of scientific attention the Mosaic account of the descent of Mankind from a single pair may be deemed,--the universality of the Noachian Deluge,--the destruction of the Cities of the plain,--the fate of Lot's wife,--Jonah in the fish's belly,--and so forth,--to all these (supposed) unscientific statements our Blessed Lord commits Himself unequivocally." (Dean John William Burgon, *Inspiration and Interpretation*, p. 135)

VIII
SERMON V.
"Interpretation of Holy Scripture--Inspired interpretation--the Bible Is not to be Interpreted Like any Other Book--God, (not man,) the Real Author of the Bible."

Sermon #5 begins Dean Burgon's discussion of proper interpretation of the Bible. It is not sufficient to have a Bible that has been verbally and plenarily inspired if the interpretation of it is improper. Dean Burgon offered helpful suggestions on Biblical interpretation in this sermon.

A. The Bible Is a Unique Book.

1. It Is Unlike Any Other Volume in the World

"... but beware how you apply your purely human notions to the utterance of the Ancient of Days; for that utterance, enshrined in one particular volume, clearly makes that one volume essentially unlike any other volume in the world." (Dean John William Burgon, *Inspiration and Interpretation,* p. 147)

2. Bible Writers Interpret it as No Other Book

"... the two chief propositions concerning Holy Scripture ... And first, I assert that it may be regarded as a fundamental rule, that the Bible is not to be interpreted like any other book. *This I gather infallibly from the plain fact, that* the inspired Writers themselves *habitually interpret it* as no other book either is, or can be interpreted.

Next, I assert without fear of contradiction that inspired Interpretation, whatever varieties of method it may exhibit, is yet uniform and unequivocal in this one result; namely, that it proves Holy Scripture to be of far deeper significancy than at first sight appears." (Dean John William Burgon, *Inspiration and Interpretation,* p. 160)

B. Some Important Rules in Bible Interpretation

1. Don't Deny the Literal Sense of Scripture

"I am not denying (God forbid!) the literal sense of Scripture. Rather am I, above all, contending for it. We may never *play tricks with the letter.*

Those Six Days of Creation, depend upon it, were six days: and the Tree of Life, and the Tree of Knowledge, and the Serpent, were the very things they are called,--and no other things. So of every other part of the Bible." (Dean John William Burgon, *Inspiration and Interpretation*, pp. 160-61)

2. Nothing is Ever Allegory or May Be Explained Away

"The literal sense of what has been revealed, is, for all that, to be depended on. All is sincere History: nothing is ever allegory,--nothing may ever be evacuated or explained away! We have our Lord's own word for it." (Dean John William Burgon, *Inspiration and Interpretation*, p. 161)

3. There Are Often Deeper Meanings of Scripture

"But I am proving that Scripture itself, literally understood, compels us to believe that under the letter of Scripture, (which of course is to be interpreted literally,) there lies a deeper and sometimes a far less obvious meaning; . . ." (Dean John William Burgon, *Inspiration and Interpretation*, p. 161)

C. The Holy Spirit's Role in Bible Interpretation

1. The Holy Spirit Is the True Author of Old and New Testaments

". . . it is the Holy Ghost who, in the New Testament, interprets what the same Holy Ghost had delivered in the Old. This, believe me, is the true key, the only intelligible solution, to all those difficulties respecting places of the Old Testament, whether interpreted, or only quoted, in the New, which have so exercised the ingenuity of learned men. We are always to remember, in a word, that the true Author of either Testament,--the real Author of every part of the Bible, is (not Man, but) God!" (Dean John William Burgon, *Inspiration and Interpretation*, p. 173)

2. The Whole Bible Is Inspired by the Holy Spirit

". . . the whole of the Bible is inspired by one and the self-same Spirit; so that one part may always be safely compared with any other part of it, you please. Nay, by no other method can you hope to understand the Bible, than by such a laborious comparison of its several parts." (Dean John William Burgon, *Inspiration and Interpretation*, pp. 174-75)

3. The True Method of Interpretation

"And the true method,--the only true method--must be that which was adopted by our Saviour, by His Evangelists, and by His Apostles: a method which they taught to their first disciples, . . ." (Dean John William

Burgon, *Inspiration and Interpretation,* p. 180)

4. Grasp the Torch of Truth and Run With It

"*O let it be our great concern,--yours and mine,--to preserve with undiminished lustre the whole deposit of Heaven-descended teaching which is the Church's treasure! . . . Like runners in a certain ancient race of which we all have read, let it be* our *pride and joy,--yours and mine,--to grasp the torch of Truth with a strong unwavering hand; to run joyously with it as long as the days of this earthly race shall last; and dying, to hand it on to another, who, with strength renewed like the eagle's, may again,--swiftly, steadily, exultingly,--run with it, till he fails! . . . So when the Judge of quick and dead appeareth,--so let Him find* you *occupied,--O young men, (many of you, my friends,) who are already the hope of half the English Church!*" (Dean John William Burgon, *Inspiration and Interpretation,* pp. 180-81)

IX
SERMON VI.
"The Doctrine of Arbitrary Scriptural Accommodation Considered"

In this sermon #6, Dean Burgon refuted the fallacy of "Scriptural Accommodation." This error has been promulgated even today by most apostates, some neo-evangelicals, and even some who call themselves fundamentalists.

A. We Must Recognize That the Source of the Bible Was God Himself.

1. God Was Speaking With Human Lips

"The view of Inspiration which Scripture itself gives us,--namely, that God is therein speaking by human lips; *so that 'holy men of God' delivered themselves as they were 'impelled,' 'borne along,' or 'lifted up' (φερόμενοι) by the Holy Ghost';--this plain account of the matter, I say, which converts 'all Scripture' into something 'breathed into by God,' (θεόπνευστος,)--men are singularly slow to acknowledge."* (Dean John William Burgon, *Inspiration and Interpretation*, pp. 183-84)

2. The Holy Spirit's Meaning Must Be Accepted

"But the most subtle enemy of all remains yet to be noticed. It is he, who,--finding the plain Word of God against him: finding himself refuted in his endeavour to fix one intention only on the words of the Holy Ghost, and that intention, the most obvious and literal one; finding himself refuted even by the express revelation of the same Holy Ghost, elsewhere delivered;--bends himself straightway to resist, and explain away, that later revelation of what was the earlier meaning." (Dean John William Burgon, *Inspiration and Interpretation*, p. 185)

3. Arbitrary "Accommodation" of the Holy Spirit's Words Is Rejected.

"Now I altogether *reject this principle of arbitrary 'Accommodation.' I hold it to be a mere dream and delusion. And I reject it on the following grounds:--1. It is evidently a mere excuse for Human ignorance,--a transparent deceit.... 2. The 'theory of Accommodation,' (as it is called,) is attended with this fatal inconvenience,--... it altogether fails of its object."* (Dean John William Burgon, *Inspiration and Interpretation*, p. 189)

4. The Same God Gave Old and New Testaments

"The same God who gave us the Scriptures of the Old Testament, gave us the New Testament also. The Bible is one." (Dean John William Burgon, *Inspiration and Interpretation*, p. 195)

B. Some Special Considerations for Bible Interpretation.

1. Humbly Address Yourself to the Bible

"We say,--The Bible is the word of God. Fill your heart with this conviction, and then humbly address yourself to the study of its pages." (Dean John William Burgon, *Inspiration and Interpretation*, p. 197)

2. Remember that Divine Language Never Needs To Be "Accommodated"

"Human language will sometimes require to be 'accommodated.' Divine language, never! May not the Holy Spirit lay His finger on whatever parts of His ancient utterance He sees fit? may He not invert clauses, and (in order to bring out His meaning better) even alter words?" (Dean John William Burgon, *Inspiration and Interpretation*, p. 213)

3. The Lord Jesus Christ Did Not Accommodate" Psalm 9:2

"Our Lord, being indignantly asked by the Jews if He heard what the children, crying in the Temple, said of Him,--made answer by quoting the 2nd verse of the ninth Psalm: 'Yea, have ye never read, 'Out of the mouth of babes and sucklings Thou hast perfected praise'?"--Pray was this 'accommodation,' or what was it? It was deemed a sufficient answer, at all events, by the Anointed Jehovah; whatoever men may think!" (Dean John William Burgon, *Inspiration and Interpretation*, p. 214)

4. The Lord Jesus Christ Was Spoke to Moses in the Bush.

"How, by the popular method,--how, by any of the new lights which have lately been let in on Holy Scripture,--was the Resurrection of the dead to have been proved by the words which the Second Person in the Trinity spake to Moses 'in the Bush?' And yet we behold that same Divine Personage in the days of His humiliation, proposing from those words, uttered by Himself 1500 years before, to establish the doctrine in dispute!" (Dean John William Burgon, *Inspiration and Interpretation*, p. 215)

5. There Is No Arbitrary Accommodation of Old Testament in the New.

"--no such thing as arbitrary Accommodation of the Old Testament Scriptures, in the New:" (Dean John William Burgon, *Inspiration and Interpretation*, p. 218)

6. Unbelief Must Not Blur our Bible Interpretation.

"Those who watch 'the signs of the times' attentively, will hear me witness that unbelief is one fearful note of the coming age. . . . Unbelief is no less the cause why so many have forsaken the Church of their Fathers, to run after the blasphemous fables and dangerous deceits of the Church of Rome, . . . At intervals, hoarse sounds, from a distance, are known to smite upon the listening ear; signals of the coming danger,--sure harbingers of the approaching storm.--Holy Scripture is the stronghold against which the Enemy will make his assault, assuredly: nor can we employ ourselves better than by building one another up in reverence for its Inspired Oracles: opposinig to the crafts of the Evil One the simplicity of a child-like faith; and resolutely refusing to see less than God, in God's Word!" (Dean John William Burgon, *Inspiration and Interpretation*, p. 219)

X
SERMON VII.
"The Marvels of Holy Scripture--Moral and Physical--Jael's Deed Defended--Miracles Vindicated"

Dean Burgon's final sermon, #7, supported all of the Biblical miracles. There is no reason for a Bible believing Christian to deny any of the miracles of Scripture.

A. The Miracles Must Be Taken With the Entire Bible.

1. Accept the Bible as a Whole Or Reject It as a Whole

"... either accept the Bible as a whole, or else reject it as a whole; for that there is no middle course open to them. The New Testament stands committed irrevocably to the Old. Every Book of the Bible stands committed to all the other Books. Not only does our Lord quote the Canon in its collected form, and call it 'the Law and the prophets,'-- or simply 'η γραφή, 'the Scripture.'--and so set His soul upon it, as one undivided and indivisible roll of Inspiration; but He and His Apostles single out the very narratives which the imbecility of Man was most likely to stumble at, and employ them for such purposes, and in such a manner, that escape from them shall henceforth be altogether hopeless." (Dean John William Burgon, Inspiration and Interpretation, p. 233)

2. There Are 30 New Testament References to the First Two Chapters of Genesis.

"It is a favourite device of these last days to hint at the allegorical character of the beginning of Genesis. But I find upwards of thirty references in the New Testament to the first two Chapters of Genesis." (Dean John William Burgon, Inspiration and Interpretation, p. 235)

3. All Parts of the Bible Stand or Fall Together.

"What I am insisting upon is, that the sacred Writers plainly say,--We stand or we fall together. They reach forth their hands, and they hold one another fast. ... They recognize one another's voices, and they interpret one another's thoughts, and they adopt one another's sayings. Verily the Bible is not 'like any other Book!' The prophets and Apostles and Evangelists of either covenant reach out one to another; and lo, among them is seen the form of One like the Son of God." (Dean John William Burgon, Inspiration and Interpretation, p. 236)

B. Miracles Must be Accepted As the Bible Gives Them and Not Doubted.

1. Miracles Should not Be Explained Away or Pared Down.

"3. Another favourite recipe there is for escaping from the bondage of Miracles, . . . These men, in a word, try to explain them away *where they can: where they cannot, they* pare them down *as much as they are able, or rather as much as they dare. Demoniacle possession? Symptoms like those described are known to accompany epilepsy. Manna? Something like it falls in the wilderness of Sinai to this hour. The Red Sea parted? Well, but a strong East wind blew all night. Stilling the storm, and healing Peter's wife's mother? Every storm is stilled if let alone; and a fever will burn out, often without occasioning death."* (Dean John William Burgon, *Inspiration and Interpretation*, p. 242)

2. Miracles' Historical Reality Must not Be Denied by Ideology.

"4. There remains to notice one subtle and most treacherous method of dealing with the marvels of Scripture,--(moral and physical alike,) . . . which I would brand with burning words if I had them at command. I allude to what is called 'Idiology,'--the plain English for which term is, a denial of the historical reality of Scripture.*"* (Dean John William Burgon, *Inspiration and Interpretation*, p. 243)

3. Miracles Are Historically True.

"All this, I say, you and I,--with the whole Church Catholic for 1800 years, --have been taught to believe as plain historical truths, mere matters of fact; past telling wonderful indeed, but yet as historically true, *as that I am standing here and you are sitting yonder,--neither more nor less."* (Dean John William Burgon, *Inspiration and Interpretation*, p. 244)

4. Miracles Are Historically True, Not Merely Ideologically True

"We are assured that every one of these things, or at least that some of them, are only ideologically *true: that* Historically, they are false. *In plain language, we are requested to believe that they never occurred at all."* (Dean John William Burgon, *Inspiration and Interpretation*, p. 244)

5. Denial of Bible Miracles Is Blasphemous Folly.

"Not only will I not *treat men with tenderness who put forth such blasphemous folly, . . . but I will hold them up to ridicule, to the very utmost of my power. Nay, I would make them objects of unqualified reprobation to all, if I could, as they deserve to be reprobated, for they are the worst*

enemies of the Gospel of Christ." (Dean John William Burgon, *Inspiration and Interpretation*, p. 249)

C. Dean Burgon's Final Words of Challenge

1. Ministers Have a Battle for Christ to Fight.

"My sympathy shall be reserved for those who have never so offended, but are, on the contrary, full of precious promise;--for the young and as yet inexperienced,--for you, who will have the battle of Christ and His Church to fight, when we shall be mouldering in the grave. Let those who do not know me, deem me uncharitable if they will. I care not. The uncharitable man,--mark me, Brethren!--the truly uncharitable man, is he, who shows no consideration for weak and unstable souls; who does not regard the trials and perils of the young; who beguiles unsteady feet to the edge of the precipice, and there forsakes them; whose destructive method, (for constructiveness is no part of that man's philosophy!)--whose destructive method leaves the young without chart and compass,--aye, without moon or stars to sail by; who labours hard to communicate the taint of his own foul leprosy to those who were before unpolluted; who dims the eye, and deadens the ear, and defiles the thoughts, and darkens the hope of as many as have the misfortune to come in his way, and feels no pity!--Yes, yes! The man who sows his own vile doubts broadcast over two continents,--doing his very best to destroy the faith of those for whom Christ died,--he, he is the uncharitable man!" (Dean John William Burgon, *Inspiration and Interpretation*, pp. 250-51)

2. Ministers Must Rise Above Perpetual Disputings.

"Friends and brethren,--(I am still addressing the younger men present!)--Divinity is not debate; and Religion is not controversy; and Life is not long enough for perpetual disputings. 'He that cometh unto God must believe that He is.' The heart dries up, and the affections wither away, and the soul faints, amid an atmosphere of cloudy doubts, and captious difficulties, and perverse disputations. You must rise above it, if you would discern the colours on the everlasting hills, and behold the beauty of the promised Land, and see objects as they really are. O put away from yourselves, (if any of you are so unhappy as to have acquired it,) a habit of mind which will effectually unfit you for profiting by what you read in Holy Scripture: and you, who are free from such dreadful bondage, beware lest, by the indulgence of some sin,--whether of the flesh or of the spirit,--you darken that spiritual eye by which alone spirituial things are to be discerned. It is like talking about colours to the blind, or about sounds to the deaf, to discuss with a certain class of persons the Inspiration, or the Interpretation, or the Marvels of Scripture." (Dean John William Burgon, *Inspiration and Interpretation*, p. 252)

3. Ministers Must Make Use of the Wealth of the Celestial Armoury.

"Begin betimes to acquaint yourselves with the wealth of that celestial armoury which contains a weapon which must prove fatal to every foe; but which it depends on yourselves whether you shall have the skill to wield or not. Suffer not yourselves to be cheated of your birthright, the Bible, either by the novel fictions of unstable men, or by the exploded heresies of a bygone age, revived and recommended by living unbelievers. You, especially who aspire to the Ministerial office, and are destined herafter to undertake the cure of souls, O do you be doubly watchful! Give to the Bible the undivided homage of a childlike heart; and bow down before its revelations with a suppliant understanding also; and let no characteristic of its method by any means escape you. Notice how it is indeed all one long narrative, from end to end; and see therein God's provision that nothing shall be idealized, nothing explained away. . . .The Bible, I repeat, is all severest history, from the Alpha to the Omega of it." (Dean John William Burgon, *Inspiration and Interpretation*, p. 253)

4. Ministers Must Have a Desire to Understand the Bible.

(speaking of the Bible) "*Let it quicken you in your desire to understand that Book out of which you will have hereafter to preach, reprove, rebuke, exhort,--sometimes to bethink yourselves of the flocks which already are expecting you; and among which God already sees your future going out and coming in; your faithful teaching, or (God forbid!) your betrayal of a most sacred trust.*" (Dean John William Burgon, *Inspiration and Interpretation*, p. 254)

5. Ministers Must Accept the Divine Origin and Power of the Bible.

". . . *you will be convinced of its Divine origin, when you have become the adoring witnesses of its Divine power. Truly, that must be from God which can so change the life and effect the heart; which can sustain the spirit under bereavement, and become the soul's satisfying portion under every form of adversity!*" (Dean John William Burgon, *Inspiration and Interpretation*, p. 254)

6. Ministers Must Realize that the Bible Is the Only Thing that Deserves Man's Attention

"*The Bible in truth, as one grows older,--(to me at least it seems so,)-- becomes almost the only thing in the world really deserviing of a man's attention. . . . There is but a step between us and death* (1 Samuel 20:2); *and assuredly when we wake up after his likeness, we shall be satisfied with it* (Psalm 17:16)! *. . . Already 'the shadows of the evening are stretched out.'*

(Jeremiah 6:4) *Be patient, O my soul, 'until the day break, and the shadows flee away.!'"* (Song of Solomon 2:17; 4:6) (Dean John William Burgon, *Inspiration and Interpretation,* p. 255)

Introducing the "INDEX OF WORDS AND PHRASES"

The next six pages are an important part of this "**Summary.**" By using this "**INDEX**" the reader will be enabled to come up with quotations by Dean Burgon on a number of important beliefs and suggestions.

It must be remembered that this "**INDEX**" is not an index of Dean Burgon's *Inspiration and Interpretation*, but rather only an index of this "**Summary.**" Though this is true, it still enables the reader to find the pages in the original book because each quotation from the book gives the page or pages on which it occurs.

As I read through the 31 pages of the "**Summary**," I came up with what I considered to be key words or phrases which would enable the reader to find quickly the exact source of these quotations.

For example, if you were interested in finding where the *Essays and Reviews*, are referred to, you will look on page "iii" and pages "2-7" in the "**Summary.**" When you look up these pages, you will find that comments on these *Essays and Reviews* occupy pages i-ccxxviii. Specific comments are mentioned by Dean Burgon on the following pages: pp. ix-x; xi, xii-xiii, xvii, xix, xxiv, and xxvi.

It is hoped that the readers will find this "**INDEX**" to be helpful in discovering many tiny details that are of interest in Dean Burgon's volume. With the use of computers these days, there is little reason not to have an index. Even after reading a book it doesn't take long before you forget where you read some interesting point. With the help of a good index, you can find what you are looking for long after reading the book.

A Most Remarkable Stand on Inerrancy! The Inerrancy of Every Letter of the Bible Must Be Defended.

"*--this Day's Sermon has had for its object to remind you, that THE BIBLE is none other than* the voice of Him that sitteth upon the Throne! *Every Book of it,--every Chapter of it,--every Verse of it,--every word of it,--every syllable of it,--(where are we to stop?)--every letter of it--is the direct utterance of the Most High!*--Πᾶσα γραφή θεόπνευστος. '*Well spake the HOLY GHOST, by the mouth of the many blessed Men who wrote it.--The Bible is none other than* the Word of God: *not some part of it, more, some part of it, less; but all alike, the utterance of Him who sitteth upon the Throne;--absolute,--faultless,--unerring,--supreme!*" (Dean John William Burgon, *Inspiration and Interpretation*, p. 89)

INDEX OF WORDS AND PHRASES

1 Samuel 20:2 30
1,000 years .... iv, 11
1500 years 25
1800 years 28
1861 .... 1, 3, vii, 14
1999 .... 2, ii, vii
21st Annual meeting ii
228 pages 2, 4, 6, 7
228 pages to answer 2
279-page advice 7
279 7
30 New Testament
    references .... vi, 27
433 .... iii, 3, 4, 6
433-page book 3
6,000 years .... iv, 12
absolute .... v, 15, 16, 20
absolute authority .... v, 20
absolutely infallible 13
accommodation ..... v, vi, 24, 26
accurate science .... iv, 12
adversity 10, 30
alarm of war 14
all Scripture 13
allegorized .... iv, 12
allegory .... v, 11, 22
Almighty 18
Alpha to the Omega . iv, 14, 16, 30
amazing ignorance .... v, 18
anchored 10
Ancient of Days 21
ancient writing .... v, 19
Anglican .... iii, 3
Anglican Clergymen ...... iii, 3
Anointed Jehovah 25
antidote .... v, 19
any other book .... v, 21, 27
Apocryphal books 14
apostasy 2, 3, 6
Apostles 5, 22, 27
APPENDIX ii
approaching storm 26
arbitrary .... v, vi, 24, 26

arbitrary accommodation ... vi, 26
Ark of God .... iv, 14
articles 4
ascension 4
assessment .... iii, 4
astounding ignorance 9
attitudes .... iii, 8
authority .... v, 20
avoid Commentaries .... iii, 8
B.F.T. #1220 vii
babes and sucklings 25
baseness 5
battle for Christ to fight .... vi, 29
battle of Christ 29
begin it tomorrow 9
begin with prayer .... iii, 8
beginning of Genesis .. 11, 12, 27
best ascertained .... v, 19
betrayal 30
betrayal of a most sacred trust . 30
Bible 2-vii, 3-22, 24-28, 30
Bible as a whole .... vi, 27
Bible can be trusted .... v, 17
Bible For Today Press 2
Bible is inspired entirely ... iv, 14
Bible miracles .... vi, 28
Bible reading .... iii, iv, 8-10
Bible study .... iii, 3, 7
Bible writers .... v, 21
Biblical inspiration must
    be defended .... iv, 14
Biblical orthodoxy 2
blasphemous .... vi, 26, 28
blasphemous fables 26
blasphemous folly .... vi, 28
blasphemy .... iii, 5
Blessed Lord 20
Book of Books 10
boredom .... iv, 9
boredom in the congregation ... 9
bread alone 18
brief memoranda .... iii, 8
Burgon .... 1, 3, ii, vii, 2-31

bush .... vi, 25
C. W. Goodwin 6
Canon 27
careful study 9
casket which contains thy
    treasure (the Bible) 20
Causes of Corruption 6
Celestial Armoury 30
challenge .... vi, 29
chaplains 4
chapter .... iii, 7, 8, 14, 18
chapter a day .... iii, 7
chapters .... vi, 13, 14, 27
chart and compass 29
childlike study of the Bible .. v, 19
Christ ..... v, vi, 5, 10, 20, 25, 29
Christian soldier 10
chronology .... v, 12, 20
chronology of the Bible 12
chronology of the world 20
Church of England 2, 4, 6
Church of Rome 26
cities of the plain 20
clauses 25
cloudy doubts 29
Collingswood .... 2, vii
Collingswood, New Jersey 2
come and go .... v, 17
coming danger 26
Commentaries ...... iii, iv, 8, 10
consecutive 8
consecutively .... iii, 7, 8
conspiracy .... iii, 3
conspiracy against the Faith . iii, 3
Copyright 2
creation ..... iv, 4, 11, 12, 20, 22
creation days .... iv, 11
creation days of 1,000 years iv, 11
creeds 4
cross 17
crude remarks 9
cure of souls 3, 30
curiosity 9
daily .... iv, 7-10, 18
daily task 7

danger 26
dangerous deceits 26
day of judgment 4
days of creation 11, 22
Dean Burgon ...... ii, vii, 2-9, 11
                  13, 14, 16, 21, 24
Dean Burgon Society ... ii, vii, 6
Dean John William
    Burgon ... 1, 3, ii, vii, 3-31
deeper meanings .... v, 22
defender of the Faith 6
definitions .... iv, 13
Demoniacle possession 28
denial .... vi, 6, 28
denied by ideology .... vi, 28
denomination 2, 6
depository .... v, 20
detail .... v, 17
devotion to the Words of God ... 6
disputings .... vi, 29
Divine language .... vi, 25
Divine origin .... vi, 30
Divine Personage 25
Divine power 30
Divine Truth .... iii, 5
Divinity of the Second Person .. 4
do not put it off 9
doctors of divinity 4
don't read Commentaries for three
    years .... iv, 10
Dr. F. Temple 6
dream and delusion 24
Dukes of Edom .... v, 17
dull sermons 9
duty 7
each day .... iii, 7
earlier pages of the Bible 12
eloquence of silence .... v, 18
enemies of the Gospel of
    Christ 29
enemy 24, 26
England's youth 4
Essays and Reviews ...... iii, 2-7
eternal punishment 4
Evangelists 5, 22, 27

evening and a morning 11	heaven 4, 5, 11, 12, 14, 16, 17, 23
every word 14, 18	hell 4
evil one 26	helps .... iii, 8
explained away .... v, vi 11, 22, 28, 30	heresies .... 30 heresy 3, 6
exploded heresies 30	Heritage Baptist University . ii, vii
expound an uninspired Text . v, 19	high heaven 14, 17
fall .... v, vi, 4, 17, 27	His glory is inexplicable 18
fallacies 4	His likeness 30
fallacy 4, 24	historical reality .... vi, 28
falsities 4	historically true .... vi, 28
falsity 4, 19	history ...... v, 4, 11, 20, 22, 30
fatal inconvenience 24	Holy Scripture . v, vi, 8-10, 12, 16
faultless 15, 16	20, 21, 25-27, 29
fellows 4	Holy Spirit iv, v, 14, 16, 17, 22, 25
fight .... vi, 29	honey .... iii, 9
final words of challenge .... vi, 29	honey in the Bible .... iii, 9
find honey .... iii, 9	hopeless scepticism 19
first page of his Bible 12	human ignorance 24
first two chapters of Genesis .. 27	human language 25
fixed time 9	humbly .... vi, 25
flood 5, 12	ideologically true .... vi, 28
flower 9	ideology .... vi, 28
foul 5, 29	ignorance .... v, 9, 18, 24
foul leprosy 29	inattentive congregations 9
foundation of faith 5	incarnation 4, 12
general problem .... iii, 3	incarnation of our Lord 12
Genesis ... iii, iv, vi, 8, 11, 12, 27	inerrancy .... iv, 14
Genesis to Revelation ...... iii, 8	inerrancy of every letter of the
geology 11	Bible .... iv, 14
God speaking to us 14, 17	inerrant 7
God was speaking with	infallible .... iv, 7, 13
human lips .... v, 24	infamous book 5
God's Truth 11	infidel 12
God's Word 3	infidelity 5
Goodwin 6	inner life 10
grasp the Torch of Truth ... v, 23	insidious 5
green spot 10	insight 8
Greenwood, Indiana .... ii, vii	*Inspiration and*
guarded half-hour .... iv, 10	*Interpretation* . ii, vii, 2-31
half hour .... iii, 7	inspiration and non-
half-hour daily .... iv, 10	inspiration .... iv, 16
heads of colleges 4	inspiration of Scripture ..... iv, 13
heart 18, 19, 25, 29, 30	inspired Book ...... v, 13, 16, 18
heaven-descended teaching ... 23	inspired interpretation 21

inspired Oracles 26
inspired words .... iv, 13
inspired writers 21
instructors of England's youth .. 4
interpretation .. 1, 3, ii, iv-vii, 2-31
interpretation of Genesis ... iv, 12
Introductory Remarks ..... iii, vii
invert clauses 25
irreligion 5
ISBN 2
Jeremiah 6:4 31
Jesus Christ ...... v, vi, 5, 20, 25
Jewish history 4
Jowett 6
Judge of quick and dead 23
justification 4
key of faith .... v, 20
Last Twelve Verses of Mark 6
Law and the Prophets 27
letters 13, 14, 16
like any other book .... v, 21
likeness 30
limitation of the Summary .. iii, 2
literal and solar .... iv, 11
literal sense .... v, 21, 22
liturgies 4
Lord from heaven 12
Lord Jesus Christ .... v, vi, 20, 25
Lord of Hosts 19
lustre 23
Majesty of Heaven 5
manna 28
man's creation .... iv, 12
man's dearest hopes 5
man's salvation 12
maps .... iii, 8
margin of your Bible 8
mercilessly 5
method of inspiration ...... v, 18
method of reading 10
middle course 12, 27
middle ground .... iv, 16
mind like Samuel .... iii, 9
ministerial office 30
ministers ...... vi, 2, 4, 5, 29, 30

ministers of the Gospel 5
miracles ...... iv, vi, 4, 12, 27, 28
miracles vindicated 27
moon or stars 29
Mosaic account 20
Moses .... vi, 25
Moses in the bush .... vi, 25
Most High 14
myth 11
never neglect Bible reading .. iv, 9
never to abridge 7
New Testament .... vi, 22, 25, 27
new to you .... iii, 7
no absolute authority .... v, 20
no middle course 12, 27
no middle ground .... iv, 16
no other book .... v, 21
Noachian deluge 20
noblest study 3
non-inspiration .... iv, 16
nothing is ever allegory ..... v, 22
Old and New Testaments v, vi, 22
Old Testament v, vi, 20, 22, 25, 26
once a day 9
open Thou mine eyes 9
ordination vows 4
Oriel College 2, 3, 7
orthodoxy 2
parable 11
Paradise of God 9
pared down .... vi, 28
Pastor D. A. Waite, Th.D.
  Ph.D. .... 1, 3, vii
Pastors .... iii, iv, 9, 10
Patriarchs 8
Pattison 6
perpetual disputings ...... vi, 29
perverse disputations 29
plain Word of God 24
Powell 6
prayer .... iii, 8, 19
professors 3, 4
professors of theological science 3
promised land 29
proper attitude .... v, 8, 18

proper attitudes . . . . iii, 8	sentences 13, 14, 16
proper interpretation . . . . iv, 12, 21	Sermon I . . . . iii, 7
prophecy 4	Sermon II . . . . iv, 11
Providence 18	Sermon III . . . . iv, 13
Psalm 17:16 30	Sermon IV . . . . iv, 16
Psalm 9:2 . . . . vi, 25	Sermon V . . . . v, 21
purpose . . . . iii, vii, 10	Sermon VI . . . . v, 24
questionings 19	Sermon VII . . . . vi, 27
quote the Canon 27	sermons 7, 9
quoted 2, 22	Serpent 22
race 23	servant delivering a message . . . iv
read every book . . . . iii, 8	seven rules for Bible study . . iii, 7
read the Bible consecutively iii, 8	severest history 30
read the whole Bible 7	silence . . . . v, 3, 18
Real Author . . . . v, 22	sincere history 22
reason 12, 27	six Anglican clergymen . . . . iii, 3
Red Sea 28	six days 22
redemption 4	six days of creation 22
regeneration 4	six thousand years 12
reinterpreted . . . . iv, 12	skipping . . . . iii, 8
resent any dishonour . . . . . . v, 19	solar . . . . iv, 11
resurrection 4, 25	soldier 10
resurrection of the dead 25	sole depository . . . . v, 20
Rev. H. B. Wilson 6	solemn duty 7
Rev. Mark Pattison 6	Son of God 27
Rev. Professor Baden Powell . . . 6	Song of Solomon 2:17 31
Rev. Professor Jowett 6	sound of the trumpet 14
Rev. Rowland Williams 6	Source of the Bible . . . . v, 24
Reviewers iii-5	species of treason 5
Revision Revised 6	speech of a sovereign . . . . . . iv, 17
Rock of Ages 10	stand or fall as a whole . . . . . v, 17
sacred trust 30	stand or fall together . . . . . . vi, 17
safest eloquence of silence . . v, 18	step between us and death 30
safety of the Ark of God . . . iv, 14	stilling the storm 28
salvation 4, 12	storm 26, 28
Samuel . . . . iii, 9, 30	study . . . . iii, v, 3, 7-10, 18, 19, 25
sap the foundation of faith 5	study of God's Word 3
scepticism 19	study of the Bible . . iii, v, 7, 9, 19
science . . . . iv, 3, 11, 12	sum without figures 19
sciences . . . . iv, 13	summary . . . . 1, iii, vii, 2, 6
scientific . . . . iv, 11, 20	supreme 15, 16
Scriptural accommodation 24	surrenders 12
Scripture chronology 12	surrenders all 12
Second Person 4, 25	surrenders the first page 12
Second Person in the Trinity . . 25	suspicion . . . . iv, 11

suspicion of Genesis ...... iv, 11
Sword of the Spirit .... iv, 10
syllable 14
syllables 13, 14, 16
system of unbelief .... iii, 3
Temple 6, 25
The Preface .... iii, 2, 3, 6
theological instruction 3
theological science 3
theory of verbal inspiration 13
thought inspiration .... v, 19
thoughts being inspired 19
thousand years 11, 12
three years .... iv, 10
title on the cross 17
Traditional Text 6
treason 5
treason against Him 5
Tree of Knowledge 9, 22
Tree of Life .... iv, 9, 22
true .... v, vi, 11, 19, 22, 28
True Author .... v, 22
true history 11
true method of interpretation v, 22
trumpet 14
truth .. iii-v, 3-5, 11, 12, 14, 23, 30
tune without notes 19
unaffected curiosity 9
unbelief .... iii, vi, 3, 26
unbelieving age 13
uncharitable 5, 29
uncharitable man 29
uncompromisingly 5
uncover their baseness 5
undergraduate ...... iii, 2, 3, 6, 7
undergraduate students 3
undiminished lustre 23
unerring 15, 16
uninspired writing .... v, 20
universality of the Noachian deluge
University pulpit 3
unlock the Bible treasure .... v, 20
unscientific statements 20
unsound remarks 9
Utterance of the Holy Spirit, 16, 17

Utterance of the Most High 14
verbal inspiration .... iv, 13
verses 6, 13, 14
vision 11
Waite, Dr. D. A. .... 1, 3, vii
war 14
wealth of the Celestial
    Armoury 30
weapon 30
whole Bible is inspired ..... v, 22
Williams 6
Wilson 6
without chart and compass 29
without moon or stars 29
without skipping .... iii, 8
word .... iii-v, 2-4, 6, 10
        13-20, 22, 24-26, 28
word inspiration v
Word of God ... iii, iv, 2, 4, 6, 10
        13, 15-17, 24, 25
words .... iii, 6, 7, 13, 14
        16-19, 24, 25, 28, 29
words of the Bible 14
young 7, 23, 29
younger clergy 9
younger men 10, 29

About the Author

The author of this book, Dr. D. A. Waite, received a B.A. (Bachelor of Arts) in classical Greek and Latin from the University of Michigan in 1948, a Th.M. (Master of Theology), with high honors, in New Testament Greek Literature and Exegesis from Dallas Theological Seminary in 1952, an M.A. (Master of Arts) in Speech from Southern Methodist University in 1953, a Th.D. (Doctor of Theology), with honors, in Bible Exposition from Dallas Theological Seminary in 1955, and a Ph.D. in Speech from Purdue University in 1961. He holds both New Jersey and Pennsylvania teacher certificates in Greek and Language Arts.

He has been a teacher in the areas of Greek, Hebrew, Bible, Speech, and English for over thirty-five years in nine schools, including one junior high, one senior high, three Bible institutes, two colleges, two universities, and one seminary. He served his country as a Navy Chaplain for five years on active duty; pastored two churches; was Chairman and Director of the Radio and Audio-Film Commission of the American Council of Christian Churches; since 1971, has been Founder, President, and Director of THE BIBLE FOR TODAY; since 1978, has been President of the DEAN BURGON SOCIETY; has produced over 700 other studies, books, cassettes, or VCR's on various topics; and is heard on both a five-minute daily and thirty-minute weekly radio program IN DEFENSE OF TRADITIONAL BIBLE TEXTS, presently on 25 stations. Dr. and Mrs. Waite have been married since 1948; they have four sons, one daughter, and, at present, eight grandchildren.

A Brief Summary of *Inspiration and Interpretation*

Defending the King James Bible--by Dr. D. A. Waite; 352 pp. hardback.; a four-fold superiority of the KJB is given: Superior TEXTS, TRANSLATORS, TECHNIQUE, and THEOLOGY. 251 review questions in the appendix plus a listing of all the complete English Bibles and New Testaments since 1300. 5th printing.
☐ BFT #1594-P @ $12.00

Four Reasons for Defending the King James Bible--by Dr. D. A. Waite. 28 pp. This is a brief summary of the KJB's superior texts, translators, technique, and theology elaborated upon in *Defending the King James Bible*. Reference is made to the larger book for more details on each point.
☐ BFT #2423 @ $2.00

The Revision Revised--by Dean John William Burgon, 640 pp. hard-back; a beautifully printed book, in which Dean Burgon does four things: (1) He attacks the false Greek text of Westcott and Hort; (2) He demolishes the theory behind that text; (3) He refutes the E.R.V. of 1881 and (4) He defends the King James Bible!
☐ BFT #611 @ $25.00

Westcott & Hort's Greek Text & Theory Refuted--by Dr. D. A. Waite, 36 pp., a summary from Dean Burgon's *Revision Revised* of the serious defects both in Westcott and Hort's Greek text as well as the false and unfounded theory on which that false text was based. Reference is made extensively to the larger book.
☐ BFT #2695 @ $3.00

The Last Twelve Verses of Mark--by Dean John William Burgon, 400 pp., perfect bound, with powerful and convincing documentation. Dean Burgon vindicates and establishes Mark 16:9-20 as genuine. In his day, the only manuscripts (with few exceptions) that omitted these verses were the false Vatican & Sinai MSS.
☐ BFT #1139 @ $15.00

Dean Burgon's Vindication of the Last Twelve Verses of Mark--by Dr. D. A. Waite, 36 pp.; a summary of Dean Burgon's *Last Twelve Verses of Mark*. The extensive arguments of Dean Burgon are placed in easy to follow chart and table form so that the abundant proof in favor of these verses can be easily seen.
☐ BFT #2506 @ $3.00

The Traditional Text of the Holy Gospels--by Dean John William Burgon, 384 pp. hardback. A careful survey of the historical supremacy of the N.T. Greek text that has been preserved from the first century until the present. Dean Burgon shows the superiority of this text and the inferiority of B and Aleph and others.
☐ BFT #1159 @ $16.00

A Brief Summary of Dean Burgon's Traditional Text of the Holy Gospels--by Dr. D. A. Waite, 36 pp., a brief summary of the major arguments of Dean Burgon's book, *The Traditional Text*, outlining his seven tests of truth, the superiority of the traditional text, and the inferiority of the Westcott & Hort N.T. text.
☐ BFT #2771 @ $3.00

The Causes of Corruption of the Traditional Text--by Dean John William Burgon, 360 pp. hardback; detailed illustrations of five accidental causes and ten intentional causes of the corruption of the original traditional text. The book is replete with condemnation of the B/Aleph, Vatican/Sinai & Westcott and Hort N.T. Greek text.
☐ BFT #1160 @ $15.00

A Brief Summary of the Causes of the Corruption of the Traditional Text--by Dr. D. A. Waite, 40 pp.; a brief summary of Dean Burgon's *Causes of Corruption*, illustrating briefly the five causes of accidental corruption and the ten causes of intentional corruption of the original traditional text.
☐ BFT #2780 @ $3.00

☐ BFT #2764VC1-4 @ $45.00--FOUR, 6-hour Videos
King James Bible Seminar Videos--420 Transparencies

 **Foes of the King James Bible Refuted**—by Dr. D. A. Waite, 158 pp.; a refutation of six leading foes of the KJB taken from the television script of the John Ankerberg program. The arguments are as old as the Westcott and Hort errors. They deserve clear answers and receive them in this booklet.
☐ BFT #2777 @ $9.00

 **The Comparative Readability of the Authorized Version**—by Mr. D. A. Waite, Jr., 84 pp.; an objective, computer generated comparison of the readability of seven versions: KJB, ASV, RSV, NASV, NIV, NKJV, & NRSV. The King James Bible wins in readability in most categories based on current readability formulas.
☐ BFT #2671 @ $5.00

 **The Theological Heresies of Westcott and Hort**—by Dr. D. A. Waite, 52 pp.; 125 direct quotations from three of Bishop Westcott's books and two of Professor Hort's books, showing their apostasy in all ten areas of theological thought. Don't believe those who tell you they were "conservative" theologians!
☐ BFT #595 @ $3.00

 **Bishop B. F. Westcott's Clever Denial of Christ's Bodily Resurrection**—by Dr. D. A. Waite, 56 pp.; an analysis of two of Westcott's books on the resurrection of Christ showing clearly his heretical denial of Christ's bodily resurrection. He also denies Christ's bodily ascension and bodily second coming. Beware!
☐ BFT #1131 @ $4.00

 **Dean Burgon's Confidence in the King James Bible**—by Dr. D. A. Waite, 36 pp.; an answer to the lie of James White that Dean Burgon would not use ONLY the King James Bible. The booklet is replete with quotations from Dean Burgon's *Revision Revised* in which he defends the KJB forcefully and accurately!
☐ BFT #2591 @ $3.00

 **The Paraphrased Perversion of the Bible—Analysis of the Living Version N.T.**—by Dr. Gene Nowlin, 344 pp. perfect bound; a detailed analysis from a theological and translational standpoint of the *Living Version New Testament*. This should be given to those who still think there is spiritual value in the LV.
☐ BFT #127 @ $6.00

 **A Brief Analysis of the NIV Inclusive Language Edition ("NIVILE")**—by Dr. D. A. Waite, 56 pp.; In spite of the plan of the NIV to go gender-inclusive and then the withdrawl of that plan, the NIV has published in England such an edition. 136 examples of faithless treatment of God's Words are given!
☐ BFT #2768 @ $4.00

 **The Contemporary English Version (CEV), An Antichrist Version (ACV)?**—by Dr. D. A. Waite, 34 pp.; The latest perversion from the American Bible Society is analyzed and condemned. 29 doctrinal words and 22 other important words have been dropped out of this CEV. Destined to be the pattern for the world!
☐ BFT #2721 @ $3.00

 **The Case for the King James Bible, A Summary of the Evidence and Argument**—by Dr. D. A. Waite, 96 pp.; this booklet is a brief summary from three different books of the favorable evidence for the Hebrew and Greek texts that underlie the King James Bible. An update of the author's 1971 work.
☐ BFT #83 @ $7.00

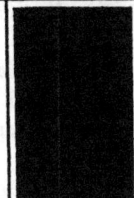 **The Textus Receptus Greek New Testament Underlying the KJB**—printed by The Trinitarian Bible Society, 487 pp.; this is a reprint of Dr. Frederick Scrivener's Greek text which exactly underlies the King James Bible. It is based on Beza's 5th edition of 1598 and should be the basis for any New Testament translation in any language.
☐ BFT #471 @ $14.00

Get our NEW BOOK on *Foes of the KJB Refuted*--$9.00!!

Order Blank (p. 1)

Name:_____

Address:_____

City & State:_____Zip:_____

Credit Card #:_____Expires:_____

[ ] Send *Inspiration and Interpretation* by Dean Burgon ($25+$5 S&H) A hardback book, 523 pages in length.

[ ] Send *The Last 12 Verses of Mark* by Dean Burgon ($15+$4) A perfect bound paperback book 400 pages in length.

[ ] Send *The Revision Revised* by Dean Burgon ($25 + $4) A hardback book, 640 pages in length.

[ ] Send *The Traditional Text* hardback by Burgon ($16 + $4) A hardback book, 384 pages in length.

[ ] Send *Causes of Corruption* hardback by Burgon ($15 + $4) A hardback book, 360 pages in length.

[ ] Send <u>all five</u> of Dean Burgon's books (*Last 12 verses, Revision Revised, Traditional Text, Causes of Corruption, & Inspiration and Interpretation*). ($96 value for $75+S&H)

[ ] Send Summary defending *Mark 16:9-20* by DAW $3 + $3)
[ ] Send *Westcott & Hort's Greek Text & Theory Refuted by Burgon's Revision Revised--Summarized* by Dr. D. A. Waite ($4.00 + $3 S&H)
[ ] Send *Summary of Traditional Text* by Dr. Waite ($3 + $2)
[ ] Send *Summary of Causes of Corruption*, DAW ($3+2 S&H)
[ ] Send *Summary of Inspiration and Interpretation* by Dr. Waite ($4 + $2)

Send or Call Orders to:
THE BIBLE FOR TODAY
900 Park Ave., Collingswood, NJ 08108
Phone: 609-854-4452; FAX:--2464; Orders: 1-800 JOHN 10:9
E-Mail Orders: BFT@BibleForToday.org; Credit Cards OK

Order Blank (p. 2)

Name:_____

Address:_____

City & State:_____Zip:_____

Credit Card#:_____Expires:_____

Other Materials on the KJB & T.R.

[ ] Send *Defending the King James Bible* by Dr.Waite $12+$4
   A hardback book, indexed with study questions.

[ ] Send *The Case for the King James Bible* by DAW ($7 +S&H) A perfect bound book, 112 pages in length.

[ ] Send *Foes of the King James Bible Refuted* by DAW ($9 +$4 S&H) A perfect bound book, 164 pages in length.
[ ] Send *Burgon's Warnings on Revision* by DAW ($7+$3 S&H) A perfect bound book, 120 pages in length.

[ ] Send *Westcott's Denial of Resurrection*, Dr. Waite ($4+$3)

[ ] Send *Four Reasons for Defending KJB* by DAW ($2+$3)

[ ] Send *Contemporary Eng. Version Exposed*, DAW ($3+$2)
[ ] Send *Guide to Textual Criticism* by Edward Miller ($7 + $4)
[ ] Send *Dean Burgon's Confidence in KJB* by DAW ($3+$3)
[ ] Send *Readability of A.V. (KJB)* by D. A. Waite, Jr. ($5 +$3)
[ ] Send *NIV Inclusive Language Exposed* by DAW ($4+$3)
[ ] Send *23 Hours of KJB Seminar* (4 videos) by DAW ($50.00)

[ ] Send *Defined King James Bible* lg.prt. leather ($40+S&H)
[ ] Send the "DBS Articles of Faith & Organization" (N.C.)
[ ] Send Brochure #1: "1000 Titles Defending KJB/TR"(N.C.)

Send or Call Orders to:
THE BIBLE FOR TODAY
900 Park Ave., Collingswood, NJ 08108
Phone: 609-854-4452; FAX:--2464; Orders: 1-800 JOHN 10:9
E-Mail Orders: BFT@BibleForToday.org; Credit Cards OK

Order Blank (p. 3)

Name:_____

Address:_____

City & State:_____Zip:_____

Credit Card#:_____Expires:_____

More Materials on the KJB &T.R.

[ ] Send *Heresies of Westcott & Hort* by Dr. Waite ($4+$3)

[ ] Send *Scrtvener's Greek New Testament Underlying the King James Bible*, hardback, $14+$4 S&H

[ ] Send *Scrivener's Greek New Testament withWestcott & Hort Changes to the Textus Receptus*, edited by Dr. K. D. DiVietro, hardback, c. 800 pages, $35+$4 S&H

[ ] Send *Why Not the King James Bible?--An Answer to James White's KJVO Book* by Dr. K. D. DiVietro, $9+$4 S&H

[ ] Send *Forever Settled--Bible Do*cuments & History Survey by Dr. Jack Moorman, $21+$4 S&H

[ ] Send *Early Church Fathers & the A.V.--A Demonstration* by Dr. Jack Moorman, $6 + $4 S&H.

[ ] Send *When the KJB Departs from the So-Called "Majority Text"* by Dr. Jack Moorman, $16 + $4 S&H

[ ] Send *Missing in Modern Bibles--Nestle-Aland & NIV Errors* by Dr. Jack Moorman, $8 + $4 S&H

[ ] Send *The Doctrinal Heart of the Bible--Removed from Modern Versions* by Dr. Jack Moorman, VCR, $15 +$4 S&H

[ ] Send *Modern Bibles--The Dark* Secret by Dr. Jack Moorman, $3 + $2 S&H

[ ] Send *Early Manuscripts and the A.V.--A Closer* Look, by Dr. Jack Moorman, $15 + $4 S&H

Send or Call Orders to:
THE BIBLE FOR TODAY
900 Park Ave., Collingswood, NJ 08108
Phone: 609-854-4452; FAX:--2464; Orders: 1-800 JOHN 10:9
E-Mail Orders: BFT@BibleForToday.org; Credit Cards OK

The Defined King James Bible

With Uncommon Words Defined

Deluxe Genuine Leather
◆Large Print◆

1 for $40.00+S&H

◆Case of 12 for◆
$30.00 each+S&H

Order Phone:
1-800-JOHN 10:9

CREDIT CARDS WELCOMED

Send Gift Subscriptions
All gifts to Dean Burgon Society are tax deductible!
THE DEAN BURGON SOCIETY
Box 354 - Collingswood, Now Jersey 08108, U.S.A.,
Phone; (609) 854-4452; FAX: (609) 854-2464

Membership Form

I have a copy of the "Articles of faith. Operation and Organization" of The Dean Burgon Society, Incorporated. After reading these "Articles," I wish to state, by my signature below. that I believe in and accept such "Articles." I understand that my "Membership" is for one year and that I must renew my "Membership" at that time in order to remain a "Member" in good standing 6f the Society.

[ ] I wish to become a member of The Dean Burgon Society for the first time.

[ ] I wish to renew my membership subscription which has expired as of: _____

SIGNED:_____
DATE:_____
I enclose: **Attention: The Dean Burgon Society**
Box 354 - Collingswood, Now Jersey 0810&
*Membership Donation ($7.00/year) $_____
*Life Membership Donation ($50.00) $_____
*Additional Donation To The Society $_____
                        TOTAL: $_____

.Please PRINT In CAPITAL LETTERS your name and address below:
NAME:_____
ADDRESS:_____
CITY:_____
STATE:_____ ZIP:_____

Although I am not a member of **The Dean Burgon Society**, I do wish to subscribe to the **Newsletter**, by making a gift of $3.50 to the Society.
NAME:_____
ADDRESS:_____
CITY:_____
STATE:_____ ZIP:_____

*1 understand that, included in my first **$3.50 gift** accompanying any donation or order regardless of the amount of the order or donation, is my year's subscription to **The Dean Burgon Society NEWSLETTER**.
Canada & All Foreign Subscriptions $7.00 Yearly

www.ingramcontent.com/pod-product-compliance
Lightning Source LLC
Chambersburg PA
CBHW071429300426
44114CB00013B/1364